BASIC MICROECONOMICS

BASIC MICROECONOMICS
SECOND EDITION

EDWIN G. DOLAN
GEORGE MASON UNIVERSITY

THE DRYDEN PRESS•HINSDALE, ILLINOIS

Text and cover design by Stephen Rapley
Copy editing and indexing by Jo-Anne Naples
Photo research by Mili Ve McNiece

Credits and Acknowledgments
Print of Adam Smith, page 11, reproduced from the collection of the Library of Congress.
Photo of Friedrich August von Hayek, page 30, courtesy of Wide World Photos. Photo of
Alfred Marshall, page 38, courtesy of Historical Pictures Service, Inc., Chicago. Photo of
William Stanley Jevons, page 89, courtesy of Historical Pictures Service, Inc., Chicago. Photo
of Ronald H. Coase, page 107, courtesy of the University of Chicago Law School. Photo of
Joan V. Robinson, page 206, courtesy of Ramsey & Muspratt Studios, Cambridge, England.
Photo of John Kenneth Galbraith, page 220, courtesy of Professor Galbraith. Photo of Joseph
Alois Schumpeter, page 228, courtesy of the Bettmann Archive. Photo of Samuel Gompers,
page 283, courtesy of the AFL-CIO. Photo of Martin Feldstein, page 316, courtesy of the
Harvard University News Office. Print of Thomas Robert Malthus, page 373, courtesy of the
Bettmann Archive. Photo of William Arthur Lewis, page 382, courtesy of Princeton
University. Photo of Theodore W. Schultz, page 382, © Patricia Evans, 1978, courtesy of the
University of Chicago. Print of David Ricardo, page 391, courtesy of Culver Pictures, Inc.
Print of Karl Marx, page 429, reproduced from the collection of the Library of Congress.
Photo of Oskar Lange, page 430, courtesy of UPI. Photo of Ludwig von Mises, page 436,
courtesy of UPI.

P R E F A C E

Teaching economics in the 1980s is more of a challenge than ever before. A recent poll taken by *Fortune* magazine found that two out of three economics professors feel there is a sense of lost moorings in economics. Three out of four feel increasing doubt about the accuracy of macroeconomic models. Seven out of eight have less confidence than they used to in government programs as solutions to economic problems. The result is that 98 percent of all professors polled said they were teaching economics differently than they did five years ago.[1]

Despite this sense of lost moorings, most economists realize that the last decade has been a very productive one in terms of economic knowledge. In macroeconomics, great strides have been made in understanding the dynamics of inflation and unemployment, the role of monetary policy in the economy, the operation of the labor market, and the importance of expectations as a determinant of economic behavior. In microeconomics, such established fields of study as industrial organization and regulation have taken on a new life, while the fields of energy and the environment have under the pressure of events, blossomed from obscure specialties into major branches of the discipline.

All this means that teaching economics in the 1980s requires a new kind of textbook—one that brings into the classroom the new learning and new controversies of today's economic science. Students have an uncanny ability, from the first day of class, to pose exactly those questions that are being debated in the latest professional journals. They deserve the best answers that can be given; and in cases where there is no universally acceptable right answer, they deserve honest explanations of why disagreement persists.

Here, in brief, is the strategy used in *Basic Microeconomics*, second edition, to meet the challenge.

MICROECONOMICS

Microeconomics has a traditional core, represented by Chapters 3, 5, 6, 7, and 8. These chapters give a careful exposition of the theories of consumer behavior, production, cost, and perfect competition. Coverage of the growth areas of microeconomics begins with Chapter 9, which discusses pure monopoly, a traditional topic, and then applies the theory to the case of cartels, a type of market organization receiving greatly increased attention in these days of OPEC. The next three chapters explain a wide variety of market forms, with

---

[1] Walter Guzzardi, Jr., "The New Down-to-Earth Economics." *Fortune*, December 31, 1978, p. 77.

the discussion organized around the questions of when perfect competition is required for satisfactory market performance and when rivalry among a relatively small number of competing firms is enough. The chapters place considerable emphasis on recent empirical work supporting each side of this question. Chapter 13 deals with antitrust policy, making it a logical follow-up to the chapters on industrial organization. Problems such as the growing complexity of antitrust litigation, shared monopoly, and conglomerate mergers receive special attention, as do a variety of reform proposals. The economics of regulation, perhaps the most active single area in all of microeconomics at present, occupies the next chapter. Utility regulation, transportation regulation, and health and safety regulation are all discussed. Special emphasis is placed on recent empirical research, on the movement toward deregulation in many industries, and on normative issues in regulatory policy.

APPLICATIONS

Basic Microeconomics contains a number of chapters that put the students' newly acquired theoretical tools to work on problems of contemporary policy significance. Chapter 18, which deals with the economics of poverty, highlights several pieces of recent empirical research into the effects of antipoverty efforts. Chapter 19, on environmental economics, applies marginal analysis to the issue of command-and-control regulation versus economic incentives. Chapter 20, entirely devoted to the economics of energy, is divided into two parts. The first introduces the elements of the theory of the mine and applies this theory to oil and gas policy. The second discusses coal, nuclear power, and solar power as major energy alternatives to oil and gas, emphasizing the economic strengths and weaknesses of each alternative. Chapter 21 discusses the economics of population and development. International economics—especially problems of the balance of payments and exchange rate determination—is a final area of application emphasizing the latest empirical and theoretical research.

TEACHING AND LEARNING AIDS

The substantive content of a textbook is only part of what makes it usable in the classroom; for the book to be effective, its content must be taught by instructors and learned by students. To facilitate the process as much as possible, this book pays particular attention to teaching and learning aids.

The Cases According to a time-honored principle, each generalization should receive a specific illustration, and each illustration should lead to a generalization. Following this principle, numerous short case studies are included in the book. Some of them illustrate general statements about economic policy with specific episodes—for example, the regulation of pollution from steel mills. Other cases introduce empirical material supporting the discussion in the text—for example, data on economies of scale. All cases are short and to the point; and they are placed directly in the text, just where they will do the most good—not at the end of the chapters. Thus they serve as an integral part of the learning process, not just as entertainment or digression.

Readability In *Basic Microeconomics*, readability means three things. First, it means a lively writing style that draws students into the subject matter. Second, it means complete control of the level of difficulty, as measured by standard readability formulas; in this respect, the book corresponds to the actual reading abilities of today's undergraduate students. Third, it means elimination of the "alphabet soup" style of textbook writing. When terms such as average variable cost and average total cost occur, the text uses the actual words, not a thicket of AVCs and ATCs that quickly bewilder the students.

Vocabulary For many students, vocabulary is one of the big stumbling blocks to learning economics. This book uses a unique three-level reinforcement technique to handle the problem. First, each new term is printed in boldface at the point it is first used and defined. Next, the term and its definition are repeated on the same page in a marginal vocabulary box. Finally, a complete alphabetical glossary of terms appears at the end of the book.

Graphs For the benefit of students who may not be used to working with graphs, an appendix on the subject has been added to Chapter 1. This appendix does more than just explain techniques. It also addresses the most common problems students have in working with graphs. One of these problems is the tendency to memorize graphs as meaningless patterns of lines, without understanding their meaning. Another is the inability to draw original graphs when they are needed in note-taking or on examinations. The Chapter 1 appendix warns of these pitfalls and carefully explains how they can be avoided. As an added bonus throughout the book, the large page size and single-column format make it especially easy to put graphs exactly where they are needed in relation to the written text.

Chapter Front and Back Matter To further facilitate the learning process, each chapter is preceded by a brief statement of learning objectives and a list of terms for review. Each chapter is followed by a concise summary and a set of review questions, and most have an annotated list of suggestions for further reading.

Student Guide A comprehensive student guide, published separately, completes the package of learning aids. This guide was developed and written by the author of the text, which makes for unusually close coordination between the text and this important supplement. Each chapter in the student guide consists of four elements: a list of learning objectives (somewhat more detailed than those given in the chapter openings in the text), a narrative synopsis of the chapter, a programmed review requiring active student involvement and problem solving for immediate reinforcement, and a self-test. (The self-test items are carefully coordinated with the test bank in terms of format, coverage, and level of difficulty. Answers to self-test items, with explanations where necessary, are at the back of the study guide.)

Teaching Aids The text is also accompanied by a complete package of teaching aids. Foremost among them is an instructor's manual, by the author of the text. This manual contains instructional objectives, lecture notes, and answers to the text's end-of-chapter questions. It also contains a special section entitled "What's Different Here, and Why." This section compares the terminology, topic sequence, and underlying models of *Basic Microeconomics* with those of other leading textbooks to help instructors who have used other books in the past convert their courses and lecture notes. For the benefit of users of the first edition of *Basic Microeconomics*, this section of the instructor's manual also summarizes changes that appear in the second edition and explains why they were made.

Text Bank The test bank, provided on request to users of the textbook, has a number of features that make it a particularly powerful instructional tool. It is divided into two sections, A and B, each containing ten true-and-false and fifteen multiple choice questions for each chapter (two thousand test items in all). The two sections closely parallel one another in terms of coverage and level of difficulty, so that they can be used in alternate semesters or in different sections of the same course and still allow comparability for grading. The test items are distributed as evenly as possible among three levels of difficulty: recognition and understanding, simple application, and complex application. Individual items are coded in terms of level of difficulty and topic covered. The test items were developed by the author of the text and Elizabeth Craig of the University of Delaware. Before publication, they were reviewed by a panel of experienced instructors to eliminate any weak or ambiguous items.

Paperback Macro Edition and Hardbound Edition For maximum flexibility in suiting the varied requirements of instructors, a companion volume, *Basic Macroeconomics*, is also published. That book begins with the same introductory chapters as *Basic Microeconomics* so the two paperback volumes can be used in any order. In addition, there is an integrated hardbound volume, *Basic Economics*, that includes all the material in both *Basic Microeconomics* and *Basic Macroeconomics*. All ancillary items can be used with any of the three books.

Transparencies and Masters As a further teaching aid, fifty transparency acetates of the most important diagrams from the text are provided to instructors on request. In addition, transparency masters are available for the remaining diagrams. The instructor's manual contains suggestions for the use of these transparencies and transparency masters.

The Newsletter The teaching aid package is rounded out by a twice-yearly newsletter available to all instructors adopting the textbook. This newsletter serves three purposes. First, it contains fresh case studies to supplement those included in the text. Second, it updates the suggestions for further reading with brief reviews of new books suitable for use in the principles course. Finally, it updates statistical series and key diagrams of the text as new data become available.

CHANGES IN THE SECOND EDITION

The second edition of *Basic Microeconomics* is the fruit of two years of planning and effort by the author, the publisher, and dozens of reviewers and users of the first edition. Several entirely new chapters and case studies have been added, others have been thoroughly rewritten to reflect the latest developments in theory and policy. No paragraph has escaped refining and polishing, even where content is substantially unchanged. In order to maintain the relatively short overall length that was an attractive feature of the first edition, redundant material has been deleted as appropriate. Only the highlights of the revision can be mentioned here; a chapter-by-chapter discussion of revisions appears in the instructor's manual.

Core Chapters Many useful suggestions on the core chapters were made by users of the first edition. In response to them, Chapters 5 through 8 of the book have been extensively revised. A more detailed exposition of elasticity is given, along with more examples. More attention is given to the income and substitution effects in the chapter on consumer choice, and the appendix to that chapter has been expanded by the inclusion of a complete graphical derivation of the demand curve. The chapter on production and cost goes into more detail on the principle of diminishing returns and on economies of scale. More attention to long-run adjustments is given in the chapter on perfect competition, and the section on the welfare implications of perfect competition is completely rewritten. All in all, the number of examples, cases, and diagrams in these chapters has been nearly doubled, so that the exposition of this crucial material is much more detailed than before.

Industrial Organization, Antitrust, and Regulation Much more space than in the first edition is devoted to industrial organization and the related topics of antitrust policy and regulation. In part, this reflects the fact, mentioned above, that these are very active fields in the profession. In part also, it represents my own increased interest in these topics after spending a year at the antitrust division of the U.S. Department of Justice. The organization of these chapters is now as follows: Pure monopoly and cartels get a whole chapter to themselves, rather than the half chapter they had in the first edition. The chapter on agriculture is expanded to include a discussion of cartel-like agricultural marketing orders. There is an entire chapter on oligopoly, and it discusses contrasting points of view on the determinants of market concentration and the performance of concentrated markets. Chapter 12, devoted to advertising and nonprice competition, begins with some of the material on advertising and consumer behavior contained in a separate chapter in the first edition. It then proceeds to a discussion of monopolistic competition and the importance of entrepreneurship.

As in the first edition, a chapter is devoted to antitrust policy. The chapter has been thoroughly rewritten for this edition, however. It now covers a wider variety of viewpoints on antitrust issues and incorporates some new case studies based on actual antitrust cases. Regulation now gets a full chapter rather than its earlier half chapter. There are more case studies, and more attention is given to health and safety regulation.

Applied Topics Several of the applied chapters are new or thoroughly revised. The chapter on poverty has been extensively updated. An entirely new chapter on the economics of energy has been added. The material on population and development has been reorganized to fit into one tighter chapter. The chapter on international monetary issues has been rewritten from start to finish to keep up with the latest developments.

A WORD OR TWO OF THANKS

I have been extremely fortunate in getting help of many kinds from many quarters while writing this book. It is a pleasure to acknowledge that help here.

I owe the greatest thanks to David E. Lindsey, my longtime friend and professional colleague . In addition to collaborating with me on the companion volume, *Basic Macroeconomics*, he read and made suggestions on the entire manuscript of the book. Any errors or shortcomings of the book are, just as much as elsewhere, my responsibility, not his.

Next, I must thank the many reviewers who commented on various drafts of the manuscript and suggested countless improvements:

Richard K. Anderson
Texas A&M University

Robert Y. Awh
Mississippi State University

A. H. Barnett
University of South Carolina

Thomas Bible
Oregon State University

David Denslow, Jr.
University of Florida, Gainesville

Marc P. Freiman
Wayne State University

Richard M. Friedman
California State University,
Northridge

Joseph C. Gallo
University of Cincinnati

John C. Gilliam
Texas Tech University

Fred Gottheil
University of Illinois

Thomas J. Grennes
North Carolina State University

Raouf S. Hanna
Eastern Michigan University

Ziad Keilany
University of Tennessee,
Chattanooga

Calvin A. Kent
Baylor University

Robert L. Lawson
Ball State University

Lucinda M. Lewis
University of Pennsylvania

Lawrence W. Lovik
Macon Junior College

Bernard J. McCarney
Illinois State University

Roger W. Mack
DeAnza College

Allan Mandelstamm
Virginia Polytechnic Institute
and State University

Geoffrey Nunn
San Jose State University

Kent W. Olson
Oklahoma State University

Michael J. Piette
University of Hartford

John Pisciotta
Southern Colorado State College

Robert Pollard
University of Texas, Austin

Anthony A. Romeo
University of Connecticut

Francis W. Rushing
Georgia State University

Don Tailby
University of New Mexico

Edward Vento
Missouri Southern State College

Percy O. Vera
Sinclair Community College

Allen J. Wilkins
University of Wisconsin, Madison

Travis Wilson
DeKalb Community College

William J. Zeis
Bucks County Community College

In addition, I am indebted to those reviewers who made helpful comments on the first edition, the Test Bank, and the Study Guide:

Richard K. Anderson
Texas A&M University

Dwight M. Blood
Colorado State University

John A. Coupe
University of Maine, Orono

Edward J. Deak
Fairfield University

Keith D. Evans
California State University,
Northridge

Jeff D. Gibbs
Macon Junior College

Kathie S. Gilbert
Mississippi State University

Richard F. Gleisner
St. Cloud State University

Douglas A. Greenley
Moorhead State University

James Halteman
Wheaton College

Jan Hansen
Capital University

W. H. Heiman
Central Connecticut State College

Willard D. Machen
Amarillo College

Bruce McCrea
Lansing Community College

H. L. Minton
DeKalb Community College

Dennis Olson
Central Michigan University

Benjamin A. Rogge
Wabash College

Milton Shapiro
California State Polytechnic
University, Pomona

Frank Slesnick
Bellarmine College

Gerald A. Smith
Louisiana State University

Sheldon Stein
Cleveland State University

Dave Streifford
St. Louis Community College,
Forest Park

Norman Van Cott
Ball State University

Gregory H. Wassall
University of Hartford

Darwin Wassink
University of Wisconsin, Eau Claire

Last, but not least, I would like to thank Gail Cooper and Wanda Farmer of Arlington, Virginia, who typed literally thousands of pages of manuscript, working much of the time under the pressure of overly tight deadlines.

Dozens of other people who go unnamed here—publishers, editors, designers, and staff—have worked hard to make this book what it is. They will recognize their own individual contributions that have gone to make this a better book.

CONTENTS

PART FOUR / THE ECONOMICS OF LIFE ON A SMALL PLANET

AN OVERVIEW OF THE MARKET ECONOMY

C H A P T E R 1

WHAT ECONOMICS IS ALL ABOUT

WHAT YOU WILL LEARN IN THIS CHAPTER

As economists struggle to understand the dramatic economic events of recent years, they are placing increased emphasis on the basics: how individual markets work and how individual people react to changing economic conditions and policies. This chapter will begin explaining these basics with a discussion of the concepts of economic scarcity and choice. It will also distinguish between economics as a science and as policy. The Appendix to Chapter 1 will introduce the use of graphs in economics.

The 1970s were years of dramatic change for the U.S. economy. Unemployment and inflation struck in combinations that not so long ago would have been thought flatly impossible. Energy and environmental quality, long ignored or taken for granted, became subjects of national debate and targets of sweeping programs of federal regulation. The international monetary system was revolutionized, and the U.S. dollar lost, perhaps forever, its status as the strongest and most stable of currencies.

Not surprisingly, all this change and turmoil pushed public interest in economics to new heights. Enrollments in economics have never been higher. Newspapers and television have greatly increased their coverage of economic affairs. The specialized business press has prospered. People want to understand the economic events they are witnessing, and they expect economists to explain them.

Economists are trying hard to do so, and this book is part of the effort. Together with the course of which it is a part, it will help readers become more perceptive of economic news and more constructive participants in discussions of economic issues.

Economics has been undergoing a revolution, part of which has been an increase in modesty among economists. Economists are beginning to understand why the theories and forecasting methods of which they were once so proud came to grief in the 1970s, but they are not fully agreed on what to replace them with. They are beginning to understand why economic policies of the past have not always had the intended effects, but they are not fully agreed on how to design policies that will do better.

There is, however, one thing that economists today seem to agree on: More emphasis on the basics is needed. That means paying more attention to how individual markets operate and how individual people react to changing economic conditions and policies. This emphasis will be very much in evidence throughout the book. The discussion will begin with two of the most basic economic concepts of all: scarcity and choice.

SCARCITY AND CHOICE IN ECONOMICS

Learning economics means learning to look in a special way at what people do, singling out some features for close attention and placing others in the background. In this respect, economics is much like other social sciences, each of which has its particular way of looking at the world. Psychology emphasizes how people's motivations and personalities shape their behavior toward one another. Political science takes special note of how people's actions are shaped by power relationships within formal and informal political institutions. Economics emphasizes how human actions are influenced by the fact of scarcity and the necessity of choice.

Scarcity

In economics, *scarcity* means that people do not have as much of everything as they want. Economic scarcity is a subjective concept; it is not measurable by any objective, physical standard. A geologist might say that tin ore is scarce but that iron ore is abundant, meaning that the earth's crust contains much more iron than tin. But an economist would say that both are scarce because people do not have as much of either as they want. An environmentalist might say that sperm whales have become scarce, meaning that there are now barely enough of them to maintain a breeding population. But an economist would say that sperm whales are less scarce than they once were. A century and a half ago, before the discovery of kerosene, whale oil was much in demand as a lamp fuel; today, there are relatively abundant substitutes.

Scarcity as an imbalance between what people have and what they want is sometimes said to be artificial. If people could only learn to limit their wants, then they would solve the problem once and for all. But scarcity is inescapable. Suppose, for example, that you limited your material desires to a single bowl of rice a day and went out into the wilderness to meditate. As soon as you began looking for twigs to build a fire to cook your rice, you would discover that twigs are scarce. You would have to take time off from meditation to look for them. You would build your fire carefully, in such a way as to boil the water without wasting fuel. And in so doing, you would be drawn to meditate that your behavior in the wilderness was shaped by scarcity, much as it was in the world you had left.

Choice

Economics accepts scarcity as a fact of life; but what makes life interesting, economically speaking, is not scarcity itself so much as the necessity of choosing among ways of coping with it. Earthworms must live with a scarcity of good soil in which to dig their burrows, but they have no choice but to dig. As a result, economists find earthworms nowhere nearly as interesting as people, who can earn their sustenance by burrowing in the soil, by fishing in the sea, or by lecturing on economics to the burrowers and fishers.

As soon as the element of choice is added to that of scarcity, a whole world of economics opens up. How does each person decide how much time to spend fishing and how much to spend burrowing for edible roots? Is it better to fish with a pole or a net, to dig with a flat rock or a pointed stick? Why do some people specialize in fishing and others in lecturing on economics? Why is one fish traded for three roots when fishers and diggers meet at the Saturday market? These are questions about how human actions and interactions are shaped by the choices people make among alternatives for coping with scarcity.

Objectives, Alternative Activities, and Constraints

People make a number of different kinds of economic choices every day. Despite the great diversity, however, most of the situations calling for economic choice can be described in terms of three features: objectives, alternatives, and constraints.

Economic *objectives* can usually be described in terms of maximizing or minimizing something. Business firms, for example, are conventionally held to make decisions with the objective of maximizing profits. Consumers seek maximum satisfaction—or maximum "utility," as economists quaintly put it. More specialized kinds of economic decisions may aim at such objectives as minimizing the cost of transporting a given quantity of freight from a set of origins to a set of destinations. The variety of objectives pursued is endless.

In addition to having an objective, every situation calling for an economic decision must be characterized by two or more *alternative activities* by means of which the objective can be pursued. For a farmer, the activities might be growing different crops or using different techniques for growing a given crop. For a shopper in a supermarket, the different activities might be purchasing different kinds of foods. For the railroad traffic manager, the different activities might be different possible routings for trains. Whatever the particulars, the job of the decision maker is to choose that pattern of activities best serving the relevant objective.

Finally, in addition to objectives and alternative activities, economic decisions involve *constraints*. In one way or another, these constraints limit people's ability to achieve their objectives. A farmer might be constrained by the acreage available and a manufacturing firm by the size of its plant. Consumers are constrained by limited budgets. The railroad traffic manager is constrained in minimizing costs by the fact that a certain quantity of freight must somehow be moved to certain points. Constraints, in short, represent the element of scarcity always present in economic life.

Pure Economizing and Entrepreneurship

Objectives, alternative activities, and constraints are present in all situations calling for economic decisions, but they are not always equally well-defined or inflexible. In the simplest case, the objectives, alternative activities, and constraints are all clearly defined and known with certainty by the person making the decision. Economic decision making then becomes a matter of solving a problem with mathematical precision—of identifying from among the available alternatives the pattern of activities that best serves the objectives, given the prevailing constraints. There is one best solution, and an independent check can be made to determine whether a particular solution is the right one. This kind of economic decision making, which consists of finding the

Pure economizing The aspect of economic decision making that consists of choosing a pattern of activities from among a given set of alternative activities that will best serve a well-defined objective, subject to known constraints.

right answer when objectives, alternative activities, and constraints are given, can be called **pure economizing.**

In practice, economic decisions are rarely so clear-cut. People do not always know what all of their alternatives are; they have to explore the world around them, be alert to new possibilities, even actively invent new possibilities. They do not always know exactly what constraints they face or whether today's constraints will change tomorrow, so they have to take risks and rely on guesswork. People do not always even know what their own objectives are; they may question the goals they have set for themselves and may experiment with new ones. These activities—exploration, experimentation, alertness to changing circumstances, guesswork, and risk-taking—are all important parts of economic decision making, but they do not fit within the narrow framework of pure economizing. Lumped together, they can be referred to as **entrepreneurship.**

Entrepreneurship The aspect of economic decision making that consists of exploring for new alternatives, inventing new ways of doing things, being alert to new opportunities, taking risks, overcoming constraints, and experimenting with new objectives.

Traditionally, entrepreneurship is associated with founding new business firms and pure economizing with the management of existing ones. It is easy to understand why. A Henry Ford starting off to produce a new product for a new market using new technology clearly must do a lot of exploration and experimentation and must take a lot of risks. The current manager of a Ford Motor Company assembly plant, by comparison, has a much more clear-cut problem—meeting a specified schedule of deliveries at minimum cost, using known production techniques and working within known constraints. In practice, of course, entrepreneurship and pure economizing are never completely separated. Even in the most standardized situation, something unexpected can occur. Then the manager must become an entrepreneur and discover a way of coping with changed circumstances. Similarly, even the most innovative entrepreneur must begin to manage the new enterprise on a day-to-day basis—or hire someone to manage it—as soon as it is set up.

Despite the fact that pure economizing and entrepreneurship always get mixed together in the real world, it can be useful for purposes of discussion to separate the two. This book will often pose the question of what consumers, managers, or investors would do if they were faced by a given, well-defined set of objectives, alternative activities, and constraints. Answering that sort of question frequently provides a solid basis for understanding the more complicated entrepreneurial aspects of economic activities as well.

Opportunity Cost

The concept of *cost* is central to all economic decision making, including entrepreneurial decision making and pure economizing. The key to understanding how cost enters into economic decisions is the concept of **opportunity cost.**

Opportunity cost The cost of doing something measured in terms of the loss of the opportunity to pursue the best alternative activity with the same time or resources.

To economists, the opportunity cost of doing something means the loss of opportunity to pursue the best alternative activity with the same time or resources. In many cases, the opportunity cost of doing something is properly measured in terms of money out of pocket. For example, the opportunity cost of spending a dollar for a hamburger is the loss of the opportunity to spend the same dollar on something else. In other cases, activities that have no money cost have an important opportunity cost in terms of time. For example, an hour spent studying economics is an hour unavailable for studying biology or French. The following case study uses a familiar situation to illustrate the concept of opportunity cost.

Case 1.1
The Opportunity Cost of a College Education

How much does it cost you to go to college? If you are a resident student at an average four-year private college in the United States, you will probably answer this question by drawing up a budget like the one shown in Exhibit 1.1a. This budget bears the heading "out-of-pocket costs" because it includes all the items, and only those items, for which you or your parents will actually have to pay during the year.

Your own out-of-pocket costs may be considerably higher or lower than these average figures, but chances are that the items in this budget are the ones that will come to your mind if you are asked about the matter. As you begin to think in economic terms, however, you may want to revise your budget in accordance with the concept of opportunity costs. Which of the items in Exhibit 1.1a represent opportunities foregone in order to go to college? Are there any foregone opportunities that are missing from the table? To see the answers, compare this out-of-pocket budget with the opportunity cost budget shown in Exhibit 1.1b. The first three items in the out-of-pocket budget show up again in the opportunity cost budget. In order to spend $3,017 on tuition and fees and $246 on books and supplies, you have to give up the opportunity to buy other goods and services, say a car or a house. In order to spend $271 getting to and from college, you have to pass up the opportunity to travel somewhere else or to spend the money on something other than travel. But the last two items in the out-of-pocket budget are not opportunity costs of college. By spending $2,228 on room, board, and personal expenses during the year, you are not really giving up an opportunity to do something that you could have done if you had not gone to college. Whether you went to college or not, you would have to eat, to live somewhere, to buy clothing. Because these are expenses you would have to meet in any case, they are not specific opportunity costs of going to college.

Thinking about what you would have done if you had not gone to college suggests one major item that must be added to your opportunity cost budget and that does not show up at all in the out-of-pocket budget. If you had not gone to college, you probably would have taken a job and started earning money soon after leaving high school. The level of average weekly earnings for sixteen to twenty-four year olds is about $175. Multiplying this by thirty-two weeks (assum-

Exhibit 1.1
Budget for one year at college

a. Budget of Out-of-Pocket Costs[a]

Tuition and fees	$3,017
Books and supplies	246
Transportation to and from home	271
Room and board	1,704
Personal expenses	524
Total out-of-pocket costs	$5,762

b. Budget of Opportunity Costs

Tuition and fees	$3,017
Books and supplies	246
Transportation to and from home	271
Foregone income	5,600
Total opportunity costs	$9,134

[a] Based on average costs for private four-year colleges, as reported in *Student Expenses at Postsecondary Institutions, 1978–79* (New York: College Entrance Examination Board, 1978), Tables 1–5, projected to 1980–81 using factors given in Tables 11 and 13.

ing you work during vacation if you go to college) comes to $5,600 per year of college. These potential earnings are something you have to forego to go to college, so the item appears in the opportunity cost budget.

Which budget you use, of course, depends on what kind of decision you are making. If you are already committed to college and are simply doing your financial planning for the year, then you will use the out-of-pocket cost budget to make sure you have enough in savings, scholarships, loans, and parents' contributions to make ends meet. But suppose you are making the more basic economic decision of whether to go to college or to pursue some alternative career pattern that does not require college. Then it is the opportunity cost of college that you should take into account, weighing this cost against the benefit of greater earnings or greater personal satisfaction that you expect to get from a college degree.

Trade-offs The discussion of opportunity cost offers a good chance to show how economists use diagrams to put their ideas across vividly.[1] Case 1.1 shows that a college education involves certain opportunity costs, which suggests that for the economy as a whole, there is a trade-off between producing education and producing other desired goods. The simple diagram in Exhibit 1.2 can give a visual image of what that trade-off is like. The horizontal axis of the figure measures the quantity of education produced in terms of the number of college graduates produced per year. The vertical axis measures the production of all other goods in billions of dollars per year. Any combination of education and other goods that is produced in the economy in some year can be shown as a point in the space between the two axes. For example, the production of 10 million college graduates and $500 billion worth of other goods is represented by Point E.

[1]For a quick brush-up on how to work with graphs, see the Appendix to Chapter 1.

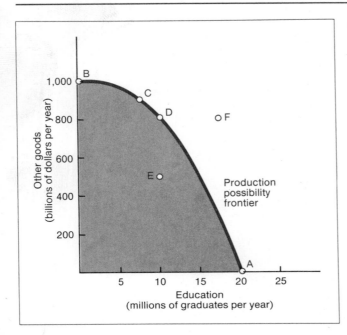

Exhibit 1.2

A production possibility frontier for education and other goods

This diagram shows a production possibility frontier for education and other goods. Point A represents the maximum production of education if no other goods are produced, and Point B represents the maximum production of other goods if no education is produced. A, B, C, D, and all other points along the frontier, as well as points such as E in the shaded area under it, are possible. Points such as F, outside the frontier, are not possible given the quantity and quality of resources available.

The Production Possibility Frontier Even if all people devoted all their time and resources to education, there would be a limit to the quantity of education that could be produced each year. For the sake of illustration, suppose that the limit is 20 million graduates per year. The extreme possibility of producing 20 million graduates and nothing else is shown by Point A in Exhibit 1.2. The maximum rate of output of other goods if no resources at all are put into education is $1,000 billion, shown by Point B. Between these two extremes is a whole range of possibilities for producing education and other goods in combination. These intermediate possibilities are represented by points such as C and D, which fall along the curve in the diagram. This curve is called a **production possibility frontier.**

It is a *frontier* because it is a boundary between the combinations of education and other goods that can be produced and the combinations that cannot possibly be produced. Points A, B, C, and D, which lie right on the curve, represent combinations of education and other goods that can be produced. A combination such as that represented by Point E in the shaded area under the production possibility frontier can be produced even if some resources remain unemployed or are used wastefully. In contrast, a combination of education and other goods such as that represented by Point F cannot possibly be produced in one year. All the points outside the shaded area are impossible.

At any point along the production possibility frontier, there is a trade-off between education and other goods. More of one cannot be produced without giving up some of the other. For example, suppose we began at Point C, where 8 million students were graduating from college each year and $900 billion of other goods were being produced. If we wanted to increase the output of graduates by 10 million per year, we would have to give up some other goods and use those resources to build classrooms, print books, and staff lecture halls. What is more, we would lose the output those students could have produced if they had taken jobs rather than going to class nine months out of the year. That would move us to Point D, which represents 10 million graduates and only $800 billion of other goods.

Now we can see how the production possibility curve allows us to visualize the concept of opportunity cost. In moving from C to D on the production possibility frontier, 2 million extra graduates can be obtained at the opportunity cost of $100 billion in other goods. Putting this on a per student basis, the opportunity cost of college education (in the range between C and D) is approximately $50,000 per additional graduate. Geometrically, the opportunity cost of education in terms of other goods is given by the slope of the production possibility frontier.

Why Is the Frontier Curved? Why is the production possibility frontier a curve rather than a straight line? If it were a straight line, that would mean that the opportunity cost of educating an additional college graduate, measured in terms of other goods, would be the same no matter how people chose to divide their efforts and resources between education and other activities. Why is this not the case?

The answer is that not all resources are **homogeneous.** That is, individual units of any resource are not all alike. Most importantly, people are not all alike. Some are suited to specializing in the production of one thing; others are

Production possibility frontier A curve showing the possible combinations of goods that can be produced by an economy, given the quantity and quality of factors of production available.

Homogeneous Having the property that every unit is just like every other unit.

suited to something else. It is easy to see why this puts a curve in the production possibility frontier.

Imagine that starting today we wanted to increase the output of college graduates. The first thing we would need would be more teachers. The opportunity cost of getting the first few teachers would be low. We could call on professors who had just retired, on their spouses who were qualified but not currently working, or on graduate students who could combine teaching with learning. Few other goods would be lost by engaging these people. Next we might turn to industry and hire chemists, engineers, or economists working there to staff additional classrooms. These people might make equally good teachers, but they would be sorely missed by the firms that had employed them, and there would be a noticeable drop in the output of other goods. The opportunity cost of education would rise, and the production possibility curve would begin to bend as we moved along it.

Pretty soon we would have to start calling in people who were not even well-qualified to be teachers, even though they might be doing a good job at something else. These people would not add much to the output of education, but a lot would be lost elsewhere. The production possibility frontier would bend still more sharply. In short, differences of ability and specialization among people (and differences among units of other factors) can be counted on to give the production possibility frontier its typical bowed-out shape.

The Division of Labor Because people are not interchangeable parts, we must pay careful attention to the division of labor—who gets which job—if we are to do well in our struggle against scarcity. Once again we can use the production possibility frontier to show why. Suppose that for some reason or other we chose to devote half the nation's labor power to producing education and half to producing other goods, but that we used the wrong half in each place. Skilled

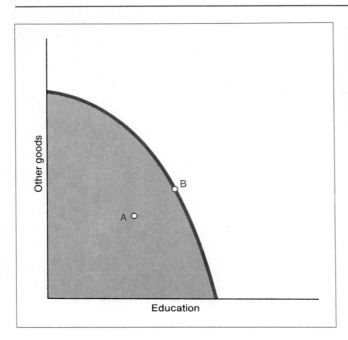

Exhibit 1.3
Effects of a poorly organized division of labor
Poor organization of the division of labor can cause the economy to drop off the production possibility frontier and end up at an interior point such as A in this diagram. This could happen even if all resources were fully employed, just because the right people were not doing the right jobs. With an improved organization of the division of labor, the economy could end up at Point B.

production workers would awkwardly mumble their way through lecture notes on Greek history, while professors got their thumbs jammed in delicate factory machinery. We would not produce as much as possible of either education or other goods. The economy would drop right off the production possibility frontier and end up at some interior point, such as Point A in Exhibit 1.3. Just by using the proper division of labor, we could produce the output combination indicated by Point B and have more of both goods.

More than two hundred years ago, Adam Smith began the most famous economics book of all time with an example emphasizing the importance of the division of labor. Smith had visited a pin factory and had seen that when one worker specialized in putting heads on the pins, another in sharpening the points, another in placing them on cards, and so on, they all could produce a hundred times more than could the same number of people working separately. Smith went on to show how free markets and private enterprise solve the problem of the division of labor simply by attracting people into the occupations where their potential earnings are greatest. Beginning with Chapter 2, this book will spend many chapters doing the same thing and will have time left over for a look at how governments sometimes try to improve on the market by substituting their own judgments concerning the division of labor.

Adam Smith was born in Kirkaldy, on the east coast of Scotland. He studied first at Glasgow University and then at Oxford. In those days, the universities of Scotland were greater centers of learning than those of England, so Smith returned to the north after finishing his studies at Oxford and obtained a chair at Glasgow. It was not, of course, a chair in economics. Economics had not yet been invented as a distinct discipline, and besides, it was not yet Smith's major interest. His specialty was moral philosophy.

During his long career, Smith wrote just two books. It was his good fortune, however, to have both bring him immediate fame. His first book was *The Theory of Moral Sentiments,* published in 1759. His second, *The Wealth of Nations,* appeared seventeen years later, in 1776. David Hume, a friend of Smith's, commented that "the reading of it necessarily requires so much attention, and the public is disposed to give so little, that I shall still doubt for some time of its being at first very popular." Hume, however, was wrong. The book sold well from the start.

The task Smith set himself first of all was to explain the workings of the economic system—that is, the sources of the "wealth of nations." The greatest source, he discovered, was the division of labor. Chapter 1 opened with the observation that "the greatest improvement in the productive powers of labor, and the greater part of the skill, dexterity, and judgment with which it is anywhere directed, or applied, seem to have been the effects of the division of labor." He then went on to give his famous pin factory example.

Adam Smith (1723–1790)

It was not enough for Smith to just describe the division of labor, however. He wanted to explain how it came about. His explanation was highly characteristic:

This division of labor, from which so many advantages are derived, is not originally the effect of any human wisdom, which foresees and intends that general opulence to which it gives occasion. It is the necessary, though very slow and gradual consequence of a certain propensity in human nature which has in view no such extensive utility; the propensity to truck, barter, and exchange one thing for another.

Here, for the first time in the book, Smith emphasized the importance of the unintended consequences of human action: Each person acting in the marketplace has only narrow ends in mind, but the joint result of the actions of everyone is a general benefit that none intended.

As *The Wealth of Nations* progressed, Smith added another theme, that of the benefits of economic liberty. The free, spontaneous interaction of people in the marketplace is not just one way to bring about the general benefit of mankind; it is the best way. Government attempts to guide or regulate the market end up doing more harm than good. Smith especially attacked the privileges of legally protected monopolies, the Poor Laws (which he saw as inhibiting the mobility of labor), and the apprenticeship system (which worked against free entry into occupations). All such restraints on the market tended to force trade into "un-natural" and less beneficial channels.

Smith's book has meant various things to various people. To some it has been a handbook of laissez-faire liberalism. To others, it has been the fountainhead of economic science. Still others have found it, not without reason, to be unoriginal and crammed with errors. Whatever its faults, it is a book that continues to be read and debated. In 1976, its bicentennial brought leading economists from all over the world to Glasgow to pay tribute to the absentminded professor of moral philosophy who had lectured there so long before.

The Margin

Margin, marginal Terms referring to the effects of making a small increase in any economic activity. See glossary entries *Marginal cost, Marginal product,* and so on.

We have not yet mentioned one concept that has wide applicability to economic decision making: the idea of the **margin.** Whenever economists talk about the margin or use the adjective *marginal,* they are referring to the effects of making a small increase or decrease in some economic activity. *Margin* is an idea that is hard to define abstractly but easy to illustrate. When we talk about the "marginal cost" of producing cars at General Motors, we are referring to the added cost of producing one more car beyond the limit of the number currently being produced. When we speak of the "marginal benefit" of sewage treatment in a certain river basin, we mean the extra benefit of making a small increase in the effort put into sewage treatment in the area. These terms and quite a few others will be defined more precisely in later chapters. For now, though, one example will give a general idea of why thinking in terms of the margin is important.

Case 1.2
Marginal Cost Pricing of Domestic Oil

In the winter of 1978–79, political turmoil in Iran threatened the United States with a new energy crisis. This caused people to become more concerned than ever about the price of oil and the cost of obtaining it. But what was the cost of oil? The matter was obscured by a complex system of oil price controls that had been in force since the early 1970s.

Under the system of price controls, so-called old oil—that produced from wells drilled before 1972—could be sold to refiners for no more than about $5.80 per barrel. New oil from more recently drilled wells could be sold for as much as $12.85 per barrel. Because there was not enough of either old or new oil to supply the energy needs of the U.S. economy, huge quantities of oil were being imported at the world market price, which stood at about $16.25 per barrel in the spring of 1979. The regulations required that the price paid by the public for products refined from this oil be based on the *average* cost to the refiners of oil from all the various sources. That average worked out to about $10 per barrel.

As the world oil price rose higher, this system of average cost pricing for petroleum products came under increasingly strong attack from economists. Instead of being priced at the average cost from all sources, they said, prices should reflect the *marginal* cost of oil to the U.S. economy—that is, the cost of getting the extra barrel of oil needed to replace each barrel consumed. For all practical purposes, an extra barrel of oil consumed could be replaced only with imported oil. That meant the marginal cost of oil to the economy was the world market price of $16.25 per barrel. (A small amount of additional oil could be produced domestically using exotic secondary recovery technology, but this too was very expensive.)

By keeping the price of petroleum products below the marginal cost of replacing what was consumed, the critics argued, price controls were causing oil to be used wastefully. Some plants that would have switched to coal if they had had to pay $16.25 a barrel for oil were content to continue burning oil at $10 per barrel. With heating oil selling for a price below its marginal cost, homeowners and builders did not find it worthwhile to insulate homes as well as they would have if fuel prices had been higher. And with gasoline prices based on an artificially low cost for crude oil, motorists had little incentive to change their driving habits or buy small cars.

After listening to these arguments, the Carter administration decided in April that average cost pricing would have to go. Because raising domestic oil prices to the world level would add to inflationary pressures, at least in the short run, the decision was a sensitive one. But inflation seemed less of an evil than was the ever-increasing reliance on imported oil. So the administration began a delicate process of political negotiation and compromise that, it was hoped, would lead to a timetable for gradually introducing marginal cost pricing of oil to the U.S. economy.

ECONOMIC SCIENCE AND ECONOMIC POLICY

A great part of what one reads about economics in the newspapers or hears about it on television is focused on specific problems of economic policy. Should the federal government spend more money and run a larger budget deficit? Should price controls on oil be lifted in the hope of increasing production and decreasing consumption? Should the government encourage or discourage exports of U.S. agricultural products? If we are to learn the economic way of thinking, we must learn how economists think about policy issues as well as how they think about pure theory.

The mention of economic policies such as price controls or budget deficits tends to set little lights labeled ''hurrah'' or ''ugh'' flashing in our minds. Sometimes our mental circuits work so fast that we do not notice that, between the mention of the policy and the flashing of the lights, a chain of thinking somewhat like the following must occur:
1. If Policy X is followed, Outcome Y will result.
2. Outcome Y is a good (or bad) thing.
3. Therefore, hurrah (or ugh) for Policy X.
In order to understand the contents of this book and how to put them to work, it is important to understand the logic of the three-step chain of thinking. To that end, we will go through it one step at a time.

Positive Economics
Economic science cannot foretell the future, but it can offer predictions of the ''if, then'' form: ''If A occurs, then B will occur, other things being equal.'' An economist might, then, make the assertion: ''If government spending were increased, then unemployment would decline, as long as no other changes in economic conditions occurred in the meantime.'' Such a statement is sometimes called a **scientific prediction.** It is a statement of cause and effect but one that is valid only under specified conditions. In making scientific predictions of this form, economists rarely attempt to foretell whether A will actually occur or whether other things will actually remain constant.

Scientific prediction A conditional prediction having the form ''if A, then B, other things being equal.''

Positive economics The part of economics limited to making scientific predictions and purely descriptive statements.

When economists limit their attention to statements that are pure scientific predictions, they are said to be practicing **positive economics.** All sound analysis of economic policy must begin with positive economics as step 1.

Resolving Disagreements Of course, economists sometimes disagree about whether a certain scientific prediction is valid. In fact, a great deal of the day-to-day work in which economists engage is directed toward resolving disagreements on matters of positive economics. Some scientific disagreements concern matters of pure theory and are much like the disagreements among mathematicians concerning whether some unproved theorem is true or false. These disputes can, in time, be resolved by a process in which each party tries to state the reasoning as carefully as possible or to detect logical errors.

Empirical A term referring to data or methods based on observation of actual past experience or on controlled experiments.

Econometrician A specialist in the statistical analysis of economic data.

Frequently, economists try to resolve disputes over matters of positive economics by using **empirical** methods. That means looking at evidence—statistical or otherwise—based on observation of past experience. Much of this work is done by specialists in the statistical analysis of economic data who are called **econometricians.** Suppose that the scientific prediction in dispute said: "If government spending were to increase, then unemployment would decline, other things being equal." An econometrician might enter the debate with the announcement that, according to a study of postwar data on the U.S. economy, an increase in government expenditure has, in fact, been consistently associated with a decline in unemployment, taking into account the probable influence of other factors. Or the econometrician might assert that the data reveal no systematic association at all between government spending and unemployment when advanced statistical techniques are used to eliminate the influence of other changes in economic conditions. Questions of this sort are not usually resolved by a single empirical study, but repeated studies and the gradual accumulation of evidence serve to narrow areas of disagreement and contribute to scientific progress in economics.

Normative Economics

A positive economic statement of the type "if Policy X, then Outcome Y" cannot by itself resolve the issue of whether Policy X is desirable. To come to a conclusion on the desirability of the policy, one must decide whether Outcome Y is good or bad. When economists make statements of the type "Outcome Y is good," they are engaging in **normative economics.**

Normative economics The part of economics devoted to making value judgments about what economic policies or conditions are good or bad.

Most economists do not consider themselves experts in ethical theory, and few would be prepared to defend their normative statements with the same rigor and clarity they would use to defend their positive economic analysis. Nonetheless, economists who wish to speak persuasively on the subject of economic policy should be able at least to point to some general ethical principles on which their normative conclusions might plausibly be based. Economists who base their like or dislike of a particular policy on arbitrary whims are less likely to be listened to than are those who speak in terms of consistent and well thought out values. With this in mind, we will look at a few basic ideas that frequently arise in discussions of normative economics.

Efficiency The property of producing or acting with a minimum of expense, waste, and effort.

The Efficiency Standard The standard of **efficiency** occupies a prominent place among those standards by which economists judge the performance of the systems they observe. In its most general sense, the word *efficiency* means the property of producing or acting with a minimum of expense, waste, and effort. A good economic example of the difference between efficiency and inefficiency appeared in Exhibit 1.3. That diagram showed how a badly organized division of labor could cause the economy to drop off the production possibility frontier and end up at an *inefficient* interior point. A better division of labor would have permitted the production of more output with the same quantity of inputs and thus would have been more efficient.

Efficiency and Equity Most economists think that efficiency itself is a good thing. This does not mean, however, that any policy promoting efficiency is automatically a good policy. Other norms and values must be introduced into policy analysis to supplement the efficiency standard. Among the most important of the supplementary standards are those referred to in everyday speech as equity, merit, and justice.

The standard of equity has two roles to play in relation to the standard of efficiency. First, it may be used to supplement the efficiency standard in cases where the choice is between policies that are equally efficient. Efficiency alone defines not a single, unique pattern of economic life but only a range of possible patterns. Different but equally efficient patterns often involve different distributions of welfare among specific individuals. In one efficient state of the world, Jones may be rich and Smith poor; in another, Smith may be rich and Jones poor; in a third, Jones and Smith may be equally well-off. When such alternatives confront us, we may be led to reason like this:

1. Policies X and Y produce equally efficient outcomes but imply different distributions of individual welfare.
2. The distributional outcome of Policy X is more equitable.
3. Therefore, let us undertake Policy X.

A second possible use for the criterion of equity is to override the criterion of efficiency. For many people, efficiency is a goal that should not be pursued at the expense of equity but that should, if needed, be sacrificed to the pursuit of equity. In such cases, the logic might run as follows:

1. Policy X would be bad for efficiency but would help achieve greater equity.
2. The loss of efficiency is unfortunate, but the gain in equity outweighs it.
3. Therefore, in the absence of a policy that will serve both goals at once, go ahead with Policy X.

A Difficulty Whichever way it is used, the concept of equity plays an important role in policy analysis. Using it, however, involves a difficulty that did not occur in the case of efficiency. The difficulty is that equity has no universally agreed-upon meaning. It means different things to different people, depending on the values they hold and the ideologies they profess. Few things are more harmful to intelligent debate on questions of economic policy than for the parties to a discussion to use the same word to mean different things. The word *equity* and the associated words *merit* and *justice* may be the cause of more misunderstandings than any other terms in economics.

In the interest of avoiding such misunderstandings, we might wish to establish beyond doubt that a particular meaning of *equity* is the right one. But to attempt it would take us deep into details of philosophy and far from the main subject of this book. Instead we will simply suggest two meanings of the equity concept (or two classes of meanings within which are many minor variations) without choosing between them.

Distributive justice The principle of distribution according to innate merit. Roughly, the principle of "from each according to abilities, to each according to needs."

Equity as Distributive Justice The first meaning of *equity* equates it to **distributive justice.** The phrase "from each according to abilities, to each according to needs" gives a rough idea of what the principle of distributive justice means. The concept is based on the idea of innate merit; that is, all people are presumed—solely by virtue of their birth, their existence, and their common humanity—to merit some share of the total stream of goods and services turned out by the economic system. An improvement on the phrase is "to each according to innate merits."

Just what each person's innate merits are is a point that gives rise to many variations on the idea of distributive justice. For example, some people believe that all economic goods should be distributed equally among all members of society. Others think that a person's innate claims on economic goods ought to be limited to some minimum standard of living and are willing to see any surplus above this minimum distributed according to other principles. Still others conceive of innate merits as being limited to certain specific types of goods. Each person might have, for example, an innate claim to a share of food, shelter, medical care, and education, but no such claim to even a minimum share of tobacco, imported wine, or manufacturing services.

Market justice The principle of distribution according to acquired merit. The observance of property rights and the honoring of contracts. Roughly, the principle of "value for value."

Equity as Market Justice The second meaning of *equity* makes it equivalent to what can be called commutative justice, or, more simply, **market justice.** The justice of the marketplace is *value for value;* market justice is based on the idea of acquired merit. Individuals have no innate claim to a share in the total economic output but merit only whatever share they acquire through production, exchange, or voluntary donation.

The idea of market justice gives a special significance to the concepts of property and contract. Suppose that the entire mass of economic goods is divided up as the properties of specific individuals (or voluntary associations of individuals), so that for every loaf of bread, some person stands ready to say, "This bread is mine—my property to use and to exclude others from using." Then the central meaning of *market justice* becomes the movement of property from hand to hand only by fair contract (except for voluntary gifts). *Fair contract* means that each party must be satisfied that the value to him or her of the property received is at least as great as the value of the property given up. So market justice can be summed up as the observance of property rights and the honoring of contracts.

Economic Ideology

Economic ideology A set of judgments and beliefs concerning efficiency, market justice, and distributive justice as goals of economic policy, together with a set of prejudices or beliefs concerning matters of positive economics.

Each person carries out the job of policy analysis, whether in a systematic or a casual way, within a personal framework of thought that can be called an **economic ideology.** An economic ideology includes a person's judgments concerning the relative priority (and exact interpretation) of distributive justice and market justice and attitudes toward the relative importance of equity and efficiency as goals of economic policy. Often, it also includes a set of prejudices and more or less rationally founded beliefs concerning matters of positive economics. Liberalism, Marxism, libertarianism, conservatism—these and many other "isms" are the labels we use to refer to economic ideologies.

To deal with every policy issue from all possible ideological points of view would be too much to attempt in this book. Instead, we will content ourselves for the most part with pointing out the implications of various policies in terms of the standards of efficiency and equity just discussed. People will have to reach their own conclusions on the ideological level.

Why Distinguish between Positive and Normative Economics?

When policy analysis is broken down into a three-step process in which positive and normative elements are clearly separated, orderly debate on important economic issues is made easier in several ways. First, the breakdown of policy analysis into positive and normative components makes it clear that disagreements on policy questions can arise from two different sources. If you and I disagree as to whether Policy X is good or bad, it may be either because we disagree on the positive issue of whether Policy X will, in fact, result in Outcome Y or because we disagree on the normative issue of whether Outcome Y is good or bad. Our analysis also indicates that a particular sort of spurious agreement could arise between us: You might think that Policy X will cause Outcome Y and that Y is good, whereas I might think Y is bad but that X will not cause it! This sort of thing occurs surprisingly often. In any event, it is clear that intelligent policy analysis requires careful thinking.

Second, if a positive statement is associated with an unpopular normative position, it is less likely to gain acceptance. Critics must be persuaded that both are valid. People are less likely to pay serious attention to the claim that fluoridation of water harms their bodies when its opponents also claim that fluoridation is an evil communist plot. A positive statement divorced from any normative view is not disadvantaged in this way.

Third, when a positive statement is associated with a popular normative position, it may be accepted too uncritically. Why? Because reactions to value judgments are much more pronounced than are reactions to positive statements, so that value judgments surreptitiously tend to dominate thought. People are all too likely to accept a "what is" statement from someone who agrees with them about "what ought to be." This natural reaction helps explain the inability of economists to persuade politicians that increases in the legal minimum wage have worsened the employment opportunities of poor people. Politicians say they want to help the poor and resent being informed that a method they support has not worked. Perhaps they even suspect that economists critical of minimum wages do not share their values. They apparently believe that minimum wage laws help the poor simply because they believe that the poor ought to be helped.

CONCLUSIONS

In a once-over fashion, this chapter has tried to give some idea of the kinds of things to which economists are sensitive when they look at the world around them. It has shown that economists think in terms of scarcity, choice, and trade-offs. It has offered some simple examples of how economists use diagrams to make it easier to visualize abstract concepts in a concrete form. It has explained how to distinguish between positive and normative economics and why that distinction is important. What can be said now to sum it all up?

If there is one single feature of overriding importance about the economic way of thinking, it is this: *Economics is about people.* Individual people are the units of analysis in all economic theory. Every economic principle developed in this book must be a statement about the way individuals make choices, struggle with the problem of scarcity, and respond to changes in their environment. And all economic policies must be judged in terms of their impact on the welfare of individual people.

This does not mean that economists are all rugged individualists, in the sense that they are indifferent to social issues, or that they are political know-nothings who do not care about the national interest. What it does mean is that economic science (and all valid social science, for that matter) is based on the recognition that society and the nation have no existence and no importance apart from the individual people of which they are composed. Society is not a super-being, and the nation is not a sentient creature capable of feeling pain when a pin is stuck in the national thumb. They are only the names of groups of which all people are equal members. *We* are what economics is all about.

SUMMARY

1. Learning economics means learning to look at human actions and interactions in a special way, singling out some features for close examination and placing others in the background. The economic way of thinking places particular emphasis on how people's actions are influenced by the fact of scarcity and the necessity of choice.

2. All economic decisions can be described in terms of objectives, alternatives, and constraints. The terms are not equally well-defined in all decision making situations, however. Economic decision making in which objectives, alternatives, and constraints are all well-defined and known to the decision maker is called pure economizing. Economic decision making in which they are less well-defined may require the decision maker to explore the situation, be alert to new possibilities, develop new ways of overcoming constraints, take chances, and so on. These activities are referred to as entrepreneurship.

3. The production possibility frontier shows which combinations of goods can be produced and which cannot. Its slope shows the opportunity cost of the good measured on the horizontal axis in terms of the good measured on the vertical axis. The position of the production possibility frontier depends on the quantity and quality of resources available to an economy. Over time, the frontier may expand, and the economy may grow. If the division of labor is not organized efficiently, the economy may drop off the production possibility frontier and end up at an interior point.

4. Positive economics cannot foretell the future, but it can offer scientific predictions in the form "if A occurs, then B will occur, other things being equal." Disputes in positive economics can, in principle, be resolved by reasoned discussion or by the examination of statistical data.

5. Normative economics is concerned with statements about what ought to be. Most economists think that efficiency is, in itself, a worthy goal of economic policy. The efficiency standard must, however, be supplemented by considerations of equity when policy decisions are to be made. There is no

universal agreement on what equity means. Some economists maintain that equity is primarily a matter of distributive justice; others emphasize market justice. Partly because of such disagreements on the meaning of *equity*, economists try to distinguish carefully between their positive statements and their normative statements.

6. Economics is about people. All economic principles must be framed in terms of the way individuals make choices and respond to changes in their environment, and all economic policies must be judged in terms of their impact on the welfare of individual people.

DISCUSSION QUESTIONS

1. Suppose you want to get as high a grade-point average as you can this term; yet your time and abilities are limited. Would it be possible to look at the way you spend your time as an economic problem? What constraints and alternative activities do you face? What is the opportunity cost of getting higher grades?

2. Suppose you won a lottery prize of $20 million. Would this solve all your personal economic problems of scarcity? Explain.

3. Can you give some real-world examples of how the economy, a firm, or even an individual might be operating inside the production possibility curve?

4. Can it be said that economics is about money or about goods and services rather than about people? Explain.

5. Do the animals in a forest face an economic problem? What are their objectives, constraints, and alternatives? What has happened to their economic problems as people have impinged on their habitat? Is economics about nonpeople too?

6. Should we all be entitled to our fair share of the earth's produce? Would this question be better stated if we replace "the earth's produce" with "the goods and services that Smith and Jones and Jansen and M'Boye and Li Ha Ching and . . . [listing all the earth's 4 billion people by name] produce"? To make it still easier, suppose that Smith and Jones are the only two people on earth. Is Smith entitled to a fair share of what Jones produces and vice versa?

7. Review Case 1.2. Looking at the oil situation from an economy-wide point of view, what is the opportunity cost of consuming a barrel of oil? Under price controls, is the opportunity cost of oil to the individual consumer the same as the opportunity cost of oil as seen from an economy-wide viewpoint?

8. Refer again to Case 1.2. Try to cast the argument of price control critics in terms of the three-step chain of reasoning given later in the chapter. Some people opposed marginal cost pricing of oil on the ground that higher prices would be particularly burdensome to low-income consumers. State this argument in terms of the three-step chain of reasoning.

APPENDIX TO CHAPTER 1
WORKING WITH GRAPHS

HOW ECONOMISTS USE GRAPHS

At one of our country's well-known colleges, the students have their own names for all the courses. They call the astronomy course "stars," the geology course "rocks," and the biology course "frogs." Their name for the economics course is "graphs and laughs." This choice of names indicates two things. First, it shows that the students think the professor has a sense of humor. Second, it shows that in the minds of students, economics is a matter of learning about graphs in the same sense that astronomy is a matter of learning about stars or geology a matter of learning about rocks.

To begin, then, we can say that economics is not about graphs; it is about people. It is about the way people make choices, use resources, and cooperate with one another in an effort to overcome the universal problem of scarcity. Economics is a social science, not an offshoot of analytic geometry.

The skeptical reader may reply, "If economics is not about graphs, why are there so many of them in this book?" The answer is that economists use graphs to illustrate the theories they develop about people's economic behavior in order to make them vivid, eye-catching, and easy to remember. Everything that can be said in the form of a graph can also be said in words, but saying something two different ways is a proven aid to learning. The purpose of this appendix is to show how to make maximum use of an important learning aid by explaining how to work with graphs.

PAIRS OF NUMBERS AND POINTS

The first thing to learn is how to use points on a graph to represent pairs of numbers. Consider Exhibit 1A.1. The small table in that exhibit presents six pairs of numbers. The two columns are labeled x and y. The first number in each pair is called the x *value*, and the second is called the y *value*. Each pair of numbers is labeled with a capital letter A through E. Pair A has an x value of 2 and a y value of 3; Pair B has an x value of 4 and a y value of 4, and so on.

Next to the table is a diagram. The lines placed at right angles to one another along the bottom and the left-hand side of the diagram are called *coordinate axes*. The horizontal axis is marked off into units and is used for measuring the x value, while the vertical axis is marked off into units for measuring the y value. In the space between these axes, each lettered pair of numbers from the table can be represented as a lettered point. For example, to put Point A in place, go two units to the right along the horizontal axis to represent the x value of 2 and then three units straight up, parallel to the vertical axis, to represent the y value of 3. The other points are placed the same way.

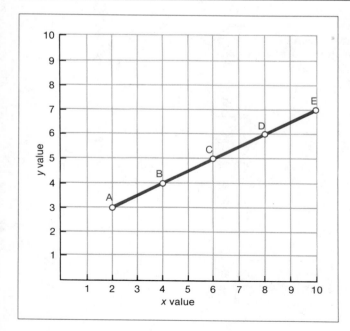

Exhibit 1A.1

Pairs of numbers and points
Each lettered pair of numbers in the table corresponds to a lettered point on the graph. The x value of each point corresponds to the horizontal distance of the point from the vertical axis, and the y value corresponds to the vertical distance from the horizontal axis.

	x	y
A	2	3
B	4	4
C	6	5
D	8	6
E	10	7

Usually, the visual effect of a graph is improved by connecting the points with a smooth line or curve. When this is done (as shown in the diagram), it can be seen at a glance that as the x value increases, the y value also tends to increase.

COMMON ECONOMIC GRAPHS

Economics is interested not in abstract relationships between x's and y's but in relationships concerning people and the things they do under various conditions. This means that graphs in economics are labeled in terms of the ideas used in putting together economic theories. Exhibit 1A.2 shows three common ways of labeling coordinate axes. Each of these will be encountered many times in this book.

Exhibit 1A.2a represents the relationship between the price of subway tokens in some city and the number of people who choose to ride the subway each day at any given price. The table shows that as the price of tokens goes up, fewer people choose to ride the subway. The graph shows the same thing. As a matter of tradition in economics, whenever a graph involves both money values and quantity units, the vertical axis is used to measure the money value (in this case, the price of subway tokens) and the horizontal axis to measure the quantity units (in this case, the number of riders per day).

Exhibit 1A.2b uses quantity units on both axes. Here, the problem is to represent the various combinations of milkshakes and hamburgers that can be bought at the local carry-out when milkshakes cost $.50 each, hamburgers cost $.50 each, and the buyer has exactly $2.50 to spend on lunch. The table shows that the possibilities are five burgers and no shakes, four burgers and one shake, three burgers and two shakes, and so on.

The graph offers a visual picture of the "menu" to choose from, given limited money to spend. The points from the table are drawn in and labeled, and any can be chosen. A diagonal line has been sketched in to connect these points, and if the purchase of parts of hamburgers and milkshakes is allowed, the buyer can choose from among all the points along this line (for example, 2.5 burgers and 2.5 shakes). The buyer who wanted to have some money left over could purchase a lunch represented by a point within the shaded area, such as Point G (which stands for two burgers and one shake and costs just $1.50). But unless the buyer gets more money, points outside the shaded area cannot be chosen.

Exhibit 1A.2c illustrates still another kind of graph frequently used in economics—one showing how some magnitude varies over time. This graph indicates what happened to the unemployment rate of nonwhite teenage males over the years 1969–78. The horizontal axis is used to represent the passage of time and the vertical axis to measure the percentage of nonwhite teenage males officially classified as unemployed. Graphs like this are good for getting a quick idea of trends over time. Although teenage unemployment has had its ups and downs in recent years, the trend during the 1970s was clearly upward.

SLOPES

When talking about graphs, it is frequently convenient to describe lines or curves in terms of their *slopes*. The slope of a straight line drawn between two points is defined as the ratio of the change in the y value to the change in the x value between two points. In Exhibit 1A.3, for example, the slope of the line drawn between Points A and B is 2. The y value changes by six units between these two points, while the x value changes by only three units. The slope is the ratio $6/3 = 2$.

When a line slants downward like the line between Points C and D in Exhibit 1A.3, the x value and the y value change in opposite directions. Going from Point C to Point D, the y value changes by -2 (that is, it decreases by two units), while the x value changes by $+4$ (that is, it increases by four units). The slope of this line is the ratio $-2/4 = -1/2$. A downward-sloping line such as this is said to have a negative slope.

The slope of a curved line, unlike that of a straight line, varies from point to point. The slope of a curve at any given point is defined as the slope of a straight line drawn tangent to the curve at that point. (A tangent line is one just touching the curve

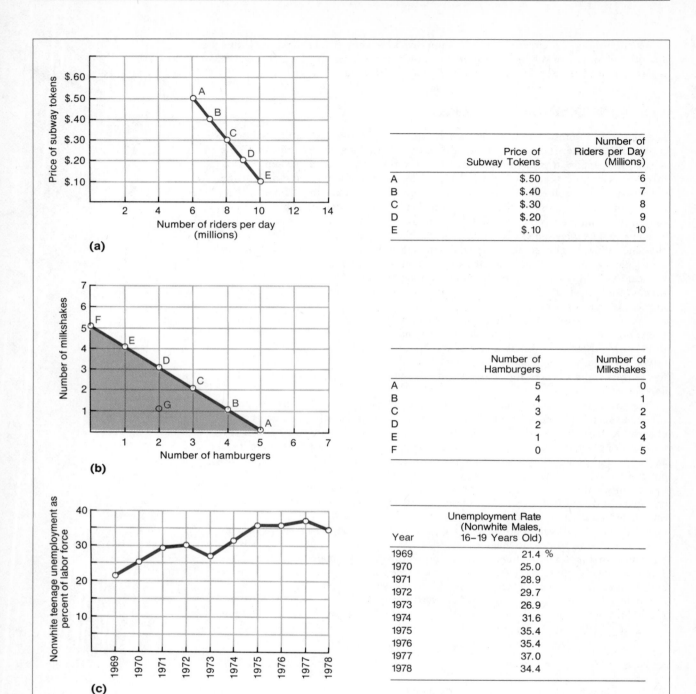

	Price of Subway Tokens	Number of Riders per Day (Millions)
A	$.50	6
B	$.40	7
C	$.30	8
D	$.20	9
E	$.10	10

(a)

	Number of Hamburgers	Number of Milkshakes
A	5	0
B	4	1
C	3	2
D	2	3
E	1	4
F	0	5

(b)

Year	Unemployment Rate (Nonwhite Males, 16–19 Years Old)
1969	21.4 %
1970	25.0
1971	28.9
1972	29.7
1973	26.9
1974	31.6
1975	35.4
1976	35.4
1977	37.0
1978	34.4

(c)

Exhibit 1A.2

Three typical economic graphs

This exhibit shows three graphs typical of those used in economics. Part a shows the relationship between the price of tokens and the number of riders per day on a certain city subway system. When a graph shows the relationship between a price and a quantity, it is conventional to put the price on the vertical axis. Part b shows the possible choices open to a person who has $2.50 to spend on lunch and can buy hamburgers at $.50 each or milkshakes at $.50 each. Part c shows how a graph can be used to represent change over time.

Source: Part c is from President's Council of Economic Advisers, *Economic Report of the President* (Washington, D.C.: Government Printing Office, 1979). Table B–30.

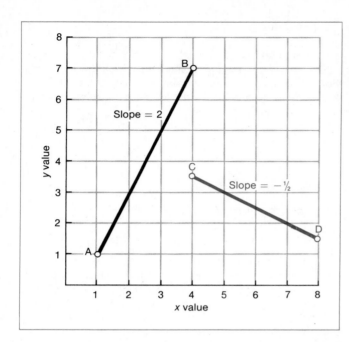

Exhibit 1A.3
Slopes of lines
The slope of a straight line drawn between two points is defined as the ratio of the change in the *y* value to the change in the *x* value between the two points. For example, the line drawn between Points A and B in this exhibit has a slope of +2, whereas the line drawn between Points C and D has a slope of −1/2.

without crossing it.) Consider the curve in Exhibit 1A.4. Applying the definition, the slope of this line at Point A is 1, and the slope at Point B is −2.

ABSTRACT GRAPHS

In all the examples so far, we have had specific numbers to work with for the x and y values. Sometimes, though, we know only the general nature of the relationship between two economic magnitudes rather than specific numbers. For example, we

Exhibit 1A.4
Slopes of curves
The slope of a curve at any given point is defined as the slope of a straight line drawn tangent to the curve at that point. A tangent line is one that just touches the curve without crossing it. In this exhibit, the slope of the curve at Point A is 1, and the slope of the curve at Point B is −2.

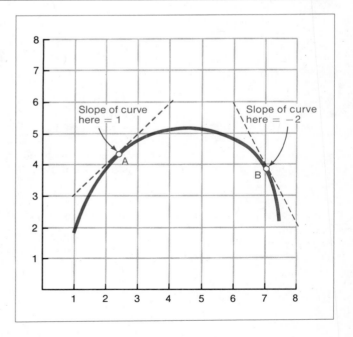

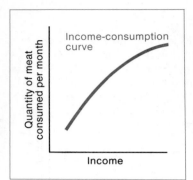

Exhibit 1A.5
An abstract graph
When we know the general form of an economic relationship but do not know the exact numbers involved, we can draw an abstract graph. Here, we know that as people's incomes rise, their consumption of meat increases rapidly at first, then levels off. Because we do not know the exact numbers for meat consumption or income, we have not marked any units on the axes.

might know that when people's incomes rise, they tend to increase their consumption of meat rapidly at first. But then, as they reach very high incomes, their meat consumption levels off. If we want to represent a relationship like this without caring about the numbers involved, we draw a graph like that shown in Exhibit 1A.5. The vertical axis is labeled "quantity of meat consumed per month," without any specific units. The horizontal axis is labeled "income," again without specific units. The curve, which rises rapidly at first and then levels off, tells us the general nature of the relationship between income and meat consumption: When income goes up, meat consumption rises, but not in proportion to the change in income. We will use abstract graphs like this one very frequently in this book. Abstract graphs express general principles, whereas graphs with numbers on the axes summarize specific known information.

STUDY HINTS FOR GRAPHS

When you come to a chapter in the book that is full of graphs, how should you study it? The first and most important rule is not to worry about memorizing graphs. I have never taught economics without having at least one student come to me after failing an exam and say: "But I learned every one of those graphs! What happened?" I always tell the students that they should have learned economics instead of learning the graphs.

Here are some specific study hints for working with graphs: After reading carefully through a chapter that uses graphs frequently, go back through the graphs one at a time. Place your hand over the explanatory note that appears beside each graph and try putting what the graph says into words. If you cannot say at least as much about the graph as the explanatory note does, read the text over again.

If you do all right going from graphs to words, half the battle is won. Next, try covering up the graph, and, using the explanatory note as a guide, sketch the graph on a piece of scratch paper. If you understand what the words mean and can comfortably go back and forth between the words and the graphs, you will find out that the two together are much easier to remember and apply than either would be separately. If you "learn the graphs" as meaningless patterns of lines, you are lost.

CONSTRUCTING YOUR OWN GRAPHS

For some students, the hardest kind of question to answer on an exam is the kind that requires construction of an original graph as part of an essay answer. Here are some hints for constructing your own graphs:
1. Put down the answer to the question in words. If you cannot do that, you might as well skip to the next question without wasting time on the graph. Try underlining the most important quantities in what you have written. The result might be

Exhibit 1A.6
Constructing a graph
To construct a graph, first put down in words what you want to say: "The larger the *number of students* at a university, the lower the *cost per student* of providing them with an education." Next, label the coordinate axes. Then, if you have exact numbers to work with, construct a table. Here we have no exact numbers, so we draw an abstract graph that slopes downward to show that cost goes down as numbers go up. For graphs with more than one curve, repeat these steps.

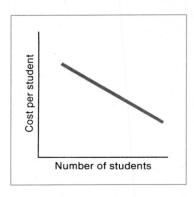

something like: "The larger the *number of students* who attend a university, the lower the *cost per student* of providing them with an education."

2. Decide how you are going to label the coordinate axes of your graph. In our example, because it is conventional to put money values on the vertical axis, we label the vertical axis "cost per student" and the horizontal axis "number of students."

3. Do you have exact numbers to work with? If you do, your next step should be to make a table showing what you know and then to use that to sketch your graph. If you do not have numbers, you will be drawing an abstract graph. In this case, all you know is that the cost per student goes down when the number of students goes up. Sketch in any convenient downward-sloping line (as in Exhibit 1A.6), and you will have done as well as can be done.

4. If your graph involves more than one relationship between pairs of economic quantities, repeat steps 1 to 3 for each relationship that you want to represent by a line or curve. When sketching graphs with more than one curve, pay particular attention to points where you think two curves ought to intersect (which will happen whenever both the x and y values of the two relationships are equal) and where you think they ought to be tangent (which will happen whenever the slopes of two curves are equal).

5. After your graph is completed, try translating it back into words. Does it really say what you wanted it to say?

A REMINDER

As you work through this book and are introduced to various specific kinds of graphs, turn back to this appendix now and then. Do not commit the fatal error of memorizing graphs as meaningless pictures. Remember that if you can go back and forth between graphs and words, the underlying theory that both are trying to express will stay with you more vividly than if you rely on either graphs or words alone. Remember that economics is about *people*, not graphs.

SUGGESTIONS FOR FURTHER READING

Bowen, William G. "Econometrics." In *Perspectives in Economics*, edited by Alan A. Brown, Egon Neuberger, and Malcolm Palmatier. New York: McGraw-Hill, 1971. *An introductory description of the important role of econometrics in modern economics. The essay on "Scope and Method of Economic Analysis" by Alan Brown and Egon Neuberger in the same volume is also useful.*

Fusfeld, Daniel R. *The Age of the Economist*. Glenview, Ill.: Scott, Foresman, 1977, chap. 3.
More on Adam Smith.

Goodman, John C., and Dolan, Edwin G. *Economics of Public Policy*. St. Paul: West Publishing, 1979, chaps. 1 and 2.
Chapter 1 provides additional perspective on the relationship between positive and normative economics. Chapter 2 uses the military draft in an extended case study of the production possibility frontier.

Kirzner, Israel M. *The Economic Point of View*. Princeton, N.J.: Van Nostrand, 1960.
A commentary on the nature and history of economics by a leading representative of the "Austrian" school.

Koopmans, Tjalling C. "Economics among the Sciences." *American Economic Review* 69 (March 1979): 1–13.
A thought-provoking presidential address to the American Economics Association, organized around several fascinating case studies.

Robbins, Lionel C. *An Essay on the Nature and Significance of Economic Science*, 2d ed., rev. London: Macmillan, 1935.
The classic treatment of the topic.

C H A P T E R 2
THE PRICE SYSTEM AND THE MARKET ECONOMY

WHAT YOU WILL LEARN IN THIS CHAPTER

This chapter will introduce the role played by markets in determining what is produced, how it is produced, and for whom it is produced. The chapter will explain each of three functions of markets: transmitting knowledge, providing incentives, and distributing income. It will show how the price system broadcasts information on opportunity costs and relative scarcities to buyers, how prices at the same time provide incentives to resource owners and entrepreneurs to put resources to best use, and how the incentive system operates to determine individuals' incomes. It will also introduce the questions of whether the market distributes income fairly and why it does not always operate perfectly. These questions will recur frequently as the discussion of economics progresses.

FOR REVIEW

Here are some important terms and concepts that will be put to use in this chapter. If you do not understand them, review them before proceeding.
- *Pure economizing and entrepreneurship (Chapter 1)*
- *Opportunity cost (Chapter 1)*
- *Positive and normative economics (Chapter 1)*
- *Market justice and distributive justice (Chapter 1)*

Modern economies are based on a vast division of labor, and each person within them makes a contribution to the whole system. One person installs hubcaps on Ford station wagons. Another keeps accounts in a New England branch of Woolworth's. Still another serves coffee, tea, or milk on Eastern Airlines. All these jobs have to be coordinated with others. When a team of auditors visit the branch of Woolworth's, someone must make sure that they will not run out of coffee on the airplane, that their rented Ford will not be missing a hubcap, and that the books they want to see will be balanced and ready when they arrive.

In the U.S. economy, markets play a central role in providing the necessary coordination. **Markets** are the various arrangements people have for trading with one another. They may be elaborately organized, like the New York Stock Exchange with its computers and ticker tape machines, or informal, like the word-of-mouth network that puts teenage babysitters in touch with the people who need their services. But however markets are organized, they perform

Markets All the various arrangements people have for trading with one another.

certain common functions: transmitting information, providing incentives, and distributing income.

THE FUNCTIONS OF MARKETS

Information and Its Value

Information is the most precious good in any economy. Economic prosperity depends on putting resources to their best uses, and to do this, the people who make decisions on how resources are to be used must know which uses are best. Like water, economic information is taken for granted when it is cheap and abundant. Its importance becomes apparent only when it is scarce, as the following case study illustrates.

Case 2.1
The Role of Information in the Bazaar Economy

At the foot of the Atlas Mountains in Morocco sits the ancient walled town of Sefrou. Once an important stop on the caravan route from Fez to the Sahara, it has been, for about a century now, an important *bazaar,* or market center, for some 15,000 to 30,000 people. Since the mid 1960s, anthropologist Clifford Geertz of the Institute for Advanced Study has been observing the bazaar at Sefrou. What he has discovered is instructive.

According to Geertz, information in the bazaar is poor, scarce, maldistributed, inefficiently communicated, and intensely valued. The level of ignorance about everything from product quality and going prices to market possibilities and production costs is very high. The name of the game in the bazaar is the search for information a person lacks and the protection of information a person has. As in any other economy, capital, skill, luck, privilege, and hard work contribute to individual success; but in the bazaar they do it not so much by increasing the efficiency of production as by enabling a person to secure a strategic location in the market's communications network. The primary problem facing participants in the bazaar is not to balance options but to find out what they are.

Geertz interprets the central features that distinguish the bazaar from a modern, industrialized market economy as responses to the scarcity of information. One of these features is bargaining. In a system where virtually nothing is packaged, standardized, or regulated, every transaction must be preceded by elaborate bargaining over price, quantity, quality, and credit terms. During the bargaining, buyers and sellers naturally try to conceal their minimum acceptable terms from one another, but at the same time they must manage to reveal enough information to form a basis for a mutually advantageous trade.

At this point, the efficiency of the bazaar is apparently improved by a second characteristic feature, which Geertz calls "clientalization." By this he means a tendency of buyers to return repeatedly to the same seller to engage in intensive bargaining rather than to search quickly but extensively among many sellers for the best price. Evidently, repeated bargaining within a stable client-seller relationship improves information exchange by enough to offset any loss of information resulting from frequent examination of alternative sources of supply.

In Geertz's view, the whole structure of the bazaar can be viewed as a set of communications channels designed to serve the needs of people whose interests are opposed in the act of bargaining but joined by the need to coordinate their economic activities. The same is true of any economic system; but since information is relatively scarce in the bazaar, its value is more prominently displayed.

Source: Based on Clifford Geertz, "The Bazaar Economy: Information and Search in Peasant Marketing," *American Economic Review* 68 (May 1978): 28–32. Used by permission.

The Price System

In the U.S. economy of today, bargaining and client-seller relationships are by no means unknown. Their importance as channels for the transmission of information, however, is completely overshadowed by another mechanism that exists only in rudimentary form in the bazaar economy. This mechanism is the *price system*. In the modern economy, prices typically are not subject to bargaining on a one-to-one basis between buyer and seller every time a transaction is made. Instead, they are widely advertised and published as an invitation to any buyer to enter the market on equal terms with other buyers. The price system is essentially a system for broadcasting information on opportunity costs and on the relative scarcity of various goods and services. A rise in the price of any good relative to the price of other goods signals increasing scarcity of that good. A fall in the price of any good (or, in times of inflation, a failure of its price to rise as fast as the prices of other goods) signals increasing abundance. Buyers can adjust their behavior accordingly.

The following case, supplied by Nobel prize–winning economist F. A. Hayek, brings out the contrast between the price system and the bazaar system. In Hayek's example, prices are the cheap and easily available source of information used by buyers to adjust to complex events occurring far away.

Case 2.2
Information and the Price System

Assume that somewhere in the world a new opportunity for the use of some raw material, say tin, has arisen, or that one of the sources of supply of tin has been eliminated. It does not matter for our purpose—and it is very significant that it does not matter—which of these two causes has made tin more scarce. All that the users of tin need to know is that some of the tin they used to consume is now more profitably employed elsewhere, and that in consequence they must economize tin. There is no need for the great majority of them even to know where the more urgent need has arisen, or in favor of what other needs they ought to husband the supply. If only some of them know directly of the new demand, and switch resources over to it, and if the people who are aware of the new gap thus created in turn fill it from still other sources, the effect will rapidly spread throughout the whole economic system and influence not only the uses of tin, but also those of its substitutes and the substitutes of these substitutes, the supply of the things made of tin, and their substitutes, and so on, and all this without the great majority of those instrumental in bringing about these substitutions knowing anything at all about the original cause of these changes. The whole acts as one market, not because any of its members survey the whole field, but because their limited individual fields of vision sufficiently overlap so that through many intermediaries the relevant information is communicated to all.

Source: Reprinted by permission from F. A. Hayek, "The Use of Knowledge in Society," *American Economic Review* 35 (September 1945): 519–530.

By informing people of the value and scarcity of tin, wheat, forklift trucks, and hundreds of thousands of other commodities, the price system reduces countless decisions to the level of pure economizing. Producers and consumers can observe market prices, combine them with their own knowledge of local circumstances, and arrive at valid judgments about the advantages and disadvantages of various production and consumption activities. To be sure, there is more to economic decision making than pure economizing, and the price system does not supply the answers to all economic questions. But entrepreneurial talents and energies, which in a bazaar economy are used up merely in finding out how much things cost, are now liberated to deal with the problem of finding new and better ways of doing things.

Incentives in the Market Economy

Knowledge of the best use of resources is a necessary condition for efficient coordination of economic activity, but it is not by itself sufficient. In addition to knowing the uses to which resources should be put, the people controlling them must have incentives to devote them to the known best use. Providing those incentives is the second major function of markets. As Adam Smith wrote more than two hundred years ago:

It is not from the benevolence of the butcher, the brewer, or the baker that we expect our dinner, but from their regard to their own interest. . . . Every individual is continually exerting himself to find out the most advantageous employment for whatever capital he can command. . . . By directing that industry in such a manner as its produce may be of the greater value, he intends only his own gain, and he is in this,

**Friedrich August von Hayek
(1899–   )**

In 1944, a slim volume entitled *The Road to Serfdom* burst onto the world's best seller list. This book warned that an enthusiasm for economic planning and strong central government was leading Western democracies down a path that, if not checked, could end in Soviet- or Nazi-style totalitarianism. The author of the book was as surprised as anyone to find it a best seller. He was Friedrich von Hayek, then a professor at the London School of Economics.

Hayek, born and educated in Vienna, by 1944 already had a first-class international reputation as an economic theorist. He had written widely on monetary theory and on the subject now known as macroeconomics. In contrast to many of his contemporaries, he did not believe that the Great Depression of the 1930s signaled the final failure of the market economy. The market would and could work, he held, if it were freed of the distortions introduced by ill-advised government policies. Most of all, what the economies of the world did not need as a cure for their troubles was comprehensive economic planning. Planning could never replace the market as a method for utilizing knowledge and guiding the division of labor. The attempt to make it do so would lead only to a loss of political freedom, not greater economic prosperity.

In 1950, Hayek left London for the University of Chicago, where he taught for twelve years as professor of social and moral science. Much of his time he now spent writing on broad issues of law and social philosophy. His major work of the University of Chicago period was *The Constitution of Liberty*. In this book, he defended the classical liberal ideal of the limited state based on a free market economy and a written constitution.

In 1962, Hayek saw that the University of Chicago's mandatory retirement age was fast approaching. Retirement seemed such an impossible idea to him that he returned to Europe, where professors could serve for a lifetime. He is now visiting professor at the University of Salzburg in Austria and professor emeritus of the University of Freiburg in Germany. In 1974, the name Friedrich von Hayek was back in the international headlines once again. The Swedish Academy of Science had awarded him the Nobel Memorial Prize in Economics—the highest professional distinction there is. A fitting time to retire from a distinguished career? Not for Hayek. The first volume of his new work, *Law, Legislation, and Liberty*, had just appeared the year before, and there were two more volumes to complete. Asked what he would do when the job had been finished, Hayek indicated that he would then, after a detour of many years, be ready to get back to some unfinished problems of economic theory.

as in many other cases, led by an invisible hand to promote an end which was no part of his intention.

The market offers different kinds of incentives to different people. Consumers who keep themselves well informed and spend their money judiciously are rewarded by the satisfaction of more needs with their limited budgets. Workers earn higher incomes if they stay alert to job market opportunities and work where their productivity is highest. Real estate brokers earn higher commissions the more efficiently they match suitable buyers and sellers. In every case, people who acquire economic information have an incentive to act on that information and not just file it away.

No doubt the most famous of incentives in the market economy is the profit motive. Profits make up a relatively small part of all income received by individuals. As officially measured by government statisticians, wages and salaries outweigh corporate profits by more than ten to one. But profits have an importance entirely out of proportion to their magnitude because they are the reward earned by entrepreneurs for properly coordinating the contributions of workers and other resource owners. A business firm earns a profit by buying inputs at their market prices and using them to produce a product that can be sold for more than the cost of all the inputs. And just as the market rewards firms that use resources productively, it penalizes those who use them wastefully. If the value of the inputs a firm buys exceeds the value of the product it makes out of those inputs, that firm will suffer a loss and will eventually disappear from the market.

Distributing Income

As a by-product of providing incentives, markets distribute income and wealth. People who possess skills and talents or who own resources that are scarce and highly valued get richly rewarded for putting them to their best use. People whose talents or resources are less scarce or of poor quality get less well rewarded even if they use what they have as wisely as possible. Entrepreneurs who take risks and guess right make large profits; entrepreneurs who take risks that looked just as prudent at the outset but who have guessed wrong suffer losses. In short, the market tends to distribute income in proportion to the contribution each person makes to the process of production.

The distributional function of the market is a source of great controversy, much of it over the normative question of whether the distribution of income in a market economy is *fair*. Not surprisingly, the answer depends largely on what is meant by *fairness*. To those for whom fairness is the observation of market justice, the distribution of income in a market economy does appear equitable. People receive what they earn from their own labor and from the voluntary exchange of property with others. All that is required for fairness, in this view, is that the contracts and exchanges be voluntary so they will work out to the mutual benefit of buyers and sellers.

To those who view fairness in terms of distributive justice, the distribution of income in the market economy is not inherently fair. Because skills, talents, and resource ownership are not distributed equally among people, the market does not distribute income equally either.

Is Distribution Separable? The controversy over the distributive function of markets also raises an important question of positive economics: Can the function of distributing income be separated from the functions of transmitting information and providing incentives? Answers differ to this question as well.

One answer is a flat no—the distributional function cannot be separated from the others. The reasoning behind this answer begins with the observation that there are only two ways to alter the distribution of income produced by the market—either to take from some people part of what they earn in order to give it to others or to manipulate prices so that some people earn more and some earn less than they otherwise would have earned. The first alternative interferes with incentives; if people know that part of what they earn will not be theirs to keep, their incentive to put their resources to best use will be correspondingly diminished. The second alternative interferes with the transmission of information through the price system; if prices are manipulated for the purpose of affecting income distribution, they cannot at the same time carry accurate signals regarding the relative scarcity of resources.

Despite the apparent reasonableness of this argument, not everyone accepts it on a practical level. It may be true, critics say, that attempts to redistribute income always carry the danger of distorting incentives or sending false signals regarding scarcity; but in practice, the distortions can be held to an insignificant level. Many think, for example, that people will not work much less or invest their capital much differently if they are subject to income taxes than if they are not. To take another kind of example, if rents on urban housing are held down to make housing more accessible to the poor, the distortion of the incentive to build such housing can be offset with other regulations or subsidies.

IMPERFECTIONS IN THE MARKET SYSTEM

Are markets perfect? Economists from Adam Smith to Milton Friedman sometimes get so enthusiastic about the principles according to which markets operate that they forget to point out that in the real world these principles operate only as tendencies. Imperfections in the market economy stem from a number of sources. By far the most important is the fact that although the price system *cheapens* the process of transmitting information to a large degree, it does not make information *free*.

Even after the price system has done its best, there is an irreducible minimum of ignorance in the world. Producers and consumers remain at least partly ignorant of what is happening in other places and substantially ignorant of what is likely to happen in the future. They may conceal their preferences for strategic reasons when dealing with others and at the same time remain ignorant of the preferences of others. A modern industrial market economy is worlds ahead of the bazaar at Sefrou in terms of the quality of information available; but as long as information is less than perfect, mistakes will be made.

Transactions Costs

Transactions costs All costs of finding buyers or sellers to transact business with and of negotiating terms of exchanges, drawing up contracts, guarding against involuntary default or foul play, and so on.

The cost of obtaining information is only one of a number of transactions costs that prevent markets from operating perfectly in the real world. By **transactions costs,** economists mean any of the costs of finding people to do business with, negotiating terms, drawing up contracts, guarding against involuntary default or foul play, and so on. Examples of market imperfections resulting from transactions costs are easy to find.

Have you ever had the experience of trying to get tickets to a play or ball game and being turned away because all the tickets were sold? Have you ever stayed away from such an event because the ticket price was too high, even though some seats remained unsold? If you have had either of these experiences, you have witnessed a market imperfection. If ticket prices accurately reflected the scarcity of seats relative to demand for them, there would be no unsold seats and no one turned away. But the transactions costs of trying to adjust ticket prices for every performance to exactly match supply and demand are evidently prohibitive. Predicting the correct price, informing the public of it each night, settling disputes, printing tickets, and a hundred other things would become so complex and costly that trying to fine tune market performance in this way just would not pay.

A second example: Have you ever been annoyed by smokers or annoyed that you were not permitted to smoke at some particular time or place? The perpetual battle between smokers and nonsmokers could, in principle, be efficiently resolved if there were a market in smoking rights. Every time two or more people got together in a room, they could hold an auction for the right to smoke. Nonsmokers could sell smokers a permit to light up or could pay them not to light up; the rules could be set either way. Whatever the rules, with such a market in operation, smoking would take place when, and only when, the benefit to smokers at least equaled the annoyance to nonsmokers. Of course, the transactions costs of holding auctions every time people walked from room to room would far outweigh the modest gains. Cruder methods, such as designating smoking and nonsmoking areas, only approximately adjust the conflicting interests of the opposing camps, but they are enormously cheaper to administer.

Property Rights

Just how seriously transactions costs interfere with the efficient use of resources often depends on the structure of the property rights that underlie the market system. Consider, for example, the problem of efficiently exploiting a common property fishing ground, say one in international ocean waters, that is open to all comers without restriction. Overharvesting is likely to be a serious problem in such a fishing ground. Overall yield can be maximized by limiting the yearly catch or the size of fish taken or by using other conservation practices, but no individual operator will have the incentive to employ conservation practices unless all others agree to do likewise. And any attempt to negotiate privately a unanimous, binding conservation agreement among all fishers would run up against insurmountable transactions costs.

In comparison, overharvesting need never be a problem in privately owned fishing grounds, such as those maintained for sports fishing by many clubs and commercial operators. Without elaborate negotiations, club directors or commercial owners simply establish the proper conservation rules, and those not inclined to observe them are not admitted. In this case, private property appears to decrease transactions costs greatly compared with common property, thereby improving the efficiency of resource use.

In other cases, private ownership of property may be a barrier to efficient use of resources. Consider, for example, the problem of obtaining a right-of-way for a new road or power line through a stretch of countryside owned by many individual farmers. Private negotiations with each landowner could very likely involve prohibitive transactions costs. Especially troublesome would be the fact that each landowner would have the incentive to hold out in the expectation that the last owner to settle could extort the best deal from the highway department or utility in question.

To cut transactions costs in cases like this, federal, state, and local governments are frequently given the power to condemn private land for public use. The private owner is forced to sell in return for what some independent agency or arbitrator judges to be a fair price. This power to condemn private land for public purposes is, of course, open to abuse and may, on occasion, itself lead to inefficient patterns of land use. But many economists believe that the savings in transactions costs more than outweigh the occasional abuses.

The proper mix of private and public property rights, then, can often reduce transactions costs to manageable levels and improve the efficiency of markets. In no case, however, can transactions costs be entirely eliminated.

CONCLUSIONS

This chapter has given just a few examples of how markets perform their functions of transmitting information, providing incentives, and distributing income. It has also offered a few examples of market imperfections and the sources from which they arise. The chapters that follow will give many more examples. In fact, the entire book can be read as an amplification of the themes set forth in this chapter: how markets operate to determine what is produced, who produces it, and for whom it is produced; why markets do not always perform perfectly; and what can be done to improve market performance.

SUMMARY

1. Markets play a crucial role in coordinating the division of labor in the market economy. This role includes performance of three basic functions: transmitting information, providing incentives, and distributing income.
2. In an advanced industrial market economy, the price system functions as a mechanism for broadcasting information about opportunity costs and the relative scarcity of resources. Rising relative prices signal increasing scarcity; falling relative prices signal increasing abundance.
3. Knowledge of the best use of resources is a necessary but not sufficient condition for efficient coordination of economic activity. In addition to knowing the uses to which resources should be put, the people controlling those resources must have incentives to devote them to their known best use. Consumers, resource owners, and entrepreneurs all have incentives to heed the information that comes to them through the price system, because doing so increases their satisfaction, income, and profit.
4. As a by-product of their function in providing incentives, markets perform the further function of distributing income and wealth. People who possess skills and talents or who own resources that are scarce and highly valued get richly rewarded for putting the resources to their best use. People whose talents or resources are less scarce or of poor quality get less well rewarded even if they use what they have wisely.
5. Despite their acknowledged effectiveness in coordinating the division of labor, markets are neither necessarily fair nor always perfectly efficient. Whether markets are considered fair is largely a question of normative economics that is answered differently by different individuals. Whether

markets function efficiently often depends on how seriously transactions costs impede the transmission of information, the execution of contracts, and so on.

DISCUSSION QUESTIONS

1. In your opinion, do the wages or salaries of various occupations have much influence on people's decisions about whether to go to college and what to major in? Justify your answer by explaining what it has to do with the functions of markets in transmitting information, providing incentives, and distributing income.

2. If you were the manager of a division of a major automobile manufacturer and you noticed that the price of steel had been going up relative to the prices of other materials used in the manufacturing of automobiles, how would you react? What would you do and have others do to make adjustments? How would you expect your competitors to react? Explain.

3. Even in an advanced industrial economy such as that of the United States, not all transactions take place in accordance with uniform, published prices. What sorts of transactions do you know of that are still subject to bargaining between buyer and seller? Why do you think they are carried out by means of bargaining rather than by fixed prices?

4. Review Case 1.2, in which it is explained that certain U.S. energy policies have the effect of holding the market price of oil below its marginal cost. What you have learned in this chapter should give you additional insights into the effects of that policy. How does it affect the ability of the price system to transmit accurate information about opportunity costs and relative scarcities? How does it affect the distribution of income?

5. Suppose you think that you and your neighbors are being overcharged by your local supermarket, which happens to be the only one in town. You decide that you will organize a consumer owned food cooperative to provide competition and low prices. What transactions costs might you have to overcome in setting up and operating the cooperative?

6. Presuming that continually repeated auctions of smoking rights are impractical, the following approach to resolving the conflict between smokers and nonsmokers is proposed: In public places, the government should set rules permitting smoking only in designated areas and guaranteeing nonsmokers a right to clean air. In private places, rules should be established and enforced by the owners of the private property. Do you find this a reasonable approach to the problem? How would you distinguish between public and private places? Would you do it strictly on the basis of legal ownership? Or would you consider such places as restaurants, theaters, and airplanes to be "public" enough, despite private ownership, to justify government imposed rules?

SUGGESTIONS FOR FURTHER READING

Coase, R. H. "The Problem of Social Cost." *Journal of Law and Economics* 3 (October 1960): 1–44.
The classic treatment of property rights and transactions costs in economics.

Hayek, F. A. "The Use of Knowledge in Society." *American Economic Review* 35 (September 1945): 519–530.
The source of Case 2.2, worth reading in its entirety.

Manne, Henry G., ed. *The Economics of Legal Relationships.* St. Paul: West Publishing, 1975.
A collection of papers on property rights and transactions costs in economics, many accessible to beginning students. Chapter 9 reproduces Coase's article on social cost, listed above. Chapter 24 is a detailed analysis of the problem of the fishery.

C H A P T E R 3
SUPPLY AND DEMAND —THE BASICS

WHAT YOU WILL LEARN IN THIS CHAPTER

Common experience suggests that the quantity of a good that buyers are willing to purchase tends to increase as the price of the good decreases, other things being equal. Similarly, the quantity of a good that suppliers are willing to sell tends to increase as the price increases, other things being equal. This chapter shows how these commonsense ideas form the basis for supply and demand analysis—one of the most useful analytical tools in all of economics. A final section introduces the concept of elasticity as a way of measuring the responsiveness of the quantity of a good supplied or demanded to a change in the price of that good.

FOR REVIEW

Here are some important terms and concepts that will be put to use in this chapter. If you do not understand them, review them before proceeding.

- *Opportunity cost (Chapter 1)*
- *Working with graphs (Appendix to Chapter 1)*

The number of markets in the U.S. economy is as large as the number of different kinds of goods and services produced—and that is very large. Despite the great diversity of markets, though, there are some economic principles so powerful that they are useful in understanding all of them. The principles of supply and demand fit into this category.

The fundamental ideas of supply and demand have long been known to practical merchants and traders. For as long as there have been markets, sellers have realized that one way to encourage people to buy more of their product is to offer it at a lower price, and buyers have known that one way to get more of the goods they want is to offer to pay more for them. Only in the last hundred years, though, have economists made systematic use of the principles of supply and demand as the central basis of their science. In the English-speaking world, Alfred Marshall deserves much of the credit for showing how useful the ideas of supply and demand can be. This chapter—and the corresponding chapters in all modern textbooks—is little more than a rewrite of the principles he taught in his own famous *Principles of Economics*.

Alfred Marshall (1842–1924)

Alfred Marshall was born in London in 1842, the son of a Bank of England cashier. His father hoped that he would enter the ministry, but young Marshall had other ideas. He turned down a theological scholarship at Oxford to study mathematics instead. He received an M.A. in mathematics from Cambridge in 1865.

While at Cambridge, he joined a philosophical discussion group. There, he became interested in promoting the wide development of the human mind. He was soon told, however, that harsh economic reality would prevent his ideas from being carried out. Britain's productive resources, it was said, could never allow the mass of the people sufficient leisure for education. This disillusioning episode appears to have first turned Marshall's attention to economics.

At the time, British economics was dominated by the so-called classical school. Marshall had great respect for the classical writers. Initially, he saw his own work as simply using his mathematical training to strengthen and systematize the classical system. It was not long, however, before he was breaking new ground and developing a system of his own. By 1890, when he brought out his famous *Principles of Economics*, he had laid the foundation of what is now called the neoclassical school.

Attempting to explain the essence of his approach, Marshall included this passage in the second edition of his *Principles:*

In spite of a great variety in detail, nearly all the chief problems of economics agree in that they have a kernel of the same kind. This kernel is an inquiry as to the balancing of two opposed classes of motives, the one consisting of desires to acquire certain new goods, and thus satisfy wants; while the other consists of desires to avoid certain efforts or retain certain immediate enjoyment. . . . In other words, it is an inquiry into the balancing of the forces of demand and supply.

Marshall's influence on economics, at least in the English-speaking world, was enormous. His *Principles* was the leading text for decades, and the modern student can still learn much from reading it. As a professor at Cambridge, he taught a great many of the next generation of leading economists. Today the neoclassical school he founded continues to dominate the profession. It has received many challenges but so far has weathered them all.

THE LAW OF DEMAND

Law of demand The law that the quantity of a good demanded by buyers tends to increase as the price of the good decreases and tends to decrease as the price increases, other things being equal.

The analysis begins with the **law of demand,** which says simply that, in the market for any good, the quantity of that good demanded by buyers tends to increase as the price of the good decreases and tends to decrease as the price increases, other things being equal. This law corresponds so closely to what common sense tells us about the way markets work that we could simply state it without further elaboration. But a few additional comments will ensure that it is properly understood.

Effective Demand

Effective demand The quantity of a good that purchasers are willing and able to buy at a particular price.

First, what is meant by *quantity demanded?* It is important to understand that the quantity demanded at a given price means the **effective demand**—the quantity purchasers are willing and able to buy at that price. The effective demand at a particular price may be different from the quantity consumers want or need. I may *want* a new Jaguar XJ-6; but given my limited financial resources, I am not willing actually to offer to buy such a car at its current price of $20,000. My want does not count as part of the quantity demanded in the market for Jaguars. Similarly, I might *need* corrective dental surgery to avoid premature loss of my teeth, but I might be very poor. If I were unable to pay, and no other person or agency were willing to pay, my need would not be counted as part of the quantity demanded in the market for dental services.

Other Things Being Equal

Second, why is the phrase *other things being equal* attached to the law of demand? The reason is that a change in the price of a product is not the only thing that affects the quantity of that product demanded. If people's incomes go up, they are likely to increase the quantities they demand of a great many goods, even if prices do not change. If people's basic tastes and preferences change, the quantities of things they buy will change. If their expectations about future prices or their own future incomes change, they may change their spending patterns even before those price and income changes actually take place.

Above all, in the law of demand, the "other things being equal" condition indicates that the prices of other goods remain unchanged. What really counts in determining the quantity demanded of some good is its price *relative* to the prices of other goods. If the price of gasoline goes up and consumers' incomes and the prices of all other goods go up by the same proportion, the law of demand does not suggest any change in the quantity of gasoline demanded. But if the price of gasoline goes up 10 percent while the price of everything else goes up 20 percent, an increase can be expected in the quantity of gasoline demanded, because its relative price has fallen.

Why?

Now that the meaning of the law of demand is clear, we can ask why it works. Three explanations are worth considering.

First, when the price of a good falls while the prices of other goods remain unchanged, we are likely to substitute some of that good for other things. For example, if the price of fish falls while the price of meat remains the same, we are likely to put fish on the menu a few of the times when we would have used meat had the price of fish not changed.

Second, when the price of a good changes, other things being equal, our effective purchasing power changes even though our income measured in money terms does not. For example, if the price of clothing rises while nothing else changes, we will feel poorer, very much as if a few dollars a year had been trimmed from our paycheck or allowance. Feeling poorer, it is likely that we will buy a bit less of many things, including clothing.

Third—and this reason is not quite distinct from the other two—when the price of a good falls, new buyers who did not use a product at all before are drawn into the market. There was a time, for example, when tape recorders were playthings for the rich or technical tools for businesses. Today, they can be bought very cheaply. Rich people are not buying ten or twenty tape recorders apiece at the lower prices, but sales have gone up ten- or twentyfold because many people are buying them who never had entered that market at all before.

Exceptions to the Law

Are there exceptions to the law of demand? Are there cases in which an increase in the price of a good causes people to use more of it? Theoretically, such exceptions are possible, although in practice they are quite rare. One kind of exception can occur if the change in the price of a good has such a strong impact on effective purchasing power that it causes a radical change in people's whole pattern of consumption. Imagine a family that lives in Minnesota and habitually spends January each year vacationing in Florida. One year, the price of home heating fuel jumps dramatically. The family reacts by turning down the thermostat a little, but the fuel bills for September through December still go up so much that the family cannot afford to take its Florida vacation in January. Yet, staying at home, even though it is cheaper than going to Florida, requires the family to burn more fuel than during the previous winters, when it left the house unheated for that month. The total effect of the rise in fuel prices is therefore an *increase* in the consumption of the product.

Perhaps other rare kinds of exceptions to the law of demand are also possible. The point is, though, that we have to think so hard to come up with examples that we end up being more convinced than ever of the validity of the law.

Demand Schedules and Curves

The law of demand, like so many other economic ideas, can usefully be illustrated with numerical tables and graphs. Suppose, for example, that we want to study the operation of the law of demand in the market for wheat.[1] One way to express the relationship between the price of wheat and the quantity of wheat demanded by all buyers in the market is in the form of a table like that given in Exhibit 3.1a.

From the first line of the table, we learn that when the price of wheat is

---

[1] In this chapter, we ignore a number of federal government policies—price supports, acreage controls, and so on—that affect the price, quantity supplied, and quantity demanded of wheat. These policies will be discussed in detail in Chapter 10.

Exhibit 3.1

A demand schedule and a demand curve for wheat
Both the demand schedule and the demand curve show the quantity of wheat demanded at various possible prices. Both show, for example, that when the price is $2 per bushel, the quantity is 2 billion bushels per year.

(a) Demand schedule

Price of Wheat (dollars per bushel)	Quantity of Wheat Demanded (billions of bushels per year)
$3.20	1.4
3.00	1.5
2.80	1.6
2.60	1.7
2.40	1.8
2.20	1.9
2.00	**2.0**
1.80	2.1
1.60	2.2
1.40	2.3
1.20	2.4
1.00	2.5
.80	2.6

(b) Demand curve

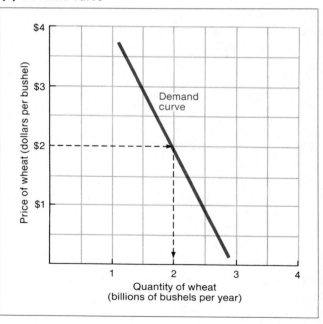

$3.20, the quantity demanded per year will be 1.4 billion bushels. Reading further, we see that as the price decreases, the quantity demanded increases. At $3 per bushel, buyers are willing and able to purchase 1.5 billion bushels per year; at $2.80, the quantity demanded is 1.6 billion bushels. The complete table is called the **demand schedule** for wheat.

The information given by the demand schedule can be expressed just as easily in graphical form. This is done in Exhibit 3.1b. The diagonal line of the graph is called the **demand curve** for wheat. Suppose that we want to use the demand curve to determine what quantity will be demanded when the price is $2 per bushel. Beginning at $2 on the vertical axis, we follow across as shown by the arrow until we reach the demand curve. We then go down from that point to the horizontal axis, where we read off the answer—2 billion bushels per year. This, of course, is the same answer given in the tabular demand schedule.

Demand schedule A table showing the quantity of a good demanded at various prices.

Demand curve A graphical representation of the relationship between the price of a good and the quantity of it demanded.

Movements along the Demand Curve

To repeat what has been said before, the demand curve shows how the quantity demanded changes in response to a change in price, *other things being equal*. When a change in the quantity of wheat demanded occurs as a result of a change in the price of wheat, acting alone, that change is represented graphically as a movement along the demand curve for wheat. If something other than the price of wheat changes, a different graphical representation is required.

Consider Exhibit 3.2. The demand curve labeled D_1 is the same as that shown in Exhibit 3.1. It is based on certain assumptions about household income, the prices of other goods, and buyers' expectations about future changes in price. Given those assumptions, the quantity demanded at a price

Exhibit 3.2

A shift in the demand curve for wheat
The effect of a change in the price of wheat, other things being equal, is represented by a movement along the demand curve for wheat, as from Point A to Point B along Demand Curve D_1. The effect of a change in something other than a change in the price of wheat (say a change in household income) must be represented by a shift in the entire demand curve, as from the position D_1 to the position D_2.

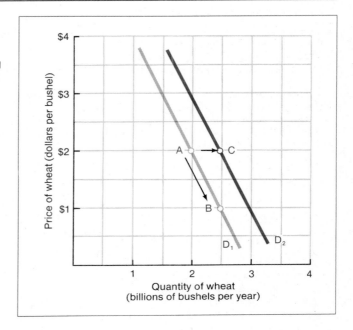

of $2 per bushel will be 2 billion bushels per year, as at Point A on Demand Curve D_1. A fall in the price from $2 per bushel to $1 per bushel, other things being equal, will cause the quantity demanded to increase to 2.5 billion bushels per year. This change in price is represented by a movement along Demand Curve D_1 from Point A to Point B.

Shifts in the Demand Curve Return now to Point A. Suppose that the price does not change but that something else changes—say, household income rises. A sufficiently large increase in household income could cause consumers to demand an additional half billion bushels per year, even without a change in the price of wheat. This change is represented by a movement from Point A to Point C in the diagram—a movement *off* Demand Curve D_1 rather than along it. With household income established at its new, higher level, changes in *price* would now cause movements up or down along the new demand curve, D_2, which passes through Point C and lies everywhere to the right of the old demand curve, D_1. The new demand curve indicates that, whatever the price of wheat, the quantity demanded, given the new, higher level of household income, will be larger than it would have been at the same price, given the old level of income.

A similar story could have been told if the prices of other goods or buyers' expectations, rather than income, had changed. The general point to be established is this: When the demand for some good changes for a reason *other* than a change in the price of the product itself, the change is represented graphically by a *shift* in the entire demand curve to a new position.

It is a rather widely established convention among economists to refer to a shift in a demand curve as a *change in demand*. The phrase *change in quantity demanded* refers to a movement along a given demand curve.

Normal and Inferior Goods Economists use some special terms in discussing the sources of shifts in demand curves. Changes in income are one source of such shifts. When a rise in buyers' incomes causes the demand curve for a good to shift to the right (as happened in Exhibit 3.2), the good is called a **normal good.** People tend to reduce their consumption of some goods when their incomes go up. Such goods, called **inferior goods,** are those goods for which there are more desirable but also more costly substitutes. Hamburger and intercity bus travel are examples. An increase in buyers' incomes causes the demand curve for an inferior good to shift to the left.

Substitutes and Complements The position of the demand curve for a good may also be affected by changes in the prices of other, closely related goods. For example, salads can be made from lettuce or from cabbage. An increase in the price of lettuce is likely to cause not only a decrease in the quantity of lettuce demanded (represented graphically by a movement up and to the left along the lettuce demand curve) but also an increase in the demand for cabbage (represented graphically by a shift to the right of the entire cabbage demand curve). When an increase in the price of one good causes an increase in the demand for another good, those two goods are said to be **substitutes** for one another. Photographic film and flashbulbs tend to be used together. If the price of film were to rise, we would expect not only a decrease in the quantity of film sold but a decrease in the demand for flashbulbs also. The

Normal good A good for which an increase in the income of buyers causes a rightward shift in the demand curve.

Inferior good A good for which an increase in the income of buyers causes a leftward shift in the demand curve.

Substitutes A pair of goods for which an increase in the price of one causes an increase in the demand for the other, other things being equal.

effect of the change in the price of film is represented graphically as a movement along the film demand curve and as a leftward shift of the flashbulb demand curve. When an increase in the price of one good causes a decrease in the demand for another good, the two goods are said to be **complements.**

Complements A pair of goods for which an increase in the price of one causes a decrease in the demand for the other, other things being equal.

SUPPLY

The next step in the analysis of markets will be to examine the relationship between the price of a good and the quantity of it that suppliers are willing and able to provide for sale. Everyday experience suggests that, in order to induce sellers to increase the quantity of a good supplied, it is necessary, other things being equal, to offer them a higher price. When this is true, the supply curve for the good in question slopes upward. Exhibit 3.3 shows a **supply schedule** and a corresponding upward sloping **supply curve** for wheat.[2]

Why exactly is the supply curve for wheat expected to slope upward? There are a number of possible reasons, any or all of which may operate in a particular case. For one thing, a higher price gives farmers a greater incentive to devote more of their time and energy to wheat production. In addition, it may

Supply schedule A table showing the quantity of a good supplied at various prices.

Supply curve A graphical representation of the relationship between the price of a good and the quantity of it supplied.

[2]Exceptions to the rule that supply curves slope upward are not so rare as exceptions to the rule that demand curves slope downward. A few examples of negatively sloped supply curves will occur later in this book. For the present, however, we will stick to upward sloping curves.

Exhibit 3.3
A supply schedule and supply curve for wheat
Both the supply curve and supply schedule for wheat show the quantity of wheat supplied at various prices. An increase in the price of wheat induces farmers to supply a greater quantity of it. This is partly because they have an incentive to devote more time and energy to the crop, partly because they substitute wheat for other crops grown previously, and partly because new resources (and even new farmers) may be drawn into wheat production.

(a) Supply schedule

Price of Wheat (dollars per bushel)	Quantity of Wheat Supplied (billions of bushels per year)
$3.20	2.6
3.00	2.5
2.80	2.4
2.60	2.3
2.40	2.2
2.20	2.1
2.00	2.0
1.80	1.9
1.60	1.8
1.40	1.7
1.20	1.6
1.00	1.5
.80	1.4

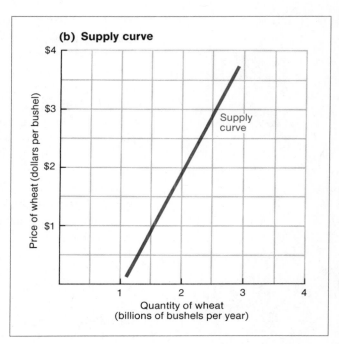

(b) Supply curve

induce them to substitute wheat for other crops they had been producing. Finally, the higher price may make it possible to attract resources into wheat farming from other lines of production, perhaps even leading to the establishment of new farms. Chapters 7 and 8 will discuss in some detail the assumptions that underlie the upward sloping supply curve. For now, these common-sense observations will suffice.

Shifts in Supply Curves

As in the case of demand, changes in the quantity supplied of a good, represented by movements along a given supply curve, are distinguished from changes in the supply of a good, represented by shifts in the supply curve. A change in the quantity supplied comes about as the result of a change in the price of the good, other things being equal. A shift in the supply curve requires a change in some other factor affecting supply.

One thing that can produce a change in the supply of a good is a change in production technology. If new technology permits more output to be produced from the same quantity of inputs, the supply curve will shift to the right. A second factor that can cause a change in supply is a change in the price of inputs used to produce a good. If input prices go up, for example, suppliers will probably want a higher price than before in order to offer the same quantity of output for sale. This effect is represented by a leftward shift in the supply curve. Finally, the supply curve for one good can be shifted as the result of a change in the price of another good, other things being equal. For example, a rise in the price of soybeans might well cause the supply curve for wheat to shift to the left, as farmers pull land out of wheat production and plant it in the newly profitable soybeans. Some examples of shifting supply curves will be given later in this chapter.

THE INTERACTION OF SUPPLY AND DEMAND

Market Equilibrium

Chapter 2 showed how the market transmits information in the form of prices to the people who are potential buyers and sellers of any good. Taking the price of the good into account, together with the other knowledge they possess, these buyers and sellers form plans. Each one decides to enter the market and buy or sell a certain number of units of the good.

Commonly, large numbers of buyers and sellers formulate their market plans independently of one another. When buyers and sellers of some particular good actually meet and engage in the process of exchange, some of them may find it impossible to carry out their plans. Perhaps the total quantity of planned purchases will exceed the total quantity of planned sales at the expected price. In this case, some of the would-be buyers will find their plans frustrated and will have to modify them. Perhaps, instead, planned sales will exceed planned purchases. Then, some would-be sellers will be unable to sell all they had expected to and will have to change their plans.

Sometimes no one will be disappointed. Given the information that market prices have conveyed, the total quantity of the good that buyers plan to purchase may exactly equal the quantity that suppliers plan to sell. The separately formulated plans of all market participants may turn out to mesh exactly when tested in the marketplace, and no one will have frustrated expectations or be forced to modify plans. When this happens, the market is said to be in **equilibrium.**

If we have supply and demand schedules for a market, we can describe more exactly the conditions under which that market will be in equilibrium. Take the market for wheat as an example. In Exhibit 3.4, Columns 1 to 3 give the supply and demand schedules. Reading down Column 2, we see how much wheat producers will plan to sell at each price. Reading down Column 3, we see how much wheat buyers will plan to purchase at each price. Comparing the two, it does not take long to discover that only when the price is $2 do the separately formulated plans of buyers and sellers exactly mesh. Thus $2 per bushel is the price at which this market is in equilibrium. If all buyers and sellers make their market plans in the expectation that the price will be $2, none of them will be disappointed, and none will have to change plans.

Shortages

What if, for some reason, buyers and sellers expect the market price to be something different from $2? Suppose, for example, that a price of $1 per bushel somehow becomes established in the market. Column 2 of Exhibit 3.4 tells us that, at this price, producers will plan to supply wheat to the market at the rate of 1.5 billion bushels per year. Column 3 tells us that buyers will plan to purchase at a rate of 2.5 billion bushels per year. When the quantity demanded exceeds the quantity supplied, the difference between the two is called an

Market equilibrium A condition in which the separately formulated plans of buyers and sellers of some good exactly mesh when tested in the marketplace, so that the quantity supplied is exactly equal to the quantity demanded at the prevailing price.

Exhibit 3.4
Supply and demand in the market for wheat
When the quantity of a product demanded exceeds the quantity supplied, there is an excess quantity demanded, or shortage, of the product. A shortage puts upward pressure on the price of the product. When the quantity supplied exceeds the quantity demanded, there is an excess quantity supplied, or surplus, of the product. A surplus puts downward pressure on the price. Only when the price of wheat here is $2 per bushel is there no shortage or surplus and no upward or downward pressure on price. At $2 the market is in equilibrium.

Price per Bushel (1)	Quantity Supplied (billions of bushels) (2)	Quantity Demanded (billions of bushels) (3)	Shortage (billions of bushels) (4)	Surplus (billions of bushels) (5)	Direction of Pressure on Price (6)
$3.20	2.6	1.4	—	1.2	Downward
3.00	2.5	1.5	—	1.0	Downward
2.80	2.4	1.6	—	0.8	Downward
2.60	2.3	1.7	—	0.6	Downward
2.40	2.2	1.8	—	0.4	Downward
2.20	2.1	1.9	—	0.2	Downward
2.00	2.0	2.0	—	—	Equilibrium
1.80	1.9	2.1	0.2	—	Upward
1.60	1.8	2.2	0.4	—	Upward
1.40	1.7	2.3	0.6	—	Upward
1.20	1.6	2.4	0.8	—	Upward
1.00	1.5	2.5	1.0	—	Upward
.80	1.4	2.6	1.2	—	Upward

Excess quantity demanded
The amount by which the quantity of a good demanded exceeds the quantity supplied when the price of the good is below the equilibrium level.

Shortage As used in economics, an excess quantity demanded.

excess quantity demanded or, more simply, a **shortage.**[3] In the case of wheat, the shortage (shown in Column 4 of the exhibit) is 1 billion bushels per year when the price is $1 per bushel.

In most markets, the first sign of a shortage is the depletion of inventories of the product available for sale. If inventories run out entirely, or if the market is for a good or service that cannot be stored in inventory at all, a queue of potential buyers may form. Under such circumstances, either sellers take the initiative to raise prices or buyers take the initiative to offer higher prices in the hope of getting part of the available quantity. In either event, the shortage puts upward pressure on price.

As the price of the product rises, producers begin to plan to sell more and buyers begin to plan to purchase less. The higher the price, the smaller the shortage. When the price of wheat in Exhibit 3.4 reaches $2 per bushel, the shortage is entirely eliminated. With its elimination, there is no further upward pressure on prices. The market is in equilibrium.

Surpluses

Suppose that, for some reason, the price of wheat becomes established at a level higher than the equilibrium price, say at $3 a bushel. At this price, according to Exhibit 3.4, producers will plan to sell 2.5 billion bushels per year, but buyers will plan to purchase only 1.5 billion bushels. When the quantity supplied exceeds the quantity demanded, there is an **excess quantity supplied** or a **surplus.** As Column 5 of the exhibit shows, the surplus of wheat is 1 billion bushels per year when the price is $3 a bushel.

Excess quantity supplied
The amount by which the quantity of a good supplied exceeds the quantity demanded when the price of the good is above the equilibrium level.

Surplus As used in economics, an excess quantity supplied.

When there is a surplus of the product, some producers will be disappointed, since they will not be able to make all their planned sales at the expected price. Inventories of unsold goods will begin to accumulate. Although the details may vary from market to market, the generalization can be made that a surplus puts downward pressure on the product price. Exhibit 3.4 shows that as the price falls, the quantity supplied decreases and the quantity demanded increases. Gradually, the surplus is eliminated until, when the price reaches $2 per bushel, the market returns to equilibrium.

Graphical Presentation

A graphical presentation of the material just covered will help reinforce the points made. Exhibit 3.5 shows both the demand curve (taken from Exhibit 3.1) and the supply curve (taken from Exhibit 3.3) for wheat. With both curves on the same diagram, the quantity demanded and the quantity supplied at any price can be directly compared. The distance from the vertical axis to the demand curve measures the quantity demanded, and the distance from the vertical axis to the supply curve measures the quantity supplied. It follows that the horizontal gap between the two curves measures the surplus or shortage at any price.

As we saw when working through the numerical example for this market, a surplus tends to put downward pressure on the price, and a shortage tends to

---

[3]We introduce two equivalent terms—*shortage* and *excess quantity demanded*—in order to make it clear that economists use the term *shortage* in a somewhat narrower sense than it is used in everyday speech. In this book, the word *shortage* will be used most of the time when it is clear that the economic meaning is intended. But sometimes, to avoid possible ambiguity, the more precise term *excess quantity demanded* will be used instead. The same considerations apply to the terms *surplus* and *excess quantity supplied*.

Exhibit 3.5

Supply and demand in the market for wheat

In this diagram, a surplus or shortage is indicated by the horizontal distance between the supply and demand curves. A surplus puts downward pressure on price, and a shortage puts upward pressure on it, as indicated by the arrows following the supply and demand curves. The market is in equilibrium at the point where the supply and demand curves intersect. Compare this diagram with the table in Exhibit 3.4.

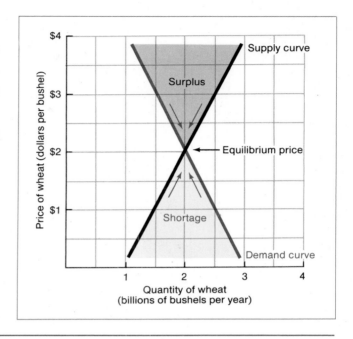

put upward pressure on it. These pressures result from the actions of frustrated buyers and sellers, who must change their plans when they find they cannot buy or sell the quantities they had intended at the price they had expected. The pressures are indicated by the arrows pointing along the supply and demand curves toward equilibrium.

There is only one price where neither upward nor downward pressure is in force—the price of $2 per bushel, the point where the supply and demand curves intersect. There is neither shortage nor surplus at that point. The quantity that buyers plan to purchase exactly equals the quantity that suppliers plan to sell. Both can carry out their plans exactly as intended, and the market is in equilibrium.

Changing Economic Conditions

When underlying economic conditions change, supply and demand curves can shift to new positions. These shifts upset the plans of buyers and sellers, who may have adjusted to some previous market equilibrium, and they bring about changes in prices and quantities. The following example describes an episode that is typical of the way markets work every day. Particular attention should be paid to the distinction between the kinds of changes that cause shifts in supply or demand curves and the kinds that cause movements along curves.

Case 3.1
Supply and Demand for Cobalt

Cobalt is a metal with important industrial applications in hardening turbine blades for aircraft engines, making high power magnets, cementing tungsten-carbide cutting tools, and manufacturing paints and varnishes. It is produced as a by-product of refining nickel and copper. About 60 percent of the world's output comes from the African country of Zaire.

In May 1978, cobalt was selling for under $10 per pound. By the end of 1978, the price had shot up to over $40 per pound. Many separate events, all happening at once, contributed to the sharp rise in price. Exhibit 3.6 shows how this complex tangle of events can be interpreted in terms of shifts in and movements along supply and demand curves.[4]

Let the supply and demand curves S_1 and D_1 in Exhibit 3.6a represent market conditions as of early 1978. These curves intersect at the equilibrium E_1, giving a market price of about $10 per pound. The first major shocks to hit the cobalt market came from the supply side. There was a strike in the mines of Zaire, and then fighting broke out in the mining region between government troops and Katangan rebels. These events had the effect of *shifting* the supply curve for cobalt to the left. S_2 represents the new position of the supply curve.

The decrease in supply at first created a shortage, thereby pushing up the price. Users of cobalt began to look for ways to conserve it. Allegheny Ludlum Steel, one of the largest cobalt users, developed a recycling program that cut the consumption of new cobalt 10 to 15 percent. Makers of high-fidelity audio systems began looking for designs that would substitute ceramic magnets for cobalt magnets. Conservation moves such as these correspond to a movement along Demand Curve D_1 in Part a. If nothing else had happened, the market would have reached a new equilibrium at E_2, with a price of about $25 per pound.

However, things were happening on the demand side of the cobalt market too. The aircraft industry was rapidly stepping up output to satisfy demand for its new models. Use of cobalt in paints and varnishes nearly doubled from 1977 to 1978. And a fad developed for a new type of earring held in place by powerful miniature cobalt magnets, making it unnecessary for wearers to pierce their ears. These events on the demand side of the market are represented in Part b as a shift in the demand curve from D_1 to D_2.

---

[4]The slopes of the supply and demand curves were chosen arbitrarily for the sake of illustration.

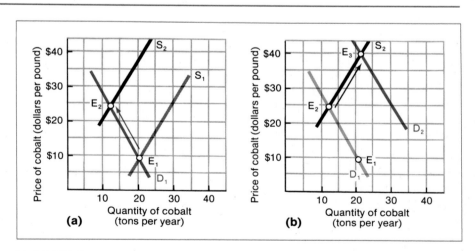

Exhibit 3.6

Changing conditions in the market for cobalt during 1978

In early 1978, cobalt was selling for about $10 per pound, represented here by the intersection between Demand Curve D_1 and Supply Curve S_1 in Part a of the exhibit. A strike and rebellion in Zaire, the world's leading producer, shifted the supply curve to the left to the position S_2. The price rose toward the point E_2 as buyers moved along Demand Curve D_1. Then a boom in the aerospace industry and other events caused the demand curve to shift to the right, as shown by D_2 in Part b of the exhibit. The price rose further as suppliers moved along the new supply curve toward its intersection with the new demand curve at E_3.

This demand shift intensified the shortage of cobalt and increased the rapidity with which the price was bid up. In response, suppliers outside Katanga did what they could to step up production. For example, Inco Ltd., the world's largest nickel producer, added new equipment that would double the amount of cobalt it could recover. These output increasing responses are represented in Part b by a movement along Supply Curve S_2 toward the final equilibrium, E_3, at a price of about $40 per pound.

Sources: Based on Agis Salpukas, "Scarcity of Cobalt Spurs Conversion," *New York Times*, December 18, 1978, and William Gilmer, Jr., "Magnetic Earrings Join Katangan Rebels as Factors in Cobalt's Recent Price Rise," *Wall Street Journal*, June 21, 1978, p. 48.

Markets in Disequilibrium

We have seen that when a market is not in equilibrium, an excess quantity demanded or supplied will put upward or downward pressure on the price. If the price is free to respond to this pressure, a new equilibrium will be established at a higher or lower price. Sometimes, though, market prices are not free to fluctuate. The forces of supply and demand must then work themselves out in some other way, as the following example shows.

Case 3.2
Coping with Gasoline Shortages: Rationing by Waiting

In the winter of 1974 and again in the spring of 1979, significant gasoline shortages struck the United States as political events in the Middle East drastically cut the supply of oil exported from that region. Because there was no immediate alternative source of oil, the supply curve for gasoline could be considered almost vertical, as shown in Exhibit 3.7.

According to this exhibit, a sufficiently high price ($2 per gallon as the graph is drawn, but this is only a guess) would have put the gasoline market in equilibrium. However, government price controls in force at the time kept the price from rising much above $1 per gallon. There was a substantial excess quantity of gas demanded; and instead of making itself visible in terms of rising prices, it made itself visible in the form of long lines at gas stations.

Exhibit 3.7

A gasoline shortage with price controls
This exhibit shows the effect of a restricted supply of gasoline when price controls are in effect. Instead of causing the price to rise toward its equilibrium level (here estimated at $2 per gallon), the shortage caused long lines to form at gas stations. The lines continued to grow until the opportunity cost per gallon of waiting in line became great enough to reduce the quantity demanded to the quantity supplied.

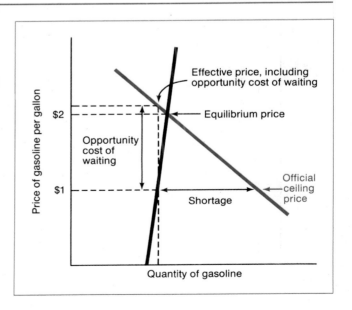

People who waited in line for gasoline had lots of time to think, and anyone who had studied a little economics could have figured out that the forces of supply and demand were still at work in a roundabout way. There were opportunity costs of waiting in line. Some people missed work. Others sacrificed valuable leisure hours. As the lines grew, the opportunity cost of waiting in them grew also, until at some point the total cost of gasoline—the money cost plus the opportunity cost of waiting—rose high enough to restrict the quantity demanded to the quantity supplied. As the exhibit is drawn, this required a total price slightly higher than the $2 per gallon to which the money price would have risen without controls. At that point, the lines stopped growing longer, and a sort of rough-and-ready equilibrium was established.

Consumers, on the average, did not gain much from price controls during these shortages. What they saved in money, they wasted in time spent in line. To get around this problem, it has been proposed that in the event of such shortages, rationing tickets limiting gas consumption to, say, two gallons per vehicle per day should be issued to motorists. People who did not use all their tickets could sell them to others who had a greater demand for gasoline. (As Exhibit 3.7 is drawn, what price do you think motorists would have been able to get for their extra rationing tickets?) Others think that the best way to handle shortages is simply to let the price rise to its equilibrium level, no matter how high it might be. As of this writing, the debate over how to handle the problem is still unresolved.

ELASTICITY

Elasticity and Changes in Revenue

The chapter has so far emphasized the effects of changes in price on the quantity of a good demanded. This section shifts focus somewhat to look at the effects of price changes on the total revenue generated by the sale of a good—total revenue being calculated as the quantity of the good sold multiplied by the price at which it is sold.

As Exhibit 3.8 shows, a change in the price of a good can have one of three effects on total revenue, depending on the shape and position of the demand curve. In the case of good A, a decline in price from $5 per unit to $3 per unit increases the quantity demanded from three units to six units. Total revenue thus increases from $15 to $18 as the price falls. In the case of good B, the same decline in price from $5 to $3 is shown as increasing the quantity demanded by only one unit, from three units to four units. Total revenue thus decreases from $15 to $12. Finally, in the case of good C, a drop in price from $5 to $3 increases the quantity demanded from three units to five units, leaving total revenue unchanged at $15.

The effects of changes in price on total revenue illustrated in Exhibit 3.8 can be expressed in terms of the relationship between the percentage by which the quantity demanded changes and the percentage by which the price changes. The ratio of the percentage change in the quantity demanded of a good to the percentage change in the price of the good is known as the **price elasticity of demand**, or simply the **elasticity of demand**, for that good. If quantity changes by a larger percentage than price, as in Exhibit 3.8a, so that

Price elasticity of demand (elasticity of demand) The ratio of the percentage change in the quantity of a good demanded to the percentage change in the price of the good.

Exhibit 3.8
Elastic, inelastic, and unit elastic demand
This exhibit illustrates the relationship between changes in price and changes in revenue for three different demand curves. As the price of good A decreases from $5 to $3, revenue increases from $15 to $18; the demand for good A is elastic. As the price of good B decreases over the same range, revenue falls from $15 to $12; the demand for good B is inelastic. As the price of good C decreases, revenue remains unchanged; the demand for good C is unit elastic.

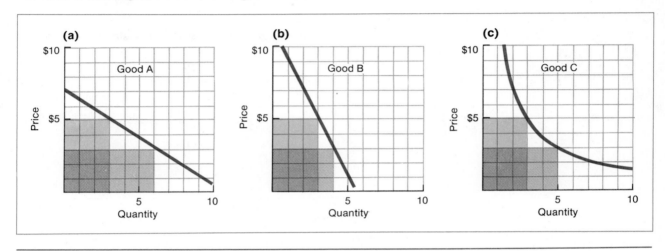

total revenue increases as the price decreases, demand for the good is said to be **elastic.** If quantity changes by a smaller percentage than price, so that total revenue decreases as the price decreases, as in Exhibit 3.8b, demand is said to be **inelastic.** And if price and quantity change by the same percentage, as in Exhibit 3.8c, so that total revenue remains unchanged, demand is said to be **unit elastic.**

In addition to the cases of elastic, inelastic, and unit elastic demand illustrated in Exhibit 3.8, there are two limiting cases illustrated in Exhibit 3.9. Exhibit 3.9a shows a demand curve that is perfectly vertical. No matter what the price, the quantity demanded is a constant five units—no more, no less. Such a demand curve is referred to as **perfectly inelastic.** Exhibit 3.9b shows a demand curve that is perfectly horizontal. Above the price of $5, none of the good can be sold. But as soon as the price drops to $5, producers can sell as much of the good as they care to produce without cutting the price any more. A horizontal demand curve such as this one is described as **perfectly elastic.**

The Importance of Elasticity

If elasticity were nothing more than another way of describing the shape and position of demand curves, it would not deserve a great deal of attention. But what makes elasticity an important concept is not so much its descriptive usefulness as its analytic usefulness. A great many business and public policy decisions depend crucially on judgments regarding the elasticity of demand for various goods and services, as the following three-part case study illustrates.

Elastic demand The situation where quantity changes by a larger percentage than price along the demand curve, so that total revenue increases as price decreases.

Inelastic demand The situation where quantity changes by a smaller percentage than price along the demand curve, so that total revenue decreases as price decreases.

Unit elastic demand The situation where price and quantity change by the same percentage along the demand curve, so that total revenue remains unchanged as price changes.

Perfectly inelastic demand The situation where the demand curve is a vertical line.

Perfectly elastic demand The situation where the demand curve is a horizontal line.

Exhibit 3.9
Perfectly elastic and perfectly inelastic demand
Part a of this exhibit shows a demand curve that is a vertical line. No matter what the price, the quantity demanded is a constant five units. Such a demand curve is referred to as perfectly inelastic. Part b shows a perfectly elastic demand curve, which is a horizontal line. Above the price of $5, none of the good can be sold. At the price of $5, suppliers can sell as much of the good as they want without further reductions in price.

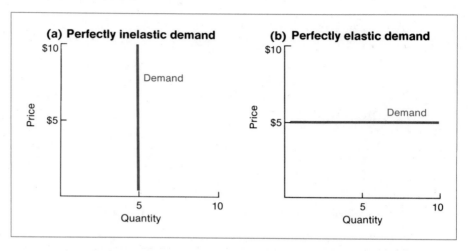

Case 3.3
The Importance of Elasticity of Demand to Business and Government Decision Making

In 1977, Congress passed legislation granting airlines substantially increased freedom from government regulation in setting air fares. For the most part, airlines initially used their newly granted pricing flexibility to cut fares for vacation travel. The demand for vacation travel, they found, was quite elastic; revenues rose as fares were cut. But most airlines remained reluctant to cut fares for business travel. They judged the demand for business air travel to be inelastic and thus feared that cutting fares for that part of their clientele would reduce rather than increase their revenues.

In the spring of 1979, President Carter made a decision to decontrol the price of domestically produced petroleum. His reasoning was based in part on a judgment about the elasticity of demand. Higher prices, his advisers persuaded him, would significantly reduce the quantity of petroleum demanded, helping to reduce U.S. dependence on foreign sources of supply. Critics of the decontrol decision, in contrast, believed the demand for oil to be almost perfectly inelastic. There would be no significant decline in the quantity demanded, they felt; the only effect would be to increase the revenues of the oil companies enormously.

Another major public policy issue widely debated during 1979 was national health insurance. One detail to be decided in designing a national health insurance system was the so-called *coinsurance rate*—the percentage of medical bills that would be paid by the consumer. Testifying before the Senate Health Subcommittee, economist Martin Feldstein of the National Bureau of Economic Research argued that the coinsurance rate ought to be no less than 30 percent, at least up to some catastrophic ceiling. His recommendation was based on his estimate of the elasticity of demand for medical care. As the coinsurance rate is reduced toward zero, Feldstein argued, the demand for medical care becomes highly elastic. A national health insurance program with too low a coinsurance rate would thus tend to swamp hospitals and doctors with more work than they could handle, and the cost to government would grow out of control.[5]

Measuring Elasticity of Demand

For some purposes, it is useful to put a numerical value on elasticity of demand, rather than simply to classify demand as elastic or inelastic. The basis for such numerical measurements is the definition of the *elasticity of demand* as the ratio of the percentage change in quantity demanded to the percentage change in price.

Percentage Changes In order to apply this definition to the measurement of elasticity, we need to be somewhat more precise than before about how to calculate percentage changes. Suppose, for example, we are dealing with a $.25 increase in the price of strawberries, from $.75 per pint to $1 per pint. In everyday usage, we would call this a 33 percent increase in price ($.25/$.75 = 0.33). However, if we observed a $.25 decrease in the price of strawberries, from $1 per pint to $.75, we would call it a 25 percent decrease ($.25/$1 = 0.25).

In measuring elasticity, it would be awkward to have to specify whether we were dealing with a price increase or a price decrease before calculating the percentage change. To get around this difficulty, we will adopt the convention of using the midpoint of the price range as a basis for calculating the percentage. The midpoint in this case is ($.75 + $1)/2 = $.875, so the percentage change, as we define it, becomes $.25/$.875 = 0.285 (approximately). Calculated this way, the percentage is the same for an increase as for a decrease over the specified range of price.

Using P_1 to represent the price before the change and P_2 the price after the change, this convention for calculating the percentage change in price can be written in terms of a general formula as:

$$\text{Percent change in price} = \frac{P_1 - P_2}{(P_1 + P_2)/2}.$$

The same problem arises in defining the percentage change in the quantity demanded that results from a given change in price. Suppose that when the price of strawberries falls from $1 to $.75, the quantity demanded increases from 100 pints per day to 150 pints. We can use the average of the higher quantity and the lower quantity to calculate the percentage change in quantity. If Q_1 and Q_2 are the quantities before and after a change in price, the formula for the percentage change can be written as:

$$\text{Percentage change in quantity} = \frac{Q_1 - Q_2}{(Q_1 + Q_2)/2}.$$

Applying this formula to the example just given, we would say that either an increase in quantity from 100 to 150 or a decrease in quantity from 150 to 100 represented a 40 percent change in quantity:

$$\text{Percentage change in quantity} = \frac{150 - 100}{(150 + 100)/2} = 0.40.$$

---

[5]Reported in "Consequences of Hospital Controls," *Wall Street Journal*, April 12, 1979.

An Elasticity Formula Defining percentage changes in this way allows us to write a practical formula for calculating elasticities. The formula can be applied to the elasticity of either supply or demand. Using P_1 and Q_1 to represent price and quantity before a change and P_2 and Q_2 to represent price and quantity after the change, the formula is:[6]

$$\begin{array}{l} \text{Price} \\ \text{elasticity} \\ \text{of demand} \end{array} = \frac{(Q_1 - Q_2)/(Q_1 + Q_2)}{(P_1 - P_2)/(P_1 + P_2)} = \frac{\begin{array}{c}\text{Percentage change} \\ \text{in quantity}\end{array}}{\begin{array}{c}\text{Percentage change} \\ \text{in price}\end{array}}.$$

The following problem illustrates the use of this formula.

Problem: A change in the price of strawberries from $1 per pint to $.75 per pint causes the quantity demanded to increase from 100 pints per day to 150 pints per day. What is the price elasticity of demand for strawberries over the range of price and quantity indicated?

Solution:
P_1 = Price before change   = $1
P_2 = Price after change   = $.75
Q_1 = Quantity before change = 100
Q_2 = Quantity after change   = 150

$$\begin{aligned} \text{Elasticity} &= \frac{(100 - 150)/(100 + 150)}{(\$1.00 - \$.75)/(\$1.00 + \$.75)} \\ &= \frac{-50/250}{\$.25/\$1.75} \\ &= \frac{-0.2}{\$.1428} \\ &= -1.4. \end{aligned}$$

Note that when the formula is applied to a good having a negatively sloped demand curve—as most, if not all, goods do—it yields a negative value for elasticity. The reason is that the quantity changes in the opposite direction to the change in price. It will be the practice in this book to drop the minus sign, however, and to speak of price elasticity of demand as a positive number; that is, the elasticity of demand for a good will be given as 2 or 0.5 or whatever rather than as -2 or -0.5. This convention of dropping the minus sign is widely used in economic writing, although it is not followed universally. If this convention is applied to the preceding problem, the elasticity of demand for strawberries will be said to be 1.4 over the range of price and quantity shown.

---

[6]Given the definition of percentage changes, we could write the elasticity formula as:

$$\frac{\dfrac{Q_1 - Q_2}{(Q_1 + Q_2)/2}}{\dfrac{P_1 - P_2}{(P_1 + P_2)/2}}.$$

This is unnecessarily complicated, however, because the 2's cancel out. The formula given in the text is the simplified equivalent of this one.

Elasticity Values and Changes in Revenue

The chapter earlier introduced the terms *elastic, inelastic, unit elastic, perfectly elastic,* and *perfectly inelastic demand.* They were defined in terms of the relationship between change in price and change in total revenue. Each of these elasticity terms corresponds to a certain numerical value or range of numerical values of elasticity as calculated according to the elasticity formula. A perfectly inelastic demand curve has a measured elasticity of 0, because any change in price produces no change in quantity demanded. The term *inelastic* (but not perfectly inelastic) *demand* applies to measured elasticities in the range from 0 up to, but not including, 1. *Unit elasticity,* as the name implies, means a numerical elasticity of exactly 1. *Elastic demand* means any value for elasticity greater than 1. *Perfectly elastic demand,* corresponding to a horizontal supply curve, is not defined numerically; as the demand curve approaches horizontal, the denominator of the elasticity formula approaches 0, so that the measured value of elasticity approaches infinity.

Varying and Constant Elasticity Demand Curves

The formula just given for calculating the elasticity of demand shows the elasticity of demand over a certain range of price and quantity. Measured over some other range of price and quantity, the elasticity of demand for the same good may or may not be different. Whether the elasticity of demand for a good changes along the demand curve turns out to depend on the exact shape of the curve. This is illustrated in Exhibits 3.10 and 3.11.

A Linear Demand Curve First consider Exhibit 3.10a, which shows a straight-line demand curve like most of those drawn in this book. The elasticity of demand is not constant for all ranges of price and quantity along this curve. Measured over the price range $8 to $9, for example, the elasticity of demand is 5.66. Measured over the range $2 to $3, it is 0.33. (The full calculations are shown in the exhibit.)

This illustrates the general principle that elasticity declines as one moves down along a straight-line demand curve. It is easy to see why: With a straight-line demand curve, a $1 reduction in price always produces the same absolute increase in quantity demanded. At the upper end of the demand curve, though, a $1 change in price is a small percentage change, while the absolute change in quantity, as a percentage of the small quantity already demanded, is large. At the lower end of the curve, the situation is reversed. A $1 change is now a large percentage of the price, while the constant absolute increase in quantity has now become smaller in percentage terms. Because it is percentages, not absolute amounts, that count in elasticity calculations, the demand curve is less elastic near the bottom than near the top. Because elasticity changes along a straight-line demand curve, it makes sense to apply the formula only to small changes.

Note the relationship between the elasticity of demand and total revenue, as shown by Exhibit 3.10b. In the elastic range of the demand curve, total revenue increases as price decreases. Total revenue reaches a peak at the point of unit elasticity and declines again in the range of inelastic demand.

A Constant Elasticity Demand Curve If the demand curve is not a straight line, the above results need not always apply. There is an important

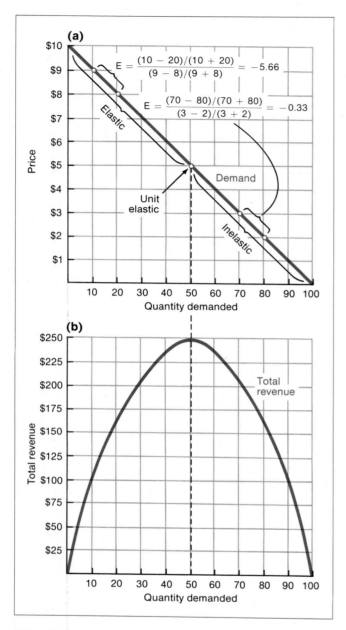

Exhibit 3.10

Variation in elasticity along a straight-line demand curve

This exhibit shows how elasticity varies along a straight-line demand curve. At low quantities, demand is elastic; for example, in the range from ten to twenty units, the elasticity of the demand curve shown in Part a of the exhibit is 5.66. At fifty units of output (half-way down the curve), a point of unit elasticity is reached. From there to a hundred units of output, demand is inelastic; in the range seventy to eighty units, for example, elasticity is 0.33. Part b of the exhibit shows that total revenue increases as quantity increases over the elastic portion of the demand curve and decreases as quantity increases over the inelastic portion. Total revenue reaches a maximum at the point of unit elasticity.

special case in which the demand curve has just the curvature needed to keep elasticity constant throughout its length. Such a curve is shown in Exhibit 3.11. As the calculations in the exhibit indicate, elasticity is exactly 1.0 everywhere on this curve. It is possible to construct demand curves with constant elasticities of any desired value. Such curves are often used in statistical studies of demand elasticity, as the following case study illustrates.

Case 3.4
Measuring Elasticity of Demand in the Cotton Market

The market for cotton has tended to be relatively unstable in the postwar period. Price changes from one year to the next have been very great. It is thought that one of the reasons for this instability is a very inelastic demand for cotton. With an inelastic demand, the price must fall a long way for producers to dispose of a relatively small surplus, and a considerable rise in price can occur when there is a shortage. Kenneth Lewis, an economist at Boston University, thought it would be useful for those concerned with the cotton market to know just how inelastic demand was.

Lewis began by assembling data on the price of cotton and the quantity of cotton purchased in sixteen industrialized countries during the period 1949 to 1964. To simplify his calculations, he followed a standard econometric practice and assumed that the cotton demand curve would have the shape needed to give constant elasticity throughout the normal range of prices. Next he had to deal with the problem of "other things being equal." A demand curve tells how the demand for cotton responds to the price for cotton when nothing else changes, but in the wide range of countries and years represented in Lewis's data, "other things" could hardly be expected to stand still. To deal with this problem, he used a statistical technique known as multiple regression analysis. This allowed an approximate correction for changes that had occurred over time in population, per capita consumer income, and the prices of other closely related products—particularly wool and synthetic fibers.

Lewis's statistical results confirmed that the demand for cotton was very inelastic—only 0.095, as nearly as he could estimate. This meant that more than a 10 percent change in price from one year to the next would be required to change the quantity demanded by 1 percent. Lewis suggested two reasons for the low elasticity of demand. One was that cotton is a raw material that often accounts for only a small portion of the value of a final product. For example, a 10 percent change in the price of cotton would have far less than a 10 percent effect on the price of a cotton shirt if the cost of manufacturing, labor, transportation, retailing, services, and the like remained unchanged. Second, the products made from cotton were necessities rather than luxuries, for the most part, and hence they too could be expected to have low elasticities of demand.

Source: Based on Kenneth Lewis, "Multi-Market Demand Functions in the Presence of Supply Constraints: International Demand for Cotton and Wool," *Southern Economic Journal* 38 (October 1971): 200–208.

Exhibit 3.11

A demand curve with constant elasticity
It is possible for a demand curve to have constant elasticity throughout its length. The calculations in the exhibit show that this curve has an elasticity of 1.0 wherever it is measured. This particular demand curve is a rectangular hyperbola with the formula $P \times Q = 100$.

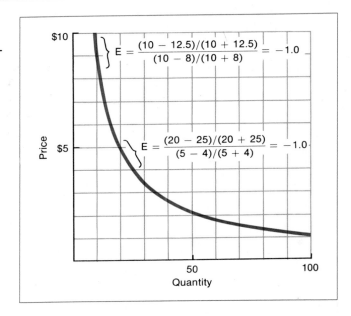

$$E = \frac{(10 - 12.5)/(10 + 12.5)}{(10 - 8)/(10 + 8)} = -1.0$$

$$E = \frac{(20 - 25)/(20 + 25)}{(5 - 4)/(5 + 4)} = -1.0$$

It is important to recognize the limitations of statistical estimates of demand elasticity. To say that the elasticity of demand for cotton is 0.095 is not to measure any inherent quality of the good itself. Neither is the measured elasticity really a constant of consumer behavior. The actual measurement is just a capsulized fragment of economic history. It tells us that at certain times and places in the past, a 1 percent change in price appears to have been associated with approximately a 0.095 percent change in quantity demanded.

Despite their limitations, however, statistical estimates of elasticity can be of considerable practical use. Economic decision makers in business and government must take past experience into account when planning for the future even though they know that market conditions in the future will not be exactly like those in the past.

Determinants of Elasticity of Demand

Why is the price elasticity of demand high for some goods and low for others? One thing helping to determine the elasticity of demand for a good is the availability of substitutes or complements. If a good has close substitutes, demand for that good tends to be elastic, because when its price rises, people can switch to something similar. For example, the demand for olive oil is more elastic than it would be if other salad oils were not available as substitutes. Similarly, the demand for cars is less elastic than it would be if good public transport were available everywhere, because cars and public transportation are reasonably close substitutes for each other. On the other hand, if something is a minor complement to an important good, its demand tends to be inelastic. For example, the demand for motor oil tends to be inelastic, because it is a complement to a more important good—gasoline. The price of gasoline is much more likely to influence the amount of driving a person does than is the price of motor oil.

Elasticity is also influenced by the portion of a person's budget spent on a good. Matches, for example, are no longer really a necessity, and good substitutes exist. Nonetheless, the demand for matches is thought to be very inelastic, just because people spend so little on them that they hardly notice a price change. In contrast, the demand for things like housing and transportation is not perfectly inelastic, even though they are necessities. Since they occupy a large part of people's budgets, changes in prices just cannot be ignored.

Finally, elasticity of demand is influenced by the time perspective being considered. Demand is often less elastic in the short run than in the long run. Consider the demand for home heating fuel, for example. In the short run, people find it hard to cut back the quantity they use when the price goes up. They are accustomed to living at a certain temperature, dressing a certain way, and so on. Given time, though, they may find ways to economize. They can put better insulation in their homes, get in the habit of dressing more warmly, or even move to a warmer climate.

Other Elasticities

The concept of elasticity has, up to this point, been applied only to the price elasticity of demand for a good; but there are many other common applications of the concept. All of them are based on the idea of the ratio of the percentage change in one variable to the percentage change in another. Two of the most commonly used types of elasticity, in addition to the price elasticity of demand, are price elasticity of supply and income elasticity of demand.

Price Elasticity of Supply The definition of the **price elasticity of supply** for a good closely resembles that of the price elasticity of demand: It is the percentage change in the quantity of the good supplied divided by the percentage change in the price of the good. The formula for price elasticity of supply is exactly the same as that for price elasticity of demand. Because price and quantity change in the same direction along a positively sloped supply curve, the formula gives a positive value for the elasticity of supply. Exhibit 3.12 applies the elasticity formula to two supply curves, one having constant elasticity and the other having variable elasticity.

> **Price elasticity of supply (elasticity of supply)** The ratio of the percentage change in the quantity of a good supplied to the percentage change in its price.

Income Elasticity of Demand As shown earlier in this chapter, changes in consumer income can cause changes in the demand for a good. Such changes are represented by shifts in the demand curve. The concept of elasticity, in the form of the income elasticity of demand, can be applied to measure the size and direction of such changes. The **income elasticity of demand** for a good is defined as the ratio of the percentage change in demand for the good to the percentage change in income. In measuring the income elasticity

> **Income elasticity of demand** The ratio of the percentage change in the demand for a good to the percentage change in the per capita income of buyers.

Exhibit 3.12
Calculating price elasticities of supply
This exhibit gives four examples of how supply elasticities are calculated—two for each of the two supply curves shown. The supply curve S_1, which is a straight line passing through the origin, has a constant elasticity of 1.0. The supply curve S_2, which is curved, is elastic for low quantities of output and inelastic for larger quantities. For example, in the range from twenty to thirty units of output, the elasticity of S_2 is 3.4, and in the range from eighty to ninety units of output, the elasticity is 0.41.

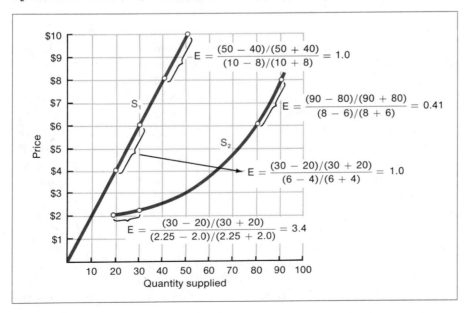

of demand for a good, the price of the good is assumed not to change. Income is usually measured in per capita terms. Using Q_1 and Q_2 to represent quantities before and after the income change and y_1 and y_2 to represent per capita income before and after the change, the formula for income elasticity of demand can be written as follows:

$$\text{Income elasticity of demand} = \frac{(Q_1 - Q_2)/(Q_1 + Q_2)}{(y_1 - y_2)/(y_1 + y_2)} = \frac{\text{Percentage change in quantity}}{\text{Percentage change in income}}.$$

Income elasticity of demand is positive for a normal good and negative for an inferior good. Suppose, for example, that a study of meat buying habits showed that for each 10 percent increase in income, the typical U.S. household tended to consume 12 percent more steak, 5 percent more chicken, and 2 percent less hamburger. One would conclude from these numbers that the income elasticity of demand was 1.2 for steak, 0.5 for chicken, and −0.2 for hamburger. Steak and chicken would thus be classified as normal goods and hamburger as an inferior good.

CONCLUSIONS

This completes the presentation of the basics of supply and demand analysis. The chapter will conclude with a few remarks that relate supply and demand to the role of markets as a mechanism for utilizing knowledge and that concern the scope of applicability of supply and demand analysis.

Information and Equilibrium

There is a simple connection between the idea of equilibrium and the idea of the market as a mechanism for distributing information. The connection is found in the fact that the market can be in equilibrium when, and only when, it has entirely completed its job of distributing information among buyers and sellers.

It is easy to see why this is true. First, if buyers and sellers have incomplete knowledge of prices and of other economic conditions, it is unlikely that their separately formulated market plans will exactly mesh. It may be that both buyers and sellers expect the price tomorrow to be higher (or lower) than it actually will be. It may be that buyers have one idea about what the price will be and sellers another. Whatever the case, someone is bound to be disappointed, and disappointed plans are the stuff of which disequilibrium is made.

On the other hand, if both buyers and sellers have complete and accurate knowledge of both present and future prices and market conditions, how can their plans fail to mesh? No one will plan to sell knowing that there will be no one to buy. With perfect information, people will formulate only such market plans as they know can be carried out on the expected terms, and that is what *equilibrium* means.

Saying that markets are in equilibrium only when all buyers and sellers have perfect information leads to a conclusion that may seem strange. The conclusion is that, in the real world, we can hardly ever expect to find a market in equilibrium! To paraphrase a famous saying, all people know something some of the time, and some people know a great deal all of the time, but everybody does not know everything all of the time. In real markets, prices are always being pushed this way or that by changes in underlying economic conditions. Some people learn of these changes right away, and the buying and selling they do telegraphs that information, via the price system, to others. But the market telegraph does not work with the speed of light. Before everyone who is directly or indirectly interested in what goes on in a particular market learns of some change, other changes have occurred. The whirling stream of human knowledge never quite catches up with an even more fluid reality.

Applicability

The fact that markets are never really in equilibrium is, in a sense, a limitation on the applicability of supply and demand analysis. There are other limitations too. As Part 2 of this book will show, supply and demand analysis applies in its pure form only to markets where the number of buyers and sellers is very large and where the products offered by one seller differ very little from those offered by another. Some real world markets fit the conditions fairly well. The markets for agricultural products such as wheat are an example. But the markets for many other products do not look exactly like the idealized markets of economic theory.

For now, though, there is no need to be overly concerned with differences between the real and the ideal. The theory of supply and demand may not *exactly* fit any market at any particular moment in time; yet, in a general sense, thinking in terms of supply and demand can give extremely useful insights into the way almost all markets work. The usefulness of these tools will be proved in application as we work through this book. Fine points can be left for more advanced courses.

SUMMARY

1. The law of demand says that the quantity of a good demanded by buyers tends to change in a direction opposite to any change in price, other things being equal. By *quantity demanded*, economists mean effective demand, as distinguished from wants or needs not backed up by willingness and ability to buy. By *other things being equal*, they have in mind such things as buyers' incomes, the prices of other goods, and buyers' expectations about future price changes.
2. A change in the quantity of a good demanded that results solely from a change in the price of that good is represented graphically as a movement along a demand curve. When something other than its price changes (for example, buyers' incomes, the prices of substitutes or complements, or buyers' expectations), the result is a change in demand, represented graphically as a shift of the entire demand curve.
3. A supply curve shows the relationship between the price of a good and the quantity of it supplied, other things being equal. Unless there is some particular reason to do otherwise, economists usually draw supply curves with upward slopes. A change in the price of a good produces a change in the quantity supplied, shown by a movement along a supply curve. A change in some other factor—technology, input prices, prices of other goods—produces a change in supply, shown by a shift of the supply curve.
4. Market equilibrium is a condition in which the separately formulated plans of buyers and sellers exactly mesh, so that the quantity supplied is equal to

the quantity demanded. If the price of a product is too high for equilibrium, there will be a surplus of the good, which, in turn, will tend to push the price down. If the price is below the equilibrium, there will be a shortage, which will tend to drive the price up. Equilibrium is possible only when the market has completely carried out its job of distributing information among buyers and sellers.

5. For some goods, a 1 percent change in price produces more than a 1 percent change in quantity demanded, so that revenue increases as price decreases. Such goods are said to have elastic demand. Similarly, goods are said to have an elastic supply if a 1 percent change in price produces more than a 1 percent change in the quantity supplied. At the extreme, where supply or demand curves are horizontal, supply or demand is said to be perfectly elastic. For other goods, a 1 percent change in price will cause less than a 1 percent change in quantity demanded, so that revenue decreases as price decreases. Such goods are said to have inelastic demand. Similarly, goods are said to have an inelastic supply if a 1 percent change in price produces less than a 1 percent change in the quantity supplied. Perfectly inelastic demand or supply means a vertical supply or demand curve.

6. The formula for calculating the elasticity of supply or demand between two points on a supply or demand curve is:

$$\text{Elasticity} = \frac{(Q_1 - Q_2)/(Q_1 + Q_2)}{(P_1 - P_2)/(P_1 + P_2)}.$$

In applying this formula to demand, it is conventional to drop the minus sign from the result and consider elasticity to be a positive number.

7. Changes in per capita income can cause shifts in demand curves. The ratio of the percentage change in quantity to the percentage change in per capita income is known as the income elasticity of demand. Income elasticity of demand is positive for a normal good and negative for an inferior good.

DISCUSSION QUESTIONS

1. The *law of demand* states that there is an inverse relationship between the price of a good and the quantity that people will be willing and able to pay for. How is this "law" like the law of gravity? How is it different? Explain.
2. Illustrate the supply of McDonald's hamburgers to an individual consumer. What is the slope of the supply curve?
3. Suppose there were a drought in the Midwest, where much of the nation's wheat is grown. What would be the impact of the drought on the demand and supply of wheat? What would happen to the price of wheat? Why? How would this be likely to affect the individual consumers of products containing wheat?
4. If you drop a marble into a bowl, it will eventually come to rest at the bottom. You can then say that the marble is at equilibrium at the bottom of the bowl. What is meant by *equilibrium*? In what ways is equilibrium in a market similar to the equilibrium of the marble? In what ways is it different?
5. If you were a wholesaler and you could see sooner than your competitors when the demand curve for the product you deal in was about to shift to the right, how could you use this advance knowledge to make money? Would you be benefiting anyone besides yourself in getting rid of the disequilibrium? Explain.
6. Suppose you read the following news item in the daily paper: "Frost in Brazil has caused a severe shortage of coffee, which has driven the price well above normal levels. The shortage is expected to persist for several years, until new coffee bushes

can be planted and reach maturity." Do you think the writer is using the word *shortage* in the same sense that it has been used in this chapter? Explain.

7. Suppose that the opportunity cost of time spent waiting in line to buy gasoline were uniformly $5 per hour for all consumers. Would imposing price controls on gasoline to deal with a sudden decrease in supply then benefit anyone at all? Would it make anyone worse off than if the price were simply allowed to rise to a higher equilibrium level? Should the owners of gas stations and oil companies be counted as "anyone" in answering this question?

8. If you were the president of a union bargaining for a new contract and asking for higher wages, would you prefer that the demand for your firm's product were relatively elastic or relatively inelastic? Explain.

9. Suppose that again, as in 1974, Middle Eastern governments cut off imports of petroleum products into the United States and that the U.S. government imposed a price ceiling. Do you think the lines that formed at gas stations would be longer if the demand for gasoline were relatively elastic or if it were relatively inelastic? (You may wish to refer to Exhibit 3.7 on page 49.)

10. The town manager of River City calls you in as a consultant to explain something puzzling. Last year, the city doubled its fares on its downtown buses. For a few months, the bus line reported a strong increase in revenues, but then the revenues began falling off and ended up lower than they had been to begin with. Does what you have learned about elasticity of demand and the determinants of that demand help you explain what happened?

11. Why would the slope of a demand curve not be just as good a measure as elasticity for the responsiveness of demand to price changes? Can you formulate a simple generalization relating the slope of a demand curve to the way in which total revenue changes when price changes?

SUGGESTIONS FOR FURTHER READING

Breit, William, and Ransom, Roger L. *The Academic Scribblers.* New York: Holt, Rinehart and Winston, 1971, Chapter 3.
An essay on Alfred Marshall. The preceding two chapters provide useful background.

Campbell, Colin D., ed. *Wage-Price Controls in World War II: United States and Germany.* Washington, D.C.: American Enterprise Institute, 1971.
Vivid descriptions and insightful analysis of what happens when governments get serious about wage and price controls.

Marshall, Alfred. *Principles of Economics.* Various editions.
First published in 1891, this book served as the definitive treatise on economics in the English-speaking world for generations. It remains remarkably accessible to browsing, even by the beginning student. For a start, look up Marshall's treatment of the determinants of demand or his discussion (and dismissal) of cases of apparently upward sloping demand curves.

THE ROLE OF GOVERNMENT IN THE ECONOMY

WHAT YOU WILL LEARN IN THIS CHAPTER

Not all economic decisions in the U.S. economy are made in the marketplace; many are also made in government at the federal, state, and local levels. This chapter provides an overview of the role of government in the economy— what distinguishes government from other actors in the economy and what the major functions of government are. It also provides an overview of how federal, state, and local governments levy taxes and what each level of government spends money on. Finally, it explains how to apply supply and demand theory to help determine who bears the real economic burden of taxation.

FOR REVIEW

Here are some important terms and concepts that will be put to use in this chapter. If you do not understand them, review them before proceeding.
- *The margin, marginal (Chapter 1)*
- *Incentives in the market economy (Chapter 2)*
- *Supply and demand analysis (Chapter 3)*

The forces of supply and demand, acting through markets, affect every significant economic decision in the U.S. economy. Nonetheless, the United States is not a pure market economy. There are other economic forces as well that affect how resources are used. By far the most important of the nonmarket forces is that of government.

As an actor on the economic stage, government differs in a number of important ways from other actors. Three characteristics in particular distinguish it from the individuals and firms constituting the market sector.

First, government can legitimately use force in economic affairs. In the private sector, firms and individuals are limited by law and custom to peaceable means of production and exchange that require the voluntary consent of everyone involved. Governments, on the other hand, are able to employ force, coercion, and involuntary expropriation in pursuit of their economic goals. When the government taxes incomes, regulates prices, drafts soldiers, or outlaws gambling, it does not require the immediate, explicit consent of the individuals taxed, regulated, conscripted, or outlawed. Although in a democracy these uses of government power are supposed to rest, at least indirectly, on the consent of the voters, they are binding on minorities and nonvoters as well. Without the use or threat of force, government could do very few of the things it does.

A second characteristic setting governments apart from other economic agents is the fact that the great bulk of goods and services produced by governments are provided to users without charge. In most cases, people do not have to pay directly for defense services, highway use, education, or police protection. Instead, they pay for these things indirectly, through taxes. In only a few cases do the taxes paid vary according to the quantity of public service consumed. The fact that governments do not charge users directly for most of their services has important implications for measuring the total contribution of government to the national product and for measuring the degree of efficiency with which government services are utilized. More on this will appear in later chapters.

A third way governments differ from other economic agents is in how they arrive at economic decisions. The system of voting and bargaining by which public decisions are made is much more complex and hard to analyze than the decision processes of private business firms and consumers. As a result, economists have not gotten as far in formulating simple rules or theories to explain resource allocation in the public sector. In the past, economists traditionally treated government decisions as givens for purposes of economic analysis and did not try to explain why one government decision rather than another was made at a particular time. In recent years, though, some progress has been made in formulating an economic theory of "public choice" to parallel the theory of private choice with which economists have traditionally worked.

Despite the peculiarities of government, market forces of supply and demand do make themselves felt to a degree even within the public sector of the economy. The principal reason is that governments have to purchase most of the inputs they require on the open market. The U.S. Department of Justice cannot hire a new clerk unless it pays at least the wage determined by supply and demand for workers with the required skills. The City of Chicago cannot buy police cars unless it pays something pretty close to what private individuals would pay for the same vehicles. The necessity of purchasing inputs at market prices makes government aware of the relative cost of various programs and helps constrain total public spending.

Of course, particular government agencies sometimes ignore the messages the market sends to them via the price system. Corrupt bidding practices, for example, result in government purchases from politically favored firms at higher than market prices. Sometimes devices such as eminent domain or the draft are used to obtain resources without paying their full market value. In such instances, the degree of market influence on government is less than usual.

A large part of the remainder of the book will be devoted to exploring the interactions between government and the private market economy. This chapter will provide some useful background material about what government does and how its expenses are paid.

WHAT DOES GOVERNMENT DO?

Some Comparisons

Just what government does varies greatly from time to time and place to place. Before looking at the functions of government in detail, and before raising the question of whether it does too much or too little or the wrong mix of things, an idea of the overall size of government is needed. Some comparisons may help.

Exhibit 4.1 gives an indication of how government has grown over time. The chart shows what has happened to federal, state, and local **government purchases of goods and services** since the early years of the century. Government purchases of goods and services (or **government purchases,** for short) include all the finished products purchased by government (everything from submarines to typewriter ribbons) plus the cost of hiring the services of all government employees (everyone from the president to the courthouse janitor). These purchases are shown as a percentage of gross national product (GNP), a measure of the economy's total output of goods and services. By this measure, government has clearly grown over time. Before World War I, government purchases averaged less than 10 percent of GNP. Except for wartime peaks, they followed a steady trend upward from about 1920 until 1970. During the 1970s, total government purchases appear to have leveled off at about 20 percent of GNP.

Exhibit 4.2 provides a different kind of comparison. This graph gives data for several countries on total government expenditures, including transfer payments as well as government purchases. **Transfer payments** are all payments made by government to individuals that are not in return for goods or services currently supplied. They include such things as social security benefits, welfare payments, and unemployment compensation.

Government purchases of goods and services (government purchases) Expenditures made by federal, state, and local governments to purchase goods from private firms and to hire the services of government employees.

Transfer payments All payments made by government to individuals that are not made in return for goods or services currently supplied. Social security benefits, welfare payments, and unemployment compensation are major forms of transfer payments.

Exhibit 4.1

Growth of government purchases in the United States

The percentage of total government purchases in GNP has grown substantially over time. In the early years of the century, government purchases averaged less than 10 percent of GNP. Government purchases hit peaks in war years and by the 1950s had grown to the present peacetime average of about 20 percent of GNP.

Sources: Data for 1929 to the present are from President's Council of Economic Advisers, *Economic Report of the President* (Washington, D.C.: Government Printing Office, 1979), Table B–1. Data for years before 1929 are from U.S. Department of Commerce, Bureau of the Census, *Historical Statistics of the United States: Colonial Times to 1970* (Washington, D.C.: Government Printing Office, 1975).

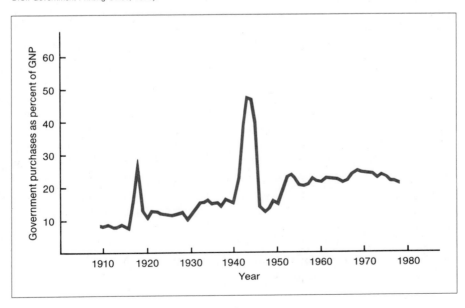

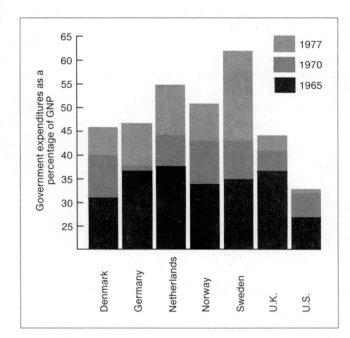

Exhibit 4.2
Total government expenditures as a percent of GNP for selected countries
The data in this graph refer to total expenditures of central and local government units, including both government purchases of goods and services and transfer payments. By this measure, the size of government relative to the rest of the economy is larger than when only government purchases are taken into account. Note that although government expenditures in the United States are growing, they are still considerably lower in relation to the size of the economy than for the other countries shown.

Source: Data from Theodore Geiger, *Welfare and Efficiency: Their Interactions in Western Europe and Implications for International Economic Relations* (Washington, D.C.: National Planning Association, 1979), Table 1–1. Used by permission. Note that the 1977 percentage for the Netherlands is actually based on 1976 data.

Using total expenditures rather than government purchases as a measure makes the public sector look somewhat larger. Government purchases plus transfer payments now equal about a third of GNP in the United States. In comparison with the advanced industrial countries of Western Europe, however, the public sector in the United States is not a particularly large percentage of GNP. In Sweden, a country with roughly the same level of per capita income as the United States, government expenditures are equal to nearly two-thirds of GNP; and in Norway and the Netherlands, government expenditures are equal to more than half of GNP.

The Functions of Government

Governments use the third to two-thirds of GNP that passes through their hands to perform a wide variety of functions. These functions can be classified under five general headings: provision of public goods, transfer of income, economic stabilization, regulation of private businesses, and administration of justice.

Provision of Public Goods The first function of government is to provide what economists call **public goods**—goods or services having the properties that (1) they cannot be provided to one citizen without being supplied also to that citizen's neighbors, and (2) once provided for one citizen, the cost of providing them to others is zero. Perhaps the best example of a public good is national defense. One citizen cannot very well be protected against foreign invasion or nuclear holocaust without having the protection "spill over" on neighbors. Also, it costs no more to protect a single resident of a given area than to protect an entire city.

Public goods are traditionally provided by government because their special properties make it hard for private business to market them profitably. Imagine

Public goods Goods or services having the properties that (1) they cannot be provided to one citizen without being supplied also to that person's neighbors, and (2) once they are provided for one citizen, the cost of providing them to others is zero.

what would happen if someone tried to set up a commercially operated ballistic missile defense system. If you subscribed, I would have no reason to subscribe too and would instead play the "free rider," relying on the spillover effect for my protection. But you would not subscribe, hoping that I would, so that you could be the free rider. The missile defense company would soon go bankrupt.

Transfer of Income The second function of government consists of making transfers of income and wealth from one citizen to another. Income or wealth is usually taken from citizens by means of taxation; but sometimes, as in the case of the military draft or jury duty, it is taken by conscription of services. Benefits are distributed either in the form of direct cash payments or in the form of the free or below-cost provision of goods and services. Among the more familiar types of cash transfers are social security payments, welfare benefits, and unemployment compensation. Goods and services used for transfers include public education, public housing, fire protection, and subsidized mass transit systems. They are provided at low or zero cost on the basis of political decisions rather than at market prices on the basis of ability to pay.

From the viewpoint of economic theory, the subsidized services used as vehicles for income transfers are different from the true public goods discussed above. They are consumed individually by selected citizens and do not share the two special properties of public goods. It sometimes happens, though, that services provided primarily as transfers may be public goods in part. For example, consider the fraction of fire protection devoted to preventing general conflagration as opposed to putting out fires in individual private buildings or the fraction of public health services devoted to controlling epidemic diseases as opposed to treating individual patients. A variety of transfer programs will be discussed in detail in Chapter 18.

Economic Stabilization Economic stabilization is a third major function of government. Economic stabilization policies are all policies aimed at promoting price stability, full employment, and economic growth. The government first became officially committed to a policy of stabilizing the economy at a high level of employment with the Employment Act of 1946.

Regulation of Private Businesses A fourth major function of government is the regulation of private businesses. Regulatory control is exercised through a network of dozens of specialized agencies and takes a variety of specific forms. Some agencies set maximum prices at which certain products can be sold, whereas others set minimum prices. The Food and Drug Administration and the Federal Communications Commission exercise considerable control over what can be produced by the firms they regulate. Agencies such as the Occupational Health and Safety Administration and the Environmental Protection Agency regulate how things are produced. Finally, the Equal Employment Opportunity Commission exercises a major say over who will produce which goods. Regulation is a subject of widespread research and controversy. Chapter 14 will take a look at some major issues in the economics of regulation.

Administration of Justice The fifth major function of government is the administration of justice. Usually, the police and courts are not thought of as part of the economic area of government; but their activities do, in fact, have important economic consequences.

Consider what happens, for example, when a judge makes a decision in a case involving an unsafe product, a breach of contract, or an automobile accident. The decision has an immediate effect on resource allocation in the particular case, because one party must pay damages to the other or make some other form of compensation. More importantly, other people will observe the outcome of the decision and , as a result, may change the way they do things. If the courts say that buyers can collect damages from the makers of unsafe products, firms are likely to design their products differently. If certain standards are set for liability in automobile accidents, car makers, road builders, and insurance companies will take notice.

In recent years, an entire field of research has opened up in the law and economics area. Although space in this book does not permit much discussion about the field, readers interested in practical applications of economic thinking may wish to pursue this area on their own or in advanced courses.[1]

One further area of economic policy combines the judicial and regulatory functions of government: the field of antitrust policy and the control of monopoly. Chapter 13 in Part 2 of this book will take up the problem of public policy toward monopoly.

Overlapping Functions

The classification of government activities by function helps provide a theoretical understanding of the role of government in the economy, but it does not correspond very well to any breakdown of government activities by program or agency. Particular programs and agencies often perform a number of different functions at the same time. For example, the main business of the Defense Department appears to be the provision of a public good—national defense—but it performs other functions as well. In wartime it performs a transfer function by shifting part of the cost of wars from the general taxpayer to young lower-class males via the draft. In peacetime it provides an instrument of economic stabilization through the way it administers its huge budget for the purchase of goods and services.

A full picture of the role of government, then, comes from looking at a breakdown of its activities not only by function but also by levels, agencies, and programs.

Public Expenditures by Type of Program

Exhibit 4.3a shows the pattern of federal government expenditures in 1978. The biggest single category was income security, which includes the social security program, unemployment compensation, public assistance (welfare), and federal employee retirement and disability benefits. Income security began to take the largest share of the federal budget only in 1974. Before that, defense had been the largest category. Throughout the 1960s, defense consistently took over 40 percent of the budget, peaking at 45 percent in 1968, at the height of

---

[1]See, for example, Suggestions for Further Reading at the end of this chapter.

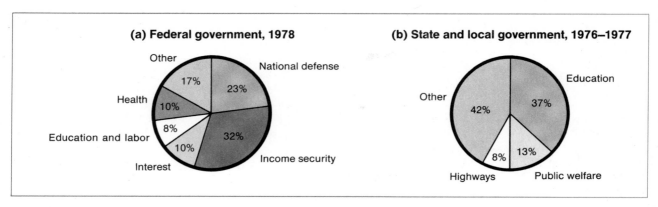

Exhibit 4.3
Patterns of government expenditure: Federal versus state and local
This exhibit shows the pattern of government expenditure at the federal, state, and local levels. The federal government bears the major burden of expenditures for national defense and income security, whereas education is by far the largest category of expenditure at the state and local levels.

Source: President's Council of Economic Advisers, *Economic Report of the President* (Washington, D.C.: Government Printing Office, 1979), Tables B–70 and B–75.

the Vietnam War. By 1978, the defense share of the budget was down to 23 percent. The other federal expenditures are largely self-explanatory.

Exhibit 4.3b shows the pattern of state and local expenditure. (State government accounted for about two-fifths of this, local government for three-fifths.) Here, by far the biggest item was education, which absorbed over a third of all expenditures. Public welfare and highways were the other largest categories.

To complete the picture, some idea of the relationship between the federal government on the one hand and state and local governments on the other is needed. Exhibit 4.4 shows that this relationship has been changing, as Washington has assumed a rapidly increasing burden of aid to state and local governments. This aid takes many forms, including job aid programs, sewage treatment construction grants, medicaid, income security programs, community development block grants, and general revenue sharing. Federal aid has been particularly concentrated in the nation's big cities. Direct federal aid to big cities increased more than tenfold between 1967 and 1977. These cities now receive more than fifty cents from the federal government for each dollar they raise from their own sources. This is more than the cities receive from their own states.

WHO PAYS FOR GOVERNMENT?

In recent years, people have become increasingly conscious of the costs as well as the benefits of a large, economically active public sector. In one sense, this is nothing new; people have grumbled about taxes ever since taxes were first invented. Nonetheless, in the late 1970s, citizens began to do more than grumble. In 1978, politicians who had paid lip service to limiting the burden of

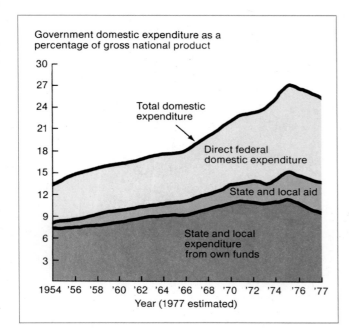

Government domestic expenditure as a percentage of gross national product

Exhibit 4.4

The changing relationship between the federal government and state and local governments

As this exhibit shows, Washington has assumed a rapidly increasing burden of aid to state and local governments in the last decade. Large cities in particular have received massive infusions of federal aid. Such cities now get more than fifty cents from the federal government for each dollar they raise from their own sources.

Source: U.S. Advisory Commission on Intergovernmental Relations, *Significant Features of Fiscal Federalism, 1976–77, Part 3: Expenditures* (Washington, D.C.: Government Printing Office, 1977).

taxes got something of a shock when voters in Alabama, Arizona, California, Hawaii, Idaho, Illinois, Massachusetts, Michigan, Missouri, North Dakota, South Dakota, and Texas imposed legal limits on state spending or taxes. Since that year of the taxpayers' revolt, economists have been paying increasing attention to the revenue side of government budgets and to the effects of taxation on the private sector. The remainder of this chapter will provide a brief tour of the economics of taxation.

What Kinds of Taxes?

We can begin by looking at the kinds of taxes that federal, state, and local governments use to raise revenue. Exhibit 4.5 gives the breakdowns. On the federal side, individual income taxes are the largest revenue raising item, although social insurance taxes and contributions have grown rapidly in recent years and are now not far behind. The corporate income tax used to be the second largest source of federal revenue, but it is now much less important than formerly.

The revenue side of the state and local government budget is quite different from that of the federal budget. State and local income taxes are in fifth place, with only 10 percent of revenues. Some states do not use the income tax at all. The largest source of revenue for state budgets is the sales tax, and for local government, property taxes are the largest item. As noted previously, an increasing share of state and local revenues comes directly from the federal government.

The Problem of Tax Incidence

Exhibit 4.5 shows the kinds of taxes paid to support various levels of government but not who really pays them. Economists refer to the question of who actually bears the burden of taxation as the problem of *tax incidence*. This

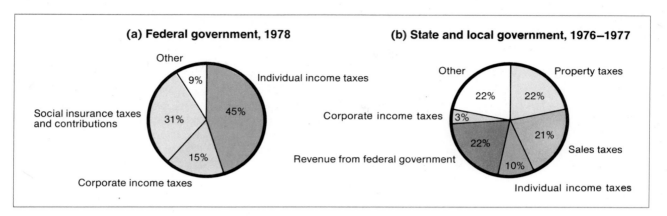

Exhibit 4.5
Sources of government revenue: Federal versus state and local
This exhibit shows the major sources of government revenue at the federal, state, and local levels. Individual income taxes and social insurance taxes are the major sources at the federal level. Local governments rely heavily on property taxes, while state governments use sales taxes and, to a lesser extent, income taxes. Notice that federal government grants are a major source of revenue for state and local governments.

Source: President's Council of Economic Advisers, *Economic Report of the President* (Washington, D.C.: Government Printing Office, 1979), Tables B–70 and B–75.

problem is not at all an easy one to solve. It is not enough just to look up the tax records of federal, state, and local governments. That would reveal only who had handed over the tax money to the authorities, not who actually bore the economic burden of the taxes. What makes tax incidence a difficult problem is the fact that the party who is obligated by law to pay the tax can often shift the burden of it to someone else.

An Illustration of Tax Incidence For a simple example, suppose a law is passed that requires all retailers to make a tax payment of ten cents to the government for each pack of cigarettes they sell. Who will bear the economic burden of this tax? A simple supply and demand analysis will provide the answer.

Look at the supply and demand curves shown in Exhibit 4.6. Without the tax, the equilibrium price of cigarettes would be twenty cents per pack, and 200 million packs per day would be sold. The tax upsets this equilibrium. In effect, the requirement of paying a ten cent per pack tax adds ten cents per pack to sellers' cost of doing business, which shifts the supply curve upward by ten cents. Buyers respond to this "artificial" shift in the supply curve in the same way they would to a genuine increase in the cost of producing cigarettes. They move up and to the left along their demand curve, cutting consumption. A new equilibrium is reached at twenty-five cents per pack—the intersection of the demand curve with the new supply curve.

Comparing the pretax with the posttax equilibrium, we see that although sellers must hand over ten cents to the government for each pack they sell, they receive only five cents per pack less than they did before the tax. Thus

Exhibit 4.6

The effects of a ten cent per pack sales tax on cigarettes

Before the sales tax is imposed, the equilibrium price for cigarettes is twenty cents per pack. The ten cent per pack sales tax can be treated as the sellers' added cost of doing business. It pushes the supply curve up by ten cents, as shown. After the shift in the supply curve, the price paid by buyers rises to twenty-five cents per pack, and the price received by sellers falls to fifteen cents. Thus, when the slopes of the supply and demand curves are equal, as shown in this exhibit, half the burden of the tax falls on sellers, and half is shifted to buyers.

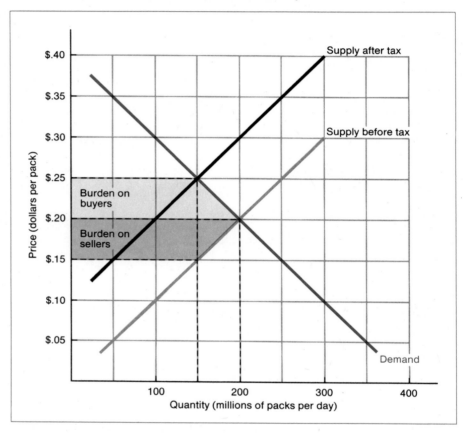

half the burden of the tax has been shifted to the buyers in the form of a price increase of five cents per pack. In the new equilibrium, the price paid by buyers is ten cents per pack more than what sellers receive after the tax.

In this example, the economic burden of the tax is divided equally between buyers and sellers, but the division need not always work out that way. If the demand curve had happened to be a little steeper and the supply curve a little flatter, the major share of the burden would have fallen on buyers. If the supply curve had been steeper than the demand curve, sellers would have borne the bigger share of the incidence of the tax. A large part of solving the puzzle of tax incidence, then, is determining just what the shapes of the supply and demand curves really are for the goods and services that are taxed.

Progressive tax A tax that takes a larger percentage of income from people whose income is high.

Overall Tax Incidence Taxes can be classified in terms of their incidence as progressive or regressive. A **progressive tax** takes a larger percentage of income from people whose incomes are high, and a **regressive tax** takes a larger percentage of income from people whose incomes are low. One of the most interesting questions about the economics of taxation is whether the overall effect of federal, state, and local taxes is progressive, regressive, or somewhere in between.

A recent study by economist Joseph Minarik of the Brookings Institution attempts to bring together evidence on the incidence of several important kinds of taxes in an attempt to show whether the U.S. tax system as a whole is progressive or regressive. The results of his study are shown in Exhibit 4.7.

The federal income tax, as expected, is progressive. As people's incomes increase, they pay not only a higher percentage of their total income but also a higher percentage of each added dollar of income. (The percentage of each added dollar of income paid in tax is known as the **marginal tax rate.**) The social security payroll tax, in contrast, is regressive. The marginal tax rate is constant for all workers who pay the tax up to a certain maximum income ($25,900 in 1980); then it drops to zero on income above the maximum. According to Minarik's calculations, state and local taxes—including income, sales, and property taxes—are on balance slightly regressive. Adding the three

Regressive tax A tax that takes a larger percentage of income from people whose income is low.

Marginal tax rate The percentage of each added dollar of income paid in taxes.

Exhibit 4.7

Tax incidence by income level in the United States, 1977

According to the data displayed in this exhibit, the U.S. tax system as a whole is neither markedly progressive nor markedly regressive over the range of income experienced by most households (66 percent of households had incomes between $5,000 and $30,000 in 1977). The progressiveness of the federal income tax offsets the regressiveness of the social security payroll tax and state and local taxes. Note that only personal contributions to social security are counted; if employer contributions were counted, the burden of this tax would be roughly doubled. The burden of state and local taxes at very low income levels is somewhat exaggerated by the presence of households whose incomes are only temporarily low.

Source: Joseph Minarik, Brookings Institution, unpublished tabulations. Reprinted by permission.

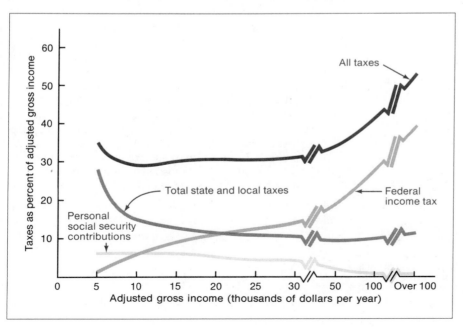

types of taxes together produces an almost flat tax schedule for the vast majority of taxpayers. It appears that the U.S. tax system as a whole is neither very progressive nor very regressive.

Incentive Effects of Taxes

Perhaps the liveliest controversy to hit the study of the economics of taxation in recent years concerns not the incidence of taxes but their effects on incentives. By far the most controversial taxes in this regard are income and payroll taxes. Let's look at both the traditional view of the incentive effects of income and payroll taxes and some recent challenges to that view.

The Traditional View   Traditionally, income and payroll taxes were thought to have only minor incentive effects, because the supply curve of labor services was believed to be very steep. The reasoning behind this view is illustrated in Exhibit 4.8. That figure shows a very steep labor supply curve, indicating that the after-tax wage or salary received makes very little difference to the quantity of labor services supplied.

Two labor demand curves are also drawn. The upper one is the curve as it looks from the point of view of the employer. It shows the quantity of labor services demanded for any given level of total labor cost, including all income and payroll taxes. The lower one is the curve as it looks from the point of view of employees. It shows the after-tax earnings corresponding to each quantity of labor and each total labor cost to the employer. Employers make their decisions on how many workers to hire in terms of the upper curve; workers decide whether to accept the jobs offered in terms of the lower curve. If there were no income or payroll taxes, the two curves would coincide. As the tax rate rises, the after-tax demand curve is pushed down farther and farther from the tax-inclusive demand curve. As the figure is drawn, the quantity of labor supplied in equilibrium and the total labor cost per worker paid by employers would be virtually the same with or without the tax.

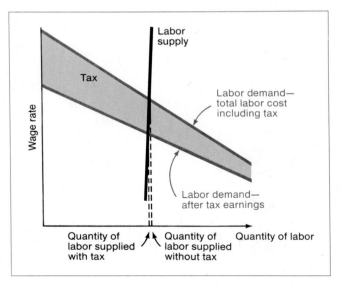

Exhibit 4.8
**Incentive effects of an income tax—
vertical labor supply curve**
Traditionally, income and payroll taxes have been thought to have relatively minor incentive effects. The reason is that the labor supply curve, as drawn here, has been thought of as nearly vertical. Even a large gap between the employers' total labor cost (represented by the upper demand curve) and the employees' after-tax income (represented by the lower demand curve) would lead to little withdrawal of work effort by employees.

Note that with the supply curve as steep as the one shown, essentially all of the burden of the tax falls on employees. Furthermore, it makes no difference whether payroll taxes are formally paid by the employee or the employer. In 1980, for example, the social security system was financed by payroll "contributions" of 6.13 percent each from the employer and the employee. That created a 12.26 percent spread between the employer's total labor cost and the employee's after-tax earnings. The economic effect of the tax would have been no different had the employer or the employee been responsible for the entire 12.26 percent. However the responsibility for payment is divided, the economic burden of a payroll tax falls on the employee, as long as the labor supply curve is vertical, or nearly so.

The Revised View Recently, some economists have begun to question this traditional analysis of the burdens and incentive effects of income and payroll taxes. They suggest that when the income tax burden gets large enough, it may in fact begin to have significant incentive effects. One way to interpret their arguments is to draw the labor supply curve with the shape shown in Exhibit 4.9. As long as income and payroll taxes are relatively moderate, they have little incentive effect, as in the traditional analysis. But after-tax earnings eventually fall to such a small percentage of pretax earnings that people no longer find it worthwhile to work as much as before. When the after-tax demand curve falls as low as the one shown in Exhibit 4.9, incentive effects become substantial.

The Laffer Curve Under certain circumstances, the incentive effects of a tax can become so pronounced that an increase in the tax rate actually produces a decrease in the total tax revenue collected. Consider the hypothetical example of Exhibit 4.10. The vertical axis in this figure measures total income tax revenue. The horizontal axis measures the income tax rate as a percent of income. With a tax rate of zero, no revenue is collected; there is a maximum incentive to work, because workers keep everything they earn (so income is

---

Exhibit 4.9

Incentive effects of an income tax—curved labor supply curve

If the labor supply curve is not vertical, at least over part of its range (as drawn here), a high enough income tax rate can produce significant negative incentive effects. The high tax rate in this diagram is shown by the large gap between the tax-inclusive and after-tax demand curves. Substantially less labor is supplied with the tax than without it.

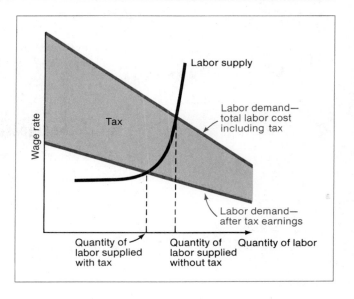

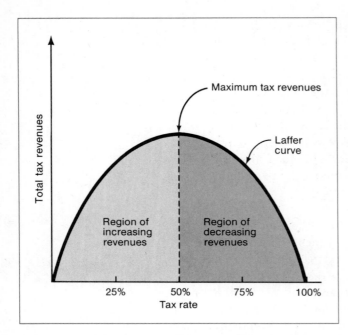

Exhibit 4.10
A Laffer curve
This Laffer curve shows the relationship thought to exist between the income tax rate and total income tax revenues. At a zero tax rate, no revenue is collected, even though incentives and total income are at their maximum. With a 100 percent tax, there is no incentive to work, so income drops to zero, and again no revenue is collected. In between, varying amounts of revenue are collected. The relationship shown is a hypothetical one. The point of maximum tax revenue need not occur at a tax rate of exactly 50 percent.

high). At the other extreme, with a tax rate of 100 percent, workers keep nothing of what they earn; there is no incentive to work, hence no income and again no tax revenue collected. In between, varying amounts of income are generated, and varying amounts of revenue are collected. At low rates, the disincentive effect is small enough that an increase in the tax rate increases total revenue. Beyond a point, however, the disincentive effect becomes large enough that an increase in the rate reduces total revenue.

Laffer curve A curve showing the relationship between a tax rate and the total revenue raised by the tax. At a zero or 100 percent tax rate, no revenue is raised; at some intermediate rate, tax revenue reaches a maximum.

The curve shown in Exhibit 4.10 has become known as a **Laffer curve,** after University of Southern California economist Arthur Laffer. Most economists accept the idea behind the Laffer curve in the abstract. There is considerable controversy, however, about just where the United States is now on the Laffer curve. Laffer and some others think that income tax rates in the United States are already so high that a reduction in tax rates would actually increase total tax revenue. But this is by no means a majority opinion among economists. There are indications that some European countries, where tax rates are higher, are experiencing substantial negative incentive effects from their tax systems. The following case study sheds some light on this problem.

Case 4.1
Incentive Effects of Income and Payroll Taxes in Europe

In 1979, the National Planning Association of Washington, D.C., published a study by Theodore Geiger of the tax and welfare systems of six European countries. One part of the study focused on the incentive effects of the high taxes required to finance the extensive welfare benefits available in most European countries. As Exhibit 4.11 shows, tax rates in Europe are considerably higher, for the average worker, than those in the United States. The percentage of income paid in taxes by the average European worker ranges from 27 percent in Germany and Norway to 35 percent in Sweden, compared with just 17 percent in the United States. Mar-

Exhibit 4.11

Average and marginal tax rates in Europe and the United States

As this exhibit shows, European workers face significantly higher tax rates than do U.S. workers. The average tax rates are based on the income and taxes of an average manufacturing worker with a family of four. The marginal tax rates are computed for the next 10 percent of income above average earnings in manufacturing.

Country	Taxes as Percent of Total Earnings	Marginal Tax Rate (percent)
Denmark	33	55
West Germany	27	34
Netherlands	31	42
Norway	27	42
Sweden	35	63
United Kingdom	26	41
United States	17	32

Source: Theodore Geiger, *Welfare and Efficiency: Their Interactions in Western Europe and Implications for International Economic Relations* (Washington, D.C.: National Planning Association, 1979), p. 28. Reprinted by permission.

ginal tax rates are even higher, ranging from 34 percent of each added dollar of income in Germany to a remarkable 63 percent of each added dollar in Sweden. The marginal tax rate for the average worker in the United States is a relatively moderate 32 percent.

In the course of his research, Geiger identified at least five perceptible negative incentive effects of these high tax rates. Most of the effects are most pronounced in Sweden, where taxes are the highest. The five incentive effects are:

1. In most of the countries studied, including the United States, there are rising pressures for a shorter workweek, longer vacations, more holidays, and new kinds of leisure (such as paid sabbaticals) for workers.
2. In the Netherlands and the Scandinavian countries especially, absenteeism rates are very high. In some large Swedish companies, absenteeism exceeds 20 percent of the labor force, partly as the result of very liberal sick leave benefits combined with high taxes on earned income.
3. In most countries, there is a perceived reduction in the difference between the after-tax disposable income obtained for work performed and the income in cash and in kind of nonworking welfare recipients. This strengthens the incentive to live on welfare.
4. High marginal tax rates foster a booming "underground economy" in several countries. Everything from repair services to legal and dental work are being done either for cash or on a barter basis. Some workers are taking leave from their regular jobs or refusing to work overtime in order to work in the underground economy.
5. In some countries, especially the United Kingdom, the tax system, together with other policies, is eroding the difference in after-tax income between skilled and unskilled workers. This is believed to be having an adverse effect on the supply of skilled workers and on the incentive to undertake certain kinds of training and education.

If the United States and Western Europe hope to maintain their high standards of living and to experience further economic growth, Geiger concluded, the interactions between tax and welfare systems on the one hand and economic efficiency on the other can no longer be neglected.

Source: Based on Theodore Geiger, *Welfare and Efficiency: Their Interactions in Western Europe and Implications for International Economic Relations* (Washington, D.C.: National Planning Association, 1979), pp. 27–30. Used with permission.

CONCLUSIONS

This chapter has explained something of the services government performs and something of who bears the costs of providing these services. But one major question not asked is *how well* the vast machinery of government does its job. This important question involves both normative and positive economics. The normative element comes in deciding what goals the government ought to pursue and the positive element in measuring how closely it meets those goals. This question of *how well* is one to which we shall return repeatedly throughout the book. Chapter 10 will examine the success of government agricultural policy; Chapters 13 and 14 will look at the regulation of business. Chapter 18 will examine the problem of poverty and evaluate the performance of a number of income transfer programs. Chapters 19 and 20 will look at policy in the areas of the environment and energy.

Until we get to all these later chapters, we will at least draw the preliminary conclusion that government is there and that it is important. In our theorizing, we may often speak of how markets work, as if the public sector were not there, but we will always come back to questions of government policy.

SUMMARY

1. The U.S. economy has a large and important government sector. Government purchases are nearly a quarter of gross national product, and taxes take over a third of it. But as large as government is in absolute terms, it is small as a fraction of GNP in comparison to the government sectors in many European countries.

2. Government differs from individuals and firms in several ways. Government can legitimately use force in the pursuit of its economic goals, while private individuals and firms cannot. Government gives away most of the services it produces without directly charging for them; the services are paid for indirectly through taxation. Also, political decision-making processes differ substantially from those of the private sector. Still, because government must go to markets to buy most of what it needs, market forces do exercise some influence over the public sector.

3. Five major economic functions of government are the provision of public goods, the carrying out of transfers, the stabilization of the economy, the regulation of the private sector, and the administration of justice.

4. The determination of the incidence of various kinds of taxes is a difficult problem of applied economics. The burden of many taxes can be shifted from those who bear the legal obligation of paying them to other parties. When all kinds of shifting are taken into account, it appears that the combined federal, state, and local tax systems are neither progressive nor regressive overall. Instead, the burden of taxes is shifted to some degree from middle-income groups to both the very rich and the very poor.

5. In recent years, a controversy has developed over the incentive effects of income and payroll taxes. At the tax rates experienced by workers in Europe, negative incentive effects do appear to be noticeable. A few economists believe that tax rates even in the United States are so high that cutting them would actually increase tax revenues.

DISCUSSION QUESTIONS

1. What would happen to U.S. society if we did away with the federal government? In which cases could state and local governments fill in? In which cases would they be unable to do so?

2. List the major goods and services provided by the government at different levels. Then determine the extent to which these goods are public goods. Which level of

government tends to supply the most public goods? Which one the least? (Can you determine which?)

3. How can a government respond to changes in the relative prices of the goods and services it buys and provides for its constituents? How is it subject to the same forces as a business? How not?

4. Would you prefer living where income taxes are progressive or regressive? Why?

5. When a tax is imposed on cigarettes, the price paid by consumers goes up and the price received by sellers goes down. The government benefits by the amount of the difference on each pack sold. There is also a second effect of the tax; fewer packs are sold. Who benefits and who is hurt by the second effect? Does the fact that cigarettes are harmful to people influence your answer? What if they were good for people?

SUGGESTIONS FOR FURTHER READING

Buchanan, James, and Tullock, Gordon. *The Calculus of Consent.* Ann Arbor: University of Michigan Press, 1962.
The seminal treatment of the economics of public goods and public choice.

Geiger, Theodore. *Welfare and Efficiency: Their Interactions in Western Europe and Implications for International Economic Relations.* Washington, D.C.: National Planning Association, 1979.
The source of Case 4.1 and an analysis of the interactions of tax and welfare systems in Europe with the efficiency of the economic systems of which they form a part.

Musgrave, Richard A., and Musgrave, Peggy B. *Public Finance in Theory and Practice.* 2d ed. New York: McGraw-Hill, 1975.
The theory of public finance is the economist's term for the economics of the government sector. This is one of the most widely used and authoritative treatments of the subject.

Phelps, Edmund S., ed. *Private Wants and Public Needs.* New York: W. W. Norton, 1965.
A collection of readings on the economics of government, compiled specifically for the use of beginning students.

Posner, Richard A. *Economic Analysis of Law.* Boston: Little, Brown, 1973.
A good introduction to the economic analysis of legal issues, written primarily for beginning law students. Highly recommended for any readers who may be contemplating a career in law. After this book, the reader may want to refer to some of the more advanced papers in Henry G. Manne, ed., The Economics of Legal Relationships, *listed at the end of Chapter 2.*

THE THEORY OF PRICES
AND MARKETS

C H A P T E R 5

THE LOGIC OF CONSUMER CHOICE

WHAT YOU WILL LEARN IN THIS CHAPTER

According to the law of demand, people tend to buy more of a good when its price goes down. This chapter discusses some of the principles of consumer choice that lie behind the law of demand. It explains how consumers, facing the necessity of choosing among alternatives and having limited budgets, balance the relative satisfactions they get from various goods against the prices they must pay for those goods.

FOR REVIEW

Here are some important terms and concepts that will be put to use in this chapter. If you do not understand them, review them before proceeding.
- *Pure economizing (Chapter 1)*
- *Law of demand (Chapter 3)*
- *Normal and inferior goods (Chapter 3)*
- *Substitutes and complements (Chapter 3)*

People are used to the idea that when the price of a good goes down, the quantity of that good demanded by consumers tends to go up. The law of demand is easy to accept, because common sense and everyday experience show that it is the way things are. Still, knowing that a thing is so does not keep people from asking *why* it is so. In Newton's day, everyone knew that when apples fell from trees, they fell down and not up; but Newton asked why, and this led him to some valuable new insights about the laws of gravitation. In the same way, economists have often asked *why* people buy more of a good when its price falls. Trying to answer that question leads to some useful insights.

CONSUMPTION AND UTILITY

The most basic question one can ask about the law of demand is why people demand goods and services at all. The answer seems to be that people want material goods and services because they get pleasure and satisfaction from them. A loaf of bread to eat, a warm bed to sleep in, or a book to read—each serves needs or desires in one way or another. Economists have their own term for this sort of thing. They say that the use or consumption of material goods gives people **utility.**

Utility The economist's term for the pleasure, satisfaction, and need fulfillment that people get from the consumption of material goods and services.

Utility and Psychological Needs

To a psychologist, just saying that people want things because they get utility from them would sound very shallow. Some psychologists, at least, would want to go into detail about the nature and sources of human wants. Followers of Abraham Maslow, for example, find it useful to think in terms of five basic kinds of needs: (1) physiological needs, (2) safety and security needs, (3) affection and belongingness needs, (4) the need for self-esteem and the esteem of others, and (5) the need for "self-actualization" or self-fulfillment.[1] For each person, the order of importance of the five needs is different.

This simple list of needs raises some important questions for psychologists. Is there a hierarchy among needs? Why is any given need more important to some people than to others? What factors in people's upbringing affect the needs they seek to satisfy in later life? Questions like these, however, get very little attention from economists. Smith may buy a tennis racket to satisfy a physiological need for exercise. Jones may buy one in order to gratify a belongingness need by joining a tennis club. Baker may buy one in order to gain the esteem of others by playing in tournaments. What is true of tennis rackets is true of other goods and services too. People with very different psychological hang-ups all have one thing in common. They get utility of one sort or another from material goods. Most economists feel that they do not really need to know any more psychology than that.

Utility and Demand

Economists may not be interested in the origins of human wants, but they are interested in the intensity of those wants. The reason is that the intensity of people's wants for some goods relative to the intensity of their wants for others determines the quantity of those goods they will demand in the marketplace. Whether a person wants a new car intensely enough to pass up the opportunity to spend the same funds on a three-week Caribbean cruise is clearly an economic as well as a psychological question. It is a question about the demand for automobiles.

Marginal utility The amount of added utility obtained from a one-unit increase in consumption of a good.

Principle of diminishing marginal utility The principle that the greater the rate of consumption of some good, the smaller the increase in utility from a unit increase in the rate of consumption.

Diminishing Marginal Utility Economists made a major step forward in their understanding of the relationship between utility and economic behavior when, in the late nineteenth century, they first clearly formulated the principle of diminishing marginal utility. The **marginal utility** of a good to a consumer means the amount of added utility obtained from the consumption of one additional unit of the good in question. The **principle of diminishing marginal utility** says that the greater the quantity of any good consumed, the less the marginal utility from a unit increase in consumption.

For a simple but vivid example of the principle of diminishing marginal utility in action, imagine yourself in a blackberry patch eating berries by the handful. As you eat more and more berries, you get more and more satisfaction; but at the same time, the satisfaction from each additional handful diminishes. If you eat enough, you may even get to a point where more berries give you no additional utility at all. Then you stop eating berries, at least until the next day.

---

[1]See Abraham Maslow, *Motivation and Personality*, 2d ed. (New York: Harper & Row, 1970).

Utility, to be sure, is a very subjective concept. No one has yet invented a "utility meter" that can be hooked up to a person's skull to read utility like blood pressure. But suppose, to indulge in a bit of science fiction, that there is such a utility meter. If you allow yourself to be hooked up to the meter during your spree in the blackberry patch, the results can be recorded in numerical or graphical form, as in Exhibit 5.1. The table and the graphs in this exhibit use the "util" as an imaginary unit for measuring utility. Both the table and the graphs show that as the quantity of berries consumed per day increases, total utility increases—but at a decreasing rate. Marginal utility—that is, the added utility obtained from each additional handful of berries—falls as the rate of consumption increases. For example, the third handful of berries increases utility by two units, from 5.5 to 7.5, whereas the fourth handful gives only 1.5 units more.

The Consumer as Economizer For better or for worse, the world is not all one big blackberry patch where people can eat as much as they want without

---

Exhibit 5.1

Diminishing marginal utility

As the rate at which a person consumes some good increases, the utility derived from one additional unit decreases. The table and figures here show that as the rate of consumption of berries increases, total utility increases—but at a decreasing rate. In Part b, a smooth curve is drawn through the stair-step total utility line, which is based on the table. Part c shows a marginal utility curve. The height of this curve at each point is equal to the slope of the smooth curve in Part b.

(a)

Quantity of Berries (Handfuls per Day)	Total Utility (Utils)	Marginal Utility (Utils per Handful)
1	3.0	
		2.5
2	5.5	
		2.0
3	7.5	
		1.5
4	9.0	
		1.0
5	10.0	
		0.5
6	10.5	

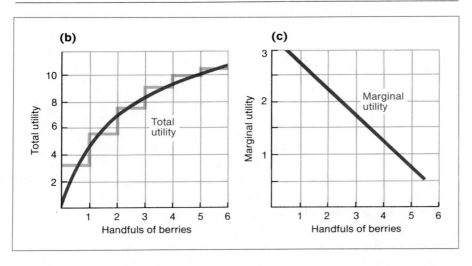

making choices. To put the principle of diminishing marginal utility to work in understanding consumer demand, one must look at a world more like the one that really exists. In particular, this is a world in which:

1. There are many different desirable goods.
2. Consumers must pay known prices for the goods they want.
3. Consumers have limited budgets.
4. Consumers try to get the greatest satisfaction they can from their limited budgets.

In such a world, consumers are faced with a classic problem in *pure economizing:* to maximize an objective (their own satisfaction) subject to known constraints (the prices of the goods and their budgets) by choosing among alternative activities (the consumption of various kinds of goods). In such a world, consumers have to make choices, and each choice involves an opportunity cost. If people spend more on one good, they have less to spend on something else. What can be said in a general way about how consumers economize their scarce resources?

Solving the Consumer Problem   Begin with the consumer you know best—yourself. Suppose you are deciding how to divide your monthly spending between, say, food and clothing. If you spend an extra dollar a month on food, you get a certain added utility from doing so. At the same time, though, you must bear an opportunity cost equal to the utility you could instead have obtained by spending the dollar on clothing. Whether or not you actually think consciously in such terms, then, your choice will depend on which utility is greater—the extra dollar's worth of food or the extra dollar's worth of clothing.

Which is greater depends in turn on how much of each good you consume. If, relatively speaking, you have a lot of clothing and not much food, the marginal utility of clothing will tend to be low and that of food to be high. By shifting a dollar from clothing to food, you can give up a small utility and gain a large one, which will increase your total utility.

If, instead, you have relatively much food and little clothing, the marginal utilities may be reversed. You will gain a lot of utility from spending an extra dollar on clothing and only a little from spending an extra dollar on food. Again, you can gain in total utility by shifting your pattern of expenditure without spending any more over all.

Consumer Equilibrium   It is clear, then, that if the marginal utility of a dollar's worth of clothing is different from that of a dollar's worth of food, you have an incentive to change your pattern of consumption. The only condition in which you will not have an incentive to change your pattern of spending on food and clothing will be if the marginal utility per dollar's worth of the two goods is exactly the same.

Generalizing from this example, it can be said that consumers tend to shift their expenditures from one kind of good to another as long as they can increase their total utilities by doing so. When consumer expenditures are distributed among the various available goods in such a way that, for each consumer, the marginal utility of a dollar's worth of each good consumed is equal to the marginal utility of a dollar's worth of each other good consumed, no further increase in utility is possible within the given budget constraint. A state of **consumer equilibrium** is then said to prevail.

Consumer equilibrium A state of affairs in which consumers cannot increase the total utility they obtain from a given budget by shifting expenditure from one good to another. (In consumer equilibrium, the marginal utility of a dollar's worth of one good must be equal to the marginal utility of a dollar's worth of any other good.)

An Alternative Statement There is another, equivalent way to state the conditions for consumer equilibrium. Suppose that a person is consuming just the right quantities of, say, chicken and beef to make the marginal utility of a dollar's worth of chicken equal to the marginal utility of a dollar's worth of beef. It must be true, then, that the marginal utility of a pound of chicken divided by the price of chicken per pound is equal to the marginal utility per pound of beef divided by the price of beef per pound. In equation form, this comes out as:

$$\frac{\text{Marginal utility of chicken}}{\text{Price of chicken per pound}} = \frac{\text{Marginal utility of beef}}{\text{Price of beef per pound}}.$$

Suppose, for example, that chicken costs $1 per pound and beef costs $3. If the equation just given holds, then an extra pound of beef will give the consumer three times as much utility as an added pound of chicken. This means, as in the earlier statement of the conditions for consumer equilibrium, that the marginal utility of a dollar's worth (one pound) of chicken is equal to the marginal utility of a dollar's worth (one-third of a pound) of beef.

The equation can be extended to a world with any number of goods and

---

The English economist William Stanley Jevons is generally credited with the first systematic exposition of the theory of marginal utility and with its first application to the problem of consumer equilibrium. Jevons was trained in mathematics and chemistry. With this background, it is not surprising that when his interest turned to economics, he would try to strengthen that science by restating its theories in mathematical form. It was the mathematical reworking of economics that led him to the theory of marginal utility.

Although Jevons wrote many books and papers, he is best remembered for his *Theory of Political Economy,* published in 1871. There he set forth the principle of diminishing marginal utility using this illustration:

Let us imagine the whole quantity of food which a person consumes on an average during twenty-four hours to be divided into ten equal parts. If his food be reduced by the last part, he will suffer but little; if a second tenth part be deficient, he will feel the want distinctly; the subtraction of the third part will be decidedly injurious; with every subsequent subtraction of a tenth part his sufferings will be more and more serious until at length he will be upon the verge of starvation. Now, if we call each of the tenth parts *an increment,* the meaning of these facts is, that each increment of food is less necessary, or possesses less utility, than the previous one.

Jevons was the first to put the new theory in print, but he shares credit for the "marginal revolution" in economics with at least three others who were working independently along the same lines at the same time. The Austrian Karl Menger published his version of marginal utility theory in 1871 also. Three years later, the Swiss economist Leon Walras, who did not know of either Jevons's or Menger's work, came out with still another version. Finally, Alfred Marshall worked out the basics of marginal analysis about the same time, although his own major work was not published until 1890.

Jevons had a strong interest in applied economics as well as in pure theory. He wrote on Australian gold mining, on the problem of Great Britain's coal reserves, on monetary questions, and on issues of social reform. As a consultant to the British government, he successfully recommended the abolition of the import duty on corn. In 1880, he resigned his teaching position at the University of London to devote full time to research. Sadly for the science of economics, however, this prolific writer died in a boating accident just two years later, at the age of forty-seven.

William Stanley Jevons (1835–1882)

services. MU_A, MU_B, and so on stand for the marginal utilities of goods A, B, and so on. Likewise, P_A, P_B, and so on stand for the prices of the various goods. The general expression for consumer equilibrium then becomes:

$$\frac{MU_A}{P_A} = \frac{MU_B}{P_B} = \frac{MU_C}{P_C} = \frac{MU_D}{P_D} = \cdots$$

From Consumer Equilibrium to the Law of Demand The concepts of consumer equilibrium and diminishing marginal utility can be combined to give an explanation of the law of demand that is intuitively appealing, if not altogether precise. The explanation goes like this: Suppose you have adjusted your pattern of consumption until you have reached an equilibrium in which, among other things:

$$\frac{MU \text{ of chicken}}{\$1} = \frac{MU \text{ of beef}}{\$3}.$$

As long as this equality holds, it will not be to your benefit to increase your consumption of beef; to do so would, according to the principle of diminishing marginal utility, quickly push down the marginal utility of beef. The marginal utility per dollar's worth of beef would drop below the marginal utility per dollar's worth of chicken, and you would be better off to switch back toward more chicken.

But what if the price of beef were to drop, say to $2.50 per pound, upsetting the equality given above? To make the two ratios equal again, given the new price of beef, either the marginal utility of chicken would have to rise or the marginal utility of beef would have to fall. According to the principle of diminishing marginal utility, one way to get the marginal utility of beef to fall is to consume more beef, and one way to get the marginal utility of chicken to rise is to consume less chicken. Because chicken and beef are substitutes to most people, probably you would do a little of both—that is, cut back a little on chicken and consume a little more beef. In doing so, you would be acting exactly as the law of demand predicts: A fall in the price of beef would have induced you to buy more beef.

SUBSTITUTION AND INCOME EFFECTS AND THE LAW OF DEMAND

The argument just given links the principle of diminishing marginal utility to the law of demand in an intuitively appealing way, but it leaves a few too many loose ends dangling to suit all economists. Is there a way to rationalize the law of demand without relying directly on the slippery, unmeasurable concept of utility? There is. The alternative approach relies on a breakdown of the effects of a change in price into two separate components, known as the substitution and income effect.

The Substitution Effect

Go back in the earlier example to the point where you had adjusted your purchases to an equilibrium, given a price of beef of $3 per pound and a price of chicken of $1 per pound. As before, suppose that the price of beef dropped to $2.50 per pound. With beef relatively cheaper than before, you would tend to substitute beef for chicken in your diet. You might substitute beef for other things too; with the price of a steak dinner cheaper, you might substitute an evening in a restaurant now and then for an evening at the movies. This effect of the change in the price of beef is known as the substitution effect. In general terms, the **substitution effect** of the change in the price of a good is that part of the change in the quantity demanded attributable to the tendency of consumers to substitute relatively cheap goods for relatively expensive ones.

The Income Effect

The substitution effect is not, however, the only reason that a drop in the price of beef would be likely to increase your consumption of beef. Suppose that with the price of beef at $3 per pound, you bought ten pounds per month. The decline in the price to $2.50 per pound would be welcome to you not only because it would allow you to substitute beef for chicken in your diet, but for another reason as well: It would increase the purchasing power of your monthly budget. With beef at $2.50 per pound, you could buy the same quantities of all goods, including beef, and now have $5 left over at the end of the month to spend as you pleased. In short, a fall in the price of any good, other things being equal, produces an increase in real income.[2]

With your increased real income, you would tend to buy more of all normal goods and less of any inferior goods. For most people, beef is a normal good. Some of your new-found $5 in real income, then, would presumably go to the purchase of more beef. This effect of the change in the price of beef on the quantity of beef demanded is known as the income effect. In general terms, the **income effect** of a change in the price of a good is that part of the change in the quantity of the good demanded attributable to the change in real income resulting from the change in price.

The Law of Demand for Normal and Inferior Goods

The concepts of the substitution and income effects of a price change are very helpful in understanding the law of demand itself and in understanding why the law of demand might, under rare circumstances, permit exceptions. Consider separately the cases of normal and inferior goods.

For a normal good, the law of demand holds absolutely, because the substitution and income effects work together to produce an increase in quantity demanded when the price of a good falls. The example given above is a case in point. When the price of beef dropped, you bought more beef partly because you substituted beef for chicken and for other goods and services that were now relatively more expensive than before. In addition, you bought more beef still because you spent part of your increased real income on beef—a normal good. Taking the two effects in combination, there is no doubt that a decline in the price of beef would increase the quantity of beef you demanded.

In the case of an inferior good, things are not quite so simple. Suppose that instead of considering a drop in the price of beef in general, you considered the effect of a drop in the price of hamburger only—with the price of all other cuts of beef held constant. Suppose further that you considered hamburger an

Substitution effect The part of the increase in quantity demanded of a good whose price has fallen that is attributable to the tendency of consumers to substitute relatively cheap goods for relatively expensive ones.

Income effect The part of the change in quantity demanded of a good whose price has fallen that is attributable to the change in real income resulting from the price change.

---

[2]Real income means income adjusted for changes in prices to reflect actual purchasing power. The same number of dollars represents more real income when prices fall and less real income when prices rise.

inferior good—one that you would tend to phase out of your diet as your real income rose. A drop in the price of hamburger, as before, would tend to make you substitute hamburger for other foods that had become relatively more expensive. By itself, this would increase the quantity demanded. However, a drop in the price of hamburger would also produce a slight increase in your real income; and that, considered by itself, would tend to make you buy less hamburger. For an inferior good, then, the substitution and income effects operate in the opposite direction. The law of demand holds for an inferior good only if the size of the substitution effect is larger than that of the income effect.

Are There Really Exceptions to the Law of Demand?

No one has ever come up with a fully convincing real-world case of an exception to the law of demand. It is reasonably certain that there are genuine examples of inferior goods. An earlier chapter cited intercity bus travel and shoe repair services as two likely examples. But as far as anyone knows, in all important cases, the substitution effect outweighs the income effect even for inferior goods, so that demand curves slope downward.

It is possible, however, to construct hypothetical examples of exceptions to the law of demand that, although perhaps farfetched, are logically possible. Chapter 3 suggested the following hypothetical case: A family living in Minnesota spends each January in Florida. One year the price of home heating fuel goes up sharply. The family turns its thermostat down a little; but even so, the heating bills go up so much that it cannot afford to go to Florida that year. Staying home in January means that the house must be kept heated during that month. The extra fuel burned during January is more than what the family has been able to save with a lower thermostat setting in the other months. Thus the total quantity of fuel burned in the season increases as a direct result of the increase in the price of fuel.

This curious case can be analyzed in terms of the income and substitution effects as follows: When the price of fuel goes up, the substitution effect works normally. The family turns its thermostat down, substituting warm clothes for heating fuel as a source of winter comfort. The weekly demand for heating fuel, however, is inelastic; even though the quantity burned per week to heat the house is slightly reduced, total expenditures on it rise, cutting sharply into the real income that the family has to spend on other goods. Now comes the "gimmick" that makes the case work. Heating fuel may not be an inferior good for most families, but this family is different. For this family, winter vacations spent in Minnesota are an inferior good; the higher the family's income, other things equal, the less time it spends in Minnesota in the winter. Heating fuel is a complement to winter vacations in Minnesota, and this complementarity makes heating fuel too an inferior good for this particular family. Other things being equal (including the price of heating fuel), the higher the family's real income, the more time it spends in Florida and the less fuel it burns per year.

With heating fuel an inferior good, the slope of the family's demand curve depends on the relative size of the income and substitution effects of the increase in the price of heating fuel. Assume that the substitution effect, although it does act to decrease consumption, is small. Sweaters are something of a substitute for a warm house, but not a particularly good substitute. Assume also that the income effect, which takes the form of spending January, the coldest month of the year, at home, is quite large. More fuel is burned in

January than the total of what is saved by wearing sweaters all the rest of the year. The increase in the price of fuel thus increases the consumption of fuel. This is a logically sound, although strictly hypothetical, exception to the law of demand.

CONCLUSIONS

Much of the available evidence concerning the theories of consumer behavior set forth in this chapter is subjective. The principle of diminishing marginal utility, the substitution effect, income effects, and the law of demand are plausible largely because they reflect the way people behave as consumers.

Many economists are content to let the theory of consumer behavior stand on a foundation of subjective evidence. But others are not. Over the years, there have been repeated attempts to expose the theory to various empirical tests. Most of these attempts at testing have used human subjects. Experimenters have set up games or artificial economies in which subjects "buy" goods or services with tokens, or something of the sort. The results of such experiments have been clouded by certain difficulties, though. Human subjects are hard to use. It is impossible to find subjects free of past experience with a market economy. It is also impossible for the subjects not to know that they are only playing a game. It is difficult or very expensive to continue the experiments for long. And it is hard to shut out all outside influences.

A few years ago, in an attempt to surmount these difficulties, a group of experimenters at Texas A&M University and the State University of New York at Stony Brook took a dramatic new approach. Instead of using human subjects to test the theory of human behavior, they used ordinary laboratory rats. Their methods and some of their results are sketched in the following case study.

Case 5.1
Testing Consumer Demand Theory with White Rats

Two white male albino rats were placed in standard laboratory cages, with food and water freely available. At one end of each cage were two levers that activated dipper cups. One dipper cup provided a measured quantity of root beer when its lever was depressed; the other provided a measured quantity of Collins mix. Previous experimentation had shown that rats prefer these beverages to water.

Within this setup, each rat could be given a fixed "income" of so many pushes on the levers per day. The pushes could be distributed in any way between the two levers. Experimenters could also control the "price" of root beer and Collins mix by determining the number of pushes the rat had to "spend" to obtain one milliliter of liquid.

In an initial experimental run lasting two weeks, the rats were given an income of three hundred pushes per day, and both beverages were priced at twenty pushes per milliliter. Under these conditions, Rat 1 settled down to a pattern of drinking about eleven milliliters of root beer per day and about four milliliters of Collins mix. Rat 2 preferred a diet of almost all root beer, averaging less than one milliliter of Collins mix per day.

Next came the crucial test. By manipulating incomes and prices, could the rats be induced to shift their consumption patterns in the way economic theory predicts? To see if they could, the experimenters proceeded as follows. First, the price of root beer was doubled, and the price of Collins mix was cut in half. At the same time, each subject's total income of pushes was adjusted to make it possible for each to afford to continue the previous consumption pattern if it should be chosen. (This adjustment in total income was made in order to eliminate any possible income effect of the price change and to concentrate solely on the substitution effect.) Economic theory predicts that under the new conditions, the rats would choose to consume more Collins mix and less root beer than before, even though they would have the opportunity not to change their behavior.

The rats' behavior exactly fitted these predictions. In two weeks of living under the new conditions, Rat 1 settled down to a new consumption pattern of about eight milliliters of root beer and seventeen milliliters of Collins mix per day. Rat 2, which had chosen root beer almost exclusively before, switched over to about nine milliliters of root beer and twenty-five milliliters of Collins mix.

Source: Adapted by permission from John H. Kagel and Raymond C. Battalio, "Experimental Studies of Consumer Demand Behavior," *Economic Inquiry* 8 (March 1975): 22–38.

This fascinating experiment can hardly be taken as the ultimate proof of the economic theory of consumer choice. Further experiments carried out with the same rats pointed to possible limitations of the theory and suggested important directions for more research. In its way, though, the experiment gave more impressive evidence in favor of the theory than any experiment with human subjects could. The complete control over the subjects' environment permitted the problem of consumer choice to be reduced to its absolute basics. The results of the experiments certainly correspond to our subjective feelings about what *we* would do under similar circumstances.

But even if theories of consumer behavior can be verified empirically, the skeptic might ask what good they are. The answer may be that, in terms of practical applications, they are not very useful. The theories do not describe the way consumers actually think about the choices they make; nor do they permit policy makers to help consumers make the right choices. If they could actually measure utility (perhaps, as suggested earlier, by hooking people up to a utility meter), such practical applications might be possible. Without a utility meter, they are not.

The value of the theories of marginal utility and consumer equilibrium, then, lies elsewhere. Rather than producing practical applications, these theories produce insight and understanding. They help us understand how consumers deal with the universal economic problem of choosing among alternative uses for scarce resources. They give a deeper insight into the logic of the familiar law of demand. These things are important enough to keep the ideas of marginal utility and consumer equilibrium alive as a basic part of modern economics.

SUMMARY

1. People demand goods and services because they get utility from them. Psychologists are able to identify many different reasons that material goods and services give people utility. The same good may fulfill different needs for different people. Economists do not usually find it necessary to distinguish the various possible sources of utility. They are interested primarily in whether people want a good enough to pay for it, not in why they want it.
2. The increase in utility from a one-unit increase in the rate of consumption of some good is called the marginal utility of that good. As the rate of consumption of any good increases, the marginal utility of that good tends to decrease.

3. Consumer equilibrium is a state of affairs in which people cannot increase the utility they get from a given budget by shifting expenditure from one good to another. Consumer equilibrium requires that the marginal utility of a dollar's worth of any good be equal to the marginal utility of a dollar's worth of any other good. Alternatively, the condition for consumer equilibrium can be expressed in the form of the equation:

$$\frac{MU_A}{P_A} = \frac{MU_B}{P_B} = \frac{MU_C}{P_C} = \frac{MU_D}{P_D} = \ldots$$

4. The effect of a change in the price of a good on the quantity of that good demanded can conceptually be broken into a substitution effect and an income effect. For normal goods, the substitution and income effects of a price decrease both act to increase the quantity demanded, guaranteeing that the demand curve for the good will have a negative slope. For inferior goods, the income effect of a price decrease tends to offset the substitution effect. With few, if any, exceptions, however, the substitution effect is stronger, so that demand curves even for inferior goods have negative slopes.

DISCUSSION QUESTIONS

1. Is it true for all goods that more is always better than less, or are there some situations in which marginal utility could become negative? Discuss.
2. Suppose you have a room that will require eight rolls of wallpaper to decorate. If someone gives you seven rolls of wallpaper, you will not get much satisfaction. The eighth roll, however, will be very much appreciated. Do you think this is a valid counterexample to the law of diminishing marginal utility?
3. Who is your favorite classical or popular musician? Do you think a concert by this person that lasted thirty minutes would give you more than ten times as much satisfaction as a concert lasting just three minutes? More than sixty times as much satisfaction as a concert lasting just thirty seconds? Would you bother to go to a concert lasting just thirty seconds even if it were free? What does all this have to do with diminishing marginal utility?
4. Martha Smith consumes two pounds of pork and five pounds of beef per month. She pays $1.50 per pound for the pork and $2 per pound for the beef. What inference can you draw about the ratio:

$$\frac{\text{Martha's marginal utility per pound of pork}}{\text{Martha's marginal utility per pound of beef}}?$$

Is this ratio equal to 3/4, 4/3, 5/2, 2/5, or none of those alternatives?
5. What would happen to the quantity you demanded of each of the following if its price rose while all other prices remained unchanged:
   a. Your favorite soft drink
   b. All forms of transportation
   c. Greyhound bus tickets
   d. Levis (the genuine brand only)
   In each case, how much of the change in quantity demanded would be attributable to the income effect and how much to the substitution effect?
6. Imagine a very poor country in which people spend most of their income on food. They eat bread when they can afford it, but they cannot afford to eat bread all the time; more than half of their diet is made up of cheaper, but less palatable, oatmeal. One year, the price of oatmeal rises substantially, while the price of bread does not change; despite the price rise, however, oatmeal remains cheaper than bread. Does it seem reasonable to you that the people just described might respond by increasing the quantity of oatmeal they consume? Try to explain how this might happen in

terms of the income and substitution effects. If you want to, make up an example with specific prices and quantities.

7. Imagine that you are the director of a slave labor camp and that you are a thick-skinned, antihumanitarian person with absolutely no regard whatsoever for the comfort or welfare of your charges. Do you think you can design an experiment to test the laws of consumer behavior using your prisoners as subjects? What possible pitfalls might you encounter that an experimenter using rats would not encounter? What advantages or disadvantages might you have compared with an experimenter who is restricted to the use of paid human volunteers?

APPENDIX TO CHAPTER 5
AN INTRODUCTION TO INDIFFERENCE CURVES

Chapter 5 gave two versions of the theory of consumer choice underlying the law of demand—one based on marginal utility, the other on income and substitution effects. This appendix gives a third version, using what are known as indifference curves. Indifference curves are not featured in this book, but they are used very frequently in intermediate and advanced level economic writing. Many students and instructors find it worthwhile to cover them at least briefly as part of an introductory course. This appendix will serve the needs of those who are interested.

CONSTRUCTING AN INDIFFERENCE CURVE

Begin by supposing that I am an experimenter and you are my experimental subject. I want to find out how you feel about consuming various quantities of meat and cheese. It would be convenient if I had a utility meter, but I do not. In order to find out your attitudes toward the consumption of meat and cheese, I instead present you with a number of food baskets (two at a time) containing various quantities of the two goods.

As I present each pair of baskets, I ask: Would you prefer the one on the left to the one on the right? The one on the right to the one on the left? Or are you indifferent between the two? If you play your role of experimental subject in good faith, I have a reasonable hope of getting a meaningful answer from you. In any event, I certainly have a better chance of getting a meaningful answer than I would have if I asked you how many utils you would get from each basket.

At some point in the experiment, I offer you one basket (A) containing, say, eight pounds of meat and three pounds of cheese and another basket (B) containing, say, six pounds of meat and four pounds of cheese. I ask you the usual questions, and you answer that you are indifferent between the two baskets. The extra pound of cheese in Basket B, you feel, just makes up for the fact that it has two pounds less of meat than does Basket A. This gives me a very useful bit of information: It tells me that, for you, Basket A and Basket B belong to an **indifference set**—a set of consumption alternatives each yielding the same amount of satisfaction, so that no member of the set is preferred to any other. Exploring the matter further, I discover that two other baskets (C and D) also belong to the same indifference set, which now has the following four members:

Indifference set A set of consumption alternatives each of which yields the same utility, so that no member of the set is preferred to any other.

Basket	Meat (pounds)	Cheese (pounds)
A	8	3
B	6	4
C	5	5
D	4	7

With this information in hand, I thank you for participating in my experiment and get out a piece of graph paper. First, I draw a set of coordinate axes, as in Exhibit 5A.1. Pounds of meat are measured on the horizontal axis and pounds of cheese on the vertical. Each basket of goods can be shown as a point on the area between the two axes. The points representing Baskets A through D are shown in their proper spots in the diagram. These points and all the points in between them lying on the smooth curve that has been sketched in joining them are members of the same indifference set. The curve itself is an **indifference curve**—a curve composed entirely of points that are all members of a single indifference set.

Indifference curve A graphical representation of an indifference set.

SOME PROPERTIES OF INDIFFERENCE CURVES

Indifference curves have properties that reflect certain basic regularities in patterns of consumer preferences. Five of these properties are of particular interest.

1. *Indifference curves normally have negative slopes.* For example, the curve sketched in Exhibit 5A.2 is not a possible shape for an indifference curve if both meat and cheese are desirable goods. The consumption basket shown by Point A contains more of both goods than the one shown by Point B. This implies that if greater quantities of meat and cheese give greater satisfaction, A must be *preferred* to B. It cannot then be a member of the same indifference set as B.

2. *The absolute value of the slope of an indifference curve at any point represents the ratio of the marginal utility of the good on the horizontal axis to the marginal utility of the good on the vertical axis.* For an example, refer back to Exhibit 5A.1. Between D and C, the slope of the curve is approximately −2 (or simply 2 when the minus sign is removed to give the absolute value). This shows that the marginal utility of meat is approximately twice the marginal utility of cheese for the consumer—when the quantities consumed are in the area of Baskets C and D. Because the marginal utility of meat is twice that of cheese in this region, the consumer will feel neither gain nor loss in total utility in trading Basket D for Basket C—that is, in giving up two pounds of cheese for one extra pound of meat. Because it shows the rate at which meat can be substituted for cheese without gain or loss in satisfaction, the slope of the indifference curve is called the **marginal rate of substitution** of meat for cheese.

Marginal rate of substitution The rate at which one good can be substituted for another without gain or loss in satisfaction (equal to the slope of an indifference curve at any point).

Exhibit 5A.1

An indifference curve

Each point in this diagram stands for a basket of meat and cheese. A, B, C, and D are all baskets among which a certain consumer is indifferent. All give equal utility. Those points and all the others on a smooth curve connecting them constitute an indifference set. An indifference curve, such as the one shown here, is a graphical representation of an indifference set.

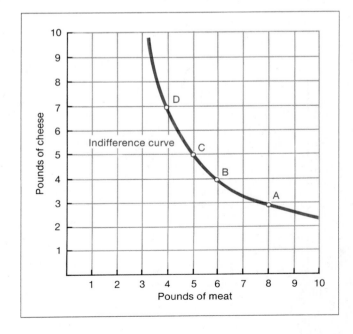

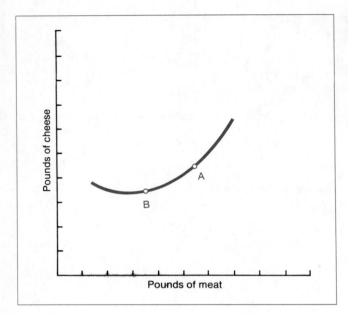

Exhibit 5A.2
Indifference curves normally slope downward
Indifference curves normally have negative slopes. The upward-sloping portion of the indifference curve shown here is impossible if both goods give increased satisfaction with increased quantity. A has more of both goods than B. Point A should thus be preferred to Point B, and therefore it could not lie on the same indifference curve.

3. Indifference curves are convex; that is, their slope decreases as one moves down and to the right along them. This implies that the ratio of the marginal utility of meat to the marginal utility of cheese (also known as the marginal rate of substitution of meat for cheese) diminishes as one moves down and to the right along the curve. Look once more at Exhibit 5A.1. In the region between D and C, the slope of the curve is approximately -2, indicating that the ratio of the marginal utility of meat to that of cheese is approximately $2:1$. By comparison, in the neighborhood between B and A, the slope is only about $-1/2$. The ratio of the marginal utility of meat to the marginal utility of cheese is now approximately $1:2$.

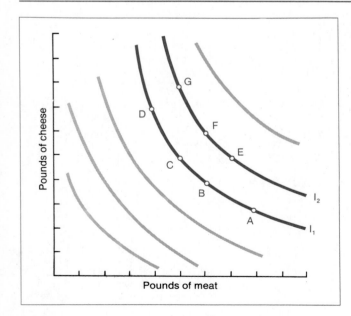

Exhibit 5A.3
Multiple indifference curves
An indifference curve can be drawn through any point. Here the indifference curve I_1 represents an indifference set containing points A, B, C, and D, while I_2 represents a set containing Points E, F, and G. All points on I_2 are preferred to all points on I_1. A representative selection of indifference curves like the one shown here can be called an indifference map.

Exhibit 5A.4
Crossing indifference curves contradict the assumption of transitive preferences
Because consumer preferences are transitive, indifference curves do not cross. The impossible indifference curves shown here represent contradictory preferences. A and B are both on I₁, so the consumer must be indifferent between them. A and C are both on I₂, so the consumer must be indifferent between them too. Transitivity implies that the consumer is indifferent between B and C, but this is impossible, because C contains more of both goods than does B.

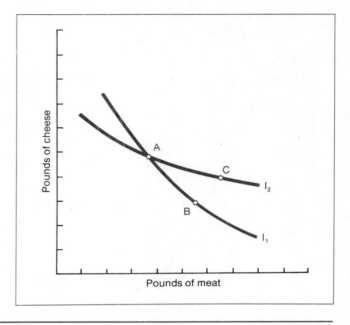

4. *An indifference curve can be drawn through the point that represents any basket of goods whatsoever.* Consider Exhibit 5A.3. Here is the same indifference curve as in Exhibit 5A.1, but labeled I₁. Point E, representing a basket with seven pounds of meat and five pounds of cheese, is not a member of the indifference set represented by this curve. Because it lies above and to the right of Point B and has more of both products than B, it must be preferred to B. There are other points, such as F and G, that have more cheese and less meat than E and, on balance, give the same satisfaction as E. The consumer is indifferent between E, F, G, and all other points on the curve I₂ and prefers all of these points to any of the points on I₁.

Any point taken at random, together with the other points that happen to be equally satisfactory, can form an indifference curve. Several other such curves, unlabeled, are sketched in Exhibit 5A.3. If all possible curves were drawn in, they would be so close together that the ink of the lines would run into a solid sheet entirely filling the space between the axes. A representative selection of indifference curves, showing their general pattern but leaving enough space to make the diagram easy to read, is called an **indifference map**.

5. *Indifference curves do not cross, because consumer preferences are* **transitive**—which means that if you prefer A to B and B to C, you will prefer A to C. Looking at Exhibit 5A.4, you can see that crossed indifference curves contradict this assumption of transitivity. Consider Points A, B, and C. A and B both lie on the same indifference curve, I₁; hence the consumer is indifferent between them. A and C both lie on I₂; hence the consumer is indifferent between them also. From the property of transitivity, if B is as good as A and A is as good as C, C is as good as B. But C lies above and to the right of B. It represents a combination of goods with more of both meat and cheese. If more is better, the consumer must prefer C to B. Since crossed indifference curves imply a contradictory set of preferences, the conclusion is that they cannot cross.

Indifference map A representative selection of indifference curves for a single consumer and pair of goods.

Transitivity The situation where if A is preferred to B and B is preferred to C, then A must be preferred to C.

THE BUDGET LINE

The range of consumption opportunities open to a consumer with a given budget and with given prices can be shown on the same kind of graph that has been used for indifference curves. Exhibit 5A.5 shows how this can be done. Suppose that you have

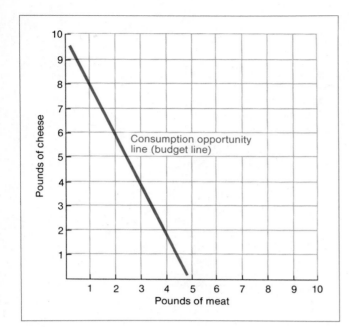

Exhibit 5A.5
The budget line
Suppose you have a budget of $10 per week. You can spend your money on meat at $2 per pound, on cheese at $1 per pound, or on some combination of the two goods. The consumption opportunity line (budget line) shows all the possible combinations available to you, given these prices and your limited budget.

Budget line A line showing the various combinations of goods that can be purchased at given prices within a given budget.

a food budget of $10 per week, that the price of meat is $2 per pound, and that the price of cheese is $1 per pound. If you spend all your money on meat, you can have up to five pounds of meat; if you spend all your money on cheese, you can have up to ten pounds of cheese. Combinations such as two pounds of meat and six of cheese or four pounds of meat and two of cheese are also possible. Taking possible purchases of fractional pounds of meat and cheese into account also, these consumption opportunities can be shown on the diagram as a diagonal line running from 10 on the cheese axis to 5 on the meat axis. This diagonal line is called the **budget line** under the assumed conditions.

Using m to stand for meat and c to stand for cheese, the equation for the budget line can be written as $2m + 1c = 10$. This equation simply says that the number of pounds of meat bought times the price of meat plus the number of pounds of cheese bought times the price of cheese must add up to the total budget if no money is left unspent. Expressed in more general terms, the equation for a budget line for goods x and y—with P_x the price of x, P_y the price of y, and B the consumer's total budget—is $P_x x + P_y y = B$. The slope of such a budget line is $-P_x/P_y$. In the case illustrated in Exhibit 5A.5, where the price of meat is $2 per pound and the price of cheese is $1 per pound, the slope of the budget line is -2.

A GRAPHICAL REPRESENTATION OF CONSUMER EQUILIBRIUM

Indifference curves and the budget line can be used to give a graphical representation of consumer equilibrium. Exhibit 5A.6 shows the budget line from Exhibit 5A.5 superimposed on an indifference map similar to that shown earlier in Exhibit 5A.3. Preferences and consumption opportunities can thus be compared easily. For example, Point B is preferred to Point A because it lies on a "higher" indifference curve (one that at some point like C passes above and to the right of A). By similar reasoning, Point D is inferior to Point B. Of all the points on or below the budget line, it is clear that Point E, representing 2.5 pounds of meat and 5 pounds of cheese, is the most preferred, because all the other points on the budget line lie on lower indifference

Exhibit 5A.6

Graphical demonstration of consumer equilibrium

E is the point of consumer equilibrium, given the indifference curves and budget line shown. All points that are better than E (such as F) lie outside the boundary of the budget line. All other points for goods that the consumer can afford to buy (such as A and D) lie on lower indifference curves than E and are thus less preferred.

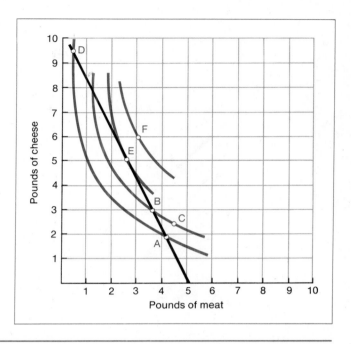

curves. Every point that, like F, is better still lies outside the range of consumption opportunities.

Because E is the point giving the highest possible satisfaction under the conditions set, it is the point of consumer equilibrium. At E, the relevant indifference curve is just tangent to the budget line; this means that the slope of the indifference curve and the budget line are the same at this point. The slope of the indifference curve, as shown earlier, is equal to the ratio of the marginal utility of meat to the marginal utility of cheese. The slope of the budget line is equal to the ratio of the price of meat to the price of cheese. It follows that in consumer equilibrium:

$$\frac{\text{Marginal utility of meat}}{\text{Marginal utility of cheese}} = \frac{\text{Price of meat}}{\text{Price of cheese}}.$$

This is the condition for consumer equilibrium given in Chapter 5.

GRAPHICAL DERIVATION OF THE DEMAND CURVE

This appendix concludes with Exhibit 5A.7, which shows how a demand curve for meat can be derived graphically from a set of indifference curves. Together with the indifference curves, Exhibit 5A.7 shows a whole family of budget lines. Each budget line is based on the assumption that the price of cheese is $1 per pound and that the consumer's budget is $10, as before. Now, though, each budget line assumes a different price, P, of meat. The budget line running from 10 on the vertical axis to 2.5 on the horizontal axis assumes P = $4. The budget line running from 10 on the vertical axis to 5 on the horizontal axis assumes P = $2. (This is the same budget line drawn in Exhibits 5A.5 and 5A.6.) The other two budget lines are based on P = $1.50 and P = $1, respectively.

The equilibrium consumption pattern for the consumer will be different for each price of meat, other things being equal. When P = $4, Point A, representing six pounds of cheese and one pound of meat, is the best the consumer can do; when P = $2, Point B is the most preferred point; and so on.

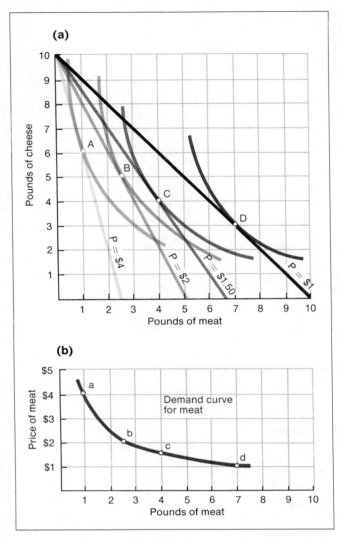

(a)

Exhibit 5A.7
Graphical derivation of a demand curve
Part a of this exhibit shows a consumer's indifference map for meat and cheese and a set of budget lines. Each budget line corresponds to a different price, P, of meat, as shown. All four budget lines assume the price of cheese to be $1 and the total budget to be $10. Points A, B, C, and D in Part a show the choices the consumer makes at meat prices of $4, $2, $1.50, and $1, respectively. In Part b of the exhibit, the information on consumption of meat at the various prices is plotted on a new set of axes. The smooth line connecting Points a, b, c, and d is the consumer's demand curve for meat.

(b)

Given this information on consumer equilibrium under different price assumptions, it is a simple matter to draw the consumer's demand curve for meat. Exhibit 5A.7b shows a new set of axes, with the quantity of meat on the horizontal axis as before, but with the price of meat now on the vertical axis. From Exhibit 5A.7a, when P = $4, the consumer chooses the consumption combination A, which includes one pound of meat. In Exhibit 5A.7b, Point a is thus marked as the quantity of meat demanded at a price of $4. Then Point b (corresponding to Point B in Part a) is added, and so on. Drawing a smooth line through Points a, b, c, and d in Exhibit 5A.7b thus gives the consumer's demand curve for meat. As expected, it has the downward slope consistent with the law of demand.

SUGGESTIONS FOR FURTHER READING

Blaug, Mark. *Economic Theory in Retrospect*. Rev. ed. Homewood, Ill.: Richard D. Irwin, 1968.
Chapter 8 discusses the origins of utility theory and the work of William Stanley Jevons. Chapter 9 discusses Alfred Marshall's refinements of utility theory and the modern restatement in terms of preference and indifference.

Leftwich, Richard H. *The Price System and Resource Allocation.* 7th ed. Hinsdale, Ill.: Dryden Press, 1979.
Chapter 5 provides an intermediate level treatment of the topics covered in this chapter and its appendix.

Nicholson, Walter. *Intermediate Microeconomics and Its Application.* 2d ed. Hinsdale, Ill.: Dryden Press, 1979.
Chapters 3 and 4 treat utility analysis and indifference curves in somewhat more detail than Leftwich does.

THE NATURE
OF THE FIRM

WHAT YOU WILL LEARN IN THIS CHAPTER

The firm is the basic unit of production in the market economy. This chapter explores the nature of the firm and of the economic decision making that takes place within it. Among the issues raised are those of why firms exist at all, how the division of labor is coordinated within and among firms, why some firms have different legal forms of organization than others, and who really controls large corporations.

FOR REVIEW

Here are some important terms and concepts that will be put to use in this chapter. If you do not understand them, review them before proceeding.
- *Pure economizing and entrepreneurship (Chapter 1)*
- *Transactions costs (Chapter 2)*

The firm is the basic unit of business in the market economy, but up to now, little has been said about what a firm really is or how it works. Firms come in a great variety of sizes and shapes. There are mom-and-pop corner stores, giant automobile and steel corporations, and powerful partnerships of lawyers and stockbrokers. Despite their different purposes and different legal forms of organization, all firms have many things in common. This chapter will explore their common ground, beginning with a look at the most basic task the firm must perform—that of coordinating economic activity.

COORDINATING ECONOMIC ACTIVITY

Market versus Managerial Coordination

Production in any modern economy, as emphasized in Chapters 1 and 2, is based on a vast division of labor. Many people make individual contributions to the whole effort that must somehow be coordinated. It must be determined what goods are to be produced, who is to produce them, and how they are to be produced. There are fundamentally two kinds of coordination for this vast division of labor: market coordination and managerial coordination.

Market coordination relies on the price system as a source of incentives and a communications network. As relative prices vary in response to the forces of supply and demand, users are induced to substitute low-priced goods

Market coordination Coordination of economic activity using the price system to transmit information and provide incentives.

and services for scarcer and more expensive alternatives. At the same time, changing relative prices continually create new profit opportunities for entrepreneurs who can devise ways of expanding the output of whatever is particularly scarce and thus particularly valuable to users. All of this is accomplished in a decentralized fashion, with no central authority making decisions or issuing demands.

There are substantial areas of economic activity, however, that do not rely directly on market coordination. Consider, for example, the internal organization of work within, say, a furniture factory. Individual employees do not decide each morning, in response to changing relative prices, that they will spend the day making end tables rather than TV cabinets. Instead, they make end tables because that is what their immediate boss tells them to do. This is the realm of **managerial coordination,** which operates on the principle of direct instruction from manager to subordinate. What makes the instruction effective is the fact that subordinates have pledged obedience to the manager (at least within certain agreed limits) as a condition of employment.

Managerial coordination Coordination of economic activity through directives from managers to subordinates.

Coordination in the Firm

In a famous essay on the nature of the firm, Ronald Coase posed a question about these two ways of coordinating the division of labor: If the market principle works as well as economists say it does, why is the managerial principle ever used at all?[1] Why do the workers in a furniture factory have to be employees taking orders from a boss? If the market principle were applied everywhere, TV cabinets and end tables would all be built by independent artisans. Changes in the relative prices of various items of furniture would keep the right number of workers at each job.

Coase found an answer to his question. He said that the market is not used for every situation where coordination is required because there are transactions costs to using it. There are costs of finding out what prices are. There are also costs of negotiating contracts, writing bills and receipts, and straightening things out when market contracts are not carried through. If, say, a potential car buyer had to negotiate separately with each person who worked on the car, the costs of coordination would make the car too expensive. If the buyer saved negotiating costs by having one or two local mechanics build the car from scratch, the advantages of mass production and the division of labor would be lost, and the vehicle would still cost too much. But when Ford Motor Company acts as an intermediary between the buyer and the workers, thousands of market transactions are eliminated. Cars are sold on the market, but everything in between is coordinated by the managerial principle of simply giving orders and expecting them to be obeyed.

Coase realized, though, that in answering one question, he had just raised another. If managerial coordination works so well, why use the market at all? Why not run the entire economy as one big firm, with all people as employees and a single, central manager running the whole show? Then it would be a matter of not only giving furniture workers or auto workers orders about what to do that day but also giving high school graduates orders about whether to be auto workers or cabinet makers. Not only would the matter of how many end

[1]Ronald H. Coase, "The Nature of the Firm," *Economica*, new series, 4 (November 1937): 386–405.

Ronald Coase is the intellectual founder of the "new institutional economics." Through his own writings and his editorship of the *Journal of Law and Economics,* Coase has fostered a unification of institutional economics and analytical economics, once separate and even antagonistic branches of the discipline. The method of the new institutional economics is simple and productive of great insights. One selects an economic institution and poses two related questions: What are the effects of this particular institution on the allocation of resources? And how can one account for the evolution and continued existence of the institution *in terms of* an analysis of its effects on resource allocation?

Coase, born and educated in London, began his studies of economic institutions early in his career. In the 1930s he studied the British postal system and the British broadcasting system as well as other public utility industries. The results of these studies were set out in a number of articles and in his book, *British Broadcasting: A Study in Monopoly,* which was published in 1951.

Coase's famous paper on the nature of the firm was published in 1937 and brought him international recognition. He came to the United States in 1951 to teach first at the University of Buffalo, then at the University of Virginia, and finally at the University of Chicago. In 1961, his most famous paper of all, "The Problem of Social Cost," appeared in the *Journal of Law and Economics.* At that time, the journal was new, and the study of law and economics hardly existed as an independent specialty within either profession. Coase's probing analysis of the nature of the law as an economic institution sparked such enormous interest among both economists and lawyers that law and economics soon became one of the most exciting fields of study around. Within little over a decade, all leading law schools had economists on their staffs and were offering courses in the new institutional economics as applied to legal institutions.

One subject on which the new institutional economics has had much to say is government regulation of industry. Coase himself has written extensively on the regulation of broadcasting, and articles on regulation of other industries appear regularly in his journal. Traditionally, the economics of regulation was concerned largely with how regulation ought to be conducted and what beneficial effects would emerge from it under ideal conditions. Coase shifted the focus to an analysis of regulatory institutions as their structure and effects actually exist. The result, on balance, has been highly critical. Coase himself has gone so far as to write, "It is now generally accepted by all students of the subject that most (perhaps almost all) government regulation is anticompetitive and harmful in its effects."

Ronald H. Coase (1910–)

tables and how many TV cabinets be handled by the managerial principle, but so would matters such as how many firms should be in the industry and where they should be located.

Managerial coordination, however, has transactions costs of its own, as well as savings of transactions costs. Under the managerial system, the person actually doing a job does not need to know all the reasons behind the decision to do it, and that is a saving. Offsetting this is the fact that *managers* have to know a great deal about all the different jobs they coordinate, and that is a cost. Sometimes the costs of supplying information to a manager or other central decision maker are greater than the costs of supplying information to people close to the job. When this is the case, managerial coordination loses its advantage over market coordination.

The Limits of the Firm

Coase saw that the two coordination principles give the key to understanding the nature of the firm and its role in the economy. A firm, he said, is an organization that uses the managerial principle of coordination internally and uses the market to coordinate its activities with those of other firms and individuals. Each firm tends to grow until the transactions cost of organizing one extra task within the firm becomes equal to the cost of organizing the same task outside the firm through the market. In some industries (as will be shown shortly), this rule dictates that firms grow to enormous size. In others, the limit to the growth of the firm occurs at a very small size. By allowing each firm to grow to its optimal size and by leaving coordination among firms to the market, the total costs of organizing economic activity can, in principle, be minimized.

Coase's insights into the nature of the firm have survived the test of time well. They should be kept in mind as the chapter turns from abstract principles to some of the practical details of the organization of business firms.

ALTERNATIVE FORMS OF BUSINESS ORGANIZATION

Textbook discussions of economic theory inevitably tend to portray business firms as well-defined, homogeneous units of analysis. In the real world, however, they take on a very wide variety of forms. Some firms are tiny, consisting of a single individual doing all production and managerial jobs. At the other extreme are corporate giants like General Motors or ITT. These firms employ more people and dispose of more assets than the governments of all but the world's largest countries. Firms differ not only in size but in their legal form of organization as well. The following three sections will discuss the advantages of the three main types of firms—sole proprietorships, partnerships, and corporations.[2]

Sole Proprietorships

Sole proprietorship A firm owned and usually managed by a single person, who receives all profits of the firm and who personally bears all of the firm's liabilities.

A **sole proprietorship** is a firm that is owned and usually managed by one person. In most cases this person is also an operative employee. Responsibility for the success or failure of the firm rests solely on the proprietor's shoulders. From a legal point of view, he or she owns all the assets and owes all the debts of the organization.

A good way to get a perspective on the organization of a sole proprietorship is to look at such a firm's balance sheet. The balance sheet shown in Exhibit 6.1 is that of Van Appleman's grocery store. All the property Appleman owns for use in his business is listed on the left-hand side of the balance sheet under the heading "assets." All the debts he owes in connection with his business are listed on the right-hand side of the balance sheet under the heading "liabilities and equity." The difference between the firm's assets and liabilities is its net worth, which represents Appleman's equity in the business. It is, in principle, the sum he would have left over if he sold all the firm's assets at the values listed and paid all the listed debts. In this case, Appleman has business assets of $34,000 and debts of $5,500; his equity in the firm is thus $28,500.

Advantages One of the most important advantages for the owner of a sole proprietorship is the complete ownership of all the assets and the right to all

---

[2] Much of the material in this section is adapted from Robert D. Hay, *Introduction to Business* (New York: Holt, Rinehart and Winston, 1968), pp. 140–148. Reprinted by permission of the author.

Exhibit 6.1

Balance sheet of Van Appleman's sole proprietorship

In a sole proprietorship, all assets are owned by one person, and that person is solely liable for all debts. The difference between the firm's assets and its liabilities is the proprietor's equity—that is, the proprietor's own stake in the business.

Assets		Liabilities and Equity	
Cash	$ 2,000	Accounts payable	$ 500
Inventory on the shelves	10,000	Mortgage payable	5,000
Equipment	2,000	Total debts	$ 5,500
Land and buildings	20,000	Appleman's equity	28,500
Total assets	$34,000	Total liabilities plus equity	$34,000

the profits of the business. The sole proprietor is legally entitled to 100 percent of any rewards. This right to all the profits is a powerful incentive to the owner to invest money and to work hard to get the revenue from customers from whom profits are derived.

Another of the reasons the sole proprietorship is so widely used is because it is relatively easy to organize. There are very few legal requirements to meet. Consequently, little or no costs of organization are involved. Practically anyone can develop an idea into a sole proprietorship form of organization. (Of course, the firm may not succeed, but at least it can be formed with little effort.) To an owner of private property wishing to manage a business, the advantage of ease of organization may be a factor in choosing this form of legal organization.

Still another factor in choosing the sole proprietorship may be the advantage of receiving a high degree of personal satisfaction from the management of the firm. People who like to have the freedom to exercise their personal judgment in management decisions and who want to be able to make decisions promptly without the consultation or approval of other owners or managers derive great personal satisfaction from the sole proprietorship of a firm. So do people who do not work well with other managers or under supervision.

Finally, ease of dissolution may be an important advantage of the sole proprietorship. Just as there are few legal complications about going into business, there are very few in going out of business. Dissolution may simply mean selling the inventory, paying the debts, and locking the door. Ease of dissolution allows the owner to retire or enter another type of business quickly and easily.

Disadvantages The sole proprietorship form of organization also has some disadvantages, however. First and foremost among them is unlimited financial liability. This means that in the event of bankruptcy, the sole proprietor's personal property may have to be sold to pay business debts.

Also, because the expansion of a sole proprietorship is limited by what the owner can contribute or borrow, he or she may find it difficult to expand. This difficulty is magnified by the sole proprietor's inability to get into other lines of business because of a lack of capital or of managerial ability. Expansion often increases financial risks, and the owner's refusal or inability to bear these risks may make expansion impossible. If the minimum amount of capital required is more than one person can safely provide, the sole proprietorship will not work.

Finally, the death, injury, imprisonment, or bankruptcy of the owner may terminate the legal life of the firm. This lack of continuity stems from the legal fact that the individual and the business are one and the same in a sole proprietorship.

Partnerships

Partnership A firm formed by two or more persons to carry on a business as co-owners. Each partner bears full legal liability for the debts of the firm.

As defined by the Uniform Partnership Act, a **partnership** is an association of two or more persons who will carry on a business as co-owners by voluntary legal agreement (called the Articles of Co-Partnership). Instead of one person being the owner, there are at least two who own all the assets, owe all the liabilities, and have an equity in the business. For example, imagine that Janet Kerwich and Alice Appleman decide to go into business together. If Kerwich and Appleman each put $28,500 cash into the business, the balance sheet might look like the one in Exhibit 6.2. Note that Appleman and Kerwich together own $62,500 worth of assets and owe $5,500; and each has an equity of $28,500, for a total equity of $57,000.

Advantages Like the sole proprietorship, the partnership as a form of legal organization enjoys simplicity and ease in getting started and, in some cases, savings in income taxes. The partnership is able to obtain more equity capital than the sole proprietorship, because the amount available is determined by the personal fortunes of the partners. Many sole proprietorships evolve into partnerships in order to raise more equity capital. For example, a person with a new idea may find another person who is willing to contribute a major share of the needed capital to turn the idea into a profitable business operation for both of them. Thus the necessary amount of capital is acquired through the formation of a partnership.

An advantage closely related to raising equity capital is the enlarged credit standing, or ability to borrow capital, of the partnership. Because the personal wealth of all the partners is available to pay debts of the business organization, a partnership may enjoy a higher credit rating than a sole proprietorship.

Many partnerships are formed to take advantage of greater managerial ability. Because numerous functions are involved in the operation of a business, partners proficient in different functions may complement each other. This combined effort leads to the greater managerial ability.

Exhibit 6.2

Balance sheet of the Kerwich and Appleman partnership

In a partnership, all assets are owned jointly by the partners. Each partner is individually liable for all the firm's debts. The difference between the firm's assets and its liabilities is the owners' equity, shared among the partners.

Assets		Liabilities and Equity	
Cash	$30,500	Accounts payable	$ 500
Inventory	10,000	Mortgage payable	5,000
Equipment	2,000	Total debts	$ 5,500
Land and building	20,000	Alice Appleman's equity	28,500
		Janet Kerwich's equity	28,500
Total assets	$62,500	Total liabilities plus equity	$62,500

Disadvantages A partnership form of organization does not offer all the answers because it too has certain disadvantages. As in the sole proprietorship, the chief disadvantage is the unlimited financial liability. In the case of a partnership, the responsibility for the debts of the business is shared individually as well as jointly. Consequently, the unlimited financial liability could result in one partner being forced to pay not only his or her own share but all the debts of the firm.

Suppose, for example, that the Kerwich and Appleman partnership finds itself unable to operate at a profit and must go out of business in order to avoid further losses. At the time of liquidation, suppose that the firm still has $62,500 in assets, as shown in Exhibit 6.2, but has in the meantime incurred total debts of $100,000. This leaves the partners with a negative equity of $37,500—the amount by which liabilities exceed assets. Suppose further that Appleman has no significant personal assets but that Kerwich does. In the process of liquidating the firm, Kerwich could be forced to sell $37,500 of her personal assets to cover debts of the partnership in addition to losing her original $28,500 investment in the firm. Her partner would lose only the original investment.

One further disadvantage of a partnership is that one partner cannot easily withdraw without the cooperation of the others. The partner who wants to withdraw must either find a new partner willing to buy his or her share in the partnership or get the other partners to agree to buy the share. Meanwhile, although the partner wishing to withdraw continues to own a share of the partnership's equity, that equity is "frozen"—it cannot be turned into cash or invested in another undertaking.

In forming a partnership, each partner must accept the others for better or for worse. Although better decisions usually result from the combined judgments of the partners, the division of decision making can cause personal difficulties. More partnerships have been dissolved because of such difficulties than for any other reason.

Any change in the combination of partners automatically causes a dissolution of the firm; thus the partnership has limited life. Like the sole proprietorship, the death, incapacity, or withdrawal of any of the partners terminates the original partnership agreement. The admission of a new partner or the sale of a partner's interest also ends the old partnership. Simply because there are more people involved, the limited life poses a larger problem in the partnership than in the sole proprietorship.

Corporations

Unlike a sole proprietorship or partnership, a **corporation** is a legal entity separate and apart from its owners. The ownership of a corporation is divided into equal parts called shares of stock. Persons who own the shares are called shareholders or stockholders. They elect officers to manage the business. Of course, if they own the majority of voting stock, they can, and often do, elect themselves as managers.

A major legal feature of the corporation is that it can be dealt with separately just like an individual. This means that the corporation serves as a buffer between the firm's owners and their customers, employees, suppliers, and creditors, as well as between the owners and the government and community. The corporation can hold, buy, sell, and exchange property in its own name. In

Corporation A firm in which the ownership is divided into equal parts called shares, with each shareholder's liability limited to the amount of his or her investment in the firm.

a sole proprietorship or partnership, property must be held in the name of the individual owners.

Suppose that the partnership of Kerwich and Appleman decides to incorporate. It can transfer its owners' equity from a partnership interest to a stockholder interest. The balance sheet will appear as in Exhibit 6.3.

Notice that the $57,000 of owner's equity (in a sole proprietorship and partnership) is now called capital stock. The ownership remains essentially the same but is called something else. Why would an owner prefer a corporation as the legal form of organization?

Advantages The main advantage of having the firm as a separate entity is that the owners carry only limited financial liability. This means that creditors can look only to the assets of the corporation for settlement of their claims. They cannot hold the owners liable for the debts of the corporation. If the corporation fails, the shareholders lose only the amount of their investment; their personal assets cannot be attached to pay the corporate debts.

This is not the case for a sole proprietorship or a partnership, where the owners are held liable for all the debts and are forced, when necessary, to pay them out of their personal assets. In a corporation, the owners' liability is limited only to their investment.

A corporation can grow to a larger size than a sole proprietorship or partnership because it can attract capital from thousands of individuals. It can expand or increase its size because the advantage of limited financial liability makes investors more willing to purchase additional shares of stock. It is easier for a corporation to raise $1 million by having a thousand people invest $1,000 each than it is for a sole proprietorship to have one person invest $1 million.

The transfer of ownership in a corporation is easily accomplished, especially for those corporations whose capital stock is listed and traded on the major stock exchanges and in the over-the-counter market. Millions of shares of capital stock change hands daily. As a general rule, corporations allow shareholders to transfer their ownership to anyone at any time (assuming that the price is agreeable to both buyer and seller) without the approval of the other shareholders.

The transferability of ownership of a corporation contributes to the continuity of the firm. Shareholders may withdraw by selling their shares or may die, leaving their shares to their heirs without disturbing the legal existence of the corporation.

Exhibit 6.3

Balance sheet of a corporation
A corporation owns all its assets in the name of the firm. Ownership of the firm's capital stock is the equity. Shareholders are liable for the firm's debts only to the extent that they have invested money in the firm.

Assets		Liabilities and Equity	
Cash	$30,500	Accounts payable	$ 500
Inventory	10,000	Mortgage payable	5,000
Equipment	2,000	Total debts	$ 5,500
Land and buildings	20,000	Capital stock (equity)	57,000
Total assets	$62,500	Total liabilities plus equity	$62,500

Disadvantages First among the disadvantages of the corporation is that it is subject to higher taxes than other forms of legal organizations. A corporation has to pay a tax to the state when it is incorporated. In addition to this so-called franchise tax, large corporations are required to pay the federal corporate income tax. (Some small corporations escape the corporate income tax under special exemptions; they are taxed in the same way as are sole proprietorships and partnerships.) In most states, corporations are also required to pay a state income tax. The owners of a corporation must then pay individual income taxes on all the dividends received from the corporation. This double taxation (on the corporate profits and on the dividends) is a major disadvantage of corporations as far as owners are concerned.

Corporations are also closely regulated. The regulations usually take the form of special reports, permits, and licenses. In large corporations, preparation of these reports requires the services of at least one full-time employee or even a whole department. Close regulation can add to the costs of doing business and is therefore a distinct disadvantage to the corporate form of organization.

Some Data on Business Organizations

According to Coase's theory, described earlier in this chapter, a firm exists because some business tasks are more easily coordinated by managerial directive than by prices and markets. The theory predicts that each firm will grow until the cost of coordinating one more task within the firm exceeds the cost of coordinating one task via the market. This limit to growth occurs at vastly different stages of development for different firms.

In 1974 there were 13.9 million firms in the United States, earning receipts (total revenues) of $3.5 trillion. Almost 11 million of the firms were sole proprietorships, 2 million were corporations, and just 1 million were partnerships. Exhibit 6.4 shows that the relatively small number of corporations accounted for the overwhelming share (87 percent) of business receipts. The

Exhibit 6.4

Distribution of firms by type of organization
In examining the various forms of legal organization available to the firm, it was shown that the proprietorship had advantages for small firms and the corporation had advantages for large ones. The data given in these charts confirm this. The top figure shows that proprietorships constitute more than three-quarters of the number of all firms, but the bottom figure shows that only 9.2 percent of all business receipts accrue to proprietorships. The vast majority of receipts are earned by the relatively small number of corporations.

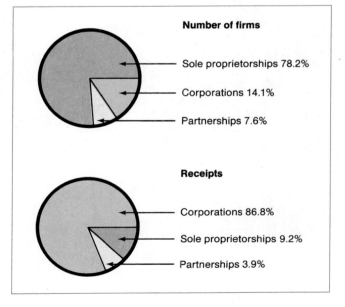

Number of firms

Sole proprietorships 78.2%

Corporations 14.1%

Partnerships 7.6%

Receipts

Corporations 86.8%

Sole proprietorships 9.2%

Partnerships 3.9%

Source: U.S. Department of Commerce, Bureau of the Census, *Statistical Abstract of the United States*, 98th ed. (Washington, D.C.: Government Printing Office, 1977), Table 892, p. 550. Data are from 1974.

reason is that, as explained in the previous section, many small firms are sole proprietorships, while large firms are usually corporations. Exhibit 6.5 confirms this impression. Some three-quarters of all sole proprietorships had receipts of less than $25,000 per year. Over half of all partnerships, but only about a quarter of all corporations, were below the same mark. Corporations with $1 million or more in annual receipts numbered less than 2 percent of all firms but accounted for nearly 80 percent of all business receipts. The relative advantages of the three types of firms vary greatly from one industry to another, as Exhibit 6.6 reveals.

The categories of manufacturing, mining, transportation and utilities, and finance and insurance are heavily dominated by corporations. Agriculture, at the other extreme, is dominated by the sole proprietorships of family farms. Proprietorships are also very important in services (27 percent of receipts) and have a strong representation in wholesale and retail trade (13 percent of receipts). Partnerships are the least common type of firm in every industry but finance, insurance, and real estate.

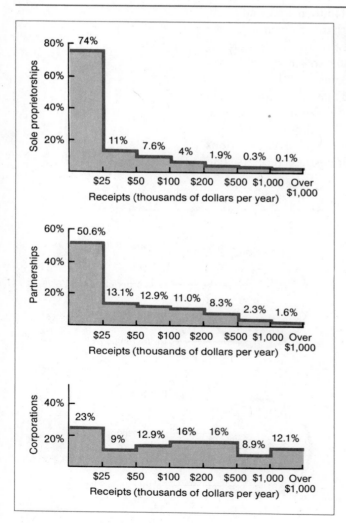

Exhibit 6.5
Size distribution of firms by type of organizational form
This exhibit presents further evidence that the proprietorship is favored as a form of legal organization predominantly by small firms. Note that the size profile of corporations is the reverse of that for proprietorships and partnerships.

Source: U.S. Department of Commerce, Bureau of the Census, *Statistical Abstract of the United States*, 98th ed. (Washington, D.C.: Government Printing Office, 1977), Table 894, p. 551. Data are from 1974.

Exhibit 6.6

Distribution of types of firms in various industries

Firms of all types find their place in every industry, but some forms of organization suit some industries better than others. The corporation dominates all major industrial groups except agriculture, where proprietorships dominate. Proprietorships are also important in services, trade, and construction. Only in the fields of finance, insurance, and real estate do partnerships hold a larger share of the industry than proprietorships.

Industry	Percentage of Receipts		
	Proprietorships	Partnerships	Corporations
Agriculture, forestry, and fisheries	64%	12%	23%
Mining	4	5	91
Construction	18	6	76
Manufacturing	1	1	98
Transportation, communication, electrical, gas, and sanitary services	4	1	95
Wholesale and retail trade	13	4	83
Finance, insurance, and real estate	3	8	89
Services	27	14	59

Source: U.S. Department of Commerce, Bureau of the Census, *Statistical Abstract of the United States*, 98th ed. (Washington, D.C.: Government Printing Office, 1977), Table 893, p. 550. Data are from 1974.

OWNERSHIP AND CONTROL OF CORPORATIONS

Sole proprietorships are owned and controlled by their proprietors and partnerships by their partners. Corporations are legally owned by their shareholders, but the matter of control is much less clear-cut than for other types of firms. Because corporations account for such a large part of the United States' business, no discussion of the nature of the firm would be complete without some mention of the controversy over control of the corporation.

Shareholder Rights

One of the advantages of the corporate form of business organization is that capital can be raised from many thousands of separate individuals, who need not invest a large share of their own portfolios in any one firm. Legally, those shareholders have the power to control the corporation. The principal channel for control is the shareholders' power to elect the corporation's board of directors, who decide company policy.

However, most shareholders do not actively exercise their ownership rights. Small shareholders are not really in a position to know what goes on inside their corporation and why decisions are made as they are. They tend to accept the policies set by managers as being for the best. If they disapprove of management policies, it is easier for them to sell their stock and buy shares in a better managed company than to try to throw their weight around at annual shareholder meetings. The result is a degree of separation of ownership from control unknown in sole proprietorships and partnerships.

Shareholders versus Managers

Why is the separation of ownership and control an important issue? The answer given by many economists is that the interests of shareholders and managers may differ. Most shareholders have only one interest in the corporation whose stock they own—that the corporation earn a maximum profit for them. Managers do not always think of their relationship to the corporation in such simple terms.

For one thing, managers are naturally concerned about the security of their own jobs. They know that they must earn at least a respectable minimum of profits or the shareholders may rebel and throw them out. But when it comes to delicate decisions involving marginal trade-offs between risk and profitability, their interests and those of the shareholders may diverge. Shareholders do not normally put all their eggs into one basket. They hold diversified portfolios. If by taking prudent risks they can earn higher average returns, an occasional failure is no disaster. Because a manager's career is more closely tied up with the fate of a single corporation, or even a single project of a corporation, managers may tend to be excessively cautious from the shareholders' point of view.

Corporate growth is another possible area of conflict of interest. Shareholders are interested in growth to the extent that growth means more profit per share, but managers may sometimes favor growth purely for its own sake. The power and prestige of managers, the number of employees they have working under them, and even their salaries are enhanced by growth, regardless of whether that growth increases profit per share.

Finally, it is claimed that managers who identify personally with their firms may be more willing than shareholders to spend money to improve their corporation's image. Lavish headquarters, charitable contributions, community relations projects, and the like may in some cases attract customers and swell profits; but because they also swell managerial pride, there can be a temptation to carry such expenditures too far.

In short, the picture offered by some observers of the corporate scene is one of contrast between the traditional firm singlemindedly pursuing the goal of profit maximization and the modern management controlled corporation for which profits are only one goal among many—and not always the highest ranking one.

Constraints on Managers

How much truth is there in this picture? The picture offered so far cannot be regarded as complete. There are strong reasons to believe that managers cannot really act as independently of the profit maximizing interests of owners as the preceding arguments might suggest.

For one thing, many corporations have plans that permit management to share directly in company profits. One of the most important types of profit sharing plans is the stock option. Stock options give managers the right to buy a certain number of shares of stock in the corporation at a guaranteed price at some time in the future. For example, say that in July 1980, a manager is given the option to buy a thousand shares of the company's stock in July 1981 at the 1980 price of, say, $25. If the manager, together with other managers, does a good job running the firm in the meantime, the price of the stock stands a good chance of rising. If the market price rises to $35 by July 1981, the option to buy a thousand shares at $25 will be worth $10,000, and the manager will reap a rich reward. But if the company is poorly managed and the share price falls, the option is worthless.

A second important constraint on the power of managers to slacken their pursuit of profits is the threat of a takeover. It is true that when ordinary shareholders do not like a corporation's policy, they may simply sell out and buy other stocks rather than attempt to exercise their influence directly. But what if a great many shareholders sell out? If they do, the price of the stock falls below the value it would have if the corporation were managed by profit maximizers. When this happens, an alert stock market entrepreneur can engineer a takeover bid. The takeover may be made by an individual, a group, or, often, another corporation. The idea is to buy a controlling percentage of the corporation's shares and use the power thus gained to replace current managers with more profit-minded ones. If the gambit succeeds, the listed value of the stock's price will rise as the new management policies attract other buyers. Then the original takeover group will reap very handsome gains.

In periods when stock prices are low by historical standards (for example, during the late 1970s), corporate takeovers become common. Large conglomerate firms that make a specialty of them go on the prowl, and weakly managed companies whose stock is selling at prices not reflecting their long-run profit potential are particularly likely to be bought up. Often, the managers of companies threatened with unfriendly takeovers cast around for a "white knight"—an alternative buyer that will take over the company and let the managers keep their jobs, provided they can convince the white knight of their competence.

The effectiveness of the corporate takeover as a device for keeping management on the profit maximizing track should not be measured solely in terms of the number of takeovers that actually occur. The threat of takeover is a powerful disciplinary device that can work without being used every day.

CONCLUSIONS

This chapter has offered just a glimpse of some of the complexities lying behind the simple concept of the firm. In many branches of economic theory, firms are treated as simple, homogeneous building blocks. In reality, they are neither simple nor homogeneous. Except for the smallest one-person operations, each firm is an organization of separate individuals united for a common purpose—the purpose of carrying out the division of labor effectively. Depending on circumstances, this purpose may best be served by the legal form of a sole proprietorship, a partnership, or a corporation. The next few chapters will set aside most of these details and complexities and will treat firms as simple units devoted to the maximization of profits. This simplifying assumption may not be altogether appropriate in each individual case, however. The information given in this chapter will be of help in keeping the firm in perspective and in avoiding acceptance of the simplifications of theory as the whole picture.

SUMMARY

1. There are two major forms of coordination for the division of labor—market coordination and managerial coordination. Market coordination uses the price system for communication and the profit motive as a source of incentives. Managerial coordination proceeds through directives from

superiors to subordinates. It organizes the division of labor within a firm, while market coordination organizes the division of labor among firms. Firms tend to grow until the cost of organizing one more task by managerial means exceeds the costs of organizing that task through the market.

2. Firms may be organized as sole proprietorships, partnerships, or corporations. Proprietorships are very common among small firms. They are easy to set up and have the advantage of giving the proprietor rights to all of the firm's profits. They have the disadvantage of unlimited liability. Partnerships also suffer from unlimited liability, but they can allow a firm to grow by bringing in new partners with new skills and new capital. Corporations protect their shareholders with limited liability and permit huge sums of capital to be raised. They suffer the disadvantages of higher taxes and closer regulations than other kinds of businesses, however.

3. It is sometimes argued that managers, rather than shareholders, exercise effective control over corporations. This is an important issue, because the interests of managers and shareholders sometimes conflict. Managers may be less willing than owners to take risks and may sometimes pursue growth at the expense of profits. There are limits to the ability of managers to pursue policies opposed to shareholder interests, though. The most important single constraint is the threat of takeover if profits are too much neglected.

DISCUSSION QUESTIONS

1. Your college or university uses a type of managerial coordination to determine which courses should be offered and which professors should teach them. In principle, market coordination could be used instead. The college or university could limit itself to providing classrooms, dormitories, library facilities, and so on. Professors would then be independent businesspeople, advertising certain courses for so much per credit hour and collecting fees directly from the students. Compare the advantages and disadvantages of each system. Why do you think the managerial system predominates? As far as you know, is the market system ever used in education? Explain.

2. Dryden Press, the publisher of this book, does not perform "in house" all the operations necessary to bring out the book. Instead, many particular jobs, such as manuscript typing, copy editing, drawing the artwork, composition, and printing are done on a subcontract basis by independent firms. How does Coase's theory of the firm help you understand why Dryden does not maintain on its own payroll all the necessary artists, compositors, printers, and so on?

3. On graduation, a classmate whom you barely know suggests that you go into business together selling sports equipment to the students in your university town. He wants to make the business a partnership. "You supply the brains; I'll put up the money," he says. Do you think you might be better off if he set the business up as a sole proprietorship, with you as his employee? As a corporation, with the two of you holding some of the stock? What would be the advantages and disadvantages to you of each alternative?

4. Why are corporations dominant in some lines of business and not in others? As the economy becomes more service oriented, do you think the importance of the corporation will decline? Explain.

5. Corporation law varies from state to state. Sometimes states make changes in the law in the hope of attracting new businesses and creating new jobs. Suppose the state where you live wants to change the law so that it will be almost impossible to make a successful takeover bid against a corporation located there. Do you think

this will work as a means of attracting corporations, assuming that other states do not do the same thing? Why and how will it work? Do you think it would be good for the economy as a whole if all states passed such legislation?

SUGGESTIONS FOR FURTHER READING

Coase, Ronald H. "The Nature of the Firm." *Economica*, new series, 4 (November 1937): 386–405.
The seminal article on the nature of the firm, it explains why there are such things as firms at all.

Galbraith, John Kenneth. *The New Industrial State*. Boston: Houghton Mifflin, 1967.
In this provocative and decidedly unorthodox book, Galbraith develops the thesis that the market plays little or no role in coordinating economic activity in the U.S. economy and that the corporation is run not by its stockholders but by something called the technostructure.

Gordon, Scott. "The Close of the Galbraithian System." *Journal of Political Economy* 76 (July–August 1968):635–644.
A short but trenchant critique of Galbraith's view of the economic system and the corporation.

Weston, J. Fred, and Brigham, Eugene F. *Essentials of Managerial Finance*. 5th ed. Hinsdale, Ill.: Dryden Press, 1979.
Chapter 3 discusses the forms of business organization and briefly explains their tax structure.

C H A P T E R 7
THE THEORY OF COST

WHAT YOU WILL LEARN IN THIS CHAPTER

Further exploration of microeconomic theory requires a better understanding of what lies behind the supply curve, which in turn requires a theory of cost. This chapter explains exactly what economists mean by cost. *Then it discusses the relationship between costs and the quantity of output produced by a firm and shows why this relationship depends on (among other things) the time horizon under consideration.*

FOR REVIEW

Here are some important terms and concepts that will be put to use in this chapter. If you do not understand them, review them before proceeding.
- *Opportunity cost (Chapter 1)*
- *The margin (Chapter 1)*

Many upward-sloping supply curves have been presented in earlier chapters. These curves have indicated that suppliers are willing to offer more of their product for sale when prices are high than when they are low. In a general way, it has been suggested that the positive slope of supply curves has something to do with costs; now it is time to take up that suggestion in more detail. The theory of cost developed in this chapter will be used as a basis for the construction of supply curves in Chapter 8 and for the analysis of many kinds of business decisions in later chapters.

THE NATURE OF COSTS

One of the most basic principles of economics is that all costs arise from the necessity of choosing among alternative uses of scarce resources. All costs of producing goods or services are opportunity costs; the true measure of the cost of doing something is always the value of the best alternative use of the same resources.

Implicit and Explicit Costs

In practical terms, the opportunity costs that a firm incurs in the course of business consist of the payments the firm must make to suppliers and the incomes it must provide to resource owners in order to attract labor, capital, and natural resources away from their alternative uses. These costs, in turn, fall into two categories—explicit costs and implicit costs.

Explicit costs Costs taking the form of explicit payments to nonowners of a firm.

Explicit costs are costs that take the form of payments to nonowners of the firm. They include payments made for the labor and raw materials used in actual production operations, the services of hired managers and salespeople, insurance, legal advice, transportation, and a great many other things.

Implicit costs The opportunity costs to a firm of using resources owned by the firm itself or contributed by owners of the firm.

Implicit costs are the opportunity costs to the firm of using resources owned by the firm itself or contributed by owners of the firm. Like explicit costs, they represent real sacrifices to the firm; but unlike explicit costs, they do not take the form of explicit payments to outsiders. For example, when a firm occupies a building or uses machinery that it owns, it forgoes the opportunity of using that building or machinery in some other way. For another example, the proprietor of a small firm who works alongside the firm's hired employees forgoes the opportunity to work elsewhere. Firms do not normally record costs of this sort in their accounts because no explicit payments are made to outsiders, but that does not make the costs any less real. Implicit costs represent the sacrifice of income that could have been earned by selling or hiring out the firm's resources to others.

Costs and Profits

Pure economic profit The sum remaining after both explicit and implicit costs are subtracted from total revenue.

The proper distinction between explicit and implicit costs is very important for understanding the concept of *profit* as it is used in economics. **Pure economic profit** means the difference between a firm's total revenues and total costs, including both explicit and implicit costs; the term *profit* as used in this book always means pure economic profit.

Much to the confusion of generations of economics students, the everyday language of business and accounting uses the term *profit* in another, quite different, sense—namely, to mean the sum remaining after only explicit costs are subtracted from total revenue. This kind of profit will be referred to as

Accounting profit Total revenue minus explicit costs.

accounting profit to distinguish it from the pure economic profit defined above. Putting the two definitions together produces the relationship:

Pure economic profit = Accounting profit − Implicit costs.

A Numerical Example The numerical example given in Exhibit 7.1 further illustrates the difference between pure economic profit and accounting profit for a firm called the Rogers Tool Company. The firm was formed when Andrea and Ralph Rogers left their jobs at a large corporation (where he had

Total revenue	$500,000
Less explicit costs:	
Wages	200,000
Salaries	100,000
Materials and other	50,000
Equals accounting profit	$150,000
Less implicit costs:	
Forgone salary, Andrea Rogers	40,000
Forgone salary, Ralph Rogers	40,000
Interest forgone on invested savings	20,000
Equals pure economic profit	$ 50,000

Exhibit 7.1
Accounts of Rogers Tool Company, 1980
Accounting profit is a firm's total revenue less its explicit costs. The accounting profit of Rogers Tool Company for 1980 is thus $150,000. To arrive at pure economic profit, implicit costs must also be subtracted from revenue. In this case, the implicit costs consist of income forgone by Andrea and Ralph Rogers, owners of the company—including $80,000 in forgone salaries and $20,000 in forgone interest on their invested savings. After these items are deducted, it can be seen that pure economic profit for the firm in 1980 is just $50,000.

worked as a manager and she as an engineer) to set up a small firm of their own. Initial capital for the new firm was provided by $200,000 in personal savings that the Rogerses had accumulated while working for their corporate employer.

During its first year, 1980, Rogers Tool Company earned total revenues of $500,000. Total explicit costs, consisting of purchased materials and wages and salaries paid to persons other than the owners, came to $350,000, which left an accounting profit of $150,000.

The explicit costs of the new firm, however, did not represent all of the opportunity costs incurred by the firm during its first year of operation. Both Andrea and Ralph Rogers gave up high-paying jobs to start the firm. Their combined former salary of $80,000 is listed in Exhibit 7.1 as an implicit cost of production because it represents the income they had to expect to derive from the firm in order to be attracted away from their former jobs.[1] Also listed as an implicit cost in Exhibit 7.1 is $20,000 of forgone interest income. This item is discussed in the next section.

After both implicit and explicit costs are subtracted from the firm's income, the firm is left with a pure economic profit of $50,000. This sum is profit, not cost, because it represents what the Rogerses earned from their new company over and above the $100,000 assumed to be necessary to attract their labor and capital away from the best alternative use. It is their reward for acting as entrepreneurs—that is, for recognizing and entering a potentially profitable niche in the machine tool market that no other entrepreneur had yet exploited.

Profit and Return to Capital

For some purposes, it is useful to calculate a firm's earnings in relation to the capital invested in the firm. In order to attract funds for investment, a firm must be able to provide prospective investors with the expectation of earning at least as much income as they would expect to earn from the best alternative use of their funds. Stated in terms of percent per year, this amount can be called the **normal rate of return to capital.** The normal rate of return represents the opportunity cost of capital to the firm. In the case of the Rogers Tool Company, the normal rate of return to capital was assumed to be 10 percent per year. The Rogerses could thus have earned $20,000 per year by putting their $200,000 of savings at the disposal of other firms in which they did not participate in an entrepreneurial capacity—for example, by using their savings to buy stocks and bonds of other companies.

As things worked out, the success of the Rogers Tool Company permitted Andrea and Ralph Rogers to earn much more than they would have if they had put their savings at the disposal of other firms. To be precise, they earned not only the $20,000 listed in Exhibit 7.1 as the opportunity cost of capital but also $50,000 in pure economic profit. The opportunity cost of capital plus pure economic profit, expressed as a percentage of capital invested in the firm, can be called the **total rate of return to capital** for the firm. In the case of the

Normal rate of return to capital The opportunity cost of capital to a firm—that is, the rate of return necessary to attract funds for investment from their best alternative uses.

Total rate of return to capital The opportunity cost of capital plus pure economic profit, expressed as a percentage of the capital invested in a firm.

---

[1] The $80,000 combined former salary is really only an approximation of what would have been required to attract the Rogerses away from their former jobs. Perhaps, because starting a new firm is a risky venture, the true opportunity cost—including lost peace of mind—would be more. Or perhaps, because the Rogerses place some value on being their own boss, the true opportunity cost would be less.

Rogers Tool Company, the total rate of return to capital for 1980 was 35 percent:

$$\frac{\$20,000 + \$50,000}{\$200,000} = 0.35.$$

From these definitions, it follows that a firm earning a total rate of return to capital greater than the normal rate of return is earning a positive pure economic profit; a firm earning a total rate of return less than the normal rate of return is earning a negative pure economic profit (that is, a pure economic loss); and a firm earning a total rate of return just equal to the normal rate of return is earning zero pure economic profit.

PRODUCTION AND COSTS IN THE SHORT RUN

Now that the economic meaning of cost is clear, the next step is to build a theory of cost. The main purpose of such a theory is to explain how costs vary as the quantity of output produced by a firm varies. The exposition of the theory of cost will be divided into two parts corresponding to two time perspectives—the short run and the long run. The distinction between these two perspectives requires just a bit more preliminary explanation before the theory of cost itself is presented.

The Long Run and the Short Run

A firm uses many kinds of inputs to produce its output. By varying the quantities of inputs it uses, the firm can vary the quantity of output produced. The quantities of some things a firm uses can often be adjusted very quickly, whereas others are not so easy to adjust. The inputs that cannot easily be varied as the level of output changes define the size of plant the firm must work with. The physical size of structures, the production capacity of major items of machinery, and specialized or not easily replaceable employees are among the inputs determining the size of a firm's plant. These inputs are known as **fixed inputs.** They can be distinguished from **variable inputs**—inputs that can be varied quickly and easily to adjust the quantity of output produced within a plant of a given size. Raw materials, energy, and hourly labor are among the major variable inputs for most firms.

The distinction between fixed and variable inputs in turn forms the basis for the distinction between the short run and the long run in cost theory. The **short run** is a time perspective too short to change the size of a firm's plant, so that variations in output can come only from changes in the quantities of variable inputs used. The **long run,** in contrast, is a time horizon long enough to permit changes in the quantities of fixed inputs and the size of the firm's plant.

Production in the Short Run and Diminishing Returns

Production with One Variable Input With these preliminaries out of the way, the discussion of short-run cost theory can begin with a simple story about the relationship between inputs and outputs in the short run for the Rogers Tool Company. Imagine, for the sake of discussion, that the company has only one input that is variable in the short run—namely, labor—and that it produces only one product—say, a small, portable drill press. Beginning from a

Fixed inputs Inputs to the production process that cannot easily be increased or decreased in a short period of time (the quantity of fixed inputs employed by a firm defines the size of the firm's plant).

Variable inputs Inputs to the production process that can quickly and easily be varied to increase or decrease output within a plant of a given size.

Short run A time perspective within which output can be adjusted only by changing the quantities of variable inputs within a plant of fixed size.

Long run A time perspective long enough to permit changes in the quantities of all inputs, both fixed and variable.

zero level of output, imagine that the rate of production of this tool is to be gradually increased, varying the quantity of labor while keeping the size of the plant fixed.

Initially, the firm might hire just one worker. This worker would have to walk from machine to machine, doing every step in the production process alone. The worker would lose time moving from machine to machine and would not become skilled at any particular task. This would not be very efficient, so costs would be relatively high in relation to output.

As more workers were taken on, output would increase rapidly. In fact, because workers could become more productive by specializing in particular tasks, it is very likely that the quantity of output produced per added unit of variable input would increase initially.

However, the rate of output per added unit of variable input could not continue to rise indefinitely. Eventually, a point would be reached beyond which the useful possibilities for specialization and division of labor within the plant would be exhausted. More workers might still increase output, of course. Each worker standing at a machine could be given a helper to pass along materials and carry away finished parts. Still more helpers could be added to pick up metal shavings for recycling or wave fans to keep the machine operators more comfortable and productive. Musicians could be hired to play string quartets to keep up morale in the stockroom. But obviously, long before that point were reached, each additional unit of variable input would be adding less and less to output. The fixed quantity of inputs other than labor would become increasingly inadequate to support the growing labor force. Eventually, additional workers would contribute nothing at all.

A Numerical Example The preceding story, although somewhat fanciful, is put more precisely in the numerical example of Exhibit 7.2. This exhibit, like the story on which it is based, assumes that labor is the firm's only variable input. Columns 1 and 2 show the quantity of output, measured in units (drill presses) per day, and the quantity of the variable input, measured in labor hours per day. Output reaches one unit per day only after labor input reaches 38 hours per day. Seventy-two labor hours per day suffice to raise output to two units per day; 102 labor hours are enough to produce three units per day, and so on. By the time labor input rises to 880 hours per day, output has risen to twenty-four units per day.

Columns 3 and 4 of Exhibit 7.2 illustrate the relationship between inputs and outputs in marginal terms. Column 3 shows the number of added labor hours required to produce each added unit of output. Column 4 shows the number of units of output added by each added unit of labor. The entry in Column 4 is thus the reciprocal of the entry in Column 3. For example, to increase output from four units to five units requires that labor input be increased from 130 hours per day to 155 hours per day, an increase of 25 labor hours. In the range between four and five units of output, then, each added labor hour contributes 1/25th of a unit (0.04 units) of output.

For present purposes, the entries in Column 4 are of particular interest. The quantity of output added per unit of added labor is called the **marginal physical product of labor.** Exhibit 7.3a, based on Columns 1 and 2 of Exhibit 7.2, shows how the total physical product of labor (that is, the total quantity of output) varies as the total quantity of labor varies. Exhibit 7.3b,

Marginal physical product (of an input) The quantity of output, expressed in physical units, produced by each added unit of the input.

Exhibit 7.2

Short-run inputs and outputs for the Rogers Tool Company

This exhibit shows hypothetical input and output data for the Rogers Tool Company. One variable input (labor) and one output (drill presses) are assumed. As the quantity of the variable input is increased—the quantities of fixed inputs remaining constant—output increases. Column 4 shows the additional output produced by each added labor hour for each one-unit range of output up to twenty-four units; this is called the marginal physical product of labor. Note that the marginal physical product of labor first rises but after nine units of output begins to fall again.

Quantity of Output (units per day) (1)	Quantity of Labor (labor hours per day) (2)	Added Labor Hours per Added Unit of Output (3)	Added Units of Output per Added Labor Hour (marginal physical product of labor) (4)
1	38.0		
		34.0	0.029
2	72.0		
		30.5	0.032
3	102.5		
		27.5	0.036
4	130.0		
		25.0	0.040
5	155.0		
		23.0	0.043
6	178.0		
		21.5	0.047
7	199.5		
		20.5	0.049
8	220.0		
		20.0	0.050
9	240.0		
		20.5	0.049
10	260.5		
		21.5	0.047
11	282.0		
		23.0	0.043
12	305.0		
		25.0	0.040
13	330.0		
		27.5	0.036
14	357.5		
		30.5	0.032
15	388.0		
		34.0	0.029
16	422.0		
		38.0	0.026
17	460.0		
		42.5	0.024
18	502.5		
		47.5	0.021
19	550.0		
		53.0	0.019
20	603.0		
		59.0	0.017
21	662.0		
		65.5	0.015
22	727.5		
		72.5	0.014
23	800.0		
		80.0	0.013
24	880.0		

based on Columns 2 and 4 of Exhibit 7.2, shows how the marginal physical product of labor varies as the quantity of labor used varies. Both graphs are based on the same assumption as the table in Exhibit 7.2—namely, that labor is the only variable input; the size of the plant and the quantities of all other inputs are assumed to remain fixed.

The Law of Diminishing Returns Notice that in Exhibit 7.3b, as the quantity of labor input varies, the marginal physical product of labor at first rises but then falls. This increase and, then, decrease in marginal product gives the total physical product curve its characteristic S-shape. The curves shown in Exhibit 7.3 illustrate a principle known as the **law of diminishing returns,** which says that as the quantity of one variable input used in a production process is increased, with the quantities of all other inputs remaining fixed, a point will eventually be reached beyond which the quantity of output added per unit of added variable input (that is, the marginal physical product of the variable input) will begin to decrease.

The law of diminishing returns is quite general. It applies to all known production processes and to all variable inputs. In the example above, the law was illustrated by the case of a manufacturing firm, with labor as the variable input. It could have been illustrated equally well by an example from farming, with, say, fertilizer as the variable input: As the quantity of fertilizer used per acre of land increases, all other inputs remaining fixed, the number of bushels of output per acre increases; but beyond some point, the quantity of output

Law of diminishing returns
The law stating that as the quantity of one variable input used in a production process is increased (with the quantities of all other inputs remaining fixed), a point will eventually be reached beyond which the quantity of output added per unit of added variable input (that is, the marginal physical product of the variable input) begins to decrease.

Exhibit 7.3
**Total and marginal physical product curves for
Rogers Tool Company**
The curves in this exhibit are drawn from the data given
in Exhibit 7.2. Part a shows the total quantity of output
produced by various quantities of the variable input
labor, given the size of the firm's plant as defined by
the quantities of fixed inputs. It is labeled the total
physical product curve. Part b shows how much extra
output is produced by each additional unit of labor. It is
labeled the marginal physical product curve. Note that
after labor input reaches approximately 230 hours per
day, the marginal physical product of labor begins to
decline. The downward-sloping section of the marginal
physical product curve illustrates the law of diminishing
returns.

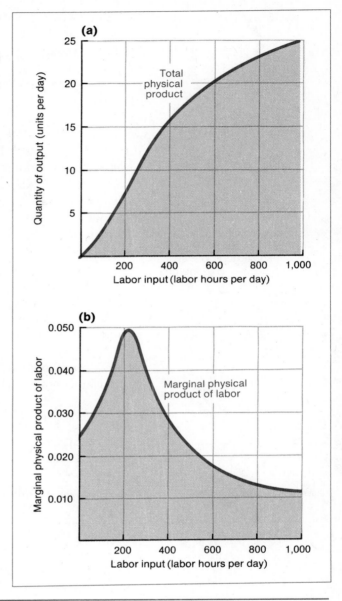

added per added unit of fertilizer begins to decrease. Or an example from the
energy industry could have been used: As the number of tons of coal burned
per week in a power plant of a given size increases, the output of electricity
increases; but beyond some point, the capacity of the plant is approached, and
the added output of electricity per added ton of coal per week decreases. In
every case, the limited quantity of fixed input is unable, after a certain point,
to adapt to increasing quantities of the variable input without a decline in
marginal physical product of the variable input.

Diminishing Returns and Short-Run Costs

It is a short step from the law of diminishing returns to an analysis of the
short-run relationship between output and costs. To explore this relationship,

return to the example of the Rogers Tool Company. Assume that the company is able to hire production workers at a constant wage of $10 per hour. If, beyond a point, each added hour of labor adds less to output than the previous one, and each added labor hour costs the same as the previous one, it follows that beyond the point where diminishing returns begin, variable costs per unit of output must rise.

Marginal Costs and Total Costs The relationship between the law of diminishing returns and the behavior of short-run variable costs is illustrated numerically in Exhibit 7.4 and graphically in Exhibit 7.5, Exhibit 7.4 is based directly on Exhibit 7.2, assuming a labor cost of $10 per hour. Column 3 shows the total variable cost, at $10 per labor hour, of producing any given level of output. Column 4 shows the amount of added cost incurred to produce each added unit of output. This cost increase is known as the short-run **marginal cost** of production at that level of output. Note that the entries in Column 4 are equal to the differences between successive entries in Column 3.

Marginal cost The increase in cost required to increase output of some good or service by one unit.

Exhibit 7.5 is derived directly from the numbers given in Exhibit 7.4. A comparison of Exhibits 7.3 and 7.5 shows that the marginal cost and total cost curves are, roughly, the mirror images of the marginal product and total product curves. In particular, over the range of diminishing returns, marginal product falls and marginal cost rises. Correspondingly, the slope of the total product curve becomes flatter as one moves to the right in the range of diminishing returns, while the slope of the total cost curve becomes steeper.

Exhibit 7.4

Total variable cost and marginal cost for the Rogers Tool Company

The data given in this exhibit are based on those given in Exhibit 7.2; they assume a labor cost of $10 per hour. Column 3 gives the total variable cost (assuming labor to be the only variable input) of producing a given quantity of output per day. Column 4 shows the marginal cost at each level of output—that is, the added cost of increasing the level of output by one unit.

Quantity of Output (units per day) (1)	Quantity of Labor Input (labor hours per day) (2)	Total Variable Cost ($10 per labor hour) (3)	Marginal Cost (4)
1	38.0	$ 380	
2	72.0	720	$340
3	102.5	1,025	305
4	130.0	1,300	275
5	155.0	1,550	250
6	178.0	1,780	230
7	199.5	1,995	215
8	220.0	2,200	205
9	240.0	2,400	200
10	260.5	2,605	205
11	282.0	2,820	215
12	305.0	3,050	230
13	330.0	3,300	250
14	357.5	3,575	275
15	388.0	3,880	305
16	422.0	4,220	340
17	460.0	4,600	380
18	502.5	5,025	425
19	550.0	5,500	475
20	603.0	6,030	530
21	662.0	6,620	590
22	727.5	7,275	655
23	800.0	8,000	725
24	880.0	8,800	800

Exhibit 7.5

Total variable and marginal cost curves for Rogers Tool Company

The total variable and marginal cost curves shown in this exhibit are plotted from data given in Exhibit 7.4. Because marginal cost measures the amount by which total cost increases each time output is increased by one unit, the height of the marginal cost curve at each quantity of output is equal to the slope of the total variable cost curve at that output. Notice in particular that just at the point of minimal marginal cost, the total variable cost curve stops getting flatter and begins to get steeper.

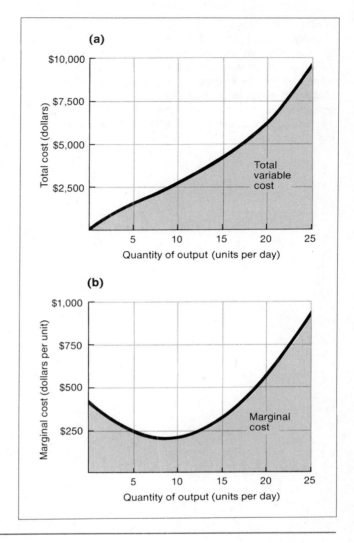

A Family of Short-Run Cost Curves

The marginal cost and total variable cost curves shown in Exhibit 7.5 are only two of a whole family of short-run cost curves that can be constructed for the Rogers Tool Company. The complete family is shown in numerical form in Exhibit 7.6c and graphically in Exhibits 7.6a and 7.6b.

Total variable cost, from Exhibit 7.4, appears in Column 2 of Exhibit 7.6c. Not all costs are variable in the short run. Fixed cost, which represents the costs of maintaining the plant within which the variable input labor is put to work, is assumed to amount to $2,000 per day in the case shown. Adding fixed cost (Column 3) to variable cost gives short-run total cost, shown in Column 4. The three total cost curves—total variable, total fixed, and total cost—are shown graphically in Exhibit 7.6a. Because fixed cost by definition does not vary as output varies, the total fixed cost curve is a horizontal line at a distance equal to $2,000 above the horizontal axis. Adding fixed cost to variable cost gives total cost, so the total cost curve parallels the total variable cost curve at a level exactly $2,000 higher.

Exhibit 7.6

A family of short-run cost curves

A whole family of short-run cost curves can be derived from the cost data shown in Part c of this exhibit. Three kinds of total cost curves are shown in Part a, while average and marginal cost curves are shown in Part b. Note that the marginal cost curve intersects the average total cost and average variable cost curves at their lowest points.

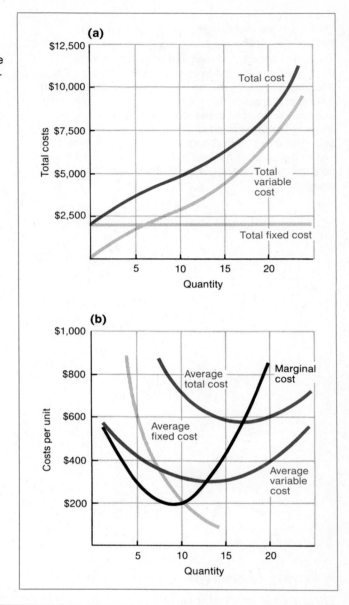

The next entry in Exhibit 7.6c is again a familiar one—marginal cost. The marginal cost data given here are the same as those in Exhibit 7.4. They again appear on lines between the total cost entries to emphasize that marginal cost shows how total cost changes as the level of output changes. The marginal cost curve drawn in Exhibit 7.6b is the same as the one appearing in Exhibit 7.5.

The last three columns in Exhibit 7.6c are all average cost concepts: average variable cost, average fixed cost, and average total cost. Average variable cost is equal to total variable cost divided by the quantity of output; average fixed cost is equal to total fixed cost divided by output; and average total cost is equal to total cost divided by output. The three average cost curves are also drawn in Exhibit 7.6b.

(c)

Quantity of Output (units) (1)	Total Variable Cost (2)	Total Fixed Cost (3)	Total Cost (4)	Marginal Cost (dollars per unit) (5)	Average Variable Cost (dollars per unit) (6)	Average Fixed Cost (dollars per unit) (7)	Average Total Cost (dollars per unit) (8)
0	$ 0	$2,000	$ 2,000		—	—	—
1	380	2,000	2,380	$380	$380	$2,000	$2,380
2	720	2,000	2,720	340	360	1,000	1,360
3	1,025	2,000	3,025	305	342	667	1,009
4	1,300	2,000	3,300	275	325	500	825
5	1,550	2,000	3,550	250	310	400	710
6	1,780	2,000	3,780	230	296	333	629
7	1,995	2,000	3,995	215	285	286	571
8	2,200	2,000	4,200	205	275	250	525
9	2,400	2,000	4,400	200	266	222	488
10	2,605	2,000	4,605	205	260	200	460
11	2,820	2,000	4,820	215	256	181	437
12	3,050	2,000	5,050	230	254	169	421
13	3,300	2,000	5,300	250	254	154	408
14	3,575	2,000	5,575	275	255	143	398
15	3,880	2,000	5,880	305	259	133	392
16	4,220	2,000	6,220	340	264	125	389
17	4,600	2,000	6,600	380	271	118	389
18	5,025	2,000	7,025	425	279	111	390
19	5,500	2,000	7,500	475	289	105	394
20	6,030	2,000	8,030	530	302	100	402
21	6,620	2,000	8,620	590	315	95	410
22	7,275	2,000	9,275	655	331	91	422
23	8,000	2,000	10,000	725	348	87	435
24	8,800	2,000	10,800	800	367	80	450

Some Geometric Relationships

A careful examination of Exhibits 7.6a and 7.6b reveals some important geometric relationships among the various average, marginal, and total cost curves represented there. First compare the marginal cost curve with the total variable cost curve drawn directly above it. The bottom of the U-shaped marginal cost curve occurs at exactly the same level of output where the slope of the reverse S-shaped total variable cost curve stops getting flatter and starts getting steeper. This occurs because the slope of the total variable cost curve is the *rate* at which the total variable cost curve is rising, just as marginal cost measures the *rate* at which total variable cost is rising. In graphical terms, then, the *height* of the marginal cost curve is always equal to the *slope* of the total cost curve.

Marginal average rule The rule that marginal cost must be equal to average cost when average cost is at its minimum.

A second feature of the cost curves drawn in Exhibit 7.6 deserves special comment. The marginal cost curve intersects both the average variable cost and average total cost curves exactly at their lowest points. This is not just coincidence. It is a consequence of a relationship that can be called the **marginal average rule.** This rule can be explained as follows: Beginning at any given point, ask what will be the cost of producing one more unit. The answer is given by marginal cost. Then ask whether this cost is more or less than the average cost of all units produced up to that point. If the added cost of the next unit produced is less than the average cost of previous units, then producing it will have the effect of pulling down the average. If the next unit costs more, its production will pull up the average. It follows that whenever marginal cost is below average variable cost, the average variable cost curve must be falling (that is, negatively sloped); and whenever marginal cost is above average variable cost, the average variable cost curve must be rising (that is, positively sloped). This in turn implies that the marginal cost curve cuts the average variable cost curve at its lowest point. All this is equally true of the relationship between marginal cost and average total cost.

LONG-RUN COSTS AND ECONOMIES OF SCALE

Short-Run and Long-Run Average Costs

Shifting perspective from the short run to the long run now, take another look at the costs of production for the Rogers Tool Company. Remember the crucial distinction between the long run and the short run: In the long run, there are no fixed inputs. Not only can quantities of labor, raw materials, energy, and the like be varied, but, given time, the size of the firm's plant can be changed by building new structures, buying new capital equipment, and adding other fixed inputs as necessary.

It is sometimes said that firms operate in the short run and plan in the long run. This slogan reflects economists' distinction between variable and fixed costs: In the short run, one varies output within a plant of fixed size; and in the long run, one plans (and executes) expansions or contractions of the plant itself. Thinking of the long run as the firm's planning perspective and the short run as the firm's operating perspective makes it easier to understand the relationship between short-run and long-run average costs.

Planning for Expansion Put yourself in the position of an entrepreneur just setting out to establish a small firm such as the Rogers Tool Company. You think it will be wise to start with just a small plant, but you want to do some long-range planning too. After consulting with production engineers and other specialists, you sketch some average cost curves for various possible sizes of plant. Five such curves are drawn in Exhibit 7.7. The first one shows short-run average costs for the range of output that is feasible with a very small plant, the second one corresponds to a slightly larger plant, and so on. As you build up the market for your product, you hope to be able to expand your plant and move from one of these curves to the next.

Of course, the five short-run cost curves in the exhibit represent only a sample of plant sizes. Intermediate positions are also possible. The size of plant you actually choose to build will depend, in the long run, on the quantity of output you expect to produce. For any given level of output, you will choose

Exhibit 7.7

Alternative short-run average total cost curves
The position of the short-run average total cost curve
for a firm depends on the size of the plant it constructs.
In the long run, the firm has a choice of operating with
any size plant it chooses. Each plant size can be represented by a different U-shaped short-run average total
cost curve. Five such curves are shown in this exhibit.
A new firm might begin with a plant corresponding to a
curve such as the first one shown here. Then, as demand for its product expanded, it might move to those
farther to the right.

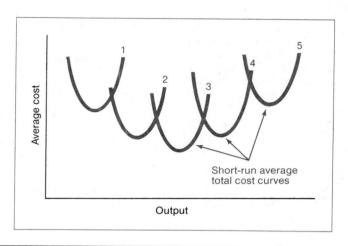

the size of plant that will permit that output to be produced at the lowest
possible average total cost.

The Long-Run Average Cost Curve As your firm gradually expands, then,
you can envision moving along a *long-run average cost curve* of the kind
shown in Exhibit 7.8. This curve is the "envelope" of all possible short-run
average cost curves. The size of plant chosen in the long run for each output
will be the one that produces a short-run average total cost curve just tangent to
the long-run average total cost curve at that point.

Economies of Scale

Economists have developed some special terminology to describe what happens
to long-run average costs as output increases. In any range of output where
long-run average cost *decreases* as output increases, the firm for which the cost
curves are drawn is said to experience **economies of scale.** In any range of
output where long-run average cost *increases*, the firm is said to experience
diseconomies of scale. Finally, if there is any range of output for which

Economies of scale A phenomenon said to occur whenever long-run average cost decreases as output increases.

Diseconomies of scale A phenomenon said to occur whenever long-run average cost increases as output increases.

Exhibit 7.8

Derivation of a long-run average cost curve
A firm can build a plant of any size, and each possible
plant size implies a different short-run total cost curve.
Here are drawn a large number of possible short-run
total cost curves, but even these curves are only a
sample of all possible curves. As the firm expands, in
the long run, it moves from one curve to another, always choosing the size of plant that minimizes the average total cost for the output the firm plans to produce
at any particular time. The path along which a firm will
expand—the firm's long-run average cost curve—is thus
the "envelope" of all the possible short-run average
total cost curves.

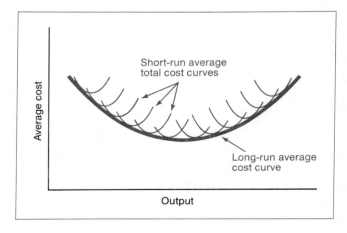

Constant returns to scale A phenomenon said to occur when there are neither economies nor diseconomies of scale.

long-run average cost does not change as output changes, the firm is said to experience **constant returns to scale** in that range.

The long-run average cost curve in Exhibit 7.8 is smoothly U-shaped, but that is not the only possible shape for such a curve. In fact, statistical studies suggest that L-shaped long-run average cost curves are the rule, at least in many manufacturing industries. Such a curve appears in Exhibit 7.9, which shows an initial range of economies of scale followed by a range of approximately constant returns to scale. The curve could turn out to be a flat-bottomed U if it were followed out far enough (as the broken extension of the curve in Exhibit 7.7 indicates). In any single industry, however, there may be no firms large enough to show diseconomies of scale. If there are none, that range of the curve remains invisible to statistical observation.

Minimum efficient scale The level of output at which economies of scale are exhausted.

Statistical studies of long-run average cost often concentrate on measuring the level of output where economies of scale are exhausted and constant returns to scale begin. This level is called the **minimum efficient scale** for the firm. As shown in Exhibit 7.9, it corresponds to the point where the L-shaped long-run average cost curve stops falling and begins to level out. If the cost curve does not have a sharp kink at this point—and there is no reason to think it must have—the minimum efficient scale can be identified only approximately. This is not a major problem, however, since statistical studies of cost must deal in approximations in any event.

Where do economies of scale come from? Why is it ever true that a large firm can produce at a lower unit cost than a smaller firm? Economists who have investigated these questions have found that there is no single source of economies of scale for all industries. Rather, there are a number of different sources, some of which are important in certain industries and others in other industries.

Economies of Scale at the Plant Level When most people think of economies of scale, what probably comes to mind first is an automobile assembly plant or a large steel mill. Costs per unit tend to decrease with the rate of output per plant per day in such industries as automobiles and steel for a

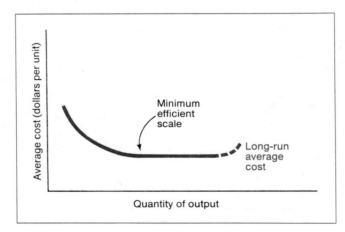

Exhibit 7.9

An L-shaped average cost curve showing minimum efficient scale

Statistical studies of long-run average cost suggest that long-run average cost curves are often L-shaped, as shown here. The point at which economies of scale are exhausted and the curve begins to flatten out is called the minimum efficient scale for the firm. Probably, if a firm continued to expand without limit, long-run average costs would eventually begin to rise. However, in many industries, there are no firms operating at a large enough scale to make the range of decreasing returns to scale visible to statistical observation. The upward-sloping portion of the curve is thus shown here as a broken line.

number of reasons. One is that a metal-forming machine or steel furnace capable of producing twice as much as another usually costs less than twice as much to build. Another is that larger plants can take advantage of more specialized division of labor. The automobile assembly line, on which each worker performs a single operation on each car as it moves by, is the classical example of this effect. Economies of scale associated with the rate of output per plant per day can be referred to as *plant-level* economies of scale. The following case study describes one attempt to measure plant-level economies of scale for a sample of twelve industries.

Case 7.1
Measuring Plant-Level Economies of Scale

In 1975, Harvard University Press published the results of an ambitious study of economies of scale in twelve major industries. The study v based on a series of interviews with engineers and industrialists of 125 c anies in six countries. The respondents were asked questions relating to the level of technology prevailing in the industry as of 1965.

Exhibit 7.10 gives some of the major findings of this study. The first column of the table shows the study's estimates of the minimum efficient scale of plant in each industry, expressed as a percentage of 1967 U.S. consumption. These numbers indicate where the flat portion of the L-shaped long-run average cost curve begins for each industry.

The second column shows the percentage increase of unit costs for a plant operating at one-third of the minimum efficient scale. These numbers give a rough indication of the steepness of the downward-sloping portion of the firm's L-shaped average cost curves. Clearly, there are big differences among the various industries in this regard. In the cement industry, a plant one-third the minimum efficient scale would incur costs per unit 26 percent above those of an efficient plant. But in cigarettes, the cost penalty for the smaller plant would be only 2.2 percent.

Source: F. M. Scherer, Alan Beckenstein, Erich Kaufer, and R. D. Murphey, *The Economics of Multi-Plant Operation: An International Comparisons Study* (Cambridge, Mass.: Harvard University Press, 1975).

Exhibit 7.10
Minimum efficient scale for twelve industries

This table presents the results of the study described in Case 7.1. The first column shows the minimum efficient scale in each industry as a percentage of 1967 U.S. consumption. It provides an indication of the point at which the L-shaped long-run average cost curve for a typical firm in each industry stops falling and begins to level out. The second column shows the cost penalty that would be paid by a firm operating at one-third the minimum efficient scale. These numbers give a rough idea of the steepness of the downward-sloping portion of the L-shaped long-run average cost curves.

Industry	Minimum Efficient Plant Size as Percent of U.S. Consumption	Percentage Increase in Cost for a Plant One-third of Minimum Efficient Scale
Ball and roller bearings	1.4	8.0
Beer brewing	3.4	5.0
Cement	1.7	26.0
Cigarettes	6.6	2.2
Cotton and synthetic fabrics	0.2	7.6
Glass containers	1.5	11.0
Paints	1.4	4.4
Petroleum refining	1.9	4.8
Refrigerators	14.1	6.5
Shoes	0.2	1.5
Storage batteries	1.9	4.6
Wide-strip steel works	2.6	11.0

Source: F. M. Scherer, Alan Beckenstein, Erich Kaufer, and R. D. Murphey, *The Economics of Multi-Plant Operation: An International Comparisons Study* (Cambridge, Mass.: Harvard University Press, 1975), Table 3.11, p. 80. Copyright © 1975 by the President and Fellows of Harvard College; all rights reserved.

Other Sources of Economies of Scale Not all economies of scale are associated with increases in the rate of output of a single plant. Sometimes, for example, they have their origin in the total quantity of a product or model produced rather than in the rate at which it is produced. With a long production run, costs associated with product design, equipment set-up, and specialized training can be spread over a large number of units. A comparison of General Motors with Volkswagen can serve to illustrate the difference between economies of scale associated with the rate of production and those associated with the volume of production. General Motors achieves important economies of scale through a high rate of production but changes models frequently. Volkswagen, by comparison, produces fewer cars per year but keeps each model in production longer. Its famous Beetle, for example, was produced with minor variations for more than four decades.

In addition to the rate and volume of production at a single plant, attention must be given to economies of multi-plant operation. The McDonald's hamburger chain provides a good example. The minimum efficient scale for a single plant (a single restaurant) is obviously very small in the fast food industry. Nonetheless, McDonald's apparently realizes important economies by operating many restaurants as an integrated system. Some of the economies are production economies: Individual food items and ingredients can be produced in efficient centralized kitchens, personnel can be trained at the famous "Hamburger University," and so on. A multi-plant firm such as McDonald's also realizes significant economies of scale with such functions as finance, advertising, and marketing.

CONCLUSIONS

This chapter has only scratched the surface of the theory of cost. Advanced books on the subject go into a wealth of extensions, additional details, mathematical formulations, and special cases. Nonetheless, the limited treatment given here will serve quite well as a basis for the analysis of individual firms and industries in the following chapters.

Chapter 8 will show how short-run and long-run cost curves can be used to derive supply curves for an industry in which there are a large number of competing firms. Chapter 9 will then use cost curves to analyze business behavior in markets where a single firm has a monopoly. Chapter 10 will examine agricultural markets. Then, Chapter 11 will turn to the case of markets dominated not by a single firm but by a relatively small number of firms. At that point, the discussion will return to the theme of economies of scale, which are an important factor in determining the number of firms that exist in the market for a given product. Chapters 12 through 14 will develop a variety of applications of cost theory to important questions of public policy.

SUMMARY

1. A firm's costs of production include all the sacrifices it must make in order to carry on production. Some of these sacrifices take the form of explicit payments to outsiders and are called explicit costs. Others are opportunity costs of using resources owned by the firm itself and are called implicit costs.

2. Economists use the term *profit* in a special sense: *Pure economic profit* means the difference between a firm's revenues and its total costs, including both implicit and explicit costs. In everyday language, the term *profit* is instead often used to mean the difference between total revenue and explicit costs; economists refer to this difference as *accounting profit.*

3. The short run is a time period so short that not all of a firm's inputs can be varied in response to changes in output. According to the law of diminishing returns, in the short run, there must be some point beyond which the marginal physical product of a variable input diminishes. Short-run average and marginal cost curves for the typical firm are U-shaped. The marginal cost curve cuts the average variable cost and average total cost curves at their lowest points.

4. In the long run, a firm can adjust the quantities of all inputs in response to changes in output. A firm will choose the size of plant that will allow the expected long-run output to be produced at the minimum possible average cost. A long-run average cost curve can be constructed as the envelope of a set of short-run average total cost curves, one for each possible size of plant.

5. A firm is said to experience economies of scale over any range of output where its long-run average cost curve slopes downward. Over any range of output where the long-run average cost curve slopes upward, the firm experiences diseconomies of scale. If there are flat spots on the long-run average cost curve, the firm is said to experience constant returns to scale there.

DISCUSSION QUESTIONS

1. Consider the costs of owning and operating an automobile. Which of the costs are implicit, and which are explicit? Are there any economy-wide opportunity costs of operating an automobile that do not show up at all in your tally of private costs?

2. Now divide the costs of owning and operating an automobile into fixed costs and variable costs. Suppose you were deciding whether to drive to a neighboring college to a football game or to take the bus instead. Would you take both fixed and variable costs into account? Suppose you were deciding whether to buy a house in a neighborhood where you could walk to work or a house located where you would have to buy a second car to drive to work every day. Would you then take both fixed and variable costs of the car into account?

3. What are the economies of scale and diseconomies of scale involved in running a university? Give specific examples.

4. Do you see any parallel between the law of diminishing returns and the principle of diminishing marginal utility? Do you think that both could be lumped together in a "law of diminishing marginal everything"? Try stating such a general law.

5. Take a piece of graph paper and draw, freehand, a typical reverse S short-run total cost curve. Then, as accurately as you can, construct the corresponding average total cost, average variable cost, average fixed cost, and marginal cost curves. When you have mastered these curves, try something harder. Draw some nontypical short-run total cost curves—curves with, say, funny kinks or bends or perhaps bumps like those on a roller coaster. They will not make much economic sense, but trying to draw the average and marginal cost curves for them will be an excellent test of whether you can really understand a graph like the one in Exhibit 7.6. If you cannot do this exercise successfully, you may need to review the Appendix to Chapter 1.

6. Turn to Exhibit 7.8. Copy this diagram onto a sheet of graph paper, drawing the long-run average cost curve and just one of the short-run average total cost curves. Use the curves you have drawn to construct the corresponding long-run and

short-run total cost curves. The total cost curves you get should both be reverse S-shaped and should be tangent to one another at the same level of output at which the average cost curves are tangent.

7. Suppose you had investigated the relationship between quantities of coal burned per week in a power plant of a given size and the output of electricity per week at that plant and had found the following: For tiny quantities of coal, not enough even to heat up the boiler, no electricity could be produced. After a critical minimum of coal was burned, the added electricity per added ton of coal burned was constant over a considerable range. Then, abruptly, a capacity limit was reached beyond which putting more coal in would produce no added electricity at all. Sketch the marginal and total physical product of coal curves for the plant. Do they conform to the law of diminishing returns?

8. It has been said that if it were not for the law of diminishing returns, all the food that the world needs could be grown in a flowerpot. Discuss. (Hint: Think of land as the only fixed factor and fertilizer as the only variable factor. How much food could be grown in the flowerpot if the marginal physical product of fertilizer were constant regardless of the quantity of fertilizer applied per unit of land?)

SUGGESTIONS FOR FURTHER READING

Alchian, Armen A. "Costs and Outputs." In *The Allocation of Economic Resources*, edited by Moses Abramovitz et al. Stanford, Calif.: Stanford University Press, 1959, pp. 23–40. Also reprinted in William Breit and Harold M. Hochman, eds. *Readings in Microeconomics*. 2d ed. New York: Holt, Rinehart and Winston, 1968, pp. 159–171. *An attempt to clarify certain aspects of the theory of costs. Alchian emphasizes, among other things, that cost varies in response to variations in the total expected volume of output as well as in response to variations in the rate of output.*

Blaug, Mark. *Economic Theory in Retrospect.* Rev. ed. Homewood, Ill.: Richard D. Irwin, 1968.
Chapter 10 discusses Alfred Marshall's pioneering contributions to cost theory.

Leftwich, Richard H. *The Price System and Resource Allocation.* 7th ed. Hinsdale, Ill.: Dryden Press, 1979.
Chapters 8 and 9 parallel the discussion of this chapter but use considerably more detail.

Nicholson, Walter. *Intermediate Microeconomics and its Application.* 2d ed. Hinsdale, Ill.: Dryden Press, 1979.
Chapter 6 gives a detailed treatment of the theory of production. Chapter 7 covers cost theory on a level somewhat more advanced then Leftwich's.

C H A P T E R 8
SUPPLY UNDER PERFECT COMPETITION

WHAT YOU WILL LEARN IN THIS CHAPTER

The theory of cost developed in Chapter 7 provides a foundation for a theory of the supply curve. That theory will be developed in this chapter, using the concept of a perfectly competitive market. The chapter will first explain how a typical firm adjusts its quantity supplied to short-run changes in market prices. Next, it will show how a short-run supply curve for the market as a whole can be built up from the supply curves of separate firms. Then it will develop the relationship between short-run and long-run adjustments for both the firm and the market. Finally, it will briefly discuss what is perfect about perfect competition.

FOR REVIEW

Here are some important terms and concepts that will be put to use in this chapter. If you do not understand them, review them before proceeding.
- *Pure economizing versus entrepreneurship (Chapter 1)*
- *Supply and demand (Chapter 3)*
- *Elasticity of supply (Chapter 3)*
- *Theory of cost (Chapter 7)*

The last two chapters have examined the nature of the firm and the cost structure of a typical firm. The discussion has supplied the background needed to develop a theory of what lies behind the supply curves so frequently drawn in earlier chapters. This chapter will begin with the simplest case—one in which the firm's supply decision is limited solely to determining how much to produce. Chapter 9 will extend the analysis to markets in which firms must also decide what price to put on their products as well as how much to produce.

THE STRUCTURE OF PERFECT COMPETITION

The nature of the decisions a firm must make depends in large part on the structure of the market in which it operates. **Market structure** in this sense means such characteristics as the number of firms that operate in each industry, the extent to which the products of different firms are varied, and the ease or difficulty firms have in getting into and out of the market.

There are many possible market structures. This chapter will be occupied

Market structure Important characteristics of a market, including the number of firms that operate in it, the extent to which the products of different firms are diverse or homogeneous, and the ease of entry into and exit from the market.

Perfect competition A market structure characterized by a large number of relatively small firms, a homogeneous product, good distribution of information among all market participants, and freedom of entry and exit.

with one known as perfect competition. As a market structure, **perfect competition** has four defining characteristics:

1. There are many sellers and buyers, each of which sells or buys only a small fraction of all that is bought and sold in the market.
2. The product traded in the market is entirely homogeneous; that is, the product sold by one firm is just like that sold by any other.
3. All participants in the market, buyers and sellers alike, are well-informed about prices, sources of supply, and so on.
4. Entry into and exit from the market are very easy.

The Perfectly Competitive Firm as Price Taker

Price taker A firm that sells its outputs at fixed prices that are determined entirely by forces outside its own control.

These four characteristics of perfect competition, taken together, ensure that all firms in the market will be **price takers**—firms that sell their outputs at fixed prices determined entirely by forces outside their own control. If a firm makes, say, steel nails, and steel nails sell for $1.50 a pound, that is that. The firm makes all its decisions and all its plans as if nothing it can do will change the $1.50 price tag.

It is easy to understand why firms operating in a perfectly competitive market are price takers. Because each producer contributes only a small fraction of the total output, its individual supply decisions will have no significant effect on the total quantity supplied in the market—and thus no significant effect on the market price as determined by supply and demand. Because the product is homogeneous, buyers are just as happy to buy from one firm as another. Thus a firm that raised its price even a fraction above what its competitors were charging would quickly lose all its customers. And because all buyers and sellers are well-informed, no one would, out of ignorance, be willing to pay or be able to get a price higher than the prevailing one.[1]

Under perfect competition, then, the decisions facing individual firms are very simple. The firm does not have to decide at what price to sell because price is completely beyond its control. It does not have to worry about product design or marketing decisions because, by definition, the product is the same for all firms and never changes. The only decision the firm needs to make is about quantity—how much to produce.

Perfect Competition: The Ideal and the Reality

Perfect competition, as defined here, is an abstraction or ideal. Economists study it because it is a theoretically interesting benchmark, useful in judging the performance of real-world industries. No industry exactly fits all the conditions of perfect competition. Nonetheless, some industries fit the pattern fairly closely. The following case study reports on one such example.

Case 8.1
Perfect Competition in Trucking

The next time you are out on the highway, take a close look at the trucks that are passing you. You will see many that belong to large firms, such as PIE and Yellow Freight, that haul large numbers of small shipments, mostly of manufactured

---

[1] The fourth feature of perfect competition—easy entry and exit—is not strictly necessary, in the short run, to make firms price takers. But, as will be explained later in the chapter, it has considerable importance for how competitive markets work in the long run.

goods, all over the country on regular schedules. Many other trucks will bear the names of companies like Sears or Sun Oil, for which transportation is only a sideline. These firms use their own trucks to haul their own products. Largely as a result of government regulatory policy, the markets these trucks operate in are far from perfectly competitive.

If you look closely, though, you will see that about one truck in four looks a little different. The tractors, often brightly painted and highly chromed, are likely to have sleepers attached to them. The refrigerated trailers, usually with no identifying name, are filled with agricultural produce moving to market. These are the trucks of independent owner-operators. Exempt from federal regulation so long as they haul only fresh farm goods, they work in a market that comes about as close to perfect competition as any to be found in the U.S. economy.

Each firm in this market consists of a man or woman who typically owns and drives just one truck. There are a large number of such firms—some 35,000 by the best available estimates. Each clearly contributes only a tiny fraction of the total market output.

The owner-operator's product is about as homogeneous as one can imagine. For the shipper of fresh produce, one refrigerated van is about as good as another, so long as it is headed in the right direction. And most operators will go anywhere the traffic takes them.

Although there is no such thing as ''perfect'' information in this imperfect world, a widespread information network keeps independent truckers pretty well-informed of where the loads are and what rates are being paid. A key element in this network is the truck broker—an information specialist who matches the needs of farmers for trucks with the needs of owner-operators for loads in return for a 5 or 10 percent commission. A call to a broker from a truck stop can give the trucker a tip that rates have moved a few dollars per load, so the time has come to switch from hauling Florida citrus to hauling California lettuce.

Finally, entry into and exit from this market are very easy. Some people go into business with a used truck and an investment of as little as $5,000. Most operators buy their trucks on credit and have less than $20,000 invested in their business. Experts can be hired to help the prospective trucker obtain the necessary state licenses and permits. Some independent truckers complain that entry and exit are, in fact, too easy and that too many operators soon go broke. But statistical studies suggest that the turnover rate is no higher than in other markets dominated by small businesses.

The people who run the giant trucking companies that haul manufactured goods often look down their noses at the independent truckers with their loads of apples and potatoes. They call them ''gypsies,'' or worse. But this highly competitive market succeeds every day in putting fresh produce on the dinner table in every town.

A Digression on Competition and Perfect Competition

Before going on, it is important to take note of a paradox associated with perfect competition. The paradox is that perfect competition, as defined, is in many respects the exact opposite of competition as many people think of it in everyday business life.

When we think of business competition, we ordinarily think of rivalry and struggle. We think of Ford and General Motors battling for shares of the market. We think of advertising people talking up one product and putting down another. We think of Kodak working in secrecy to build an instant camera as good as Polaroid's.

Perfect competition, though, is none of these things. In a perfectly competitive market, there is no reason to battle for market shares because there is plenty of room for each small firm to sell as much as it wants at the going price.

There is no advertising in such a market, because buyers are already well-informed, and goods are perfectly homogeneous—not only in fact but in the eyes of their consumers as well. There is no need for secrecy about techniques or innovations, because all technological knowledge is widespread and there are no innovations. The market environment is still competitive in the sense that any firms that fail to make their cost and supply decisions as accurately as their rivals may be forced out of the market. Firms are not sheltered from that kind of competition by any special privileges. Nonetheless, many more colorful or personalized aspects of competition are absent. Much more will be said about the relationship of "perfect" competition to real-world competition in the next few chapters.

SHORT-RUN SUPPLY UNDER PERFECT COMPETITION

Short-Run Profit Maximization for a Typical Firm

Now that the concept of perfect competition has been introduced, it is time to turn to the main subject of the chapter—what lies behind the supply curve in a perfectly competitive market. The investigation will begin at the level of the individual firm, using the Rogers Tool Company as a typical example. The discussion will assume throughout that this firm and all others in the market make their production decisions with the object of earning maximum economic profits for the firms' owners, given prevailing prices of inputs and outputs and the production technology available. If prevailing market conditions make it impossible to earn positive economic profits, the firms will try to minimize losses.

A simple numerical example will show how a perfectly competitive firm adjusts the quantity of output it supplies to maximize profits. Exhibit 8.1a shows short-run cost data for Rogers Tool Company (as first given in Chapter 7). It also shows the revenue earned by Rogers Tool from the sale of each quantity of output, assuming a constant price of $500 per unit. The price per unit does not vary as output per day varies because it is assumed, for the sake of discussion, that the drill press produced by Rogers Tool is essentially the same as that produced by a large number of other companies in this perfectly competitive market. The company is thus a price taker.

Subtracting total cost in Column 3 from total revenue in Column 2 gives the total profit the firm earns at each level of output. The maximum is reached at nineteen units per day, where a profit of $2,000 per day is earned. Nineteen units per day is thus the quantity the firm will choose to supply at the price of $500 per unit, assuming that it wants to earn the maximum profit.

This profit maximizing quantity of output is also identified graphically in Exhibit 8.1b. In that diagram, the firm's total profit is indicated by the vertical distance between the total revenue and total cost curves. As shown, that distance is greatest at nineteen units of output.

A Marginal Approach As an alternative to comparing total cost and total revenue, a marginal approach can be used to determine the profit maximizing level of output for the competitive firm. Turn first to Columns 5 and 6 of Exhibit 8.1a. Column 5 gives data on marginal cost. As in Chapter 7, these data are printed on lines between the entries in the first four columns to indicate that marginal cost is the change in cost as output moves from one

Exhibit 8.1

Short-run profit maximization under perfect competition—Rogers Tool Company

This exhibit shows the profit maximizing quantity of output chosen by a perfectly competitive firm—Rogers Tool Company. The output can be found by comparing total cost and total revenue in Columns 2 and 3 of Part a. This approach is shown graphically in Part b, where total profit appears as the gap between the total revenue and total cost curves. Alternatively, the profit maximizing output can be found by comparing marginal cost and marginal revenue in Columns 5 and 6 of Part a. Profit increases up to the point where marginal cost begins to exceed marginal revenue and declines thereafter. Part c of the exhibit gives a graphical representation of the marginal approach. Whatever approach is used, the profit maximizing output is seen to be nineteen units per day, and the maximum profit per day is seen to be $2,000.

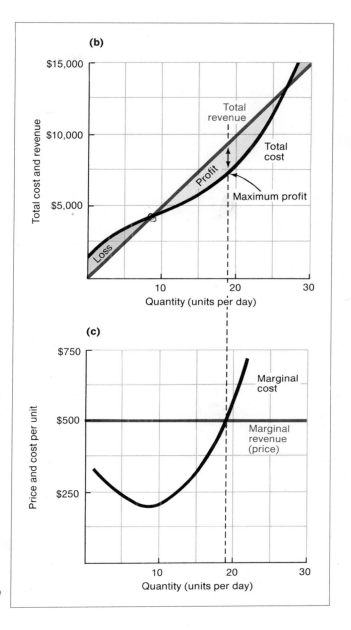

(b)

(c)

(a)

Quantity of Output (1)	Total Revenue (2)	Total Cost (3)	Total Profit (2) − (3) (4)	Marginal Cost (5)	Marginal Revenue (6)
1	$ 500	$ 2,380	−$1,880		
				$340	$500
2	1,000	2,720	−1,720		
				305	500
3	1,500	3,025	−1,525		
				275	500
4	2,000	3,300	−1,300		
				250	500
5	2,500	3,550	−1,000		
				230	500
6	3,000	3,780	−780		
				215	500
7	3,500	3,995	−495		
				205	500
8	4,000	4,200	−200		
				200	500
9	4,500	4,400	100		
				205	500
10	5,000	4,605	395		
				215	500
11	5,500	4,820	680		
				230	500
12	6,000	5,050	950		
				250	500
13	6,500	5,300	1,200		
				275	500
14	7,000	5,575	1,425		
				305	500
15	7,500	5,880	1,620		
				340	500
16	8,000	6,220	1,780		
				380	500
17	8,500	6,600	1,900		
				425	500
18	9,000	7,025	1,975		
				475	500
19	9,500	7,500	2,000		
				530	500
20	10,000	8,030	1,970		
				590	500
21	10,500	8,620	1,880		
				655	500
22	11,000	9,275	1,725		
				725	500
23	11,500	10,000	1,500		
				800	500
24	12,000	10,800	1,200		

level to another. Column 6 presents a new concept—marginal revenue. **Marginal revenue** is the amount by which total revenue increases when output increases one unit. For a firm that is a price taker, as this one is, marginal revenue is equal to the price of the product. Each extra unit of output sold by the Rogers Tool Company thus adds $500 to total revenue.

As Exhibit 8.1 is constructed, every unit increase in output adds to both total cost and total revenue. If the increase in revenue exceeds the increase in cost (that is, if marginal revenue is greater than marginal cost), increasing output by one unit increases total profit. If the increase in cost exceeds the

Marginal revenue The amount by which total revenue increases as the result of a one-unit increase in quantity.

increase in revenue (that is, if marginal cost is greater than marginal revenue), increasing output by one unit reduces profit. It follows that in order to maximize profit, a competitive firm should expand output so long as marginal revenue exceeds marginal cost. It should stop as soon as marginal cost begins to exceed marginal revenue. A comparison of Columns 5 and 6 of Exhibit 8.1 shows that for Rogers Tool Company, this means producing nineteen units of output per day—the same number arrived at through a comparison of total cost and total revenue.

The marginal approach to short-run profit maximization is represented graphically in Exhibit 8.1c. Up to nineteen units of output, the marginal cost curve lies below the marginal revenue curve, so that each added unit of output increases profit. Beyond nineteen units, the marginal cost curve is above the marginal revenue curve, so that each added unit of output reduces profit. Note that the point of profit maximization, where the marginal cost and marginal revenue curves intersect, corresponds exactly to the point in Part b where the spread between total revenue and total cost is greatest.

Minimizing Short-Run Losses In the example just given, Rogers Tool Company was able to make a comfortable profit at the prevailing market price of $500 per unit. But market conditions need not always be so favorable. Suppose, for example, the market price were to drop to $300. The firm, being a price taker, could do nothing about the price and would simply have to adjust its quantity of output as best it could to meet the new situation. The necessary adjustments can be determined from the table and diagrams of Exhibit 8.2. The table shows that there is no level of output at which the firm can earn a profit. *Unable to earn a profit, the firm must turn its attention to minimizing losses.* With a price of $300 per unit, the minimum loss occurs at fourteen units of output. As in the previous case, this is the level of output beyond which marginal cost begins to exceed the price of the product.

The two diagrams in Exhibit 8.2 give additional insight into the loss minimizing supply decision under the given market conditions. Exhibit 8.2b shows clearly why the firm cannot earn a profit: The total cost curve is everywhere higher than the total revenue curve. Nonetheless, total revenues come closest to meeting total costs at fourteen units of output.

Exhibit 8.2c is perhaps the most helpful of all for understanding why it is worthwhile for the firm to produce fourteen units of output even though it loses money by doing so. In addition to the marginal cost and marginal revenue curves, it shows average variable cost and average total cost curves. Notice that the point where marginal cost is equal to price lies between the two average cost curves. The vertical distance between the average variable cost and average total cost curves is equal to average fixed costs. Thus, at fourteen units of output, the price of $300 is more than enough to cover each unit's share of variable costs but not quite enough to cover each unit's share of fixed costs.

Without referring to technical terminology, it is easy to see that the firm's loss minimizing decision corresponds to simple common sense. Assume that the only variable input for Rogers Tool Company is labor, and substitute the term *payroll* for the term *variable cost*. Similarly, assume that the firm's only fixed input is its factory building, and substitute *mortgage payment* for *fixed cost*. Clearly, with a price of $300, the firm is better off producing fourteen

Exhibit 8.2

Short-run loss minimization under perfect competition—Rogers Tool Company

If the product price is too low for the firm to earn a profit, the firm must turn its attention to minimizing losses. The same techniques illustrated in Exhibit 8.1 can be used to find the loss minimizing level of output, which is fourteen units of output for a price of $300 per unit, as shown here. Part c of this exhibit shows that the marginal revenue curve intersects the marginal cost curve at a point higher than average variable cost but lower than the average total cost. Each unit of output sold earns more than its share of average variable cost but not enough to pay its share of average total cost (including its share of average fixed cost).

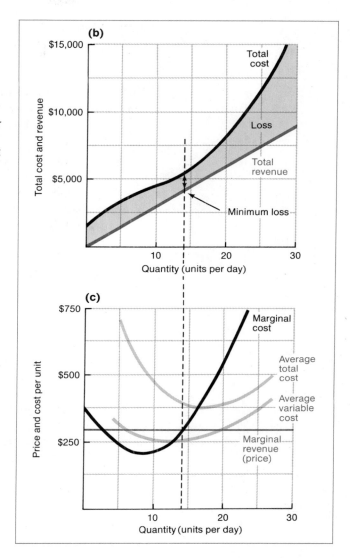

(a)

Quantity of Output (1)	Total Revenue (2)	Total Cost (3)	Total Profit or Loss (4)	Average Total Cost (5)	Average Variable Cost (6)	Marginal Cost (7)	Marginal Revenue (8)
0	$ 0	$ 2,000	−$2,000	—	—	$380	$300
1	300	2,380	−2,080	$2,380	$380	340	300
2	600	2,720	−2,120	1,360	360	305	300
3	900	3,025	−2,125	1,009	342	275	300
4	1,200	3,300	−2,100	825	325	250	300
5	1,500	3,550	−2,050	710	310	230	300
6	1,800	3,780	−1,980	629	296	215	300
7	2,100	3,995	−1,895	571	285	205	300
8	2,400	4,200	−1,800	525	275	200	300
9	2,700	4,400	−1,700	488	266	205	300
10	3,000	4,605	−1,605	460	260	215	300
11	3,300	4,820	−1,520	437	256	230	300
12	3,600	5,050	−1,450	421	254	250	300
13	3,900	5,300	−1,400	408	254	275	300
14	4,200	5,575	−1,375	398	255	305	300
15	4,500	5,880	−1,380	392	259	340	300
16	4,800	6,220	−1,420	389	264	380	300
17	5,100	6,600	−1,500	389	271		

units of output than no units of output, because each unit more than pays for its share of the payroll and makes at least some contribution toward paying the mortgage.

Shutting Down to Minimize Short-Run Losses What would happen if the price dropped even lower? Would it always be worthwhile for the firm to keep grinding out drill presses, even though it was losing money? The answer, as shown in Exhibit 8.3 is no.

Exhibit 8.3 is based on an assumed price of $225 per unit. The table in Part a shows that there is no way for the firm to make a profit with the price so low. Any supply decision will produce a loss. But this time, the loss can be minimized at a zero level of output. The best thing for the firm to do in the short run is to shut down. If things get better and the price rises again, the firm can restart production. If things never do get better, then, in the long run, the firm will have to wind up its affairs and go out of business altogether.

Notice that in this case it can be misleading to look only at the marginal revenue and marginal cost columns of the table. After seven units of output, marginal cost drops below the price of $225 and stays below until an output of eleven units is reached. *If* the firm were to stay in production, eleven units of output would give it a lower loss than any slightly greater or smaller level of output. But in this case the firm takes a still smaller loss by not producing at all.

As in the previous examples, the graphs tell the same story as the table. Exhibit 8.3b shows once again that the total revenue curve never reaches the total cost curve. It comes fairly close at eleven units of output but not as close as it comes at zero output.

Exhibit 8.3c shows that marginal cost and price are equal at eleven units of output. However, even at eleven units, the price does not cover average variable cost. Losses are minimized by shutting down. Once again, it may help to put the problem in payroll and mortgage terms. If the firm produced eleven drill presses per day and could sell them for only $225 apiece, it would not earn enough even to meet its payroll. Better to send the workers home, suffer a loss equal to the mortgage payment, and hope for things to get better.

The Firm's Short-Run Supply Curve

The preceding examples supply everything needed to construct a short-run supply curve for the profit maximizing firm in a perfectly competitive market. Exhibit 8.4 shows how this curve is constructed.

Work through this exhibit beginning with a price of $500. As before, Rogers Tool Company would choose to produce nineteen units of output at this price. Point E_1 of the firm's short-run marginal cost curve must therefore be a point on the firm's supply curve.

Suppose now that the market price of the firm's product begins to fall as a result of forces beyond its control. As it does, the point where price equals marginal cost moves down along the firm's marginal cost curve. Soon Point E_2 is reached—the point where marginal cost and average total cost are equal. This occurs at an output of approximately seventeen units and a price of approximately $385. At this price, the best the firm can do is break even. Either a greater or a smaller output would result in a loss.

If the price falls still lower, the firm's problem becomes one of minimizing

Exhibit 8.3
Shutting down Rogers Tool Company to minimize short-run losses

Sometimes the price of a firm's output may drop so low that the firm must shut down altogether to minimize short-run losses. That possibility is illustrated here at the price of $225 per unit. Notice that eleven units of output yield a smaller loss ($2,345 per day) than any slightly greater or smaller output. However, the loss can be reduced to just $2,000 per day if the firm shuts down. Notice also that in Part c of the exhibit, the marginal cost curve intersects the marginal revenue curve at a point below minimum average variable cost. That is the signal to shut down.

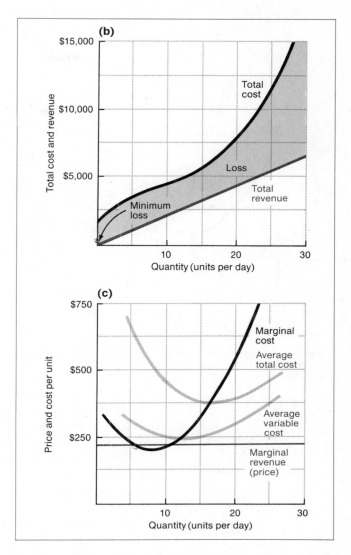

(b)

(c)

(a)

Quantity of Output (1)	Total Revenue (2)	Total Cost (3)	Total Profit or Loss (4)	Average Total Cost (5)	Average Variable Cost (6)	Marginal Cost (7)	Marginal Revenue (8)
0	$ 0	$ 2,000	−$2,000	—	—		
1	225	2,380	−2,155	$2,380	$380	$380	$225
2	450	2,720	−2,270	1,360	360	340	225
3	675	3,025	−2,350	1,009	342	305	225
4	900	3,300	−2,400	825	325	275	225
5	1,125	3,550	−2,425	710	310	250	225
6	1,350	3,780	−2,430	629	296	230	225
7	1,575	3,995	−2,420	571	285	215	225
8	1,800	4,200	−2,400	525	275	205	225
9	2,025	4,400	−2,375	488	266	200	225
10	2,250	4,605	−2,355	460	260	205	225
11	2,475	4,820	−2,345	437	256	215	225
12	2,700	5,050	−2,350	421	254	230	225
13	2,925	5,300	−2,375	408	254	250	225
14	3,150	5,575	−2,425	398	255	275	225
15	3,375	5,880	−2,505	392	259	305	225
16	3,600	6,220	−2,620	389	264	340	225
17	3,825	6,600	−2,775	389	271	380	225

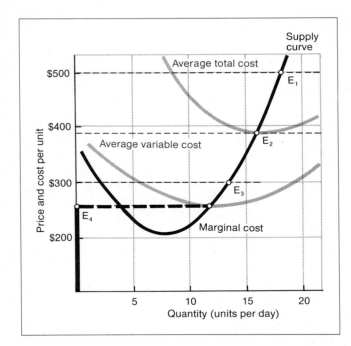

Exhibit 8.4

Derivation of the short-run supply curve for Rogers Tool Company

This diagram traces Rogers Tool Company's short-run supply curve. When the price is $500, the firm will produce at Point E_1. As the price falls, the firm moves down along its short-run marginal cost curve, as shown by Points E_2 and E_3. The firm will continue to produce where price equals marginal cost, until marginal cost falls below average variable cost. At that price, the firm will do just as well to shut down—that is, to produce at Point E_4.

loss rather than maximizing profit. At a price of $300, for example, the firm minimizes losses by producing fourteen units, at Point E_3. In the range of prices lying between minimum average total cost and minimum average variable cost, the supply curve continues to follow the marginal cost curve.

Below a price of about $254, a change occurs. As before, when price is lower than the lowest point on the average variable cost curve, the firm minimizes losses by shutting down, rather than continuing to produce up to the point where marginal cost begins to exceed price. For a price of $254, then, Point E_4 on the vertical axis is the preferred point of operation. This point must then be a point on the firm's short-run supply curve. As the diagram shows, for this and all lower prices, the supply curve coincides with the vertical axis.

All that has been learned so far about the firm's short-run supply decision can now be stated in the form of an important generalization: *The short-run supply curve for a profit maximizing firm operating in a perfectly competitive market coincides with the upward-sloping part of the marginal cost curve lying above its intersection with the average variable cost curve.*

The Short-Run Industry Supply Curve

The supply curve for a whole industry can now be constructed on the basis of the supply curves of the individual firms. As a first approximation, an industry supply curve can be obtained by the horizontal addition of individual firms' supply curves, as shown in Exhibit 8.5. It is necessary to make one qualification, though. The assumption has been that any individual firm can expand output without any change in input prices; but if all firms in an industry expand simultaneously, input prices will rise unless the supply curve of the input is perfectly elastic. If input prices rise as industry output expands, the short-run industry supply curve will be somewhat steeper than the sum of the individual supply curves.

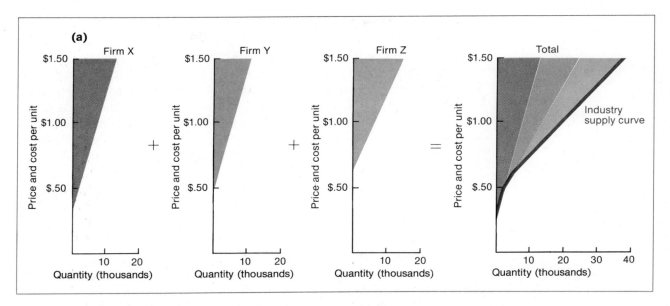

(b)

	Quantity Supplied			
Price	Firm X	Firm Y	Firm Z	Total
$ .40	1,500			1,500
$ .80	5,500	3,000	3,333	11,833
$1.20	9,500	7,000	10,000	26,500
$1.50	12,500	10,000	15,000	37,500

Exhibit 8.5
Approximate derivation of short-run industry supply curve
An approximation to the short-run industry supply curve can be obtained by horizontal summation of individual firms' supply curves. Here the method of summation is shown for an industry with just three firms. If the prices of inputs vary as industry output varies, it will be necessary to make an adjustment in the industry supply curve.

LONG-RUN EQUILIBRIUM UNDER PERFECT COMPETITION

Entry and Exit

For the individual firm, the long run is distinguished from the short run by the fact that all, not just some, inputs can be varied. In the long run, firms can go out of business entirely. (Sometimes firms go peaceably, with the owners selling off the assets and banking what is left. Other times they go with a crash, leaving their creditors to collect perhaps only pennies on the dollar for the mortgages, bonds, and other debts they hold.) Also in the long run, new firms can come into a market, building new plants and buying new equipment, which then become their short-run fixed inputs. As firms enter and exit, whole industries expand and contract.

One of the defining characteristics of perfect competition is that there must be no barriers to this free flow of firms into and out of the industry. This characteristic played no direct role in the discussion of a firm's short-run supply decision, but free entry and exit are crucial to explaining how a competitive market works in the long run.

Equilibrium

Equilibrium, as explained here in many different contexts, is a state of affairs in which economic decision makers have no incentive to change their current patterns of behavior. In a perfectly competitive industry, short-run equilibrium means that each firm must have no incentive either to increase or to decrease its quantity of output. That requires the firm to adjust its output to the point where marginal cost is equal to the price of the product. (Keep in mind that a perfectly competitive firm is a price taker, so price and marginal revenue are always equal.) In the long run, equilibrium in a perfectly competitive industry requires two other things as well. One is that each firm have no incentive to change the size of plant it uses to produce its current output, and the other is that firms have no incentive either to enter or to leave the industry.

Exhibit 8.6 shows graphically how all these requirements are satisfied simultaneously in long-run equilibrium for a perfectly competitive firm. First, marginal cost is equal to price at the equilibrium quantity of output. This equality ensures that there is no incentive in the short run either to increase or to decrease output.

Second, the firm is operating with a plant of just the size necessary to make short-run average total cost equal to the minimum possible long-run average cost at the equilibrium quantity of output. No change in the quantity of fixed inputs employed can reduce average cost, so the firm has no long-run incentive to change its plant size.[2]

Third, average total cost (both long-run and short-run) is equal to price at the equilibrium quantity of output. As always, average total cost includes an allowance for a normal rate of return on capital—no more, no less. Thus, when average total cost is equal to price, there is no incentive for firms either to enter

---

[2]The reader may wish to review Exhibits 7.7 and 7.8, which show the relationship between short-run and long-run average cost curves for various plant sizes.

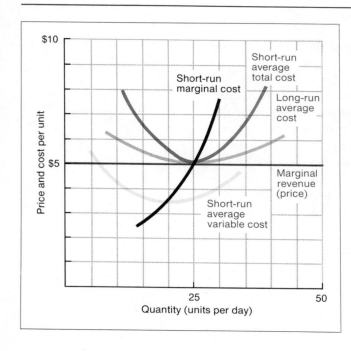

Exhibit 8.6
The typical perfectly competitive firm in long-run equilibrium
Long-run equilibrium in a perfectly competitive industry requires that the typical firm (1) have no short-run incentive to change the quantity of output currently produced, (2) have no long-run incentive to change the size of plant used to produce its current output, and (3) have no long-run incentive to enter or leave the industry. This requires that price, short-run marginal cost, short-run average total cost, and long-run average cost all have the same value in equilibrium, as shown.

the industry (to seek pure economic profit in excess of the normal rate of return on capital) or to leave the industry (in order to avoid pure economic loss—that is, a rate of return on capital less than the normal rate).

The long-run equilibrium conditions shown graphically in Exhibit 8.6 can also be expressed in the form of the following equation:

$$\text{Price} = \frac{\text{Marginal}}{\text{cost}} = \begin{array}{c} \text{Short-run} \\ \text{average} \\ \text{total cost} \end{array} = \begin{array}{c} \text{Long-run} \\ \text{average} \\ \text{cost.} \end{array}$$

If any part of this equation does not hold, there will be an incentive for firms to change the quantity of output they are producing within their current plants, to change the size of the plants they are using to produce their current output, or to enter or leave the industry. That is, unless all parts of the equation hold, the market cannot be in long-run equilibrium.

Industry Adjustment to Falling Demand

A particular position of long-run equilibrium, such as the one shown in Exhibit 8.6, can continue undisturbed only so long as outside conditions remain unchanged. Exhibit 8.7, for example, shows how a perfectly competitive industry reacts to a long-run decrease in the demand for its product.

The exhibit consists of two parts. Part a shows a set of cost curves, much like those shown in Exhibit 8.6, for a typical individual firm in the industry. Part b

---

Exhibit 8.7

Long-run adjustment to a decline in demand

In this exhibit, Part a represents a single typical firm and Part b the entire industry. Initially, both the firm and the industry are in long-run equilibrium at a price of $5. Then something happens to shift the demand curve leftward from D₁ to D₂. In the short run, the price falls to $4, at the intersection of D₂ and S₁. The firm's short-run reaction is to retreat down along its marginal cost curve. Eventually, some firms (not the one shown) get tired of taking losses and exit from the industry. Their exit causes the supply curve to shift toward S₂ and the market price to recover. The typical firm returns to breakeven operation. The market has traced out part of its long-run supply curve, as shown by the large arrow.

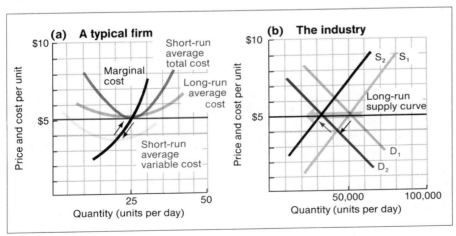

is a simple supply and demand diagram representing the market in which the typical firm sells its output. The curves drawn there are short-run industry supply curves built up from the short-run supply curves of all the individual firms in the market (see Exhibit 8.5). The demand curves are short-run market demand curves of the usual kind.

Suppose that, initially, short-run supply curve S_1 and short-run demand curve D_1 applied. That would produce a market equilibrium price of $5. The individual firm would take this price as given and adjust its output accordingly, producing twenty-five units of output, as shown. At this price and output, it would be just breaking even. Remember, though, that breaking even in the economic sense means earning enough to cover all costs including the implicit cost of a normal rate of return on the owner's invested capital.

Suppose now that something happens—say, a change in consumer tastes or incomes—that shifts the demand curve to the new position, D_2. The short-run result of this demand shift will be a drop in the market price to $4 per unit. The individual firm, being a price taker, will consider this decline in price as something beyond its control and will adjust to it as best it can. As shown in Part a of the exhibit, this means cutting back output a little to minimize loss but not shutting down completely. The movement of each individual firm back down along its marginal cost curve is what produces the movement of the market as a whole down and to the left along short-run supply curve S_1.

But the situation that the market is now in cannot prevail in the long run. The reason is that the typical firm and its fellows are operating at a loss. They are not giving their owners the normal rate of return they need to make an investment in this industry worthwhile. If the demand curve does not show any hope of shifting back to the right, some owners will become discouraged and will pull their capital out of the industry. Perhaps their firms will actually go bankrupt, or perhaps they will sell off their plant and equipment and get out while the going is good. Perhaps they will keep their firms intact but set to work to produce other goods for other, more profitable, markets. The particular form of exit does not much matter.

There is no real way to tell which firms will be the first to go; but for convenience, assume that the typical firm shown in the exhibit is not one of the first. Look what happens to it now as some of the others leave. As some firms withdraw, the market loses their contribution to the total supply. The market supply curve, now added together from fewer individual supply curves, shifts to the left toward S_2. As it does so, the market price begins to rise up along demand curve D_2. When the price gets all the way back up to $5, the firms still left in the industry will no longer be losing money. The exodus from the industry will stop, and the market will have reached a new long-run equilibrium. In the new equilibrium, price, marginal cost, short-run average total cost, and long-run average cost will once again be equal.

The entire sequence of events has traced out a portion of this industry's *long-run* supply curve, as shown by the arrow. A long-run supply curve for an industry shows the path along which equilibrium price and quantity move in response to persistent changes in demand, given time for individual firms to adjust the sizes of their plants, if necessary, and given time for entry and exit to occur. The long-run supply curve shown in Exhibit 8.7 is perfectly elastic, at least in the region shown. In the long run, the leftward shift of the demand curve causes no change in price, only a decrease in the quantity supplied.

Industry Adjustment to Rising Demand

Freedom of entry plays the same role in the long-run adjustment of a perfectly competitive market to rising demand as freedom of exit plays in the adjustment to falling demand. This is illustrated in Exhibit 8.8.

The starting position in this exhibit is exactly the same as in Exhibit 8.7. Short-run supply curve S_1 and demand curve D_1 give an equilibrium price of $5. The individual firm just breaks even producing twenty-five units of output at this price. Now follow what happens as the demand curve shifts, this time to position D_2, to the right of D_1.

The short-run result of the shift in the demand curve is an increase in the market price to $6. The typical firm adjusts to this new price by moving up along its marginal cost curve to a somewhat higher level of output. As all firms do this, the market moves up and to the right along short-run supply curve S_1.

But again, this short-run adjustment does not result in a state of affairs that can last in the long run. For now, all the firms are making profits in excess of the minimum needed to attract capital to the industry. Entrepreneurs elsewhere in the economy will soon spot this healthy, expanding market as a prime investment opportunity. Some of them may start brand new firms to produce for this market. Others may shift plants and equipment previously used to produce something else to making goods for this industry. It does not matter whether the entry is by brand new firms or by firms already existing in other industries that devote part of their capital to this particular market for the first time. In either case, new entry will cause the supply curve to shift to the right, toward S_2.

Exhibit 8.8

Long-run adjustment to an increase in demand

In this exhibit, both the firm and the industry are again initially in equilibrium at a price of $5. Then something happens to shift the demand curve rightward to D_2. In the short run, the price rises to $6, at the intersection of D_2 and S_1. The firm's short-run reaction is to move up along its marginal cost curve, earning better than normal profits. These high profits eventually attract new firms into the industry. As new firms enter, the supply curve shifts toward S_2. Profits for the typical firm return to normal, and entry activity ceases. Again, the market has traced out part of its long-run supply curve, as shown by the large arrow.

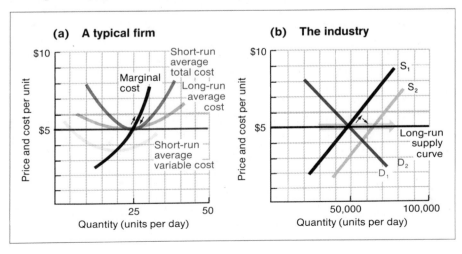

As the supply curve shifts, the price falls. It does not fall far enough to drive the new entrants back out again, but it does fall enough to drive everyone's profits back to the normal level. Entry will stop, and the market will be in a new long-run equilibrium at the intersection of S_2 and D_2.

Once again, a portion of the long-run supply curve for the industry has been traced out, as shown by the large arrow. And once again, this long-run supply curve is horizontal in the region investigated. A rightward shift in the demand curve has, in the long run, produced an increase in quantity supplied but no increase in price.

Other Long-Run Supply Curves

In the examples just given, the industry long-run supply curve was a horizontal straight line, at least in the region examined. That is not the only possible shape such a supply curve can take, however. Exhibit 8.9 shows some other possibilities—upward-sloping, downward-sloping, and U-shaped.

Which shape the long-run industry supply curve takes depends primarily on what happens to the industry's input prices in the long run as output expands. If the long-run supply curve for all inputs is perfectly elastic, the price of those inputs will not change as the quantity of them demanded by the industry increases. Or perhaps the industry will use such a small part of the total supply of each unspecialized input that whatever change in input price

Exhibit 8.9

Possible long-run supply curves for a competitive industry
The shape of an industry's long-run supply curve depends largely on what happens to the prices of the industry's inputs as demand and output expand in the long run. If input prices do not change significantly, the long-run supply curve will be horizontal, as in Part a of this exhibit. If input prices rise, the long-run supply curve will slope upward, as in Part b. Falling input prices will produce a downward sloping long-run industry supply curve, as in Part c. Finally, mixed cases, where the long-run supply curve first falls and then rises, are possible, as in Part d.

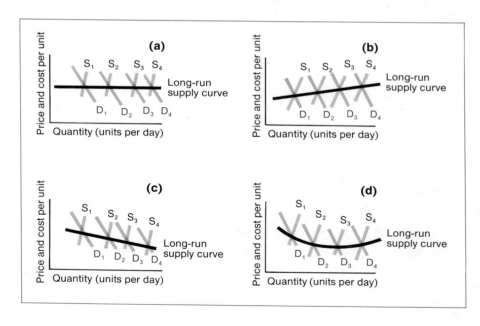

does occur will be negligibly small. Industry output can thus expand without affecting the underlying costs of the individual firms. Thus the long-run supply curve of the industry using the outputs will be perfectly horizontal (that is, perfectly elastic) too. This is the case in Exhibits 8.7 and 8.8. Exhibit 8.9a shows a succession of short-run supply and demand curves lying along such a horizontal long-run supply curve. Each pair of short-run curves represents one stage in the industry's long-run expansion.

Suppose, though, that the industry uses some specialized input, the supply of which cannot easily be increased. Perhaps some special skilled labor is needed, and more workers can be induced to acquire the skill only by bidding up the wage rate. The rising price of this important input will cause an upward shift in the cost curves of all the firms in the industry as new firms enter the industry and output expands. In this case, the industry long-run supply curve will slope upward, as in Exhibit 8.9b.

It is also possible that the price of some important input can decrease as output of the industry expands. For example, as sales of electronic equipment expand, the firms making the components that go into that equipment may be able to adopt cheaper methods of production. If this occurs, the cost curves for all firms will drift downward as new firms enter the industry. The long-run supply curve will then be downward-sloping, as in Exhibit 8.9c.

Finally, it is possible that a combination of forces can be at work. In the industry shown in Exhibit 8.9d, long-run supply is at first influenced by the falling price of one specialized input; but beyond a point, some other specialized input becomes a bottleneck that causes the long-run supply curve to bend upward. Many variants are possible. Only actual observation of particular industries can determine which possibility applies.

WHAT IS PERFECT ABOUT PERFECT COMPETITION?

The discussion of perfect competition is now very nearly complete. We have a fairly good picture of how perfectly competitive markets work. But there is one remaining question that deserves more attention than it has yet been given: What is so perfect about perfect competition?

As suggested early in the chapter, the answer is not that such a market is the perfect place to observe all forms of business rivalry. Far from it. Many familiar forms of rivalry are completely absent from perfectly competitive markets. Under perfect competition, business managers go blandly about their pure economizing without caring a whit what any particular other firm in the industry does. After all, those other firms cannot, by definition, be big enough to have any individual impact on market prices. They cannot, by definition, be getting ready to introduce a new, distinctive version of the industry's product. And they cannot, by definition, have any secrets. So it is not in any of these senses that perfectly competitive markets are perfect.

They are instead perfect in another sense. Think, for a moment, about just what a market really is. Very simply, it is a mechanism for getting buyers and sellers together to carry out mutually beneficial transactions. It would seem to make sense, then, to say that *a perfect market is one in which all potential mutually beneficial transactions are in fact carried out—a market in which none is missed.* That is exactly the sense in which perfectly competitive markets are perfect.

To see why, look at Exhibit 8.10. This is a quite ordinary supply and demand diagram (long-run variety) just like many shown before. But now look at it in a slightly different way.

Start with the demand curve. Usually, one thinks of a demand curve as showing the quantity that consumers are willing and able to buy at any given market price. But the demand curve can also be thought of as showing the maximum amount consumers are willing to pay for a marginal unit of the good, given the quantity already available. This particular demand curve, for example, has a height of $12 at 100 units of output. That means someone is willing to pay barely $12 for the marginal 100th unit and someone is willing to pay almost, but not quite, that much for the 101st.

The supply curve can be interpreted in much the same way. Usually, one thinks of it as showing how much producers are willing to supply at a given price. But it also shows the minimum amount necessary to induce producers to supply the marginal unit. The supply curve in this exhibit, for example, has a height of $6 at an output of 100 units. That means someone is barely willing to supply the 100th unit for $6 and that no one will supply a 101st unit unless offered just a little bit more.

Now, suppose that for some reason, producers in fact are supplying goods to this market at a rate of only 100 units per period. At that level of output, the demand curve is above the supply curve. Some consumer out there is willing to pay nearly $12 for the 101st unit. And some producer is willing to supply it for anything just over $6. If production stops at 100 units, then, buyers and sellers will be passing up an opportunity for a mutually beneficial transaction. The market will not be perfect.

The same will be true, to a slightly lesser degree, if output stops at 101, 110, or 149 units. Even the production and sale of the 150th unit represents a mutually beneficial exchange, although only barely so. It can be said, then, that

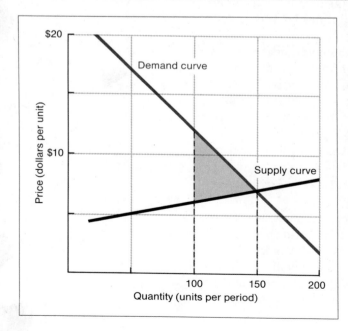

Exhibit 8.10
Why perfectly competitive markets are perfect
Think of the demand curve in this diagram as showing how much consumers would be willing to pay for additional units of output and the supply curve as showing how much producers would have to be offered to supply them. If production were limited to a rate of 100 units per period, mutually beneficial opportunities for exchange would be passed up. Consumers would be willing to pay nearly $12 for the 101st unit, while producers would have to be given barely more than $6 to produce it. Not all such worthwhile trades would take place until output were raised to 150 units. The shaded area provides a rough measure of the opportunities for mutual benefit that would be wasted if production were limited to 100 units. But a competitive market would carry output all the way to 150 units.

the whole shaded area in the diagram gives a measure of the accumulated potential for mutual benefit that will be wasted if production stops short at 100 units.

Now we can see the sense in which perfectly competitive markets, when they are in equilibrium, are perfect. In such markets, production is carried out up to, but not beyond, the point where the long-run supply and demand curves intersect. All possible mutually beneficial transactions between consumers and producers are thus carried out. And, as shown in the previous section, each firm in long-run perfectly competitive equilibrium produces at the minimum possible average total cost. That means no further gains are possible on the production side, at least within the limits of current technology. With no improvements possible through changes in either the quantity of output traded or the way that output is produced, the market does as well as it can in satisfying the needs of consumers. In that sense, it is a perfect market.

CONCLUSIONS

It would be tempting to draw broad generalizations from the preceding section. Would not an economy in which all markets displayed all the structural characteristics of perfect competition be a perfect one in every economic respect? There is a sense in which this proposition is true, but its truth is hedged with a number of qualifications.

One very important qualification is that technology does not cooperate. Economies of scale make it altogether impractical in many industries to scatter production among a large number of very small firms.

A second qualification is the refusal of consumers to be indifferent between the products of different firms. Consumers demand variety, not homogeneity, from the firms they patronize. To enforce homogeneity in the name of perfect competition would be to pass up many mutually beneficial opportunities for firms to cater to the differing individual tastes of consumers.

A third qualification is inherent in the whole concept of perfect competition. General propositions about the efficiency of perfect competition place little weight on the entrepreneurial element in business life. The theories set forth in this chapter say little about how efficiently resources are allocated in a world where change occurs, where knowledge is not perfectly distributed, and where markets are not always in equilibrium. Do markets with large numbers of small firms guarantee efficient entrepreneurial decision making in a world of change and uncertainty? Are such markets most productive of new and better ways to satisfy human wants? The theory of perfect competition says nothing one way or the other in answer to these questions. Later chapters will return to them.

When all is said and done, perfect competition is one of the great abstractions of economics. As such, it produces many valuable insights. It makes it possible to think more clearly about what lies behind the law of supply and demand. It makes it easier to understand the element of pure economizing in business decision making—an important part of the real world of business but not all of it. It provides some insights into economic efficiency that, if not overgeneralized, can be of real use in comparing alternative economic policies. And, finally, for some kinds of markets, it is not so very far from the mark in a descriptive sense.

SUMMARY

1. A firm is a price taker if it can do nothing to affect the prices of the outputs it sells. The characteristics of perfect competition are sufficient to make firms behave as price takers. Firms are too small to influence output prices by varying their own quantities supplied. The fact that consumers are indifferent between the products of different individual firms makes it impossible for those firms to raise their prices above the prevailing level without losing all their customers. The "other things being equal" assumption applies in a particularly strong way to the price taking, perfectly competitive firm, which makes all its managerial calculations as if whatever it did would not affect in any way what others did.

2. Perfect competition, as the technical name of a particular market structure, must be carefully distinguished from real-world business competition. Many common types of business rivalry among entrepreneurs are absent in perfect competition.

3. For the typical firm with U-shaped short-run cost curves, the short-run supply curve is that upward-sloping portion of the short-run marginal cost curve that lies above the average variable cost curve. If price falls below average variable cost in the short run, the firm minimizes its losses by temporarily shutting down. The short-run industry supply curve is approximated by the summation of the supply curves of individual firms. An adjustment must be made, though, for any change in input prices that may occur when all firms in the industry expand or contract simultaneously.

4. In long-run equilibrium, product price, short-run marginal cost, long-run average cost, and short-run average total cost must all be equal for the competitive firm. If price rises above long-run average cost, new firms will be attracted to the industry, driving the price back down. If price is below long-run average cost, some firms will leave the industry, allowing the price to rise again. In the long run, variations in industry output take place primarily through the entry or exit of firms rather than through changes in the quantity produced by each individual firm.

5. Competitive markets are perfect in the sense that when they are in equilibrium, they leave no unrealized opportunities for mutually beneficial transactions between producers and consumers. One must, however, be cautious about generalizing from the perfection of particular markets, in this sense, to broad propositions about the economy as a whole.

DISCUSSION QUESTIONS

1. Instead of saying that a perfectly competitive firm is a price taker, it is sometimes said that such a firm faces a perfectly elastic demand curve. Why are these two ways of putting the matter equivalent?

2. The concept of being a price taker can apply to consumers as well as producers. A price taking consumer is one who cannot influence the price paid for a product by changing the quantity purchased. For which of the goods and services that you buy are you a price taker? Are there any goods or services you buy for which you are not a price taker?

3. If the government imposes a price ceiling on some product, does that make the firms that sell the product price takers, regardless of whether their industry fits the market structure of perfect competition? Explain.

4. Make a list of half a dozen products that you purchase frequently. Do you buy any

of these things from firms that are perfect competitors? If the firms you buy from are not perfect competitors, do they compete, in some other sense, with rivals for your business?

5. Explain the role that the free entry and exit assumption plays in determining the nature of long-run equilibrium in a competitive industry.

6. Here is a definition of efficiency that economists often use: An economy is said to be operating efficiently if and only if there is no possible change that will make at least one person better off and no person worse off. Can you show that perfectly competitive markets are efficient in this sense?

SUGGESTIONS FOR FURTHER READING

Henderson, James M., and Quandt, Richard E. *Microeconomic Theory: A Mathematical Approach.* 2d ed. New York: McGraw-Hill, 1971.
Chapter 5 parallels the subject matter of this chapter in a treatment requiring a knowledge of elementary calculus.

Leftwich, Richard H. *The Price System and Resource Allocation.* 7th ed. Hinsdale, Ill.: Dryden Press, 1979.
Chapter 10 offers an intermediate level discussion of the topics covered in this chapter.

Nicholson, Walter. *Intermediate Microeconomics and Its Application.* 2d ed. Hinsdale, Ill.: Dryden Press, 1979.
Chapter 9 roughly parallels this chapter. Chapter 8 contains an interesting discussion of the profit maximization assumption and some alternative assumptions.

Robinson, Joan. "What Is Perfect Competition?" *Quarterly Journal of Economics* 49 (November 1934): 104–120. Also reprinted in William Breit and Harold M. Hochman, eds. *Readings in Microeconomics.* 2d ed. New York: Holt, Rinehart and Winston, 1971, pp. 197–206.
This classic paper, nearly a half-century old now, attempts to pin down some of the fine points of the concept of perfect competition. Not all the issues raised in it have yet been laid to rest.

C H A P T E R 9
THE THEORY OF MONOPOLY

WHAT YOU WILL LEARN IN THIS CHAPTER

This chapter is devoted to the analysis of pure monopoly, a market structure in which the entire quantity sold is supplied by a single firm. It will show that under pure monopoly a firm can potentially earn pure economic profits, even in long-run equilibrium. At the same time, it will show that pure monopoly is a less efficient market structure than perfect competition. In addition to the theory of pure monopoly, the chapter will discuss the closely related problems of price discrimination and cartels.

FOR REVIEW

Here are some important terms and concepts that will be put to use in this chapter. If you do not understand them, review them before proceeding.

- *Pure economizing (Chapter 1)*
- *Price elasticity of demand (Chapter 3)*
- *Perfect competition (Chapter 8)*
- *Pure economic profit (Chapter 7)*
- *Normal rate of return on capital (Chapter 7)*
- *Marginal revenue (Chapter 8)*

Perfect competition, with its very large number of very small firms, is one polar extreme of market structure. The other extreme is **pure monopoly**—the name given to a market structure in which one firm supplies 100 percent of industry sales.

Pure monopoly A market structure in which one firm accounts for 100 percent of industry sales.

As the sole supplier to its market, the pure monopolist is assumed not only to have no current competitors but also to be protected against the potential competition of new entrants into the market. Various kinds of barriers to entry can protect a pure monopolist from potential competition. In some cases, the barriers are technological, as when the nature of the product makes it inefficient for more than one firm to serve a market. Local utilities—such as the electric power, gas, water, and telephone companies—are the classic examples, in that it is likely to be wasteful for competing firms to provide duplicate lines or mains to any one neighborhood. Monopolies protected by technological barriers to entry are called **natural monopolies.** Monopolies based on the ownership of a unique natural resource can also be considered natural monopolies.

Natural monopoly A monopoly protected from competition by technological barriers to entry or by ownership of unique national resources.

Other monopolies are created or perpetuated by government grants of monopoly privilege that make it illegal for new firms to enter even when it is

Franchised monopoly A monopoly protected from competition by a government grant of monopoly privilege, such as an exclusive license, permit, or patent.

technologically feasible for them to do so. Monopolies protected by law against the entry of new competitors are called **franchised monopolies.** The U.S. Postal Service is the classic example of a franchised monopoly. The law permits private carriers to compete with the Postal Service in the transportation of parcels, but competition in first class mail has been prohibited. Monopolies based on patented inventions or processes can also be considered franchised monopolies.

The barriers to entry protecting natural and franchised monopolies from competition have their origin in technological or legal factors not directly created by the monopolistic firm itself. In addition, it may sometimes be possible for a firm or a group of firms acting in concert to erect other, artificial barriers to the entry of new competitors. This possibility will be discussed in Chapter 11, which examines certain market structures that are intermediate between perfect competition and pure monopoly.

Having defined pure monopoly, the chapter will turn now to an analysis of how a pure monopolist decides what quantity to supply to the market it dominates. As in the case of perfect competition, it will look first at the short run and then at the long run.

PROFIT MAXIMIZATION FOR THE PURE MONOPOLIST
The Monopolist Is Not a Price Taker

The short-run profit maximization decision for a pure monopolist, like that for a perfectly competitive firm, is a problem in pure economizing. With market demand conditions, the technology of the production process, and the prices of inputs given, the problem is to determine the quantity of output to supply in order to earn the maximum profit or minimum loss.

The supply decision for the pure monopolist, however, does differ from that of the perfectly competitive firm in one major respect: The pure monopolist is not a price taker. The perfectly competitive firm is assumed to be so small in relationship to its market that its individual supply decision has no noticeable impact on the market price. Not so for a monopolist. The pure monopolist, as the sole supplier to the market, must take into account the fact that the market demand curve has a negative slope. As the monopolist increases output, it must reduce the price at which it offers its product for sale in keeping with the law of demand.

Output and Revenue Consider Exhibit 9.1a for example. Columns 1 and 2 give market demand for a typical pure monopolist. Exhibit 9.1b presents the same demand graphically. This demand curve provides the relationship between the quantity of output that the monopolist chooses to supply and the price at which that quantity can be sold. The greater the output, the lower the maximum price the monopolist can charge without leaving an excess supply unclaimed by any buyer.

The information contained in the demand curve can be used to determine what happens to the firm's revenue as its output changes. For any output, total revenue is equal to price times quantity. Column 3 of Part a and the graph in Part c of the exhibit show that as output increases, total revenue first rises, then reaches a maximum at about seventeen units of output, and then falls.

Exhibit 9.1

Demand, total revenue, and marginal revenue for a pure monopolist

This exhibit shows the relationships among demand, total revenue, and marginal revenue for a typical monopolist. Total revenue is found by multiplying price times quantity at each point on the demand curve. Marginal revenue is the increase in total revenue resulting from a one-unit increase in output. Part b of this exhibit shows the demand curve and marginal revenue curve in graphical form. Note that for a straight-line demand curve, the marginal revenue curve lies halfway between the demand curve and the vertical axis and that it cuts the horizontal axis at the point where price elasticity of demand is equal to zero. This point corresponds to the point of maximum total revenue, as shown in Part c.

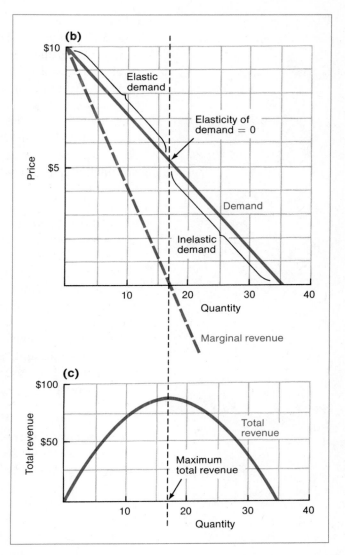

(a)

Quantity (1)	Price (2)	Total Revenue (3)	Marginal Revenue (4)
1	$10.00	$10.00	
2	9.70	19.40	$9.40
3	9.40	28.20	8.80
4	9.10	36.40	8.20
5	8.80	44.00	7.60
6	8.50	51.00	7.00
7	8.20	57.40	6.40
8	7.90	63.20	5.80
9	7.60	68.40	5.20
10	7.30	73.00	4.60
11	7.00	77.00	4.00
12	6.70	80.40	3.40
13	6.40	83.20	2.80
14	6.10	85.40	2.20
15	5.80	87.00	1.60
16	5.50	88.00	1.00
17	5.20	88.40	.40
18	4.90	88.20	−.20
19	4.60	87.40	−.80
20	4.30	86.00	−1.40
21	4.00	84.00	−2.00
22	3.70	81.40	−2.60
23	3.40	78.20	−3.20
24	3.10	74.40	−3.80
25	2.80	70.00	−4.40
26	2.50	65.00	−5.00
27	2.20	59.40	−5.60
28	1.90	53.20	−6.20
29	1.60	46.40	−6.80
30	1.30	39.00	−7.40
31	1.00	31.00	−8.00
32	.70	22.40	−8.60
33	.40	13.20	−9.20
34	.10	3.40	−9.80
35	.00	.00	−3.40

Notice the similarity between this exhibit and Exhibit 3.11, which appeared as part of the discussion of price elasticity of demand. There it was demonstrated that when demand is *elastic*, a decrease in price causes total revenue to increase. (The reason is that in percentage terms, the quantity sold increases by more than the price decreases, so the product of the two increases.) In contrast, when demand is *inelastic*, revenue falls when the price goes down. (That is because, with inelastic demand, the percentage increase in quantity is less than the percentage decrease in price.) With a straight-line demand curve like that of Exhibit 9.1b, the upper half is elastic and the lower half inelastic. That accounts for the shape of the "revenue hill" in Part c of this exhibit.

Marginal Revenue The relationship between output and revenue for the pure monopolist can also be viewed in marginal terms. Chapter 8 defined *marginal revenue* as the change in total revenue resulting from a one-unit increase in a firm's output. Column 4 of Exhibit 9.1a gives data on marginal revenue for the firm in this example. Notice that the figures in this column are simply the differences between successive entries in Column 3. Part b of the exhibit shows a graph of marginal revenue. Notice that the marginal revenue curve is above the horizontal axis when total revenue is increasing (elastic demand) and below the axis when total revenue is decreasing (inelastic demand). It intersects the horizontal axis just at the point of maximum total revenue.[1]

Profit Maximization

The relationship between output and revenue for the pure monopolist forms the basis for an analysis of short-run profit maximization. Profit maximization for a pure monopolist can be demonstrated by means of a numerical example similar to that used for the case of perfect competition.

Exhibit 9.2 incorporates the demand and revenue data for a typical pure monopolist from Exhibit 9.1 and gives total and marginal cost data for the same firm. One way to determine the profit maximizing quantity of output for the firm is to compare total cost and total revenue, as given in Part a of the exhibit. Subtracting total cost in Column 6 from total revenue in Column 2 gives total profit in Column 7. A glance down Column 7 shows the profit maximizing level of output to be thirteen units. The total-revenue, total-cost approach to profit maximization is shown graphically in Exhibit 9.2b. Total profit appears in that exhibit as the vertical gap between the total cost and total revenue curves; it reaches a maximum at thirteen units of output, where the two curves are the maximum distance apart.

Note that maximizing profit is not the same thing as maximizing revenue. Between thirteen and seventeen units of output, total revenue continues to rise; but total cost rises even faster, so profit declines.

The Marginal Approach Alternatively, the profit maximizing level of output for the pure monopolist can be found by comparing marginal cost and

---

[1] Here is an easy rule that will help in sketching the marginal revenue curve corresponding to any straight-line demand curve: *The marginal revenue curve for a straight-line demand curve always cuts the horizontal distance from the demand curve to the vertical axis exactly in half.* This rule does not work for curved demand curves, but the examples in this book will be kept simple.

Exhibit 9.2

Profit maximization for a pure monopolist

This exhibit demonstrates that a pure monopolist maximizes profits by producing that quantity of output for which marginal cost is equal to marginal revenue. Notice that maximizing profit is not the same as maximizing revenue. As this example is constructed, the profit maximizing output is thirteen units. In the range from thirteen to seventeen units of output, total revenue continues to increase. But because total cost increases even faster in this range, profits decline. Notice also that the profit maximizing price for the monopolist is determined by the height of the demand curve (not the marginal cost or marginal revenue curve) at the profit maximizing quantity of output.

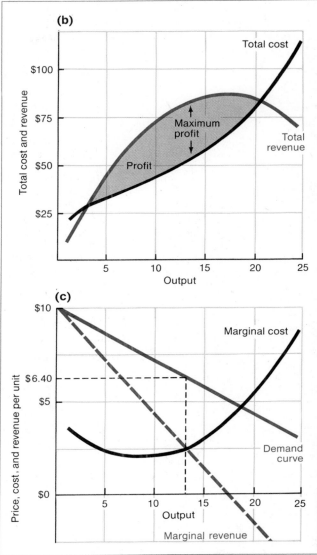

Output (1)	Price (2)	Total Revenue (3)	Marginal Revenue (4)	Marginal Cost (5)	Total Cost (6)	Total Profit (7)
1	$10.00	$10.00			$ 23.80	−$13.80
			$9.40	$3.40		
2	9.70	19.40			27.20	−7.80
			8.80	3.05		
3	9.40	28.20			30.25	2.05
			8.20	2.75		
4	9.10	36.40			33.00	3.40
			7.60	2.50		
5	8.80	44.00			35.50	8.50
			7.00	2.30		
6	8.50	51.00			37.80	13.20
			6.40	2.15		
7	8.20	57.40			39.95	17.45
			5.80	2.05		
8	7.90	63.20			42.00	21.20
			5.20	2.00		
9	7.60	68.40			44.00	24.40
			4.60	2.05		
10	7.30	73.00			46.05	26.95
			4.00	2.15		
11	7.00	77.00			48.20	28.80
			3.40	2.30		
12	6.70	80.40			50.50	29.90
			2.80	2.50		
13	6.40	83.20			53.00	30.20
			2.20	2.75		
14	6.10	85.40			55.75	29.65
			1.60	3.05		
15	5.80	87.00			58.80	28.20
			1.00	3.40		
16	5.50	88.00			62.20	25.80
			.40	3.80		
17	5.20	88.40			66.00	22.40

marginal revenue, as shown in Columns 4 and 5 of Exhibit 9.2a. Marginal revenue is the amount by which total revenue increases as the result of a one-unit increase in output, and marginal cost is the amount by which total cost increases. It follows that so long as marginal revenue exceeds marginal cost, adding one more unit of output will add more to total revenue than to total cost and will hence add to total profit. Beyond thirteen units of output, marginal revenue falls below marginal cost, so further expansion of output reduces total profit.

Exhibit 9.2c makes the comparison between marginal revenue and marginal cost graphically. The profit maximizing quantity is found where the marginal cost and marginal revenue curves intersect. It corresponds to the point of maximum profit, shown in Exhibit 9.2b as the point where the gap between the total revenue and total cost curves is greatest.

The intersection of the marginal cost and marginal revenue curves in Exhibit 9.2c gives the profit maximizing quantity of output for the pure monopolist; the corresponding profit maximizing price is given by the height of the demand curve for this quantity. For the pure monopolist, this price is always above marginal cost. Marginal cost at thirteen units of output for the firm in the example is $2.50 per unit, but according to the demand curve, consumers would be willing to buy thirteen units of output for as much as $6.40. The price of $6.40 is thus what the monopolist will charge for the thirteen units of output in order to earn the maximum profit.

Profit Maximization or Loss Minimization?

Just as for a perfectly competitive firm, profit maximization for a monopolist can sometimes mean loss minimization, at least in the short run. Whether there are actual profits to be made or only losses to be minimized depends on

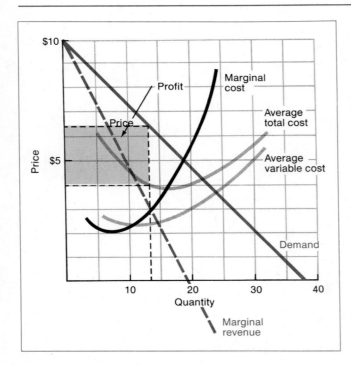

Exhibit 9.3

A pure monopolist earning positive profits
The profit actually earned by a pure monopolist depends on the relationship of price to average total cost. In this example, the monopolist's demand curve is high enough to enable a pure economic profit to be earned. Total profit is shown in the diagram as the shaded rectangle with a height equal to the difference between price and average total cost and a width equal to the profit maximizing quantity of output.

the position of the demand curve relative to the monopolist's average cost curves.

One possibility is illustrated in Exhibit 9.3. Here, demand is high enough relative to average cost for the monopolist to make a pure economic profit, above and beyond the normal rate of return on capital that is built into the definition of average total cost. As in Exhibit 9.2, the profit maximizing quantity, at the intersection of the marginal cost and marginal revenue curves, is roughly thirteen units of output. The demand curve indicates that the profit maximizing price for that quantity of output is approximately $6.40 per unit.

At thirteen units of output, average total cost is only $4 per unit. That means the monopolist earns a pure economic profit of $2.40 per unit above and beyond all costs, including the implicit cost of a normal rate of return on invested capital. At thirteen units of output, total profit is $31.20. This is shown graphically in Exhibit 9.3 as the shaded rectangle. The base of the rectangle is equal to the quantity of output (thirteen units). Its height is equal to the difference between the price of $6.40 per unit and the average total cost of $4 per unit—that is, to the $2.40 average profit the firm earns.

Under less favorable demand conditions, however, the same firm may be able to do no better than to minimize losses. This possibility is illustrated in Exhibit 9.4. The demand curve in the diagram lies below the average cost curve at all points. This can happen, for example, during a severe recession, when consumer incomes are abnormally low. Following the usual rule, the profit maximizing quantity of output is found to be about ten units, as Exhibit 9.4 is drawn. According to the demand curve, that much output can be sold for $4 per unit, but average total cost at ten units of output is $4.75. At a price of $4 per unit, the monopolist will lose $.75 on each unit sold. This total loss is shown in the exhibit by the shaded rectangle.

Exhibit 9.4
Short-run loss minimization for a pure monopolist
Sometimes demand may not be sufficient to permit a pure monopolist to earn a pure economic profit. As this exhibit is drawn, for example, the demand curve lies below the average total cost curve at all points. The best the monopolist can do, in the short run, is to minimize losses by producing at the point where marginal cost equals marginal revenue. If the demand curve were to shift downward even farther, so that the firm could not obtain a price covering average variable cost, the short-run loss minimizing strategy would be to shut down.

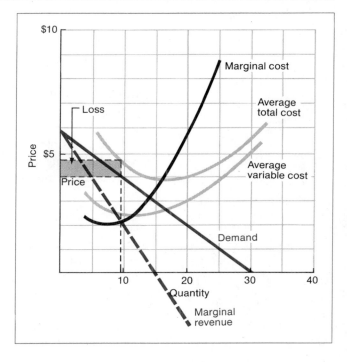

Although the monopolist suffers a loss at ten units of output, no other choice of output will yield a smaller loss. As Exhibit 9.4 is drawn, $4 per unit is more than enough to cover average variable costs. The monopolist, like the perfectly competitive firm, is better off staying in production in the short run, even at a loss, so long as the price at which the output can be sold is greater than the average variable cost. If the demand curve shifts so far to the left that it falls below the average variable cost curve at all points, the pure monopolist, like the perfectly competitive firm, will minimize short-run losses by shutting down. In the long run, if demand conditions do not improve, the firm will go out of business.

Long-Run Profit Maximization under Pure Monopoly

One of the most important conclusions reached in Chapter 8 was that, in the long run, pure economic profits are impossible under perfect competition. The reason is that if an increase in demand for the product raises the market price above average total cost, new firms will be attracted into the industry. As the new firms enter, the total quantity supplied to the market increases, driving the market price back to the level of average total cost.

Under pure monopoly, in contrast, pure economic profits can continue indefinitely if demand conditions are favorable. The reason is that a monopolist is assumed to be protected against competition by barriers to entry. Even if short-run demand conditions permit a higher than normal rate of return on capital, as in Exhibit 9.3, no other firm can enter the market. If nothing happens to disturb the favorable position of its cost and demand curves, a pure monopolist can earn pure economic profits above and beyond the normal rate of return even in the long run.

Indirect Competition and Long-Run Profits

Although protection from direct competition makes it possible in some cases for pure monopolists to earn pure economic profits in the long run, there are other cases in which long-run profits are eroded by indirect competition. In one limiting case, a monopolist faced with indirect competition might find itself in the position pictured in Exhibit 9.5. In that exhibit, the demand curve just touches the average total cost curve at the quantity of output for which marginal revenue equals marginal cost, so that the best the firm can do is break even. It earns sufficient revenue to cover all its costs, including a normal rate of return on capital, but nothing more.

Two kinds of indirect competition in particular might push a monopolist toward this long-run breakeven position. One is competition in the process of establishing a monopoly in the first place. A firm may have to bid competitively for a key patent or for access to a key natural resource in order to establish its monopoly. Perhaps it will have to hire expensive lawyers and consultants to convince a government agency that it, and not some other firm, should get a key license or permit. If entrepreneurs compete vigorously to establish a monopoly, it may very well turn out that the winner never does better than break even. Its initial efforts, although successful, may cost so much that it ends up in the position shown in Exhibit 9.5.

Competition from substitute products can also force a monopolist to the breakeven position. A firm with a monopoly of steel production, for example, may find that, over time, clever entrepreneurs in the aluminum or plastics

Exhibit 9.5

The breakeven position for a pure monopolist
Being a pure monopolist in a market may make it possible to earn a pure economic profit in the long run, but it does not guarantee that positive profits will be earned. This exhibit shows a monopoly that is only breaking even (that is, earning only a normal rate of return on invested capital). Among other possibilities, this could be the result of high costs of obtaining or defending the firm's monopoly position or of erosion of demand through indirect competition from substitute products.

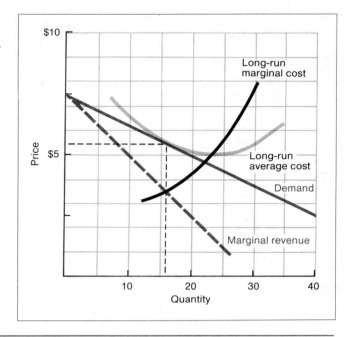

industries are stealing away more and more of its customers. The competition of substitutes may gradually erode demand for the monopolist's own product until, in the limiting case, the demand curve falls all the way to tangency with the average cost curve.

The likelihood of actually reaching the limiting position of zero profits depends on the closeness of the substitutes offered by other firms. For example, a firm whose monopoly consists in owning the only Italian restaurant in town will clearly feel more competitive pressure than will a firm owning the only restaurant of any kind. In fact, when a firm's "monopoly" is so narrowly based that many competing firms offer products that are very close substitutes, economists no longer classify the firm as a pure monopolist. Instead, they call a market structure in which a large number of firms offer products that are relatively close substitutes for one another **monopolistic competition.** Chapters 11 and 12 will have more to say about monopolistic competition and about other forms of competition lying between pure monopoly and perfect competition.

Monopolistic competition A market structure in which a large number of firms offer products that are relatively close substitutes for one another.

MONOPOLY, CONSUMER WELFARE, AND PRICE DISCRIMINATION

Pure Monopoly as an Imperfect Market Structure

Chapter 8 showed that production is carried out in a perfectly competitive market up to the point where price is equal to marginal cost. This, it was argued, makes perfect competition a "perfect" market form in the sense that all potential mutually beneficial transactions are carried out. Beyond the point of competitive equilibrium, consumer welfare cannot be further improved without imposing an actual loss on producers.

Under pure monopoly, in contrast, production stops short of the quantity necessary to bring market price down to the level of marginal cost. Consider Exhibit 9.6, for example. There, the monopolist maximizes profit by producing 2,000 units of output per month and selling each unit for $3. At a rate of output of 2,000 units per month, marginal cost is only $1 per unit. There is a $2 gap between marginal cost and the market price. This gap represents a market imperfection; it indicates that some potential mutually beneficial transactions are not being carried out.

One way to understand the nature of this market imperfection is to think of the monopolist as a middleman standing between the consumer and resource owners. The height of the demand curve at 2,000 units of output in Exhibit 9.6 represents what consumers are willing to pay for the 2,000th unit of output. The height of the marginal cost curve at this point represents what the firm has to pay resource owners for the various inputs necessary to produce the 2,000th unit. Clearly, production of the 2,000th unit is worthwhile; consumers value it at $3, and resource owners value the resources used up in producing it at only $1.

Reasoning in the same way, it would also be worthwhile to produce a 2,001st unit of output. Consumers would value the 2,001st unit at only slightly less than $3, and resource owners would be willing to release the necessary inputs for only a little more than $1. If it were feasible for consumers to negotiate directly with resource owners for production of the 2,001st unit, it would presumably be produced at a mutually agreeable price, such as $2. In this case, however, consumers do not deal with resource owners directly. They deal instead through the monopolist as an intermediary, and it is not worthwhile for the monopolist to produce a 2,001st unit of output. Even though the 2,001st unit could be sold at a price higher than its marginal cost, the marginal revenue earned by the monopolist from the transaction would be less than marginal cost. And it is not profitable for the monopolist to increase output beyond the point where marginal revenue falls below marginal cost.

What is true of the 2,001st unit is also true of the 2,002nd, the 2,003rd, and all units up to and including the 3,000th. Each of these units could be produced and sold at a price higher than marginal cost—that is, at a price high enough to fully compensate resource owners and low enough to still be agreeable to consumers. But so long as consumers deal with resource owners only at arm's length, through the agency of the monopolist, this potential mutual benefit, represented in Exhibit 9.6 by the shaded triangle, will not be realized. It is in this sense that pure monopoly is an imperfect market structure.

Price Discrimination

This is a good place to emphasize an assumption that has been only implicit in the discussion to this point—the assumption that the pure monopolist sells all units of output at a uniform price. Such a pricing policy is forced on the monopolist whenever the nature of the product makes resale among buyers possible. For example, it is highly unlikely that your campus bookstore (a monopoly on many campuses) could get away with selling economics texts at list price to seniors and at a 25 percent discount to everyone else. If it tried to do so, it would not be long before some enterprising freshman went into

Exhibit 9.6

Why monopoly markets are imperfect
A perfect market is one in which all potential mutually beneficial exchanges are carried out and none is missed. Monopoly markets are not perfect in this sense. In the case illustrated here, a pure monopolist will maximize profits at a quantity of 2,000 units per month and a price of $3 per unit. But at that price and quantity, there is a gap between the demand curve and the marginal cost curve, which indicates that, in principle, further production can be carried out to the mutual benefit of consumers and resource owners. The shaded triangular area indicates the value of potential benefits forgone.

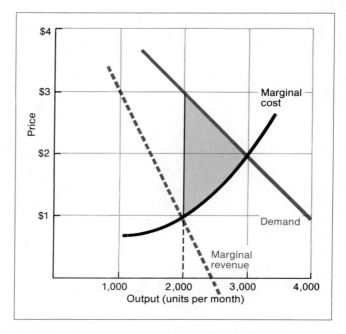

business buying books for resale to seniors at some split-the-difference price. The bookstore's list-price sales would soon fall to zero.

Some firms, however, do not sell their product to all customers at the same price. Such sellers are said to practice **price discrimination.** Two things are required if price discrimination is to be possible. First, resale of the product among consumers must be impossible, or at least inconvenient. And second, the seller must be able to classify potential customers into groups with highly inelastic demand, who can be charged high prices, and groups with more elastic demand, who will be driven away unless offered low prices. The following case study illustrates price discrimination in action.

Price discrimination The practice of charging more than one price for different units of a single product, when the price differences are not justified by differences in the cost of serving different customers.

Case 9.1
Price Discrimination in Higher Education

In contrast to campus bookstores, which ordinarily must sell at uniform prices, colleges and universities themselves very commonly practice price discrimination in selling their main product—education. Usually, it works this way. First, the business office sets tuition at some ambitiously high level. Then, the admissions office gives its stamp of approval to a certain number of qualified applicants. After this is done, the financial aid office gets busy working out a price discrimination strategy. The strategy consists of offering selective price rebates, called scholarships, to those students who it thinks will not be willing or able to attend if charged full tuition.

A college or university is in an ideal position to practice price discrimination. For one thing, the product is completely nontransferable. If you get admitted to both Harvard and Dartmouth, you can't sell your Dartmouth admission to someone who didn't get into either place! Furthermore, the college collects a great deal of information that allows it to classify students according to willingness and ability to pay. For example, most colleges require you to submit a family financial statement when you apply for financial aid. Each college then calculates the "family contri-

Exhibit 9.7
Guidelines for family contribution to a student's higher education

Many colleges and universities practice a form of price discrimination in which some students are expected to contribute a large share of the cost of their education while others have their contribution reduced through scholarships or other forms of financial aid. The table reproduced here from a student guide to scholarships and loans is representative of pricing practices in higher education during the 1978–79 school year.

Parents' Contribution						Student's Contribution			Family Contribution
Family Size	Number in College	Income	Assets	Contribution		Assets	Summer Wages	Contribution	
2	1	$ 8,000	$ 500	$ 0		$ 100	$500	$535	$535
3	1	10,000	1,000	210		400	500	640	850
3	1	17,000	5,000	1,560		500	500	675	2,235
3	1	24,000	20,000	4,810		800	600	880	5,690
3	1	31,000	40,000	6,910		1,000	500	850	7,760
4	1	12,000	3,000	145		100	500	535	680
4	1	20,000	15,000	1,810		400	500	640	2,450
4	1	28,000	35,000	5,230	+	600	600	810	= 6,040
4	2	36,000	65,000	5,400 each		700	500	745	6,145 each
5	1	13,000	5,000	176		200	600	670	846
5	2	18,000	10,000	600 each		300	600	705	1,305 each
5	2	27,000	30,000	2,315 each		400	700	840	3,155 each
5	2	37,000	75,000	5,680 each		900	500	815	6,495 each
6	2	19,000	15,000	560 each		600	600	810	1,370 each
6	3	30,000	30,000	1,700 each		400	500	640	2,340 each
7	3	33,000	50,000	2,450 each		500	600	775	3,225 each

Source: Adapted by permission from Robert Leider, *Don't Miss Out: The Ambitious Student's Guide to Scholarships and Loans,* 3rd ed. (Alexandria, Va.: Octameron Associates, 1978), Table 1, p. 3.

bution'' toward your education (in plain terms, the price that it will charge) according to a table such as the one reproduced in Exhibit 9.7..

If the price discrimination strategy is successful, everyone involved may benefit. Students who would not have been able to attend college at all without financial aid probably benefit most. Students who pay full tuition find their college experience enriched by the diversity of a student population with a wider variety of backgrounds and abilities than could have been attracted without a scholarship program. Meanwhile, the college itself benefits by keeping its classrooms full with the help of scholarship students and its budget balanced with tuition and fees collected from those without scholarships.

Pros and Cons of Price Discrimination

Price discrimination is widely perceived as unfair, especially by those who pay a high price while others pay less. Attempts have been made to outlaw price discrimination in some markets. However, as the preceding case study suggests, price discrimination should not be condemned without considering the alternatives.

The key question to ask in evaluating any price discrimination scheme is whether it moves the market closer to or farther from the ideal state in which all potential mutually beneficial trades are carried out. When price discrimination allows buying by those who are willing to pay a price at least equal to marginal cost but not as high as what a nondiscriminatory monopolist would charge, it may very well be beneficial. For example, price discrimination makes it possible for some students to attend colleges they otherwise could not afford. It allows parents to take their young children to the movies. And it makes it possible for standby passengers, who could not afford the full fares business travelers pay, to fill airplane seats that would otherwise go empty. These forms of price discrimination almost certainly represent improvements in market performance compared with what would realistically be possible under uniform pricing.

On the other hand, price discrimination can sometimes be carried too far. In particular, it is important that the lowest price charged not fall below marginal cost. If that were to happen, another kind of market imperfection would be introduced: Output would be too large, rather than too small, in comparison with a perfectly competitive market. Too many, rather than too few, resources would be attracted to the industry in question. For example, public utility commissions in some states encourage electric utilities to discriminate against industrial users and in favor of residential users even to the point that some power for residential use is sold below long-run marginal cost. Many economists believe that this has encouraged wasteful use of electricity by homeowners and has thus made it necessary for utilities to overexpand their generating capacity.

Later chapters will discuss a number of additional examples of price discrimination. Case by case evaluations will show that some are good and others bad.

CARTELS

Pure Monopolies and Cartels

To the extent that it is motivated by profit maximization, every firm would like to be a monopolist. But most firms have no realistic chance of becoming pure monopolists. In most markets, firms face competitors that are far too numerous and far too vigorous ever to be bought up or driven away. Furthermore, in most markets, decreasing returns to scale would make it highly inefficient to concentrate all production in a single firm.

For would-be monopolists in such markets, there is a tempting alternative to the pure, single-firm monopoly. That alternative is a **cartel**—an agreement among a number of independent firms to stop competing and, instead, to coordinate their supply decisions so all of them will earn a monopoly profit.

Cartel An agreement among a number of independent suppliers of a product to coordinate their supply decisions so all of them will earn monopoly profits.

How Cartels Work

A simple example will show just how cartels work. Imagine an industry composed of one hundred identical small firms. For simplicity, assume that the marginal cost of production for all firms in the industry is a constant $1 per unit, regardless of the quantity produced. Because marginal cost is the same for all units of output, the marginal cost curve also serves as the long-run average cost curve and the long-run supply curve for the industry. This perfectly elastic long-run supply curve is shown, together with a hypothetical demand curve for the industry, in Exhibit 9.8.

The equilibrium price and quantity of output of the industry depend on how the market is organized. Suppose initially that all firms behave as perfect

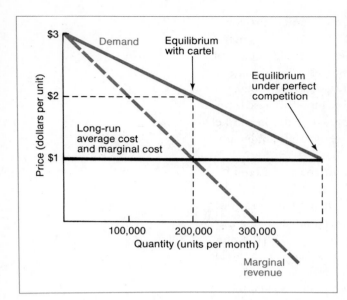

Exhibit 9.8
The effects of a cartel
This exhibit represents an industry composed of one hundred identical firms, each producing at constant long-run average and marginal cost. If the firms behave as perfect competitors, the industry will be in equilibrium where the demand curve and marginal cost curve intersect. If the firms form a cartel, however, they can jointly earn profits by restricting output to the point where marginal cost is equal to marginal revenue and by raising the product price from $1 to $2.

competitors. Under the theory set forth in Chapter 8, this situation will result in an equilibrium in which the market price is $1 per unit (equal to long-run average cost and long-run marginal cost) and in which 400,000 units of output are produced each month. In this equilibrium, each firm earns a normal rate of return on its capital and earns no pure economic profit.

Suppose now that one day the heads of the hundred firms get together to form a cartel. It is their hope that by replacing competition with cooperation, they can advance their mutual interests. They elect one of their number as cartel manager. The manager is instructed to work out a production and marketing plan that will maximize total profits for the industry and to share these profits fairly among the members.

The profit maximizing problem faced by the cartel manager is exactly the same as that faced by a pure monopolist. Industry profits are maximized at the output where marginal revenue for the industry equals marginal cost. That output is 200,000 units per month for this example. By restricting output to that quantity, the price can be raised to $2 per unit, and $200,000 per month of pure economic profit will be generated. To share this profit among all cartel members, each firm will be given an output quota of 2,000 units a month, half as much as it had been producing as a competitor. By this arrangement, the member firms will reap the benefits of pure monopoly despite their small size and large numbers.

The Stability Problem for Cartels

For its members, a successful cartel is a wonderful thing. Each firm is able to share in the profits of a monopoly while maintaining its organizational independence. But for buyers of the product, a cartel is clearly no blessing. In this example, buyers end up spending the same amount of money on the product as under competition but getting only half the quantity.

Fortunately for consumers, relatively few markets are organized as cartels. Partly, this is because most cartels are illegal under U.S. law. (More on this subject in Chapter 13.) Even more importantly, though, cartels suffer from two big built-in problems that prevent most potential cartels from being formed at all and keep others from surviving for long if they are formed.

Control over Entry The first problem that cartels suffer from is control over entry. As long as competition in an industry keeps price down to the level of long-run average cost, membership in the industry tends to be stable. As soon as a cartel raises price above this level, however, the industry becomes a magnet for new entrants. The entry of new firms does not increase the total quantity that the cartel can sell at the profit maximizing price. It increases only the number of members among which profits have to be shared. Unless there is a way for a cartel to control entry into its market, it cannot effectively serve the interests of its members.

Enforcement of Output Quotas The second, even more serious, built-in problem of cartels is the enforcement of output quotas. In every cartel, each individual member always has an incentive to cheat on its quota by producing extra, unauthorized output. Take the cartel in Exhibit 9.8. The quota for each of the one hundred members is 2,000 units per month, just half of what each firm would produce under competitive conditions. What would happen if any single firm cheated on its quota by stepping up output to the precartel level while the others continued to play by the rules?

The answer is simple. An extra 2,000 units per month by one firm would have a negligible effect on the market price, because it would represent only a 1 percent increase in industry output. By producing 4,000 units a month, the cheater would double its monthly profit—as long as others did not cheat too.

What if the others did cheat? What if all the other ninety-nine firms stepped up output to 4,000 units while only one firm stuck to its quota? With industry output at 398,000 units, the price would be forced down virtually all the way to the competitive level of $1. The firm that played fair would gain nothing for its honesty.

Because cartels are potentially so profitable, cartel organizers sometimes undertake elaborate measures to suppress cheating and enhance stability. In the case of illegal cartels, these efforts go on behind locked doors, and outside observers rarely have a chance to learn the details. Not all cartels are illegal, however. Ocean shipping conferences (cartels of international freight liners) are an example of legal cartels. The Federal Maritime Commission (FMC) is empowered to approve ocean shipping cartels under a special exemption from the antitrust laws, provided, among other things, that the members publicly file a full written statement of their rules and regulations. The following case study, taken from evidence submitted in a recent FMC proceeding, shows that even legally sanctioned cartels suffer chronically from the stability problems identified here.

Case 9.2
Instability in an Actual Cartel

The West Coast of Italy—North America Conference (WINAC) is a cartel composed of shipping lines carrying cargo from Italy to ports on the Northeast Atlantic coast of the United States. From its formation in 1934 until the mid-1960s, it was apparently able to function to the general satisfaction of its members. In the 1960s, however, WINAC was disrupted by a major technological revolution—the trend to containerization of cargo. Because it reduced the number of workers needed to load and unload ships, containerization greatly increased productivity. This in turn gave rise to a severe problem of excess capacity. As a result of a competitive struggle among carriers to fill their excess capacity, discipline in the cartel broke down almost completely.

Although the conference continued to meet to establish prices, it found itself unable to agree upon or enforce a division of output among its members. This failure encouraged two practices on the part of members that proved very damaging to profits. One was competition in scheduling. Each carrier tried to attract cargo by putting more and more ships in service, until each ship was traveling only partly loaded and at a high cost per ton of cargo carried. The other practice was a form of under-the-table price cutting in which carriers gave large rebates to shippers, in violation of conference rules.

By 1978, members had been driven to a virtually zero profit position. Some even left the trade altogether. The remaining members felt that the time had come to make a major new effort to put the cartel back together. After many months of delicate negotiations, they came up with an agreement that would establish what is called a *pool.* Under the terms of the pool, any member that carried more than its agreed share of the total cargo available would have to pay a penalty into a common fund. The fund would be used to compensate members who were cheated out of their agreed share. The agreement itself was more than fifty pages long and defined types of cargos, organization, penalties, arbitration arrangements, and many other matters in exhaustive detail.

The FMC, traditionally sympathetic to ocean shipping conferences, granted WINAC permission to give the pool a try. In the course of the FMC proceedings, however, even the strongest proponents of the pool had to admit that success was by no means guaranteed. Although they hoped that the pool would end cheating and rebating by members, they were concerned about the loss of traffic to nonmember carriers. At the time of writing, it is too early to tell how long WINAC's latest efforts will hold up, but one thing appears certain: Even with full legal protection, cartels rarely face smooth sailing.

The Exception: OPEC

Despite the very serious problems that cartels encounter, there are a few known exceptions to the rule that cartels are unstable and short-lived. In modern times, by far the most conspicuously successful cartel has been the Organization of Petroleum Exporting Countries, commonly known as OPEC. When OPEC quadrupled the price of oil in 1974, many prominent economists believed that it had overreached itself and would soon collapse. Instead, it remained strong and at this writing appears to be in no immediate danger of falling apart.

Why has OPEC been able to succeed as a cartel when many other cartels have failed? All observers agree that its success has been aided, more than anything, by the enormous time and expense required to develop alternative sources of supply. True, non-OPEC supplies, such as Alaskan and North Sea oil, did appear in response to the escalation of world prices; but at least through the 1970s, these new supplies were barely enough to offset a part of the increase in world oil demand and did not cut seriously into OPEC revenues. Development of such enormous potential non-OPEC reserves as those of Mexico and China appears to be many years in the future.

Beyond this primary advantage of very high barriers to entry, certain other factors have enhanced OPEC's stability. One of these is that a single producer, Saudi Arabia, is so large that it is able to make production cutbacks single-handedly when other members are tempted to supply more than they ought to. Another advantage is the unity of political purpose of the Arab members of OPEC, which dominate the cartel. Still another advantage is a very inelastic demand for the cartel's output. Finally, OPEC has sometimes been rescued by sheer good luck. In the winter of 1978–79, for example, just as OPEC seemed to be threatened by a temporary world oil glut, the revolution in Iran took the cartel's second largest producer temporarily out of action and led to renewed upward movement of world prices.

In short, although OPEC is to some degree subject to the same problems as other cartels, it is better equipped than most to cope with those problems. Someday, no doubt, it will go the way of most of its fellow cartels throughout history, but economists have grown cautious about predicting the day and the hour.

CONCLUSIONS

It would be tempting to conclude this chapter with some sweeping comparisons of monopoly and competition. Competition is perfect; monopoly is flawed. So three cheers for competition, and down with monopoly! But not so fast. The implications that can legitimately be drawn from a comparison of the two market structures are more limited than they initially appear. And a lot more groundwork must be laid before even those limited conclusions can be drawn.

For one thing, remember that all of the analysis of perfect competition and pure monopoly has taken place on the level of pure economizing. We should be reluctant to draw any conclusions about the relative merits of alternative market structures until we know something about how they affect entrepreneurial decision making as well. That is a topic to be taken up in Chapters 11 and 12.

Second, even within the realm of pure economizing, we have seen only how to compare two *different* markets—one competitive and the other monopolistic. That is not at all the same thing as making an evaluation of how a single market would perform under two alternative forms of organization. In practice, it is rarely, if ever, possible to change the structure of a market without making other changes in it as well. In particular, any change in market structure that involves increasing or decreasing the number of firms among which production is divided is very likely to affect costs and product characteristics as well. If competition reduces costs and improves product characteristics, its degree of superiority over monopoly may be very much greater than the little triangle in Exhibit 9.6 indicates. On the other hand, if excessive fragmentation of production has adverse effects on cost or product quality, those effects may more than outweigh competitive benefits of the type looked at so far.

Finally, it would simply be premature to make any comparisons between perfect competition and pure monopoly until we have examined many other market structures that are neither one nor the other. That job will occupy most of the next five chapters.

SUMMARY

1. Pure monopoly is a market structure in which one firm accounts for 100 percent of market supply. A firm operating as a pure monopolist is poten-

tially much more profitable than one operating as a perfect competitor. Any short-run profits earned by a competitive firm will soon be eaten away by new entrants. But under pure monopoly, a price high enough to allow short-run profits need not immediately be driven down by competitors because, by definition, there are no competitors in that particular market.

2. The monopolist is not a price taker. Because the firm can expand sales only by lowering the price at which the product is sold, marginal revenue is always less than price. With a straight-line demand curve, the marginal revenue curve always lies exactly halfway between the demand curve and the vertical axis.

3. Once the demand curve, marginal revenue curve, and cost curves are given, profit maximization for the monopolist can be treated as a problem in pure economizing. To find the profit maximizing quantity, locate the point where marginal cost and marginal revenue curves intersect. Then, to find the profit maximizing price, go vertically up from that point to the demand curve.

4. Whether the profit maximizing supply decision actually yields a profit over and above the normal rate of return on invested capital or merely minimizes losses depends on the location of the demand curve relative to the average cost curves. If the demand curve is above the average total cost curve at the point where marginal cost and marginal revenue are equal, the firm will earn a positive profit. If the demand and average total cost curves are tangent at that point, the firm will break even. If the demand curve passes below the average total cost curve but above the average variable cost curve, the firm will minimize losses in the short run by producing where marginal cost equals marginal revenue. If the demand curve is everywhere below average variable cost, the firm will minimize losses by shutting down.

5. A perfect market is one in which all potential mutually beneficial transactions are carried out. Pure monopoly is not perfect in this sense. At the profit maximizing quantity of output, there is a gap between the demand curve and the marginal cost curve; this indicates that further production will be beneficial to both consumers and resource owners. Sometimes these additional gains from trade, wasted under pure monopoly, can be realized if the monopolist engages in price discrimination. Price discrimination may result in some buyers paying even higher prices than under pure monopoly, but it also may permit buying by some who would be shut out of the market altogether under nondiscriminating monopoly.

6. A cartel is an agreement among a number of independent suppliers in a market to stop competing and, instead, to coordinate their activities in order to earn a monopoly profit. The profit maximizing rule for a cartel is the same as that for a pure monopolist: Produce where industry marginal cost equals industry marginal revenue. Cartels are less common than they might otherwise be partly because they are often illegal and partly because they are often unstable. They are unstable because each firm has an incentive to cheat on the cartel's price and output decisions in order to earn more than its agreed-upon share of the cartel's total profits.

DISCUSSION QUESTIONS

1. One sometimes hears it said that a firm with a monopoly in its particular market will charge "the highest price it can get" for its product. What is the fallacy in this statement?

2. The common form of price discrimination involves charging different prices to different customers when the price difference is not justified by differences in the cost of serving those customers. Can you think of any examples where the different prices a firm charges *are* justified by differences in the cost of service? Alternatively, can you think of any instances in which a firm charges the same price for all units it sells, even though the cost of serving various customers is not the same? Should this too be considered price discrimination? Explain.

3. The U.S. Postal Service has traditionally maintained a special low rate for shipments of books. Can you think of any likely economic reasons for this particular instance of price discrimination? Do you think the policy is a desirable one? Explain.

4. In what respects do you think labor unions resemble cartels? In what respects do they differ from cartels? Do you think labor unions ever suffer from the instability problems that plague product market cartels?

5. What is the best example you know of a pure monopoly? What protects this monopoly from the entry of direct competitors? How significant is the indirect competition by substitute products that this monopoly faces?

6. What kinds of transactions costs prevent consumers from dealing directly with resource owners and thus overcoming market imperfections under pure monopoly? (See Chapter 2 for a discussion of the concept of transactions costs.)

SUGGESTIONS FOR FURTHER READING

Bork, Robert H. *The Antitrust Paradox: A Policy at War with Itself.* New York: Basic Books, 1978.
Chapter 4 of this influential book on policy toward monopoly is devoted to an excellent nontechnical summary of the economic theory of monopoly, emphasizing its implications for efficiency.

Leftwich, Richard H. *The Price System and Resource Allocation.* 7th ed. Hinsdale, Ill.: Dryden Press, 1979.
Chapter 11 presents an intermediate level analysis of pure monopoly.

McGee, John S. "Ocean Freight Rate Conferences and the American Merchant Marine." *University of Chicago Law Review* 27 (Winter 1960): 191–314.
This book-length article provides an excellent general discussion of cartels and their problems (with many useful references) and applies the general analysis to the particular problem of ocean shipping conferences.

Nicholson, Walter. *Intermediate Microeconomics and Its Application.* 2d ed. Hinsdale, Ill.: Dryden Press, 1979.
Chapter 11 discusses monopoly and includes a diagrammatic analysis of price discrimination.

C H A P T E R 10

COMPETITION
AND PUBLIC POLICY
IN AGRICULTURE

WHAT YOU WILL LEARN IN THIS CHAPTER

This chapter discusses U.S. agriculture and agricultural policy. First, it explains why farmers regard the almost perfectly competitive structure of agricultural markets as a mixed blessing. Next it analyzes selected farm policies, applying the theories of competition and monopoly described in previous chapters. It shows how agricultural marketing orders permit price discrimination in the markets for fresh fruit, produce, and dairy products. It also shows how to analyze the economic effects of price supports, acreage controls, and target prices.

FOR REVIEW

Here are some important terms and concepts that will be put to use in this chapter. If you do not understand them, review them before proceeding.
- *Price and income elasticity of demand (Chapter 3)*
- *Perfect competition (Chapter 8)*
- *Pure monopoly (Chapter 9)*
- *Cartels (Chapter 9)*
- *Price discrimination (Chapter 9)*

The theories of perfect competition and pure monopoly are two of the most important items in the economist's tool kit. They provide patterns for thinking about the complex and varied market structures of which the U.S. economy is composed.

This chapter applies the theories to agricultural markets. Agriculture is a sufficiently important sector of the U.S. economy to be worth studying for its own sake. Consumers in the United States devote nearly a quarter of their consumption expenditure to farm products, despite the fact that only 4 percent of the population actually lives on farms. But the chapter is not just descriptive. It has a theme as well as a subject. This theme is the tension between the inherently competitive structure of agricultural markets and the departures from perfect competition introduced by government agricultural policy.

THE STRUCTURAL ORIGINS OF THE FARM PROBLEM

The Mixed Blessings of Perfect Competition

Many agricultural markets come very close to fitting the four structural requirements of perfect competition: large numbers of small firms, homogeneous products, good information flows, and easy entry and exit. In the United

States, there are some 2.7 million farms altogether, almost 90 percent of which are sole proprietorships—traditional family farms. Nearly half of all agricultural output is produced on farms whose annual sales are less than $100,000. Large corporate farms are gradually becoming more common, but they still contribute less than 20 percent of total output. Most agricultural markets are characterized by a high degree of product homogeneity. Only rarely do consumers know or care about which particular farm produced the products they buy. The flow of information in agricultural markets is accomplished through highly organized commodity exchanges for major crops, supplemented by the information services of the U.S. Department of Agriculture. The last structural requirement for perfect competition, easy entry and exit, is also well satisfied in agriculture.

As explained in Chapter 8, perfectly competitive markets have some important virtues. Whenever consumers are willing to pay more for a good than its marginal cost, a competitive market will bring forth the additional supply. If existing firms cannot handle the demand, new firms will enter. Similarly, if consumers are unwilling to buy all that is produced at a price at least equal to marginal cost, competition will accomplish the required reduction in supply. If a long-run reduction in supply is needed, some firms will withdraw from the market. In every case, the necessary adjustments occur in response to changes in the market price of the good, as determined by supply and demand. No central planner is needed to give orders; Adam Smith's "invisible hand" is at work.

Left alone, agricultural markets really do work in something quite close to this ideal fashion. But for farmers the ideal is a mixed blessing. In the short run, competition means unpredictable prices and unstable incomes as supply and demand curves shift with the weather and with patterns of world trade. In the long run, competition has driven more and more farmers from the land as new technology has increased crop yields per worker. So not despite but because of the perfectly competitive structure of agricultural markets, there is a farm problem.

The farm problem, it must be added, is a problem for *farmers*. From the consumer's point of view, and even more so from the detached point of view of the economist, fluctuating prices and declining farm population may not be problems at all; they may be merely the healthy functioning of competitive markets. Nonetheless, the farmer's point of view has traditionally dominated the U.S. government's farm policy. That being the case, it is worth examining more closely the cause of the problem, in order to evaluate the policies designed to cure it.

Instability and Price Inelastic Demand

In a competitive market, the response of price and revenue to changes in the quantity supplied depends on the price elasticity of demand. This response is illustrated by Exhibit 10.1 Market A in the exhibit is characterized by relatively low price elasticity of demand and Market B by relatively high elasticity.

Very short run A time horizon so short that producers are unable to make any changes in input or output quantities in response to changing prices.

In both markets, the time horizon is the **very short run**—a time so short that producers cannot make any adjustments in inputs or outputs in response to a change in price. This is the case in the market for a perishable agricultural good after the crop has been harvested and before the farmers have a chance to respond to prices by adjusting their supply decision for the next year.

Exhibit 10.1

Demand elasticity and price instability

The stability of prices and revenues in the face of changing supply conditions depends on the price elasticity of demand for the product. In Market A, where demand is relatively inelastic, an increase in supply from 100,000 units to 125,000 units brings the price down from $2 to $1 and revenue down from $200,000 to $125,000. In Market B, where demand is relatively elastic, the same increase in supply causes the price to drop to $1.80 and revenue to increase from $200,000 to $225,000.

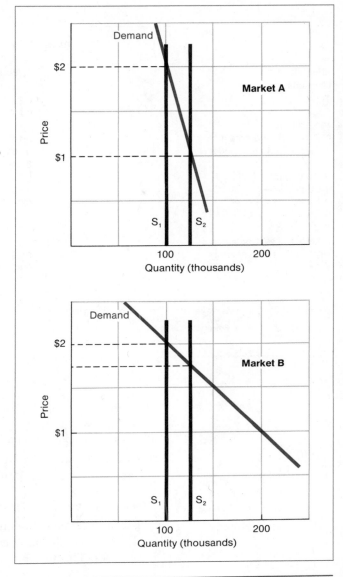

Suppose now that in the first year, 100,000 units of each crop are harvested. When that quantity of output is brought to market, an equilibrium price of $2 is established for both goods. The next year, because of improved weather, increased planting, or some other reason, output in both markets increases to 125,000 units. This is represented in the exhibit by a shift in the short-run supply curve from S_1 to S_2. What happens to price and revenue?

In Market A, where demand is inelastic, a large decrease in price is necessary to bring about the required increase in quantity demanded. As the price falls from $2 to $1, total revenue earned from the sale of the crop declines from $200,000 to $125,000. In Market B, however, a relatively small decline in price, from $2 to $1.80, is sufficient to increase the quantity demanded to 125,000 units. Because the price declines by a smaller percentage than the quantity of output increases in this market, revenue rises from $200,000 to $225,000.

Farm Product	Demand Elasticity
Cattle	0.68
Calves	1.08
Hogs	0.46
Sheep and lambs	1.78
Chickens	0.74
Turkeys	0.92
Eggs	0.23
Milk used for:	
Fluid milk and cream	0.14
Evaporated and condensed	0.26
Cheese	0.54
Ice cream	0.11
Butter	0.66
Other use	0.36
Soybean	0.61
Cottonseed	1.03
Potatoes, sweet potatoes	0.11
Dry beans, peas, peanuts	0.23
Wheat	0.80
Corn	0.50
Oats	2.00

Source: G. E. Brandow, "Interrelations among Demands for Farm Products and Implications for Control of Market Supply," *Bulletin 680* (University Park, Pa.: Pennsylvania State University Agricultural Experiment Station, 1961), pp. 59, 64, 80, 81, and 96. Reprinted by permission.

Exhibit 10.2

Price elasticity of demand for selected farm products
This table shows estimated price elasticities of demand for selected farm products. The low demand elasticities for many major products are a factor contributing to chronic price instability.

Studies of actual agricultural markets indicate that they are more like Market A than Market B. Exhibit 10.2 presents some statistical estimates of elasticity for farm products. The striking thing about this table is how low most of the elasticities are. With the exceptions of sheep, calves, cottonseed, and oats, all the elasticities listed are less than 1.

The Historical Instability of Prices

Because demand for farm products is price inelastic, changing supply and demand conditions result in disproportionately large year-to-year price changes. The instability of agricultural prices is evident from Exhibit 10.3,

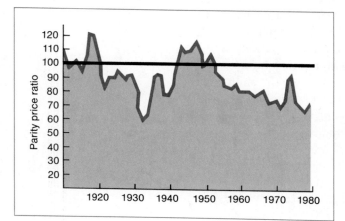

Exhibit 10.3

The parity price ratio
The parity price ratio is the ratio of an index of prices that farmers receive to an index of prices that farmers pay. The index is based on prices that prevailed in 1910–1914, a period of unusual peacetime farm prosperity. Since then, the index has been above 100 only in time of war. Even in peacetime, as the experience of the 1930s and the 1970s shows, the index can undergo wide swings over periods of only two or three years.

Sources: President's Council of Economic Advisers, *Economic Report of the President* (Washington, D.C.: Government Printing Office, 1977); and *Survey of Current Business*, August 1979.

which shows the historical record of the **parity price ratio.** This statistic is the ratio of an index of prices that farmers receive to an index of prices that farmers pay. The ratio uses the years 1910–1914 as a base period, since they have long been considered to represent the best period of peacetime farm prosperity in this century.

As the diagram shows, the parity price ratio has had its ups and downs. In the worst episode, from 1929 to 1932, the ratio fell from 92 to 58 in just over three years. The collapse of domestic demand in these early years of the Great Depression pushed all prices down; but with agricultural demand so inelastic, farmers were hit worse than anyone else. The index of prices paid by farmers sank substantially over this period, from 160 to 112; but the index of prices received fell catastrophically, from 149 to a mere 65.

Farm prices recovered together with the rest of the economy during World War II. Then, during the 1950s and 1960s, farm prices, as measured by the parity price ratio, declined steadily but without such sharp year-to-year fluctuations as in earlier periods. Any hope that agricultural markets had become permanently more stable, however, was proved premature by the experience of the 1970s.

In 1973, a combination of circumstances, ranging from bad weather in the Soviet Union to a failure of the Peruvian anchovy catch, created a worldwide food shortage. Farm prices skyrocketed. The parity price ratio rose to an average of 91 for 1973, and in August of that year it briefly touched the 100 mark for the first time in two decades. After that, prices collapsed almost as swiftly as they had risen. By 1977, the ratio had reached 66, its lowest level since the Great Depression, before recovering somewhat in 1978 and 1979.

Long-Term Adjustment and Rural Poverty

The parity price ratio tells the story of one part of the farm problem— short-term instability. There is a second part of the farm problem as well— long-term adjustment to rising productivity and its resulting rural poverty.

The long-term problem too is a product of inelastic demand. Demand for farm products is not only price inelastic but income inelastic as well. As per capita income grows, the quantity of agricultural output increases, but proportionately less than the increase in income.

The result of slowly growing demand and rapidly growing farm productivity has been a steady decline in the farm population required to meet the demand for agricultural goods. The record of this decline is given in Exhibit 10.4.

The competitive market knows just one way to bring about the exit of resources from an industry where they are no longer needed: Reduce the amount those resources are paid. Not surprisingly, then, per capita farm income has been lower than per capita nonfarm income throughout this long period of declining farm population.[1] Furthermore, the transfer of population from farm to nonfarm occupations has not everywhere been a smooth one. Skills, education, and capital are not distributed equally in the farm population. The marginal farmers who have been least able to benefit from technological advances have often also been the least mobile and the least able to find

Parity price ratio The ratio of an index of prices that farmers receive to an index that farmers pay, using the years 1910–1914 as a base period.

---

[1] The long-standing gap between farm and nonfarm incomes is gradually being closed, however. In 1977, per capita farm income stood at 84 percent of per capita nonfarm income, up from just over 50 percent as recently as 1960.

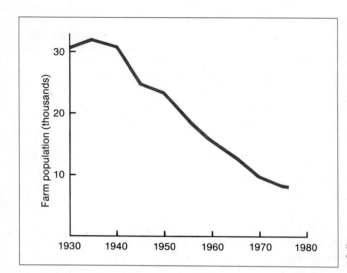

Exhibit 10.4
Declining farm population in the United States
Demand for most farm products is income inelastic as well as price inelastic. Over the years, this demand has grown much more slowly than farm productivity. The result has been a steady decrease in the farm population required to produce what the nonfarm population consumes.

Source: U.S. Department of Commerce, Bureau of the Census, *Statistical Abstract of the United States*, 98th ed. (Washington, D.C.: Government Printing Office, 1977), Table 1132.

satisfactory nonfarm work. As a result, poverty rates in rural areas have persistently remained above those in cities, even after differences between the urban and rural cost of living are taken into account.

If Only . . .

Such then are the dimensions of the farm problem. How have farmers reacted to their troubles? Although few farmers are also economists, it appears that they very well understand that the origins of the farm problem are to be found in the structure of the markets they operate in. Understanding this, their very sensible response has been to wish: *If only these markets were not so competitive!*

Their wishes have not gone unheeded. Helpful policy makers in Washington have heard the farmers' complaints and agreed that something should be done. Piece by piece, over the past half-century, has emerged a farm policy that has at its heart a series of restrictions on competition. As a result, U.S. agriculture not only supplies textbook writers with some good illustrations of perfect competition in action but also gives them a chance to develop some applications of the theory of monopoly.

FARM POLICY: MARKETING ORDERS AND PRICE DISCRIMINATION

Competition versus Coordination

Farmers could solve many of their own problems if only they could coordinate their activities instead of competing with each other. The theory developed in Chapter 9 suggests that one way to do this would be to form a comprehensive system of agricultural cartels. The cartel for each crop could limit the quantity supplied to the market and hold prices up. It could also carry one year's surplus over for sale at a higher price in a year when the crop was not so abundant. If there were more farmers than required to produce the profit maximizing output, the cartel could assign each member a fair share of the limited production while planning an orderly withdrawal of unneeded resources.

But organizing such a system of agricultural cartels on a private, voluntary basis would be a completely hopeless undertaking. As Chapter 9 showed, cartels have built-in stability problems of their own. To be successful, a cartel must be able to restrict the entry of nonmembers into the industry, and it must be able to enforce its rules among its own members. Because the number of farms is so large and the barriers to entry are so low, these problems would quickly prove fatal for any privately organized agricultural cartel.

Unable to overcome their problems through voluntary coordination, then, it is not surprising that farmers have turned to the government for help. The government has one overwhelming advantage over any private cartel manager: The rules it sets have the force of law. However, the government is subject to political pressure from other interest groups too, so the rules it sets are not always those of a perfect cartel designed with only the needs of the farmer in mind.

The Origins and Principles of Marketing Orders

The first farm policies to be looked at are those embodied in the Agricultural Marketing Agreement Act of 1937. This act, like much depression-era legislation, reflects the then prevailing view that the economic problems of the time were caused by excessive competition. The particular solution to the problem adopted in the 1937 act was to permit farmers, upon a two-thirds majority vote of producers in a given region, to establish marketing orders as a means of coordinating their supply decisions. **Agricultural marketing orders,** stripped to their essentials, are agreements, enforced by the Department of Agriculture, to control the quantities of particular farm products flowing to particular markets.

Marketing orders are best understood in terms of the theory of price discrimination. Chapter 9 showed that price discrimination is often a profitable market strategy for a single firm monopoly or cartel. For discrimination to be possible, however, the buyers must be divisible into two identifiable submarkets—one with high demand elasticity and the other with low demand elasticity. Buyers in the low elasticity market are made to pay a very high price for a restricted quantity, while additional units are supplied at a lower price to the high elasticity market.

The markets for milk, citrus fruit, and many types of fresh produce can be divided in this way. The low elasticity submarket consists of those buyers who intend to consume the product fresh, and the high elasticity submarket consists of those who intend to buy it for further processing. Thus the demand for fresh milk by households has been found to be less elastic than the demand for milk to be processed into ice cream or dried milk products, the demand for fresh lemons for table use is less elastic than the demand for lemons to be processed for flavoring concentrates, and so on.

The possibility of dividing markets, however, is only a necessary, not a sufficient, condition for the practice of price discrimination. Such discrimination is not actually possible unless competition among alternative suppliers can be eliminated. For unless competition is eliminated, sellers will try to undercut one another's prices in order to get a share of the high price market until the

Agricultural marketing orders Agreements authorized by the Agricultural Marketing Agreement Act of 1937 that allow farmers collectively to control the quantities of particular farm products flowing to particular markets.

difference in prices disappears. The voting and enforcement provisions of the 1937 act are designed to prevent this kind of competition.

A Simple Example of Marketing Orders

The operation of marketing orders can be illustrated with a simplified example based on the market for lemons. Consider Exhibit 10.5, which contains two demand curves for lemons. Demand curve D_f represents the demand for fresh lemons and is moderately inelastic. MR_f is the marginal revenue curve for the fresh lemon market. Demand curve D_p represents the demand for processed lemons. To keep the diagram simple, D_p has been made perfectly elastic (although all that is really required is that it be more elastic than D_f). Because marginal revenue and price are equal when demand is perfectly elastic, marginal revenue curve MR_p for this market exactly coincides with the demand curve. The exhibit has been completed with a supply curve, S, which reflects the marginal cost of producing lemons.

Suppose now that lemon producers are organized as a perfect cartel and that spillover of lemons from the processed market into the fresh market is completely prohibited. What will be the cartel's profit maximizing strategy?

For a cartel that does not practice price discrimination, profits will be maximized by setting marginal cost equal to marginal revenue. This rule will also work for a price discriminating cartel, provided that each unit of the product is sold in the market where marginal revenue is the highest. To find the profit maximizing quantity, then, proceed as follows: Begin by selling lemons in the fresh market, as long as that is where they earn the highest marginal revenue. After output reaches 5 million boxes per year, the marginal revenue from fresh lemons drops below $2 per box. At that point, switch to selling in the processed market. Continue producing for the processed market until marginal cost and marginal revenue are equal, at a total output of 15 million boxes. Of this 15 million boxes, then, 5 million will be sold in the fresh

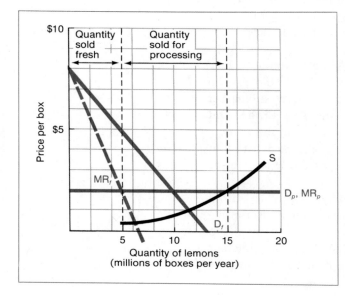

Exhibit 10.5

Profit maximization for a perfect price discriminating cartel

This exhibit shows how a perfect price discriminating cartel maximizes profits in the lemon market. To do so, it must set marginal cost equal to marginal revenue; at the same time, it must sell each box of lemons in the submarket where it will earn the highest possible marginal revenue. To find the right level of output, move down along the marginal revenue curve for the fresh market, MR_f, until it cuts the marginal revenue curve for processed lemons, MR_p. Then move along MR_p until marginal revenue and marginal cost are equal. The level is 5 million boxes of fresh lemons at $5 per box, plus 10 million boxes for processing at $2 per box.

market at $5 per box, and the remaining 10 million will be sold in the processed market at $2 per box.

This outcome, clearly, is highly beneficial to lemon growers. Under competition, it would be impossible to separate the two markets, so the 15 million boxes of lemons would all be sold at $2 per box.[2] With the aid of the marketing order, farmers are able to earn $15 million in pure profit by jacking up the price of fresh lemons to $5 per box.

Some Practical Difficulties

In practice, things do not work quite as smoothly as this for all marketing orders. Many of them are not able to function as perfect cartels in the important area of entry limitation. They can control the flow of lemons (or whatever) into the fresh and processed markets, but they cannot control the flow of farmers into lemon production.

Exhibit 10.6 shows what happens in a market operating under a marketing order but without entry control. The exhibit is identical to the previous one, except for the addition of an *average revenue curve*. This curve shows the average price of all lemons sold for each level of output, assuming that 5 million boxes are always sold fresh at $5 per box and the rest are sold for processing at $2 per box.[3]

Now, in any market where there is free entry, producers will come in as long as the revenue they expect to earn is sufficient to cover their cost. When

---

[2]Under competition, 10 million boxes would be sold fresh and only 5 million would be processed. Can you see why?

[3]It is easy to construct such a curve. When only 5 million boxes are produced, all are sold fresh, so the average revenue is $5. When 10 million are produced, half are sold fresh, so the average revenue is halfway between the processed price of $2 and the fresh price of $5. When 15 million are produced, a third are sold fresh, so the average revenue is one-third of the way between the two prices, and so on.

Exhibit 10.6

A price discriminating cartel without entry control

Some marketing orders are less than perfect cartels, because they are unable to restrict entry. This exhibit shows how such a cartel would work. Each grower would be allowed to sell the same amount of fresh lemons at $5 per box and would have to sell the rest at $2 per box. Average revenue per box would thus be between $5 and $2, depending on the total market output, as shown by the average revenue curve. New growers would enter the market, producing lemons on marginal land, until cost rose to the level of average revenue. Although that would leave no further profit opportunities for the marginal entrant, growers with superior land would still earn higher returns than under perfect competition.

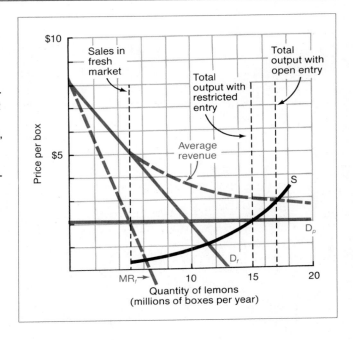

output is 15 million boxes (which is the profit maximizing level) for a cartel that cannot control entry, average revenue exceeds marginal cost, so more people will start growing lemons. Not all land is equally suited to growing lemons, however. Presumably, the best lemon growing land will already have been put to that use, so the new entrants must use inferior land where the marginal cost of growing lemons is more than $2 per box. When output has expanded to 17 million boxes, the land remaining available is so unsuitable for lemon growing that cost exceeds average revenue. Entry therefore ceases at the point where the supply curve intersects the average revenue curve.

This outcome is not really too bad for the original group of lemon growers. True, the average price of lemons is a little lower than it would have been without the new entrants, but it is still well above the cost of growing lemons on the best land. All but the marginal entrants continue to earn a better than normal rate of return on their resources.

From the economist's all-embracing point of view, however, the new equilibrium involves a troublesome waste of resources: Two million boxes of lemons are being grown and dumped in the processed market at less than their marginal cost of production. The resources used to produce those extra lemons would give greater consumer satisfaction if used to grow some other crop. The only reason they are produced is that they give a few marginal farmers an entry ticket into the cartel, which then allows them to sell part of their crop at the inflated fresh lemon price.

All in all, then, marketing orders are an effective but wasteful method of raising farmers' incomes. Even with entry control, a marketing order distorts the allocation of the product between its high valued fresh use and its lower valued processed use. And without entry control, there is the further waste of attracting inefficient producers to supply output that no one really wants. What is true of the lemon example is true of about half of all fruit, vegetable, and nut production in the United States—and of milk production as well. In these markets, the farm problem is solved, but only at a high cost to consumers.

FARM POLICY: PRICE SUPPORTS, ACREAGE CONTROLS, AND TARGET PRICES

Not all agricultural markets are suitable for the practice of price discrimination, and not all crops come under the Agricultural Marketing Agreement Act of 1937. But the growers of wheat, feed grains, cotton, rice, peanuts, and a host of other farm products want high prices and market stability just as much as do citrus and dairy farmers. For these markets, government policy makers have devised an entirely different set of restrictive policies to accomplish the same objectives. These too date back to depression-era legislation—the Agricultural Adjustment Act of 1933. For wheat, feed grains, cotton, and several other products, the three main policy instruments are price supports, acreage controls, and target prices.

Price support A program under which the government guarantees a certain minimum price to farmers by undertaking to buy any surplus that cannot be sold to private buyers at the support price.

Price Supports

Price supports are the most venerable of all instruments of farm policy. Exhibit 10.7 shows how they work, taking the market for wheat as an example. As the figure is drawn, the competitive equilibrium price is $2 per bushel, and the equilibrium quantity of output is 2 billion bushels per year.

Exhibit 10.7

The effects of direct price supports

To carry out its price support policy, the government agrees to pay $3 per bushel for all wheat that cannot be sold at that price in the open market. Because the support price is above the equilibrium price for a competitive market, this policy will reduce the quantity of wheat demanded and increase the quantity of wheat supplied. The resulting surplus will be purchased by the government and put into storage or otherwise disposed of.

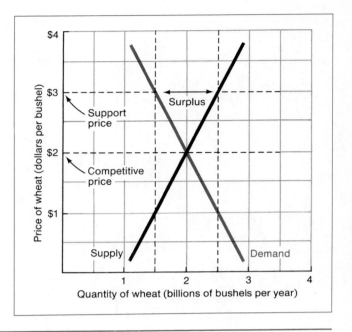

Suppose now that in order to raise farm incomes, the government declares a support price of $3 per bushel. At this price, farmers will produce 2.5 billion bushels of wheat, but consumers will buy only 1.5 billion. The government will maintain the price at the support level by buying the 1 billion bushels of surplus wheat at the support price and putting it in storage.[4]

But what is to be done with the surplus wheat? During the 1950s and 1960s, the quantities of wheat stored by the government became a national scandal. Luckily, most of the vast accumulation (or at least the part of it that had not spoiled) was cleared out during the 1973 world food crisis. Since that time, the government has tried to place greater emphasis on two other instruments of farm policy that potentially avoid the problem of surpluses.

Acreage Controls

Acreage controls are one of the instruments intended to avoid the problem of surpluses. Exhibit 10.8 shows how they work. The demand curve, D, and supply curve S_1 in this exhibit are the same as in Exhibit 10.7. The objective of government policy is also the same: Raise the price of wheat from its equilibrium level of $2 per bushel to the desired level of $3 per bushel.

The method of pushing the price up is different this time, however. Instead of offering to buy any wheat that goes unsold at the price of $3 per bushel, the government attempts to restrict the quantity of wheat produced in order to

Acreage controls Policies designed to raise agricultural prices by limiting the acreage on which certain crops can be grown.

[4]In practice, the government employs a curiously indirect method of purchasing the surplus wheat. Suppose a farmer harvests 100,000 bushels of wheat and cannot immediately find a buyer at $3 per bushel. The farmer can store the wheat and apply for a loan of $300,000—an amount equal to the value of the wheat at the support price—from a government agency called the Commodity Credit Corporation. Later, the farmer can sell the wheat and repay the loan if the price rises above $3 per bushel. If the price does not rise, the farmer can repay the loan by delivering the wheat itself to the Commodity Credit Corporation, which will then take over the problem of storing it. For all practical purposes, the effect of this complicated scheme is identical to that of a simple government promise to buy all surplus wheat at the support price.

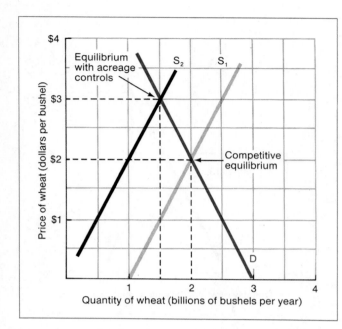

Exhibit 10.8
The effects of acreage controls
This exhibit shows how the government can raise the price of wheat to the desired level of $3 per bushel through the use of acreage controls. Acreage controls raise the cost of producing wheat, shifting the supply curve from S_1 to S_2. The effect is to push up the price of wheat without creating a surplus. However, more resources must be used to produce each bushel of wheat than would have been the case without acreage controls.

drive the price up to the desired level. It does this by requiring each farmer to take some land out of wheat production.

The effect of the artificial restriction of acreage is to raise the marginal cost of producing wheat. Ordinarily, farmers who want to grow more wheat will minimize their cost of production by adding a little more land, a little more labor, and a little more capital (machinery and fertilizer) in certain cost minimizing proportions. Now those same farmers face a new constraint: They can use more labor and capital but not more land. It is still possible to grow more wheat if the price is high enough to justify the added cost, so the new supply curve, S_2, still has an upward slope. But the increased marginal cost resulting from the constraint on farming practices pushes the supply curve to a higher level. If acreage is restricted by just the right amount, as it is in Exhibit 10.8, the same price ($3 per bushel) will be reached as was reached through direct price supports in the previous example.

Target Prices

Neither price supports nor acreage controls offer much to consumers but the prospect of spending more and getting less. With policy makers becoming more sensitive to consumer complaints, a third instrument of farm policy, **target prices,** has received increased attention.

Exhibit 10.9 shows how target prices work. It begins with the same supply and demand curves as before and the same goal of getting the revenue received by farmers up to $3 per bushel. Now, however, the government does not try to control either the quantity of wheat produced or the actual market price. Instead, it sets a target price of $3 per bushel and promises farmers a "deficiency payment" equal to the difference between the target price and the market price for each bushel produced. Knowing they will receive $3 per bushel regardless of how low the market price falls, farmers follow their supply

Target price A price guaranteed to farmers by the government; if the market price falls below the target price, the government pays the farmers the difference.

Exhibit 10.9

The effects of target prices

Target prices are a third way of raising the price of wheat to the desired level of $3 per bushel. The government announces a target price of $3 per bushel but does not actually offer to buy any wheat at this price. Farmers responding to the target price increase the quantity they supply from 2 to 2.5 billion bushels. The increased quantity drives the market price down to $1 per bushel. The government then makes a "deficiency payment" to farmers equal to the difference between the market price and the target price.

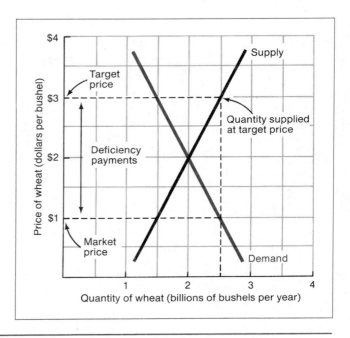

curve up to an output of 2.5 billion bushels. When this quantity of wheat is thrown on the market, the price falls to $1 a bushel. Consumers get lots of cheap wheat, and the government pays most of the bill.

Alternative Policies Compared

Which of these three policy instruments—price supports, acreage controls, or target prices—is the best? The answer turns out to depend on whose viewpoint is taken—the farmer's, the consumer's, the taxpayer's, the economist's, or the Washington policy maker's.

From the farmer's point of view, direct price supports and target prices tie for best, and acreage controls are clearly inferior. As the examples here have been constructed, both price supports and target prices raise total farm revenues from $4 billion to $7.5 billion, without any adverse impact on productivity. Acreage controls, in contrast, raise revenues to only $4.5 billion and simultaneously raise costs per unit. Valuable labor and capital are wasted cultivating some land too intensively, while other land lies altogether idle.

From the consumer's point of view, target prices are by far the best, with price supports and acreage controls equally bad. Target prices give consumers more wheat at a lower price per unit, while the other two instruments give them less wheat at greater cost.

From the taxpayer's point of view, the three policy instruments rank still differently. Acreage controls are the cheapest, involving only administrative costs. Both price supports and target prices involve large payments directly to farmers. Which of the two is more expensive for taxpayers depends on the exact shape and position of the supply and demand curves.

It is not quite so easy to say which of the three policies looks best from the economist's point of view. The answer may again depend on the exact shape and position of the supply and demand curves. However, most economists would agree that, other things being equal, the cost required to secure a benefit of a given size should be minimized, regardless of who gets the benefit.

All three of the policy instruments discussed in this chapter involve some administrative costs. All three also distort resource allocation in that they result in the wrong amount of wheat being produced. Under target prices and price support, too much wheat is grown; and under acreage controls, too little is grown. Nonetheless, price supports and acreage controls involve certain additional costs that target prices do not have. In the case of price supports, the cost is that of keeping wheat in storage to shore up the market price, instead of letting people eat it. In the case of acreage controls, the cost is the extra labor and capital required to grow each bushel of wheat when the use of land is artificially restricted. Without the alternative of a freely competitive market in wheat, many economists would therefore choose target prices as the best of the three alternatives.

Current Wheat Policy Now comes the question of which policy instrument looks best from the point of view of policy makers in Washington. Clearly, the answer depends on which interest groups Congress and the administration want to please. Because politicians normally want to please everyone at once, it is not surprising that actual farm policy employs a mixture of all three major instruments. Consider, for example, the case of wheat policy as it stood in 1978.

Case 10.1
Wheat Policy—1978 Model

Congress made a heroic effort to balance the interests of farmers, consumers, and taxpayers in the Food and Agriculture Act of 1977. This enormously complicated piece of legislation covered wheat, feed grains, cotton, dairy products, sugar, peanuts, certain less important crops, and other agriculture related matters. The act survived unchanged for only a few months. In the winter of 1978, protesting farmers won the Emergency Agriculture Act of 1978, which shifted the balance of farm policy a bit in their favor. Simplifying everything as much as possible, and focusing on just one crop—wheat—here is how U.S. farm policy looked as of mid-1978.

Support price. The 1977 act gave the secretary of agriculture the authority to set support prices within specified ranges. The 1978 support price for wheat, which was set at $2.25 per bushel, was intended to put a floor under the market price of wheat. If the price threatened to drop below the support level, farmers could obtain Commodity Credit Corporation loans to keep their crops off the market.

Target price. The 1977 act also established a target price for wheat, originally set at $2.90 per bushel for 1978. The 1978 Emergency Agriculture Act raised the price to $3.20 per bushel. Supposedly, this target price represented the cost of growing wheat, although the costing methodology employed was severely criticized by economists.

In any event, the target price is the basis for calculating deficiency payments to farmers. If the market price is less than or equal to the support price, farmers get a deficiency payment equal to the difference between the target price and the support price. If the market price rises above the support price, they get a deficiency payment equal to the difference between the target price and the market price.

Acreage controls. The 1977 and 1978 acts provided for three separate kinds of acreage controls. Of these, the most important, in the case of wheat, is a rule saying that farmers cannot receive deficiency payments unless they set aside at least 20 percent of their wheat land for soil conservation uses. If that does not prove sufficient to prevent the accumulation of surpluses, the secretary of agriculture can implement supplementary acreage control mechanisms.

Treatment of feed grains and cotton under the 1977 act is similar to the treatment of wheat, except that the target price is not set so far above the support price. Deficiency payments are consequently expected to be less important for these crops.

Source: Based on D. Gale Johnson, "The Food and Agriculture Act of 1977: Implications for Farmers, Consumers, and Taxpayers," in *Contemporary Economic Problems,* ed. William Fellner (Washington, D.C.: American Enterprise Institute, 1978), pp. 167–210.

This completes the discussion of specific agricultural problems and policies. A great many details have been left out, of course, because of space limitations and because the details of policy change almost every year.

CONCLUSIONS

Throughout this chapter, the theme has been the tension between the inherently competitive structure of U.S. agriculture and the desire of farmers to shield themselves from what they perceive to be the mixed blessing of competition. The intent is not to condemn farmers for wanting protection. They owe no moral allegiance to the economist's abstract theory of perfect competition. But not all criticisms of farm policy by nonfarmers come down to a simple tug-of-war between contending interest groups, each wanting more for itself and less for others.

First, the critics find that current farm policies are very expensive for consumers. Furthermore, as a means for transferring income from consumers to farmers, they are a very leaky bucket. Administrative costs and misallocation of resources mean that for each dollar in cost to consumers, farmers gain only pennies in real net profits.

Second, critics claim that farm policies have lost sight of their own goal of short-term stabilization. All farm policies involve built-in trade-offs between the goal of stabilization and the goal of enhancing farm incomes. A pure stabilization policy would operate to raise prices in some years and depress them in other years, so the average price would be close to that of a competitive equilibrium. In practice, many farm policies are designed to take advantage of each year's changing supply and demand conditions to raise farm prices as high as possible in that year. That is a major reason why, despite fifty years of activist farm policies, price stability has not in fact been achieved.

Third, farm policies are criticized for giving little attention to the goals of long-term adjustment and elimination of rural poverty. The most prosperous farmers get the lion's share of all subsidies, while poor farmers get little or none. How else could it be in a system where subsidies are paid out in proportion to acres planted or bushels harvested? To be sure, there are limits on the amount of subsidies that any farmer can collect in one year; but these limits are not low. The 1977 act raised the limits for major grain programs from $20,000 per farmer to $45,000. Such generous subsidies do not encourage the orderly withdrawal of resources from farming or even the orderly transfer of resources from heavily subsidized crops (such as wheat) to other valuable crops (such as soybeans) that traditionally pay their own way.

All in all, then, U.S. farm policy is not a very inspiring picture. But at least it supplies economists with plenty of opportunities to put the tools of their trade to use.

SUMMARY

1. Many agricultural markets fit the structural requirements of perfect competition very closely. They have large numbers of small firms, homogeneous products, good information systems, and free entry and exit. Farmers, however, regard perfect competition as a mixed blessing. The demand for most farm products is price inelastic; as a result, prices fluctuate sharply as the size of the crop varies from year to year. Demand is also income inelastic, with the result that the growth of demand for farm goods has not kept pace with the growth of farm productivity. This has led to depressed farm incomes.

2. One way for farmers to enhance their incomes and stabilize prices would be to form cartels. However, it would be very difficult to form purely voluntary cartels in agriculture because of the large number of producers and the ease of entry. In some cases, government policy makes it possible for farmers to engage in cartel-like practices. Marketing orders for fruits, fresh produce, and dairy products are an example. Marketing orders allow farmers to control the flow of produce into particular markets and to practice a form of price discrimination. They enhance farm incomes but only at the expense of high consumer prices and wasteful misallocation of resources.

3. Price supports are another instrument of farm policy that can be used to stabilize prices and enhance farm incomes. The government announces a support price higher than the competitive equilibrium price. That induces farmers to move up along their supply curve, increasing total quantity supplied. To maintain the support price, the government must purchase the excess quantity supplied and keep it off the market. Price supports result in high prices to consumers and substantial storage costs for taxpayers.

4. Acreage controls are a policy sometimes used to raise farm prices without encouraging surplus production. They shift the supply curve upward, which means a higher equilibrium price and a lower equilibrium quantity than without controls. However, farmers respond to these controls by applying increased labor and capital to each acre of land, thereby raising the cost of production. These increased production costs offset the advantage that farmers get from the high prices.

5. Target prices are a method of raising farm incomes without raising consumer prices. Under this policy, the government announces a target price above the competitive equilibrium price but does not agree to buy surplus output. Farmers increase output, thereby driving down the market price. The government makes up the difference between the market price and the target price with deficiency payments to farmers.

6. U.S. farm policies are subject to many criticisms. One objection is that the policies are very expensive for consumers. Another is that they pay too little attention to the goal of short-run stabilization and place too much emphasis on raising farm incomes. Still another is that they are ineffective in dealing with the problem of rural poverty, because most subsidies go to relatively well-to-do farmers.

DISCUSSION QUESTIONS

1. What aspects of the farm problem are problems from the farmer's point of view only, and what aspects are problems from the consumer's point of view as well? Is a low average level of farm prices a problem for consumers? For a given average level of farm prices, are unstable prices a problem for consumers? Explain.

2. Turn to the table of demand elasticities for farm products that is presented in Exhibit 10.2. Can you find any examples there that seem to illustrate the rule that elasticity will be greater for products with close substitutes than for those without close substitutes? The rule that the greater the proportion of the consumer's budget spent on the good, the greater the elasticity? What other explanations of differences in the elasticities shown can you think of?

3. Consider the following profit maximization rule for a price discriminating cartel: Sell in each market up to the point where the opportunity cost of selling in that market is equal to the marginal revenue in that market. Explain why this rule works, using the example shown in Exhibit 10.5. Begin with the market for fresh lemons. What is the *opportunity* cost of selling a box of lemons in this market? Once the profit maximizing quantity for the fresh lemon market is established, what is the opportunity cost of lemons for the processed market?

4. Here is a problem for readers who enjoy working with graphs: Using Exhibit 10.5 as a starting point, redraw the graph with a new demand curve, D_p, that has a slight downward slope. (Try starting at $3 on the vertical axis and descending to $2 at 20 million boxes.) Determine the profit maximizing prices and quantities for each submarket under these changed conditions.

5. Another problem involving graphs: Using Exhibits 10.7 to 10.9 as guides, draw a single graph illustrating the operation of the wheat policy described in Case 10.1.

SUGGESTIONS FOR FURTHER READING

Food and Agricultural Policy. Washington, D.C.: American Enterprise Institute, 1977. *This volume contains the proceedings of a conference covering a wide variety of topics relating to food and agricultural policy.*

Johnson, D. Gale. "The Food and Agriculture Act of 1977: Implications for Farmers, Consumers, and Taxpayers." In *Contemporary Economic Problems,* edited by William Fellner. Washington, D.C.: American Enterprise Institute, 1978. *A penetrating analysis of the major statute governing agricultural policy today.*

MacAvoy, Paul W., ed. *Federal Milk Marketing Orders and Price Supports.* Washington, D.C.: American Enterprise Institute, 1977. *This volume, which is the condensed and edited version of a report prepared by the U.S. Department of Justice, examines the regulatory scheme under which most of the milk produced in the United States is sold.*

C H A P T E R 11

OLIGOPOLY: COMPETITION AMONG THE FEW

WHAT YOU WILL LEARN IN THIS CHAPTER

Most markets have neither a single firm, as required for pure monopoly, nor the many firms required for perfect competition. Markets in which there are only a few firms, at least some of which have a large share of industry sales, are called oligopolies. This chapter will explain how to measure the degree of concentration in an oligopolistic industry and what determines the degree of concentration. It will examine several attempts to construct formal theories of oligopoly and explain why none of these attempts has been entirely successful. It will also examine evidence regarding the relationship between profits and market concentration. Throughout the chapter, a major question will be how well oligopolistic markets perform.

FOR REVIEW

Here are some important terms and concepts that will be put to use in this chapter. If you do not understand them, review them before proceeding.

- *Economies of scale (Chapter 7)*
- *Minimum efficient scale (Chapter 7)*
- *Perfect competition (Chapter 8)*
- *Pure monopoly and cartels (Chapter 9)*

As pointed out before, the term *competition* has two distinct meanings in economics. Used in "perfect competition," it refers to market structure. A market is said to be perfectly competitive if it has large numbers of small firms, a homogeneous product, well-informed buyers and sellers, and easy entry and exit. In contrast, when used as the verb "to compete," competition refers to business rivalry. In this sense, it is a matter of conduct rather than market structure. Two firms are said to compete if they treat each other as rivals in their independent efforts to do the best they can in the marketplace.

Up to this point, the emphasis has been almost entirely on the structural side of things. Rivalry has played little role in the theories that have been introduced. There is no rivalry in perfectly competitive markets because each firm sees each other firm as too small to have much influence on market conditions. Rivalry is absent from pure monopoly because there is only one firm in the market. And in a cartel, rivalry disappears as the result of an explicit decision to replace competition with coordination.

In the vast majority of markets, however, rivalry plays too big a role to be pushed into the background. Most markets have more than a single firm but

Oligopoly A market structure in which there are two or more firms, at least one of which has a large share of total sales.

fewer than the large number required for perfect competition. Most such markets also lack explicit agreements among competing firms to refrain from business rivalry. Such markets are known as **oligopolies.**

Under oligopoly, it matters very much to each firm what its rivals do. This is true even for the simplest kind of oligopoly, in which all firms produce a homogeneous product, because each firm is so large that a change in the quantity it supplies can significantly affect the market price. It is even more true in more complex forms of oligopoly, where the products of rival firms are not exactly alike. There, each firm must be prepared to react to moves that its rivals make in terms of style changes, product innovations, and promotional techniques as well as to changes in price and quantity of output and in many other areas.

The need to focus on the interaction of many firms rather than on the behavior of each firm in isolation makes it difficult to formulate a completely satisfactory theory of oligopoly. Rather than presenting a single, unified theory, then, this chapter will look at a number of fragmentary theories all tied together by one central question: *Is perfect competition necessary for satisfactory market performance, or is competition among a few large rival firms good enough?* Some economists have argued that even without explicitly agreeing to do so, oligopolists can coordinate their actions to restrict output and raise prices almost as effectively as do members of formal cartels. Others reject this idea and argue instead that competition among the few works very efficiently to serve consumer needs. Still others hedge their bets by saying that some oligopolies seem to perform better than others for reasons that are not completely understood. Although the controversy cannot be settled here, at least a map of the territory can be provided.

MARKET CONCENTRATION AND ITS DETERMINANTS

The main purpose of this chapter is to develop some insight into the performance of oligopolistic markets, but two preliminary questions need to be asked. First, how many markets are really dominated by just a few firms (and how many is "a few")? And second, what determines the number of firms in a market and the size of their market shares? Knowing the answers to these questions will make it easier to understand both how markets work and what government policy is toward monopoly and oligopoly.

Measuring Market Concentration

Concentration ratio The percentage of all sales contributed by the four or eight largest firms in a market.

Concentration ratios provide a rough-and-ready measure of the extent to which markets are dominated by a few firms. The most common of these ratios are the four-firm concentration ratio (which measures the percentage of sales attributed to the top four firms in a given market) and the eight-firm concentration ratio (which measures the share of the top eight firms). Exhibit 11.1 gives concentration ratios for a representative selection of manufacturing industries. At the top of the figure are industries that are classic oligopolies; they consist of a handful of firms that control virtually the entire market. For other industries, shown in the middle of the chart, the top four firms account for less than half of industry sales, although these firms are clearly large enough not to fit the strict requirements of perfect competition. Only in the case of commercial lithographic printing does it appear safe to say that there are

Exhibit 11.1

Four-firm and eight-firm concentration for selected industries, 1972
Concentration ratios measure the percentage of industry output contributed by the largest firms. This representative selection of thirty-one U.S. industries shows a wide range of concentration ratios. The figures given here do not take into account foreign competition or the fact that some industries produce mainly for local markets.

Source: U.S. Department of Commerce, Bureau of the Census, *Statistical Abstract of the United States*, 98th ed. (Washington, D.C.: Government Printing Office, 1977), pp. 808–809.

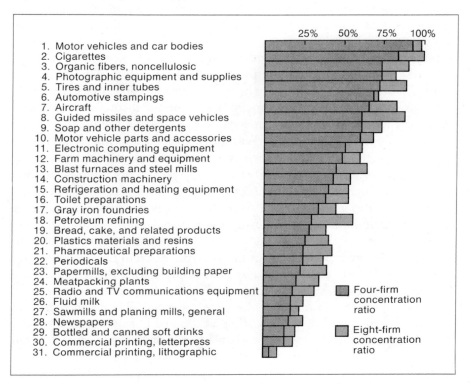

1. Motor vehicles and car bodies
2. Cigarettes
3. Organic fibers, noncellulosic
4. Photographic equipment and supplies
5. Tires and inner tubes
6. Automotive stampings
7. Aircraft
8. Guided missiles and space vehicles
9. Soap and other detergents
10. Motor vehicle parts and accessories
11. Electronic computing equipment
12. Farm machinery and equipment
13. Blast furnaces and steel mills
14. Construction machinery
15. Refrigeration and heating equipment
16. Toilet preparations
17. Gray iron foundries
18. Petroleum refining
19. Bread, cake, and related products
20. Plastics materials and resins
21. Pharmaceutical preparations
22. Periodicals
23. Papermills, excluding building paper
24. Meatpacking plants
25. Radio and TV communications equipment
26. Fluid milk
27. Sawmills and planing mills, general
28. Newspapers
29. Bottled and canned soft drinks
30. Commercial printing, letterpress
31. Commercial printing, lithographic

Four-firm concentration ratio

Eight-firm concentration ratio

"many" firms, each one of which is "small" relative to the size of the market. All in all, somewhere between a third and a half of all manufacturing output comes from markets in which the top four firms control half the markets or more.

The Determinants of Market Concentration

Exhibit 11.1 gives a rough indication of the extent of industrial concentration. The next important question is: Why are some industries more concentrated than others? The phenomenon of economies of scale provides a logical place to start answering this question.

Economies of Scale Chapter 7 introduced the concept of economies of scale. A firm is said to experience economies of scale if its long-run average costs decline as its scale of output increases. Shapes of long-run average cost curves vary from one industry to another, but statistical studies have indicated that many industries fit the pattern of an L-shaped long-run average cost curve.

Such a cost curve shows economies of scale initially, followed by a range of constant returns to scale.

The point at which the average total cost curve stops falling and begins to flatten out is known as the minimum efficient scale for the firm—an important determinant of market concentration. Some estimates of plant-level economies of scale made by F. M. Scherer, given earlier in Exhibit 7.10, are reproduced in Exhibit 11.2. To make it easier to draw implications about market concentration, two new columns have been added to the one from the original table. One of the two shows the theoretical minimum four-firm concentration ratio implied by the minimum economic scale for the industry. This is simply the minimum economic scale as a percentage of industry output, multiplied by four. The industry cannot be any less concentrated than this without forcing firms to use inefficiently small plants. The other new column in Exhibit 11.2 shows the actual 1967 four-film concentration ratio for the industry. In every case, this is much larger than the theoretical minimum. The clear implication, then, is that economies of scale *at the plant level* are not sufficient to explain the observed degree of concentration.

Economies of scale are not necessarily limited to the plant level, however. In many industries, firms operate more than a single plant. Large multi-plant firms can frequently cut costs by using longer production runs or by having each plant specialize in a limited range of products. They can also economize on such overhead functions as accounting, research, advertising, and marketing.

Another kind of adjustment also has to be made in the data shown in Exhibit 11.2 before inferences about market concentration can be drawn. Not all the industries listed operate in a single national market. Some markets are separated into regional submarkets by high transportation costs. Cement, steel, and glass bottles are examples. Others are separated into distinct product submarkets—for example, roller bearings as opposed to ball bearings. A given level of economies of scale would explain a higher degree of concentration in one submarket than in a unified national market.

Industry	Minimum Efficient Plant Size as Percent of U.S. Consumption	Theoretical Minimum Four-Firm Concentration Ratio	Actual 1967 Four-Firm Concentration Ratio
Ball and roller bearings	1.4	5.6	54
Beer brewing	3.4	13.6	40
Cement	1.7	6.8	29
Cigarettes	6.6	26.4	81
Cotton and synthetic fabrics	0.2	0.8	36
Glass containers	1.5	6.0	60
Paints	1.4	5.6	22
Petroleum refining	1.9	7.6	33
Refrigerators	14.1	56.4	73
Shoes	0.2	0.8	26
Storage batteries	1.9	7.6	61
Wide strip steel works	2.6	10.4	48

Exhibit 11.2

Plant level economies of scale and market concentration

Column 1 of this table gives estimates of the minimum efficient scale for an individual plant in twelve industries. Multiplying these estimates by four gives Column 2, the theoretical minimum four-firm concentration ratio for each industry. Comparison of Columns 2 and 3 indicates that all industries shown are substantially more concentrated than plant level economies of scale alone can explain.

Source: F. M. Scherer, Alan Beckenstein, Erich Kaufer, and R. D. Murphey, *The Economics of Multi-Plant Operation: An International Comparisons Study* (Cambridge, Mass.: Harvard University Press, 1975), Table 3.11, p. 80. Copyright © 1975 by the President and Fellows of Harvard College; all rights reserved.

Taking all these things into account, Scherer drew the following conclusions about the extent to which observed concentration ratios could be explained on the basis of economies of scale: For beer brewing and refrigerators, economies of multi-plant operation seemed sufficient to explain approximately the actual degree of market concentration. For cigarettes, concentrated oligopoly at the national level could be explained only if one placed great emphasis on economies of scale in advertising and the creation of brand image. In the case of glass containers, steel, and bearings, economies of scale appeared sufficient to explain a concentration ratio of 50 or more within particular regional or product submarkets but not within the national market. In petroleum refining and cement, such a degree of concentration might be explained by economies of scale in some sparsely populated submarkets where transportation costs played an especially large role. In the remaining four industries—fabrics, paints, shoes, and batteries—the existing degree of concentration was substantially greater than anything Scherer could explain on the basis of any kind of economies of scale.

Scherer's results are not, of course, the last word on the subject. For example, his work has been criticized for not placing sufficient emphasis on various intangible benefits of large-scale business organization that neither economists nor accountants can measure accurately.[1] Nonetheless, Scherer's belief that economies of scale do not entirely determine market concentration is probably still the majority view. It is thus worth considering other possible determinants.

Barriers to Entry One reason that an industry may be more concentrated than economies of scale alone would indicate is that there may be barriers to entry of new firms. Even if profits in the industry are unusually high, prospective entrepreneurs may for some reason be unable to duplicate the performance of existing firms. As demand for the product expands, then, growth can come only through the expansion of existing firms, even after all economies of scale have been exhausted.

As in the case of pure monopoly, barriers to entry into oligopolistic industries are sometimes created on purpose by federal, state, or local government policy. In such industries, policy stops short of creating a pure franchised monopoly but still limits the number of competitors to fewer than would exist under free entry. For example, entry into many segments of the trucking industry was for years tightly controlled by the Interstate Commerce Commission. Despite some recent reforms, these legal barriers to entry have still not been entirely dismantled. At the state level, entry into many professions—law, medicine, plumbing, hairdressing, and dozens of others—is limited by licensing boards. Entry into rental housing or retailing in many communities is limited by local zoning regulations. The list of such legal barriers to entry goes on and on.

A second kind of barrier to entry is ownership of some nonreproducible resource. For example, entry into the ski resort industry is limited by the availability of suitable mountains. Entry into extractive industries is, in at least some cases, limited by ownership of the best available natural resources by

---

[1] See John S. McGee, "Efficiency and Economies of Size," in *Industrial Concentration: The New Learning*, ed. Harvey J. Goldschmid, H. Michael Mann, and J. Fred Weston (Boston: Little, Brown, 1974), pp. 55–96.

existing firms. In other markets, the nonreproducible resources in question are human. Entry into the movie industry might be difficult, for example, if the top-quality stars were all under contract to existing firms. Whatever the reason, ownership of a nonreproducible resource gives existing firms an advantage over new entrants and thus constitutes a barrier to entry.

Patents and copyrights, another important class of barriers to entry, operate under oligopoly as well as under pure monopoly and can be placed in either of the two categories of barriers just discussed. A patent or copyright can be treated as a restrictive government regulation. Alternatively, ownership of a patent or copyright can be treated just like ownership of any other non-reproducible resource. Whichever point of view is adopted, patents and copyrights clearly can make entry difficult and thus can contribute to market concentration.

As the term is used here, a *barrier to entry* is something that prevents new entrants from duplicating the performance of existing firms in terms of cost or quality of product. It does not mean that every effort or expense that a firm must undertake to enter a market should be considered such a barrier. To start a new firm, a prospective entrepreneur must be willing to bear risks, must find investors to put up capital, must recruit a labor force, must attract customers, and so on. All these things are hard work—often hard enough to discourage less enterprising individuals from making the effort. Nonetheless, the need for hard work is not itself a barrier to entry in the economic sense. When entrepreneurs are freely able to go out and buy the various building blocks of their new firms in the same market where existing firms buy their inputs, barriers to entry are not a determinant of market structure.

Random Influences Suppose there is a market with no economies of scale and no barriers to entry. Will such a market necessarily be inhabited by a large number of firms, all of roughly equal size? Not necessarily, it seems. Even after all other factors have been allowed for, pure chance appears to play a very significant role in determining market concentration. Just how significant is suggested by the following case study based on Scherer's work.

Case 11.1
Chance as a Determinant of Economic Concentration

How much market concentration can be expected in a world from which economies of scale, mergers, government policies, and all other identifiable determinants of concentration are absent? Northwestern University professor F. M. Scherer once performed a computer simulation experiment to try to find out. The answer, he discovered, is that even in such a world, a high degree of market concentration appears not only possible but likely.

Scherer began by constructing an imaginary industry composed of fifty identical firms, each with a 2 percent share of the market. He assumed zero economies of scale. Each year the industry as a whole would grow by 6 percent, but each individual firm in the industry would have a certain random probability of growing a little faster or a little slower than the average. The average rate of growth and the variability of individual firm growth around this average were set equal to the actual rates observed for *Fortune*'s list of the five hundred top industrial corporations. Having gotten all firms off to a fair start, Scherer programmed his computer to follow the industry through 140 years of simulated history. His results for sixteen repetitions of the experiment are shown in Exhibit 11.3.

Exhibit 11.3

Concentration in a simulated market

This exhibit shows the results of a computer simulation experiment on market concentration conducted by F. M. Scherer. Scherer began by assuming a hypothetical industry of fifty firms, all identical and all experiencing no economies of scale. He assumed that the industry would grow at a rate of 6 percent per year but that, by luck, various individual firms would grow faster or slower. In sixteen repetitions of the experiment, shown here, chance alone soon resulted in a moderate to substantial degree of concentration, even when other sources of concentration, such as economies of scale and barriers to entry, were entirely absent.

Four-Firm Concentration Ratios Resulting from Sixteen Simulation Runs of a Stochastic Growth Process Model, with Mean Growth of 6 Percent per Annum and a Standard Deviation of 16 Percent

	Four-Firm Concentration Ratio at Year:							
	1	20	40	60	80	100	120	140
Run 1	8.0	19.5	29.3	36.3	40.7	44.9	38.8	41.3
Run 2	8.0	20.3	21.4	28.1	37.5	41.6	50.8	55.6
Run 3	8.0	18.8	28.9	44.6	43.1	47.1	56.5	45.0
Run 4	8.0	20.9	26.7	31.8	41.9	41.0	64.5	59.8
Run 5	8.0	23.5	33.2	43.8	60.5	60.5	71.9	63.6
Run 6	8.0	21.3	26.6	29.7	35.8	51.2	59.1	72.9
Run 7	8.0	21.1	31.4	29.0	42.8	52.8	50.3	53.1
Run 8	8.0	21.6	23.5	42.2	47.3	64.4	73.1	76.6
Run 9	8.0	18.4	29.3	38.0	45.3	42.5	43.9	52.4
Run 10	8.0	20.0	29.7	43.7	40.1	43.1	42.9	42.9
Run 11	8.0	23.9	29.1	29.5	43.2	50.1	57.1	71.7
Run 12	8.0	15.7	23.3	24.1	34.5	41.1	42.9	53.1
Run 13	8.0	23.8	31.3	44.8	43.5	42.8	57.3	65.2
Run 14	8.0	17.8	23.3	29.3	54.2	51.4	56.0	64.7
Run 15	8.0	21.8	18.3	23.9	31.9	33.5	43.9	65.7
Run 16	8.0	17.5	27.1	28.3	30.7	39.9	37.7	35.3
Average	8.0	20.4	27.0	33.8	42.1	46.7	52.9	57.4

Source: F. M. Scherer, *Industrial Market Structure and Economic Performance* (Chicago: Rand McNally, 1970), Table 4.4, p. 126. Copyright © 1970 by Rand McNally College Publishing Company. Reprinted by permission.

Why do industries become so highly concentrated when everyone has a fair start and when there are no economies of scale? The answer, according to Scherer, is pure luck. By chance, some firms get an early run of luck and grow faster than the average several years in a row. Once they lead the pack, it is hard for the followers to catch up, since, by definition, each firm has an equal chance to grow by a given *percentage* amount each year. The result is that the imaginary industries end up with just about the same degree of market concentration observed in the real world.

Source: The experiment is described in F. M. Scherer, *Industrial Market Structure and Economic Performance* (Chicago: Rand McNally, 1970), pp. 125–130.

COORDINATION AND INTERDEPENDENCE UNDER OLIGOPOLY

After this explanation of why some industries are more concentrated than others, the chapter can turn to the behavior of firms in concentrated markets. In particular, it will examine the interdependence of firms in an oligopolistic market and the conditions under which the firms may be able to coordinate their price and output decisions to their mutual advantage.

Joan V. Robinson
(1903–   )

Joan Robinson is best known as a pioneer in the study of the behavior of firms in less than perfectly competitive markets. When she was a young assistant lecturer at Cambridge University, she decided to stand the accepted procedures of economics on their head. "It is customary," she wrote, "in setting out the principles of economic theory, to open with the analysis of a perfectly competitive world, and to treat monopoly as a special case. . . . This process can with advantage be reversed. . . . It is more proper to set out the analysis of monopoly, treating perfect competition as a special case." These words and the analysis to support them appeared in her *Economics of Imperfect Competition* in 1933. The book established her reputation immediately and remains one of the basic pioneering contributions to this branch of economics. (As often happens in economics, a similar theory was developed independently and published in the same year—by E. H. Chamberlin.)

Microeconomics was not Robinson's only interest, however. She was a pioneer of macroeconomic thinking. Even as her work on imperfect competition came out, she was involved in the debate that preceded the publication of Keynes's *General Theory*. In fact, in much of her later macro work, she is critical of the very kind of "partial" analysis on which her theory of imperfect competition rests.

Robinson has always been intensely interested in policy questions. In all her policy writings, she is a vehement critic of the market. In 1945, she wrote in *Private Enterprise and Public Control*:

The system of private property in its modern developments leads to great evils. Its inequality is not only an outrage on social justice, but also on common sense. It leads to large scale waste through unemployment, while the development of monopoly creates artificial scarcities and the dominance of the interests of property over the interests of human beings twists the whole system into a form for which it is impossible to find any reasonable justification.

Her opposition to the market and her interest in broad normative questions also led her to write *An Essay on Marxian Economics* (1956), *Economic Philosophy* (1962), and *Freedom and Necessity* (1970). Now long past retirement age, Robinson continues an active life as debater, social critic, and economic heretic.

Oligopolistic Interdependence

Oligopolistic interdependence The necessity, in an oligopolistic market, for each firm to pay close attention to the behavior and likely reactions of its rivals when planning its own market strategy.

When there are only a few firms in a market, it matters very much to each firm what its rivals do. Economists call the situation **oligopolistic interdependence.** This interdependence makes it very difficult to develop a theory of pure economizing in highly concentrated markets. A simple example will explain the problem.

Imagine a market in which there are only two firms—Alpha Company and Zed Enterprises. Their product costs $1 per unit to make. If both firms set their price at $5 per unit, each will sell 100 units per month at a profit of $4 per unit, for a total monthly profit of $400. If both firms set their price at $4 per unit, each will sell 120 units at a profit of $3 per unit for a total profit of $360. Which price will the firms actually set? Clearly, $5 is the price that will maximize their joint profits; but under oligopoly, this price may not represent a stable equilibrium.

Exhibit 11.4 shows why. It presents the alternative pricing strategies available *as they appear to Alpha Company.* In addition to the two possibilities already mentioned, Alpha must consider two more. One new possibility is to cut its price to $4 while Zed holds at $5. That will allow Alpha to steal away a lot of Zed's customers and to sell 150 units, for a profit of $450. The other new possibility is for Alpha to hold its price at $5 while Zed cuts to $4. Then Zed

Exhibit 11.4

Profits for Alpha Company under different pricing strategies

This exhibit shows the profits that Alpha Company would earn under different pricing strategies for Alpha and its rival, Zed Enterprises. If both firms price at $5, each earns $400. If both cut their price to $4, they continue to split the market; and each earns $360. If Alpha cuts its price while Zed does not, Alpha steals many of Zed's customers and earns $450. If Zed cuts its price while Alpha's remains at $5, Zed steals many of Alpha's customers, leaving Alpha with only $240 in profit.

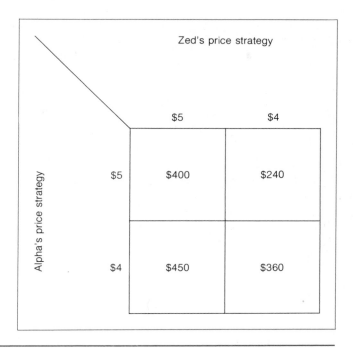

will steal a lot of Alpha's customers and leave Alpha selling only 60 units, for a total profit of $240.

So what will happen? We just don't know! The theories that have helped explain many other market structures do not work for this simple oligopoly problem. We know how the firms can maximize joint profits if they coordinate their efforts. We know how to maximize Alpha's profits if we know what Zed is going to do. We know how to maximize Zed's profits if we know what Alpha is going to do. But none of that is enough. Something is still missing. The missing link needed to solve the problem of oligopolistic interdependence is some assumption about *how Alpha thinks Zed will react* to each possible move that Alpha might make.

Types of Oligopolistic Interdependence All formal theories of oligopoly include some assumption about oligopolistic interdependence—about how each firm will react to its rival's market behavior. Although none of these can be upheld as the single correct theory, several are interesting enough to be worth describing briefly.

One very important possibility is that the rival firms in an oligopolistic market will recognize that they are all in the same boat and will tacitly coordinate their activities. Do unto others as you would have them do unto you will be the golden rule in such a market. Each firm will choose the price and output strategy that, if chosen by all the others, will maximize joint profits. In terms of the example in Exhibit 11.4, each firm will choose a price of $5. In the more general case, the golden rule will lead to a market equilibrium under oligopoly that will be the same as for a pure monopoly or a perfect cartel.

At the opposite extreme from the assumption of tacit coordination is the assumption that each firm will expect its rivals to do the worst thing possible. In the example, Alpha's managers will ask themselves what is the best they can do if Zed does the worst—that is, cuts its price. The answer is that Alpha must cut its price too. If Zed follows the same reasoning, both firms will end up charging $4.

A more general variation of this theory is based on the assumption that each firm will expect its rivals to match its price decreases but not its increases. Under this assumption, a firm will be reluctant to lower its price because it knows that will only touch off a mutually destructive price war. At the same time, the firm will be reluctant to raise its price because its rivals will keep their prices down and steal customers. This theory has the curious property of saying that, under oligopoly, prices are not likely to change—without saying why prices are at one particular level rather than another in the first place. Nonetheless, it is claimed that some oligopolists actually do have exactly these expectations about their rivals' pricing strategies.

Objection to Formal Theories

Unfortunately, all the assumptions about oligopolistic interdependence just described suffer from a common failing: They make business managers sound terribly naive.

Consider first the assumption of tacit coordination. The best evidence available is that rival firms are not likely to be able to achieve true joint profit maximization through tacit coordination alone. Cartels are explicit agreements among rivals to coordinate price and output strategies. Often cartel agreements are written up in a great detail, with elaborate enforcement and penalty clauses. Yet cartels are notoriously unstable. For each one that works, many fall apart before they get off the ground. And if explicit coordination is so difficult to achieve, how can tacit cooperation have any hope of working very well for very long?

On the other hand, it has been argued that it is just as naive for business-people always to assume that their rivals will do the very worst, when such behavior can clearly be mutually harmful. People have devised ingenious games in which, under controlled conditions, with carefully measured rewards and penalties, experimental subjects play the roles of rival managers. The results of some of these games have shown that after an initial period of all-out competition, opponents gradually learn to play cooperatively, even if they never meet or communicate directly.[2]

Informal Theories of Oligopoly

Many economists have simply given up the hope of developing a workable formal theory of oligopoly. Instead, they have resorted to various informal theories and rules of thumb that may be of some use in judging the perform-ance of oligopolistic markets. These theories can be presented simply as a list of circumstances under which tacit coordination among oligopolists is likely to be more or less successful.

Number and Size of Firms There is little doubt that the number and size of firms in a market make a lot of difference. Tacit coordination in a market with only two or three big firms of roughly equal size is surely more plausible than,

---

[2]See, for example, L. B. Lave, "An Empirical Approach to the Prisoner's Dilemma Game," *Quarterly Journal of Economics* 76 (August 1962): 424–436.

say, coordination in a market with an eight-firm concentration ratio of 40 percent. A major reason is that the larger the number of firms, the more likely it is that any one firm can cut prices under the table without its rivals' knowledge.

The relative size of the various firms in the market is probably also important. Many observers have suggested that tacit coordination of prices is easier in an industry where there is one clearly dominant firm. That firm may then be able to act as a price leader. Under the strongest form of **price leadership,** firms are no longer uncertain about how their rivals will react to price changes. The leader can be confident that the others will follow it both up and down. The others can be certain that if they follow the leader, others will too; but if they initiate price increases (or decreases) of their own, others will not follow. Ideally, this arrangement can lead to joint monopoly profits for the industry.

However, tacit coordination cannot always be inferred solely from the timing of price changes. In any industry, someone has to be the first to change prices if underlying market conditions change. Even if one particular firm is usually the first to make a move, its role may be no more than that of a barometer telling others that the pressure of demand or cost has made a change necessary.

Nature of the Product The nature of the product is also believed to affect the ease or difficulty of achieving tacit coordination. A homogeneous product with a smooth flow of orders tends to make coordination easier. A variable product with lumpy or irregular orders tends to make it more difficult. With a nonhomogeneous product, there are simply too many things to coordinate. It is not enough that all firms tacitly agree to sell at the same price. They also have to agree on a schedule of allowances above and below the basic price for changes in quality, accelerated or delayed delivery, size of the customer's order, and so on. Under these conditions, an agreement to raise the price above the competitive level, even if it can be sustained, will probably not lead to higher profits. It will more likely lead instead to an outbreak of competition in terms of quality, scheduling, volume discounts, and so on. These things will add to the cost of doing business until excess profits disappear. The next two chapters will return to this theme of nonprice competition several times.

Information Tacit coordination under oligopoly, if possible at all, is probable only in a market where firms have fairly good information about what their rivals are doing. Clearly, there can be no tacit understanding that all firms will charge the same price or follow a price leader if prices are kept secret. So there is little doubt that secrecy is an enemy of coordination under oligopoly.

There is a subtle danger in trying to reverse this formula, however. If secrecy is the enemy of coordination, does that make secrecy the friend of competition? From there it is only a short step to the proposition that bad information is the friend of good market performance. But this last statement is clearly nonsense. The primary function of the market system, after all, is to facilitate the flow of information among potential buyers and sellers. Perfect markets require perfect information, not perfect secrecy.

Growth and Innovation The rates of growth and innovation in a market are a final factor likely to affect the ease or difficulty of tacit coordination

Price leadership A situation in an oligopolistic market where increases or decreases in price by one dominant firm, known as the price leader, are matched by all or most other firms in the market.

among rival oligopolists. In a market where product characteristics, production technologies, and the personalities of individual buyers and sellers do not change from year to year, an agreement among firms, whether tacit or explicit, need never be reworked once it is established. In a market where things change rapidly, any agreement that is reached will soon be rendered obsolete by changing circumstances or disrupted when newly entering buyers or sellers have to be accommodated. Given the uncertainties of establishing tacit agreements and the illegality of establishing explicit agreements, one would expect rival firms to be able to coordinate their activities less successfully the more rapid the pace of growth and change.

MEASURING MARKET PERFORMANCE UNDER OLIGOPOLY

Neither the formal nor the informal theories of oligopoly just discussed give conclusive answers to the question asked at the outset of this chapter—namely, whether rivalry among a few firms in a concentrated market is sufficient to secure good market performance. Good market performance, in this context, means performance resembling that of a perfectly competitive market, with prices equal or close to marginal cost and all major opportunities for mutually competitive transactions among consumers, firms, and resource owners carried out. Poor performance means performance resembling that of a monopoly or cartel, in which efforts of firms to secure higher profits result in equilibrium prices higher than marginal cost and unrealized opportunities for potentially mutually beneficial trades between consumers and resource owners.

With pure theory unable to answer questions about market performance, it is natural for economists to try to answer the questions by the statistical examination of empirical data. Because it is usually difficult to measure directly whether a gap exists between a firm's output prices and its marginal costs, the most common approach taken is an indirect one. If firms in concentrated industries can be shown, on the average, to earn higher than normal rates of return on capital, it is reasoned, the inference that they are behaving more like monopolists than like perfect competitors can be drawn. If, on the other hand, firms in concentrated industries appear to earn rates of return no higher, on the average, than firms in relatively unconcentrated industries, it can be inferred that oligopolies perform about as well as more competitively structured industries.

Early Empirical Studies

The first person to try this approach in a systematic way was University of California professor Joe Bain. In 1951, he published the results of a study of forty-two selected industries for the years 1936–1940. These results are shown in Exhibit 11.5. According to Bain's interpretation of the data, industries with concentration ratios over 70 earned higher profits than less concentrated industries. The relationship between profits and concentration was not perfect and not overwhelmingly strong, but it did exist.

During the 1950s and 1960s, many of Bain's students and followers repeated his studies for other industries and other years. Most of them got the same results—a weak but persistent relationship between profits and concentration.

Exhibit 11.5

The relationship of market concentration to profits
This table shows the relationship between market concentration and profits, according to a pioneering study published in 1951. The table appears to indicate that firms in industries with concentration ratios over 70 earn higher profits, on the average, than firms in less concentrated industries. The validity of the relationship shown by the figures has been the subject of lively debate ever since.

Average of Industry Average Profit Rates, by Concentration Groups, Forty-two Selected Industries, 1936–1940

Eight-Firm Concentration Ratio	Average Profit Rate	Number of Industries
90–100	12.7	8
80–89	9.8	11
70–79	16.3	3
60–69	5.8	5
50–59	5.8	4
40–49	8.6	2
30–39	6.3	5
20–29	10.4	2
10–19	17.0	1
0–9	9.1	1

Source: Joe S. Bain, ''Relation of Profit-Rate to Industry Concentration,'' *Quarterly Journal of Economics* 65 (August 1951): 293. Copyright © 1951 by the President and Fellows of Harvard College; all rights reserved. Reprinted by permission.

It became part of the conventional wisdom of economics that the more highly concentrated an industry, the more likely its performance would resemble that of a cartel or monopoly. This would be true even if there were no conspiracy among rivals to raise prices and divide markets.

More Recent Results

As faith in this proposition grew, economists tried harder and harder to verify it, using the more powerful statistical techniques and better data that became available year by year. Curiously, the harder they tried, the more elusive the relationship became. Some studies showed that if adjustments were made for the absolute size of firms in different markets, the relationship between concentration and profits tended to disappear. Other studies showed that if adjustment were made for differences in advertising expenditures, the relationship would disappear. Still other studies seemed to show that results like Bain's held only in years of depression and recession and disappeared with prosperity.

What is more, even as the relationship between concentration and profits was becoming less certain, economists were also becoming less certain about how such a relationship should be interpreted even if it were confirmed. New reasons were discovered why firms in more concentrated industries might appear to earn higher profits than firms in less concentrated industries. These reasons had nothing to do with monopoly pricing or tacit collusion. For example, a concentrated industry that was growing rapidly might need to earn high profits to attract the new capital it needed. Or the high profits of the largest firms in each concentrated industry might simply reflect the firms' superior efficiency relative to smaller firms in the same industry. Finally, the higher profits that some concentrated industries appeared to earn might not be profits at all in the economic sense. They might reflect only the fact that the categories used by accountants to classify business transactions are different from those used by economic theorists.

It is still too early to tell which team of econometricians will have the last word in the debate over concentration and profits or which team of theorists will have the last word on what the relationship means, if there really is one. For the moment, however, it appears that the empirical approach is not much more successful than the theoretical approach in solving the riddle of oligopoly behavior.

CONCLUSIONS

This chapter began with the question of whether rivalry among the few is enough to guarantee satisfactory market performance. After reviewing the apparent determinants of market concentration, the available formal and informal theories of oligopoly behavior, and the empirical evidence on the relationship between concentration and profits, the answer is maybe yes, maybe no—it all depends.

Perhaps, though, economists are looking in the wrong place for an answer. The search for a theory of oligopoly is a search for a theory that is analogous to the theories of perfect competition and monopoly but lying somewhere in between. The theories of monopoly and competition, however, are theories of pure economizing. They deal with only a part of business reality—the search for maximum profits under *given* conditions of demand, technology, and resource availability. Perhaps economists would do better in their efforts to understand competition among the few if they broadened their focus to take into account more of the entrepreneurial elements in business decision making.

There have already been some hints that this is where they should look. The subjects of advertising competition and nonprice competition have come up more than once. These forms of competition involve entrepreneurial decision making. The question of barriers to entry has been raised. Entry of a new firm into an industry is an entrepreneurial decision. And such entrepreneurial variables as product homogeneity, growth, and innovation play major roles in determining how firms behave in concentrated markets. Without further delay, then, a new chapter will look into some of these things.

SUMMARY

1. Markets that have more than one firm but fewer than many firms are called *oligopolies.* Any study of oligopoly must pay close attention to the phenomenon of business rivalry. The conduct of oligopolistic firms is very much influenced by what each firm expects its rivals to do in the competitive struggle for sales and profits.
2. The four-firm (or eight-firm) concentration ratio for a market is the percentage of industry output contributed by the top four (or eight) firms in the market. Something between a third and a half of all manufacturing output in the United States comes from markets with a four-firm concentration ratio of 50 or more.
3. Economies of scale are one major determinant of market concentration. Plant level economies alone, however, are not enough to explain observed concentration ratios. Economies of multi-plant operation must also be taken into account. Even when multi-plant scale economies are accounted for, some market concentration remains to be explained by barriers to entry and random influences.

4. Many attempts have been made to construct a formal theory of oligopoly. Such a theory would resemble the theories of perfect competition and pure monopoly but would lie somewhere between the two. However, the formal theory of oligopoly to date has not been conspicuously successful. The reason is that it is very difficult to know how firms will react to the price and output decisions of their rivals. No simple assumption works for all cases.

5. Even in the absence of a formal theory of oligopoly, an attempt can be made to list factors that are likely to facilitate or hamper tacit coordination among rival firms. Among the most important factors are the number and size of firms in the market, the nature of the product, the availability of information about rival firms, and the rates of growth and innovation in the market.

6. Partly because oligopoly theory does not give clear answers about market performance in concentrated industries, economists have made many efforts to see whether firms in such industries are more profitable than those in less concentrated industries. If they were, that might indicate that oligopolists were able to achieve tacit coordination of their price and output decisions. Initial results reported during the 1950s appeared to indicate that concentrated industries were more profitable. More recent studies, however, have called these early results into question.

DISCUSSION QUESTIONS

1. What is the difference between rivalry and competition? What does it mean to say that rivalry is a matter of conduct, while competition is a matter of structure?

2. The data on market concentration in Exhibit 11.1 relate only to manufacturing, the sector of the economy that has been studied most closely in this respect. How highly concentrated do you think the following sectors of the economy are: Agriculture? Transportation? Services? Retail trade? Communications? What factors do you think probably account for concentration or lack of concentration in each of these sectors?

3. Evaluate the following statement: Barriers to entry are lower in the restaurant industry than in the airline industry, because a restaurant requires only a few workers and a few thousand dollars in capital, while even a small airline requires hundreds of workers and millions of dollars in capital.

4. Would you consider the market for university education to be an oligopoly? What factors do you think determine the structure of the university "industry"? How important are economies of scale? Barriers to entry? Chance factors?

5. Oligopoly has sometimes been called a game, because each player's behavior depends on thinking ahead to outguess the strategies and reactions of rivals. How does oligopoly resemble such games as chess? Bridge? Tennis? War? Would it surprise you to learn that the formal theory of games is not much more practical help in understanding actual games than formal theories of oligopoly are in understanding actual oligopoly behavior? Explain.

SUGGESTIONS FOR FURTHER READING

Brozen, Yale, ed. *The Competitive Economy.* Morristown, N.J.: General Learning Press, 1975.
Of the forty-two articles and excerpts from books collected in this volume, too many to list separately are relevant to this chapter. Brozen is skeptical of the view that concentration necessarily implies poor market performance, and many of the readings reflect this point of view.

Goldschmid, Harvey J.; Mann, H. Michael; and Weston, J. Fred. *Industrial Concentration: The New Learning.* Boston: Little, Brown, 1974.

This volume is in the form of a series of debates between very highly qualified representatives of contrasting views on many of the problems discussed in this chapter. Especially relevant are Chapter 2 (a debate between F. M. Scherer and John S. McGee on economies of scale as a determinant of concentration) and Chapter 4 (which matches Harold Demsetz against Leonard Weiss on the concentration-profits issue).

Leftwich, Richard H. *The Price System and Resource Allocation.* 7th ed. Hinsdale, Ill.: Dryden Press, 1979.

Chapter 12 presents an intermediate level treatment of the topics covered in this chapter.

Nicholson, Walter. *Intermediate Microeconomics and its Application.* 2d ed. Hinsdale, Ill.: Dryden Press, 1979.

Chapter 12 covers many of the topics covered in this chapter; an appendix presents some attempted formal theories of oligopoly pricing.

C H A P T E R **12**

ADVERTISING AND NONPRICE COMPETITION

WHAT YOU WILL LEARN IN THIS CHAPTER

This chapter introduces a number of topics in competition and market performance. First, it discusses how advertising affects consumers and why consumers, as well as businesses, sometimes act as entrepreneurs. Next, it reviews an ongoing controversy concerning the conditions under which advertising can act as a barrier to entry into a market or industry. In connection with the discussion of advertising and nonprice competition, it introduces a formal theory of monopolistic competition. Finally, it distinguishes between static and dynamic efficiency and explains why both kinds of efficiency must be considered when evaluating the effects of market structure on market performance.

FOR REVIEW

Here are some important terms and concepts that will be put to use in this chapter. If you do not understand them, review them before proceeding.
- *Positive and normative economics (Chapter 1)*
- *Pure economizing versus entrepreneurship (Chapter 1)*
- *Theory of consumer choice (Chapter 5)*
- *Pure monopoly and monopolistic competition (Chapter 9)*

There are still large pieces missing from the picture of competition drawn in the last four chapters. For one thing, up to this point the emphasis has been mainly on price and output decisions. Advertising, product innovation, and other forms of nonprice competition have remained in the background. In addition, the focus has been more on pure economizing than on entrepreneurial aspects of business conduct. This chapter will try to fill in some of the gaps and broaden the understanding of the process of competition.

It will begin with a discussion of advertising—first its effects on consumers and then its possible role as a barrier to entry into markets or industries. From there, it will move to a discussion of monopolistic competition—the market structure under which there are numerous firms and no barriers to entry but under which nonprice competition is very important. Finally, it will discuss the relationships among market structure, innovation, and competition for entrepreneurs.

ADVERTISING AND THE CONSUMER

The Consumer as Economizer and Entrepreneur

Chapter 5 presented the outlines of a long-established economic theory of consumer choice. This theory sees consumer choice as a classic problem in pure economizing. Consumers are presented with certain givens—namely, their tastes, the size of their budgets, the characteristics of available goods, and the prices of those goods. Using these givens, consumers must calculate the mix of purchases that will give them the greatest satisfaction. They do this by equalizing the marginal utility per dollar's worth of goods for all goods.

In certain important respects, this theory of consumer choice resembles the theories of perfect competition and monopoly developed in Chapters 8 and 9. All are theories of pure economizing, which is to say that all are concerned with situations in which the decision maker confronts objectives, alternative activities, and constraints as givens—clearly known and not subject to manipulation. In addition, all these theories are concerned with decision-making situations in which price and quantity are the primary variables.

In reality, though, consumer choice is a matter of more than just pure economizing. Consumers are not fully aware of prices and product characteristics. They are not givens; they are constantly changing. Consumer decision making is not costless or instantaneous. Instead, it requires significant time and effort. The practical consequence is that consumers, just as much as business managers, must constantly be making entrepreneurial decisions. They have to be alert to new information, and they have to be willing to explore innovative ways of satisfying their wants.

Recognizing the entrepreneurial element in consumer decision making is the key to understanding how advertising works. It is not possible to understand why businesses spend money on advertising until it is understood why advertising affects the way consumers spend their money.

Overcoming Consumer Ignorance

Any explanation of how advertising works must begin with the simple fact that because information is costly to acquire, consumers are always ignorant to some degree. They may have some idea of how much eggs cost, but they do not automatically know whether this week eggs are cheaper at the A&P or at Safeway. They know beds are bought in furniture stores, but they are not able to reel off a list of all the furniture stores in town—at least not if the town is very big. They know what a car is, but they do not always know which ones have front-wheel drive or which have side-window defrosters. Every firm can feel certain that there are consumers who would buy its product if they knew about it. By telling consumers of the price and characteristics of products and the places where they can be bought, advertisements attract enough customers to pay for the resources spent to produce the ads.

Inducing Changes in Demand

Other kinds of advertising are aimed not at informing consumers about prices and products but at changing their tastes. If consumer tastes are changeable, firms can make profits by changing them. Making consumers like a firm's product more can increase the demand for the product and in some cases can make the demand more inelastic. Sales or prices or both can then be increased, which will raise profits. To understand advertising, then, it is useful to know something about the mechanisms by which consumer tastes are produced and modified.

Changing Tastes   For one thing, people's tastes and preferences do not originate spontaneously. Instead, they are strongly influenced by the tastes and preferences of others. Some people are innovators and take up new styles or products of their own accord, but more people are imitators and change their buying patterns only after they see others change. The interaction of innovators and imitators in the consumer community keeps tastes and styles in flux. Through advertising, firms can hope to control the direction and pace of change. Controlled and predictable change is more profitable and less risky than random change. It can be worth the advertising resources invested to produce it.

Changing Perceptions   Changing tastes is not the whole story, though. Market researchers have found that advertising changes not only tastes but also perceptions. It can influence not only which product people will like but how well they will like a given, unchanged product. The following case study provides an interesting illustration.

Case 12.1
Advertising and the Perceived Taste of Turkey Meat

In 1965, James C. Makens of Michigan Technological University conducted an experiment to determine the effect of a well-known brand name on consumers' preferences for turkey meat. In Part 1 of the experiment, 150 subjects from Detroit were presented with two plates, each containing a slice of turkey meat. Although the two slices were actually from the same turkey, they were labeled differently. One bore a brand name heavily advertised and well known in Detroit, and the other bore an unfamiliar brand name. Of the 150 subjects, only 10 percent indicated that they thought the two samples tasted alike; 56 percent expressed a definite preference for the known brand, and 34 percent preferred the unknown brand. Makens concluded that in the presence of brand name clues, the subjects tended to perceive identical portions of turkey as being different, and they tended to prefer the more familiar name.

In Part 2 of the experiment, sixty-one consumers were presented with two plates. One plate contained a slice of tender turkey meat and the other a slice of tough turkey meat. This time, no brand names were used. The tender sample was marked with one symbol and the tough sample with another. Forty-nine subjects said they preferred the tender meat, four said they preferred the tough meat, and eight said they could not tell the difference. The conclusion was that, in the absence of brand name clues, consumers generally can perceive an actual difference in quality.

In the final part of the experiment, the sixty-one subjects who had tasted the samples marked with symbols were asked to indicate which brand they thought each sample belonged to—after they had said which they preferred. Thirty-four subjects said that the turkey they preferred must have been the known brand; eighteen identified the preferred turkey as probably the unknown brand; and one did not express an opinion. The conclusion was that consumers tended to think it likely that the high quality product was the one with which they were familiar.

Makens summarized his results in these terms: "Brand preference for one well-known turkey brand was strong enough to influence the perceived taste for turkey meat among the subjects. . . . [Also] the consumers expect a well-known brand to be of superior quality to an unknown brand" (p. 263).

Similar results have been reported elsewhere. These experiments leave us a long way from the idea that taste and preferences are a given of the consumer choice process.

Source: Based on James C. Makens, "Effect of Brand Preferences upon Consumers' Perceived Taste of Turkey Meat," *Journal of Applied Psychology* 49 (November 4, 1965): 261–263. Copyright 1965 by the American Psychological Association. Used by permission.

Brand Loyalty In the idealized world of economic theory, the decisions consumers make are neither costly nor time-consuming. In the real world, this is not so. The shortcuts consumers take to simplify the decisions they have to make sometimes create openings for advertisers. An example is the phenomenon of brand loyalty.

A brand loyal consumer keeps decision costs down by choosing the same brand again and again. Where does brand loyalty come from? It can perhaps be explained to some degree on the basis of innate differences in tastes among consumers. (Some people may just be born with a liking for Budweiser and others with a liking for Schlitz.) The following case study, though, shows that there is more to brand loyalty.

Case 12.2
An Experimental Study of Brand Loyalty

In 1968, J. Douglass McConnell of the Stanford Research Institute reported the results of an experimental study of brand loyalty. The product chosen for the experiment was beer. It was chosen because people buy beer frequently and because McConnell judged that the nature of the product would help motivate subjects to stay with the experiment over the two-month period required. A random sample of sixty beer drinkers was drawn from Stanford University students living in married student housing. The subjects were told that the experiment was part of a marketing test of three types of beer produced by a local brewer.

Once a week, the subjects were presented, in their homes, with an opportunity to choose one bottle from among three bottles labeled "M," "L," and "P." They were told that Brand M was a high-priced beer, Brand L a medium-priced beer, and Brand P a bargain-priced beer. The subjects did not actually have to pay for their beer; but to make the price difference seem realistic, the medium-priced beer had a $.02 "refund" taped to the bottle, and the low-priced beer had a $.05 "refund." The subjects could keep the refunds.

In point of fact, the three brands of beer were identical. They were all drawn from the same production run at the brewery, and they differed only in terms of the labels added by the experimenter. This, however, did not prevent the development of fierce brand loyalties by many of the subjects. One measure of brand loyalty that McConnell used was the occurrence of four consecutive choices of the same label. Although at first the subjects experimented with different brands, by the end of twenty-four trials, fifty-seven of the sixty had developed brand loyalty, as measured by the four-choice criterion. Of these fifty-seven, twenty-six chose Brand M, twelve Brand L, and nineteen Brand P.

Another measure of brand loyalty is the probability of making a switch in brands from one trial to the next. The lower the probability of switching, the more loyal. Exhibit 12.1 shows how the probability of switching decreased rapidly over the first twelve trials of the experiment.

Because the beer was actually all the same, these results could not be explained by any "given" differences in tastes. The results instead suggest that, by convincing themselves that one brand was better than another, the subjects avoided the painful task of having to make up their minds from scratch at each trial.

Exhibit 12.1

Effects of repeated tasting on brand loyalty

In the experiment, subjects were given a choice of three bottles of beer on each trial. The bottles had different labels, but their contents were the same. At first, consumers experimented, switching from brand to brand to find one they liked. Soon, though, the frequency of switching fell to a low level as brand loyalty developed.

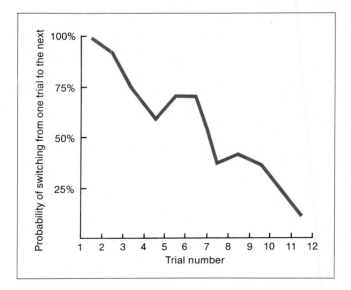

Source: J. Douglass McConnell, "The Development of Brand Loyalty: An Experimental Study," *Journal of Marketing Research* 5 (February 1968): Table 3. Reprinted from *Journal of Marketing Research* published by the American Marketing Association.

Given the nature of the choice the subjects were offered, it is remarkable how firmly set in their opinions some of them became. One girl reported, "M is a good strong malty beer, but I like L because it is lighter. Mmm!!! P would poison me—make me ill." Another subject, who developed an enthusiasm for P, once deviated to experiment with a bottle of M and reported, "Worst I've ever had; you couldn't give it away."

Source: Based on J. Douglass McConnell, "The Development of Brand Loyalty: An Experimental Study," *Journal of Marketing Research* 5 (February 1968): 13–19. Used by permission.

Normative Implications

So far, the chapter has discussed advertising and the consumer purely from the point of view of positive economics. It can, for example, be experimentally verified that external clues, such as exposure to advertising or differences in price, change consumer perceptions of unchanged products. This kind of positive analysis of the effects of advertising is all that is really needed in order to understand the role of advertising in the competitive process. In practice, though, advertising is an emotionally charged subject that invites normative as well as positive analysis. Before moving on to a discussion of advertising and market structure, then, the chapter will look at some of the normative issues that advertising raises.

The Case against Advertising It is not hard for opponents of advertising to get an audience. Anyone who has ever been interrupted in the middle of a favorite Bogart film on late-night television is an automatic convert. But the case against advertising rests on much more than just the complaint that it is intrusive, annoying, ugly, and distracting. Following are some of the most common normative objections to advertising that economists make.

Heading the list of arguments against advertising is the complaint that it violates consumer sovereignty. Producers, it is said, do not adjust their output to consumer preferences. Instead, they use advertising to force consumers to buy whatever it is that they feel like producing. Harvard professor John Kenneth Galbraith has been one of the most vocal proponents of this view. In his book, *The Affluent Society*, he put the matter this way:

Were it so that a man arising each morning was assailed by demons which instilled in him a passion sometimes for silk shirts, sometimes for kitchen ware, sometimes for chamber pots, and sometimes for orange squash, there would be every reason to applaud the effort to find the goods, however odd, that quenched this flame. . . .

Consumer wants can have bizarre, frivolous, or even immoral origins, and an admirable case can still be made for a society which seeks to satisfy them. But the case cannot stand if it is the process of satisfying wants that creates the wants. For then the individual who urges the importance of production to satisfy those wants is precisely in the position of the onlooker who applauds the efforts of the squirrel to keep abreast of the wheel that is propelled by his own effort.[1]

Advertising is identified as the chief method by which the people who satisfy the wants (that is, the economy's business firms) also create those wants. According to Galbraith, a distinction must be made between wants that are

---

[1]John Kenneth Galbraith, *The Affluent Society* (Boston: Houghton Mifflin, 1958), pp. 153–154.

John Kenneth Galbraith (1908–   )

John Kenneth Galbraith enjoys a unique distinction among U.S. economists today: His books regularly hit the best-seller list and stay there for long periods. Galbraith represents the opposite extreme from economists who, like Paul Samuelson, write primarily to gain the applause of other economists. On the contrary, his major books—*The Affluent Society* (1958) and *The New Industrial State* (1967)—are all-out attacks on conventional economics, written to be read by the widest possible nonprofessional audience.

Galbraith lumps everything he dislikes about modern economics under the heading of "the conventional wisdom." By this phrase, he means all the ideas that he claims are widely believed not because they are true but simply because they are often repeated. He saves his sharpest barbs for two particular elements of the conventional wisdom: consumer sovereignty and the law of supply and demand.

Consumers are not sovereign, Galbraith says, because their tastes and preferences are heavily manipulated by advertising. The ability of business to manipulate consumers knocks the "demand" leg out from under supply and demand theory. The "supply" leg is then knocked out with a second deftly aimed kick. The supply curve is valid only in an economy where firms aim to maximize profits. In the U.S. economy, says Galbraith, firms do not do this. How, then, can supply and demand determine price? The kinds of goods that consumers are persuaded to buy and the prices at which these goods are sold are determined by the whims of the "technostructure," Galbraith's name for the managerial-professional-academic elite who run the country.

Galbraith is many things other than an economist. He is a political activist, always promoting liberal and ultraliberal causes. He served as chairman of the Americans for Democratic Action, and he played a key role in securing the Democratic presidential nomination for George McGovern. He is also a diplomat and served as John Kennedy's ambassador to India. (At six feet eight inches, he towered almost comically over his local diplomatic counterparts there.) In a burst of self-indulgence, he once even turned his hand to writing a novel, *The Triumph*.

Few economists take the complete Galbraithian system seriously, but many admit that he is a useful critic. Economics, like other social science disciplines, is in fact always in danger of becoming excessively abstract and formalistic. Economists who talk only to other economists, and then only in mathematical language, do indeed often end up saying things that are just plain silly. Galbraith is determined that they not get away with it.

innate within the consumer and those that producers create through advertising. Consumer sovereignty means guiding production purely in accordance with innate wants. Advertising and all other means of want creation are a violation of that sovereignty.

Twenty years after the appearance of Galbraith's book, the ideas he expressed remain popular. Now they often take the form of the doctrine of consumer alienation, to use a term favored by Marxist-oriented economists. The doctrine is based on the idea that people have two sets of preferences. One set reflects their "true" wants and needs; the other reflects the "false" wants and needs created by advertising and other evils of modern capitalism. In this view, consumer sovereignty is a mockery unless preceded by consumer liberation from false needs and desires.

Another Point of View But by no means do all economists accept the view that advertising is a violation of consumer sovereignty or an attempt to exploit some shameful, perverse side of human nature. Those who adopt a less hostile attitude toward advertising usually begin by making the point that there are no such things as natural, given, or innate consumer preferences, at least not if one means by this preferences for specific kinds of goods and services. People may well be born with basic needs for food, security, affection, self-esteem, and the rest; but there is an infinite variety of particular goods that can satisfy these needs. If the advertisers of one generation persuade people that their need to keep their feet dry is best satisfied with pointy-toed boots and those of the next that square-toed boots do the job better, so what? One should not be silly enough to think that, left to their own devices, people's "true" tastes in boot-toes would magically emerge, making everyone better off.

Perhaps, some go so far as to say, the idea of true and false preferences itself poses a potential threat to consumer sovereignty. Perhaps the so-called true preferences are just the preferences of a cultural elite who do not like the lowbrow life-styles of their neighbors. Because the members of this elite prefer Beaujolais to Budweiser, or camping in the High Sierras to snowmobiling in Iowa cornfields, or "tastefully" styled European cars to "tasteless" American cars, they think that everyone else ought to share their preferences. It is a short step from a policy of forbidding the advertising of Budweiser, snowmobiles, and Buicks to forbidding their production in the name of giving the people what they really want. And then what becomes of consumer sovereignty?

ADVERTISING AND MARKET PERFORMANCE UNDER OLIGOPOLY AND MONOPOLISTIC COMPETITION

Having said this much about the normative economics of advertising, it is time to return to positive economics. For the economists' case against advertising does not consist entirely in the claim that it violates consumer sovereignty. There is also a group of issues concerning the effect of advertising on market performance under oligopoly and monopolistic competition. These issues too, as will be shown, are highly controversial.

Is Advertising a Barrier to Entry?

Perhaps the most controversial issue of all is that of advertising as a barrier to entry. If advertising does represent a barrier to entry, then it may contribute to high levels of market concentration. And as shown in the last chapter, market concentration in turn may lead to poor market performance.

Advertising as a Barrier The mechanism by which advertising acts as a barrier to entry is said to be the creation of brand loyalties. Consumers who might otherwise treat all cola drinks as very close substitutes are divided into opposing camps, some fiercely loyal to Pepsi, others to Coca-Cola. Each firm can then raise its price with little fear that doing so will cause its customers to go elsewhere. And each firm will have to worry less that the resulting high profits will attract new entrants, because the new firms will not only have to spend money to build plants and hire workers but will also have to mount fabulously expensive advertising campaigns.

In 1967, this view of the effects of advertising received a substantial boost from W. S. Comanor and T. A. Wilson, who looked at the statistical relationship between advertising expenditures and profits in forty-one industries and reached the following conclusion:

It is evident that . . . advertising is a highly profitable activity. Industries with high advertising outlays earn, on the average, at a profit rate which exceeds that of other industries by nearly four percentage points. This differential represents a 50 percent increase in profit rates. It is likely, moreover, that much of this profit rate differential is accounted for by the entry barriers created by advertising expenditures and by the resulting achievement of market power.[2]

An Alternative View of Advertising and Entry Neither the theory of advertising as a barrier to entry nor the results of the Comanor and Wilson study have been accepted by everyone, however. Other economists, notably Yale Brozen of the University of Chicago business school, see the relationship between advertising and competition in a rather different light.[3]

According to Brozen, the theory that advertising is a barrier to entry stands reality on its head: Advertising is not an impediment to competition; it is a means of competition. Existing firms have no advantage over new firms in buying advertising; ad agencies stand ready to sell their services to anyone willing to pay the proper fee. In fact, advertising is even more important for new firms than for existing firms. In Brozen's view, firms aim their advertising not so much at building loyalty in their own customers as at getting their rivals' customers to try something different. The real way to create a barrier to entry and protect established oligopolies, he says, would be to outlaw advertising. Then it would be far harder for a new firm to break into a market.

What about the Comanor and Wilson study, though? Brozen treats the apparent relationship between profits and advertising as an example of the fallacy of confusing accounting categories with the categories of economic theory. Encouraged by certain features of the tax laws, accountants treat advertising as a current expense, like wages or purchases of materials. In fact, Brozen contends, advertising is an investment having long-term effects. A brand image takes years to develop; and once developed, it is a valuable, long-lasting asset for the company that created it. If an adjustment is made to

---

[2] W. S. Comanor and T. A. Wilson, "Advertising, Market Structure, and Performance," *Review of Economics and Statistics* 49 (November 1967): 437.

[3] For a representative exposition of Brozen's views, see Yale Brozen, "Entry Barriers: Advertising and Product Differentiation," in *Industrial Concentration: The New Learning*, ed. Harvey J. Goldschmid, H. Michael Mann, and J. Fred Weston (Boston: Little, Brown, 1974), pp. 115–137.

treat advertising as an investment, companies that advertise intensively no longer appear to be more profitable than the average.

Advertising and Monopolistic Competition

Up to this point, the discussion of advertising and market performance has centered on markets that are oligopolistic in structure. Critics of advertising have charged that in such markets, advertising acts as a barrier to entry, that it contributes to market concentration, and that it is associated with excessively high rates of profit. Now attention will be given to the claim that even in markets where none of these things is true, advertising may have adverse effects on market performance. This effort will require a closer look at a type of market structure that has been mentioned before only in passing: monopolistic competition.

According to the definition given in Chapter 9, a monopolistically competitive market is one in which there are a large number of small firms, a differentiated product, and no significant barriers to entry. Examples can be found in such industries as restaurants, gasoline retailing, and personal services.

Equilibrium for the Firm under Monopolistic Competition The theory of monopolistic competition, like its definition, is a blend of monopolistic and competitive elements. The theory can be understood with the help of Exhibit 12.2, which shows short-run and long-run equilibrium positions for a typical firm under monopolistic competition.

Exhibit 12.2
Short-run and long-run equilibrium under monopolistic competition
Under monopolistic competition, each firm has a downward-sloping demand curve, but there are no barriers to entry. In the short run, a firm producing at the point where marginal cost is equal to marginal revenue can earn profits in excess of the normal rate of return, as shown in Part a of the diagram. In the long run, however, new competitors are attracted. This diverts part of the demand from firms originally in the market, and the original firms may fight to retain their market shares, using promotional techniques that add to total costs. Entry will continue until a long-run equilibrium in which profits are eliminated is reached, as shown in Part b.

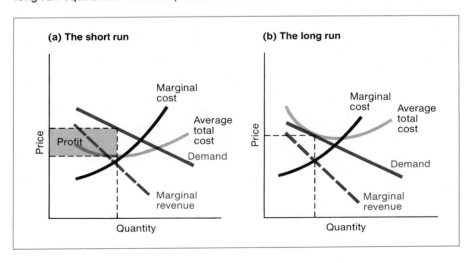

The demand curve for a monopolistically competitive firm, like that for a pure monopolist, slopes downward, although it is likely to be more elastic than that of a monopolist. Each firm's product is a little different from the products of its competitors. Each firm can therefore raise its price at least a little without losing all its customers, because some customers attach more importance than others to the special style or location or whatever that the firm offers. Given this downward-sloping demand curve, the short-run profit maximizing position shown is analytically the same as that for a pure monopolist. The quantity of output is determined by the intersection of the marginal cost and marginal revenue curves, and the price charged is determined by the height of the demand curve at that point.

But this short-run equilibrium cannot also be a long-run equilibrium under monopolistic competition. The reason is freedom of entry. In the short-run position shown in Exhibit 12.2a, the firm is earning profits in excess of the normal rate of return on investment. (This is shown by the fact that price exceeds average total cost.) High profits attract new competitors. As new competitors come in, the demand curves of firms that are already there will shift downward, because the new entrants will sell products that are reasonably good substitutes for those of the original firms. If the original firms try to resist the shift in demand by improving their products or marketing them more aggressively, those efforts will raise their average total costs. The downward shift in the demand curve of the original firms and/or the upward shift in their cost curves will continue until there are no more profits to attract new entrants. The result is the long-run equilibrium position shown in Exhibit 12.2b.

Market Performance In this long-run equilibrium position, it is claimed, markets perform poorly. For one thing, as under pure monopoly, each firm produces too little of its product. The gap between price and marginal cost indicates an unrealized potential for further mutually beneficial transactions. In addition, the monopolistically competitive firms do not operate at the minimum points on their long-run average cost curves. If there were fewer firms, each producing a greater quantity of output, the same quantity of products could be provided to consumers at a lower total cost. The hallmarks of monopolistic competition, then, are said to be too many gas stations, supermarkets, and restaurants, each operating at only a fraction of capacity and each charging inefficiently high prices, yet each earning no more than the minimum return needed to stay in business.

And what does advertising have to do with all this? Advertising is said to make the effects of monopolistic competition worse than they otherwise would be. The reason is that advertising exaggerates the differences among the products of various firms and thus makes each firm's demand curve less elastic than it would otherwise be. The performance gap between monopolistic competition and perfect competition is thus made even wider.

Are Perfect Competition and Monopolistic Competition Different?

The analysis of market performance under monopolistic competition just given has not been accepted by all economists. Many scholarly articles have been written on the subject, and many elaborate mathematical variations on the theory have been suggested. Setting aside differences in detail, most of the attempts to defend monopolistic competition come down to the simple idea that monopolistic competition and perfect competition are not really significantly different.

One argument is that the illusion of a difference comes from a mistaken idea about the nature of the product being sold. Take restaurants, for example. The restaurants in any town sell meals that are highly differentiated according to location, national cuisine, atmosphere, service, and many other characteristics. But perhaps meals are not really the relevant product. Instead, think of all restaurants as selling a homogeneous good called dining pleasure. The differences among restaurants should be thought of not as differences in product but rather as differences in the technology used to produce dining pleasure and differences in the size of the package of dining pleasure being sold. By analogy, different farmers grow potatoes in assorted sizes and use a variety of farming methods, but the potato market is still considered to be close to perfectly competitive. The dining pleasure market, according to this line of reasoning, is no different from the potato market.

A variation on this defense of monopolistic competition acknowledges differences among products but points out that product diversity is valuable in and of itself. Suppose it were true, as the theory of monopolistic competition suggests, that prices would be a little lower if there were fewer barbershops, each not quite so conveniently located, or fewer supermarkets, each a little more crowded, or fewer flavors of ice cream. Would a move in that direction benefit consumers? Not necessarily, if consumers are willing to pay something for variety. Imagine that there were some way to split the market for, say, ice cream into two markets—one for the good called ice cream and the other for the good called variety. If that were possible, then each good could have its own separate price, and each market could be perfectly competitive. But such a split is simply impossible. In the real world, a single market for both goods, having the structure described as monopolistic competition, is as close as one can come to the ideal.

Evidence on Advertising and Market Performance

As in so many cases where economic theorists disagree, attempts have been made to use empirical methods to settle the controversy about advertising and market performance under monopolistic competition. The studies on advertising and profits are not really relevant here, because firms would not be expected to earn profits under either perfect or monopolistic competition. Instead, evidence bearing more directly on the effect of advertising on market structure is needed. Is the natural state of the world one in which consumers tend to view all sources of supply as just alike and to move freely among them in response to small changes in price? Or is the natural state one in which inertia and ignorance on the part of consumers cause them to cling to familiar sources of supply, giving each firm a local monopoly vis-à-vis its own customers? And advertising—does it set up unnatural barriers between firms, thereby adding to their monopoly power, or does it break down natural barriers, thereby destroying monopoly power? A number of kinds of evidence might help answer these questions.

One kind of evidence comes from studies of consumer behavior, such as the two case studies given earlier in this chapter. But these studies by themselves do not entirely settle the issue. Case 12.1, for example, showed that advertising affected the perceived taste of turkey meat that was actually all from the same turkey. This indicates that advertising can increase brand loyalty. On the other hand, Case 12.2 showed that in the case of beer, people not subjected to advertising also perceived great differences among actually identical goods and were very reluctant to switch from one "brand" to another. This indicates that brand loyalty can arise even in the absence of advertising.

Another kind of evidence comes from studies of how advertising is actually used by firms. For example, it has been shown that new products are advertised more intensively than old products. This may indicate that makers of old products tend to depend on consumer inertia and that advertising is a way of breaking down that inertia. It has also been shown that consumers in markets where advertising is heavy are less loyal to one brand than are consumers in markets where advertising is light. This too might indicate that advertising helps overcome consumer reluctance to try substitute products.[4]

Perhaps most interesting of all, people have recently been given a chance to witness a real-life experiment—the sudden introduction of advertising into a market where it had been prohibited before. The market is that for legal services, and the initial results of the experiment are reported in the following case study.

Case 12.3
The Effects of Advertising on the Market for Legal Services

Until 1977, there was no advertising in the market for legal services. Lawyers who were so daring as to publicize the level of their fees or, in some states, the nature of their legal specialties could be thrown out of the profession by bar association ethics committees. Then, along came John Bates and Van O'Steen, partners in a legal clinic in Phoenix, Arizona. Bates and O'Steen were not content to live with the advertising ban. They ran an ad in the local paper, advertising their clinic and listing standard fees for certain services, such as filing for uncontested divorces. The state bar association pounced, but Bates and O'Steen fought their case all the way to the United States Supreme Court—and they finally won. The ban on advertising, said the court, violated their constitutional right of free speech.

Since then, advertisements for legal services, once unknown, have become commonplace. The results have been striking.

For one thing, prices have come down dramatically. In Phoenix, according to O'Steen, the fee for an uncontested divorce has dropped from about $350 to the range of $150 to $200. In New York City, a legal name change, which used to cost $150 to $200, can now be obtained for about $75. Similar price decreases have been noted for the preparation of wills, title searches, and other routine services.

A second effect of the Supreme Court decision has been the development of lawyer referral services. These organizations offer no legal services themselves but simply act as go-betweens, helping people with legal problems find the right attorney to handle their problems for a price they can afford.

Perhaps even more importantly for the long run, the increased vigor of competition has acted as a spur for the introduction of many innovative kinds of legal services. John Bates, for example, has now quit the legal clinic to concentrate on designing and selling self-help packages for consumers with routine legal problems. For $16.95, he now sells a do-it-yourself divorce kit complete with all neces-

---

[4]The article by Brozen, cited in footnote 3, contains references to and discussions of these and several similar studies.

sary instructions and forms. In another city, an outfit calling itself The Law Store gives its customers a telephone consultation for $9.95; for another $10, it will follow up with a letter or phone call.

In this instance, at least, advertising has clearly brought improved market performance.

MARKET DYNAMICS AND COMPETITION AMONG ENTREPRENEURS

Static Efficiency versus Dynamic Efficiency

Up to this point, the discussion of market structure and economic performance has focused almost entirely on the problem of **static efficiency**—the ability of an economy to get the greatest output of consumer satisfaction from given resources and technology. Static efficiency is a measure of how close an economy operates to its production possibility frontier. But market structure may also have an important impact on the economy's **dynamic efficiency**—its success in achieving growth in the rate of output per unit of resources. Dynamic efficiency is thus a measure of the rate at which the production possibility frontier of an economy shifts outward over time.

Of the two kinds of efficiency, dynamic efficiency is by far the most important in the long run. During the 1960s, the U.S. real gross national product grew at an average rate of about 4.6 percent per year. The most important single factor contributing to this growth was the improvement of knowledge—that is, innovation and technological change. Improvement in knowledge accounted for about a third of all economic growth, or 1.5 percent per year. The remaining economic growth is attributable to capital accumulation, population growth, increased education, and other factors. The contribution of innovation and technological change is very large compared to the estimate of the loss in static efficiency caused by monopolistic and oligopolistic market imperfections. The largest estimate of the static efficiency loss ever seriously put forward is about 2.5 percent of gross national product. Innovation and technological change add more than that to GNP each two years.

The Schumpeter Hypothesis

If every policy promoting static efficiency also contributed to dynamic efficiency, the distinction between the two would not be important in a chapter dealing with market structure and economic performance. Unfortunately, however, it is not certain that things work out that way. In fact, there is a widely shared hypothesis according to which some sources of dynamic efficiency are to be found in just those concentrated markets that are suspected to be sources of static inefficiency. This will be referred to as the Schumpeter hypothesis, after economist Joseph Schumpeter, who first brought it to widespread attention.

According to Schumpeter, the source of innovation and growth is competition—but not the kind of competition found in those markets classified as perfectly competitive. Instead, he wrote:

The competition that counts is the competition from the new commodity, the new technology, the new source of supply, the new type of organization (the largest scale unit of control, for instance)—competition which commands a decisive cost or quality advantage and which strikes not at the margins of the profits and the outputs

Static efficiency The ability of an economy to get the greatest consumer satisfaction from given resources and technology.

Dynamic efficiency The ability of an economy to increase consumer satisfaction through growth and innovation.

**Joseph Alois Schumpeter
(1883–1950)**

Joseph Schumpeter was born in Trietsch, Moravia, then a part of Austria. He studied law at the University of Vienna, also attending the seminars of the leading economists of the Austrian school of the day. In 1906, he received a doctor of laws degree and briefly practiced law before turning to teaching as a career. He taught at several European universities, taking time out in 1919–1920 to serve as the Austrian minister of finance. In 1932, he emigrated to the United States. There, he accepted a post at Harvard University, which he held until his death in 1950. In 1948, he was honored with the presidency of the American Economic Association.

Schumpeter's writings are characterized by a broad scope rare in twentieth century economics. In his writings on economic development, business cycles, the history of economics, and economic systems, he attempted to portray the whole of the economic process. He had little use for the kind of economics that reduces everything to problems of managerial calculations and then reduces those problems to an arid set of mathematical equations. To him, the crucial figure in economic life was the entrepreneur, not the clerk or manager. What is more, he saw the entrepreneur as operating in an environment shaped as much by history, politics, and religion as by simple forces of supply and demand.

Although his *History of Economic Analysis* is probably Schumpeter's greatest scholarly achievement, it is *Capitalism, Socialism, and Democracy* that holds the most interest for the general student of economics. The book is, among other things, Schumpeter's reply to Karl Marx. The opening chapters of the book contain one of the most lucid and perceptive analyses of Marx's system ever written. Schumpeter went on to explain why he believed that capitalism would inevitably come to an end and be replaced by socialism. Unlike Marx, however, Schumpeter believed that capitalism would be killed not by its failures but by its successes. In the process of explaining this paradoxical proposition, he offered an analysis of the role of the entrepreneur in the market economy and explained why, in the twentieth century, the entrepreneur has come to face an increasingly hostile intellectual environment. A minor but significant role in the downfall of capitalism, Schumpeter believed, would be played by the economic profession's myopic focus on the fairyland of perfect competition and its blindness to the nature and importance of entrepreneurship.

of the existing firms, but at their foundations and their very lives. This kind of competition is as much more effective than the other as a bombardment is in comparison with forcing a door, and so much more important that it becomes a matter of comparative indifference whether competition in the ordinary sense functions more or less promptly; the powerful lever that in the long run expands output and brings down prices is in any case made of other stuff.[5]

"In this respect," he added in another place, "perfect competition is not only impossible but inferior, and has no title to being set up as a model of ideal efficiency."[6]

Just how is it that market concentration can actually promote, rather than retard, the kind of competition on which dynamic efficiency depends? There appear to be two mechanisms at work.

First, monopoly power is often the goal of competition among entrepreneurs and the chief incentive to engage in such competition. The first firm to seize on new knowledge and put it to use is able to make profits in excess of the normal rate of return precisely because its new discovery establishes a temporary monopoly that it can exploit until its competitors successfully imitate or

[5]Joseph Schumpeter, *Capitalism, Socialism, and Democracy* (New York: Harper & Bros., 1942), pp. 84–85.
[6]Ibid., p. 106.

outflank it. If each new product had to be introduced at a price that just covered costs, or if each cost-reducing innovation had to be followed immediately by a matching reduction in price, there would be little reason to introduce such innovations at all. If the first firm to adjust to changing circumstances were not able to increase the gap between its costs and its revenues by doing so, there would be no incentive to be first. Competition among entrepreneurs is competition for monopoly power of at least a temporary kind. In this sense, monopoly is not the opposite of competition but a normal result of it.

Second, monopoly power, once achieved, acts as a spur to competition. This is not only true in the now familiar sense that an industry where monopoly profits are being made tends to attract new entrants. It also applies to competition among different industries and product groups for the consumer's dollar. The OPEC countries' exploitation of their oil monopoly has subjected oil to greatly intensified competition from other sources of energy. The rate of innovation in methods of energy production and the rate of introduction of known energy-conserving technology have been greatly speeded up. Even if the oil cartel were now to be broken up, world energy markets would not return to their former equilibrium pattern. In this sense, monopoly is not the opposite of competition but a spur to it.

Can the Schumpeter Hypothesis Be Tested?

The Schumpeter hypothesis poses a sweeping challenge to economic theory and policy. Not surprisingly, many attempts have been made to verify or refute it by examining the available data on economic growth, market concentration, and innovative activity. The results to date, however, are somewhat inconclusive.[7]

The major difficulty with testing the Schumpeter hypothesis lies in measuring innovative activity. Schumpeter had a fairly broad concept of innovation in mind. Inventing new products or processes, developing practical applications of new inventions, working out new forms of business organization, discovering new ways of financing investment, and creating new methods of marketing and distribution were, to Schumpeter, all equally important sources of dynamic efficiency. But clearly, most of these sources can be measured only indirectly, and some not at all. As a result, attempts to test the Schumpeter hypothesis have had to make do with rather crude approximations to the central concepts involved.

One favorite indirect test has relied on formal research and development (R&D) spending as an approximation of the innovative effort of various firms. The answer to the simple question, "Do large firms in concentrated industries account for more than their share of all R&D spending?" appears to be a straightforward yes. The four hundred to five hundred largest firms, having five thousand or more employees, account for 80 to 90 percent of R&D spending and only 25 to 30 percent of all output. This alone is enough to suggest that the Schumpeter hypothesis cannot be dismissed out of hand.

However, many more sophisticated statistical studies have added a host of qualifications to this conclusion. For example, using patented investments

---

[7]For a survey of the most important efforts, see Jesse W. Markham, "Concentration, Stimulus or Retardant to Innovation," in Goldschmid, Mann, and Weston, eds., *Industrial Concentration*, pp. 247–272.

rather than R&D spending as a measure of innovative activity appears to reduce the strength of the relationship between concentration and innovation. Also, such factors as the nature of the product that the industry produces or the scientific environment in which the industry operates appear to account for a substantial part of the differences in innovative activity among firms. Finally, some studies have suggested that firm size and market concentration contribute to innovative activity only up to a certain threshold, with super-giant firms having no advantage relative to merely large firms.

Perhaps the safest conclusion to reach is that innovation—in Schumpeter's sense—is simply too complex a phenomenon to be subjected to rigorous statistical analysis. Looking at all the studies in perspective, it appears that firms of all sizes in markets of all levels of concentration are, under favorable circumstances, able to contribute positively to the dynamic efficiency of the economy. This implies that neither a policy of indiscriminately breaking up large firms into smaller ones nor a policy of indiscriminately welding small firms into larger ones can be counted on to speed the pace of innovation. The ability of the largest corporations to mass huge R&D teams on a difficult technical problem is important, but so is the flash of insight that may come to a lone inventor. In short, for all we know, the present mix of large and small firms may be just about right from the point of view of dynamic efficiency.

CONCLUSIONS

Much of this chapter and the preceding one have been devoted to describing unresolved issues of market structure and performance, and they have been unable to offer firm conclusions. In preparation for the next chapter, which discusses public policy toward competition and market structure, it will be useful to summarize what has been covered up to this point in terms of two major areas of controversy.

The first area concerns the extent to which perfect competition, or something reasonably close to it, can be regarded as the natural state of the economy. If a substantial degree of concentration is necessary in most markets in order to take advantage of economies of scale, perfect competition appears to be an exceptional market structure, unattainable in most cases. On the other hand, if most market concentration can be explained on the basis of artificial barriers to entry, such as government franchises or the advertising and marketing strategies of firms dominating the market, public policies aimed at reducing such barriers may realistically be expected to be effective. Somewhat similarly, in the case of unconcentrated but monopolistically competitive industries, one can ask whether the existing degree of product differentiation is natural or contrived.

The second area of controversy concerns the question of whether perfect competition, or something closely approximating it, is a necessary or even a sufficient condition for good market performance. If, in concentrated markets, tacit or explicit cooperation among firms is the exception and vigorous rivalry is the rule, perfect competition may not be necessary. And if, at least in some markets, economic concentration and large-scale operations are necessary to ensure dynamic efficiency, perfect competition may not be even a sufficient condition for good market performance.

Disagreements over these analytical issues, as will be shown in the next chapter, underlie many of today's public policy debates.

SUMMARY

1. The traditional theory of consumer choice, introduced in Chapter 20, assumes that consumers have established tastes, complete information about products, and the ability to make decisions instantly and without cost. In such a world, advertising would not only be unnecessary—it would not work. Advertising works because consumers are continuously developing new tastes and acquiring new information and because consumers cannot make decisions without incurring costs.

2. Some economists think that advertising may act as a barrier to new competition in concentrated industries. Their argument is twofold: (1) that advertising creates strong brand loyalties, thereby making the demand for each firm's product less elastic; and (2) that the necessity of mounting an advertising campaign adds to the start-up costs of a new firm. Other economists disagree; they see advertising as a means of competing rather than a barrier to competition. They argue that advertising is a way of attacking established brand loyalties and facilitating the entry of new firms.

3. A monopolistically competitive market is one in which there are large numbers of small firms, no significant barriers to entry, and a strongly differentiated product. Each firm in such a market faces a downward-sloping demand curve and maximizes profits at the point where marginal cost and marginal revenue are equal. If firms earn profits in the short run, then new firms will enter the market until those profits are eliminated. In long-run equilibrium under monopolistic competition, price must be equal to average total cost.

4. Economists disagree about market performance under monopolistic competition. Some argue that, in equilibrium, there will be too many firms in the market, each producing too little output. Others think that there is really little or no difference between monopolistic competition and perfect competition.

5. An economy's static efficiency is its ability to get the most out of given resources and technology; its dynamic efficiency is its ability to grow through innovation and technical change. According to the Schumpeter hypothesis, large firms in concentrated industries are the economy's major source of dynamic efficiency.

DISCUSSION QUESTIONS

1. The Jack Daniels distillery sells its black label whisky for $1 more per bottle than its green label whisky. Black label is aged one year longer, but even officials of the distillery admit that few, if any, ordinary consumers can tell the two apart in a blind tasting. Why, then, does black label outsell green label by a wide margin? For that matter, why does it sell at all? Do you think consumers would be better off if Jack Daniels discontinued its expensive advertising campaign for black label and put all its production into the lower priced green label? Would you answer any of these questions differently if the whisky sold under the two labels came out of the same vat, without even a difference in aging?

2. Discuss the following statement in the light of what you have learned in this chapter: Many people argue that advertising deceives consumers and makes them buy things they don't really want; but few people will admit that they themselves are deceived by advertising or that the things they themselves buy are not the things they really want.

3. Discuss the controversy over advertising as a barrier to entry in terms of the following statement: A barrier to entry is something that prevents new entrants

from duplicating the performance of existing firms in terms of cost or quality. Nonetheless, the need for hard work is not in itself a barrier to entry in the economic sense. When entrepreneurs are freely able to go out and buy the various building blocks of their new firms in the same markets where existing firms buy their inputs, barriers to entry are not a determinant of market structure.

Do you think it is important that the market for advertising services is itself highly competitive?

4. In downtown Moscow, there are many fewer restaurants than in comparable U.S. cities. These restaurants are, on the average, much larger and much more crowded than their U.S. counterparts. The quality of food served is high, although service leaves something to be desired by U.S. standards. Do these facts suggest to you that the central planners who control Moscow's restaurants have designed their system to perform better than the restaurant market in most U.S. cities? Using what you have learned about monopolistic competition, make a serious attempt to argue both sides of this question.

5. A landmark study found that eyeglasses were cheaper in states where advertising was freely permitted than in states where it was restricted. Where advertising was completely banned, glasses cost an average of $37.48 per pair; where there were no restrictions, the average was $17.98.[8] Explain these results in terms of what you have learned in this chapter.

6. Evaluate the following argument in terms of what you have learned in this chapter: The apparent association between dynamic innovation and large firm size is an artificial result of the patent system, which allows firms to grow fat on the monopoly profits of their inventions. Without patents, new inventions could be equally shared among a large number of small firms, and there would be just as much dynamic efficiency without the need to suffer the present degree of market concentration.

SUGGESTIONS FOR FURTHER READING

Galbraith, John Kenneth. *The Affluent Society.* Boston: Houghton Mifflin, 1958.
Contains Galbraith's well-known attack on advertising as a violation of consumer sovereignty.

Goldschmid, Harvey J.; Mann, H. Michael; and Weston, J. Fred. *Industrial Concentration: The New Learning.* Boston: Little, Brown, 1974.
Chapter 3 is a debate between Yale Brozen and H. Michael Mann on the topic of advertising as an impediment to competition. In Chapter 5, Jesse W. Markham discusses market concentration and innovation, citing several attempts to bring empirical evidence to bear on the Schumpeter hypothesis.

Hayek, Friedrich A. von. "The Non Sequitur of the Dependence Effect." *Southern Economic Journal* 27 (April 1961).
A reply to Galbraith's views on advertising and consumer sovereignty.

Schumpeter, Joseph. *Capitalism, Socialism, and Democracy.* New York: Harper & Bros., 1942.
Part 2 of this book contains Schumpeter's famous discussion of the relationship between market concentration and dynamic efficiency.

Trivoli, G. William. "Has the Consumer Really Lost His Sovereignty?" *Akron Business and Economic Review,* Winter 1970, pp. 33–39.
Attacks Galbraith's arguments on a broad front and cites some important empirical evidence that advertising does not always succeed in manipulating consumer behavior.

---

[8]Lee Benham, "The Effect of Advertising on the Price of Eyeglasses," *Journal of Law and Economics* 15 (October 1972): 337–352.

GOVERNMENT AND BUSINESS: ANTITRUST POLICY

WHAT YOU WILL LEARN IN THIS CHAPTER

This chapter will discuss antitrust policies—government policies intended to control market structure and the competitive behavior of firms. It will show that such policies are shaped by the goals of promoting efficiency and preserving small business. Particular attention will be given to the Sherman Act of 1890 and the Clayton Act of 1914—two acts that have evolved into a specific set of constraints on mergers and competitive tactics. Antitrust policy has many critics, but the chapter will describe how the critics do not always agree among themselves as to the changes that are necessary. A concluding section will show two possible directions for the evolution of antitrust policy.

FOR REVIEW

Here are some important terms and concepts that will be put to use in this chapter. If you do not understand them, review them before proceeding.
- *Monopoly (Chapter 9)*
- *Price discrimination (Chapter 9)*
- *Oligopoly (Chapter 11)*
- *Barriers to entry (Chapter 11)*

This chapter turns from a study of how market structure and competitive behavior affect market performance to a study of how public policy affects market structure and competitive behavior. The policy is embodied in a set of laws known as **antitrust laws.**

There is a connection between the antitrust laws and economists' concern with the performance of concentrated markets, but the connection is not as close as one might think. The antitrust laws are not simply economic theory translated into legislation. The foundations of these laws were laid in the last century, before the modern economic theory of monopoly had seen the light of day. Today, as then, antitrust policy is as much a reflection of broad social concerns as of narrow economic analysis.

In the United States of the nineteenth century, people were hostile toward the "trusts," as they called the big businesses of their day, not because they were inefficient but because they were rich and powerful. If they were efficient as well, that made them richer and more powerful still. Consider, for example,

Antitrust laws A set of laws, including the Sherman Act of 1890 and the Clayton Act of 1914, that seek to control market structure and the competitive behavior of firms.

the attitudes reflected in this famous passage from an 1897 Supreme Court decision:

[Large business combinations] may even temporarily, or perhaps permanently, reduce the price of the article traded in or manufactured, by reducing the expense inseparable from the running of many different companies for the same purpose. Trade or commerce under those circumstances may nevertheless be badly and unfortunately restrained by driving out of business the small dealers and worthy men whose lives have been spent therein and who might be unable to readjust themselves to their altered surroundings. Mere reduction in the price of the commodity dealt in might be dearly paid for by the ruin of such a class.[1]

Clearly, the concerns of a judge who would dismiss the benefits of "mere" price reductions in favor of the interests of "small dealers and worthy men" are different from the concerns of modern writers on market structure and economic performance.

The relationship between the social and political purposes of the antitrust laws on the one hand and their economic effects on the other will be a major theme of this chapter. It will try to explore just how much of an overlap there is between the kind of antitrust policy that actually exists and the kind that economic analysis suggests ought to exist. Of course, there are differences of opinion as to how large the overlap is. In part, these differences reflect the unresolved issues in positive economic analysis discussed in Chapters 11 and 12. But the differences should not be exaggerated. What follows will be concerned as much with areas of broad agreement among economists as with areas of disagreement.

ANTITRUST LAWS AND POLICIES

The Sherman Act

The logical starting point for a description of antitrust laws is the Sherman Antitrust Act of 1890. This act is the cornerstone of antitrust policy in the United States. It outlaws "every contract, combination in the form of a trust or otherwise, or conspiracy in restraint of commerce among the several states, or with foreign nations." It also declares that "every person who shall monopolize, or attempt to monopolize, or combine or conspire with any other person or persons, to monopolize any part of the trade or commerce among the several States, or with foreign nations, shall be deemed guilty of a misdemeanor." (In 1974, the act was strengthened by making violation of it a felony.)

Under the Sherman Act, the government can sue offending firms and ask for any of several forms of relief. It can ask for fines or jail sentences. (The latter, once rare in antitrust cases, have become much more common now that violations are felonies.) Alternatively, it can obtain an *injunction* (a court order preventing the offending firm from continuing the anticompetitive practice in question). In extreme cases, it can even ask the court to order the offending firm to be broken up into smaller, competing units.

In addition, private parties who claim to be injured by anticompetitive practices in violation of the Sherman Act can initiate suits of their own. If successful, they can obtain damages equal to three times the value of any loss they can prove to have suffered. Private antitrust suits are quite common.

---

[1] *United States v. Trans-Missouri Freight Ass'n,* 166 U.S. 323 (1897).

The Clayton Act and the Federal Trade Commission Act

Antitrust authorities won some notable early victories under the Sherman Act, the most spectacular of which were the breakups of Standard Oil and American Tobacco in 1911. Nonetheless, many people felt that the Sherman Act was not enough. For one thing, the act was unclear about the status of monopolies achieved through merger. In addition, people felt that the law should identify more precisely the kinds of business practices that were likely to have anti-competitive effect. The product of these concerns was the Clayton Act of 1914, which has four major provisions:

1. It outlaws price discrimination among purchasers of goods, except when such discrimination is based on grade, quality, and quantity of the product sold or on tangible differences in selling costs. To discriminate otherwise is illegal if the effect is to lessen competition substantially or to tend to create a monopoly.

2. It forbids sellers from making *tying contracts*—contracts for the sale of a firm's products that include an agreement that the purchaser will not use or deal in the products of a competitor—when the effect of such contracts is to lessen competition.

3. An antimerger section of the act forbids any corporation engaged in commerce from acquiring the shares of a competing firm or from purchasing the stocks of two or more competing firms. Again, the prohibition is not absolute; it applies only when the effect is to lessen competition substantially.

4. The one unconditional provision of the Clayton Act outlaws *interlocking directorates*—situations where the same person is on the board of directors of two or more firms: (a) if the corporations are competitive, (b) if any of them has capital, surplus, and undivided profits of more than $1 million, and (c) where elimination of competition will violate the antitrust laws. Such interlocks are illegal whether or not proof of a reduction of competition can be found.

In the same year as the Clayton Act, Congress passed the Federal Trade Commission Act, which supplements it. This act declares broadly that "unfair methods of competition in commerce are illegal." It leaves the determination of what constitutes unfair methods to the Federal Trade Commission, which the act established as an independent government agency having the goal of attacking unfair practices. (The FTC also has some regulatory functions in protecting the public against false and misleading advertisements for foods, drugs, cosmetics, and therapeutic devices.) The importance of the Federal Trade Commission Act lies not so much in broadening the scope of illegal business behavior as in providing an independent antitrust agency with the power to initiate court cases.

Since 1914, the Clayton Act has received two important amendments. One is the Robinson-Patman Act of 1936, which has strengthened the law against price discrimination. The other is the Celler-Kefauver Antimerger Act of 1950, which, as the name implies, has strengthened the law against mergers. These important amendments will be examined in the next section.

Antitrust Policy

It would be impossible to determine the actual nature of U.S. antitrust policy from a reading of the antitrust statutes alone. The laws are vaguely written.

What is an "attempt to monopolize"? A "substantial lessening of competition"? An "unfair method of competition"? Congress left these questions to be answered by the courts. In addition, the government's two major antitrust enforcement agencies—the Federal Trade Commission and the antitrust division of the Department of Justice—also have considerable discretion in determining the direction of antitrust policy. Within the framework of the statutes and prior court decisions, it is their job to decide just what kinds of business conduct should be prosecuted as anticompetitive.

Antitrust policy has not pursued a completely steady course over the years. The courts and the enforcement agencies have often disagreed on important points. It is difficult to give a brief description of antitrust policy without conveying a false impression of unity and precision. With this warning, however, an attempt will be made anyway. The discussion will be organized under the headings of price fixing, mergers, vertical restraints, and price discrimination.

Price Fixing Whatever else the Sherman Act may or may not do, no one disputes that it outlaws price fixing. Competing firms must make their pricing decisions independently; they cannot cooperate to establish prices more to their liking than those resulting from independent action. The modern tendency of the courts and antitrust authorities is to treat price fixing as a per se violation of the law—which means that only the fact of a price fixing arrangement need be proved in order to secure a conviction. It is not necessary to prove that the price fixing attempt was successful or that the prices established were unreasonable. It also means that accused price fixers cannot defend themselves on the ground that their activities might have had beneficial effects.

In addition to making price fixing illegal, the law as presently interpreted also reaches other forms of cooperative conduct that might indirectly have an effect on prices. For example, such traditional cartel practices as agreements to restrict output or divide markets are treated just as severely as agreements on prices. Generally, however, the law has not made much headway against purely tacit coordination of prices. Enforcement agencies have often argued that such things as price leadership or the exchange of pricing information among competitors also constitute illegal price fixing, but the courts have not consistently ruled against these practices.

Mergers Not long after passage of the Sherman Act, the question of what to do about monopolies created through merger arose. There appeared to be a danger that competing firms could get around the law against cartels simply by merging into one big firm. That would make price fixing and output restrictions matters of internal policy, beyond the reach of the law.

In an early case involving the merger of two railroad companies, the Supreme Court took the position that the merger of direct competitors was a combination in restraint of trade and therefore a violation of the antitrust laws. This precedent was not followed consistently, however. Neither did the antimerger section of the Clayton Act prove very effective in its initial form. Not until the Clayton Act was amended by the Celler-Kefauver Act in 1950 did control of mergers become an important part of antitrust law enforcement.

As presently interpreted, the law still does not make all mergers illegal per se.

Almost all mergers today, however, are at least examined for possible anti-competitive effects. And sometimes, as the following case study shows, seemingly small anticompetitive effects are enough to persuade the courts to block a merger.

Case 13.1
Von's Grocery

On March 28, 1960, Von's Grocery Company of Los Angeles, a large supermarket chain, merged with a direct competitor, Shopping Bag Food Stores. The government had opposed the merger even before it was consummated; and in 1966 the case found its way to the Supreme Court. The Supreme Court, in a decision that is regarded as a landmark in antimerger law, ruled that the merger was a violation of the Clayton Act.

In terms of economic concentration, the facts of the case are not very impressive. Von's was the third largest supermarket chain in Los Angeles; but even as such, it accounted for only 4.7 percent of sales. Shopping Bag was even smaller. Together, the merged firms controlled just 7.5 percent of the market, slightly less than the leader, Safeway. At the time of the merger, in addition to the various competing chains, there were also some 3,818 single store operators in the Los Angeles retail grocery market.

What impressed the court, however, was not the large absolute number of competitors in the market but the fact that the number of single store operators appeared to be on the decline. Justice Black's decision noted that in 1950 there had been 5,365 such stores. Not persuaded by the argument that even 3,000 stores was enough to ensure competition, he instead cited the nineteenth century court's concern with the fate of "small dealers and worthy men." "The basic purpose of the 1950 Celler-Kefauver Act," he wrote, "was to prevent economic concentration in the American economy by keeping a large number of small competitors in business. . . . Thus where concentration is gaining momentum in a market, we must be alert to carry out Congress' intent."

Source: *U.S. v. Von's Grocery Co.*, 384 U.S. 270 (1966).

Although many observers doubt that today's Supreme Court would be willing to enforce the standard of *Von's Grocery* literally, the government continues to pursue a vigorous antimerger policy. In addition to opposing **horizontal mergers** (such as Von's with Shopping Bag)—mergers where both firms operate in the same market—the government also often opposes **vertical mergers**—mergers of firms having a supplier-customer relationship. **Conglomerate mergers**—mergers of firms operating in unrelated markets—also frequently draw government opposition.

Horizontal mergers Mergers between firms that are direct competitors in the same market.

Vertical mergers Mergers between firms that stand in a supplier-purchaser relationship to one another.

Conglomerate mergers Mergers between firms that operate in unrelated markets.

Vertical Restraints Vertical restraints on trade, like vertical mergers, involve agreements between a supplier and a customer. They are distinguished from horizontal restraints, which involve agreements between competing suppliers. Many kinds of vertical restraints have been attacked under the antitrust laws, although not always successfully. Among the kinds most often attacked are resale price maintenance, territorial restrictions, tying agreements, and exclusive dealing.

Resale Price Maintenance Under resale price maintenance agreements, retailers agree not to sell a good below a price set by the manufacturer. Such agreements have been held to be unlawful restraints on trade. The reasoning is that they limit price competition among the various retailers carrying a manufacturer's product. In practice, the prohibition of resale price maintenance is not watertight; agreements that indirectly accomplish the same thing have sometimes survived court tests.

Territorial Restrictions Restrictions imposed by a manufacturer on the territory in which a retailer can sell also limit competition at the retail level. Antitrust authorities view such restrictions with suspicion; but as in the case of resale price maintenance, the prohibition is not watertight.

Tying Agreements Tying agreements are explicitly outlawed by the Clayton Act where their effect is substantially to limit competition. The Supreme Court has found that "tying arrangements serve hardly any purpose beyond the suppression of competition."[2] Among the tying agreements declared illegal by the court was one in which IBM required buyers of its business machines also to buy IBM-brand punchcards.

Exclusive Dealing In an exclusive dealing agreement, a manufacturer extracts from a retailer a promise that the latter will not deal in products of the manufacturer's competitors. Many exclusive dealing agreements have been overturned by the courts, although the practice of exclusive dealing survives in some industries.

Price Discrimination Price discrimination was listed as an objectionable practice in the original Clayton Act, but this section was not widely or successfully enforced for a time. Things changed in 1936 when the Clayton Act was amended by the Robinson-Patman Act, which considerably strengthened the law against price discrimination. Although the act is so complex as to defy accurate summary, its basic purpose is to prohibit sellers from offering discriminatory price discounts unless those discounts can be shown to reflect cost savings or to be efforts to meet competition.

Both the Federal Trade Commission and the Department of Justice can bring suits under the Robinson-Patman Act, although, as a practical matter, the FTC has always done most of the enforcement work. Private suits for triple damages are also possible in price discrimination cases.

This completes the brief sketch of what the antitrust laws do. The next section turns to the more lively subject of whether what they do is good or bad.

CRITICAL PERSPECTIVES ON ANTITRUST LAW AND POLICY

Antitrust laws and policies are the subject of an enormous number of books and articles by economists, many of whom are highly critical of antitrust efforts. The critical commentary does not come only from those economists who think that the market system is inherently competitive and will function quite adequately without active intervention from government. There are also

---

[2]*Standard Oil Co. of California and Standard Stations Inc. v. U.S.*, 337 U.S. 293, 305 (1949).

many critics who favor a strong antitrust policy but who think that past efforts have been ineffective, misdirected, or even counterproductive. Some of the criticism centers on the complexities of antitrust procedures. Certain writers are concerned that a policy designed with monopolies and cartels in mind works poorly in the area of oligopoly. Others complain that antitrust policy pays too little attention to questions of economic efficiency and too much to protecting individual firms against allegedly unfair methods of competition.

The critical literature on antitrust policy is hard to summarize, partly because many of the criticisms are inconsistent with one another. Nonetheless, without worrying too much about consistency for the time being, the next section will survey some of the major points that have been raised. The chapter will conclude by putting the proposed solutions into some kind of order.

The Problem of the "Big Cases"

One problem of antitrust policy that is obvious even to nonprofessionals is the sheer size and complexity of many modern antitrust cases. Consider some examples:

1. In 1969, on the last day of the Johnson administration, the government filed a massive antitrust suit against IBM, accusing the firm of monopolizing the computer business through a variety of unfair practices. It took the government six years to get the case ready for trial and then three years to present it to the single judge appointed to render a decision. In 1978, defense lawyers for IBM finally got their turn, and at last report the two sides were still at it.
2. A private antitrust case against the Xerox Corporation reached trial after just four years. Unlike many antitrust cases, this one was tried before a jury. The trial took exactly one year to complete, making it one of the longest jury trials in history. Initially decided in 1978, the case will continue through many years of appeals.
3. After the jury in another five-year private antitrust suit failed to reach a verdict, the presiding judge dismissed the case, commenting that "the magnitude and complexity of the present lawsuit render it on the whole beyond the ability and competency of any jury to decide rationally."[3] The case is now on appeal.
4. In 1973, after a three-year investigation, the Federal Trade Commission brought a suit against Exxon and seven other oil companies, accusing them of monopolizing the oil market east of the Rockies. The trial is expected to start in 1982 or 1983, and an initial decision is expected about 1988. Appeals could drag on into the next century.

Everyone seems to agree that the enormous time and expense involved in such trials is a scandal, but opinions differ on what should be done. Some proposals focus on streamlining procedures to get the cases to trial faster. Others suggest the appointment of special judges who are experts in antitrust matters. Procedural reforms might help, but it appears that the nature of the antitrust laws themselves is largely to blame for the length and complexity of many trials. And that leads to the next set of criticisms.

---

[3] *Memorex v. IBM*, 458 F. Supp. 423 (1978), U.S. District Court, Northern District of California.

Antitrust and Oligopoly

The antitrust laws, especially the Sherman Act, appear to have been designed with such relatively simple problems in mind as open price fixing and pure monopoly. Pure monopoly is quite rare. Open price fixing, although not uncommon, does not usually result in lengthy, complex litigation. The problems appear to come when antitrust law is stretched thin in an attempt to make it fit the complicated problems of modern oligopoly. It is just not always easy to decide whether particular practices of rival firms represent vigorous competition or tacit cooperation. It is no wonder that such questions take many years to resolve in court; as indicated in earlier chapters, economists cannot even resolve them in their textbooks.

Given this analysis, two solutions suggest themselves. One is that if it is so hard to prove that the practices in question are really monopolistic, they cannot really be very harmful. The implication is that the solution to the "big case" problem is not to bring such cases in the first place. The second solution is to supplement the present antitrust laws with a law aimed specifically at oligopoly. If the government were empowered to break up any firm exceeding a given size or market share, the facts at issue in the big cases would be greatly simplified and the trials consequently shortened. Both proposals are examined in the next section.

Competition versus Efficiency

Almost all economists would agree that, under given conditions of cost, competitive markets perform more efficiently than markets in which competition is restricted. But a major problem with antitrust policy, according to many critics, is that cost conditions are not always given. If the very practice that the courts condemn as anticompetitive also decreases the costs of doing business, the consumer may end up paying higher, rather than lower, prices as a result of antitrust enforcement.

The law on vertical restrictions is often singled out as a case in point. Suppose your company makes high quality stereo equipment, which you want to market to discriminating buyers. You have a number of competitors who produce less expensive equipment that looks much the same as yours. The only difference is that it does not sound as good. But how are you going to convince buyers?

Your best strategy might be to line up a network of sophisticated dealers who would draw in customers with local advertising, hire knowledgeable salespeople to demonstrate your equipment in acoustically perfect surroundings, and build customer loyalty with quality repair services. But there would be problems: Unless your dealers had exclusive local rights to sell your product, they might not be willing to advertise. Unless they sold only your product line, they might spend their time selling some competitor's equipment instead. And unless they could be sure customers would not listen to demonstrations in their expensive showrooms and then buy the equipment from a discount warehouse on the edge of town, they might not be willing to sign on as dealers at all.

In short, unless you could impose vertical restrictions on your dealers, you might have to resort to a less efficient way of selling your product. You might, for example, have to reach potential buyers through expensive national advertising, even though on-the-spot selling efforts would be cheaper and more informative. Consumers would ultimately have to foot the bill for the less efficient distribution system or end up with inferior equipment.

It might, of course, be worth depriving consumers of the benefits of the distribution method just described if the result of the vertical restraints were to create significant monopoly power. But, say critics of the laws against vertical restraints, there is no such danger. The fallacy of present policy is that it focuses on the apparent restriction of competition among individual retailers, when the important issue is competition among manufacturers. If there are many firms making stereo equipment, some will no doubt choose the market strategy described above. Others will build equipment aimed at price-conscious users who are willing to sacrifice a little quality. Those firms will be happy to sell their equipment through discount houses because, for them, that will be the most efficient means of distribution. There will be all the competition that consumers need.

Efficiency and Mergers

Much of what the critics say about the law of vertical restraints can also be said about the law of mergers. Vertical and conglomerate mergers are unlikely to have significant anticompetitive effects; therefore, blocking them will be a mistake if they will bring even small cost savings. Horizontal mergers obviously have greater potential to be anticompetitive, but they also have greater potential to bring cost savings.

The *Von's Grocery* case is often cited as an example of antimerger policy gone astray. That merger occurred at the end of a decade of radical changes in transportation patterns and life-styles of the people of Los Angeles. These changes made supermarket chains more cost-effective and more attractive to consumers than were the old-fashioned neighborhood groceries. The role of antitrust policy in such a situation should not have been to try to turn back the clock or to prescribe one distribution strategy rather than another. Instead, it should simply have been to ensure that the conditions for free entry into the market were maintained and that firms already in the market did not openly rig prices or divide up markets.

In addition to bringing possible benefits through cost savings in production and distribution, mergers play a variety of important roles in financial markets. For one thing, a merger may be the only practical way for an owner/ entrepreneur to sell a small corporation. Such a person might wish to sell out in order to realize the profits of a successful venture and move on to something new. An aging owner might seek a merger because no heir or buyer could be found to run the firm as an independent entity. In effect, the possibility of an eventual merger reduces the risk that an entrepreneur faces in starting a new firm. By encouraging the entry of such firms into a wide variety of markets, mergers fill a procompetitive, not an anticompetitive, function.

Of course, not all mergers are friendly arrangements between the managements of two firms with complementary interests. Many hostile mergers also take place; in these mergers the acquiring firm goes over the head of the present management of a corporation and appeals directly to its stockholders to sell out. As explained in Chapter 6, takeovers of this kind—and, even more, the threat of such takeovers—are the market's best guarantee against too great a separation of ownership from managerial control. Incompetent managers or those who pursue their own interests in perquisites at the expense of their stockholders' interests in profits can survive only until the value of their company's stock drops so low on the market that someone comes in to buy them out.

In sum, the critics contend that antimerger policy has become so restrictive that it does more harm than good. Most mergers, they suggest, should automatically be given the benefit of the doubt. Only horizontal mergers between large, direct competitors in markets with substantial barriers to entry should properly remain the target of antitrust action.

Protection of Competitors

Sometimes, according to yet another criticism, the law appears to confuse the protection of individual competitors with the protection of the competitive process itself. It has already been shown how a concern with "small dealers and worthy men" played a role in the *Von's Grocery* merger case. But the area of antitrust law that draws the most fire from economists in this regard is the law on price discrimination under the Robinson-Patman Act. The following case study describes what many economists regard as one of the most misdirected antitrust decisions ever reached by the Supreme Court.

Case 13.2
Utah Pie

In 1958, the Utah Pie Company, a local bakery in Salt Lake City, built a new frozen pie plant. The frozen pie market in that city was expanding rapidly. It more than quadrupled in size between 1958 and 1961. Through an aggressive campaign featuring low prices, Utah Pie was able to capture fully two-thirds of this market almost immediately after starting its operation.

Utah Pie's main competitors were three national food product companies—the Pet Milk Company, the Carnation Milk Company, and the Continental Bakery Company. Nowhere else in their operation had these firms faced the kind of vigorous competition that Utah Pie was giving them. But rather than simply retreating from the Salt Lake City market, they decided to fight back. By cutting prices on their own pies and making special deals with local supermarkets to sell pies under house brand labels, they succeeded in cutting Utah Pie's slice of the market back to 45 percent by 1961. (In absolute terms, however, Utah Pie's sales increased steadily throughout the period.)

Angered by the actions of the three outside companies, Utah Pie sued them under the Robinson-Patman Act. Its lawyers claimed that Pet, Carnation, and Continental were practicing illegal discrimination by selling pies at lower prices in Salt Lake City than elsewhere. When the case reached the Supreme Court, it was decided in favor of Utah Pie. Pet, Carnation, and Continental, in the words of the court, "contributed to what proved to be a deteriorating price structure over the period covered by this suit," to the injury of the local firm. And that, said the court, was just the sort of action the Robinson-Patman Act was designed to prohibit.

Source: Information from Ward S. Bowman, "Restraint of Trade by the Supreme Court: The Utah Pie Case," *Yale Law Journal* 77 (November 1967): 70–85. *Utah Pie v. Continental Baking Co.*, 386 U.S. 685 (1967).

It is hard to imagine a decision more completely at odds with any economic theory on which antitrust law might be based. Utah Pie was a virtual local monopolist in 1958. The only sin of Pet, Carnation, and Continental was to try to encroach on its monopoly. Their efforts resulted in lower prices and greater quantities of pies for consumers, although prices remained high enough to give all four companies a profit throughout the period. True, the three national companies did discriminate in selling their pies more cheaply in Salt Lake City than elsewhere. But if that was a sign that something was wrong, the solution surely should have been to encourage more competition in the other markets, not less competition in Salt Lake City.

Partly because of the tendency of the Robinson-Patman Act to produce bizarre results like that in the Utah Pie case, the government in recent years has sharply cut back its enforcement efforts. In 1976, the Department of Justice issued a report advocating repeal of the act, but legislative efforts in this direction have not made much headway. Private suits are still possible, and small businesses apparently still perceive Robinson-Patman as a valuable weapon with which to defend themselves against the competition of larger and more efficient rivals. Despite reduced enforcement, the act continues to influence competitive price behavior throughout the economy.

CONCLUSIONS

This brief survey of antitrust policy and its critics makes it clear that there are pressures for change from many quarters. There is less than complete agreement, however, as to what direction change should take. Perhaps the best way to conclude this chapter, then, is to draw two alternative sketches of what the antitrust policy of the future might look like.

The View from Within

The basis for the first sketch will be a point of view from within the government's antitrust enforcement agencies. What would the antitrust policy of the future look like if these agencies were able to shape it free of legislative, judicial, and political constraints?

One change—a change that is already taking place—would be an increased emphasis on what has become known as the shared monopoly problem. The term *shared monopoly* is loosely used to refer to any industry that behaves more or less like a monopolist even though its structure is that of an oligopoly. When antitrust enforcers speak of a "problem" of shared monopoly, they are simply expressing their belief that many, if not most, oligopolistic industries work that way and that something should be done about it.

Just what should be done is not yet clearly decided. Conventional antitrust suits in oligopolistic industries are liable to turn into just the kind of decade-long "big cases" that both defendants and prosecutors would like to avoid. It appears likely, then, that a really vigorous attack on shared monopolies would require new legislation aimed directly at controlling market structure. One recurrent suggestion is to give the government power to break up any firm holding a market share of 15 percent or larger, unless that firm can defend its size on the basis of efficiency.

Another area in which antitrust authorities would like a freer hand is that of conglomerate mergers. Authorities have found the existing antitrust laws ineffective in preventing large conglomerate mergers, primarily because such mergers usually can be shown to have few, if any, adverse economic effects. Nonetheless, in pursuit of what FTC chairman Michael Pertschuk calls a "Jeffersonian preference for dispersed power," legislation has been introduced to prohibit certain conglomerate mergers whether or not they can be shown to have adverse economic effects. Typical of several currently pending pieces of legislation is Senator Edward Kennedy's proposed Small and Independent Business Protection Act of 1979. This act would prohibit mergers (1) between all companies with assets or annual sales of $2 billion each, (2) between companies with assets or sales over $350 million unless they could show that the transaction would have the "preponderant effect of substantially enhancing competition," and (3) between one company with over $350 million in assets or sales and another with 20 percent or more of any market having at least $100 million in annual sales. These prohibitions could be avoided only if the larger of the two merging firms sold off one or more subsidiaries equal in size to the smaller of the two merging firms. The Kennedy bill has been supported, with some variations, by both the FTC and the antitrust division of the Department of Justice.

One additional change in the emphasis of antitrust enforcement that is already underway—and that is likely to gather momentum in the future—is the application of antitrust concepts to regulated industries and industries enjoying antitrust immunities. There is a widespread feeling that the regulatory commissions that control such key industries as energy, transportation, and communications have not done all they can to encourage competition in the markets under their control. (The next chapter will discuss some of the reasons for this.) The Department of Justice and the Federal Trade Commission now appear routinely in regulatory proceedings to argue in favor of increased competition. In addition, some industries are directly shielded by law from antitrust action. The agricultural marketing orders discussed in Chapter 10 are an example. Antitrust authorities would very much like legislative authority to move against such legalized price fixing.

In sum, the vision of the future from within the enforcement agencies is one of an increasingly activist and comprehensive antitrust policy. This new activism would be guided in part by economic considerations. But in the words of the Carter administration's chief antitrust official, it would also be guided by "the rich blend of American themes—diversity, opportunity, local ownership, economic liberty—that play eloquently through the legislative history of the antitrust laws and subsequent antitrust jurisprudence."[4]

The View from Outside

Outside the government, in the schools of business, law, and economics of major U.S. universities, one can find some people who hold very different views of the proper future of antitrust policy. Outside critics do endorse a few changes that are presently underway in antitrust policy—for example, the increased emphasis on competition in regulated industries and the decreased emphasis on price discrimination. But in many major respects, the critics not only oppose the initiatives now being taken by the authorities but want actually to move in the opposite direction.

One of the most eloquent of these critics is Robert H. Bork, former solicitor general of the United States and now professor of law at Yale University. In his recent book, *The Antitrust Paradox*, Bork makes the following recommendations concerning the future direction of antitrust policy.

---

[4]Testimony of John H. Shenefield, assistant attorney general, antitrust division, U.S. Department of Justice, before the Antitrust Subcommittee of the Senate Judiciary Committee, July 28, 1978.

First, the only goal that should guide antitrust policy is the economic welfare of consumers. The idea that the antitrust laws are there to protect small businesses from competition and economic change should be buried once and for all.

Second, in judging consumer welfare, the possible beneficial effects that any behavior might have for the efficiency of production or distribution should explicitly be weighed against possible anticompetitive effects of that behavior.

Third, antitrust enforcers should focus their energies on just three categories of anticompetitive behavior: (1) horizontal conspiracies to fix prices or divide markets, (2) horizontal mergers creating very large market shares, and (3) deliberately predatory actions undertaken to damage competitors (with care taken to distinguish deliberate predation from mere vigorous competition).

Fourth, there are a number of kinds of behavior with which antitrust law ought not to be concerned at all: (1) vertical restraints that are incidental to achieving an efficient organization of economic activity, including resale price maintenance, tying contracts, and exclusive dealerships; (2) small horizontal mergers and all vertical and conglomerate mergers; (3) price discrimination; and (4) any firm size or industry structure created by internal growth or merger more than ten years old.[5]

"These are not prescriptions for the nonenforcement of the antitrust laws," notes Bork, "but rather for their enforcement in a way that advances rather than retards competition and consumer welfare."[6]

SUMMARY

1. Antitrust policy is the area of public policy intended to control market structure and the competitive behavior of firms. There is a connection between the antitrust laws and economists' concern about the performance of concentrated markets, but the connection is not an exact one. Other goals too, particularly the goal of maintaining a strong small business sector in the economy, have influenced the historical development of the antitrust laws.

2. The foundations of antitrust policy are the Sherman Act of 1890 and the Clayton Act of 1914. These acts, together with amendments and subsequent court interpretations, place constraints on business behavior. The prohibition of price fixing and the control of mergers are the two most important antitrust constraints on what firms can and cannot do. In addition, antitrust laws prohibit certain kinds of vertical restraints—such as tying contracts and resale price maintenance—as well as many forms of price discrimination.

3. Many economists are critical of one or more aspects of contemporary antitrust policy. One reason for the critical attitude is that many big antitrust cases brought in recent years have required five to ten years or even longer to resolve. The complexity of modern antitrust cases appears partly to stem from the difficulty of applying the law to problems of modern oligopoly.

4. Other economists find that antitrust policy is not sufficiently concerned

---

[5] Adapted from Robert H. Bork, *The Antitrust Paradox* (New York: Basic Books, 1978) pp. 405–406.
[6] Ibid., p. 406.

with costs and efficiency. Sometimes seemingly anticompetitive behavior may result in cost savings to the consumer. Overly rigid application of antitrust laws may actually leave consumers worse off if potential cost efficiencies are not balanced against the potential anticompetitive effects of mergers or vertical restraints.

5. Sometimes antitrust laws have been used to protect individual firms from the competition of more efficient rivals, rather than protecting competition itself. This is a particularly important problem in the area of price discrimination law as it has developed under the Robinson-Patman Act.

6. The economic critics of antitrust law are far from united on what course antitrust policy should take in the future. Some consider extending antitrust policy to the control of oligopoly to be the most important direction for change. Others think that antitrust enforcers should concentrate their efforts on preventing price fixing and large horizontal mergers while paying less attention to areas such as vertical mergers and price discrimination, where present policy is seen as counterproductive.

DISCUSSION QUESTIONS

1. Both Congress and the courts have shown strong interest in protecting "small dealers and worthy men" from competition by large and powerful rivals, whether or not such protection contributes to economic efficiency or to low prices for consumers. Why does small business receive such sympathetic treatment? Do you agree that the protection of small business should be a goal of antitrust policy, quite apart from the consideration of economic efficiency? Explain.

2. According to economist Milton Friedman, the best antitrust law of all would be a law permitting completely free international trade in all goods and services. In what ways would such a law promote competition?

3. Explain why you agree or disagree with the following statement: Each person should have the unrestricted right both to sell goods or services in any market and to withhold goods or services from sale.

    Does antitrust policy violate this principle? If so, how?

SUGGESTIONS FOR FURTHER READING

Bork, Robert H. *The Antitrust Paradox.* New York: Basic Books, 1978.
A detailed critique of the antitrust laws by a former solicitor general of the United States.

Goldschmid, Harvey J.; Mann, H. Michael; and Weston, J. Fred. *Industrial Concentration: The New Learning.* Boston: Little, Brown, 1974.
Chapter 7, which deals with the public policy implications of the new learning, is particularly relevant to the topics discussed in this chapter.

Posner, Richard A. *Economic Analysis of Law.* Boston: Little, Brown, 1972.
Chapters 6 and 7 examine the relationships between the legal and economic concepts of monopoly and antitrust. Chapter 11 discusses the problem of conglomerates.

Stelzer, Irwin M. *Selected Antitrust Cases.* 5th ed. Homewood, Ill.: Richard D. Irwin, 1976.
Surveys the application of economic reasoning in the antitrust area through the examination of actual antitrust cases.

Wilcox, Clair, and Shepherd, William G. *Public Policies toward Business.* 5th ed. Homewood, Ill.: Richard D. Irwin, 1975.
Part 2 reviews antitrust laws and policies in a more favorable way than do Bork and Posner.

C H A P T E R **14**

GOVERNMENT AND BUSINESS: REGULATION

WHAT YOU WILL LEARN IN THIS CHAPTER
This chapter considers several important areas of public regulation of private business, including the regulation of public utilities, transportation, and industrial health and safety. A major theme is the distinction between the actual and the intended effects of regulation. A secondary theme is the use of regulation to redistribute income and wealth in ways different from how the market would distribute them. Several cases and examples will show why economists are frequently critical of regulation, at least as currently practiced.

FOR REVIEW
Here are some important terms and concepts that will be put to use in this chapter. If you do not understand them, review them before proceeding.
- *Normative and positive economics (Chapter 1)*
- *Minimum economic scale (Chapter 7)*
- *Normal rate of return to capital (Chapter 7)*
- *Natural and franchised monopoly (Chapter 9)*
- *Cartels (Chapter 9)*

It is very difficult to write a single chapter on government regulation of private business; the chapter threatens to swallow the entire book. Regulation is everywhere: Farm policies are a form of regulation. Antitrust law is a form of regulation. Banks are closely regulated by the Federal Reserve System and other federal agencies for both macroeconomic and microeconomic reasons. Periodically, the government subjects all sectors of the economy to wage and price regulation in the name of fighting inflation. In short, all government policy is regulation, and there is no real way to distinguish between regulated and unregulated sectors of the economy.

Nonetheless, there are three reasons to have a separate chapter on regulation. First, without a separate chapter, some important kinds of government policy toward private business would slip through the cracks and escape attention altogether. One kind is policy toward what are traditionally called the regulated industries—in particular, public utilities and transportation. Another is health and safety regulation. Also, without this chapter, there would be no opportunity to make some points about regulation in general—what it can hope to accomplish and what constraints stand in the way of achieving its goals.

The second reason for having a chapter on regulation is that the topic is too big to ignore. According to one respected estimate, in fiscal year 1978, the cost of issuing and complying with government regulations reached $96.7 billion.[1] That sum is greater than the contributions to national income of the steel, automobile, and communications industries combined. The $96.7 billion included $666 added to the cost of every new car sold that year, and $2,000 added to the cost of every new house. It also included the cost of 143 million hours of work the businesses spent filling in over 4,400 different federal forms.

A third reason for having a separate chapter on regulation is that as regulation grows, it becomes more controversial. Today, economists, businesspeople, and consumers are increasingly raising questions about regulation. Are people getting their money's worth from all those billions? Do the regulations increase their welfare by more than enough to offset the cost? Are there less expensive ways to achieve the goals of government regulation? Are the goals themselves those that people really want? These questions will set the theme for the chapter.

In what follows, several particular kinds of regulation will be examined: first the regulation of natural monopolies, then the regulation of inherently competitive industries, and finally health and safety regulation. The last part of the chapter will tie the rest together in the form of some general principles of regulation.

REGULATING A NATURAL MONOPOLY

A natural monopoly is an industry in which total costs are minimized by having just one producer serve the entire market. Residential gas, electric, water, and telephone services are frequently cited examples. It is easy for one utility to hook up extra customers in a neighborhood once it has run its basic lines, but it is wastefully expensive for separate companies to run duplicate sets of lines down each street.

The Problem

The policy problem raised by natural monopoly is how to keep the single supplier from exploiting its monopoly position to raise prices and restrict output to inefficient levels. Ordinary antitrust policies of the type discussed in the last chapter are ineffective against natural monopoly because, by definition, markets that are naturally monopolistic cannot be made competitive. Consider the example shown in Exhibit 14.1. The firm represented there has constant marginal costs and an L-shaped long-run average cost curve. The demand curve intersects the long-run average cost curve at Quantity Q_1, not far above the minimum economic scale of production. If this output were divided between even two firms, each producing half of Quantity Q_1, the cost per unit would be substantially higher.

If a single firm operates in the market, it will tend to behave as a pure monopolist. Instead of producing Q_1, it will produce Q_2, which corresponds to the intersection of the firm's marginal revenue curve with its marginal cost curve. The price corresponding to this output is P_2, which is far in excess of

---

[1]Murray L. Weidenbaum, testimony before the Joint Economic Committee, U.S. Congress, Washington, D.C., April 11, 1978.

Exhibit 14.1
Regulation of a natural monopoly
This exhibit shows the cost and demand curves for a
typical natural monopoly. As an unregulated monopolist,
the firm will maximize profits by charging Price P_2 and
producing Quantity Q_2. If regulators impose a maximum
price of P_1, the firm will find it worthwhile to produce
the larger quantity, Q_1. This assumes, however, that
regulation does not have an adverse effect on the
firm's incentive to minimize cost.

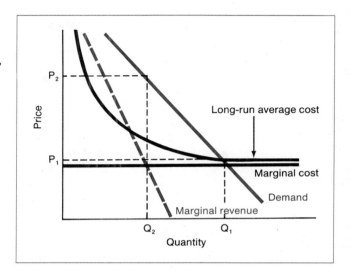

marginal cost. This is a smaller output and higher price than efficient resource
allocation requires.

The Regulatory Solution

The analysis to this point indicates that under conditions of natural monopoly,
competition by two or more firms is wasteful, and monopoly pricing by a single
firm is wasteful too. The standard solution is to allow just one firm to operate
and to regulate the price at which it can sell its output. For example, the firm
may be limited to charging a price no higher than P_1, the price at which the
demand curve intersects the long-run average cost curve in Exhibit 14.1. With
this price ceiling in force, the firm becomes a price taker for quantities of
output up to Q_1, because restricting output below that quantity no longer
enables it to raise the price. Maximum profit is earned under the regulated
price by producing Q_1 units of output. This is a larger price and greater
quantity than would result either from an unregulated pure monopoly or from
dividing production among two or more competing firms.[2]

The Rate of Return as a Focus of Regulation It is easy to identify the
appropriate regulated price in Exhibit 14.1, given the shapes and positions of
the demand and cost curves for the firm. In the real world, however, regulators
typically do not have complete demand and cost information. Lacking this
information, they proceed to set the regulated price indirectly by focusing on
the rate of return earned by the firm. The reasoning used is simple and
straightforward: If the price is set above average cost, the firm will earn a higher
than normal rate of return on capital. If the price is set too low, the firm will
earn a lower than normal return. Therefore, if a price that will allow the firm
to earn just the normal rate of return can be found, that is the price to charge.

[2]Actually, in order to make the market function at perfect efficiency, the price would have to be reduced to
the level of marginal cost, which is slightly lower than P_1. At any price less than P_1, however, the firm would
suffer a pure economic loss and would eventually be driven out of production (if not offered a public subsidy).
By allowing the firm to charge the price P_1, which is high enough to cover all costs including a normal rate of
return on capital, the regulators avoid the need for an explicit subsidy at only a small cost in terms of efficiency.

Armed with this reasoning, the rate setting process proceeds in five steps:

1. The regulators measure the value of the firm's capital, which for the hypothetical firm in the exhibit is, say, $1,200,000. This is called the firm's rate base.
2. They measure the average rate of return for the economy, which turns out to be, say, 10 percent per year. (In practice, neither of the first two steps is quite as easy as it sounds, but for present purposes the regulators can be given the benefit of the doubt.)
3. They multiply the rate base by the permitted rate of return to figure out a total return target for the firm.
4. They ask the firm to propose a price or schedule of prices that it thinks will allow it to earn the target return.
5. As time goes by, the regulators monitor the firm's actual rate of return, cutting the price if it rises too high and allowing the price to rise if returns fall below the target.

Limits on the Effectiveness of Rate of Return Regulation For a variety of reasons, rate of return regulation may not always be effective in achieving its objective of lower prices and larger output for consumers. One possibility is that regulators may lack the will to limit the profits of regulated firms. This may occur, for example, if regulated firms exercise sufficient political power to control appointments to regulatory commissions or if commissioners follow lax policies in the hope of securing well-paid jobs in the industry after their terms expire. Another possibility is that regulators may not know enough about the industry to control its rate of return effectively. It is by no means easy to measure such economic magnitudes as the regulated firm's stock of capital, its rate of return on capital, and the normal rate of return to be used as a benchmark. The more regulators have to rely on guesswork, the less likely their efforts are to be effective.

Furthermore, even if regulators have the will and the knowledge to constrain the regulated firm's rate of return effectively, it is by no means certain that the result will be lower prices and larger outputs than would prevail without regulation. To the extent that regulators succeed in putting regulated firms on a cost-plus basis, they distort incentives, regardless of the particular rate of return they permit. If a firm is permitted to earn revenues that exceed its cost by a certain amount and no more, why should it bother to minimize costs at all? Minimizing costs is hard work for managers. Why not relax and take things easy? Why not take Wednesday mornings off for golf? Install new carpets on the boardroom floor? Give a job to the president's incompetent nephew? Generally make life more pleasant at the expense of operating efficiency?

In addition to just slacking off, a regulated firm may be tempted to over-expand its stock of capital. An unregulated firm will invest in additional capital only if the value of the extra output is sufficient to cover the cost of the investment. For a regulated firm, investment can be profitable whether or not the particular investment project undertaken is productive, provided only that the rate of return allowed by regulators exceed the cost of borrowing capital for expansion. As an extreme case, imagine a regulated utility that spends $1 million on an investment project that adds absolutely nothing at all to output. The next time it goes before the regulatory commission, it can point to a million-dollar increase in its rate base and legitimately ask for a corresponding increase in the revenue it will be permitted to earn. Of course, because the new investment does not produce any new output, the only place the added revenue can come from is a price increase. The increase is not good for consumers; but from the firm's point of view, profits from overexpansion of capital are just as good as any other kind of profits.

Empirical Studies of Utility Regulation

How important are all these limitations on the effectiveness of regulation? That question was not usually asked by earlier generations of economists, who were interested primarily in what regulators ought to do. Since the early 1960s, however, economists have become much more interested in what regulators actually accomplish. The article summarized in the following case study marked an important turning point in regulatory economics.

Case 14.1
What Can Regulators Regulate? The Case of Electricity

The October 1962 issue of the *Journal of Law and Economics* carried a pioneering article by University of Chicago economists George Stigler and Claire Friedland. It began with this impertinent sentence: "The literature of public regulation is so vast that it must touch on everything, but it touches seldom and lightly on the most basic question one can ask about regulation: does it make a difference in the behavior of an industry?"

The authors set out to find an answer for the case of electricity. Their method was the straightforward one of comparing data from regulated and unregulated states in selected years from 1912, when electric rates were regulated in only six states, to 1937, when thirty-four states had adopted regulation.

They looked first at differences in the level of rates between regulated and unregulated states. In making their comparison, they used the statistical technique known as multiple regression analysis to adjust for the influence on electric rates of population density, per capita income, fuel prices, and the availability of hydroelectric power. When the proper adjustments had been made for the effects of these four variables, Stigler and Friedland found no statistically significant difference in electric rates between regulated and unregulated states.

As a check on this result, the authors studied the experience of stockholders who had invested in utilities that had come under regulation early with the experience of investors whose firms had gone unregulated for a long time. If regulation had served as an effective check on the realization of monopoly profits by utilities, they reasoned, stockholders whose firms had escaped regulation should have earned higher returns on their investment. Again, however, they found no statistically significant relationship between stockholder experience and the date at which utilities came under regulation.

Stigler and Friedland thus reached the conclusion that in the case of electric utilities, at least, and for the years studied, the regulators simply did not regulate much of anything. Although they went through the legal forms of imposing constraints on utility prices, the rate ceilings they established apparently were not much different from what would have been charged had they never made the effort. Stigler and Friedland did not conclude specifically whether it was a lack of will to control profits or a lack of information that led to the regulatory failure, but one or both of these factors seems to have been at work.

Source: Based on George Stigler and Claire Friedland, "What Can Regulators Regulate? The Case of Electricity," used with permission from the *Journal of Law and Economics* 5 (October 1962): 1–16. Copyright 1962 by the University of Chicago Law School.

Not all studies of regulation have found it to have no effect on the industries regulated. However, economists who followed the new direction for research suggested by Stigler and Friedland began to find that the effects of regulation—where there were measurable effects—were often quite different from traditional ideas of what regulation ought to do. Further examples can be found in the regulation of other kinds of markets and industries.

REGULATING INHERENTLY COMPETITIVE INDUSTRIES

Regulation in the U.S. economy is not limited to natural monopolies. At one time or another, many important industries have been brought under regulation in spite of, or even because of, the fact that they are inherently competitive.

Historical Origins

Regulation of competitively structured industries got a particularly big boost during the 1930s. One tends to think of the Great Depression of the 1930s mainly in terms of high unemployment, but the high rates of unemployment were accompanied by low prices. Between 1929 and 1933, the consumer price index actually dropped by some 25 percent. Today, most economists would explain both the high unemployment and the falling prices in macroeconomic terms. At the time, however, people tended to blame the high levels of unemployment on low prices. If only prices could be raised, business leaders said, it would become profitable to put more workers on the payroll.

In the atmosphere of those times, it is not surprising that competition, which has the microeconomic effect of keeping prices in particular markets low, was not very popular. In fact, excessive competition was seen as a barrier to economic recovery. In 1933, Congress passed the National Recovery Act, which encouraged firms to employ cartel-like methods to prop up prices. That act was soon declared unconstitutional by the Supreme Court, but more narrowly drawn legislation applying to particular industries survived. Two of the most important industries that were regulated in order to limit competition were trucking, which was brought under control of the Interstate Commerce Commission (ICC) in 1935, and airlines, which were brought under control of the Civil Aeronautics Board (CAB) in 1938.[3]

Rate and Entry Regulation in Transportation

The regulatory schemes imposed on these two transportation industries differed in two major respects from the regulation of natural monopoly. First, they made control of entry a major focus of regulation. (In the nature of things, regulators of natural monopolies do not have to worry about excessive numbers of new competitors crowding into the market.) And second, they emphasized minimum rather than maximum price regulation. The traditional argument for regulation of natural monopoly was that without it, prices would rise too high. In the case of airlines and trucking, the concern instead was that without

---

[3]Agricultural marketing orders, another competition limiting device, date from the same period. (See Chapter 25.)

regulation, prices would fall too low. Both the ICC and the CAB were, however, given the power to regulate maximum as well as minimum rates.

It is generally acknowledged that regulation of trucking and airlines succeeded in its objective of raising prices and limiting the number of competitors in particular transportation markets. As the years passed, however, many economists began to have second thoughts as to whether high prices and limited competition were really worthy objectives of government policy. With the advent of the inflationary 1970s, the doubts about regulation became conviction, and the economics profession turned almost unanimously against regulation of entry and of minimum rates in competitively structured industries. Several theories of what regulation of airlines and trucks has actually accomplished are worth examining.

The Cartel Theory of Regulation

One widely advanced theory of airline and trucking regulation maintains that regulation is nothing more or less than a device permitting rival firms to form cartels. It is easy to see why this theory developed. Chapter 9 showed that two major weaknesses of most cartels are an inability to control competition from nonmembers and an inability to prevent members from cheating on price agreements. The laws giving the ICC and the CAB authority over trucking and airlines remedied these two problems. Both agencies became extremely restrictive of entry. (The CAB did not let in a single new major airline in the first forty years of its existence, and the ICC was barely more generous.) And both agencies were granted, and used, authority to prevent carriers from cutting prices below the established minimums.

True, the authority given the ICC and the CAB to set upper limits on prices did not fit in well with the cartel theory of regulation. But proponents of the theory argued that both agencies were soon "captured" by the industries they regulated, so that the power to impose the maximum rates was not used effectively. It is true that for many years trucking firms and airlines were able to use their political influence to ensure that a majority of commissioners remained friendly to the industry point of view.

A number of empirical studies appeared to support the cartel theory of regulation. Many of these studies, like the Stigler-Friedland study of electric utilities, were based on comparisons of regulated and unregulated transportation markets. One study, for example, showed that unregulated intrastate airline fares in California and Texas were only about half the level of regulated interstate fares over comparable distances. Other studies compared regulated freight rates for industrial commodities with freight rates for agricultural commodities, which had been granted a special exemption from regulation. Again, the regulated rates appeared substantially higher.

The Distributional Theory of Regulation

Despite its surface plausibility, and despite the evidence of higher prices in regulated industries, not all economists found the cartel theory of regulation acceptable, at least in its simple form. Certain pieces of evidence did not fit in. For example, despite the best efforts of the CAB, airlines were not consistently able to earn high profits. And in the trucking industry, the major users of freight service, whom one would expect to be hurt most directly by high rates, rarely complained. In fact, they generally praised the regulatory scheme for bringing about a high quality of transportation service.

Imperfection in the Cartels   In order to explain these puzzling observations, economists began to pay more attention to imperfections in the supposed cartels that regulation had established. The most glaring imperfection was the fact that while both airline and trucking regulations controlled *price* competition, neither successfully controlled *nonprice* competition. Both trucking firms and airlines were free to compete for customers by increasing the frequency and convenience of service, by advertising, and by intensive personal sales efforts. This nonprice competition was very expensive. In the case of airlines, for example, adding more flights each day to attract customers meant that each flight would carry fewer passengers. Nonprice competition thus pushed the cost per passenger up so high that no matter what level of fares the CAB allowed, no more than a normal rate of return could be earned—and sometimes not even that.

Distributional Effects   As some of these indirect effects of regulation became more fully understood, economists began to see that regulation could not be thought of simply in terms of a transfer of monopoly profits from users to producers. Instead, the effects of regulation on the way the net products of the industry were distributed were very much more complicated. Some producers, no doubt, were enabled to earn higher profits than they otherwise would have—some of the time. But most of the potential profits resulting from high fares went elsewhere.

Unionized workers appear to have been one group benefiting from regulation. Regulatory controls on entry have limited competition by nonunionized firms and have made it possible for Teamsters and airline pilots to bargain for higher wages. (Both these unions staunchly supported regulation.) Because nonprice competition sometimes put more airplanes in the skies and more trucks on the road than were strictly necessary to carry the traffic available, suppliers of transportation equipment may have been able to enjoy higher sales than they otherwise would have. And at least some transportation users were able to benefit from nonprice competition by getting a higher quality of service than would have been available without regulation. (Other users, however, would rather have had lower prices and done without some service frills.) The following case study illustrates the approach taken by proponents of the distributional theory of regulation.

Case 14.2
The Beneficiaries of Trucking Regulation

Thomas Gale Moore of the Hoover Institution at Stanford University was one of the first economists to try to measure the cost to the economy of trucking regulation. He did a number of studies based on comparisons of the regulated U.S. trucking industry with unregulated intrastate trucking and with less strictly regulated industries in other countries. These studies indicated that regulation raised freight rates some 10 to 20 percent above their competitive equilibrium level.

Having estimated that the total cost of trucking regulation was some $4 billion per year, Moore next turned to the question of how the excess revenue was distributed. Did it end up in the pockets of the carriers' stockholders? Did it disappear into thin air?

First, Moore estimated the effect of regulation on the wages of unionized trucking employees. Using a variety of methods, he concluded that members of the International Brotherhood of Teamsters earned a total of about $1.2 billion per year more under regulation than they would have been able to earn without regulation.

Next, he attempted to estimate the excess profits, if any, earned by trucking firms. He was aided in his efforts by the fact that the ICC allows truckers to buy and sell, among themselves, the "certificates" that permit them to carry certain cargos over certain routes. Moore reasoned that the price a trucking firm would be willing to pay for such a certificate would indicate the profits it expected to earn on that route, above and beyond its operating costs. From data on the value of operating certificates, then, he estimated that truckers were earning some $1.4 billion per year in pure economic profits.

Moore next considered possible benefits from regulation to suppliers of transportation equipment and to shippers. He concluded that benefits to suppliers were negligible. And although particular shippers probably gained from regulation, others presumably lost, so that shippers as a group received no net gains.

After deducting $1.2 billion for the Teamsters and $1.4 billion for the carriers from the original $4 billion, another $1.4 billion was still unaccounted for. Moore concluded that this sum was dissipated in pure waste. For example, ICC regulations sometimes force truckers to follow circuitous routes. Other times they force them to return empty to home base after a trip instead of allowing them to compete with other truckers for return loads. Such practices mean wasted time, energy, and capital equipment.

If trucking regulation is a cartel, concluded Moore, it is certainly a very imperfect one. Each $1 in monopoly profits earned by truckers appears to cost the shipping public $2.86.

Source: Based on Thomas Gale Moore, "The Beneficiaries of Trucking Regulation," used with permission from the *Journal of Law and Economics* 21 (October 1978): 327–344. Copyright 1978 by the University of Chicago Law School.

Other Theories of Regulation

By no means everyone accepts Moore's estimate of a $4 billion annual burden from trucking regulation. There are at least two other theories that have not yet been considered. One is the Stigler-Friedland theory, which says that regulation does not necessarily have any effect at all on prices, profits, or output of the regulated industry. Applied to the trucking industry, this theory suggests that, over the years, trucking firms have in one way or another been able to get around most of the apparently restrictive regulations imposed by the ICC. A decisive test of this theory would require an actual controlled experiment in which regulation were removed from all or a large part of the industry. If this were done, and if rates did not fall the 10 to 20 percent that Moore's estimates suggest, it would be clear that trucking regulation has in fact been no more effective than Stigler and Friedland estimated electric regulation to be.

Still another theory—advanced by economists working for the trucking industry but accepted by few outside of it—holds that regulation has certain important benefits not yet mentioned. The most important of these benefits, it is said, is a stabilization of freight rates and service quality. Many users of the transportation system appear to accept this theory. They do not believe that the average level of trucking rates would fall anywhere near 20 percent under deregulation. Instead, they think that rates would have about the same average level but would move up and down frequently and unpredictably, thereby hampering systematic transportation planning. This theory too appears hard to test, short of a large-scale controlled experiment.

Moves toward Deregulation

As the 1970s drew to an end, it began to appear that time had run out for many of the anticompetitive regulatory schemes that had their origins in the 1930s. The most spectacular single action was the passage by Congress in 1978 of a bill that will, after a transitional period, almost entirely deregulate the air passenger industry and abolish the CAB altogether. A companion bill the same year ended rate and entry regulation for air freight. It will be several years before the long-run impact of these actions can be evaluated, but the initial results are encouraging: In 1978, record numbers of passengers took to the air in response to low, competitive fares; and at the same time, airlines earned record profits.

Meanwhile, a new generation of commissioners began to fill seats on and chair many major regulatory agencies. At the CAB itself, Chairman Alfred Kahn had greatly relaxed regulation before Congress passed its landmark legislation. At the ICC, too, new Carter appointees moved cautiously but steadily toward regulatory reform. Eventually, Congress can be expected to pass legislation to reinforce the administrative actions that the ICC is taking. This means that some of the ''controlled experiments'' alluded to above are likely to be carried out.

The late 1970s also saw relaxation of regulation, if not always outright deregulation, in other industries discussed specifically elsewhere in this book. Congress passed legislation easing (and, in principle, eventually abolishing) regulation of natural gas prices. The Federal Reserve System issued new rules making it easier for banks and savings institutions to compete with one another for funds. And the Securities and Exchange Commission abolished regulations that had long limited competition among stockbrokers, an action that resulted in a much lower average level of brokerage fees.

But even while the regulations of the 1930s were being discarded, the 1970s saw a spectacular growth of new forms of regulation in the areas of health, safety, and the environment. No discussion of regulation would be complete without at least some mention of them.

HEALTH AND SAFETY REGULATION

Among the most rapidly growing regulatory agencies of the last decade have been the Occupational Safety and Health Administration (OSHA), the Consumer Product Safety Commission (CPSC), the National Highway and Traffic Safety Administration (NHTSA), and the Environmental Protection Agency (EPA). In addition, some long-established agencies, such as the Food and Drug Administration (FDA), have become much more active than before. These agencies are not directly concerned with prices, entry, and competition. Instead, they are concerned with what kinds of products are produced and how they are produced. Leaving environmental issues to later in the book (Chapter 19), the next section will look at what economists have to say about health and safety regulation.

Some Normative Issues

The goals of health and safety regulation are to make the world a safer, healthier, more pleasant place to live. Since these are goals that no one can argue with, why are the regulations designed to achieve them so controversial? Part of the answer is that even when goals are agreed upon, there can be disagreements about the best ways to pursue them. Such disagreements, which belong to the realm of positive economics, will be discussed shortly. Other important sources of controversy, however, are fundamentally normative. Even though virtually everyone believes that health and safety are in themselves good, there are profound normative disagreements about the relationship of these goals to other, also worthy, goals. Two such areas of disagreement often threaten to overshadow all discussion of the positive economics of health and safety regulation.

Can an Economic Value Be Put on Health and Safety? The first question is whether it is morally defensible to consider trade-offs between human health and safety on the one hand and material prosperity on the other. Many of those who support strong, strictly enforced health and safety regulations (such as Dr. Sidney Wolfe, director of the Public Citizen's Health Research Group) argue that there is no way to measure the value of human life, so regulations should be set without regard to economic trade-offs or cost-benefit ratios.[4]

Others, however, do not share this view. It is not that they are inclined to belittle the value of human life but rather, simply, that they see no point in morally condemning something that people do every day. And people do, every day, sacrifice health and safety in favor of other goals. People choose the convenience of travel by car over the annoyances of travel by bus, even though buses are known to be many times safer than cars. People take high paying jobs in cities rather than low paying jobs in the country even though city air is known to be many times less healthful than country air. People have medical checkups once a year but not twice a year or once a week because, beyond some point, the gain in terms of health is no longer worth the sacrifice of time and money.

Whose Values? A second normative question remains even if it is conceded that cost-benefit analysis can legitimately be applied in the areas of health and safety. That is the question of whose values should govern the trade-offs that are made between health and safety on the one hand and economic costs on the other. Should policy be guided by the values of the individual people who actually receive the benefits and bear the costs? Or should such decisions be reserved to the superior judgment of experts? In practical terms, this comes down to the emotionally charged question of when people should simply be warned of health and safety hazards and when they should be forced to be safe and healthy whether they want to be or not. Should people simply be warned that tobacco or saccharin are potential health hazards, or should consumption of these products be prohibited? Should people be allowed to decide for themselves whether to buckle their auto seatbelts, or should they be prohibited from buying cars not having airbags or other passive restraints?

Strictly speaking, economics as a science has nothing to say about these normative issues. As it happens, though, economists as individuals often believe strongly in the moral legitimacy of considering economic costs and benefits in health and safety decisions and of allowing well-informed individ-

---

[4]See Philip Shabecoff, ''Regulation by the U.S.: Its Costs vs. Its Benefits,'' *New York Times*, June 14, 1978.

uals to make those decisions for themselves whenever possible. When such an economist undertakes to discuss health and safety regulation with someone who believes in health and safety at any cost, whether people want it or not, what takes place is often more a fight than a rational debate. That is a pity, because there are some things that economics as a science—positive economics—can contribute to the controversy over health and safety regulation.

Minimizing the Cost of Regulation

The major area in which economists and regulators ought to cooperate rather than do battle is that of ensuring that regulatory goals, once chosen, are achieved at least cost. A constant theme in the economics of health and safety regulation is the importance of giving local decision makers maximum flexibility in choosing the least cost means of complying with regulation. One way to do this is to issue regulations in the form of performance standards rather than in the form of engineering controls. *Performance standards* are rules that specify the results to be achieved, whereas *engineering controls* are rules that specify particular techniques to be used or equipment to be installed. The following case study illustrates the issue of performance standards versus engineering controls.

Case 14.3
Regulating Worker Exposure to Cotton Dust

As of 1978, an estimated 150,000 of 800,000 cotton workers in the United States were subject to a respiratory ailment known as brown lung disease. There appeared to be little disagreement among industry and government officials that the disease was a serious health hazard and that its incidence could be significantly reduced by lowering worker exposure to cotton dust. When it came time to issue specific regulations, however, a sharp dispute broke out within the Carter administration over the issue of performance standards versus engineering controls.

On one side of the dispute were Labor Secretary Ray Marshall and Dr. Eula Bingham, director of the Occupational Safety and Health Administration. In Dr. Bingham's view, the law creating OSHA ordered the agency to ensure a safe and healthful workplace for every worker and said nothing about economics. The most effective known technique for reducing cotton dust exposure as of 1978 appeared to be elaborate equipment that would filter the dust out of the air in the factory. So OSHA proposed a directive that would require all firms to install such equipment on a specified schedule.

On the other side of the debate were Charles Schultze, chairman of President Carter's Council of Economic Advisers, and Barry Bosworth, head of the Council on Wage and Price Stability. They argued that the engineering controls proposed by OSHA showed no understanding of how the market economy worked and that they would be unnecessarily inflationary. Alternative worker protection techniques were available, they pointed out; among them were individual respirators (dust masks) for workers and frequent medical inspections that would screen highly susceptible workers out of high exposure areas. Instead of mandating expensive filtration equipment, the government should only indicate the direction firms should take and let private management decide how to get there. The engineering controls, they complained, would not only be unnecessarily expensive but would remove all incentive to develop new technology. As an example, they pointed to an improved lightweight individual respirator being developed in England. Such technology, although perhaps not yet ready for implementation, should not be frozen out, they said.

After several weeks of much publicized infighting, the regulations finally issued leaned heavily in the direction of engineering controls. The president's economists did achieve what they considered significant concessions, however. OSHA agreed to a stretched-out timetable for installing the filtration equipment and permitted individual respirators to be used in the meantime. And a provision was added to encourage the industry to develop new, less expensive technology in the future.

Commenting on these efforts to introduce notions of cost-effectiveness into the process of government regulation, one government economist said: "It's like trying to turn an aircraft carrier. We never dreamed how entrenched the bureaucracy could become in its ideas about how something should be done."

CONCLUSIONS

This chapter has covered a lot of ground, including discussions of many different regulatory agencies and industries. Everywhere it has turned, however, it has found one constant theme: Economists, more than ever before, are skeptical about regulation. As economist George Eads, a member of President Carter's Council of Economic Advisers, once put it, "The weight of economic evidence has become so great that any economist venturing to support regulation today is apt to find himself in a very lonely position. What only a short time ago was considered heresy now has assumed the status of conventional wisdom."[5]

When all the details and particulars are stripped away, why is it that economists are so critical of regulation? It appears that the economic case against regulation can be expressed in terms of two fundamental propositions.

The first proposition is that regulatory agencies and proceedings in practice come to be dominated by efforts to redistribute the product of the industry differently than the market would distribute it, and this inevitably has a negative impact on the efficiency with which the regulated industry operates. In some cases, the distributional objective may be to prevent the owners of regulated firms from earning monopoly profits. In other cases, it may be to prevent such firms from competing one another's profits away. The distributional objective may be to favor one group of customers or suppliers at the expense of other customers and suppliers. It may be to give workers in the industry higher wages than they could achieve in an unregulated market or to give them a different balance between wages and safe working conditions. Economists complain not so much about any of these particular distributional goals of regulation as about the fact that regulation is such a leaky bucket to use for transferring wealth or income from one group to another. Many dollars in costs must be dipped out in order to deliver one dollar in benefits to those the regulation intends to help.

The second proposition that underlies the economic case against regulation is one that would apply even if regulators were to put a high priority on efficiency and cost effectiveness: Regulatory efforts to improve on the workings of the market fail more often than not simply because the regulatory process is a less efficient mechanism than is the market for making decisions and utilizing information. Utility regulators fail to keep rates down because they know too little about the cost and demand conditions under which the firms they regulate operate. Transportation regulators try to second guess the market as to which carriers should be allowed to serve which segments of it and end up imposing higher costs on all carriers. Health and safety regulators impose

---

[5]George Eads, "Economists vs. Regulators," in *Perspectives on Federal Transportation Policy*, ed. James C. Miller, III (Washington, D.C.: American Enterprise Institute, 1975), p. 101.

engineering controls that leave too little leeway for local managers to make use of their superior knowledge of local conditions.

These are propositions that will be dealt with again later in the book in the discussions of environmental and energy regulation. They are propositions that will continue to underlie debates in Washington between regulators and inflation fighters. And they are propositions that will underlie much of what appears about regulation in the daily papers.

SUMMARY

1. A natural monopoly is an industry in which total costs are minimized by having just one producer serve the entire market. The policy problem raised by natural monopoly is how to keep the single producer from exploiting its monopoly power to raise prices and restrict output. The traditional solution is to impose maximum price regulation in order to limit the firm's rate of return to a normal level. In practice, however, the effectiveness of such regulation may be rather limited.

2. Other industries are regulated despite the fact that they appear to be inherently competitive. For example, the regulatory schemes introduced during the 1930s for airlines and trucking firms were designed to limit competition by controlling the entry of new competitors and limiting the freedom of firms to cut prices. Economists disagree about the actual effects of such regulations. Some think that regulation in effect sets up a cartel that delivers monopoly profits to regulated firms. Others think that the main effect of regulation is to redistribute the product of the regulated industries, with producers benefiting only to a limited extent. Still others doubt that regulation has any major effect once firms adjust completely.

3. Health and safety regulation has grown rapidly in recent years at the same time that some older types of economic regulation have been phased out. The expansion of health and safety regulation has raised controversial issues for both normative and positive economics. One important normative issue is whether it is morally acceptable to place a dollar value on human health and safety. Another is whether people should be given more health and safety protection than they might voluntarily choose. Positive economics cannot make any contribution to resolving those normative issues, but it can be brought to bear on another important issue of health and safety regulation: how to achieve given goals at minimum cost. A major recommendation here is that, where feasible, regulators should set goals and leave private managers maximum flexibility in deciding how to achieve them. This recommendation implies a preference for performance standards over engineering controls.

4. Regulation, at least as currently practiced, is not highly thought of by most economists today. The economic case against regulation can be expressed in terms of two fundamental propositions. First, regulatory agencies and proceedings become dominated by efforts to redistribute income and wealth among participants in regulated markets, and this inevitably has a negative impact on economic efficiency. Second, even when regulators consciously try to make markets work more efficiently, they more often than not fail because regulation is not as effective as the market itself for making economic decisions and utilizing economic information.

DISCUSSION QUESTIONS

1. Compare and contrast antitrust laws and regulation as alternative policies toward monopoly. Why is it that sometimes one and sometimes the other is used? In view of the criticisms of antitrust law examined in Chapter 13, do you think regulation should be used as a substitute for antitrust action in every case? Explain.

2. In the case of a true natural monopoly, do you think it would be best to have a regulated private monopoly, public ownership of the monopoly, or an unregulated private monopoly? How do considerations of efficiency enter into your choice? Considerations of equity? Considerations of the actual, as opposed to the ideal, operation of regulation and publicly owned producers?

3. Because the ICC limits the number of trucking firms allowed to serve particular routes, often the only way a new firm can get authority to serve a route is to purchase the "certificate" of a carrier already serving it. As a result, such certificates are often worth hundreds of thousands of dollars. If the trucking industry were deregulated so that any firm could serve any route it wanted, what do you think would happen to the value of these certificates? Do you think regulatory reformers should be concerned about the effects of deregulation on certificate values? If so, what could they do to mitigate those effects?

4. Why would a regulation setting a minimum fare for taxicabs (at a level above the market equilibrium fare) not by itself be likely to increase the profits of cab owners in the long run? Explain why regulations governing entry and nonprice competition would also be necessary. Once a comprehensive system of taxi regulation were in force, what groups other than cab owners might try to manipulate that system for their own purposes, and how would they do it?

5. Lowering the speed limit from seventy miles per hour to fifty-five miles per hour has reduced the number of people killed on the highways. Presumably, reducing the speed limit still further, say to forty-five miles per hour, would cut traffic deaths still more. How would you go about determining whether the further reduction in the speed limit is worthwhile? Is there any way you could make this decision without at least implicitly placing an economic value on human life?

SUGGESTIONS FOR FURTHER READING

Argyris, Chris, et al. *Regulating Business: The Search for an Optimum.* San Francisco: Institute for Contemporary Studies, 1978.
A combination of case studies of regulation and broader papers on general problems of regulation, all quite accessible to the general reader.

Kahn, Alfred E. *The Economics of Regulation,* 2 vols. New York: Wiley, 1971.
This remains the definitive treatise on the economics of regulation; the author has gone from being a Cornell professor to being chairman of the New York State Public Service Commission, the Civil Aeronautics Board, and President Carter's Council on Wage and Price Stability.

Miller, James C., III, and Yandle, Bruce. *Benefit-Cost Analysis of Social Regulation.* Washington, D.C.: American Enterprise Institute, 1979.
A selection of actual case studies in cost-benefit analysis of health and safety regulation, featuring the work in this area done by the Council on Wage and Price Stability. Includes airport noise, lawnmower safety, motorcycle emission standards, and many more subjects.

Peterson, Mary Bennett. *The Regulated Consumer.* Ottawa, Ill.: Green Hill Publishers, 1971.
A concise journalistic account of unintended effects of regulation on the people regulations are supposed to protect.

Regulation.
This bimonthly journal published by the American Enterprise Institute contains analysis and commentary on all aspects of regulation. It is written for policy makers and nonspecialists.

FACTOR MARKETS
AND INCOME DISTRIBUTION

FACTOR MARKETS AND MARGINAL PRODUCTIVITY THEORY

WHAT YOU WILL LEARN IN THIS CHAPTER

This chapter is the first of four that discuss the operation of factor markets—the markets in which labor, capital, and natural resources are bought and sold. These markets are much like the product markets studied earlier, with one major exception: In factor markets, households are the sellers and firms the buyers. Accordingly, a theory of factor supply can be developed as an outgrowth of the theory of consumer choice, and a theory of factor demand can be developed as an outgrowth of the theory of the firm. The factor market theory discussed in this chapter covers both perfectly competitive and less than perfectly competitive cases.

FOR REVIEW

Here are some important terms and concepts that will be put to use in this chapter. If you do not understand them, review them before proceeding.
- *Marginal utility and consumer equilibrium (Chapter 5)*
- *Income and substitution effect (Chapter 5)*
- *Marginal physical product (Chapter 7)*
- *Law of diminishing returns (Chapter 7)*

One very important set of markets in the economy has been referred to so far only indirectly: **factor markets**—the markets in which labor, capital, and natural resources are bought and sold. Factor markets perform two major functions in a market economy. They help determine how goods and services are produced and for whom they are produced. This chapter and the next three chapters will look at both functions.

Factor markets are important in determining how goods and services are produced because most goods and services can be produced in more than one way. Wheat, for example, can be grown by extensive cultivation of large areas of land with a lot of machinery and little labor or by intensive cultivation of small areas with little machinery and much labor. The choice of production methods depends on the relative prices of the various factors. As those prices change, production methods can change too. Factors that are relatively cheap are used intensively, while those that are relatively expensive are used sparingly.

At the same time, factor markets help determine for whom output is produced, because most people earn their incomes by selling whatever factors

Factor markets The markets in which the factors of production—labor, natural resources, and capital—are bought and sold.

Functional distribution of income The distribution of income according to factor ownership—that is, the distribution among workers, natural resource owners, and owners of capital.

Personal distribution of income The distribution of income among individuals, taking into account both the functional distribution of income and the distribution of factor ownership among persons.

of production they own. The greatest number sell their labor services. Many also sell or rent land or capital that they own. Because markets determine factor prices, they also determine how much of the total product will go to the owners of labor services, capital, and natural resources.

The distribution of income among factor owners is called the **functional distribution of income.** Functional distribution partly explains for whom output is produced, but it is not the whole story. The **personal distribution of income**—which specific people receive the income—depends both on the functional distribution of income and on the way ownership of factors is distributed among people. This chapter and the next two will be largely concerned with the functional distribution of income. First, the outlines of marginal productivity theory will be presented. Chapter 16 will apply this theory to labor markets and use it to help explain the nature and functions of labor unions. Chapter 17 will turn to two other factor markets—those for natural resources and capital—and will also discuss profits as a source of income. Finally, Chapter 18 will take up the subject of the personal distribution of income and, in particular, the problem of poverty. It will show how the operation of factor markets helps determine the incidence of poverty and will discuss various government policies aimed at reducing or eliminating poverty.

THE DEMAND FOR FACTORS OF PRODUCTION

The Firm in Factor Markets

In many ways, factor markets are much like the product markets already studied. The theories of supply and demand and the tools of marginal analysis apply to factor markets just as to product markets. But factor markets do differ from product markets in one major respect. In factor markets, it is firms that are the buyers and households that are the sellers, rather than the other way around. A theory of the demand for factors of production must be based on the same considerations of price, revenue, and profit that determine the supply of products. A theory of factor supply must be an extension of the theory of consumer choice.

In taking the first steps toward a theory of factor demand the assumption, as earlier, will be that firms aim to maximize profits. Each profit maximizing firm must take three things into account when it makes its hiring decisions. The first is the quantity of output produced by a unit of the factor in question, the second is the revenue derived from the sale of the output that will be produced, and the third is the cost of obtaining the factor.

Marginal Physical Product

Chapter 7 defined the *marginal physical product* of a factor as the increase in output resulting from a one unit increase in the input of that factor when the quantity of all other factors used remains unchanged. For example, if employing one additional worker hour of labor in a light bulb factory yields an added output of five light bulbs, when no other inputs to the production process are increased, the marginal physical product of labor in that factory is five bulbs per hour. To take another example, if giving a farmer one more acre of land makes it possible for the farmer to produce twenty more bushels of wheat per year—without any increase in the amount of work performed, the amount of machinery used, or anything else—the marginal physical product of land on that farm is twenty bushels per acre. Finally, if having one extra dollar of capital allows a taxi company to carry one extra passenger one extra mile each year, that puts the marginal physical product of capital for the company at one passenger mile per dollar's worth of capital.

Law of Diminishing Returns As Chapter 7 showed, the marginal physical product of a factor varies as the quantity of the factor used varies, other things being equal. In particular, as the quantity of a single variable factor increases, with the quantities of all other factor inputs remaining fixed, a point will be reached beyond which the marginal physical product of the variable factor will decline. This principle is known as the *law of diminishing returns.*

Exhibit 15.1 shows total and marginal physical product curves for a firm subject to the law of diminishing returns throughout the range of zero to twenty units of factor input. (At this point, it does not matter whether the factor in question is labor, capital, or natural resource; the principle is the same for all.) As the quantity of this one factor is increased, with the quantities of all other factors used held constant, output increases—but at a diminishing rate. The first unit of the factor yields a marginal physical product of twenty units of output, the second a marginal physical product of nineteen units of

---

Exhibit 15.1

Total and marginal physical product of a factor of production

As the quantity of one factor increases with the quantity of other factors remaining unchanged, total physical product increases, but at a decreasing rate. Marginal physical product, as Part c of this exhibit and Column 3 of the table in Part a show, decreases as the quantity of the factor employed increases. This decrease in marginal physical product is a direct consequence of the law of diminishing returns.

(a)

Quantity of Factor (1)	Total Physical Product (2)	Marginal Physical Product (3)
0	0	
1	20	20
2	39	19
3	57	18
4	74	17
5	90	16
6	105	15
7	119	14
8	132	13
9	144	12
10	155	11
11	165	10
12	174	9
13	182	8
14	189	7
15	195	6
16	200	5
17	204	4
18	207	3
19	209	2
20	210	1

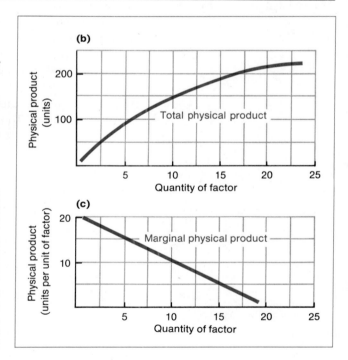

output, and so on. After the twentieth unit of output, as the example is constructed, marginal physical product drops to zero. This implies that some absolute capacity ceiling has been reached, so that adding more of the variable factor cannot produce more output unless the quantities of some of the fixed factors are also increased. For example, if the variable factor in question is labor, it may be that adding more than twenty workers will do nothing to increase output unless, say, the quantity of machinery available for use by the workers is also increased. Note that beyond twenty units of output, where the marginal physical product of the variable factor drops to zero, the total physical product curve becomes horizontal.

Marginal Revenue Product

To determine what quantity of each factor of production it should hire to maximize profit, a firm must take into account the revenue that will be earned from the sale of the product of an added unit of factor input as well as the size of the marginal physical product. Here, a new term will be useful. The change in revenue resulting from the sale of the product produced by one additional unit of factor input is called the **marginal revenue product** of that factor.

Marginal revenue product (of a factor) The change in revenue resulting from the sale of the product produced by one additional unit of factor input.

Marginal Revenue Product for a Competitive Firm

What happens to the marginal revenue product of a factor as the quantity of that factor is varied depends on what happens to both the marginal physical product of the factor and the marginal revenue earned by selling the product. The simplest case to consider is that of a perfectly competitive firm. Because such a firm is a price taker, as shown in Chapter 8, the quantity of output it produces has no effect on the price at which its output is sold. Marginal revenue for the competitive firm is thus equal to the price of the firm's output, which is constant for all quantities of output. To calculate marginal revenue product of a factor for such

Quantity of Factor (1)	Total Physical Product (2)	Marginal Physical Product (3)	Revenue per Unit (Price) (4)	Marginal Revenue Product (5)
0	0			
1	20	20	$1	$20
2	39	19	1	19
3	57	18	1	18
4	74	17	1	17
5	90	16	1	16
6	105	15	1	15
7	119	14	1	14
8	132	13	1	13
9	144	12	1	12
10	155	11	1	11
11	165	10	1	10
12	174	9	1	9
13	182	8	1	8
14	189	7	1	7
15	198	6	1	6
16	200	5	1	5
17	204	4	1	4
18	207	3	1	3
19	209	2	1	2
20	210	1	1	1

Exhibit 15.2
Marginal revenue product for a typical price taking firm
For a price taking firm, the marginal revenue product of a factor is equal to the factor's marginal physical product times the price of the product. This table is constructed on the assumption that the product price is $1 per unit and that marginal physical product is the same as in Exhibit 15.1.

a firm, then, the marginal physical product of the factor is multiplied by the price of the output.

Exhibit 15.2 gives an example of how marginal revenue product is calculated for a perfectly competitive firm. The marginal physical product schedule is the same as that given in Exhibit 15.1, and a constant price of $1 per unit of output is assumed.

Marginal Revenue Product for a Monopolist If the firm in question is not perfectly competitive, the price at which it sells its output will tend to vary as the quantity of output varies. Suppose, for example, that the firm is a pure monopolist. As Chapter 9 demonstrated, a pure monopolist must decrease the price at which its product is sold each time it wants to increase the quantity sold, in accordance with the downward-sloping demand curve for its product. Because the price per unit decreases as output increases, marginal revenue per unit of output is always less than price per unit for a monopolist.

To calculate the increase in revenue resulting from a one unit increase in factor input for a monopolist, then, requires taking changes in both marginal physical product and marginal revenue into account. Exhibit 15.3 illustrates

---

Exhibit 15.3

Marginal revenue product for a monopolistic firm

This exhibit shows how marginal revenue product varies as the quantity of factor input varies for a firm that is a pure monopolist. As Column 3 shows, price falls as outputs increase, in accordance with the demand for the firm's product. Total revenue begins to decline after ten units of output, as marginal revenue per unit of output becomes negative, even though marginal physical product remains positive. Marginal revenue product can be calculated either as the differences between successive entries in the total revenue column or as the product of marginal physical product and marginal revenue per unit of output.

Quantity of Factor (1)	Total Physical Product (2)	Price of Output (3)	Total Revenue (4)	Marginal Revenue Product (5)	Marginal Physical Product (6)	Marginal Revenue per Unit of Output (7)
0	0	—	0			
1	20	$1.40	$ 28.00	$28.00	20	$1.40
2	39	1.31	50.90	22.90	19	1.21
3	57	1.22	69.26	18.36	18	1.02
4	74	1.13	83.62	14.36	17	.84
5	90	1.05	94.50	10.88	16	.68
6	105	.98	102.38	7.88	15	.52
7	119	.91	107.70	5.32	14	.38
8	132	.84	110.88	3.18	13	.24
9	144	.78	112.32	1.44	12	.12
10	155	.73	112.38	.06	11	.01
11	165	.68	111.38	−1.00	10	−.10
12	174	.63	109.62	−1.76	9	−.20
13	182	.59	107.38	−2.24	8	−.28
14	189	.56	104.90	−2.48	7	−.35
15	195	.53	102.38	−2.52	6	−.42
16	200	.50	100.00	−2.38	5	−.47
17	204	.48	97.92	−2.08	4	−.52
18	207	.47	96.26	−1.66	3	−.55
19	209	.46	95.10	−1.16	2	−.58
20	210	.45	94.50	−.60	1	−.60

Figures in Columns 3, 4, 5, and 7 are rounded to the nearest cent.

how this is done. The exhibit is constructed using the same total physical product schedule as Exhibits 15.1 and 15.2, but this time the firm is assumed to be a monopolist. Column 3 gives the firm's demand curve, showing that the price at which output can be sold drops from $1.40 per unit at 20 units of output to $.45 at 210 units of output. Multiplying price times total physical product gives the total revenue corresponding to each quantity of factor input, shown in Column 4.

The differences between successive entries in the total revenue column give the marginal revenue product data, shown in Column 5. For example, as the quantity of factor input increases from 4 units to 5 units, the total output increases from 74 units to 90 units, while the price falls from $1.13 per unit to $1.05. As Column 4 shows, total revenue increases from $83.62 when 4 units of factor input are used to $94.50 when 5 units of factor input are used. This gives a marginal revenue product of $10.88 in the range from 4 to 5 units of factor input.

As the price continues to fall, marginal revenue eventually becomes negative. Beyond that point, additional units of factor input, even though they increase total physical product, reduce total revenue. The turning point comes at 10 units of factor input, as Exhibit 15.3 is constructed. Beyond that point, marginal revenue product is negative, even though marginal physical product remains positive.

At every level of factor input, the marginal revenue product of the factor is equal to the marginal physical product times the marginal revenue per unit of output. This relationship is shown in Columns 5 through 7 of Exhibit 15.3. Note that the marginal revenue figures in Column 7 are expressed in terms of dollars per unit of output, whereas the marginal revenue product figures in Column 5 are expressed in terms of dollars per unit of factor input.

Marginal Factor Cost

The third consideration a firm must take into account to determine the profit maximizing quantity of a factor is the cost of obtaining each additional unit of that factor—the factor's **marginal factor cost.**

Marginal factor cost The amount by which a firm's total factor cost must increase in order for it to obtain an additional unit of that factor.

To keep things simple for the moment, consider only the case where a firm is a price taker in the market where it buys its factors of production. This will happen if the firm is only one among a large number of firms competing to hire that particular factor and if the quantity of the factor it uses is only a small fraction of the total used by all firms. For a firm that buys as a price taker, marginal factor cost is simply equal to the market price of the factor. If, for example, the market wage rate for typists is $7 per hour, then the marginal factor cost for this particular type of labor is $7 per hour for any firm that is a price taker in the market for typists.

Profit Maximization

Profit maximization requires that a firm hire just enough of each factor of production to equalize marginal revenue product and marginal factor cost. If marginal revenue product exceeds marginal factor cost, hiring one more unit of the factor will add more to the revenue than to the cost and hence will increase profit. If marginal factor cost exceeds marginal revenue product, reducing input of the factor by one unit will reduce cost by more than revenue and hence will also increase profit. Only when marginal revenue product and marginal factor cost are equal will it be impossible for any change in factor input to raise profit. This rule applies both to a firm that is a perfect competitor in its output market and to a monopolist.

Exhibit 15.4 illustrates this profit maximization rule. The exhibit, which contains both a table and a corresponding diagram, is constructed on the assumption that the firm is a perfect competitor in the output market and that it sells its product at $1 per unit, as in Exhibit 15.2. The firm is also assumed to be a price taker in the factor market, buying inputs of the factor at $5 per unit. Notice that profit rises as more of the factor is hired—up to the fifteenth unit of input. The firm just breaks even on the hiring of the sixteenth unit of input, and profit declines thereafter. It is between the fifteenth and sixteenth units of factor input that marginal revenue product becomes exactly equal to marginal factor cost.

Exhibit 15.4

Profit maximization for a price taking firm

Profit maximization requires that a firm hire just enough of each factor of production to equalize marginal revenue product and marginal factor cost. Here it is assumed that the firm is a price taker, as in Exhibit 15.2. The point of profit maximization falls between fifteen and sixteen units of output.

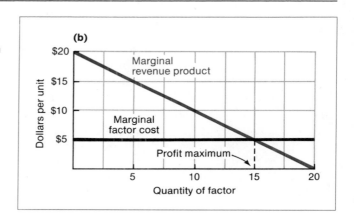

(b)

(a)

Quantity of Factor (1)	Marginal Revenue Product (2)	Marginal Factor Cost (3)	Total Factor Cost (4)	Fixed Costs (5)	Total Revenue (6)	Total Profit (7)
1			$ 5	$100	$ 20	−$85
2	$19	$5	10	100	39	−71
3	18	5	15	100	57	−58
4	17	5	20	100	74	−46
5	16	5	25	100	90	−35
6	15	5	30	100	105	−25
7	14	5	35	100	119	−16
8	13	5	40	100	132	−8
9	12	5	45	100	144	−1
10	11	5	50	100	155	5
11	10	5	55	100	165	10
12	9	5	60	100	174	14
13	8	5	65	100	182	17
14	7	5	70	100	189	19
15	6	5	75	100	195	20
16	5	5	80	100	200	20
17	4	5	85	100	204	19
18	3	5	90	100	207	17
19	2	5	95	100	209	14
20	1	5	100	100	210	10

Factor Demand Curves

It follows from this analysis of profit maximization that a firm's marginal revenue product curve for a factor is also the firm's demand curve for that factor. A demand curve must indicate the quantity demanded at each price, and it has just been shown that the quantity of the factor demanded will be whatever quantity makes the factor's price (more precisely, its marginal factor cost) equal to marginal revenue product.

Individual firm demand curves for a factor of production can be added together to get a market demand curve for that factor. Such a market demand is said to be a *derived* demand curve, because the demand for a factor of production does not arise from the usefulness of the factor services themselves. Instead it is derived indirectly from the usefulness of the products the factor can produce. The market demand for farmland is derived from the market demand for food, the market demand for printers from the market demand for books, and so on.

Changes in Factor Demand

The demand for factors, like the demand for products, changes in response to changes in economic conditions. Consider Exhibit 15.5. Suppose that the demand curve D_0 is the market demand curve for some factor of production. A change in the market price of that factor will cause the quantity of the factor demanded to change. This is represented by a movement along the demand curve. (See the arrow drawn parallel to D_0.) Changes in economic conditions other than a change in the factor's price can cause a change in demand for a factor—for example, a shift in the demand curve from D_0 to D_1 or D_2.

Three kinds of changes in particular are capable of causing shifts in the demand curve for a factor of production. First, an increase in demand for the product that the factor produces will shift the factor demand curve to the right. Similarly, a decrease in demand for the product will cause the factor demand curve to shift to the left. Second, a change in the price of another factor of

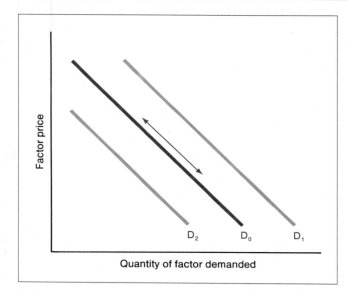

Exhibit 15.5

Movements along a factor demand curve and shifts in the curve

Changes in the price of a factor, other things being equal, will produce movements along a given factor demand curve, as shown by the arrow. Other kinds of changes can shift the factor demand curve. An increase in demand for the product produced by the factor might shift the curve from D_0 to D_1. An increase in the price of another factor that is a complement to the given factor might shift the curve from D_0 to D_2.

production used in combination with the given factor can also cause the demand for the given factor to shift. An increase in the price of a factor that is a substitute for the given factor will cause the demand curve for the given factor to shift to the right, while an increase in the price of a factor that is a complement to the given factor will cause the demand curve of that factor to shift to the left. Third, any change in technology that increases the marginal physical productivity of a factor will cause its demand curve to shift to the right, other things being equal, while a decrease in the marginal physical product of the factor will shift the curve to the left.

SUPPLY AND DEMAND IN THE LABOR MARKET

Up to this point, marginal productivity and factor demand have been discussed in general terms. It is time now to turn to the specifics of markets for particular factors. This section begins the analysis of such markets by looking at the supply and demand for labor. The discussion will be limited at first to the case where individual workers compete with one another for jobs. The next chapter will take up the case of organized labor markets, where workers join together into unions to bargain with employers rather than competing with one another for jobs on an individual basis. Finally, Chapter 17 will look at markets for capital and natural resources.

The Labor Supply Curve

The general analysis of a factor demand given in the previous section can be applied to the labor market without special modification. A labor supply curve is now needed to go with the labor demand curve. A look at the labor supply decision for an individual worker will begin the analysis.

Labor Supply for the Individual As individuals, people's decisions regarding how much labor to supply to the market are part of the general problem of consumer choice and can be analyzed in terms of the theory developed in Chapter 5. The best way to approach the problem is to think in terms of a trade-off between two alternative sources of utility—leisure and the consumption of purchased goods and services. Leisure is valued for relaxation, recreation, and the accomplishment of assorted household tasks. Time spent at leisure is time taken away from work, however, and thus is time taken away from earning income that can be used to buy goods and services. Within the limits of a twenty-four-hour day, people balance the relative advantages of work and leisure to achieve a consumer equilibrium in which, ideally, the marginal utility per hour of leisure exactly equals the marginal utility of the goods that can be bought with an hour's earnings.

The hourly wage rate can be thought of as the price—or, more precisely, as the opportunity cost—of leisure to the worker, in that it represents the dollar equivalent of the goods and services that must be sacrificed in order to enjoy an added hour of leisure. As the wage rate increases, it affects work versus leisure decisions in two ways. First, there is a substitution effect; the increased wage rate provides an incentive to work more, because each hour of work now produces more income to be spent on goods and services. In effect, purchased goods and services are substituted for leisure. Second, however, the increase in the wage rate has an income effect that tends to reduce hours worked. The higher wage rate, assuming that the prices of goods and services in general remain unchanged, increases workers' real incomes. With higher real incomes, they tend to consume more of all goods that are normal goods and less of those that are inferior goods. Leisure is a normal good. Other things being equal, people generally seek more leisure, in the form of shorter working hours and longer vacations, as their incomes rise. Taken by itself, then, the income effect of a wage increase is the reduction of the quantity of labor supplied by workers.

It can be seen, therefore, that the net effect of an increase in the wage rate on the quantity of labor supplied by an individual worker depends on the relative strength of the substitution and income effects. It is generally believed that for very low wage rates, the substitution effect predominates, so that the quantity of labor supplied increases as the wage increases. As the wage rises, however, the income effect becomes stronger. People tend to treat leisure as a luxury good; after they have assured themselves of a reasonable material standard of living, they begin to consider "spending" any further wage increases on increased time off from work. The labor supply curve for an individual to whom this generalization applies has a backward-bending shape, like the one shown in Exhibit 15.6. Over the positively sloped low wage section, the substitution effect of wage changes predominates, and over the negatively sloped high wage section, the income effect predominates.

Market Labor Supply Curves Even though the labor supply curves for all individual workers may bend backwards, at least over some range of wages, the supply curve for any particular type of labor as a whole is likely to be positively sloped throughout. Consider, for example, the supply of electrical engineers, the supply of typists in Chicago, or the supply of farm laborers in Texas. Each individual engineer or typist or laborer might, beyond some point, respond to an increased wage by cutting back on hours worked; but for the market as a whole, this tendency would be more than offset by new workers drawn into that particular labor market from other occupations or areas. Thus, other

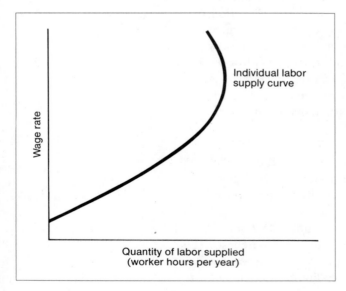

Exhibit 15.6
An individual's labor supply curve
On the one hand, a higher wage tends to increase the amount of work an individual is willing to do, because the extra money compensates for time taken away from leisure activities. On the other hand, a higher wage allows a person to take more time off work and still enjoy a high standard of living. Taken together, the two effects tend to give the individual labor supply curve the backward-bending shape shown here.

Exhibit 15.7

Hypothetical supply curve for typists

Although each individual typist may have a backward-bending supply curve, the supply curve for typists in any particular local market will have the usual upward-sloping shape. As the wage rises, people will be drawn into this occupation from other kinds of work or other localities.

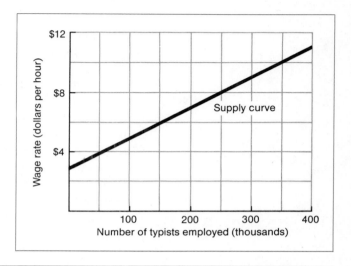

things being equal, if the wage rate for electrical engineers rose, more engineering students would take up that specialty; if the wage rate for typists in Chicago rose, more people would become typists than, say, filing clerks; and if the wage for farm laborers in Texas rose, workers would be drawn in from Arizona, Florida, and Mexico. As a result, for any discussion of the market for a particular category of labor at a particular time and place, it is reasonable to draw the labor supply curve with the usual positive slope, as in Exhibit 15.7, regardless of the shape of the individual labor supply curves underlying it.

Competitive Equilibrium

Determining the wage rate in a labor market that is fully competitive on both sides is a straightforward exercise in supply and demand analysis. Exhibit 15.8, for example, shows a supply and demand curve representing the labor market

Exhibit 15.8

Determination of the equilibrium wage in a competitive labor market

When both employers and workers are price takers in the labor market, the point of equilibrium is found where the supply and demand curves intersect. Here the equilibrium wage rate is $7 per hour, and the equilibrium quantity of labor is 200,000 typists employed.

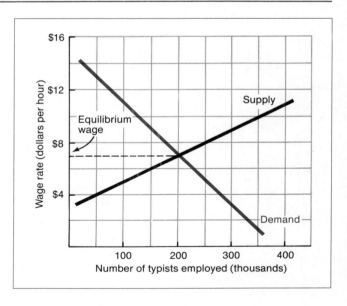

for typists in Chicago. It assumes that a large number of typists compete with one another for jobs and that a large number of employers compete with one another for typists, so that both are price takers. The demand curve for typists is the employers' combined marginal revenue curve. The supply curve is the same as that in Exhibit 15.7.

Equilibrium in this market requires a wage rate of $7 per hour, with 200,000 typists employed. If the wage rate were lower, there would be a shortage of typists. Some firms, unable to fill all their job openings, would offer premium wages to workers from other jobs or other regions. The wage rate would be driven up to the equilibrium level. If, on the other hand, the wage rate were above $7 per hour, there would be a surplus of typists. Many people would be looking for typing jobs and not finding them. After sufficient fruitless search, some would become willing to accept work at lower than expected wages, thus pushing the wage rate down toward equilibrium. Others would drift into other occupations or regions.

In a labor market such as this one, where both employers and employees are price takers, the equilibrium wage rate is equal to the marginal revenue product of labor. In the special case where all employers are price takers (perfect competitors) in the market where they sell their output as well as in the market where they purchase inputs, the equilibrium wage rate is equal to the marginal physical product of labor times the price per unit of output.

Monopsony

Not every factor market has a large number of buyers competing with one another. The extreme situation where there is only one buyer in a market is called **monopsony.**

Monopsony A market in which there is only one buyer; from the Greek words *mono* ("single") and *opsonia* ("buying").

There is an important difference between the case of competition and the case of monopsony. For a monopsonist, marginal factor cost is not equal to the price of the factor. Exhibit 15.9 shows why. The table and graph in this exhibit represent the supply side of the market for typists in a small town where there is just one big employer—an insurance company—which employs all or almost all the town's typists.

The supply schedule of typists shows that no one will work as a typist if the wage rate is $3 per hour or less. Above that wage, each extra two cents per hour will attract one more worker. Suppose that the monopsonistic employer has hired 150 typists, paying them $6 per hour. The total labor cost for a labor force of this size is $900 per hour. What will happen to the firm's total labor cost if it expands its labor force by one additional worker?

According to the supply curve, to hire 151 typists requires a wage of $6.02 per hour. That wage must be paid not just to the 151st worker but to all workers. The total cost of a labor force of 151 typists, then, is $6.02 times 151, or $909.02. The addition of one more worker has raised the total labor cost from $900 to $909.02, a marginal factor cost of $9.02. Similar results can be obtained by choosing other starting points from the table. In every case, the marginal factor cost for the monopsonist is greater than the factor price (the wage rate).

Exhibit 15.9b shows a marginal factor cost curve based on the marginal factor cost column of the table in Part a. This curve lies above the supply curve at every point. The relationship between the supply curve and the marginal cost curve for a monopsonist, as shown in this figure, is analogous to the

Exhibit 15.9

Marginal factor cost under monopsony

Under monopsony, marginal factor cost exceeds factor price. Consider an increase in quantity from 150 to 151 units of labor in this exhibit. The wage rate must be raised from $6 to $6.02 not just for the 151st employee but for all the previous 150 as well. Marginal labor cost in this range is thus $9.02 per hour, not $6.02 per hour.

(a)

Quantity of Labor Supplied (1)	Wage Rate (2)	Total Factor Cost (3)	Marginal Factor Cost (4)
1	$3.02	$ 3.02	
2	3.04	6.08	$ 3.06
3	3.06	9.18	3.10
150	6.00	900.00	
151	6.02	909.02	9.02
152	6.04	918.08	9.06
200	7.00	1,400.00	
201	7.02	1,411.02	11.02
202	7.04	1,422.08	11.06

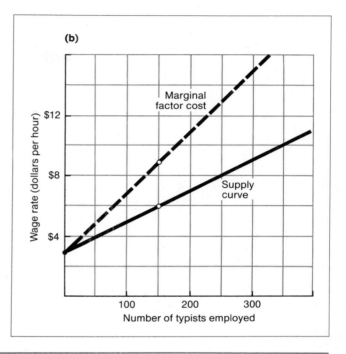

relationship between the demand and marginal revenue curves for a monopolist.

Monopsony Equilibrium

Given the monopsonist's marginal factor cost curve—derived from the factor's market supply curve—determining the equilibrium level of employment for the firm is a matter of routine. Exhibit 15.10 shows the monopsonistic em-

Exhibit 15.10

Wage determination under monopsony

Here are a monopsonist's marginal revenue product of labor curve, labor supply curve, and marginal factor cost curve. The quantity of labor required to maximize profits is found where the marginal revenue product curve and the marginal factor cost curve intersect. Note that the equilibrium wage rate is *not* shown by the intersection of the marginal factor cost and marginal revenue product curves. Instead, the rate is equal to the height of the supply curve directly below that intersection.

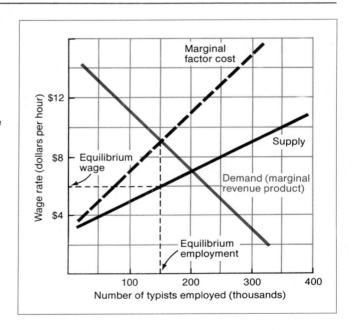

ployer's marginal revenue product curve along with the labor supply and marginal factor cost curves from Exhibit 15.9. Following the general rule that profit is maximized where marginal factor cost is equal to marginal revenue product, it can be seen that the monopsonist will hire 150 typists at a wage rate of $6 per hour.

Note that when a labor market is in monopsony equilibrium, the wage rate is lower than the marginal revenue product of labor. In the example shown, the equilibrium wage rate is $6 per hour, although the marginal revenue product is $9 per hour. Despite the gap between the wage rate and the marginal revenue product, this increase in the quantity of labor hired will not increase revenue by enough to offset higher labor costs. The reason is that the cost of hiring another worker is not just the $6.02 per hour that must be paid to the 151st worker but that sum plus the extra two cents per hour by which the wages of all 150 previously hired workers must be raised. The complete marginal factor cost for the 151st worker is thus $6.02 + $3.00, or $9.02 per hour.

CONCLUSIONS

The introduction to this chapter mentioned that factor markets determine not only how productive inputs are allocated among competing uses but also how total output is divided among individual factor owners. Consider the case in which several factors of production are used by a firm and factor markets are competitive. Profit maximization then requires that each factor be used up to the point where its marginal revenue product is equal to its price.

Marginal productivity theory of distribution A theory of the functional distribution of income according to which each factor receives a payment equal to its marginal revenue product.

This suggests that each unit of each factor receives a reward that is equal to the contribution it makes to the firm's revenue. The idea that factors are rewarded according to their marginal productivity is known as the **marginal productivity theory of distribution.** The theory applies only to cases in which all factors are purchased in competitive input markets.

In an economy where all markets are perfectly competitive—not only input markets but output markets as well—the marginal productivity theory applies in an even stronger form. It has been shown that when output markets as well as factor markets are competitive, marginal revenue product is equal to output price times marginal physical product. In such an economy, the reward that each unit of each factor receives is exactly equal to the value of its marginal physical product. If an extra hour's labor in a T-shirt factory produces two extra T-shirts, and each T-shirt sells for $5, the wage rate must be $10 per hour—no more, no less.

This principle of distribution, in which every factor receives a reward equal to the value of its marginal product, appeals to many people as the most just one possible. The reward of every worker is exactly equal to the contribution of that worker to the productive process. If a worker or factor owner were to decide to withhold a unit of productive services from the market, that person would suffer a loss of earnings exactly equal to the value of production that would be lost to the economy as a whole.

Not everyone favors distribution according to marginal productivity, however. Some people do not believe it leads to the best personal distribution of income. There are two main lines of criticism. Some critics argue that it is fine for factors to earn their marginal products but that a just personal distribution of income also requires that the ownership of factors be justly distributed among people. Others argue that productivity is completely irrelevant as a basis for distribution. Instead, distribution should be carried out on the principle of "to each according to need." These issues lie somewhat beyond the scope of this chapter, but the chapters on poverty and on capitalism versus socialism will return to them.

SUMMARY

1. In factor markets, firms are the buyers, and households are the sellers. The theory of demand for a factor of production is thus an extension of the theory of the firm. A profit maximizing firm must take three things into account when it makes a hiring decision for any factor: (a) the quantity of output produced by a unit of the factor in question (marginal physical product), (b) the revenue derived from the sale of the output that will be produced by the extra unit of the factor (marginal revenue product), and (c) the cost of obtaining an extra unit of the factor (marginal factor cost).

2. A profit maximizing firm will hire just enough of each factor of production to equalize marginal revenue product and marginal factor cost. In the special case where a firm is a price taker both in the market where it buys its inputs and in the market where it sells its outputs, profit maximization requires that each factor's price be equal to its marginal physical product times the product price. So long as the firm is a price taker in the factor market, its demand curve for a factor of production is that factor's marginal revenue product curve.

3. The theory of labor supply for an individual household is an extension of the theory of consumer choice. Given the alternatives of work and leisure, each consumer works just enough that the marginal utility per hour of leisure exactly equals the marginal utility of the goods that can be bought with an hour's wage. The labor supply curve for a single individual tends to have a backward-bending shape. The market labor supply curve for a particular occupation or locality, however, ordinarily has the conventional upward-sloping shape.

4. In a market where both workers and employers are price takers, the equilibrium wage rate and equilibrium quantity of labor are found at the intersection of the labor supply and labor demand curves. If the workers are price takers but their employer is a monopsonist, the equilibrium quantity of labor is found at the intersection of the marginal revenue product curve and the marginal factor cost curve, and the equilibrium wage rate is determined by the height of the supply curve directly below this intersection.

5. In a competitive market where there are several factors of production, profit maximization requires that each factor be used up to the point where its marginal product is equal to its price. Each factor thus receives a reward equal to its marginal revenue product. This distribution is thought by some to be the most just distribution of income possible.

DISCUSSION QUESTIONS

1. What is meant by the statement that factor markets help determine for whom things are produced? Is it that workers consume exactly the things they produce? Do

they ever do this? When they do not, what other markets also help determine for whom things are produced?

2. The text examined only factor markets where the buyers are firms. Are households ever the buyers of factors of production? Are you the direct purchaser of a factor of production when you hire someone to type a term paper for you? When you get your hair cut? When you buy or rent a plot of land for a vegetable garden? What changes would have to be made in the theory of factor markets to take into account the case where both buyers and sellers are households?

3. In his historical novel *Chesapeake* James Michener at one point describes the unsuccessful efforts of early European colonists to run their plantations with hired native American labor. Among the many problems contributing to the breakdown of relationships between the planters and the local tribes were some of an economic nature. In one instance, for example, Michener reports the frustration of a planter who finds an offer of higher wages ineffective in preventing his native workers from quitting their jobs in the fields. The planters, of course, eventually resorted to importing black slave labor. Does what you have learned in this chapter shed any light on these events? Explain.

4. Is a monopsonist necessarily a monopolist, and vice versa? Try to imagine a firm that is a monopolist in its product market but not a monopsonist in its factor markets. Then try to imagine a firm that is a monopsonist but not a monopolist.

5. Do you think there is any close connection between the value of what somebody produces and the amount that person earns? Consider these specific examples: an auto worker; a real estate salesperson; a rock star; your economics professor; a member of the Civil Aeronautics Board; an owner of New York City municipal bonds. Why does the connection between earnings and product seem closer in some cases than in others?

6. Suppose a friend said to you that it was just fine to let factor markets determine how things were produced, but the matter of for whom ought to be handled according to the principle of "to each according to need." Sketch a reply to this remark that begins: "But that won't work. If you don't let markets determine for whom, they won't be able to determine the how. . . ."

SUGGESTIONS FOR FURTHER READING

Leftwich, Richard H. *The Price System and Resource Allocation.* 7th ed. Hinsdale, Ill.: Dryden Press, 1979.
Chapters 14 and 15 of this intermediate level text discuss pricing in factor markets.

Nicholson, Walter. *Intermediate Microeconomics and Its Application.* 2d ed. Hinsdale, Ill.: Dryden Press, 1979.
Chapters 13 to 15 cover factor markets, including some interesting applications (monopsony in baseball, racial discrimination) and some advanced topics.

Scitovsky, Tibor. *Welfare and Competition.* Rev. ed. Homewood, Ill.: Richard D. Irwin, 1971.
Chapter 5 of this authoritative treatise on economic theory discusses efficiency in the labor market and the worker's trade-off between work and leisure. A knowledge of indifference curves is required (see Appendix to Chapter 5).

LABOR UNIONS AND COLLECTIVE BARGAINING

WHAT YOU WILL LEARN IN THIS CHAPTER

This chapter completes the discussion of labor markets begun in the previous chapter. It explains how labor markets operate when workers organize into unions and bargain collectively with their employers. It begins with a brief history of the union movement in the United States. Next, it shows how to interpret the effects of unionization in terms of supply and demand curves. Finally, it reviews the history of public policy toward labor unions and discusses some contemporary issues in labor union economics.

FOR REVIEW

Here are some important terms and concepts that will be put to use in this chapter. If you do not understand them, review them before proceeding.
- *Sherman Antitrust Act (Chapter 13)*
- *Monopsony (Chapter 15)*

The discussion of the last chapter was limited to labor markets in which workers are not formally organized—those in which they compete openly with one another for jobs. Not all labor markets operate that way. About a fifth of all U.S. workers are organized into labor unions, which allow workers to present a united front to employers and to bargain collectively with them.

Although the extent of unionization in the United States is not as high as in many European countries, and although the unionized sector of the labor force, now 20 percent, has been falling for more than a generation, unions are still important enough to deserve the attention of a separate chapter. Indeed, they have economic importance out of proportion to their numerical strength. Partly this is because they are strongest in such strategically important industries as transportation, steel, and automobile manufacturing. (The Teamsters, United Steelworkers, and United Auto Workers are three of the largest unions.) Partly also it is because union wage settlements are believed to set patterns followed by many nonunion employers. Without further introduction, then, the chapter will look at what labor unions are and how they work, beginning with a brief historical survey.

THE HISTORY OF U.S. UNIONISM

Earliest Beginnings

U.S. unionism began toward the end of the eighteenth century. In the 1790s, craft workers, including printers, shoemakers, and carpenters, formed local associations to further their economic interests. By the end of the century, printers and shoemakers in Boston, Philadelphia, New York, and other cities of the eastern seaboard were bargaining collectively with employers.

Craft union A union of skilled workers all practicing the same trade.

These earliest labor groups, called **craft unions,** were organizations of skilled workers, all in the same trade. Their skills and common interests made it relatively easy for them to work together in union activities and gave their organizations some degree of monopoly power in dealing with employers.

But the early local craft unions were usually short-lived. They faced many problems. It was not until 1842, for example, that the courts recognized unions as being legal; and even after that date, the courts were often unfriendly. Furthermore, few of the early local unions were strong enough to survive the recurrent business depressions of the period. As soon as business fell off, they lost most of their bargaining power with employers. They then faded away, to be organized again in the next period of prosperity.

Knights of Labor

Unionism did not begin seriously on a national scale until after the Civil War. At that time, national unions began to appear, and local unions joined them as chapters. The most prominent of the national labor organizations in the post–Civil War period had the colorful name of the Noble Order of the Knights of Labor. This organization was founded as a secret society in 1869, but its growth began only after it abandoned secrecy in 1878. Membership reached a peak of more than 700,000 workers in 1886.

Many local unions of skilled craft workers were affiliated with the Knights of Labor, but the Knights' principles went far beyond the narrow bounds of craft unionism. The Knights welcomed anyone who worked for a living, including farmers, agricultural workers, and unskilled laborers. Only such "undesirables" as bankers, liquor dealers, Pinkerton detectives, and lawyers were excluded. The Knights' program was not limited to strictly economic concerns. It also stressed worker education and producer cooperatives as means to help counteract the "evil of wealth."

The breadth of organization and purpose of the Knights of Labor permitted rapid growth but also led to the eventual decline of the group. After 1886, conflicts with craft unions increased. Public hostility was aroused by the killing of a policeman during Chicago's Haymarket Riot of 1886, although no connection of the Knights with that event was ever proved. From that year on, however, the Knights of Labor was increasingly overshadowed by the emergent American Federation of Labor.

The AFL

The American Federation of Labor or AFL (first called the Federation of Organized Trades and Labor Unions) was founded in 1881. Its founders included some independent craft unions and some local craft affiliates of the Knights of Labor that felt the bargaining power of skilled craft workers would be wasted in an attempt to win benefits for the unskilled. Since 1886, the AFL has played a dominant role in union history.

The AFL found strong leadership under Samuel Gompers, its president for all but one year from 1886 until his death in 1924. Gompers sought to avoid the mistakes that had led to the downfall of the Knights of Labor. The AFL owes its success largely to three features of its organization and philosophy that were prominent from its earliest years:

1. The AFL was based solidly on the principle of craft unionism. Its leaders thought that the dangers of economic depressions and employer opposition could be overcome only by relying on skilled workers who could not easily be replaced during strikes. The AFL itself was, in effect, an umbrella organization of national craft unions.

2. The AFL emphasized business unionism; that is, it devoted most of its energies to bread-and-butter issues of pay and working conditions. Unlike many European labor unions, it was content to work within the capitalist system. It did not seek the overthrow of private property or the establishment of socialism.

3. The AFL limited its political role to that of a lobbyist on labor's behalf. Again in contrast to European labor movements, it did not found a labor

---

Samuel Gompers was born in a London tenement, the son of a skilled cigar maker. When he was thirteen, his family moved to the United States and settled on the East Side of New York. Gompers followed his father into the cigar trade.

Although his formal education ended at the age of ten, Gompers was very active in the workers' self-education movement of the time. In the cigar-making shops, jobs were organized on a piecework basis. Groups of workers would have one of their members read to them while they worked, "paying" the reader by making his cigars for him. Gompers became acquainted with the works of Marx, Engels, and other European socialists in this way. Often he was chosen as the reader.

The cigar makers' union to which Gompers belonged fell apart during the depression of 1873. Gompers rebuilt it as a model of the craft unions he was later to unite under the American Federation of Labor. Key features of this union were high membership dues, central control of funds, national officers with control over local unions, and union-organized accident and unemployment benefits for members.

Gompers became disillusioned with radical socialism. The main role of unions, in his view, was to watch after the economic interests of their members. He wrote:

Unions, pure and simple, are the natural organization of wage workers to secure their present material and practical improvement and to achieve their final emancipation. . . . The working people are in too great need of immediate improvements in their condition to allow them to forego them in the endeavor to devote their entire energies to an end however beautiful to contemplate. . . . The way out of the wage system is through higher wages.

During the 1890s, a socialist faction emerged within the AFL. It adopted a program calling for the collective ownership of all means of production and other radical measures. Gompers opposed the group, and in the 1895 election for the AFL presidency, he was defeated. He fought back, however, and succeeded in regaining the presidency the next year. He remained president until his death in 1924.

Gompers was an ardent patriot throughout his career. During World War I, he opposed pacifism and supported the war effort. In 1918, he said: "America is a symbol; it is an ideal; the hopes of the world can be expressed in the ideal—America."

Samuel Gompers (1850–1924)

party. Gompers thought that excessive political involvement would lead to internal conflict within the labor movement and would weaken its ability to achieve concrete economic objectives.

The AFL grew slowly at first and then more rapidly. It reached 2 million members by 1904. Membership peaked at about 5 million in 1920 and thereafter declined to around 3 million in 1930.

Early Industrial Unions

Although the relatively conservative AFL dominated the union scene in the decades around the turn of the century, its principle of craft unionism was not universally followed. In places, there were notable early successes in organizing **industrial unions**—unions that included workers of all crafts and levels of skills within a given industry. The oldest major industrial union is the United Mine Workers, founded in 1890. After 1900, three successful industrial unions emerged in the clothing industry. The International Ladies' Garment Workers' Union was the strongest of them. Brewery workers also organized successfully. During the same years, though, industrial unionism suffered some spectacular failures. Strike efforts by steelworkers and railway workers were defeated after clashes involving Pinkerton detectives, state troopers, strikebreakers, and the jailing of labor leaders.

On another front, the AFL was challenged by unionists who were unwilling to work within the capitalist system. The most notable of their organizations was the International Workers of the World (IWW), whose members were known as "Wobblies." The IWW campaigned for "one big union" that would embrace all workers of all skills and crafts and for workers' management of industry. It was successful in organizing lumberjacks and agricultural workers, among whom conventional unionism had made few inroads. During World War I, the IWW opposed the U.S. war effort—a stand that brought it under intense political attack. Many of its leaders and members were jailed, and the organization faded rapidly in importance.

The 1930s and the CIO

Unionism had declined in the 1920s; but during the Great Depression, the decline was reversed. In large part, the revival of organized labor was brought about by favorable legislation passed during this period. The legislation (discussed in some detail later in the chapter) removed the main legal barriers to union organization and crippled the antiunion efforts of employers.

In the improved legal climate, pressures grew for organizing the mass production industries—steel, rubber, automobiles, and others—which had resisted earlier attempts. This led to serious conflicts within the AFL, whose old-line craft unionists did not believe that stable unions could be formed on the industrial principle. They also resented the efforts of industrial unions to recruit skilled workers in their industries. The AFL thought that these workers ought to join existing craft unions. As a result of this dispute, an opposition group formed within the AFL, led by John L. Lewis of the United Mine Workers. In 1938, the group was expelled from the AFL and formed the rival Congress of Industrial Organizations (originally known as the Committee for Industrial Organization).

The CIO managed some major successes during the 1930s, the biggest being unionization of the steel industry. (The industry leader, U.S. Steel, agreed to

Industrial union A union of all workers in an industry, including both skilled and unskilled workers and workers practicing various trades.

collective bargaining in 1937.) Successful organization campaigns were carried out around the same time in the rubber, automobile, electrical, meat packing, and textile industries, to name just some.

The successes of the CIO demonstrated that craft unionism was not the only workable recipe for labor organization. They also contributed to a rapid growth in union membership—although the AFL itself grew rapidly too during the period. By 1939, union membership had risen to 29 percent of nonagricultural employees, more than double the figure of just four years earlier. By 1945, over a third of nonagricultural workers had been organized.

The AFL-CIO Merger

After World War II, unions again faced difficulties. The political and legislative climate began to shift against them. Unionization drives in the South, expected to yield millions of new members, were relatively unsuccessful. During the 1950s, union membership stagnated. The CIO was more seriously affected, and it fell in membership to about half the size of the AFL.

Many union leaders felt that feuding between the AFL and the CIO accounted for a large part of labor's problems. At the same time, leadership of both unions passed into the hands of men who had not been so directly involved in the bitter disputes that had led to the original split. The distinction between craft and industrial unions seemed less important now that both types had proved to have their place. The outcome was an agreement to merge the two labor federations, signed in December 1955.

The Present and Future

Formation of the AFL-CIO did not prove successful in reversing the decline in union membership or even in preventing further gradual decline. Many factors have contributed to the difficulties of union organizers in recent decades. For one thing, blue collar workers, traditionally the easiest to organize, now make up a much smaller percentage of the labor force than earlier. Women, who make up an increasing proportion of the labor force, have never joined unions in proportion to their numbers. The labor force is also said to be becoming more transient; in particular, unions have not successfully followed the shift of jobs from the industrial Northeast and Midwest to the Sunbelt states. Finally, it is thought by some observers that younger workers simply lack the traditional sense of unions as important to their well-being. Despite some success in the organization of state and local government workers and agricultural workers, then, the prognosis for unionization is continued gradual decline.

COLLECTIVE BARGAINING AND WAGE RATES

Union Goals

Labor unions have done many things for their members and pursued many goals. They have bargained for shorter working hours and better health and safety conditions. They have founded pension funds for their members, promoted worker education, and engaged in party politics. For U.S. unions, however, the number one goal has long been to achieve higher wages for their members. This section will look at the means unions have to achieve higher wages. Later sections will examine how successful they have been.

The Union in a Competitive Market

The discussion will begin with the case of a union that is formed in a previously competitive market and now seeks higher wages through the threat of a strike. Consider Exhibit 16.1. This figure shows a labor market in which the competitive equilibrium wage rate is $8 per hour and the equilibrium level of employment is 300,000 worker hours per year. (See Point E_1 in the exhibit.)

Suppose that the newly organized workers in this industry tell employers that they want $10 per hour, or else they will go on strike. The strike threat is shown in the diagram by a change in the shape of the supply curve. Originally, the supply curve had the usual upward-sloping shape. After the strike threat, employers face a supply curve with a kink in it. The horizontal left-hand branch of the new kinked supply curve indicates that if the employer does not pay at least $10 per hour, no workers at all will be available. Up to 400,000 worker hours will be supplied at $10 per hour. To hire more labor than that, the wage will have to be raised higher than the union is demanding.

Suppose that the employers decide they have no choice but to accept the union demand. They will react by shifting to a new equilibrium at Point E_2 in Exhibit 16.1, where the demand curve and the horizontal part of the new supply curve intersect. There they will hire 250,000 worker hours per year at $10 per hour. The union will have succeeded in raising the wage of its members, although only at the expense of reducing the amount of work available from 300,000 worker hours per year to 250,000 worker hours per year.

The trade-off in this example between increased wages and reduced employment is a rather general one when workers bargain collectively with competitive employers. Given the inevitable trade-off, just how far back along the employers' demand curve for labor should the union try to push?

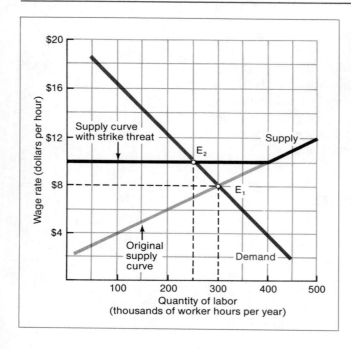

Exhibit 16.1

Effect of unionization in a competitive labor market
A union formed in a previously competitive labor market can use a strike threat to bargain for higher wages. Here, the union threatens to strike unless the wage is raised from its competitive level of $8 per hour ($E_1$) to $10 per hour. With the strike threat in force, the supply curve of labor to employers becomes horizontal at $10 per hour up to 400,000 labor hours per year, as shown. A new equilibrium is reached at E_2, where the new supply curve intersects the demand curve. The wage is higher than initially, but the quantity of labor employed is smaller.

There is no easy answer—no easy way to calculate an optimal wage demand. If the union wants to keep as many of its workers employed as possible, it may simply accept the competitive wage and confine its bargaining to nonwage issues. Perhaps, though, the union wants to raise the total income of its members. If the demand curve is inelastic in the region of the competitive wage, this can be done by pushing the wage up a bit. Although employment will fall, total labor income will increase.

In Exhibit 16.2, the labor demand curve is inelastic up to a wage of $10 per hour, unit elastic at that point, and elastic beyond. The $10 wage thus gives the largest possible total labor income—$2.5 million per year. Unfortunately, keeping the wage at this level creates a surplus of labor. Workers will be willing to supply 400,000 hours per year, but only 250,000 will be demanded. The union can simply allow workers to compete for jobs on a first-come, first-serve basis and not worry about those who cannot get a job. Alternatively, it can try to parcel out the available work among all who want a job in the industry. Each worker will then be limited in the number of hours that can be put in. Whichever route is taken, a union that keeps the wage above the equilibrium level must be well enough organized to prevent nonunion workers from undercutting it.

Sometimes a strong union will ask for a wage even higher than the one that gives the maximum labor income. Suppose, for example, that the union takes an elitist attitude, restricting membership to certain racial or ethnic groups or to friends and relatives of current members. Look at Exhibit 16.2 again. An elite group of workers may push the wage up to, say, $16 per hour, if 100,000 hours per year is all the work members of the group want. To hold a card in such a union, needless to say, will be a jealously guarded privilege.

Exhibit 16.2

The wage-job trade-off

Unions facing employers who are price takers may choose various ways of dealing with the wage-job trade-off. If the union's objective is to maximize employment, it will not bargain for a wage higher than the competitive equilibrium. If the labor demand curve is inelastic at the competitive equilibrium point, total income of union members can be increased by raising the wage to the point where the demand curve becomes unit elastic. If the union restricts membership to a limited elite group, it may push wages even higher.

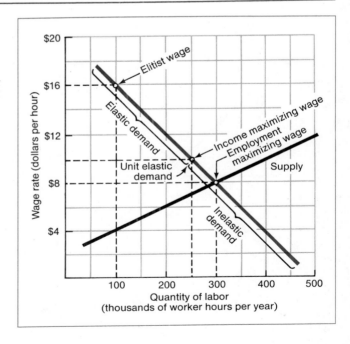

Featherbedding

Featherbedding The practice of negotiating purposefully inefficient work rules so that more workers will be needed to do a job.

Sometimes powerful unions try to get around the trade-off between wages and jobs through the practice of **featherbedding**—insisting on purposefully inefficient work rules so that more workers will be needed to do a job. There have been some notorious examples of featherbedding in U.S. industry. Railroad unions have required fire fighters on diesel locomotives. Union printers have been required to set duplicate "dummy" type for newspapers when advertisers submit copy in ready-to-print form. Electricians have had to tear apart and rewire on the job certain kinds of prewired electrical equipment.

If featherbedding simply meant that some workers stood idly by while others worked normally, it would just be another form of work sharing. To the extent that it involves technical restrictions that lower productivity, though, it creates problems that simple work sharing does not. Lowering productivity means shifting the labor demand curve to the left. In the end, total earnings for a group of featherbedding workers must be lower than earnings for an equal number of workers who practice a form of work sharing that does not restrict productivity.

Union versus Monopsonist

There is one exception to the trade-off between jobs and wages—the case where a union faces a monopsonistic employer. Consider Exhibit 16.3. This figure shows a labor market in which a monopsonistic employer faces a group of workers who are initially unorganized. The wage rate in equilibrium is $6.50 per hour, and only 220,000 hours of labor per year are hired. This point is labeled E_1.

Now consider what happens if a union confronts the monopsonist with a demand for a wage of $10 per hour and backs the demand with a strike threat. As in Exhibit 31.1, this demand puts a kink in the labor supply curve. What is

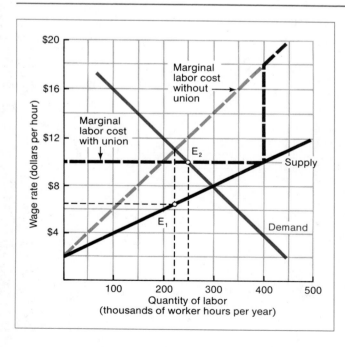

Exhibit 16.3
The effects of unionization in a monopsony labor market

When a union faces a monopsonistic employer, it can sometimes raise both wages and employment. Here, the original monopsony equilibrium wage is $6.50 per hour with 220,000 worker hours per year (E_1). A strike threat puts a kink in the monopsonist's marginal labor cost curve, because the union's take-it-or-leave-it $10 per hour bargaining position makes the employer a price taker in the labor market at that wage rate. The new marginal labor cost curve intersects the demand curve at 240,000 worker hours per year, which becomes the new equilibrium point, E_2. Both the wage rate and the quantity of labor employed are higher than at E_1.

more important, along the horizontal part of the new labor supply curve, the monopsonist's marginal labor cost is equal to the wage rate. The union says, in effect, that the firm can hire as many workers as it wishes at no more and no less than $10 per hour—which means that changes in the quantity of labor hired no longer require changes in the wage rate. One more worker hour raises total labor costs by no more and no less than $10.

Suppose that the union is strong enough to make the monopsonist accept its wage demand on a take-it-or-leave-it basis. The new equilibrium will then be found where the new marginal labor cost curve intersects the demand curve, at Point E_2. The wage rate there is $10 per hour, and 240,000 worker hours per year are employed. Both the wage rate and employment are higher than in the previous monopsonistic equilibrium.

Notice, however, that there is a limit on the power of a union facing a monopsonist to raise wages without losing jobs. This limit is set by the extent to which the original monopsony wage fell short of the competitive wage. Once the wage rate begins to exceed the level where the supply and demand curves intersect, further raises reduce employment. In fact, as Exhibit 16.3 is drawn, the wage of $10 per hour is already in the trade-off region. Maximum employment is achieved with a wage rate of $8 per hour, equal to the competitive wage.

Bilateral Monopoly

The example just given assumes that the monopsonistic employer will accept the union demand on a take-it-or-leave-it basis. Not all employers react this way. A strong employer may counter the union demand with the threat of a lockout or of some take-it-or-leave-it offer of its own. The kind of bargaining situation that develops when neither party to the labor contract acts competitively and neither passively accepts the demands of the other is called **bilateral monopoly.** The outcome of bargaining under bilateral monopoly is impossible to predict with the type of analysis used here. Economic theory can only specify a range of outcomes within which a settlement can take place. The actual outcome depends simply on the relative bargaining strength and skill of the two sides. The headline-making disputes in which "big labor" clashes with "big business" often fall into the category of bilateral monopoly.

Bilateral monopoly A market in which both buyer and seller exercise monopoly power and neither passively accepts the demands of the other.

Relative Wages

How successful unions are in raising the relative wages of their members depends primarily on three things: (1) whether the unions are strong enough to make a creditable strike threat; (2) how willing they are to sacrifice jobs in order to gain higher wages; and (3) what the demand conditions are in their sector of the labor market. No purely theoretical analysis can tell which unions will be able to win higher relative wages and which will not. This is an empirical question that has drawn the attention of many economists. The following case reviews some of the results they have reached.

Case 16.1
Labor Unions and Relative Wages

In 1963, H. G. Lewis of the University of Chicago published a study of the effects of unionism on relative wages. As part of his work, he made an exhaustive survey of previous studies of individual industries. The main results of the earlier studies, as presented by Lewis, are shown in Exhibit 16.4.

Exhibit 16.4
Effects of unionization on relative wages in selected industries
Unions vary in their ability to win higher relative wages for their members. Cases where union wages are at least 25 percent higher than nonunion wages appear to be rare. Many unions gain only a very slight relative wage advantage for their members.

Author of Study	Industry	Years Covered	Effect of Unionization on Relative Wages
Rees	Steel	1945–1948	Zero or negative
Scherer	Hotels	1939–1948	Negligible, 6–10%
Sobel	Tires	1936–1938	10–18%
		1945–1948	5–9%
Sobotka	Construction (skilled)	1939	25%
	Construction (unskilled)	1939	5%
Greenslade	Coal	1909–1957	Variable; 0–82%
Maher	Seven manufacturing industries	1950	0–7%
Craycroft	Barbers	1948	2%
		1954	19%
Rayaek	Men's clothing	1919	20%
		1926	12%
Sobotka	Airline pilots	1956	24–30%
Laurie	Local transit	1920s	15–20%
		1948	10%
Rapping	Seamen	1939–1957	6–35%

Source: Data from H. G. Lewis, *Unionism and Relative Wages in the U.S.* (Chicago: University of Chicago Press, 1963), pp. 184–186. © 1963 The University of Chicago. Reprinted by permission.

This table suggests that unions do have some measurable power over their members' relative wages. Often, however, this power is not great. Cases in which unions were found to raise relative wages more than 25 percent above the nonunion level are rare. Lower figures are common, and in more than one instance the relative wage power of unions declined over time. Their greatest impact was in the first years of organization.

Source: Based on H. G. Lewis, *Unionism and Relative Wages in the U.S.* (Chicago: University of Chicago Press, 1963), pp. 184–186.

Unions and Absolute Wages

It seems well established, then, that unions can affect relative wages. Are they also able to raise the average wages of all workers, as measured by the share of wages in national income? That is a quite separate question. This time, there is little theoretical basis for believing they can. Except in cases of true monopsony, which are likely to be temporary and purely localized, unions win their higher wages at the expense of fewer jobs. As the wage in unionized industries rises, the supply of labor to nonunionized sectors increases, keeping nonunion wages down.

National income statistics show labor's share of national income to be remarkably stable over time. Unadjusted figures show the proportion of wages in national income rising from about 60 percent in the 1920s to around 75 percent today, but this change reflects factors other than unionization. It is largely explained by the relative growth of sectors of the economy that employ much labor (especially government and services) and the decline of sectors using less labor in proportion to other inputs. When an adjustment is made for this, labor's share of national income appears to have increased by only about 2 percent over the past half-century. Since this period coincides with the period of fastest union growth, the impression left is that the impact of unionization on average wages has been minimal.

PUBLIC POLICY TOWARD UNIONS

The Problem

What should be the government's policy toward unions? This question has been a topic of impassioned political debate ever since unions began. Some have argued that all unions should be suppressed as illegal restraints on trade. Others have advocated government support for unions to promote industrial stability and high living standards for all. Still others have favored a laissez-faire policy, letting workers and management bargain without government interference. The debate has been clouded by disagreements about the true effect of unions on relative and absolute wages and on industrial efficiency. Without taking a position, the next section will survey the changing course of government policy over time, showing how first one and then another opinion has become dominant.

Early Court Hostility

Unions had trouble with the courts from their earliest days. Under precedents from English common law, they were often treated as illegal conspiracies in restraint of trade. In *Commonwealth v. Hunt*, a landmark case decided in Massachusetts in 1842, the court declared that unions were not necessarily illegal in themselves, but it restricted the aims unions could pursue and the means they could use to pursue them.

In the early twentieth century, the legal climate grew, if anything, more hostile toward unions. In a series of cases from 1908 through the 1920s, the Sherman Antitrust Act was applied to unions. This happened in spite of considerable doubt as to whether Congress had originally intended such an interpretation of the act.

In this period, the main legal weapon used against unions was the injunction. If a firm felt that union activities threatened it in any way, it could get an injunction (a court order) barring the union from striking, picketing, publicizing labor disputes, assembling to promote its interest, and virtually anything else. Often such injunctions were issued without even hearing the union side of the case.

The Norris–La Guardia Act

As union membership sank to a low point in 1932, the legal climate was changed dramatically by the passage of the Norris–La Guardia Act. This act deprived antiunion employers of the injunction, formerly their biggest weapon. The law declared, in effect, that the government should remain neutral in labor disputes. The courts could still intervene to protect tangible property and prevent the overt use of violence. As long as they remained nonviolent, however, unions would have the right to strike, picket, boycott, assemble, and persuade others to do these and other things.

The Wagner Act

The growing prolabor climate of the 1930s soon led to the passage of further labor legislation. The Wagner Act of 1935 came next. This act took government policy out of the neutral position where the Norris–La Guardia Act had left it and put the government squarely on the side of the unions.

The Wagner Act declared that "employees shall have the right to self-organization, to form, join, or assist labor organizations, to bargain collectively through representatives of their own choosing, and to engage in concerted activities, for the purpose of collective bargaining or other mutual aid or protection." The law created its own enforcement machinery in the form of a three-member National Labor Relations Board (NLRB). This board was to oversee enforcement of the act, arrange for representative elections, and preside as judge and jury when the act was violated.

The Wagner Act also outlawed a specific list of "unfair employer labor practices." Employers could no longer use lockouts, intimidation, blacklists, or spying. They could no longer force employees to sign contracts that made nonmembership in a union a condition of employment. In some cases, employers were even barred from speaking against unions.

The Taft-Hartley Act

The Wagner Act gave such a boost to labor unions that people began to worry whether it was working too well. Unions became strong and powerful. They could call strikes that could paralyze a region and even threaten national welfare. After a series of particularly damaging strikes in 1946, a Republican Congress passed new legislation, amending the Wagner Act.

The Taft-Hartley Act of 1947 tried to move public policy back toward a neutral position on labor issues. It modified the structure of the NLRB and removed its powers as a prosecutor. It kept the list of unfair employer labor practices but added a list of unfair union labor practices. The new list included restraint or coercion of employees by unions, strikes and boycotts aimed at forcing self-employed persons to join unions, and secondary boycotts. (The last are strikes or boycotts intended to force an employer to cease dealing in the product of another firm involved in a labor dispute.) The act limited the closed shop, under which union membership is a condition of employment. It also provided machinery for federal intervention in strikes that threaten to create a national emergency.

The Landrum-Griffin Act

The last major piece of legislation defining government policy toward unions was passed in 1959. The Landrum-Griffin Act of that year put government in the business of policing internal union affairs for the first time. A series of scandals and congressional hearings had brought several instances of corrupt or criminal practices of union officials to public attention. This legislation was an attempt to clean up unions.

A major provision of the act is a bill of rights for rank-and-file members. It guarantees their right of free speech, their right to vote in union elections, and so on. The act also requires union reports on finances, regulates the term of office of union officials, specifies election procedures, and strengthens the Taft-Hartley Act's provisions against secondary boycotts.

Recent Legislative Efforts

In 1978, worried by continued declines in union membership, organized labor mounted its biggest political effort in many years in an attempt to secure further revision of the Wagner Act. Union leaders argued that under existing legislation, it was too easy for employers to flout the intent of the law and stifle organizing efforts with delaying tactics and illegal reprisals against prounion employees. Among the changes sought in the law were a provision for quicker union elections to give employers less time to mount an antiunion campaign, a provision that would give union organizers increased access to workers on company premises and company time, and a provision to increase the size of the NLRB.

Despite great political efforts, and despite the attempt by unions to represent the proposed legislation as nothing more than a fine tuning of existing legislation aimed only at employers who break the law, Congress narrowly rejected the proposals. Other prolabor legislation also failed to win approval in the Ninety-fifth Congress.

CONCLUSIONS

For the moment, then, most questions of organization, representation, and labor and employer bargaining practices appear to be settled. In the 1970s, a new aspect of union activity became a center of controversy. This aspect is the role of unions in the process of inflation.

Earlier in this chapter, it was argued that unions have a limited ability to raise their members' relative wages but little power to raise the average wages of all workers, measured as a percentage of GNP. What about nominal wages, though? Can unions raise average wages measured in money terms rather than as a share of national income? If unions can succeed in raising nominal wages rather than getting their members a bigger slice of the national income pie, their actions may only cause inflation. This inflation erodes the purchasing power of everyone's income, including that of union members.

Worries over inflation have led to pressure for a new form of government intervention in collective bargaining—namely, wage and price controls. Under such controls, the government intervenes in collective bargaining not to strike a balance between labor and management but rather to contain an inflationary wage-price spiral. The United States experimented briefly with controls under President Nixon in 1971–1973. The policy was abandoned as a questionable success, but many people believe that it should be tried again.

SUMMARY

1. The first local craft unions in the United States were established toward the end of the eighteenth century. After the Civil War, a serious national union movement began, led at first by the Knights of Labor. The Knights were soon succeeded by the American Federation of Labor, which emphasized craft unionism and concentrated on the bread and butter issue of higher wages. There were some early successes in industrial unionism toward the end of

the nineteenth century, but industrial unionism became widespread only with the formation of the Congress of Industrial Organizations in the 1930s. At first, the AFL and the CIO feuded bitterly, but, in 1955, the two organizations merged. Today, about four-fifths of all union members belong to AFL-CIO affiliated unions.

2. The strike threat is a union's ultimate weapon in bargaining with employers for higher wages. A union wage demand backed up by a strike threat has the effect of bending the labor supply curve so that it becomes horizontal at the level of the wage demand. In a market where employers are price takers, a higher wage can usually be won only at the expense of jobs lost. Sometimes, featherbedding or other kinds of work sharing are used to spread available work among all union members. Within certain limits, a union can win higher wages from a monopsonistic employer and gain higher employment at the same time.

3. Empirical studies show that many unions actually do succeed in raising the relative wages of their members. Often, though, the relative wage advantage of union members is only a few percent. It is doubtful that unions have a significant effect on the average wages of all workers, as measured in terms of the share of wages in national income.

4. Public policy toward unions has gone through several phases. Until the 1930s, courts were generally hostile toward unions. In the early part of this century, the Sherman Antitrust Act was applied to unions, and employers found it easy to obtain antiunion injunctions. During the Great Depression, the legislative climate changed. First the Norris–La Guardia Act abolished the injunction as an antiunion weapon and made government a neutral party in labor disputes. Then the Wagner Act went even further, putting the government squarely on the side of the unions. After World War II, policy moved back toward the neutral position with passage of the Taft-Hartley Act. The most recent major piece of labor legislation was the Landrum-Griffin Act of 1959, which put the government in the business of policing the internal affairs of unions for the first time. In the 1970s, the most controversial issues of labor legislation concerned the role of unions in the process of inflation.

DISCUSSION QUESTIONS

1. Why are unions stronger in the Northeast than in the South? In what ways would workers in the Northeast gain if unionization became more widespread in the South? Would any workers lose if the South became more highly unionized?

2. Why has socialism never been a strong political force in U.S. unionism, even though the labor movements of almost every other country are strongly socialist or communist?

3. Is the nonteaching staff of your college or university unionized? If so, what union or unions represent them? Is the teaching faculty unionized? If not, are there any active attempts underway to unionize the faculty? Explain.

4. Why do some unions encourage wasteful featherbedding rather than simple work sharing in the form of, say, shorter hours or longer vacations?

5. In what ways do labor unions resemble cartels? Do you think labor unions deserve more public policy support than cartels of producers? Explain.

6. Do you think public employees should be allowed to form unions? Should they have the right to strike? What changes need to be made in the analysis of unions and labor markets in order for it to apply to unions of public employees? (Hint: What determines the labor demand curve of a unit of government?)

SUGGESTIONS FOR FURTHER READING

Reynolds, Lloyd G. *Labor Economics and Labor Relations*, 6th ed. Englewood Cliffs, N.J.: Prentice-Hall, 1974.
A comprehensive text in labor economics by one of the best-known theorists in the field.

Rottenberg, Simon. ''The Baseball Player's Labor Market.'' *Journal of Political Economy* 64 (June 1956): 242–258.
Before recent changes that permitted players to become free agents, the professional baseball leagues represented a near-perfect example of monopsony employers.

Rowan, Richard L., ed. *Readings in Labor Economics and Labor Relations*. Homewood, Ill.: Richard D. Irwin, 1976.
A useful collection of readings on a wide variety of topics related to this chapter.

C H A P T E R 17
RENT, INTEREST, AND PROFITS

WHAT YOU WILL LEARN IN THIS CHAPTER

This chapter completes the treatment of the functional distribution of income by considering factor markets other than the labor market. First, it discusses the meaning of pure economic rent and explains how rent is determined by the interaction of demand with perfectly inelastic supply. Next, it shows how the interest rate is determined by the demand for capital as a factor of production, operating through credit markets. After discussing these two factor markets, it reviews some theories of profit and explains why some profit often remains to provide income for entrepreneurs even after all implicit and explicit factor payments to owners of labor, natural resources, and capital have been made.

FOR REVIEW
Here are some important terms and concepts that will be put to use in this chapter. If you do not understand them, review them before proceeding.
- *Entrepreneurship (Chapter 1)*
- *Elasticity of supply (Chapter 3)*
- *Pure economic profit (Chapter 7)*
- *Normal rate of return (Chapter 7)*

Wages and salaries are a big part of the income distribution picture in the U.S. economy. In 1978, they accounted for some three-quarters of all personal income. They are not the whole picture, however.

The remaining quarter of personal income (excluding transfer payments) is composed of rent, interest, and profits. These sources of income, although relatively small, deserve the same careful analysis given in earlier chapters to wages and salaries. Rent, interest, and profits play a key role in the resource allocation process. They also play an important role in determining the overall personal distribution of income, since they are distributed somewhat less equally than labor income.

RENT

Economic Rent

Pure economic rent is the income earned by a factor of production that is in completely inelastic supply. The classic example of such a factor is land, which in this context means the natural productive powers of the earth and the locational advantages of particular sites. It does not include artificial

Pure economic rent The income earned by any factor of production that is in perfectly inelastic supply.

improvements; nor does it include such matters as destruction of the soil through erosion or creation of new land through reclamation.

Exhibit 17.1 shows how rent is determined by supply and demand in a competitive market. It considers a particular category of land—Kansas wheatland. The supply curve for Kansas wheatland is a vertical line, because the quantity of land supplied does not vary as the rent that it earns varies. The demand curve is the marginal revenue product curve for that land as seen by Kansas wheat farmers. The marginal product of land falls as more land is used in combination with fixed quantities of labor and capital because of diminishing returns. The demand curve thus slopes downward to the right.

The rent the land earns is determined by the intersection of the supply curve, representing the scarcity of land, and the demand curve, representing its productivity. If the rent is higher than the equilibrium shown, not all land will be put to use. The rent will then fall as landowners compete with one another to find tenants. If the rent is lower than the equilibrium rate, farmers will be unable to find all the land they want. They will bid against one another for the limited available supply and drive rents up.

Capitalization of Rents

The price of land is called rent; but much land, of course, is used by the person who owns it and is therefore not rented by a tenant from an owner. That use does not change the way supply and demand determine the value of land. It does mean, though, that it is sometimes useful to speak of the price of land in terms of a lump-sum sales price rather than as a rent per month or year.

Capitalized value of a rent
The amount equal to the value of the sum of money that would earn a periodic interest return equal to the rent if invested at the current market rate of interest.

There is a simple relationship between the value of a piece of land expressed as a rent and the price at which that piece can be sold in the market. The market price of a piece of land is said to be the **capitalized value of its rent**—that is, the sum that would earn an annual return equal to the annual rent if it were invested at the market rate of interest.

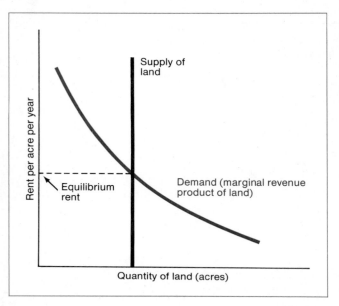

Quantity of land (acres)

Exhibit 17.1
Determination of rent by supply and demand
Pure economic rent is earned only by a factor that has a perfectly inelastic supply curve. This figure shows hypothetical supply and demand curves for Kansas wheatland. No account is taken of any possibilities for creating or destroying such land, so the supply curve is vertical. The demand curve, as for other factors, is based on the land's marginal revenue product.

Consider, for example, a piece of land with an expected real rental value of $1,000 per year in perpetuity. If the expected real rate of interest were 5 percent per year, a buyer would be willing to pay $20,000 for title to the land. If the expected real rate of interest were 2 percent per year, the price of the land would rise to $50,000, and so on. In general, the price of a parcel of land having a perpetual expected real annual rental value of R dollars per year, capitalized at the real rate of interest r is given by the formula R/r.

Other Rents

The term *rent* can refer to the market return earned by any factor of production that is unique or that is in perfectly inelastic supply. Consider the very high incomes of people with unique talents, such as singers, actors, and some executives. These incomes are more plausibly thought of as rents earned on talents rather than as wages earned for work done. Artificially created legal privileges can be said to earn rents, too. For instance, part of the earnings of a New York taxicab can be counted as rent earned from the "medallion" (license) that gives it the legal privilege to operate, so long as the supply of medallions is strictly limited by city authorities.

The hallmark of pure economic rent is inelasticity of supply. Pure economic rent should not be confused with what is loosely called the rental income earned by manufactured assets that are not in perfectly inelastic supply. Consider rental income of an apartment house owner, for example. It may in part be pure economic rent earned by some uniquely convenient site on which the building is located. In addition, though, the owner's income includes implicit wages for any custodial work done in the building, implicit interest on the money invested to build it, and so on.

What is pure economic rent and what is not depends in part on the time framework within which the income is considered. In the short run—say a period too short for new buildings to be constructed—a case could be made for considering the income earned from buildings as a pure economic rent. In the long run, however, when additional buildings can be supplied at a price, such rental income is clearly not a pure economic rent.

INTEREST AND CAPITAL

Two Aspects of Interest

The theory of capital and interest is in many ways the most complicated part of factor market theory, and care must be taken to understand the relationship between two different aspects of interest. The term *interest* is used to express both the price paid by borrowers to lenders for the use of loanable funds and the market return earned by capital as a factor of production. A person who loans $1,000 to another in return for a payment of $100 per year (plus eventual repayment of the principal) is said to earn 10 percent interest per year on the money. At the same time, a person who buys a machine for $1,000 and earns $100 a year by employing the productive services of that machine is said to earn 10 percent interest on the capital.

Consumption Loans

The discussion of interest and capital will begin by looking at how credit markets work in a simplified economy where households are the only suppliers of credit—that is, of loanable funds. Savers are households that earn incomes now but consume less than they earn in order to put something aside for expected future needs. Not all households in the economy are savers, however; some want to consume more than their current incomes permit. The latter may be households that want to tide themselves over a temporary decrease in income, or they may be households with steady incomes that just do not want to wait to buy a car or take a vacation. These and other households that borrow for any number of reasons are one source of demand for loanable funds. The loans they take out are called consumption loans.

Exhibit 17.2 shows how credit markets look in an economy where consumption loans are the only source of demand for loanable funds and personal saving is the only source of supply. Under these conditions, the willingness of savers to save, at various rates of interest, determines the shape and position of the supply curve. The eagerness of borrowers to borrow, at various rates of interest, determines the shape and position of the demand curve. The intersection of the two curves determines the market rate of interest.

The Productivity of Capital

Nothing has yet been said about production or capital. Opportunities to use capital as a factor of production are a second source of demand for loanable funds, in addition to the demand for pure consumption loans. To understand the demand for loans of this kind, it is necessary to understand why capital is productive.

Using capital means using a roundabout method of production rather than a direct method. Consider, as an example, a person whose business is making bricks. There are two ways to make bricks. The direct way is to form them by hand out of raw clay scooped up from the ground and to bake them over an

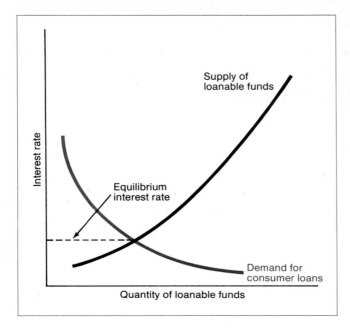

Exhibit 17.2
Determination of the interest rate for consumption loans
If consumption loans were the only kind of loans ever made, the interest rate would be determined as shown in this exhibit. The supply curve for loanable funds is determined by the willingness of savers to lend their money. The demand curve is determined by the eagerness of borrowers to consume now and pay later. The intersection of the two determines the interest rate.

open fire. Suppose that by using this method, a worker can make 100 bricks per month. The alternative way of making bricks is a roundabout one. The brickmaker first spends a month forming bricks by hand and putting them together to make a kiln. When the kiln is completed, its hotter fire and lower fuel consumption make it possible to produce 110 bricks per month from then on. The roundabout method using capital (the kiln) lengthens the period between the time work starts and the time finished bricks begin to appear. In return, it increases the eventual rate of output. That is the sense in which capital is productive.

The brickmaker's experience is repeated in a more elaborate way whenever a firm makes a capital investment. Producing automobiles on an assembly line is a roundabout method of production compared to producing them one by one with hand tools. Constructing a building in which to hold economics classes is a roundabout method of education compared with holding classes in the woods under a tree. In every case, time is taken to construct aids to production in order to produce more effectively later on.

Investment Loans

The brickmaker in the example invested directly by actually building the needed capital equipment. In a market economy, firms need not build their own capital equipment. Anyone who sees an opportunity for increasing output by using a more capital intensive (that is, a more roundabout) production process can borrow money and buy capital. The productivity of capital thus creates a source of demand for loanable funds in addition to the demand for consumption loans. Loans for increasing productivity can be called investment loans.

Exhibit 17.3 shows how the rate of interest is determined when the demand for investment loans is added to the demand for consumption loans. The

Exhibit 17.3
Determination of the interest rate with both consumption and investment loans
The demand for investment loans must be added to the demand for consumption loans to get the combined demand curve for loanable funds. Note that the equilibrium interest rate is higher in this exhibit than it would be if only consumption loans were taken into account.

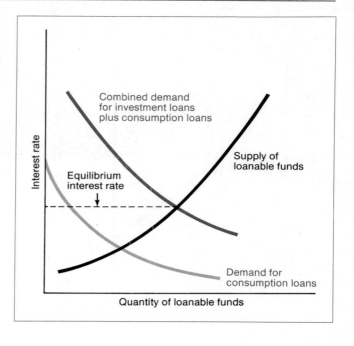

diagram reveals that the interest rate is higher when both types of loan demand are taken into account than it is when only consumption loans are considered. In practice, the investment demand for loanable funds is much greater than the consumption demand, which means that the investment demand is the most important factor determining the interest rate.

Capital and Interest

The chapter turns now from the determination of the interest rate in the credit market to the relationship between the demand for loanable funds and the demand for capital as a means of production. Exhibit 17.4 shows the short-run rental market for physical capital equipment—machines, buildings, and the like. In the short run, the supply of capital is fixed by the existing stock of capital equipment, so the supply curve is perfectly inelastic. The demand curve, as in other factor markets, is the marginal revenue product curve for the services of capital equipment. The two determine the rental value of capital equipment.

If the short-run rental price of capital equipment is high enough and the expected real rate of interest is low enough, it will pay to build more such equipment. Suppose, for example, that a car rental company can buy a car for $6,000 with funds that it borrows at a 5 percent expected real rate of interest. If its expected net income from renting the car, adjusting for inflation and allowing for operating expenses and depreciation, is $300 per year or more, it will pay the company to invest in expansion of its fleet.

Over time, as investment proceeds and capital accumulates, the short-run supply curve of capital shifts to the right. In the long run, this tends to drive down the rental price of capital equipment and reduce the incentive to invest. The investment demand for loanable funds thus diminishes, and the real rate of interest falls. Theoretically, the economy can end up in a steady-state equilibrium. In this state, all worthwhile investment projects are completed,

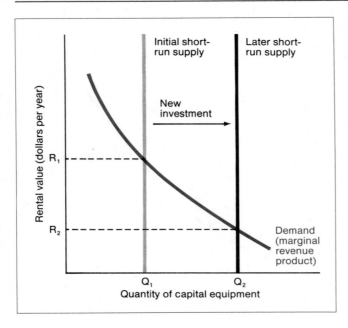

Exhibit 17.4
Short-run rental value of capital equipment and the long-run effect of investment
In the short run, the rental value of capital equipment is determined by the existing stock of capital and the demand (marginal revenue product) curve for the services of capital equipment. In the long run, new investment causes the supply curve to shift to the right. This drives down the rental value, other things being equal. In practice, however, innovations continually shift the demand curve for capital services to the right as well.

and consumption loans provide the only remaining demand for loanable funds. In practice, the steady state never arrives. Technological innovation constantly pushes up the demand curve (marginal revenue product curve) for capital services. The short-run rental value of capital equipment is thus kept high enough to justify substantial investment in new capital equipment year after year.

PROFIT AND ENTREPRENEURSHIP

The term *pure economic profit* was introduced in Chapter 7 to refer to the income, if any, remaining to owners of a firm after they deduct all implicit and explicit costs of production. Explicit costs include factor payments to workers, resource owners, and suppliers of capital, together with the cost of semifinished inputs, if any, purchased from other firms. Implicit costs include a normal rate of return on capital supplied by owners of the firm plus the opportunity costs of using natural resources or labor supplied by owners of the firm or owned by the firm itself. What is left over is pure economic profit.

This definition of profit leaves unanswered two very important questions that have not yet been raised explicitly: Why does a firm ever earn any pure economic profit at all? Why is the entire value of the product of all firms not divided up among the owners of the labor, natural resources, and capital used in the production process? These are subtle questions that have occupied the minds of many great economists, who have not yet come up with answers that everyone agrees with. Still, it will be worthwhile to look at some of the kinds of answers that have been suggested.

Theories of Profit

Risk and Profit According to one theory, profits are a reward that the owners of businesses receive for bearing risk. Every business venture is subject to the risk of failure. That is the nature of economic life in a world where the future is not known with certainty. People who merely hire out their factor services largely escape risk. A new business is usually expected to offer workers contractual guarantees that the payroll will be met even if the firm loses money. It is also expected to offer security against default to banks or bondholders who provide capital. The owner or owners of the firm (stockholders if the firm is organized in the corporate form) bear most of the risk of loss if the firm fails. In return, they get the privilege of keeping the profits if revenues turn out to be more than enough to pay off the obligations to hired factors. Why is it, though, that the profits earned by successful risk takers are not exactly offset by the losses of the unsuccessful? The answer has to do with people's attitudes toward risk.

It is possible that some people are indifferent to risk. A person who is indifferent to risk will be indifferent between the opportunity to earn $10,000 a year with absolute certainty and the opportunity to try for $20,000, subject to a fifty-fifty chance of failing and earning nothing. People who are indifferent to risk may launch new businesses even when the expected profit if the business succeeds is exactly offset by the expected loss if the business fails.

In practice, though, most people dislike risk. If they know they can earn a secure $10,000 a year, they will not launch a business with a fifty-fifty chance of failure unless that business, if successful, will pay more than $20,000.

Because most people dislike risk, somewhat fewer business ventures are launched than would be otherwise. That makes opportunities a little more favorable, on the average, for those who are willing to bear some risk. When successes and failures are averaged out over the whole economy, profits more than offset losses. The excess of profits over losses is the reward earned by the people who bear business risks. Factor owners are willing to accept less than the whole value of the product of the firm to the extent that they are shielded from these risks.

Arbitrage The activity of earning a profit by buying a good for a low price in one market and reselling it for a higher price in another market.

Profits as Arbitrage A second theory equates profits with the return to the activity of **arbitrage**—buying a good at a low price in one market and selling it at a higher price in another. Examples of pure arbitrage can be found in markets for agricultural commodities, precious metals, foreign currencies, and other markets where completely standardized goods are traded at different points in the world. Consider, for example, the gold markets in London and Hong Kong. Economic policies, daily news developments, and other events may initially affect supply and demand in these two gold markets differently.

A political crisis in the British government, for example, might prompt an increase in demand in the London market, sending the price of gold there up relative to the price in Hong Kong. Before the prices got far apart, however, alert arbitrageurs in Hong Kong would start buying gold at the low Hong Kong price for resale at the higher London price. This activity would raise demand in Hong Kong and increase supply in London until the price in the two markets was equalized. (In practice, because of various transactions costs, the prices would be only approximately equalized on any given day.) In the process of acting as a crucial link in the international transmission of information through the price system, the arbitrageurs would turn a handy profit.

Arbitrage cannot always be seen in a form so pure as the international gold market. However, New York University economist Israel Kirzner has pointed out in an influential book that there is an element of arbitrage in every profit-making transaction.[1] Consider the entrepreneur-owner-manager of, say, a small shoe factory. This person buys inputs in one set of markets at the lowest prices possible and, after combining the inputs to form finished shoes, sells the product in other markets at the highest prices possible. In a hypothetical world where all markets were in perfectly competitive long-run equilibrium, it would no more be possible to make a profit by buying labor and leather and selling shoes than it would be by buying gold in Hong Kong and selling it in London. In such a world, the price of the leather and labor would be bid up to just equal the price of the finished shoes. In the real world, though, the alert entrepreneur can find arbitrage opportunities in a great variety of markets and can earn profits accordingly.

Profits and Innovation A third theory associates profit with the activity of innovation. This theory has achieved considerable popularity through the writings of Joseph Schumpeter.[2] In subtle contrast to the entrepreneur as arbitrageur, taking advantage of spontaneously occurring opportunities to buy

---

[1] Israel Kirzner, *Competition and Entrepreneurship* (Chicago: University of Chicago Press, 1974).
[2] See, for example, Joseph Schumpeter, *Capitalism, Socialism, and Democracy* (New York: Harper & Bros., 1942). Schumpeter's theories are also discussed in Chapter 27 of this text.

low and sell high, the entrepreneur as innovator creates new profit opportunities by devising a new product, a new production process, or a new marketing strategy. If successful, the entrepreneur achieves a position of temporary monopoly that permits pure economic profits to be earned until rival firms catch on or leap ahead with innovations of their own.

Further Comments on the Nature of Profit

Entrepreneurship as a Factor of Production It is probably pointless to argue which of the three theories of profit just discussed is the correct one. The economic activity that, since Chapter 1, has been called entrepreneurship is best thought of as an inseparable blend of risk taking, alertness to opportunities for arbitrage, and innovation.

Because entrepreneurs, like workers, resource owners, and suppliers of capital, earn a reward for their contribution to production, entrepreneurship is sometimes spoken of as a fourth factor of production. In some ways, it is indeed a little like the three factors of production—labor, natural resources, and capital. First, entrepreneurship, like the others, is scarce. Not everyone possesses the ability to organize business undertakings and recognize new economic opportunities. Second, entrepreneurs do earn an income in the form of the profit that remains after all the costs of their firms have been covered. Third, as is true for labor, natural resources, and capital, production cannot take place without entrepreneurship.

There is a limit, however, to how far the parallel between entrepreneurship and other factors can be pushed. The chief problem is that entrepreneurship is an intangible, not subject to measurement. There is no quantitative unit of entrepreneurship and hence no way to determine a price per unit. Applying supply and demand analysis to this fourth factor of production just does not work.

Monopoly Profits Up to this point, no distinction has been made between the profits earned in the short run by a competitive firm (before those profits are eroded by the competition of new entrants) and the profits earned by a monopolist (which under proper conditions of demand can persist indefinitely). Some writers have suggested that monopoly profits are a separate category of income that cannot be explained either as a reward to labor, capital, or natural resources or in terms of the entrepreneurial activities of risk bearing, arbitrage, and innovation. On close inspection, however, it turns out that most, if not all, of monopoly profit can be explained without introducing a special new category of income.

Consider, for example, the case of a monopoly based on a patented invention. When explicit costs are subtracted from revenue for such a firm, more than enough will be left over to provide a normal rate of return on capital. The firm might be said to earn a pure economic profit, but it would more accurately be said to earn an implicit rent as owner of the patent. It could, after all, sell or lease the patent rights to some other firm, in which case the patent owner would earn an explicit rent and the firm using the patent would earn only a normal return on capital after paying to acquire the patent. The opportunity cost to a monopolist of not renting the patent to another firm should thus be counted as an implicit cost, not as part of pure economic profit. The same applies to firms having a monopoly based on any other unique advantage that is in perfectly inelastic supply, such as a government franchise, a uniquely suitable location, or a unique natural resource.

If a monopolistic firm does not possess any unique advantage, its monopoly cannot be more than temporary. Sooner or later, other entrepreneurs will enter into competition with the firm and begin the process of reducing its pure economic profits to zero. Temporary monopoly profits of this type are not a separate category of income; they are simply the return earned by the monopolistic entrepreneur who was alert enough to get into the market before any competitors did so.

Windfall Profits   So-called windfall profits might appear to be another category of income not yet accounted for. *Windfall profit* is not a well-defined term of economic science but rather is a popular way of describing almost any kind of unexpected or fortuitous increase in the income of an individual or firm. Often, use of the term is accompanied by the normative implication that the income in question is undeserved or should not be permitted.

Perhaps the most familiar use of the term is in reference to the increase in the rental income of a natural resource owner that occurs when the demand for the resource unexpectedly increases or when the supply from other sources unexpectedly decreases. Consider, for example, the case of U.S. oil well owners when, in 1979, the Iranian revolution and related events sent the world price of oil up sharply. Oil well owners, through no action of their own, reaped great financial gains, which were popularly referred to as windfall profits; in the technical economic sense, however, they were really windfall increases in rent.

Widespread sentiment for subjecting the windfall to a stiff tax immediately developed. The tax was proposed partly on the normative ground that the income was undeserved and partly on the positive ground that such a tax would have no adverse effect on production, provided it was limited to wells already in production at the time the price rose.

It is not always true, however, that taxes on windfall gains have no effect on quantities supplied. In particular, it is important to distinguish between windfall gains that arise from events that are genuinely unforeseen and those that arise from events that were known in advance to be possible but were not certain. Again an illustration can be drawn from the oil industry. After the Iranian revolution sent the world price of oil up from about $15 per barrel to $20 or so, people began to think about what might happen if there were a similar revolution in Saudi Arabia, the world's largest producer. Suppose wildcat oil well drillers judged that a Saudi Arabian revolution would send the price up to $40 and that there was a fifty-fifty chance that such a revolution would occur. If they expected to be able to sell their oil for $40 if the revolution did come, they would drill in somewhat less promising locations than if they were certain that the price would stay permanently at $20 per barrel. The U.S. domestic oil supply would thus be somewhat greater than it would have been if no one had taken the possibility of a Saudi Arabian revolution into account.

If, however, wildcatters got the idea that every time a revolution sent the price of oil up, the government would impose a new windfall tax on existing wells, they would no longer consider it worthwhile to drill in anticipation of such an event. The oil supply would be smaller than it would have been without the expectation of a windfall tax. This scenario suggests, then, that a tax on windfall gains can sometimes have an adverse effect on supply after all.

Profits and Loot One final kind of financial gain that is sometimes confused with profit is the acquisition of wealth not through production and voluntary exchange, as in the case of profit and factor incomes, but coercively, through the expropriation of other people's property. Suppose, for example, that a service station owner, instead of paying a mechanic the market wage of $10,000 per year, hires a gang of thugs to threaten to burn the worker's house and molest the worker's children unless the wage is reduced to $6,000. The station's accounting profit will then appear to be $4,000 greater than otherwise. The extra $4,000 is not really pure economic profit, however, but something else. The vocabulary of economics lacks an accepted general term for the proceeds of coercive activity, but perhaps the word *loot* can serve as well as any. Looting need not be as crude as in the example just given. If a firm earns money by misrepresenting its product and defrauding consumers, that money is loot, not profit. If it gets rid of industrial wastes by dumping them on unwilling bystanders, then part of the firm's apparent profit is really loot. Loot is not only not profit; properly speaking, it is not a form of income because it is not a payment for newly produced goods or for services currently rendered.

CONCLUSIONS

This chapter began by discussing rent, interest, and profit purely in terms of positive economics. By the time it arrived at the topics of monopoly profits, windfall profits, and loot, however, it became apparent that not all controversies concerning the origin and distribution of income depend on purely positive analysis. Once the normative side of these matters is broached, a whole new set of issues concerning poverty and the personal distribution of income is raised. These issues are important enough to merit a separate chapter.

SUMMARY

1. Pure economic rent is the income earned by any factor of production that is in completely inelastic supply. Land is the classic example of a factor that earns a pure economic rent. Rent can be expressed in terms of either a periodic payment or a lump-sum price paid when a piece of land is transferred from one owner to another. The market price of a piece of land is the capitalized value of the rent it can earn. Rent can also be said to be earned by other factors that are in perfectly inelastic supply. The special talents of uniquely gifted persons earn rents, as do artificially created legal privileges.

2. The term *interest* expresses both the price paid by borrowers to lenders in credit markets and the income earned by capital as a factor of production. The interest rate is determined in credit markets. The supply of credit depends on the willingness of savers to lend. The demand for credit is composed of the demand for consumption loans plus the demand for investment loans. There is a demand for investment loans because capital using, roundabout methods of production are more productive than direct methods.

3. In the short run, supply and demand determine a rental price for the services of capital equipment. If the rental value of newly produced capital equipment (expressed as a percentage of the cost of producing the equip-

ment) is higher than the interest rate, it will pay firms to expand their stocks of capital. As the stocks of capital expand, the rental value of new capital—other things being equal—will tend to fall, thereby reducing the investment demand for credit and driving down the interest rate. In principle, these tendencies will eventually bring the economy to a steady state in which there is no new investment and the interest rate is determined entirely by the supply and demand for consumption loans. In practice, technological innovation constantly pushes up the marginal productivity of capital services, so there is always an incentive to invest.

4. There are several theories about the true nature of profits. One theory holds that profit is the reward that entrepreneurs earn for performing the function of bearing risks. Another sees profits as earned primarily through arbitrage. Still another emphasizes innovation. In practical terms, profit usually appears to arise from a mixture of these three sources.

DISCUSSION QUESTIONS

1. In 1974, U.S. farmers earned a gross income of $101 billion. Part of this income went to cover explicit private costs of $74 billion, leaving farmers with $27 billion of net income. Is that net income best thought of as wages, rent, interest, or profit? How can one go about making a rough breakdown of net farm income into these categories? Do you think that any farm income ought to be considered loot?

2. The chapter has suggested that part of the income of persons with exceptional talents might best be considered pure economic rent earned on those talents. Suppose a certain opera singer makes $100,000 per year. How could you tell what part of that income is wages and what part is rent? Here are three possible tests for finding what part is rent: (a) Ask how big a pay cut the singer would take before switching to a job where singing talent would be of no use. (b) Measure the difference between this singer's income and the income of a singer with the same training but only average natural talent. (c) Measure the difference between the singer's income in opera and the income he or she could earn in the next-best nonsinging job available. Which test is best? Do they all give about the same answer? Explain.

3. Turn back to Chapter 4 and Exhibit 4.6, and refresh your memory about the theory of tax incidence. How would the burden of a tax on pure economic rent be divided between resource owners and consumers? What about a tax on the "rental" income of apartment house owners?

4. Suppose you decide to start a Christmas tree farm. You already own a suitable piece of land. You get seeds from pine cones picked up in the woods. You plant the seeds with your bare hands, using no tools or equipment of any kind. Five years later, you harvest the trees, breaking them off with your hands rather than using any tools whatsoever. You sell the trees and earn a handsome income. How should that revenue be divided into wages, rent, interest, and profit? Did you use any capital? If so, what form did it take? (Hint: Did you use a roundabout method of production?)

5. Suppose a contractor places an ad for laborers in the newspaper, offering to pay them $1 per cubic yard for removing rocks and dirt from a cellar hole. Four workers show up and start the job. Alice is a person of average build. She uses a simple shovel and bucket for the job and manages to earn $2 a day. Baker, a giant of a man, also uses a shovel and bucket but earns $5 a day. Charles brings a wheelbarrow with him and earns $6 a day even though he is no stronger than Alice. Donna uses a bucket and shovel and, like Alice, earns only $2 a day at first. Not satisfied with this, she takes a month off to go through an intensive course of physical conditioning. When she comes back, she can earn $5 a day. How should the income of each worker be categorized in terms of wages, rent, income, and profits?

6. The term *loot* means income earned by someone through the use of coercion, fraud, theft, or intimidation. Is loot then a synonym for *income earned illegally?*

What kinds of legally earned income should perhaps be counted as loot? What kinds of illegally earned income should perhaps be counted as ordinary wages, rent, interest, or profits?

SUGGESTIONS FOR FURTHER READING

Böhm-Bawerk, Eugen von. "The Nature of Roundabout Production." In *Contemporary Economics: Selected Readings,* 2d ed. Edited by Reuben E. Slesinger, Mark Perlman, and Asher Isaacs. Boston: Allyn & Bacon, 1967.
A classic statement of the nature of capital and production by the turn-of-the-century Austrian economist.

Kirzner, Israel. *Competition and Entrepreneurship.* Chicago: University of Chicago Press, 1974.
Kirzner's own theory of profits, which emphasizes the element of arbitrage in entrepreneurial behavior. The book also contains a comprehensive critique of alternative theories.

Nicholson, Walter. *Intermediate Microeconomics and its Application.* 2d ed. Hinsdale, Ill.: Dryden Press, 1979.
Chapter 13 discusses rent; Chapter 16 covers capital.

Scitovski, Tibor. *Welfare and Competition.* Rev. ed. Homewood, Ill.: Richard D. Irwin, 1971.
Chapter 19 of this classic and wide-ranging treatise discusses capital and entrepreneurship.

C H A P T E R **18**

THE PROBLEM
OF POVERTY

WHAT YOU WILL LEARN IN THIS CHAPTER

This chapter turns from the functional to the personal distribution of income. First, it discusses various alternative ways of defining and measuring poverty. Next, it reviews the major efforts that have been made to alleviate poverty, distinguishing between event conditioned and income conditioned transfers, explaining what both types of transfer programs have accomplished, and looking at what critics and reformers have to say about them. It also considers job market strategies for helping the poor.

FOR REVIEW

Here are some important terms and concepts that will be put to use in this chapter. If you do not understand them, review them before proceeding.

- *Tax incidence (Chapter 4)*
- *Progressive and regressive taxes (Chapter 4)*
- *Functional distribution of income (Chapters 15 to 17)*

The personal distribution of income, as pointed out in the introduction to Chapter 15, depends on the distribution not only of income among factors according to marginal productivity but also of factor ownership among individuals. Ownership of factors of production is by no means equally distributed. Reportedly the wealthiest 1 percent of the population owns some 40 percent of all capital. Natural resources are presumably also unequally distributed, although accurate statistics are hard to come by. Labor—in terms of the sheer potential to contribute labor hours—is distributed fairly equally; but the quality of labor services, and hence earned income, varies widely among individuals. Taking all sources of cash income into account, the wealthiest 20 percent of U.S. citizens earn some 40 percent of all personal income, while the poorest 20 percent must make do with only 5 percent of the total.

Behind these simple statistics lies a whole host of economic policy issues. In the United States today, it is widely accepted that one of the major functions of government is to influence the distribution of income. But just why income is distributed as it is, how it should be distributed, and the means by which it should be redistributed, if at all, are extraordinarily controversial. This brief chapter will try to raise the major subjects of controversy, although there is little hope that any of them can definitely be resolved.

POVERTY AND THE NATURE
OF THE INCOME DISTRIBUTION PROBLEM

Three Views of the Nature of Poverty

There is no doubt that poverty exists in the United States today, despite the fact that its people—by many, if not all, measures—continue to have the highest average incomes in the world. Poverty is plainly seen in vast neighborhoods in every large city. It is tucked away only slightly less visibly in small towns and rural areas throughout the country. Yet there is surprisingly little agreement as to just what poverty is. At least three major points of view can be identified.

First is the view that poverty means not having enough income to provide some objectively defined decent standard of living. According to this view, people are poor if they cannot afford the simple necessities of life—food, clothing, and shelter. Implicit in this viewpoint is the idea that people can be raised out of poverty by lifting their incomes above the objectively defined threshold.

A second view resembles the first in that it identifies poverty with low incomes, but it maintains that what constitutes low income must be defined in subjective terms, relative to the incomes of others in society. For example, it is often suggested that a poverty-level household income should be defined as one equal to less than half of the median income for all households. (In 1978, the median household income was about $17,000; some 20 percent of all households had cash incomes less than half that amount.) This view makes poverty level income a moving target rather than an objectively defined threshold. Nonetheless, like the first view, it implies that poverty can be overcome by raising the incomes of the poor.

A third view is somewhat different from the other two. It makes poverty a matter not so much of low incomes but of how people cope with the fact of having them. Some low income households honestly, industriously, and successfully make do with what they have, keep families together, and keep children out of trouble. Others—including many who, statistically speaking, have been raised above the poverty threshold—are for one reason or another unable to cope. They fall into a pattern of social pathologies ranging from juvenile crime and teenage pregnancy to drug and alcohol abuse. They turn newly constructed public housing into instant slums and, in a variety of ways, frustrate the hopes of those who aspire to the elimination of poverty through generous public spending and giving. Implicit in this view is the idea that no amount of income distribution can by itself eliminate poverty. If poorly conceived government programs foster dependency and destroy self-respect, they may even make things worse.

Poverty as Officially Defined

Of these three possible approaches to defining poverty, the one officially chosen by the U.S. government is the first: an objectively defined standard based on the cost of necessities. This approach begins with the idea of an economy food plan devised by the Department of Agriculture. The plan provides a balanced nutritive diet at the lowest possible cost, given prevailing market prices. The cost of the plan varies according to the size of a family, the age of its members, and their place of residence. In 1978, the cost of a minimal diet was approximately $2,172 for an urban family of four, with the two children aged 6 to 11 years.

By itself, a total income equal to the cost of the economy food plan is not sufficient to keep a family well-nourished. Other needs must be satisfied too. To take the other needs into account, the government sets the low income level—the dividing line between the poor and the nonpoor—at three times the cost of the economy food plan. Below that income level, the pressure of a family's needs for shelter, clothing, and other necessities tends to become so great that the family will forgo buying the needed food in order to get other things instead. Exhibit 18.1 shows low income levels set for farm and nonfarm families of various sizes in 1977.

How Many Poor?

Part of the reason for selecting an objective, need-based official definition of poverty in the first place was to provide a benchmark against which to measure progress toward the elimination of poverty. On the basis of the official definition, the incidence of poverty fell rapidly during the 1960s—from 22.4 percent of the population in 1959 to 12.1 percent in 1969. During the 1970s, however, there was essentially no further reduction in the number of officially measured poor families. The percentage of such families fluctuated between a low of 11.1 in 1973 and a high of 12.3 in 1975, with no discernable trend upward or downward. What went wrong?

The answer, recent studies suggest, is that government policy changed course in the 1970s in a way that made the official definition of poverty increasingly inaccurate as a measure of material well-being. More specifically, government programs in aid of the poor began to rely increasingly on such in-kind transfers as public housing, food stamps, and Medicaid, while the official poverty statistics continued to count only cash income. Increasing numbers of people whose standard of living was lifted above the low income level by in-kind transfers continued to be reported as poor in the official series.

Recently a number of efforts have been made to adjust the official figures to take in-kind transfers into account. For example, a recent paper by Robert Plotnick of Dartmouth College and Timothy Smeeding of the University of Utah reports that when food stamp, Medicare, and Medicaid programs are taken into account, the number of people living in poverty fell from 10.1

Exhibit 18.1

Official low income levels for farm and nonfarm families, 1977

Official low income levels are calculated on the basis of an economy food plan devised by the Department of Agriculture. The cost of this food plan is then multiplied by three to allow for the purchase of things other than food. The low income level for farm families is set at 85 percent of the level for nonfarm families.

Number of Family Members	Nonfarm Income	Farm Income
2	$ 4,072	$3,461
3	4,833	4,108
4	6,191	5,262
5	7,320	6,222
6	8,261	7,188
7 or more	10,216	8,684
Unrelated individuals	3,152	2,679

Source: U.S. Department of Commerce, Bureau of the Census, *Statistical Abstract of the United States*, 100th ed. (Washington, D.C.: Government Printing Office, 1979), Table 732.

percent of the population in 1968 to 6.5 percent in 1976.[1] Another study, by Morton Paglin of Portland State University, considers additional in-kind transfers, including public housing programs and food and nutrition programs other than food stamps. This study indicates that the number of people living in poverty fell to just 3 percent of the population by 1975.[2]

Do such adjusted figures, which show poverty to be substantially eradicated, mean that people live in the best of all possible worlds? Hardly. The figures simply mean that they live in a complex and paradoxical world—one where a Greek fishing family can live picturesquely and perhaps even comfortably on an income equivalent to less than $1,000 per year, while many U.S. families with ten times that income manage to exhibit all the outward signs of desperate poverty. There seems to be little point in saying that either the prosperity of the one or the poverty of the other is illusory. The important thing is simply to keep in mind, while reviewing the mechanics of income transfer policies, that solving the poverty problem somehow involves more than just pushing dollars around.

HELPING THE POOR: TRANSFER STRATEGIES

In keeping with the orthodox view that poverty is primarily a matter of a lack of income, the predominant strategies of government aid to the poor have emphasized income transfers. According to a comprehensive inventory compiled by the Institute for Socioeconomic Studies, in fiscal 1977, the federal government spent at least $170 billion on income transfers.[3] If certain tax relief and insurance programs designed to aid the economically distressed had been included in the total (as some say they should be), the figure would have been $248 billion.

Event conditioned transfers
Social insurance programs under which transfer payments are available to all citizens, regardless of income level, upon the occurrence of a specified event such as retirement, unemployment, or disability.

Income conditioned transfers
Welfare or public charity programs under which transfer payments are available to citizens who meet some specified low income criterion.

These income transfer programs can be divided into two categories—event conditioned transfers and income conditioned transfers. **Event conditioned transfers**—often referred to as social insurance programs—are available to all citizens, regardless of income, upon the occurrence of some specific event such as retirement, unemployment, or disability. **Income conditioned transfers**—sometimes called public charity or welfare programs—are made available to citizens who meet some set low income criterion. In what follows, the major programs of each type will be discussed in turn.

Social Security

The Social Security Act of 1935 set up what has become the largest single income transfer program of the U.S. government. In fiscal 1977, the Social Security Administration spent some $135 billion. Social security itself—payments to retired workers, survivors of workers, and disabled workers—accounted for about $83 billion. Medicare added another $22 billion, and various smaller programs made up the rest.

Despite its near-sacred status among elected politicians, the social security

---

[1] Robert Plotnick and Timothy Smeeding, "Poverty and Income Transfers: Past Trends and Future Prospects," *Journal of Public Policy* 27 (Summer 1979): 259.

[2] Morton Paglin, "Transfers in Kind: Their Impact on Poverty, 1959–75," paper presented at Hoover Institution Conference on Redistribution, October 7–8, 1977.

[3] William J. Lawrence and Stephen Leeds, *An Inventory of Federal Transfer Programs* (White Plains, N.Y.: Institute for Socioeconomic Studies, 1978), p. 11.

program is the target of many criticisms, and the criticisms are gradually leading to reforms. It is worth looking at some of the major problems that social security faces in the 1980s.

Financing Problems One of the biggest problems facing social security is that it has outgrown the method used to finance it. Social security benefits are financed by a special payroll tax, half of which is deducted from the employee's gross pay and half of which is paid by the employer. (However, as pointed out in Chapter 4, all or most of the true incidence of the tax bears on employees' wages and salaries.) When the program first began, the payroll tax was a modest one—just 1 percent each for employers and employees on the first $3,000 of income. Over the years, as the program's coverage has expanded and as benefit levels have risen, the tax rate and the range of income to which it applies have risen steadily. In 1979, employers and employees were each paying 6.13 percent tax on the first $22,900 of income—nearly a fiftyfold increase since the program began. What is more, demographic trends will make it necessary to increase taxes further as the ratio of beneficiaries to workers rises.

The critics of social security complain not only that the tax is burdensome but also that it is regressive. Because the tax is levied only on earnings below a specified threshold, and because it is levied only on wage and salary income, lower and middle income households pay taxes that are higher in relation to their incomes than do higher income households.

Short of cutting benefits—which some critics in fact propose—little can be done to reduce the necessity of raising large sums of tax dollars to pay for social security. But the burden of the tax could be more equitably spread, it has been suggested, if all or part of the cost of social security were financed from general tax revenues. Bringing federal workers into the system (they now have their own retirement program and pay no social security taxes) would also help spread the tax burden more equitably.

Effects on Saving A second criticism of the social security program is based on its apparent effect of displacing private saving. Originally, the social security program itself was supposed to be a source of saving in the economy as workers paid taxes into a trust fund during their earning years and drew on the fund during retirement. The trust fund concept was long ago abandoned in all but name, however, in favor of a pay-as-you-go system. Payroll tax proceeds now go directly to pay benefits of currently retired workers, so no saving is involved.

Nonetheless, although payroll taxes no longer represent saving from the viewpoint of the economy as a whole, they are a substitute for saving from the viewpoint of individual workers. Knowing that they will receive social security benefits upon retirement, individuals feel that they need to put aside less money to finance their own retirement. Just how much private saving is displaced by each dollar of promised social security benefits is a matter of considerable dispute, but according to estimates by Harvard economist Martin Feldstein, the effect may be quite large. If so, the economy is left with less saving to finance investment; and with less investment, it is left with slower economic growth. The implication is that today's workers will retire into a world where income and living standards will be lower than they would have been if the social security system had not promised to protect those very living standards for individual future beneficiaries.

**Martin Feldstein
(1939–   )**

Martin Feldstein is a leading member of a generation of young economists who increasingly are bringing microeconomic analysis to bear on important issues of public policy. The economics of social security is one of the fields in which Feldstein's research has been particularly influential. His pioneering paper, "Social Security, Induced Retirement, and Aggregate Capital Accumulation," touched off the ongoing debate over the extent to which social security displaces private saving.[4]

After graduating from Harvard, Feldstein went to Oxford University in England as a Fulbright scholar. He received his doctorate there in 1967 and returned to Harvard as an assistant professor. In just two years—some think it was record time—he attained the rank of full professor. Currently, in addition to his Harvard post, Feldstein is president of the National Bureau of Economic Research, a sixty year old nonprofit research organization specializing in objective quantitative studies of the U.S. economy. He received the prestigious John Bates Clark medal from the American Economic Association in 1977.

Feldstein's work, like that of many of his contemporaries, is sometimes classified as conservative because it challenges preconceived notions about such traditional liberal policies as social security, unemployment insurance, income taxation, and publicly financed medical insurance. Feldstein considers himself an apolitical centrist, however. He comes upon such conservative sounding ideas as taxing unemployment compensation to get unemployed workers back on the job faster not from ideological preconceptions but simply from careful real world observations that show people behaving in the way the theory of supply and demand has long predicted they should. The thrust of Feldstein's contributions to public policy is that, whether inspired by conservative or by liberal views, public programs should always be designed in accordance with the economic facts of life if they are to have their intended results.

Treatment of Women A third major criticism leveled against social security has been its treatment of women. The system was designed originally for the household with a male breadwinner and a non-income-earning wife. Social security benefits for working women were tacked on as an afterthought. Married women have received little or nothing in the way of benefits for any contributions made while working; divorced women have been eligible for a share of their former husbands' benefits only if the marriage lasted twenty years or more.

Fortunately, it appears that this inequity is very likely to be corrected in the near future. The technical merits of alternative proposed reforms are still being debated as of this writing, but it seems probable that social security soon will begin treating men and women equally for the first time.

Income Conditioned Transfer Programs

In addition to social security and other event conditioned transfer programs, the federal government operates a number of income conditioned transfer programs. In fact, nearly half of all federal transfer programs, broadly defined, are conditioned on need at least to some extent. Some of the most important of these programs are discussed in the next section.

Aid to Families with Dependent Children (AFDC) To most people, "welfare" means Aid to Families with Dependent Children. AFDC provides

---

[4] Martin Feldstein, "Social Security, Induced Retirement, and Aggregate Capital Accumulation," *Journal of Political Economy* 82 (September–October 1974): 905–926.

assistance in covering the minimum costs of food, shelter, and clothing for needy dependent children, generally in single parent households. In fiscal 1977, the federal government spent some $5.7 billion on AFDC, plus an additional $400 million on a closely related smaller program aiding children in families with unemployed fathers.

Perhaps the most controversial aspect of AFDC is the incentive the program seems to provide for men to desert their families and for women to bear additional children. Despite attempts at reforming eligibility rules in many states, and despite the addition of the AFDC–Unemployed Father program at the federal level, this perverse incentive structure has yet to be completely eliminated. Defenders of the program are correct in pointing out that evidence of response to the troublesome incentives is largely anecdotal. Nonetheless, AFDC remains a popular target of reformers.

Medicaid Medical assistance to low income persons under the Medicaid program is the largest single federal income conditioned transfer program; fiscal 1977 expenditures on this program were $9.9 billion. Some 24 million persons receive medical care annually under the program. Unlike most other income conditioned transfer programs, Medicaid benefits are not gradually reduced as income increases. Low income families either qualify for full coverage or receive none at all. AFDC families automatically qualify for Medicaid in all states; and in some states, families with somewhat higher incomes also qualify.

Food Stamps Food stamps are a third major income conditioned transfer program. In fiscal 1977, some 17 million persons received benefits worth $5.5 billion. In some areas where a high percentage of residents are eligible for the program, food stamps have become a virtual second currency. Although they can, of course, be spent only on food, they release money for other uses that otherwise would have been spent on food. While food stamps are unquestionably important to the budgets of a great many low income families, it is far from clear that they have any more impact on nutrition than would cash grants of equivalent value.

Income Transfers and Work Incentives All income transfer programs affect work incentives to some extent by imposing either explicit or implicit taxes on earned income. The social security payroll tax, which begins with the first dollar of earned income for a low income worker, is an example of an explicit tax. The 33 percent **benefit reduction rate** built into the AFDC program is an example of an implicit tax: For each $1 of earned income in excess of $30 per month, AFDC benefits are reduced by $.33. And some transfer programs, such as Medicaid, have all-or-nothing cutoff incomes that provide additional negative work incentives.

The percentage of each additional dollar of earned income that a household loses through either explicit taxes or benefit reductions can be called the **effective marginal tax rate** for that household. At present, the combined effect of the major income transfer programs imposes very high effective marginal tax rates on low income households, as the following case study illustrates.

Benefit reduction rate The amount by which transfer benefits are reduced per dollar of earned income.

Effective marginal tax rate The percentage of each dollar of additional earned income that a household loses through all explicit taxes and benefit reductions combined.

Case 18.1
Incentive Effects of Income Transfers, Washington, D.C.

A typical AFDC family living in Washington, D.C., in 1979 consisted of a woman with three young children. If the family had no earned income, it received $3,768 per year in AFDC benefits and $1,404 per year in food stamp benefits—a total of $5,172. In addition, the family was eligible for Medicaid benefits, which can be estimated at approximately $1,600 per year on the basis of nationwide average payments to program participants. The family's total income, including in-kind transfers, was thus $6,772.

For each $1 of earned income, the woman heading this household paid $.06 in social security taxes. In addition, for each $1 in earned income, the family lost $.33 in AFDC benefits and $.22 in food stamp benefits. The effective marginal tax rate on the family, then, beginning after the first $420 per year in earned income, was 61 percent. This rate is higher than the 50 percent marginal tax rate imposed on the earned income of even the wealthiest individuals by the federal income tax.

To look at it another way, suppose the head of this hypothetical household were able to get a full-time job at the minimum wage. This job would have brought in a total earned income of $6,500 per year. After adjustments for social security payroll taxes, federal income taxes, reduced AFDC benefits, and the complete loss of food stamp eligibility, the $6,500 of earned income would leave the family only $2,627 richer than when earned income was zero. Suppose that, alternatively, the head of the household were able to get into some educational or job training program that eventually would qualify her for a job at twice the minimum wage, or roughly $13,000 per year. After adjusting for social security taxes, income taxes, the loss of remaining AFDC benefits, and the complete loss of Medicaid benefits, this very substantial jump in earned income would leave the family with just $1,526 more than when earned income was $6,500!

Source: Based on telephone interviews with various Washington, D.C., welfare officials.

This example is by no means extreme. In fact, it understates the effective marginal tax rate the household would face because it ignores such other income conditioned transfers as public housing, school lunch subsidies, and free or subsidized day-care services. It also ignores any work related expenses the wage earner might incur. When these effects are taken into account, low income families sometimes face effective marginal tax rates in excess of 100 percent over crucial ranges of earned income.

The Negative Income Tax

Economists concerned about the disincentive effects of the present welter of poorly coordinated transfer programs have long advocated "cashing out" all in-kind transfers and rolling all transfer programs into a single negative income tax program. The basic idea behind a negative income tax is very simple. Under a positive income tax—the kind currently used—individuals pay the government an amount that varies according to how much they earn. A **negative income tax** puts the same principle to work in reverse. It makes the government pay individuals an amount that varies in proportion to their earnings.

Exhibit 18.2 shows how a negative income tax could be set up. The horizontal axis of the figure measures the income a household earns. The vertical axis measures what it actually receives after payments from or to the government. The 45 degree line represents the amount of disposable income households would have if there were no tax of any kind. The negative and positive

Negative income tax A general name for transfer systems that emphasize cash benefits, beginning with a basic benefit available to households with zero earned income that is then subject to a benefit reduction rate of substantially less than 100 percent.

Exhibit 18.2
Possible schedules for a negative income tax
A negative income tax redistributes income without imposing extremely high marginal tax rates on either taxpayers or beneficiaries. In order to maintain low marginal tax rates, some benefits are given to nonpoor families, and some poor families are given more than they need to reach the low income level. The cost of a negative income tax scheme must therefore always be greater than the aggregate income deficit.

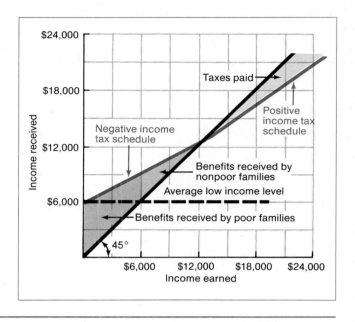

income tax schedules show the disposable income of families with the negative income tax program in force.

As the exhibit is drawn, the benefit received by a family with no income at all is just equal to the average low income level, assumed to be $6,000. That is necessary if the scheme is to eliminate officially measured poverty entirely. Starting from zero earnings, benefits are reduced by $.50 for each $1 earned. When earned incomes reach a level equal to twice the low income level, a breakeven point where no taxes are paid and no benefits received is reached. Beyond that point, a positive income tax schedule of the familiar kind takes over.

The negative income tax has the great advantage of maintaining work incentives for all beneficiaries. The marginal tax rate for poor families is only 50 percent as the exhibit is drawn. This rate is presumably low enough to prevent widespread withdrawal of effort. Note, however, that the cost of the program is still much greater than the initial size of the aggregate income deficit. All but the very poorest families receive more than the minimum they need to reach the low income cutoff. What is more, many nonpoor families—those with earned incomes in the $6,000 to $12,000 range—also receive benefits.

Many practical questions about the cost and workability of a negative income tax cannot be answered by armchair economics. They can be answered only on the basis of actual experience with running such a program. Some significant experiments have now been carried out; one of them is described in the following case study.

Case 18.3
The Seattle-Denver Income Maintenance Experiment

Between 1968 and 1978, the U.S. Department of Health, Education, and Welfare carried out a series of social experiments to test the feasibility of a negative income tax. The largest and longest running of these experiments, conducted in Seattle and Denver, ran for eight years and involved nearly five thousand families.

Exhibit 18.3
Average labor supply responses of families receiving grants under the Seattle-Denver experiment

Basic Benefit	Average Hours per Year before Response	Change in Hours	Percentage Change	Participating Families (millions)
	50 Percent Benefit Reduction Rate			
50 Percent of Poverty Line Husband-wife families:				
Husbands	1,381	−166	−12	
Wives	353	−66	−19	
Total	1,734	−232	−13	1.6
Female family heads	435	5	1	2.1
75 Percent of Poverty Line Husband-wife families:				
Husbands	1,550	−155	−10	
Wives	386	−101	−26	
Total	1,936	−256	−13	3.7
Female family heads	602	−43	−7	2.7
100 Percent of Poverty Line Husband-wife families:				
Husbands	1,716	−136	−8	
Wives	437	−149	−34	
Total	2,152	−286	−13	7.1
Female family heads	714	−84	−12	3.2
	70 Percent Benefit Reduction Rate			
50 Percent of Poverty Line Husband-wife families:				
Husbands	1,213	−246	−20	
Wives	332	−66	−20	
Total	1,545	−312	−20	1.0
Female family heads	327	−6	−2	1.9
75 Percent of Poverty Line Husband-wife families:				
Husbands	1,326	−234	−18	
Wives	343	−95	−28	
Total	1,669	−328	−20	2.1
Female family heads	468	−47	−10	2.4
100 Percent of Poverty Line Husband-wife families:				
Husbands	1,459	−223	−15	
Wives	376	−129	−34	
Total	1,836	−352	−19	3.7
Female family heads	582	−91	−16	2.8

Source: U.S. Department of Health, Education, and Welfare, *Summary Report: Seattle-Denver Income Maintenance Experiment* (Washington, D.C.: Government Printing Office, February 1978), Table 4.

The major purpose of the program was to test the effect on work incentives of replacing the major existing tax and transfer programs with a negative income tax.

Each participating household received a basic benefit at the zero earned income level; the benefit was then reduced at a specified rate as earned income increased. To ensure that the effective marginal tax rate faced by the families was exactly equal to the benefit reduction rate, participants were reimbursed for any social security payroll taxes or federal income taxes that they paid on their earned income. The participating families were divided into groups corresponding to benefit reduction rates of 50 and 75 percent. Within each group, some families were assigned to subgroups receiving a basic benefit of 50, 75, or 100 percent of the official low income level.

The results of the experiment were somewhat disappointing to economists who had hoped that replacing current AFDC, food stamp, payroll tax, and income tax programs with a single negative income tax would substantially improve work incentives. Instead, as Exhibit 18.3 shows, virtually all categories of recipients reduced their work effort in response to the grants received. The only exception to the pattern of reduced work hours was for female family heads receiving a basic grant of 50 percent of the low income level, subject to a benefit reduction rate of 50 percent. For these households, the program lowered both total transfers received and the effective marginal tax rate (compared with the combination of AFDC plus food stamps that it replaced) and thus resulted in a slight increase in work effort.

HEW analysts also conducted simulations that compared the total projected costs of a nationwide negative income tax with and without taking the labor supply response into account. These simulations found that the labor supply response would make the costs of a national program from 16 to 31 percent higher than the costs of a hypothetical program in which all participants maintained exactly their preprogram work effort.

Source: U.S. Department of Health, Education, and Welfare, *Summary Report: Seattle-Denver Income Maintenance Experiment* (Washington, D.C.: Government Printing Office, February 1978).

The significance of the preliminary experimental results on which the preceding case study is based is still under intense debate. Nonetheless, it does appear to cast doubt on the ability of a negative income tax to improve the material well-being of the poor, create work incentives, and save money for taxpayers simultaneously—a combination of virtues to which negative income tax advocates had in the past laid claim.

HELPING THE POOR: JOB MARKET STRATEGIES

Transfer strategies for helping the poor are based on the diagnosis that people are poor because they do not have enough money. The implied cure is to give them additional resources in cash or in kind. A different approach to the problem of poverty is based on the diagnosis that poverty results from a failure of factor markets to allocate human resources properly. By implication, putting wasted labor to work would make many poor households self-supporting.

The diagnosis that poverty is a matter of factor market failure must be broadly interpreted if it is to have any credibility at all. National data suggest that very few of the poor are adults in households headed by unemployed, able-bodied males aged eighteen to sixty-five. A narrowly conceived jobs-for-the-poor approach that focused just on this group would not make much of a dent on the overall poverty picture. In a broader sense, though, much more poverty is attributable to job related sources. The number of elderly poor and working poor would be reduced if the market provided higher paying jobs. The number of families headed by women, where the highest proportion of poor children are concentrated, would be less if it were not for the destructive effect on family life of men's inability to get good jobs. In the long run, job market strategies for alleviating poverty could benefit all the poor.

The Dual Labor Market Theory

Dual labor market The division of the labor market into a primary sector, containing good jobs with established firms, and a secondary sector, containing low-paid, unstable jobs with marginal firms.

Job market failure as a source of poverty is not just a matter of unemployment. According to one theory, the problem lies in the existence of a **dual labor market.** One sector of the market contains high wage jobs with profitable firms. These jobs not only pay more but are more likely to be unionized, to offer opportunities for advancement, and to be less affected by macroeconomic fluctuations. The secondary job market, in contrast, contains low paying jobs with marginal firms. These jobs are held by unorganized workers with unstable work patterns. They are largely dead-end jobs with few opportunities for advancement, and they are heavily hit by cyclical swings in unemployment.

According to proponents of the dual labor market theory, the two parts of the job market are kept separate by a complex of interacting factors. Discrimination, attitudes, motivation, and work habits determine which sector a worker is in. Once in the secondary sector, a worker develops attitudes and work habits that make discrimination more likely. The dual labor market theory has clear implications for antipoverty policy—namely, that such a policy must aim at breaking down the barriers between the two market sectors. The following section looks at some possible means of doing this.

Education Economists like to view education as an investment. By spending money and taking time away from current employment, people can improve their skills and productivity. Later, they can sell their services at higher wages in the labor market. One antipoverty strategy, then, is to make good quality education available to the poor and to the children of the poor, in the hope that this education will make them self-supporting.

There are actually two different ways in which education can have an impact on the problem of poverty. On the one hand, education benefits the particular individuals who are educated, thus taking people one by one out of poverty. On the other hand, improved education has a general impact on the equality of income distribution; by increasing the supply of highly educated workers, it lowers their relative wages. Both effects are slow, however, and far from foolproof.

Looking first at elementary education, one encounters the problem of an uncertain relationship between the quantity of educational inputs and the quality of educational outputs. Despite numerous studies, it is by no means clear that spending more on schools improves the performance of the pupils who go to them. To a considerable extent, the home and community environment may be more powerful than formal education in transmitting the crucial attitudes, motivations, and work habits that decide which sector of the labor market a person will end up in.

Increased spending on higher education appears to be an even less certain method for combating poverty. It is true that a college education gives upward mobility for many individuals from impoverished backgrounds. Those who succeed in college, however, are likely to be those with the attitudes and abilities that would bring them success in any event, even if they never had the chance to go to college. There is some evidence that in the early 1970s, salaries for college trained workers began to fall in response to an increased supply of college graduates. This may be having some effect on the inequality of income distribution. There are probably other, better ways to achieve the same effect, though. It would seem better to bring up the income of the poor rather than to push down the income of college graduates by encouraging their oversupply.

One thing remains to be said in favor of education as an antipoverty measure. Although the economic effects of subsidizing education may be difficult to measure, a good education is something that most disadvantaged parents want for their children. Improvements in education thus fill a perceived need. This may be important in itself.

Discrimination

Many economists believe that discrimination plays an important role in separating the two sectors of the labor market. During the 1960s, there was considerable occupational upgrading among blacks. Yet blacks are still less than proportionately represented in high paying jobs and more than proportionately represented in secondary sector jobs.

The level of black family income rose during the 1960s from 55 to 65 percent of white family income. During the early 1970s, however, it slipped back, as shown in Exhibit 18.4. Wages for blacks continued to rise, but the increase was more than offset in terms of family income by rising black unemployment, falling black labor force participation, and increases in the percentage of black families headed by women.

Since the Civil Rights Act of 1964, discrimination in employment has been illegal under federal law. The Equal Employment Opportunity Commission has broad powers to enforce this act. It is not clear, however, how far affirmative action to encourage minority employment can go before it becomes illegal discrimination against nonminority workers.

Antidiscrimination laws have had some effect, but there are economic limits to what can be expected from them. The market contains built-in antidiscrimination incentives of its own. Suppose it were true that the low paid secondary sector of the labor market contained substantial numbers of workers who were there only because of their race. Suppose that these workers had the

Exhibit 18.4

Black income as a percentage of white income
During the 1970s, the income of black families in the United States as a percentage of the income of white families declined. This happened despite the fact that over the most recent seven years, the earnings of individual black male workers rose from 69 percent of the level for white men to 77 percent, while the earnings of individual black female workers rose from 80 percent of the level for white women to 94 percent. These gains in individual incomes were more than offset by increased unemployment among blacks, the declining average age of the black population, and the increase in the proportion of black families headed by women.

Source: U.S. Department of Commerce, Bureau of the Census surveys in March of each of the indicated years. Reported in Alfred L. Malabre, Jr., "After Shrinking, the Gap Widens Again between Black and White Family Income," *Wall Street Journal*, March 6, 1979, p. 48.

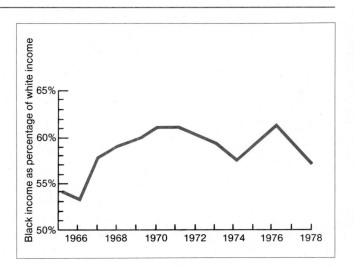

same skills, motivations, and work habits as everyone else. If this were the case, there would be potential profit opportunities in employing those workers. Not all entrepreneurs could be expected to pass them up. True, there would be some employers who, because of prejudice, tradition, or community pressure, would rather hire less competent whites than more competent blacks to do a job or who would pay whites more than equally skilled blacks. Nonetheless, other employers who ignored tradition or community pressure could cut their labor costs and gain a competitive edge. In fact, that may be why many communities in the South, in the days before civil rights legislation, felt it necessary to enforce segregation with specific "Jim Crow" laws. If they had not, market forces might have brought about a degree of integration unacceptable to their white leaders.

No one would claim that these antidiscriminatory market incentives operate so quickly or so thoroughly that they entirely eliminate all labor market discrimination. It is likely, though, that they do operate well enough to ensure that the residue of discrimination left by the market is relatively small. Removing that residue is really all that can be hoped for from equal opportunity legislation.

Other Demand Side Strategies

Elimination of discrimination is an antipoverty strategy that works from the demand side of the market. Such a program differs from programs of training and education, which try to benefit the poor by enabling them to supply more attractive services to the factor market. Instead, demand side strategies aim to increase the demand for the services that poor people are already equipped to offer. There is a feeling among some dual labor market theorists that an effective antipoverty program must emphasize demand side strategies. These economists hope that such strategies can operate more quickly and more certainly than education and job training, although the latter might still have a job to do in the long run.

Besides antidiscrimination legislation, there are two other widely discussed demand side strategies. One is the concept of public employment. In its most ambitious form, a public employment program would make the government an employer of last resort, so that all poor people, no matter how meager their skills or training, would be able to get jobs and become self-supporting.

Attractive though the idea of public employment may be, it has potential problems. A major problem is that the jobs the government sector can most easily create—service jobs requiring little capital investment and producing nonmarketed outputs—tend not to be as productive as jobs in the private sector. Thus there is a danger than an employer-of-last-resort program would transfer large quantities of labor from the high productivity private sector to the low productivity public sector. To avoid this danger, wage subsidies have been proposed as an alternative demand side strategy. These subsidies would raise the demand for labor in the private sector by paying private firms to hire impoverished workers whom they otherwise would not employ. In recent years, Great Britain has experimented with wage subsidies as an alternative to public employment, and some success has been reported.

CONCLUSIONS

The economics of poverty is, in many ways, a discouraging branch of economics to study. At first glance, the problem looks so small. Other things being equal, shifting just 1 percent of gross national product down to the poorest 20 percent of the population would serve to eliminate all officially measured poverty. But somehow, other things are not equal. Federal, state, and local governments now spend not 1 percent but more like 20 percent of GNP on income transfer programs of one kind or another; yet highly visible poverty still exists. Part of the problem appears to be that people do not have any universally accepted concept of what poverty actually is. Another part of the problem is to be found in the perverse incentives that are an inevitable by-product of any transfer program. A third part of the problem is that much of the money spent on existing transfer programs is not targeted specifically for the poorest members of the population.

Many proposals have been advanced over the years for comprehensive reform of the present income transfer program, which consists of a complex system of hundreds of major and minor programs that seems to have grown up almost by chance. One approach that has been widely discussed in recent years has emphasized cashing out some in-kind programs, consolidating as many programs as possible into something resembling a negative income tax, and offsetting the possible negative work incentives with programs to increase the supply of jobs available to the poor. As of this writing, it remains to be seen whether this set of reforms, or any other, will be adopted.

SUMMARY

1. Between 11 and 12 percent of all people in the United States are officially classified as poor, according to the federal government's low income level. This method of counting the poor, however, has been criticized for taking only cash income into account in a period when antipoverty efforts have increasingly emphasized in-kind transfers such as food stamps, public housing, and Medicaid. Attempts to evaluate the impact of in-kind transfers have led to the conclusion that the incidence of poverty may be as low as 3 percent.

2. Event conditioned transfers, or social insurance, are available to all citizens regardless of their income level. Social security, the largest income transfer program of all, is of the event conditioned variety. Unemployment insurance and Medicare are other major social insurance programs.

3. Income conditioned transfers, also known as welfare or public charity, are available only to those officially classified as in need. The largest program of this type is Aid to Families with Dependent Children. Food stamps, Medicaid, and public housing also fall into the income conditioned category.

4. All transfer programs have the unfortunate side effect of reducing work incentives for participants. When the taxes and benefit reduction rates associated with the various overlapping programs in existence today are added together, poor families are found to face effective marginal tax rates that exceed those imposed on earned income at the highest income tax brackets. Economists have long recommended a negative income tax as a way to reduce the adverse work incentives of existing transfer programs.

Recent experimental results have not been particularly encouraging to proponents of a negative income tax, however.

5. Job market strategies for aiding the poor approach poverty as a problem of factor market failure. More is involved than just unemployment. According to one theory, antipoverty efforts must aim at breaking down a dual labor market. Some think that the government should approach the problem from the supply side with education and job training programs. Others emphasize demand side programs including antidiscrimination measures and public employment.

DISCUSSION QUESTIONS

1. It is sometimes said that poverty is the fault not of individuals but of society. Do you agree? What do you think the statement means? Because society is itself composed of individuals, does it mean that certain nonpoor individuals are responsible for the poverty of poor individuals? If so, which individuals are responsible? Do you think that any of your own actions may be at fault in causing someone else to be poor? Explain.

2. According to the official definition of poverty, a family living below the low income level is likely not to be able to afford an adequate diet. Yet government statistics also show that of families at or near the official poverty line, 68 percent own one or more cars, and 12 percent own two or more; 71 percent own black and white televisions, and 37 percent own color sets; 55 percent own clothes washers, and 25 percent have clothes dryers; and 38 percent own air-conditioners. Is it natural and reasonable, in your opinion, that a poor family should own such things? How does your answer to this question relate to a choice among the varying definitions of poverty suggested early in this chapter?

3. What are the relative merits of cash versus in-kind transfers? Review Chapter 5, paying particular attention to the concepts of marginal utility and consumer equilibrium. Suppose Program A gives a family a $1,000 cash benefit, and Program B gives the family $1,000 worth of goods in kind—but in proportions not selected by the family itself. Which program would be likely to give the family greater utility? To make the question easier to answer, assume a simplified economy where there are only two goods—food and clothing. What if the two goods were food and whiskey?

4. Suppose that there were a universally effective negative income tax in force, so that measured poverty was entirely eliminated. Would you then be willing to see other social insurance programs, including social security (retirement), unemployment insurance, and Medicare abolished? Explain.

5. What are the relative merits of job market versus transfer strategies for combating poverty? Do you think either one could ever entirely replace the other? Explain.

SUGGESTIONS FOR FURTHER READING

Anderson, Martin. *Welfare: The Political Economy of Welfare Reform in the United States.* Stanford, Calif.: Hoover Institution, 1978.
A penetrating study of the entire welfare reform issue by a former adviser to Presidents Nixon and Ford.

Campbell, Colin D., ed. *Income Redistribution.* Washington, D.C.: American Enterprise Institute, 1977.
The proceedings of a 1976 conference on income redistribution that attracted papers from eminent scholars of a wide range of political persuasions. Notable in that it considers both practical questions, such as the future of social security, and broad philosophical questions, such as the nature of poverty and the case for progressive taxation.

Goodman, John C., and Dolan, Edwin G. *Economics of Public Policy: The Micro View.* St. Paul, Minn.: West Publishing, 1979.
Chapter 15 summarizes Goodman's extensive scholarly research on social security in a form accessible to nonexperts. (Goodman is highly critical of the program.)

Lawrence, William J., and Leeds, Stephen. *An Inventory of Federal Income Transfer Programs.* White Plains, N.Y.: Institute for Socioeconomic Studies, 1978.
The government apparently does not keep a systematic catalog of all the income transfer programs it runs. Lawrence and Leeds fill the gap with a comprehensive inventory of 182 programs totaling $248 billion in expenditures in 1977.

Levitan, Sar A. *Programs in Aid of the Poor.* 3rd ed. Baltimore: Johns Hopkins University Press, 1976.
A concise overview of the nation's complex system of antipoverty programs. Levitan is currently chairman of the National Commission on Employment and Unemployment Statistics.

THE ECONOMICS OF LIFE
ON A SMALL PLANET

C H A P T E R 19

THE ECONOMICS
OF POLLUTION

WHAT YOU WILL LEARN IN THIS CHAPTER

This chapter will explain how the problem of pollution, like other economic problems, can be treated as a problem of allocating scarce resources to their best uses. It will apply the concepts of opportunity cost, marginal analysis, and supply and demand to determine the optimal degree of pollution abatement. Then it will examine the advantages and disadvantages of various approaches to pollution abatement, including the command-and-control approach currently favored by environmental regulators and other approaches that place more emphasis on efficiency and economic incentives. Finally, it will explore briefly the normative as well as the positive economics of pollution.

FOR REVIEW

Here are some important terms and concepts that will be put to use in this chapter. If you do not understand them, review them before proceeding.
- *Opportunity cost and the margin (Chapter 1)*
- *Market justice and distributive justice (Chapter 1)*

In recent years, economists have devoted increasing attention to the interrelated problems of pollution, energy, population, and resource depletion. These problems take on an increased urgency as the planet earth seems to shrink year by year. Each year there seem to be fewer unpolluted areas remaining; each year the ratio of the earth's surface area to its population declines; and each year people burrow deeper into the planet's mines and wells to extract scarce resources that can never be replaced. What does the future hold in store for the planet?

Economics, as the science of scarcity, has much to say about pollution, energy, population, and resource depletion. The more tightly scarcity presses, the more important it is to use resources wisely. Economics can help in three ways: First, it can help formulate realistic standards of wise use against which to measure the actual allocation of resources. Second, it can help identify the sources of past and present errors in resource use. Third, it can help formulate improved policies that will make it possible to meet the challenge of the future successfully.

This chapter begins the job by discussing the problem of pollution. It puts the familiar tools of supply and demand to work in a novel way to analyze the demand for pollution opportunities. In doing so, it provides a framework for comparing several different strategies of pollution control.

Chapter 20 will attend to the problems of energy and resource depletion, and Chapter 21 will turn from the problems of industrialized countries to the problems of population and economic development faced by third world countries.

POLLUTION AS AN ECONOMIC PROBLEM

Pollution and Scarcity

Everyone has something to say about pollution. There are as many different ways of looking at the problem as there are people. Ecologists look at pollution in terms of the disruption of complex systems of plant and animal life. Politicians look at it in terms of votes. Moralists look at it in terms of good and evil. Economists too have a point of view.

From the economic point of view, pollution is a problem of scarcity. The critical scarce resource is the waste disposal capacity of the environment. That capacity is not unlimited. Air, water, and land areas can absorb human and industrial wastes to a certain extent without adverse effects. Some production by-products can be incorporated into natural cycles. Small amounts of pollutants can be diluted to imperceptible concentrations. However, the capacity for natural recycling and dilution is already smaller than the waste output of the economic system in many areas.

Once pollution has been identified as an economic problem, familiar tools of economic analysis can be applied to it. The discussion that follows will show how economic ideas such as opportunity cost, marginalism, and supply and demand can aid in understanding the problem of pollution and in finding ways to deal with it.

Trade-offs and Opportunity Costs

Economists think of environmental issues in terms of trade-offs and opportunity costs. Some trade-offs involve converting wastes from one form into another. Most methods of pollution abatement do not really get rid of wastes but merely change their physical form. Production and consumption are, after all, subject to the law of the conservation of matter. Scrubbing systems on factory smokestacks convert airborne wastes into waterborne wastes, but they do not reduce the total tonnage of wastes. Sewage treatment systems convert waterborne wastes into solid wastes, but some place must still be found to dump the sludge. Incineration gets rid of solid wastes but creates airborne wastes.

Recycling is often pictured as a way out of these trade-offs, since it converts wastes into useful substances rather than other wastes. Yet even recycling involves opportunity costs. To gather bottles and cans and remelt them or to remove usable sulfur from the smoke of burning coal and oil requires a lot of energy. This energy produces waste heat. Ultimately, recycling means trading off material pollution for energy pollution.

Of course, this does not mean that waste treatment and recycling are futile. It is just because wastes cannot be made to vanish that it is very important to release them into the environment in the least destructive way. Changing wastes from one form into another makes the maximum use of scarce environmental waste disposal capacities under a variety of local conditions.

There is also a second important set of trade-offs bearing on the pollution problem. Pollution can sometimes be reduced by substituting one product for another. It is possible, for example, to substitute unleaded for leaded gasoline. Fewer material goods and more services can be produced. Pollution can be reduced still further by giving up marketable goods and services in favor of such nonmarket goods as increased leisure and the direct enjoyment of nature through outdoor recreation.

Applications of the Marginal Principle

All these trade-offs mean a lot of decisions that cannot be made without some general standards. To economists, it seems natural to express many of the important standards in marginal terms. As an example, consider the decision of how much pollution should be tolerated. This decision, it can be shown, requires finding a balance between two margins.

The first margin is the **marginal social cost of pollution.** For a given type of pollution, this means the cost to all members of society of an additional unit of pollution. Suppose, for example, that in a community of 1,000 people, each additional pound of sulfur dioxide emitted costs each person 0.003 cent in the form of damage to painted surfaces and 0.004 cent in terms of personal discomfort. The marginal social cost of sulfur dioxide pollution in this community is thus:

$$1,000 \ (0.003 + 0.004) = 7 \text{ cents per pound.}$$

For most kinds of pollution, it is likely that the marginal social cost of pollution increases as its quantity increases. A graph of the marginal cost of pollution will thus have the form shown in Exhibit 19.1. Marginal social cost begins at zero for pollution within the natural absorptive capacity of the environment. As pollution concentrations become first unpleasant and then dangerous, marginal social cost rises to a high level.

The second margin is the **marginal cost of pollution abatement,** which is the economic cost of reducing pollution of a given kind by one unit. Other things being equal, the marginal cost of pollution abatement tends to rise as the level of pollution decreases. For example, in controlling automobile

Marginal social cost of pollution The total additional cost to all members of society of an additional unit of pollution.

Marginal cost of pollution abatement The added cost of reducing a given kind of pollution by one unit.

Exhibit 19.1

The marginal social cost of pollution

The marginal social cost of pollution is the total additional cost to all members of society that results from a one-unit increase in pollution. At low levels of pollution, within the natural absorptive capacity of the environment, the marginal social cost of pollution may be zero. As the quantity of pollution increases, the marginal social cost probably tends to increase for most pollutants.

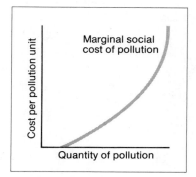

exhaust emissions, relatively cheap devices can cut pollution by half. Somewhat more complicated and expensive devices are required to cut the amount in half again, to the level of 75 percent abatement. Very elaborate and costly methods must be installed to cut it in half a third time, to 87.5 percent abatement. Given such examples, the marginal abatement cost curves are drawn with negative slopes, as in Exhibit 19.2.

The Optimal Quantity of Pollution

In Exhibit 19.3, both schedules appear in one diagram, which makes it possible to identify the point—the intersection of the two curves—where the marginal cost of abatement is equal to the marginal social cost of pollution. As far as economics is concerned, this point represents the optimal quantity of pollution. Pollution in excess of this amount represents a misallocation of resources. The damage done by additional pollution then exceeds the cost of eliminating it. Excessive abatement—that which operates to the left of the intersection point—is also wasteful. It too represents an unnecessary reduction in human welfare. If the marginal cost of pollution abatement exceeds the marginal social cost of pollution, a gain is made by trading a small reduction in environmental quality for a relatively large increase in material production.

Measurement Problems

This marginal analysis gives a simple theoretical standard for pollution control. The standard is not so easy to apply in practice, however. There are severe problems of measurement, especially on the side of social cost. Attempts to measure the social cost of pollution usually concentrate on such things as damage to property, health costs measured in terms of medical expenses and time lost from work, and the value of wildlife and crops killed. Actual estimates suffer from several defects.

First, data on the costs of pollution are at best fragmentary, and the many gaps must be filled by pure guesswork. Second, it is difficult to account for purely subjective costs, including offenses to aesthetic sensibilities and discomforts not actually resulting in damage to health. Yet these subjective costs have a very real economic value. The fact that many people spend hard-earned money to avoid the effects of pollution by leaving polluted areas shows such costs to be real. Finally, estimates of the social costs of pollution rarely give more than the average cost figures. But the marginal cost data, which are much

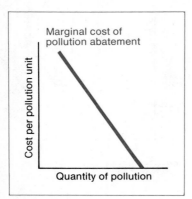

Exhibit 19.2
The marginal cost of pollution abatement
The marginal cost of pollution abatement is the added cost of reducing pollution by one unit. The marginal cost of eliminating pollution tends to increase as the percentage of all pollution eliminated increases. That gives the marginal cost of pollution abatement curve a downward slope.

Exhibit 19.3

The optimal quantity of pollution
The optimal quantity of pollution is determined by the intersection of the marginal cost of pollution abatement curve and the marginal social cost of pollution curve. To the left of that point, the benefits of further reductions in pollution do not justify the high cost of abatement. To the right of the point, the cost of abatement is less than the cost imposed on society by additional pollution.

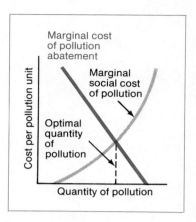

more difficult to obtain, are the really relevant data for making pollution policy decisions.

There are problems too in estimating the costs of pollution abatement. One major problem is that calculations must take into account not only the direct costs of getting rid of one form of pollution but also the social costs of any different forms of pollution that may be produced as a result. Measurement of these costs is subject to all the problems of measuring the social costs of any kind of pollution.

Nonetheless, despite the serious problems of precisely calculating marginal costs and benefits, thinking in marginal terms can often prevent serious mistakes, even when only approximate data are given. The following case study provides an illustration.

Case 19.1
New York's North River Sewage Treatment Plant:
A Case of Overzealous Cleanup?

Dr. Merril Eisenbud is a prominent environmental scientist who served as New York City's first environmental protection administrator. An example he gives of apparently overzealous environmental protection can serve as an excellent illustration of the importance of marginal thinking in the environmental area.

The example concerns the North River sewage treatment plant that New York City is building in Harlem to control wastes being dumped into the Hudson River. The plant was originally designed to remove 67 percent of organic wastes of the type that rob the river of oxygen and threaten aquatic life. During the 1960s and early 1970s, however, enthusiastic politicians enacted regulations that raised the required level of cleanup for plants like the North River installation to 90 percent.

The project encountered the problem of increasing the marginal cost of pollution abatement in the process of redesigning to meet the new standards. Cleaning up the first 67 percent of the pollution would have cost about $250 million. Getting rid of the next 23 percent cost another $750 million, which raised the total cost of the installation to $1 billion.

According to Dr. Eisenbud, redesign of the plant to meet the 90 percent abatement standard also took the project into the region of a zero or near zero marginal social cost of pollution:

What the Federal law failed to take into account, Dr. Eisenbud says, is the nature and use of the receiving water. For some water, 90 percent removal is not enough, he says, while for others it is far too much. Because the Hudson is scoured each day by tides that run as far north as Poughkeepsie and because the harbor waters getting the city's wastes are not used for drinking or washing, the 67 percent removal standard was more than sufficient, according to all technical advisers on the project.[1]

The benefit of the additional abatement was thus effectively zero. In short, the North River project, as redesigned, went past the crossover point, where the benefits of further pollution abatement were not worth the added cost.

ECONOMIC STRATEGIES FOR POLLUTION CONTROL

Supply and Demand

Controlling pollution is a problem of economic policy. As in many other cases, supply and demand can be used to explain where the problem comes from and to compare alternative solutions.

Consider Exhibit 19.4. The marginal cost of pollution abatement curve drawn in Exhibit 19.2 is now given a new name—the demand curve for pollution opportunities. It is very easy to understand why the same curve serves both purposes. Simply ask how much a firm would be willing to pay, if necessary, for the opportunity to dump an additional unit of untreated waste directly into the environment. The answer is that it would pay any sum smaller—but not any sum larger—than the cost of pollution-free waste disposal.

So much for the demand curve. Exhibit 19.4 also shows a supply curve for pollution opportunities as a straight line lying right along the horizontal axis. The line indicates that unlimited pollution opportunities are available without paying any price at all. The equilibrium quantity of pollution is found where

---

[1]Michael Sterne, "Environmentalist Questions Priorities," *New York Times*, May 12, 1978, p. B–1. © 1978 by The New York Times Company. Reprinted by permission.

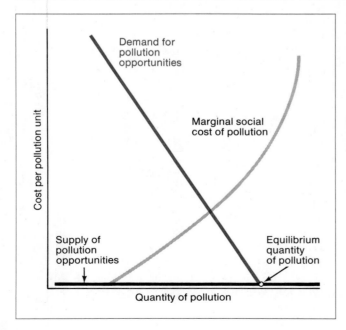

Exhibit 19.4
Supply and demand for pollution opportunities
The marginal cost of pollution abatement curve can also be called the demand curve for pollution opportunities. The position of the supply curve for pollution opportunities depends on how much firms must pay in order to discharge wastes into the environment. If they do not have to pay at all, the supply curve will coincide with the horizontal axis, as shown here, and the equilibrium quantity of pollution will be greater than the optimum quantity.

the two curves intersect. Unless the social cost of pollution is also zero (which is not the case) this equilibrium is not the optimal point. What can be done?

Command and Control

Most current government policies for controlling pollution take the so-called command-and-control approach. Congress sets up some agency with authority to control pollution of particular types or in particular areas. Sometimes, the regulators simply set a maximum amount of pollution permitted from each source and leave the choice of abatement methods up to the polluter. In other cases, the regulators specify that certain abatement procedures must be followed. Command-and-control regulations have the effect of rationing pollution opportunities. They can keep the economic system from ending up at an equilibrium like that shown in Exhibit 19.4, where there is too much pollution.

Although this approach has in many cases been effective, economists often find fault with it. For one thing, regulations can be written so rigidly that they do not give polluters enough incentive to search for the least-cost method of cleaning up their wastes. For another, regulation does not always ensure that the burden of cleaning up is efficiently allocated among various pollution sources. Critics of the command-and-control approach have suggested some alternative strategies for pollution control that use supply and demand more directly. Two important strategies are the residual charge and property rights approaches.

Residual Charges

One nonregulatory strategy for controlling pollution works by shifting the pollution opportunity supply curve with **residual charges,** which are, in effect, waste disposal taxes. Charges of a fixed amount per unit of waste are imposed on all sources of a given kind of waste. As an example, consider a residual charge on sulfur dioxide emissions. Suppose that all sources of this type of pollution had to pay a fee of $.05 per pound for all sulfur emitted into the atmosphere.

Exhibit 19.5 shows the effect of this residual charge, which shifts the pollution opportunity supply curve up from its position along the horizontal axis to a position $.05 higher. Polluters react to the tax by moving back along their demand curve to a new equilibrium where there is less pollution. They do this because it pays them to use all pollution abatement methods that can remove a pound of sulfur from the stack gases for $.05 or less.

By raising or lowering the amount of the charge, any desired degree of pollution control can be achieved. Ideally, the charge is set so that the pollution opportunity supply curve passes exactly through the intersection of the marginal abatement cost curve (demand curve) and the marginal social cost curve. This ideal situation is shown in Exhibit 19.6. (Unfortunately, there is no easy way to determine just where the intersection is and, hence, just what the charge should be. The agency responsible for setting the rate of the residual charge is faced with the measurement difficulties mentioned above.)

Objections to Residual Charges Because pollution taxes and residual charges are likely to figure prominently in future policy debates, it will be worth taking a moment to look at some often-heard objections to them. The

Residual charges Charges of a fixed amount per unit of waste imposed on all sources that discharge a given kind of waste into the environment.

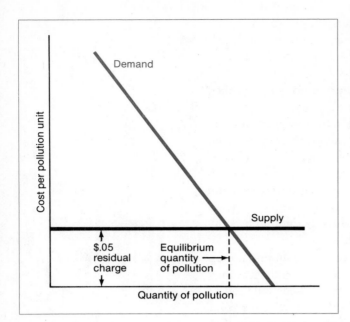

Exhibit 19.5
The effect of a residual charge
A residual charge makes it necessary for polluters to pay for the opportunity to discharge wastes into the environment. Here, the charge is set at $.05 per unit. The residual charge moves the pollution opportunity supply curve upward to the position shown and forces polluters up and to the left along their demand curve, thereby reducing the equilibrium quantity of pollution.

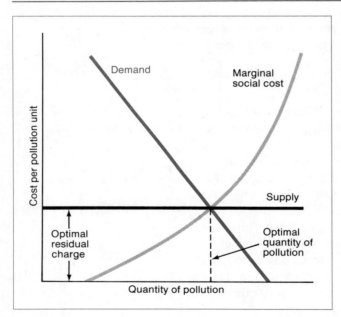

Exhibit 19.6
An optimal residual charge
Ideally, a residual charge could be set just high enough to reduce pollution by the optimal amount. Here, the supply curve for pollution opportunities cuts the demand and marginal social cost curves at their point of intersection. In practice, such fine tuning of residual charges is quite difficult.

objections come from three principal sources—industrialists, consumers, and environmentalists.

Industrialists sometimes say that residual charges impose an unfair double burden on industry, which has to pay the charge at the same time it is undergoing the expense of installing pollution abatement equipment. Consumers object that industry can pass the burden of the charge along in the form of higher product prices. Environmentalists protest that residual charges grant a license to pollute. They fear that industry will just put up the money and keep right on despoiling the environment as before. Each of these objections is discussed in the following sections.

Double Burden The double burden objection is the weakest of the three. No industry is ever forced by a residual charge to pay a double charge. Any polluter always has the option of paying the charge and making no effort at all to reduce pollution. In this case, it bears just one burden, that of the charge itself. Any money it spends on pollution abatement equipment is spent for one reason only—that it is cheaper to install the equipment than to pay to pollute. Far from being a second burden, abatement expenditures represent a way to escape from the tax and hence to reduce the total burden.

Passing on the Burden The argument that residual charges can be shifted to consumers has more truth to it. Exhibit 19.7 shows why. Let D represent the demand curve for a commodity and S_1 the market supply curve before there is any pollution control policy. These conditions give an equilibrium at E_1, with price P_1 and quantity of output Q_1. A residual charge raises the marginal cost of production. The increase is either the amount of tax paid per unit of production or the cost of the abatement equipment needed to avoid payment, whichever is smaller. This increase shifts the whole supply curve up to the new position, S_2. The vertical distance between the old and new supply curves is equal to the per unit burden of the charge. With the new supply curve, S_2, equilibrium is at E_2 with price P_2 and quantity Q_2. The difference between the new price and the old one shows the share of the burden passed along to the consumer. As the figure is drawn, this amount is about half the burden of the tax. The exact share passed on varies from product to product, depending on the shapes of the supply and demand curves.

It can be seen, then, that at least part of the burden of a residual charge can be passed along to consumers. But does this really constitute a valid criticism of the policy? A strong argument can be made that it does not. After all, someone always pays the price of pollution; different policies change only who pays for it. Under current conditions, producers and consumers of pollution-intensive goods both get a free ride. They shift the burden to innocent third parties (the victims of the pollution). If the burden is to be lifted from these third parties, why should consumers expect to be able to continue their free ride?

Exhibit 19.7
Effects of a residual charge on product price
The effects of a residual charge are shown here in terms of the supply and demand for a product produced by a firm that must pay the charge. The product supply curve is shifted up from S_1 to S_2. This causes the equilibrium price of the product to rise from P_1 to P_2. Part, but not all, of the cost increase is thus passed along to the consumer.

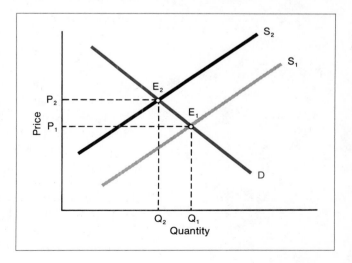

Higher prices for high pollution products are actually beneficial. They stimulate consumers to make the trade-offs that are necessary to protect the environment. If the prices of relatively dirty products rise compared to those of relatively clean products and services, consumers will shift their spending patterns accordingly. If firms cannot pass along to consumers part of the pollution taxes imposed upon them, it is not easy to see how the necessary change in consumption habits will come about.

License   The third objection—that residual charges are just a license to pollute—is open to more than one interpretation. Depending on how it is interpreted, it may be wholly invalid or partially valid.

Sometimes the argument implies that residual charges have no effect on pollution, that businesses will pay the charges and carry on as before. But this is flatly incorrect, unless one is going to deny that the law of supply and demand applies to waste disposal as it does to other business activities. At other times, the license to pollute argument is meant as an objection to the fact that the taxes eliminate only part, not all, of the pollution output. In this application, too, the argument violates good economic reasoning. To eliminate all pollution regardless of cost, as some environmentalists advocate, involves greater sacrifices of material welfare than can be justified in terms of consumer satisfaction. Instead, pollution control should proceed only up to the point where the marginal cost of pollution abatement begins to exceed the marginal social cost of pollution.

A third interpretation of the license to pollute argument makes more economic sense. The problem is that no direct compensation is offered to those downwind or downstream of any pollution sources that continue polluting even after imposition of the charges. To these remaining victims, it seems unjust that a firm can legally continue to make life miserable just by paying a fee to the government. Polluters, it is argued, should pay compensation to their victims, not taxes to the government.

Pollution Control and Property Rights

Pollution as Theft   The question of who should be compensated for pollution damage raises the whole issue of pollution and property rights. The basic idea is this: From the point of view of property rights, pollution is theft. If you use the air in and around my home as a dumping ground for your unwanted combustion products, you are stealing waste disposal services from me. If you use my living room as a reverberation chamber for noise from your truck or motorcycle, you are robbing me of my right to peace and quiet. As the owner, I should have the right to prevent you from using my property in these ways unless you negotiate with me in advance to buy my permission. If you do not, I should be able to bring civil or criminal action against you in a court of law.

In some respects, however, current law is stacked against property owners and in favor of polluters. Various changes have been recommended to redress the balance. It could, for example, be made easier for private citizens to initiate lawsuits when their property is attacked by pollution. At present, property owners often must wait for local governments to take legal action on their behalf. If the polluters have more pull in the statehouse or city hall than their victims do, the victims may wait in vain. Also, it could be made easier for large groups of citizens to act jointly, through class action suits or other means, to gain legal redress for damages done to them.

What would be the economic effect of laws permitting property owners to protect themselves from pollution? One possible effect would be the creation of a private market for pollution rights. In this market, people would sell pollution opportunities to firms in return for a price high enough to compensate them for the damage done. If all individuals sold pollution rights at prices equal to the marginal cost to them of pollution damage, the pollution market would look like the diagram in Exhibit 19.8. The pollution opportunity supply curve would follow exactly along the marginal social cost curve. The equilibrium quantity of pollution would be exactly the economically optimal amount.

Objections The legal protection of private property rights as a method of pollution control is open to certain practical objections. One objection is that not all environmental resources that are open to pollution damage are privately owned. Does this mean that polluters would retain unlimited opportunities to dump their wastes in public waterways, world oceans, publicly owned wilderness areas, and the like? One way to overcome the problem would be to auction off all rivers, oceans, national parks, and similar areas to private owners. The private owners could then protect them from damage. Short of this radical proposal, taxes and user charges could protect such public resources, while private law protected privately owned resources.

There is a second objection to giving private owners blanket rights to protect their property against pollution. Such a policy might result in excessive reduction in pollution levels. A potential polluter located in a densely populated area might have to negotiate pollution opportunity contracts with tens of thousands of individual small property owners before emitting even a single puff of smoke. The transaction costs of doing this would be prohibitive, even if the actual charges paid to each owner were in themselves reasonable; and just one holdout among the individual property owners could wreck the deal. To avoid these difficulties, a firm might spend far more than the economically optimal amount on pollution abatement. Some might argue, of course, that

Exhibit 19.8
Pollution opportunities with perfect protection of private property
If all property were privately owned and if polluters always had to compensate victims for damage to persons or property, a private market in pollution opportunities would be created. Ideally, the supply curve in this market would exactly coincide with the marginal social cost of pollution curve. The equilibrium quantity of pollution would then equal the optimal quantity.

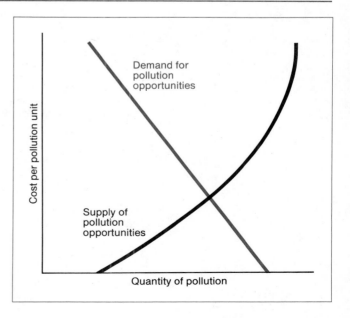

people have suffered from too much pollution for so long that it would be a pleasant novelty to suffer from too little. Speaking more practically, though, it can be conceded that the property rights approach probably works best when the impact of pollution is relatively concentrated. Some type of residual charge scheme may be a better answer when the damages are very widely dispersed.

Trends in Pollution Control Techniques

The drawbacks of the command-and-control approach to pollution abatement, compared with the theoretical elegance of the residual charge and property rights approaches, have been well known for many years. Until quite recently, however, officials engaged in the practical task of enforcing environmental protection laws were not much interested in alternatives to command and control.

Toward the end of the 1970s, however, a powerful new ingredient entered the debate over pollution control techniques. That ingredient was inflation. Everyone was concerned about rapidly rising prices, and complaints were heard increasingly often that one reason prices were going up was that environmental regulations were pushing up costs.

In some cases, regulators reacted by simply relaxing specific pollution standards that appeared to have been pushed beyond the point of optimal pollution abatement and then continuing to enforce the relaxed standards by the same command-and-control strategies. More importantly, however, some environmental officials—such as Douglas M. Costel, head of the Environmental Protection Agency—began to look seriously at new methods of enforcement that would emphasize economic incentives rather than command and control. The following case study gives an idea of some of the problems and promise of one such approach.

Case 19.2
The "Bubble" Concept in Pollution Control

The steel industry is one of the nation's dirtiest; and as such, it has been one of the hardest hit by environmental cleanup regulations. By the late 1970s, it had invested more than $6 billion in pollution control equipment, and its pollution control costs were approaching 10 percent of total operating costs. If any industry needed to find ways to clean up the air while minimizing the cost to consumers, the steel industry was it. Then, along came a brave new idea called the "bubble concept."

The bubble concept is simplicity itself. In the past, under its command-and-control strategy, the Environmental Protection Agency had been imposing specific standards on each pollution emitting piece of equipment within a plant. But that could change:

The law now says how much pollution is allowed in the air—for example, an annual average of no more than seventy-five micrograms of particulates per cubic meter. In hope of reaching this standard, the EPA limits pollution from each source it wants to control—blast furnaces, boilers, paint sprayers, etc.—in an industrial complex. Under the bubble concept, the regulators would replace these "stack by stack" rules with a single limit applied to the whole plant. In either case, the total pollution would be the same. But by operating under an imaginary bubble, the plant's engineers would have the flexibility to find the most cost-effective mix of pollution controls to meet the standard.[2]

---

[2]Peter Nulty, "A Brave Experiment in Pollution Control," *Fortune*, February 12, 1979, p. 121. © 1979. Time Inc. Courtesy of *Fortune Magazine*.

One early bubble enthusiast on the industry side was John Barker, an environmental engineer for Armco Steel:

Taking Armco's plant in Middletown as a test case, Barker found that spraying water on piles of iron ore would prevent 284 tons of particles a year (mostly dust and iron oxide) from blowing into the surrounding community. The cost per ton would be $704. By comparison, pollution-control devices on a blast furnace would reclaim 309 tons of iron oxide for $8,500 a ton, and devices on an open-hearth furnace would capture 140 tons for $35,700 a ton.[3]

Studies such as this helped convince many EPA administrators that the bubble concept was worth pursuing, but it soon became clear that there were many practical details to work out. For one thing, there is the problem that not all kinds of pollution are equally damaging. Fine particles are more damaging to lungs than coarse particles, for example. And the carcinogenic benzapyrene emitted from the steel industry's coke ovens is clearly far more dangerous per ton than mere dust of any size.

Because of this and other difficulties, the EPA to date has endorsed the bubble concept only in limited form. More than one bubble is to be placed over every plant—for example, a general bubble for particulates and a tighter bubble for carcinogens from coke ovens. No one knows yet how well the bubble concept will work out in practice or how successful bubble enthusiasts will be at overcoming the remaining bureaucratic resistance. But the whole idea is an encouraging sign that economists, environmental regulators, and industrial engineers can at least sometimes find common ground for action.

CONCLUSIONS

The main objective of pollution control, as discussed in this chapter, has been to improve the efficiency of resource allocation. A complete analysis of environmental policy should look at the normative implications of this objective as well. The discussion will conclude with a look at pollution control policies in terms of market justice and distributive justice.

By the standard of market justice, the effects of pollution control policies of almost any kind appear to be beneficial. Pollution is theft. It is a form of coercion through which producers enjoy unjustifiably high profits and consumers enjoy unjustifiably low prices. Third parties, as victims of pollution, are unwillingly forced to bear the costs without sharing in the benefits. Policies that put a price tag on pollution help to correct these injustices by making everyone pay the full cost of the things produced and consumed.

Strictly speaking, according to the standard of market justice, a policy not only should impose penalties on polluters but also should provide compensation to the victims of pollution. Policies based on enforcement of private property rights—including the right of pollution victims to sue for damages—do this, while residual charges do not.

From the point of view of distributive justice, the effects of pollution control policies are more problematical. If one's notion of distributive justice is simply increased equality of real incomes, antipollution measures may well make things worse. One would have to study carefully the exact distribution of the costs and benefits of various alternative policies in order to be certain on this point. Without such study, only conjectures can be made. These conjectures suggest, however, that low income groups might not fare well. They might bear

[3]Ibid.

a disproportionately large share of the costs of pollution control policies and might receive a disproportionately small share of the benefits.

One result of effective pollution control policies, as shown here, must be to raise the prices of goods to consumers. Low income groups spend a larger portion of their budget on material goods and devote a smaller portion to consumption of services and to saving. The burden of pollution taxes can thus be expected to rest more heavily on them in proportion to their incomes.

At the same time, it seems likely that the benefits of pollution control policies are less valuable to the poor than to the rich. Suppose that the benefits of pollution control were equally distributed in physical terms. For example, suppose that the level of air pollution were lowered just as much in low income as in high income neighborhoods. This does not mean that the benefit would be equally distributed in economic terms. Clean air and other environmental amenities are to a considerable extent luxury goods. They have a high value to those who already have a generous supply of material goods and a relatively low value to those who do not. How many pounds of beef or pairs of shoes or dollars would poor people be willing to give up in order to reduce by half the sulfur dioxide content of the air they breathed? How much would wealthy people be willing to sacrifice for the same purpose? It is easy to see that, at least beyond a certain point, pollution control policies may reflect the tastes only of the relatively well-to-do.

SUMMARY

1. Pollution can be viewed as a problem in the allocation of scarce resources. In this case, the scarce resource is the waste absorption capacity of the environment. Once this capacity is exceeded, further waste disposal must incur opportunity costs of one kind or another. If wastes are discharged untreated into the environment, the opportunity costs take the form of a less healthy and pleasant world in which to live. If costly pollution abatement techniques are used, scarce factors of production must be diverted from other uses. No policy can avoid these trade-offs altogether. The economic problem of pollution is how to balance the social cost of pollution against the economic cost of pollution abatement.

2. Supply and demand analysis can be applied to the problem of pollution control. The marginal cost of pollution abatement curve can be thought of as a demand curve for pollution. If there are no pollution controls of any kind, the supply curve for pollution opportunities is a horizontal line at zero height. The equilibrium quantity of pollution will be too high when the supply curve has that shape. All pollution control policies aim in one way or another to limit the supply of pollution opportunities.

3. The command-and-control approach to pollution abatement is, in effect, a form of administrative rationing for pollution opportunities. It has been effective in some cases, but economists often criticize it as inefficient. Residual charges are an alternate pollution control method. Under a residual charge scheme, the supply curve for pollution opportunities becomes a horizontal line at the height equal to the charge per unit of waste. Still another approach to pollution control is through the enforcement of private property rights. Ideally, if all property were privately owned and polluters had to compensate owners for all damage to persons and property, the

supply of pollution opportunities curve would coincide with the marginal social cost of pollution curve. Each approach has its advantages and its practical difficulties. For the moment, it seems worthwhile to experiment with all methods.

4. Pollution raises normative as well as positive issues. One such issue is that of compensating victims of pollution. The regulatory and residual charge approaches to pollution control do not compensate victims. Pollution control via defense of private property rights appears to be superior in this respect. Another normative question concerns the distributive impact of pollution control. In the absence of firm evidence to the contrary, it seems plausible to think that the costs of pollution control may be borne more than proportionately by the poor and that the benefits of pollution control may accrue more than proportionately to the well-to-do.

DISCUSSION QUESTIONS

1. Why has pollution become a major national policy issue only recently? Is pollution worse than it used to be? Do the cars of New York City today discharge more tons of waste each day than the horses of New York City did in 1901? Has the high standard of living in the United States actually caused more pollution, or has it made people less willing to tolerate it than they used to be? Or has it done both? Discuss.

2. Can you think of circumstances in which the marginal social cost of waste disposal for a firm is also part of its explicit private costs of production? Of its implicit private costs? Of neither its implicit nor explicit costs? Explain.

3. When does waste disposal become pollution? How do you distinguish between the two? Is the distinction a matter of positive economics or of normative economics? Explain.

4. Many environmentalists are uncomfortable with the concept of an economically optimal amount of pollution. They tend to think that less pollution is always better. Do you agree? Do you think that the difference between the environmentalist viewpoint and the viewpoint set forth in this chapter is one of values or of analysis? Explain.

5. Suppose you were a member of Congress when a bill came up to abolish all specific pollution control regulations for automobile exhausts. In place of the present regulations, there would be a residual charge of $.01 per mile placed on all driving. The charge would be reduced appropriately for drivers who could prove that their cars were equipped with effective emission control devices. Would you favor this measure? Explain. If your only objection were that $.01 per mile was too low a charge, how high would you think the rate should be?

6. Many of the Great Lakes have become seriously polluted. Among the people damaged by this pollution are the owners of lakefront property. Do you think that these owners ought to be permitted to bring suit against any company polluting the lake on which their property is located? If such suits were permitted, do you think many would be brought? Should property owners who win their cases against polluters be able to obtain a cease-and-desist order stopping all further pollution, or should they simply be awarded monetary damages? Explain.

SUGGESTIONS FOR FURTHER READING

Dorfman, Robert, and Dorfman, Nancy S., eds. *Economics of the Environment: Selected Readings.* New York: W. W. Norton, 1972.
A collection of papers by well-known economists covering the whole range of topics discussed in this chapter. Most are reprints of articles from professional journals, but none is excessively technical.

Freeman, A. Myrick, III; Haveman, Robert H.; and Kneese, Alan V. *The Economics of Environmental Policy.* New York: Wiley, 1973.
A book length, nontechnical discussion of many of the themes of this chapter, including problems of allocating common property resources and ways of putting economic incentives to work solving environmental problems.

Mills, Edwin S. *The Economics of Environmental Quality.* New York: W. W. Norton, 1978.
A thorough, up-to-date treatment of environmental problems and policies from an economic point of view. Includes a historical sketch of environmental policy in the United States and a discussion of environmental problems and policies of the rest of the world.

CHAPTER 20
THE ECONOMICS OF ENERGY

WHAT YOU WILL LEARN IN THIS CHAPTER

This chapter covers selected topics in the economics of energy. It begins by introducing a theory of the allocation of nonrenewable resources over time. It discusses both competitive markets and markets dominated by cartels. It then examines recent U.S. oil and natural gas policies in the light of this allocation theory, paying special attention to the effects of price controls and decontrol. The remainder of the chapter is devoted to the principal energy alternatives to oil and natural gas: coal, nuclear power, and solar power.

FOR REVIEW

Here are some important terms and concepts that will be put to use in this chapter. If you do not understand them, review them before proceeding.
- *Positive and normative economics (Chapter 1)*
- *Elasticity of supply and demand (Chapter 3)*
- *Monopoly and cartels (Chapter 9)*
- *Price discrimination (Chapter 9)*

Having discussed the economics of pollution, we turn now to another aspect of the economics of life on a small planet: the economics of energy. The availability of energy, like the availability of unlimited environmental sinks for the disposal of waste products, is something that used to be taken for granted. Today, however, energy—more than any other commodity—symbolizes the problem of scarcity. The United States now has a Department of Energy and a national debate over energy policy. Such diverse topics as inflation, military strategy, and international diplomacy cannot be discussed without bringing energy into consideration. It seems appropriate, then, to devote a chapter to the economics of energy and energy policy, beginning with nonrenewable energy sources and moving on to possible alternatives.

THE ECONOMICS OF OIL AND NATURAL GAS

The nonrenewable fossil fuels oil and natural gas are the most important current sources of energy in the United States. These fuels are being replenished by natural processes at imperceptible rates, if at all. The economics of oil and gas is thus a matter of allocation over time—of when it is best to use the limited stocks available.

The discussion will begin with the fairly well developed branch of eco-

Theory of the mine The branch of economics concerned with the allocation over time of nonrenewable natural resources.

nomics known as the **theory of the mine,** which deals with problems of this type. Although this chapter is interested primarily in nonrenewable energy resources, the theory of the mine applies equally well to nonrenewable resources other than energy.

Introduction to the Theory of the Mine

The key economic decision studied by the theory of the mine is that of when to extract and use the limited stock of resources that the mine contains. This decision involves a strict trade-off between the present and the future: What is used today cannot be used tomorrow, and what is conserved cannot be used today.

Both immediate and delayed use have advantages. Immediate use permits gratification of consumer demand without delay or permits use of the resource for investment purposes, thereby increasing tomorrow's supply of productive capital. Delayed use is advantageous because, to the extent that any of the resource is consumed today, what remains will be scarcer and hence more valuable in the future.

The Case of Competitive Markets The way resource owners handle the trade-off between present and future use depends, among other things, on the structure of the markets in which they operate. As often is true, the case of perfectly competitive markets provides a useful benchmark. Consider, for the sake of illustration, the market for natural gas, assuming for the present that the market is perfectly competitive, that the quantity of natural gas available for extraction is known, and that the cost of extracting it is zero.

Under these idealized conditions, the only decision left to gas well owners is whether to extract their gas and sell it now or to conserve all or part of it for the future. If the owners are motivated primarily by financial considerations, they can be expected to make the choice that will maximize their total wealth. Keeping the gas in the ground means holding that wealth in the form of a reserve of energy that can be expected to increase in value in the future. Extracting the gas and selling it today allows the conversion of the wealth to other forms—for example, corporate stocks or government bonds—that can be expected to earn their owners a normal rate of return on the invested capital.

It follows that the decision of when to sell the gas depends on a comparison of the market rate of return available outside the gas industry with the rate at which the price of gas is expected to increase in the future. Suppose, for example, that the market rate of return on alternative investments is 10 percent per year, that the price of gas today is $3 per thousand cubic feet (tcf), and that this price is expected to rise at the rate of 5 percent per year. Selling 1,000 tcf of gas at today's prices and investing the proceeds at 10 percent will give a gas well owner a sum of $3,300 at the end of a year. Alternatively, leaving the same 1,000 tcf of gas in the ground and selling it at $3.15 per tcf next year will yield a sum of $3,150. Under these assumed conditions, then, it will be most profitable to sell the gas today.

However, there is a limit to how much gas will be sold currently, because today's sales of gas tend to change the conditions initially assumed to prevail. For one thing, greater supplies of gas brought to market today will tend to depress the price below the assumed level of $3 per tcf. In addition, more sales today will reduce the stocks available for the future, thereby reducing future supplies and increasing the future price. As the price today falls and the expected future price rises, the expected percentage increase of next year's price over this year's price also rises. As soon as the expected rate of price increase becomes equal to the rate of return available on alternative investments, it will no longer be profitable to sell today. Any owners who have not yet sold will conserve their supplies for the future, because it will pay them to do so.

In short, when a resource exists in a known, fixed quantity and the cost of extraction is low, a competitive market will allocate that resource over time, as shown in Exhibit 20.1. The price will rise over time at a rate equal to the market rate of interest. Other things being equal, the rate of use will fall as the price rises.[1]

Some Qualifications The preceding argument puts a ceiling on the rate at which the price of a scarce resource will increase and the rate at which it will be used up. However, there are circumstances under which the rate of the price increase is less rapid than the interest rate because the rate of depletion is slower than implied. In particular, this will be the case if the resource is costly to extract or if high prices stimulate a search for new reserves or for substitutes.

If, for example, the current price of a resource is equal to the current marginal cost of extracting it, the quantity supplied will be limited by the quantity demanded at the current price rather than by the expected effect of current use on future prices. The quantity demanded may very well not be high enough to deplete the resource fast enough to push its future price up at a rate equal to the interest rate. Alternatively, if there are reserves of a resource that cannot be profitably extracted today but that can be used if the price rises

---

[1] If economic growth or population growth causes demand for the resource to increase as time goes by, this pattern may be somewhat modified. The rate of price increase will still not exceed the interest rate, but the rate of use can, for a time, increase before it begins to taper off.

Exhibit 20.1
Market allocation over time of a nonrenewable resource
The market price of a nonrenewable resource tends to rise over time. Supply and demand conditions limit the rate of depletion, so the price will not rise at a rate faster than the rate of interest. As the price rises, the rate of use falls, other things being equal.

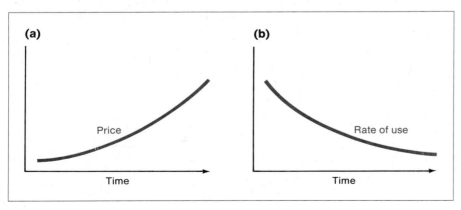

a little, the presence of those reserves will limit the rate of price increase, because it will increase expected future supply.

In practice, the usable reserves of many important resources do appear to increase quite elastically as demand and prices rise. This is partly because higher prices make it worthwhile to spend more money on exploration and partly because they make it worthwhile to exploit known low-grade reserves. Exhibit 20.2 shows how the known reserves of many important nonrenewable resources expanded between 1950 and 1970. Naturally, the rates of reserve expansion shown in the table cannot be extrapolated indefinitely into the future. They do show, however, that the assumption of absolutely fixed quantities of known reserves is a very restrictive one.

Effects of a Cartel Up to this point, it has been assumed that the markets in which nonrenewable resources are bought and sold are perfectly competitive. With the rise of the OPEC oil cartel during the 1970s, however, economists have become increasingly interested in the situation where a nonrenewable resource is controlled by a cartel rather than supplied competitively.

Chapter 9 showed that under given conditions of demand and cost, a cartel tends to supply a smaller quantity at a higher price than does a competitively organized market. By reducing the quantity supplied and raising the price, the cartel benefits its members by increasing profit per unit sold. Profits are maximized at the point where marginal cost and marginal revenue are equal. Exhibit 20.3 makes the comparison between the output chosen by a cartel and

Exhibit 20.2

The growth of reserves of nonrenewable resources, 1950–1970

In the past, known economic reserves of most (but not all) nonrenewable resources have expanded at a faster rate than those reserves have been used up. The reason is partly that new high-grade reserves are discovered and partly that higher prices and new technologies make it worthwhile to exploit reserves that were known earlier but considered to be of no commercial value. There is, however, no theoretical guarantee that reserves will continue always to grow in the future.

Ore	Known Reserves in 1950 (1,000 Metric Tons)	Cumulative Production 1950–1970 (1,000 Metric Tons)	Known Reserves in 1970 (1,000 Metric Tons)	Percentage Increase in Known Reserves 1950–1970
Iron	19,000,000	9,355,000	251,000,000	1,221
Manganese	500,000	194,000	635,000	27
Chromite	100,000	82,000	755,000	675
Tungsten	1,903	630	1,328	−30
Copper	100,000	80,000	279,000	179
Lead	40,000	48,000	86,000	115
Zinc	70,000	70,000	113,000	61
Tin	6,000	3,800	6,600	10
Bauxite	1,400,000	505,000	5,300,000	279
Potash	5,000,000	216,000	118,000,000	2,360
Phosphates	26,000,000	1,011,000	1,178,000,000	4,430
Oil[a]	75,000,000	180,727,000	455,000,000	507

[a] Thousand barrels.

Source: National Commission on Supplies and Shortages, *Government and the Nation's Resources* 16 (1976). Reprinted by permission from Stephen F. Williams, "Running Out: The Problem of Exhaustible Resources," *Journal of Legal Studies* 7 (January 1978): 166 (Table 1). Copyright 1978 by the University of Chicago Law School.

Exhibit 20.3
Comparison of a competitive market and a cartel
For the same conditions of cost and demand, producers in a competitive market will tend to supply more each period than will the same producers organized as a cartel. The competitive market produces a quantity that makes marginal cost equal to price; the cartel maximizes profits at the quantity that makes marginal cost equal to marginal revenue.

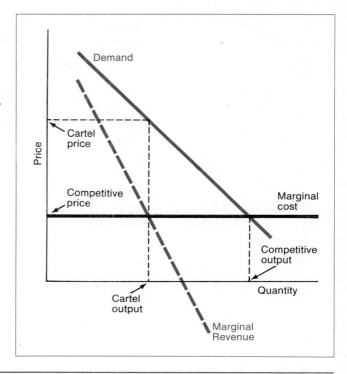

that resulting from competition under the simplifying assumption of constant marginal cost.

Because they sell a smaller quantity at a higher price, cartels are more conservational than competitive markets. If, for example, a cartel were suddenly formed in a resource market that had been perfectly competitive, its first act would be to cut back production. Only in that way could the market price be raised. As a by-product of this profit maximizing action, more of the resource would be left in the second and each subsequent year than would have been the case under competition.

What is more, an additional factor may tend to make natural resource cartels even more conservational than the preceding argument implies. That factor is the possibility that the cartels will try to practice intertemporal price discrimination. According to the theory of price discrimination, cartels will cut back production most sharply in markets with the most inelastic demand, because they can get away with raising the price most in such markets. Thus, if a cartel expects future demand for its product to be more elastic than present demand, it will discriminate against present buyers by raising the price very high initially. The high price will further slow the present rate of consumption. In the case of an oil cartel, it seems reasonable to believe that present demand is in fact less elastic than demand will be in the future, because the technology of substitute energy sources is constantly improving.

Is the Market Rate of Use Optimal?

The theory of the mine shows that the market contains a built-in conservation mechanism. In effect, it transforms predictions of future scarcity into actions for present conservation, as profit maximizing resource owners opt to sell at higher future prices rather than low present prices.

But an important question remains: Might it not be wise to be more conservational still? That is, should current resource owners do future generations a favor by leaving them an even greater endowment of nonrenewable resources than what the market forces dictate? The question of obligations toward future generations raises profound normative issues. Previous generations toiled in mines, fields, and factories, enduring great hardships to accumulate the stock of capital on which present wealth depends. Many people today feel that they themselves should do no less for their own descendants. Fortunately, it is not necessary to resolve all the great ethical questions of income distribution among the generations in order to answer the narrower question of how rapidly nonrenewable resources should be used up. The reason is that the conservation of nonrenewable resources is a question not of how much wealth should be left for future generations but of what form that wealth should be left in.

Basically, there are two tangible forms in which to leave wealth to future generations. One form is capital. It can be produced in as much quantity as people want, provided they are willing to abstain from the present consumption of income and to invest the resulting saving. The other form is natural resources. They cannot be created, but they can be conserved. Even after the decision of how much total wealth to leave to the next generation is made, there is still a need to decide how much of that wealth to leave in each of the two forms. At that point, it is surely ethically acceptable for people to think of themselves and to adjust the mix in such a way that their own sacrifices are minimized.

Once the matter is put this way, it is easy to determine, at least in principle, the optimum degree of conservation of nonrenewable resources. A dollar's worth of nonrenewable resources should be extracted today and invested in durable capital goods if and only if the future value of the resulting capital is greater than the future value of the natural resources that are left in the ground. The future value of the capital can be determined by compounding the current rate of saving at the prevailing rate of return. The rule just given can thus be restated as the instruction to extract resources in the present unless the value of those resources in the future, as measured by their market price, will be likely to rise more rapidly than will the interest rate. As previously shown, a competitive market economy operates in such a way as to ensure that this rule will not be violated. If monopolistic tendencies make markets more conservational than this rule implies, people must bear a greater than necessary burden in the present for any given endowment that they choose to pass along to the future; but the error will be one of leaving too many, not too few, natural resources.

Price Controls and Renewable Resources

The preceding discussion of the allocation of nonrenewable resources, whether in a competitive market or in one dominated by a cartel, assumed that prices would adjust flexibly to the supply decisions of producers and the demand decisions of buyers. While such price flexibility does exist in world energy markets, the U.S. markets for oil and natural gas have for some years operated under price controls. The exact nature of the controls applying to the two products differ, as do the agencies involved in administering them; but oil and gas controls have two essential features in common. First, they place a ceiling, lower than the world price, on the price that is paid to domestic producers. Second, they place a ceiling on the price paid by consumers that is roughly equal to an average of the world price and the price allowed domestic producers.[2]

The Effects of Price Controls The effects of this kind of price control are shown in Exhibit 20.4. The exhibit refers to the oil market, but that for gas is analytically similar. Part a of the exhibit shows the U.S. market as it would appear in the absence of controls, using three supply curves. One fairly inelastic supply curve represents the supply of domestically produced oil. A second curve represents the supply of imported oil, which is shown as perfectly elastic. (The perfectly elastic supply curve implies that foreign producers are willing to sell unlimited quantities at the official OPEC price, shown as P_0 in

---

[2]For oil, the averaging of domestic and import prices is accomplished by the so-called entitlement system, under which refiners buying low-priced domestic oil are required, in effect, to pay a special tax, while refiners buying high-priced imported oil receive what is, in effect, a subsidy. For gas, the averaging is accomplished through so-called roll-in pricing, under which utility commissions permit pipeline companies to sell high-priced imported gas below cost while making up the loss by selling low-priced domestic gas above cost. Details of both regulatory programs can be found in the suggestions for further reading at the end of this chapter.

Exhibit 20.4

Effects of oil price controls
This exhibit shows, in somewhat simplified form, the effects of price controls such as those prevailing for oil in the United States in the 1970s. Part a shows how the market operates without controls. Domestic users purchase domestic supplies up to the point where the domestic supply curve crosses the import supply curve and import the remainder of their needs. Part b shows the effects of price controls that set a ceiling, P_1, on the price paid to domestic producers and a ceiling, P_2, equal to the average of the domestic price and the import price, on what can be charged to users. Under controls, the equilibrium quantity of domestic production is smaller, total domestic consumption is greater, and imports are greater than without controls.

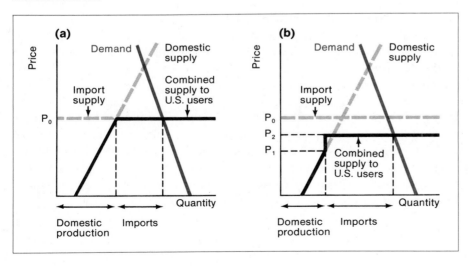

the exhibit. This is something of a simplification, but it serves as a satisfactory approximation for present purposes.) A third curve, shown as a solid line, represents the combined supply curve as it appears to U.S. users. In the absence of price controls, these users will buy from domestic producers up to the point where the domestic price begins to exceed the world price and will then begin to buy imported oil. The combined supply curve thus has a kink in it, as shown. Equilibrium occurs at the point where the demand curve intersects the combined supply curve. The quantities produced domestically and the quantities imported are shown in the diagram.

Exhibit 20.4b shows the U.S. oil market with price controls in effect. As before, P_0 is the world price of oil as set by the cartel. Domestic producers can now be paid no more than P_1, which is below the world price.[3] All oil is sold to U.S. users at price P_2, which is an average of the prices of domestic and imported oil. The combined supply curve as seen by domestic buyers is again shown by a solid line in Part b. This time it follows the domestic supply curve only up to the ceiling price, P_1, beyond which no additional domestic supplies are forthcoming. At that point, imports take over; they are bought at price P_0 but resold to domestic users at P_2. The combined supply curve as seen by U.S. users becomes horizontal at price P_2. Equilibrium is reached where this combined supply curve crosses the demand curve.

Quantities produced domestically and imported under price controls are shown in Exhibit 20.4b. Comparison with Part a of the exhibit shows that price controls decrease domestic production, increase domestic consumption, and increase total oil imports.

Moves toward Decontrol Each of these effects of controls—the decrease in domestic production, the increase in domestic consumption, and the increase in oil imports—runs contrary to professed national policy goals. In order to encourage domestic production, discourage consumption, and reduce imports, steps have recently been taken to phase out price controls on both natural gas and oil. Legislation passed by Congress in 1978, if not further modified, will gradually deregulate the price of natural gas over a period of about five years. Already, the initial phases of deregulation appear to be having a beneficial effect on the exploration for and production of natural gas. In the spring of 1979, President Carter acted under authority previously granted by Congress to begin a similar phased decontrol of domestic crude oil prices. Decontrol of oil prices will probably be accompanied by a new tax on domestic oil, which will mean that U.S. producers still will not receive the full world price. The success of the decontrol effort will depend in part on the exact nature of this tax, which is not clearly decided as yet.

Opposition to Decontrol Despite the fact that the effects of price controls seem strongly at variance with widely accepted policy goals, decontrol of oil and natural gas prices has faced—and continues to face—stiff political opposition. Setting aside such narrow considerations as regional and party rivalries within Congress, at least three economic arguments are advanced in favor of retaining controls.

---

[3]This too is a simplification. Actual price controls impose separate ceilings for various categories of oil, depending on location, time of discovery, and the recovery technology employed.

The first argument is based on the fear of inflation. As energy prices rise to the world level, they will push up the consumer price index. At a time when prices are already increasing rapidly, this idea is not welcome. Thus even some government economists who favor eventual decontrol of energy prices think any major policy change should wait until the broader problem of inflation has been solved.

The second argument against decontrol is based on the belief that the U.S. economy should not be allowed to be disrupted by the artificially high price of oil charged by the OPEC cartel. Price controls in this context are seen as shielding the domestic market from the excessive world price, thereby permitting the same high rate of energy use that could be enjoyed if the world energy market were perfectly competitive. Despite some theoretical appeal of this argument, it is not clear that a policy based on it would really work. Domestic energy prices can be kept low only at the expense of enormous payments to foreign oil producers, and these payments can be even more disruptive to the economy than high energy prices would be.

The third argument against decontrol is based on its probable distributional effects. Decontrol, it is argued, would lead to a massive transfer of income from energy users to energy producers, and the transfer would offend the sense of distributive justice of at least some policy makers. This normative argument is usually combined with the positive economic assertion that decontrol would not significantly discourage demand or encourage domestic supply. The transfer of income from consumers to producers would thus not "buy" much in the way of reduced consumption or increased production. While this is not the place to debate the normative question of whether the government should favor producers, consumers, or neither of them in its economic policies, some attention should be given to the second part of the argument—whether the supply of energy, the demand for energy, or both supply and demand are significantly elastic with respect to price.

Effects of Decontrol If demand and supply were both perfectly inelastic, price decontrol would lead only to a pure transfer from consumers to producers. If either demand or supply were not perfectly inelastic, however, the situation would be more complicated. There would still be some transfer of income from consumers to domestic producers, but there would also be a transfer from foreign producers to domestic producers and a reduction in the real cost of energy to the U.S. economy as a whole. It will be worthwhile, then, to look at least briefly at the likely supply and demand responses to higher energy prices.

Demand Price controls have protected some—but not all—U.S. energy users from the full impact of higher world prices. Where prices have risen, demand has already begun to respond. Between 1973 and 1977, total energy use in the United States increased just 0.17 percent for each 1 percent increase in GNP. This represents a radical break with the long-term trend of one-for-one energy and GNP growth.

In the consumer sector, reductions in energy use have been less dramatic, partly because price controls have shielded consumers from some price increases. Prices for heating oil, bottled gas, and coal, adjusted for inflation, rose by some 50 percent between 1973 and the end of 1978. That helped to make homeowners much more conscious of insulation, storm windows, and thermostats.

On the other hand, cutbacks in gasoline use have been disappointing, despite the fifty-five-mile-per-hour speed limit and tougher mileage standards for new cars. This is not surprising in light of the behavior of gasoline prices. As Exhibit 20.5 shows, the real price of gasoline, adjusted for inflation, was no higher at the end of 1978 than it was in 1967 and was actually lower than it was in 1957. Only after the new upsurge in world oil prices following the 1979 Iranian revolution did the price of gasoline rise above its previous peak. When gasoline prices finally did rise, the immediate result was a boom in public transportation ridership and in the demand for subcompact cars.

In sum, the available evidence indicates considerable price responsiveness of energy demand among industrial users. The potential for consumer response to higher energy prices is large, but it has not been fully tested in areas where price controls have been effective.

Supply There is mounting evidence that there are considerable reserves of fossil fuels that are not worth bringing to the market at present prices but that,

Exhibit 20.5

Gasoline prices adjusted for inflation

This exhibit shows the course of gasoline prices, adjusted for inflation, from 1957 to mid-1979. From 1957 to 1972, the trend was steadily downward; gasoline prices in current dollars rose less than 20 percent, while the consumer price index as a whole rose nearly 50 percent. The 1974 Arab oil embargo sent gasoline prices up 33 percent in a single year; but thereafter, the prices in current dollars stabilized while inflation in general accelerated. By the end of 1978, before the price of gasoline started rising again, it was as low in real terms as it had been in 1967 and actually lower than twenty years before.

The index shown in this exhibit is the ratio of the gasoline and motor oil series to the consumer price index (all items). Source: President's Council of Economic Advisers, *Economic Report of the President* (Washington, D.C.: Government Printing Office, 1979), Tables B-50 and B-51.

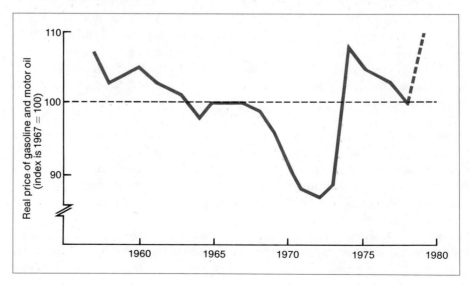

at some price, will be worth extracting. There is much debate, however, about just how much these new sources will cost to develop and which ones are likely to appear on the market first in response to rising prices.

Consider natural gas supplies, for example. In 1977, proven U.S. reserves of natural gas worth recovering at the then-prevailing price were officially calculated at 216 trillion cubic feet (Tcf). That amount was less than a ten-year supply. Yet the following other natural gas reserves were also known to exist in the United States: 300 Tcf of gas (a fifteen-year supply) trapped in coal seams, 600 Tcf (a thirty-year supply) in so-called tight sands under the Rocky Mountains, another 600 Tcf trapped in the Devonian shale formations of Ohio and neighboring states, and a stupendous 100,000 Tcf of natural gas (a theoretical five-thousand-year supply) dissolved in geopressurized brine along the Gulf Coast. No one will really know how much of all that gas can be recovered until the price rises high enough to make it worthwhile for someone to try recovering it.

No one has yet found a five-thousand-year supply of oil, but a number of more modest prospects exist for obtaining additional supplies at costs somewhat in excess of today's prices. These prospects include expanded offshore exploration, expanded use of secondary and tertiary recovery (that is, of methods for getting a higher percentage of the oil out of existing reservoirs), and the extraction of oil from tar sands and oil shale. Outside the United States, especially in China and Mexico (neither of which is a member of OPEC), there are prospects for large conventional discoveries.

The supply response to higher energy prices is by no means limited to added production of oil and gas, however. Much attention is now being given to the development of alternative energy sources. The economic prospects and problems of these sources are sufficiently different from those of oil and gas to warrant discussion in a separate section.

THE ECONOMICS OF ALTERNATIVE ENERGY SOURCES

For the immediate future, the major energy alternatives to oil and gas are coal, nuclear power, and solar power. Strictly speaking, coal and conventional nuclear power are nonrenewable energy sources like oil and natural gas, but they present rather different economic problems in that the availability of known fuel reserves is not the main barrier to their wider use. Solar power—broadly defined to include wind power, water power, and the combustion of farm and forest products (biomass)—is genuinely renewable. This section will discuss each of these alternatives in turn.

Coal

Coal, like oil and natural gas, is a fossil fuel; but unlike the latter, its use as an energy source is limited on the demand rather than the supply side. U.S. coal reserves are enormous—enough to last five hundred years at least. What is more, mining capacity already in place is not even being used fully. The major factor constraining the greater use of coal as an energy source is the cost of burning it in an environmentally acceptable way. This raises two sets of economic issues—those concerned with setting the environmental standards for use of coal and those concerned with meeting the standards.

Setting the Standards The major pollutant in coal is sulphur, which, when burned, produces sulphur dioxide. In urban areas, air pollution from unrestricted burning of coal is a major public health hazard. In agricultural and forest areas, sulphur dioxide pollution causes acid rain, which damages vegetation. And in wilderness areas, such as those of the coal-rich western states, burning coal is a threat to visibility and hence to the attractiveness of national parks and other outdoor recreation areas.

Chapter 18 discussed a number of alternative strategies for regulating air pollution, and little need be added to that discussion here. Suffice it to say that the regulation of emissions from coal combustion has until now emphasized the command-and-control approach, which is often criticized for its inefficiency. By adopting more sophisticated regulatory strategies that pay more attention to variations in local conditions and provide more incentives to employ least-cost methods of abatement, it is likely that the economic burden on coal could be eased while acceptable air quality standards are maintained.

Meeting the Standards Meanwhile, work is under way on a number of alternative technologies for the clean burning of coal. Presently, most coal is burned directly to fire boilers generating electricity, with the pollutants scrubbed out of the stack gases before they are released into the air. The major alternatives focus on preliminary conversion of coal into a clean synthetic fuel that can be burned without elaborate pollution control devices at the point of use. One technique, known as solvent refining, produces a liquid substitute for oil. Another technique bakes the coal and blasts it with air to produce a clean, flammable mixture of carbon monoxide and hydrogen known as producer gas. This gas was widely manufactured in local gasworks around the turn of the century, but it was displaced by natural gas when long-distance pipelines were built. Although producer gas is unlikely to be reintroduced in the residential market (it has a much lower energy value per cubic foot than natural gas), many industrial users are now finding it profitable to build on-site producer gas plants to meet their own needs.

Nuclear Energy

Nuclear energy, everyone's darling in the 1960s and already a major contributor to U.S. energy supplies, now faces an uncertain future. Not all the objections to this form of energy are economic. However, the economic problems of nuclear energy are, in a sense, the most threatening ones because they are producing disenchantment among its traditional friends as well as among its foes.

Because nuclear energy is used almost exclusively to produce electricity, its major competitor is coal. It is appropriate, then, to cast the discussion of the economics of nuclear power in the form of a comparison with coal.

Nuclear Power versus Coal—The Basics The basic economics of nuclear power versus coal is very simple to state: Nuclear power plants are more expensive to build but cheaper to operate.[4] According to one recent set of estimates, as of 1978, a new nuclear power plant would cost $913 per kilowatt

---

[4]Cost data given in this section, except where otherwise noted, are taken from Edmund Faltermayer, "Nuclear Power after Three Mile Island," *Fortune,* May 7, 1979, pp. 114–122.

of capacity, compared with $639 per kilowatt for coal. Once built, however, the coal plant would gulp a hundred-car trainload of fuel every two days, while the nuclear plant would consume less than half a carload of fuel per year. At 1978 prices for coal and uranium, this would make the fuel cost of nuclear power just half the fuel cost for coal.

Whether the trade-off of higher construction costs for lower fuel costs is worthwhile depends on the cost of capital and the percent of capacity at which the plant is operated. During the 1960s, the economics seems clearly to have favored nuclear power over coal. Utilities reported total generating costs per kilowatt hour, including capital costs, to be 40 percent lower for nuclear facilities of that period than for coal-fired plants of comparable age.

Today, however, the advantage is shifting. Higher interest rates and longer construction times have pushed up capital costs. Safety problems requiring more frequent shutdowns have seriously reduced the percentage of capacity at which nuclear plants have been able to operate. And although environmental regulations have increased the cost of coal-fired plants too, they have had even more of an impact on nuclear plants in that they have increased the gap in construction costs. A recent internal study by the Exxon Corporation suggests that when all of these effects are taken into account, the operating cost per kilowatt hour for plants built today is 5.07 cents for nuclear and 5.11 cents for coal—nowhere near enough of a difference to justify the enormously greater construction cost of the nuclear plant.[5] Even these figures are based on what some observers think are overly optimistic assumptions about the percentage of capacity utilization for the nuclear alternative.

Nuclear Power versus Coal—The Hidden Costs If conventional calculations such as those given above suggest that nuclear power is losing the economic advantage it once enjoyed over coal, some unconventional calculations are even more disconcerting. They focus on a number of hidden costs of nuclear power—costs that are opportunity costs from the point of view of the economy as a whole but that are not fully borne by owners of nuclear facilities or their rate payers (users of electric power). The most important of these hidden costs are in waste disposal and dismantling and in health and safety areas.

Waste Disposal and Dismantling One of the great unsolved problems of nuclear power is how to dispose of the radioactive wastes it produces. These wastes are extraordinarily toxic and must be kept isolated for thousands of years. No one really knows how the job can best be done, although there are a number of promising alternatives under exploration. Even if it is technically possible to safely dispose of nuclear wastes, however—something that many nuclear critics are willing to concede—there is no realistic way of knowing what the cost will be. The government agrees, in principle, that private nuclear utilities should be charged the full cost of waste disposal, but that is not yet being done.

A similar problem concerns the dismantling of the reactors themselves at the end of their useful life of forty years or so. Estimates of the dismantling costs range anywhere from 5 to 25 percent of the original construction costs.

---

[5]Dan Dorfman, "Nuclear Power Cost Questioned by Exxon," *Washington Post*, June 6, 1979, p. D3.

Again, no one really knows, because no big nuclear power plant has ever been dismantled. Whatever the costs, however, they are not being fully charged against nuclear power now being generated. The economic advantage of nuclear power over coal is thereby exaggerated.

Safety and Health The Three Mile Island episode of 1979 touched off a great national debate over the safety of nuclear power. Critics charged that the accident came within a hairsbreadth of a core meltdown that could have killed tens of thousands of people. Proponents of nuclear power countered that the accident injured not a single person and in fact showed that a nuclear plant could survive a much more serious combination of human errors and equipment failures than even the critics had imagined possible. This is not the place to resolve the technical arguments over nuclear safety; but however they are resolved, it is clear that after Three Mile Island, stricter safety standards will be imposed on the nuclear industry. These standards will further erode any remaining cost advantage that nuclear power holds over coal.

A further safety related issue concerns liability for nuclear accidents. Early in the nuclear power era, Congress passed the Price-Anderson Act, which set a $560 million limit on utilities' insurance liability in case of accident. Competing energy sources, in contrast, must bear full liability. The Price-Anderson Act thus constitutes another hidden subsidy of nuclear power by the government. In the wake of Three Mile Island, it is safe to say that the premiums for nuclear liability insurance, if utilities were required to carry it, would be quite substantial.

Hazards of Coal Nuclear power, to be sure, is not unique in posing health and safety hazards. Pronuclear writers often point out that coal too has major health and safety problems. The hazards to which coal miners are exposed far exceed those confronted by workers in the nuclear industry, and air pollution is a very real public health hazard in contrast to the largely speculative hazards of low-level radiation or core meltdowns. Some calculations indicate that unrestricted burning of coal might be as much as a thousand times more hazardous than widespread use of nuclear power.

There can be no doubt that a balanced economic comparison of nuclear power versus coal must take into account the full health and safety costs of both alternatives. More research needs to be done, however, before this aspect of the debate can be said to favor nuclear power conclusively. For one thing, the health and safety costs of coal mining are not hidden; they are costs that the coal industry is already bearing in its wage bills, retirement benefits, workmen's compensation premiums, and so on. As for the public health hazards of air pollution as compared with those of nuclear disasters, the question is not so much which is greater at present but which can be controlled at least cost through well-designed regulation.

Solar Energy

Solar energy represents the third major alternative to nonrenewable oil and natural gas. Solar energy—broadly defined to include wind power, hydroelectric power, alcohol, and wood—now contributes about 6 percent of the nation's total energy needs. This percentage is expected to double by the end of the century even if no major new policy initiatives are undertaken. (In 1979, the Carter administration announced plans for a Solar Development Bank, which—if created—would be the centerpiece of an effort to raise the solar contribution to 20 percent by the year 2000.) The economics of solar power can be summarized briefly under the headings of capital costs and net energy costs.

Capital Costs Replacing fossil fuels with solar power represents, even more than in the case of nuclear power, a trade-off of capital investment and operating costs. The system of dams along the Columbia River between Oregon and Washington, for example, although enormously costly to construct, produces electric power at an operating cost of around half a cent per kilowatt hour. Unfortunately, few, if any, really attractive sites remain in the United States for large-scale hydroelectric projects. For the immediate future, solar prospects appear to consist of small-scale applications that are economical given today's costs and technology and larger-scale applications that cannot yet repay their capital costs but that offer some promise for future development.

One of the best-known small-scale applications of solar energy is for residential water heating. In recent years, many companies, large and small, have begun producing practical solar hot water systems. The system produced by AMSOLHEAT, a small company in Danbury, Connecticut (see Exhibit 20.6), is typical. It uses off-the-shelf technology made economically attractive by rising energy prices. Entrepreneur Joseph Heyman of AMSOLHEAT has calculated that his sytem, which costs about $3,000 installed, can pay for itself in seven years as a replacement for electric water heating; this represents an attractive rate of return at today's interest rates.

Another example of off-the-shelf technology, once widespread and now returning to use, is low-head hydroelectric power. Low-head hydroelectric power from small dams on local streams compares to hydroelectric power from the dams of the Columbia River as a wood stove does to a 1,000 megawatt nuclear plant. Nonetheless, many small dams dating from the last century are now being put back into use with modern generating equipment.

For the future, many potentially attractive technologies exist for both large-scale and small-scale use. Wind power, photovoltaic power, and large-scale solar steam plants are in the design or pilot plant stage. All are still at least one technological generation away from being economically competitive with conventional fuels, however.

Net Energy Costs One of the most controversial aspects of solar energy sources concerns their net energy costs. Practitioners of the art of net energy analysis attempt to add up all the energy inputs needed to produce a unit of energy output from a given technology to see if more comes out than goes in. If more energy goes in than comes out, a technology clearly cannot be considered an energy "source" in the conventional meaning of the term.

Photovoltaic power is an example of a technology that is on the margin from a net energy point of view, at least given today's technology. This kind of power uses silicon wafers to convert sunlight directly into electricity. The wafers, which are manufactured by a highly energy-intensive process, have an expected life of about ten years in commercial applications. Even if located in

Exhibit 20.6

A practical application of solar power

After world oil prices began to rise in 1973, many companies began to produce domestic solar hot water heating systems. The system produced by AMSOLHEAT of Danbury, Connecticut, is typical, in that it uses off-the-shelf technology that had fallen into disuse in the 1950s and 1960s with the advent of cheap conventional fuels. At 1979 prices, the AMSOLHEAT system was calculated to save enough electricity to repay its initial cost in seven years.

Source: Courtesy of American Solar Heat Corp., Danbury, Conn.

AMSOLHEAT Introduces Free Hot Water for Two Billion Years.

Now we don't anticipate your home will be around for the projected two billion years of the sun's existence, but during the next hundred years or so isn't it reassuring to know that the price of the sun's heat will never increase (it's free), whereas the price of home fuel oil will continue to rise.

The Sun Yesterday.

Harnessing the sun's energy for productive use has been experimented with for centuries...with the introduction of a solar powered steam engine operating a printing press in 1878, an irrigation system in Egypt (1913) and a solar still delivering 6,000 gallons of water in the Chilean desert over 40 years ago.

Solar water heating systems have been commercially available in such countries as Australia, Israel, and Japan for a number of years. In Florida and Southern California, there was a thriving solar water heater business in the 1940's and 50's, which declined, of course, when conventional fuel became cheap and widely available.

The Sun Today.

In the 1970's, however, interest in solar heating and application in affordable systems has risen again, this time to stay, due in no small part to economic necessities rising out of the oil embargo.

Here in the Northeast, American Solar Heat Corporation (AMSOLHEAT) is proving the thesis that solar heat effectively and efficiently provides the necessary energy to heat domestic hot water.

With AMSOLHEAT's solar collectors, the sun's energy, unlike our natural resources of oil, gas and coal, is not only renewable but economically controllable so that your hot water heating bills can be reduced significantly. AMSOLHEAT customers have seen their hot water bills reduced by up to 70 per cent! With these savings, the AMSOLHEAT solar unit, priced at $1,260.00, will pay for itself within a short period of time (6 years plus).

This simple diagram tells you HOW the sun works for you.

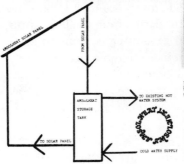

The heat of the sun is collected in the water of the copper pipes within AMSOLHEAT's solar panel. This water is circulated through the AMSOLHEAT storage tank in the basement which goes into your existing hot water system.

Testimonial—Mrs. Rose Heyman of Danbury, Conn., a satisfied AMSOLHEAT customer, said this of our solar panels "...definitely increased the amount of our hot water."

This simple panel tells you WHEN the sun is working for you.

While the roof panels are collecting solar energy and the hot water is storing in the basement tanks, this panel inside your home (installed next to your thermostat) indicates the following:

ON: When your AMSOLHEAT system is operable.
FREE HEAT: When you're getting free solar heat.
DRAIN: When the panels drain to prevent freezing.
TEMPERATURE GAUGE: Temperature of your solar panel or storage tank.
Testimonial—Barbara Wardenburg of Ridgefield, Conn., another satisfied customer, had this to say about AMSOLHEAT's panel "...simple enough operation so our children can see the practical application of science working to solve human problems."

This simple coupon will help you save money. CALL now 792-0077 or mail this coupon today for a free AMSOLHEAT installation estimate.

AMERICAN SOLAR HEAT CORPORATION
7 National Place
Danbury, Ct. 06810

☐ I am a homeowner tired of paying increasing prices for hot water heat.

☐ I am an architect, contractor, builder and want to know more about AMSOLHEAT products.

Name _____

Address _____

Telephone # _____

the sunny Southwest, more than half of the ten years would be needed just to repay the energy used in manufacturing the wafers, not counting any of the other energy used in constructing and operating the plant.

Alcohol fuel, another solar technology, has also been challenged on net energy grounds. It appears that alcohol made from grain grown in the United States by mechanized methods and produced with gas or oil fired stills consumes more energy than it yields. Alcohol cannot be entirely written off as an energy source, however. For one thing, if mixed with gasoline to make gasohol, it improves mileage and raises octane ratings, thereby contributing more than its energy value to the mix. Also, alcohol produced from raw materials other than grain or distilled using wood or crop waste as a fuel can be more energy efficient. For example, Brazil has a large program of alcohol fuel production that uses sugar cane as its raw material and burns cane waste as a fuel.

CONCLUSIONS

Perhaps the safest thing to say about the economics of energy is that it is a rapidly changing field. The prospects for oil and natural gas depend very much on supply and demand reactions to price decontrol over the next five to ten years. Nuclear power appears at the moment to be going nowhere, but existing plants contribute an indispensable one-eighth of all electric power. Coal is enormously abundant, but its wider use is being held up while cost-efficient ways are sought to overcome its environmental problems. Solar power is growing in importance but is unlikely to contribute more than a fifth of U.S. energy needs in this century. Energy economics promises to be exciting for years to come.

SUMMARY

1. According to the theory of the mine, in a competitive market, a nonrenewable resource will be depleted no faster than the rate that will cause its price to rise at a rate equal to the prevailing interest rate. Any faster rate of depletion would be self-correcting, since wealth-maximizing resource owners would begin to withhold present supplies from the market in order to sell them at higher prices later. When the market for such a resource is dominated by a cartel, the rate of depletion tends to be less than in a competitive market.

2. Price controls on oil and natural gas in the United States have partially insulated domestic markets from the effects of rising world prices. The result has been a lower rate of domestic production, a higher rate of domestic consumption, and a higher rate of imports than would have prevailed without controls. Controls on both oil and gas prices are presently being phased out.

3. The major energy alternatives to oil and natural gas are coal, nuclear energy, and solar power. All these alternatives require greater capital expenditure per unit of energy output than oil and gas if they are to meet health, safety, and environmental safeguards. From an economic point of view, all three still appear to be in the running as major energy sources for the future, although coal and solar power currently seem to be gaining at the expense of the nuclear alternative.

DISCUSSION QUESTIONS

1. Imagine that you are snowed in for the winter in a small cabin in the mountains. Your food supply consists of a sack of potatoes. There are more than enough potatoes to survive on but less than enough to eat all you want every day. How will you allocate the potatoes over the winter? Will you eat an equal amount every day? More per day at first and then gradually taper off? Fewer at first and more toward the end? What does the theory of the mine have to say about this kind of situation?

2. When this edition of this text was written, Congress had just passed legislation that was to gradually deregulate the price of natural gas over a period of about five years. Is this deregulation process proceeding on schedule, or has new natural gas legislation proved necessary since 1978?

3. Go to your library, and find a copy of the *Monthly Labor Review* or some other publication that gives a product-by-product breakdown of the consumer price index. Compare the current price index for gasoline with the price index for all goods and services for all urban consumers. Use these data to update Exhibit 20.5.

4. Is it still true, as you are reading this, that the government is subsidizing imported oil at the expense of domestic production? What has happened to the so-called entitlements program? (Hint: Use the *New York Times* index for a quick review of major energy policy changes since early 1979.)

SUGGESTIONS FOR FURTHER READING

Goodman, John C., and Dolan, Edwin G. *The Economics of Public Policy.* St. Paul, Minn.: West Publishing, 1979.
Four chapters in this book are devoted to energy-related topics. Chapter 3 deals with gasoline rationing, Chapter 7 with electric power, Chapter 9 with natural gas, and Chapter 10 with oil.

Mead, Walter J. *Energy and the Environment: Conflict in Policy.* Washington, D.C.: American Enterprise Institute, 1978.
This short monograph looks at the reasons that energy and the environment have become two of the leading political issues of the day and examines their economic relationships.

Stobaugh, Robert, and Yergin, Daniel, eds. *The Energy Future.* New York: Random House, 1979.
This study, by a group of Harvard business school professors, examines a broad spectrum of energy alternatives for the future and concludes that conservation remains the most important single hope for reducing U.S. dependence on imported oil.

Williams, Stephen F. "Running Out: The Problem of Exhaustible Resources." *Journal of Legal Studies* 7 (January 1978):165–199.
The article begins with an exposition of the theory of the mine and concludes with an examination of some of the normative issues connected with the allocation of nonrenewable resources over time.

CHAPTER 21

THE ECONOMICS OF POPULATION AND DEVELOPMENT

WHAT YOU WILL LEARN IN THIS CHAPTER

Most of the inhabitants of the planet earth are very poor, and the numbers of the poor are increasing more rapidly than those of the more well-to-do. This chapter discusses some of the economic problems faced by the inhabitants of the less developed countries. It begins with a lesson in basic population arithmetic. Then it compares population growth trends over time in the developed and less developed countries and shows why the population problem of the less developed world is in many respects more serious than that faced in earlier times by the now developed countries. Finally, the chapter turns from the population problem itself to the problem of producing sufficient food to feed the ever-growing third world population.

FOR REVIEW

Here are some important terms and concepts that will be put to use in this chapter. If you do not understand them, review them before proceeding.
- *Pure economic profit (Chapter 7)*
- *Pure economic rent (Chapter 17)*

Having dealt with pollution and energy, the discussion turns now to a third major problem of life on this planet: population. How will the ever-increasing numbers of people in the world find room to live? How are they going to be fed? These are among the most pressing worldwide problems to be faced in the closing years of the twentieth century.

Unlike the problems of pollution and energy, those of food and population have largely been solved in the world's industrialized market economies. For that reason, this chapter will focus on the less developed countries, where two-thirds of the world's people already live. It begins with a brief discussion of the nature of the economic development process itself. Next, it turns to the topic of population. Finally, it reviews the status of world food production, on which the solution of the problems of development and population so heavily depend.

THREE FACES OF ECONOMIC GROWTH

Economic Development as Growth

The less developed countries that make up what is called the "third world" differ from one another and from the developed countries in many ways, but they have one conspicuous thing in common—low per capita income. No magic number divides the rich countries from the poor; there is a spectrum of degrees of poverty, as shown in the map in Exhibit 21.1. At the very bottom of

$3,001 to more than $7,000

Australia	Gabon	Norway
Austria	Greenland	Oman
Bahamas Islands	Iceland	Qatar
Bahrain	Israel	San Marino
Belgium	Italy	Saudi Arabia
Bermuda	Japan	Spain
Brunei	Kuwait	Sweden
Canada	Libya	Switzerland
Czechoslovakia	Liechtenstein	United Arab Emirates
Denmark	Luxembourg	United Kingdom
East Germany	Monaco	United States
Faroe Islands	Nauru	USSR
Finland	Netherlands	West Germany
France	New Zealand	

$201 to $1,000

Albania	Dominica
Algeria	Dominican
Angola	Republic
Antigua	Djibouti
Belize	Ecuador
Benin	Egypt
Bolivia	El Salvador
Botswanna	French Guiana
Cameroon	Gambia
Chili	Ghana
Colombia	Gibraltar
Congo	Gilbert Islands
Cook Islands	Grenada
Cuba	Guadeloupe

$1,001 to $3,000

Andorra	
Argentina	
Barbados	
Brazil	
Bulgaria	
Costa Rica	
Cyprus	
Falkland Islands	
Fiji	
French Polynesia	
Greece	
Hong Kong	
Hungary	Portugal
Iran	Puerto Rico
Iraq	Romania
Ireland	Singapore
Jamaica	South Africa
Malta	Surinam
Martinique	Taiwan
Mexico	Trinidad and
Netherlands Antilles	Tobago
New Caledonia	Turkey
Panama	Uruguay
Poland	Venezuela
	Yugoslavia

Exhibit 21.1
Gross national product per capita, 1977 (in 1977 U.S. dollars)
The countries of the world exhibit an enormous range in per capita incomes.
There is no sharp dividing line between the developed and less developed countries. Here, four groups are distinguished. The most poverty stricken countries are
those with incomes of less than $200 GNP per capita. Those with per capita in-
comes of less than $1,000 are also very poor, but many are experiencing promis-

Guatemala
Guyana
Haiti
Honduras
Indonesia
Ivory Coast
Jordan
Kenya
Lebanon
Lesotho
Liberia
Macao
Madagascar
  Republic

Malaysia
Mauritania
Mauritius
Mongolia
Morocco
Mozambique
Namibia
Nicaragua
Nigeria
North Korea
North Yemen
Papua-New
  Guinea
Paraguay

Peoples Republic
  of China
Peru
Philippines
Rhodesia
St. Christopher-
  Nevis-Anguilla
St. Lucia
St. Vincent
Sao Tome/Principe
Senegal
Seychelles
Sierra Leone
South Korea

South Yemen
Sri Lanka
Sudan
Swaziland
Syria
Thailand
Togo
Tonga
Tunisia
Uganda
Western Sahara
Western Samoa
Zambia

Less than $201

Afghanistan
Bangladesh
Bhutan
Burma
Burundi
Cambodia
Cape Verde Islands
Central African
  Empire
Chad
Equatorial Guinea
Ethiopia
Guinea-Bissau
India
Laos
Malawi
Mali
Nepal
Niger
Pakistan
Rwanda
Somalia
Tanzania
Upper Volta
Vietnam
Zaire

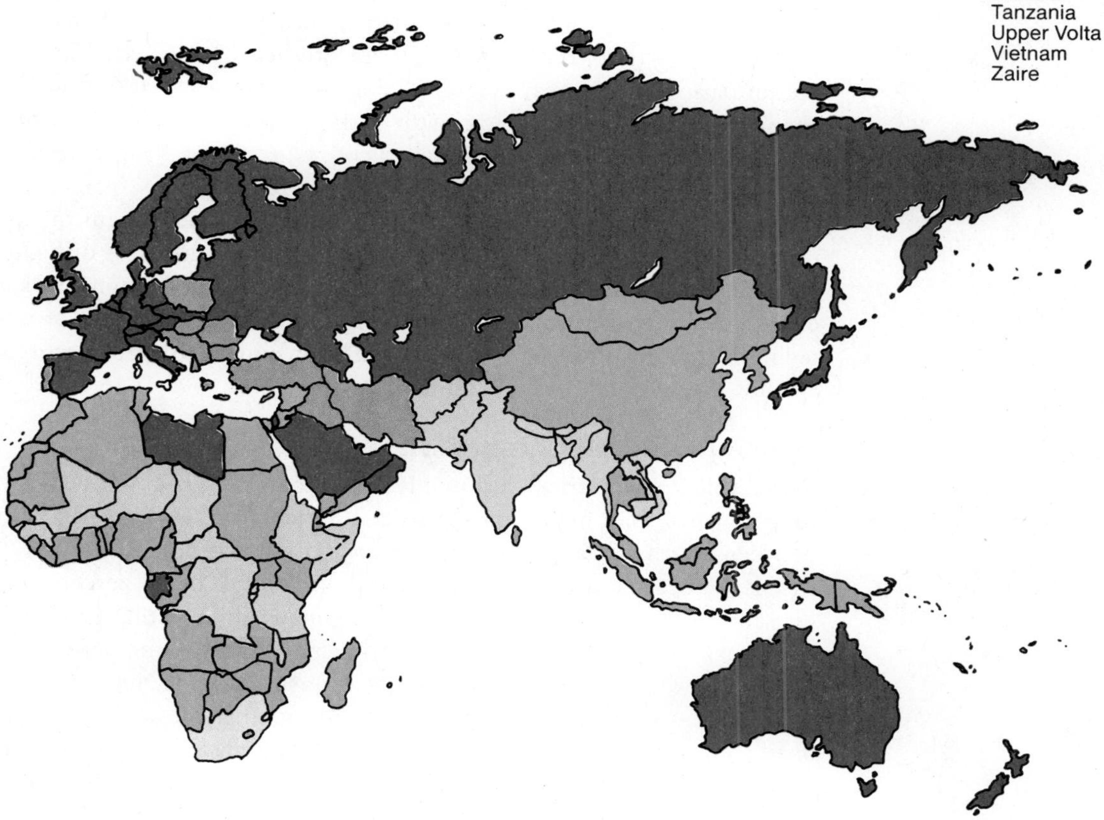

ing self-sufficient economic growth. Countries in the $1,000 to $3,000 range belong in the less developed category in some respects; but in other ways, they more closely resemble the countries with more than $3,000 per capita GNP. This last group includes the oil-rich countries of the Middle East as well as the industrialized countries of Europe and North America.

Source: Adapted from U.S. Central Intelligence Agency, National Foreign Assessment Center, *Handbook of Economic Statistics* (Washington, D.C., 1978), Figure 1, p. 1.

the spectrum are the poorest of poor countries—those with per capita GNP of less than $200 per year. These countries are found in southern Asia, from Afghanistan to Vietnam, and in a band through central Africa reaching from Guinea on the west coast to Tanzania on the east. The map also distinguishes countries with per capita GNP in the range of $201 to $1,000, clearly in the less developed group but somewhat better off. A third group, in the $1,001 to $3,000 range—including much of Latin America as well as such countries as Portugal, Yugoslavia, and Taiwan—straddles the ill-defined border between developed and less developed status. Countries with still higher levels of per capita GNP include the truly developed countries as well as the somewhat anomalous oil-rich countries of the Middle East.

To draw these distinctions in terms of per capita incomes implies that economic development equals economic growth. That is the traditional view of the matter, and it is a view that still has much truth to it. Economic growth can occur without bringing a better life to everyone, but it is hard to see how a better life for all can come without at least some growth. This is especially true for the least developed countries that have less than $200 of GNP per capita.

Much of development economics, then, focuses on ways to enable a country to grow. Growth oriented development studies usually emphasize capital accumulation as the great key. Capital accumulation has accounted for only about 15 percent of economic growth in the United States in recent years; but it is more important for less developed countries, which have a great shortage of capital. Typically, saving and investment are only 5 to 7 percent of GNP, compared to over 15 percent in the United States and 35 percent in Japan and the Soviet-type economies. Without capital accumulation, it is difficult to put unemployed and underemployed people to work. Without capital it is equally difficult to improve the level of education or to take advantage of imported technology. Yet, although capital accumulation and growth are important, they are not the whole story of economic development.

Development as Industrialization

The developed countries are not only richer than the less developed countries; they are also more highly industrialized. Developed countries typically have between a fifth and a quarter of their populations engaged in industry. In the less developed countries, the proportion is likely to be 10 percent or less. A second interpretation of economic development, then, is that it means industrializing, just as the advanced countries have done in the past.

The view that development means industrialization, like the view that development means economic growth, has much truth to it. The less developed countries have large and growing urban populations. Only industrialization offers them much hope of employment. As incomes rise in a developing country, the demand for manufactured goods increases rapidly. It makes sense to meet many of these needs with domestic sources of supply. Many less developed countries have valuable raw materials that they now export for processing; these materials could be processed domestically instead. Still, despite all this, the importance of industrialization to development should not be exaggerated.

For one thing, an overemphasis on industrialization may cause resources to be wasted on ill-conceived showcase projects. Not every less developed country needs a steel mill and an automobile plant. Even small-scale industrial projects may be inappropriate if they mean building an exact replica of some plant originally designed for Manchester or Milwaukee, where relative factor scarcities and other market conditions are completely different.

What is more, an overemphasis on industrialization can lead to the neglect of other development objectives. The third face of economic development shows why.

Development as Depauperization

It is a widely shared opinion that a major goal of economic development should be a better life for the poorest of the poor—the people at the low end of the income distribution in the poorest countries. They are the true paupers—lacking adequate food, often lacking all access to medical care, and not infrequently lacking even the most primitive shelter.

Development economists once were confident that the benefits of growth and industrialization would automatically trickle down to the poorest of the poor. Unfortunately, this optimism may not be justified, as the research of Irma Adelman and C. T. Morris has shown.[1] Their work focuses on the range of development from sub-Saharan Africa to the poorest countries of South America—that is, from about $100 to $500 per capita income. In these countries, development tends to bring both relative and absolute impoverishment to the poorest 60 percent of the population. At very low levels of development, there appears to be no trickling down at all. The poor begin to benefit only after an intermediate level of development has been reached.

Adelman and Morris have concluded that the policies needed to benefit the poor are different from those needed to maximize growth rates. The ideas of development as growth or industrialization, they say, should be replaced with the idea of **depauperization**—the provision not only of the necessary material basis for life but also of access to education, security, self-expression, status, and power. Depauperization stresses the removal of social, political, and spiritual deprivation as much as physical deprivation. It has as much to do with equity as with growth.

Depauperization Economic development of a kind that benefits the poorest of the poor, providing them not only with the material necessities of life but also with access to education, status, security, self-expression, and power.

Two Strategies

The choice of development goals strongly influences the strategy that can best promote the development process. The Soviet Union represents one extreme. For early Soviet planners, development meant industrialization above all else. Through high rates of saving, they sacrificed consumption to achieve rapid growth. Through collectivization, they sacrificed the growth of agriculture to achieve the growth of industry. Eventually, the benefits of successful industrialization began to trickle down to the population at large. Initially, though, living standards declined, and the overall distribution of income shifted in favor of industrial workers and against peasants.

Even where industrialization as an end in itself is not made a higher priority than overall growth, the benefits of development may be spread unevenly. Many less developed countries suffer from what is called a **dual economy.** In such an economy, a modern, Westernized industrial sector provides high wages for better educated workers and a tax base to pay a middle class of civil

Dual economy An economy that is sharply divided into a modern, westernized industrial sector capable of rapid growth and a traditional rural sector that remains stagnant.

---

[1]Irma Adelman and C. T. Morris, *Society, Politics, and Economic Development* (Baltimore: Johns Hopkins University Press, 1967).

servants. Meanwhile, a secondary, traditional sector remains largely untouched. Sometimes, the overall growth rate of GNP can be maximized by concentrating available development resources on the modern sector, at least in the short run. Often also foreign aid and the investments of multinational corporations are concentrated on the modern sector of dual economies.

There is a second kind of development strategy that contrasts with the industry-first approach. It emphasizes redistribution and mass education first and growth later. Redistribution in the context of less developed countries means most importantly the redistribution of land ownership. Education means mass education in literacy and general knowledge, rather than just specialized training for participation in the modern sector. If this strategy works, redistribution can provide the basis for rural development and education the basis for the growth of broadly based, labor-intensive industry. Adelman and Morris cite Israel, Japan, South Korea, Singapore, and Taiwan as countries that have successfully followed this strategy. China should probably be added to the list. In the last century, U.S. economic development followed this strategy much more than did economic development in Europe.

POPULATION AND DEVELOPMENT

Whatever development strategy they choose, all less developed countries face certain common problems that they must somehow solve. None is more serious than the problem of population growth. As background for a discussion of population problems in the less developed countries, here is a review of some basic population arithmetic.

Population Arithmetic

For a population to increase, it is obvious that more people must be born than die each year. (In this section and in what follows, immigration and emigration are ignored.) The number of people born into a population per thousand per year is the **crude birthrate** for that population. The number who die per thousand per year is the **crude death rate.** The difference between the two is the **rate of natural increase.**

Crude birthrate The number of people born into a population per thousand per year.

Crude death rate The number of people in a population who die per thousand per year.

Rate of natural increase The current growth rate of a population calculated as the crude birthrate minus the crude death rate.

Exhibit 21.2 shows crude birthrates, crude death rates, and rates of natural increase for a selection of countries, according to the latest available data. In interpreting data such as these, it sometimes helps to translate rates of natural increase into population doubling times. This is done in the last column of the table. The faster the rate of natural increase, the shorter the period of time required for the population to double in size.

Growth Curves A population that grew indefinitely at a constant rate of natural increase would double each time a fixed number of years elapsed. It would reach 2, 4, 8, 16, 32, 64 (and so on) times its original size, following the same sort of growth path as that followed by the value of a sum of money invested at compound interest.

Normally, however, living populations are not able to grow exponentially without limit. Suppose that bacteria are allowed to multiply in a glass jar of nutrient, or a population of fruit flies is allowed to grow in a glass cage or room of fixed size, or a breeding pair of dogs is introduced on an island previously inhabited only by rabbits. Under such conditions, the growth of the population of bacteria, fruit flies, or dogs typically follows the kind of S-shaped growth

Exhibit 21.2

Birthrates, death rates, and the rate of natural increase of the population for selected countries (most recent available data)

The rate of natural increase for a population is found by subtracting the current death rate per thousand from the current birthrate per thousand. If the rate of natural increase is greater than zero, it can also be expressed as the number of years that would be required for the population to double if that rate were to continue.

Country	Crude Birthrate	Crude Death Rate	Rate of Natural Increase	Doubling Time of Population (years)
Honduras	47	12	35	20
Mexico	41	7	34	20
Algeria	48	14	33	21
Nigeria	50	18	32	22
Ghana	48	17	31	22
Pakistan	44	14	30	23
Somalia	48	20	28	25
Brazil	36	8	28	25
Haiti	42	16	26	27
Ethiopia	50	25	25	28
Afghanistan	50	27	23	30
Yemen	48	25	23	30
Thailand	32	9	23	30
Argentina	22	9	13	53
China	20	8	12	58
Japan	15	6	9	77
USSR	18	10	8	87
Czechoslovakia	19	12	7	99
United States	15	9	6	116
France	14	10	4	173
Italy	13	10	4	173
Sweden	12	11	1	693
United Kingdom	12	12	0	—
West Germany	10	12	−2	—

Source: Reprinted by permission from *1979 World Population Data Sheet* (Washington, D.C.: Population Reference Bureau, 1979).

curve shown in Exhibit 21.3. At first, the population will expand at the exponential rate. The biological characteristics of the species in question determine the population doubling time under optimal conditions. Sooner or later, though, the population will begin to fill up its jar or cage or island or whatever. Then, under more crowded conditions, the time needed to double

Exhibit 21.3

Typical S-shaped curve of population growth

A living population cannot grow indefinitely in a finite environment. Under laboratory conditions, populations of bacteria or fruit flies or other organisms tend to follow S-shaped growth curves such as the one shown here. In the long run, it seems inevitable that the growth curve of human population will also begin to decrease.

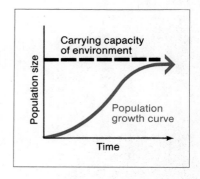

the population will increase. Eventually, overcrowding will bring population growth to a halt.

Must the growth of human population also be subject to this S-curve pattern? In the long run, it surely must. Estimates of the maximum human population of earth vary widely, but no one doubts that there is some finite ceiling. (One admittedly fanciful estimate places the limit as high as 20 million times the present world population. This would require people to live 120 to the square meter in a two-thousand-story building covering the entire earth. Even that limit would take only 890 years to reach at the present growth rate of world population!)

In the short run, though, the growth of human population has not followed the simple S-curve pattern. In fact, over as long a period as any kind of population estimates can be made, the world rate of natural increase has been accelerating, not slowing down. World population has doubled in about the last forty-five years and would double again in the next thirty-five if the current growth rate were to continue. The last preceding doubling of population took about eighty years, from 1850 to 1930. The doubling before that took some two hundred years. It is hard to imagine that this trend will continue. There are now indications that the world is reaching the bend in the population growth curve and that world population growth, for the first time, is beginning to slow.[2]

Population Equilibrium

There can be no doubt that in the long run the level of human population is headed for an equilibrium state in which births will just balance deaths. The really interesting question is: What will that equilibrium look like? Let's explore some possibilities.

First, imagine a market economy in which people earn money to buy the necessities of life only by selling factor services. The population begins to approach some fixed limit to population growth defined, for example, by the food supply. Income is distributed unequally in this society. As population nears the ceiling, the price of food rises relative to the wage rate. The lowest income groups find their standard of living reduced, and this eventually affects their birth and death rates. At some point, an excess of deaths over births will occur among the poorest classes. This will be accompanied by a balance between births and deaths for those living just at the margin of subsistence. An excess of births will be possible only among the well-to-do. When enough people have finally been pushed down to or below the margin of subsistence, population growth as a whole will cease. The result can be called a marginal subsistence equilibrium for population.

This equilibrium assumes great inequality. It implies affluence for a few against the backdrop of destitute masses whose members are continuously replenished by the excess children of the rich driven down into poverty. If the assumption of inequality is removed, the result is a second type of population equilibrium, which can be called the absolute subsistence equilibrium. Under

---

[2]For example, Donald J. Bogue and Amy Ong Tsui, in "Zero World Population Growth," *Public Interest*, no. 55 (Spring 1979): 99–113, go so far as to declare the once-feared population bomb a dud. Between 1968 and 1975, they report, fertility declined in 103 countries having a total population of 3.2 billion and increased or was unchanged in only 45 countries with a total population of 749 million.

this solution, as crowding begins to lower the living standards of a population, taxes and transfers are used to divide the burden equally among all. This equality permits population growth to go on longer; no one is starved or crowded to the point of being unable to reproduce until everyone reaches that point. The total number of people living in poverty in the absolute subsistence equilibrium is greater than in the marginal subsistence equilibrium.

Population projections like these were what once caused economics to be called the "dismal science." As long ago as 1798, Thomas Malthus forecast a marginal subsistence population equilibrium for humanity that would come about through the operation of the law of diminishing returns, as a growing population caught up with a fixed supply of agricultural land. According to Malthus's theory, only the landlords, who owned the means of producing precious food, would escape eventual poverty. Even the capitalists would eventually be ground down and their profits reduced to zero.

Malthus's prophecy has not come true for Great Britain, the United States, or other advanced industrial countries. These countries have instead achieved, or nearly achieved, a nonsubsistence population equilibrium with low birthrates, low death rates, and high living standards. The process by which this equilibrium has been achieved is a good illustration of how economic and demographic processes interact.

Thomas Robert Malthus was born in England in 1766 and received what was, for his time, a radical upbringing. His father was an admirer of Rousseau and Condorcet, and one of his tutors was imprisoned for expressing the wish that the French revolutionaries would invade and liberate England. Malthus studied at Cambridge, took holy orders, and became a curate.

In 1793, a book appeared that had a great impact on the circles in which young Malthus moved. The book was *Enquiry Concerning Political Justice and Its Influence on Morals and Happiness* by the anarchist and socialist, William Godwin. As a result of many lively debates over this book and subsequent essays by Godwin, Malthus decided to write down his own view that population growth constituted an insurmountable barrier to a society of absolute equality and abundance. This writing appeared as *An Essay on the Principle of Population* in 1798.

The heart of Malthus's argument was the doctrine that population tended to grow in geometric progression (2, 4, 8, 16, and so on) while the means of subsistence grew only in arithmetic progression (2, 4, 6, 8, and so on). As population increased, increasingly less fertile land would have to be brought into cultivation. Population would outstrip food production, and wages would be driven down to the subsistence level.

Famine, vice, misery, and war could be avoided only if people engaged in "moral restraint"—later marriages with fewer children per family. Schemes such as the Poor Laws or subsidized housing for the poor were worse than useless, according to Malthus. They simply encouraged population growth and led to an actual deterioration of conditions.

Thomas Robert Malthus (1766–1834)

Malthus's views influenced Darwin in developing his survival of the fittest doctrine in the nineteenth century. More than anyone else, it was Malthus who was responsible for earning political economy the name of the "dismal science." Not everyone has interpreted the man in such a negative light, however. John Maynard Keynes placed Malthus firmly in "the English tradition of humane science . . . a tradition marked by a love of truth and a most noble lucidity, . . . and by an immense disinterestedness and public spirit."

The Demographic Transition

In a preindustrial society, birthrates and death rates are both very high, and the rate of natural increase of population is low. With industrialization and economic development, per capita incomes begin to rise. The first demographic effect of rising income is a reduction in the death rate brought about by better nutrition, better hygiene, and better medical care. With the birthrate remaining high, the drop in the death rate increases the rate of natural increase. Population enters a phase of very rapid growth.

If there are sufficient natural resources and enough investment in new capital, economic growth can outstrip population growth. Per capita income then rises. This has happened in all the major industrialized countries of the world. In these countries, rising per capita incomes have eventually caused the birthrate to fall. Population growth has then slowed, and population equilibrium has been approached.

Demographic transition A population cycle that accompanies economic development, beginning with a fall in the death rate, continuing with a phase of rapid population growth, and concluding with a decline in the birthrate.

The whole cycle, from falling death rates to rapid population growth to falling birthrates and equilibrium is called the **demographic transition.** Exhibit 21.4 provides a graphical view of the demographic transition. Part a represents the course of the crude birthrate and death rate over time. Part b shows what happens to the rate of natural increase as it first rises and then falls. Part c shows the familiar S-curve pattern of population growth that results from the demographic transition. The human population growth curve shown in Part c differs in an important respect from that of flies in a jar or dogs on an island; it levels off at an equilibrium population below the biologically maximum level set by subsistence requirements.

The crucial part of the demographic transition is the fall in birthrates produced by rapid economic development. Demographers do not completely understand the mechanisms that bring about this decline. In large part, it is probably caused by increasing urbanization. Traditionally, a large number of children is an economic asset to a farm family, because children can contribute to production from an early age. In the city, children tend to be an economic burden. There is no guarantee of remunerative jobs for them, and

Exhibit 21.4
The demographic transition
In a preindustrial society, both birthrates and death rates are high, so that population growth is slow. The first effect of economic development is a drop in the death rate. This brings on a period of rapid population growth. As economic development continues, the birthrate begins to fall. Population growth decelerates and eventually may fall to zero.

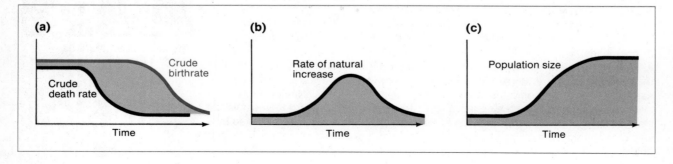

their food, clothing, and housing cannot be produced at home. More subtle changes in life-styles and attitudes toward family life, which occur as income rises, also seem to be involved in the demographic transition.

Net Reproduction

To complete the demographic transition and approach an equilibrium population takes many decades. To understand why the transition takes so long, one needs to know more about population growth than crude birthrates and crude death rates alone can offer.

Crude birthrates and death rates can be misleading because they depend on both the underlying reproductive behavior of a population and its age structure. A more direct measure of reproductive behavior is the **net reproduction rate** for a population—the average number of daughters born to each female child in the population over her lifetime. If the net reproduction rate is equal to 1, then the population is, in the long run, just replacing itself. If it is greater than 1, then the population has a long-run tendency to grow. If it is less than 1, it has a long-run tendency to shrink.

In the short run, the rate of natural increase in a population may be positive even when the net reproduction rate is 1 or less. In particular, this will happen when population growth has been slowing in the recent past. The present situation in the United States provides a case in point. The U.S. net reproduction rate is now less than 1, but it has fallen to that level only recently. The elderly people now in high mortality brackets are members of the relatively small generation born around the turn of the century. People in the high fertility range are members of the much larger generation who were born immediately after World War II. The disproportion in the size of the generations causes the crude death rate to be lower—and the crude birthrate to be higher—than will be the case in the long-run equilibrium. If there is no further change in reproductive behavior, and if the net reproduction rate remains slightly less than 1, it will take some forty to sixty years for the rate of natural increase to fall to 0. Only at that point will the demographic transition in this country be complete.

Net reproduction rate The inherent long-term growth rate of a population, measured as the average number of daughters born to each female child over her lifetime.

The Population Trap

Birthrates, death rates, economic growth, and income levels are in very delicate balance during economic development. Countries that develop successfully undergo a process called the demographic transition. During that process, rising income levels first depress death rates, causing population growth rates to accelerate, and then depress birthrates, causing population growth to slow.

Exhibit 21.5 shows what happens to per capita income and population growth, assuming steady economic growth, during the demographic transition. In Part a, the vertical axis measures the level of per capita income. When income is below Level B, people are so poor that death rates are high, and when it is above A, people are prosperous enough that birthrates are low. (Of course, things are really more complicated than this. There are not really any sharp cutoff levels of income, but this simple assumption makes the point.) In Part b, the vertical axis measures growth rates of total GNP and population. Note that population growth never exceeds the growth of GNP. The curve of per capita income in Part a always moves upward, although it rises less rapidly in the zone between A and B while the demographic transition is under way.

Exhibit 21.5
The demographic transition and economic growth

Here, the effects of the demographic transition are shown in terms of economic growth and population growth. It is assumed that death rates begin to fall once per capita income reaches Level A and that birthrates begin to fall once per capita income reaches Level B. During the transition, population growth speeds up and per capita income growth slows. Economic growth always stays above population growth, however.

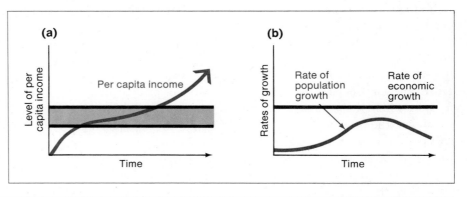

Population trap A situation in which the rate of population growth rises above the rate of economic growth, halting the growth of per capita income and aborting the demographic transition.

Can today's less developed countries complete this process as the developed countries have done? It is to be hoped that they can, but it is by no means certain. There is a real danger that they will get caught in a **population trap,** which will abort their attempt to make it through the demographic transition.

Exhibit 21.6 shows schematically how a country can fall foul of the population trap. Suppose that such a country begins development normally, as did the country represented in Exhibit 21.5. This time, though, either population growth is more rapid or economic growth is slower. At Time T, population growth begins to exceed the growth of income, and per capita income starts to fall. Instead of completing the demographic transition, the country falls back into a subsistence equilibrium with birth and death rates both high and per capita income stagnant.

Exhibit 21.6

The population trap

If at some point during the demographic transition the rate of population growth exceeds the rate of economic growth, a country may be caught in a population trap. As this exhibit is drawn, the country enters the trap at Time T. At that point, per capita income begins to fall and the demographic transition is aborted.

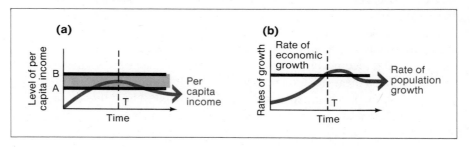

Escaping the Population Trap In the nineteenth century, when Western Europe and North America were industrializing, death rates fell only slowly—and only after living standards had already begun to improve. Population growth rates did not rise above 1 percent per year in most cases. Today, modern death control techniques have reached almost every corner of the globe, no matter how poor. That makes it more difficult for today's less developed countries to escape the population trap. During the nineteenth century, the U.S. economy experienced growth rates of GNP in the range of 3.5 to 4.5 percent per year. Growth rates in that range are no longer good enough for less developed countries, where population itself can grow as fast as 3.5 percent per year. Any growth rate for GNP slower than 6 to 7 percent per year gives little hope for escaping the population trap just by outrunning it. Countries like South Korea or Taiwan may make it, but those like Haiti, Chad, or Dahomey, where per capita incomes are already falling, will not.

The only other way to escape the population trap is to bring down the birthrate while per capita incomes are still low. Although headway has been made in some countries, serious problems remain elsewhere, as the examples in the following three-part case study show.

Case 21.1
Three Experiments in Population Control

Saying that less developed countries need to bring population growth under control is one thing; accomplishing the feat is another. Here is a report on population programs in three of the largest countries of the third world. Each has made major efforts, but the results are not uniformly encouraging.

Pakistan. Few countries have a more serious population problem than Pakistan. Development planners were thus delighted when, in 1973, Pakistan was chosen as the laboratory for a massive experiment in the "inundation" approach to family planning. Using $58 million in U.S. aid as well as local resources, the plan was literally to flood the countryside with condoms and birth control pills at a price so low—2.5 cents for a month's supply—that even the poorest people could afford them. The flood of birth control devices was to be followed by teams of "continuous motivators," who were to visit each household three or four times a year to give encouragement and instruction.

Today, the program appears to be a total failure. The birthrate has gone up, not down. Only 9 percent of fertile couples in the country have ever tried birth control, and only 6 percent practice it regularly. Why the failure? Poor administration is part of the reason, but the real flaw in the program was its assumption that families *wanted* to have fewer children. In rural Pakistan, each child, male and female, begins to contribute positively to the support of the family as early as the age of four by tending goats or chickens, running errands, or driving a bullock cart. And in this conservative Moslem society, children are a source of social prestige. The condoms were turned into children's playthings or melted down by contractors to make caulking material.

India. India, a neighbor of Pakistan, faces a population problem of much the same magnitude. Under the leadership of former Prime Minister Indira Gandhi and her controversial son, Sanjay, however, India adopted a very different approach to birth control. To make certain that families stayed on the birth control track once they got on it, the government emphasized sterilization and insertion of IUD's as the main birth control techniques. An elaborate program of incentives and disincentives was devised to persuade married men to undergo sterilization. The incentives included transistor radios; the disincentives included disqualification for government housing for men not willing to accept sterilization after two children. When even this program proved unequal to the task of getting the birthrate down to a level of 25 per 1,000, the government turned to outright coercion. At a rate of a million a month, men were herded into sterilization clinics.

It soon became apparent, though, that the Gandhi policy had gone too far. After a period of nationwide political disruption, Gandhi was swept out of office by India's voters, who feared and detested the birth control program. Under the new government, birth control efforts collapsed, and the birthrate began to creep up again. It has already risen to 35 per 1,000 from its low of 33 in 1977 and is likely to reach 40 soon unless the government takes strong action—something that is now almost impossible politically.

Indonesia. Meanwhile, on the Indonesian island of Bali, a population program is achieving heartening success. In the tiny village of Banjar Kangin, for example, 218 of the village's 243 fertile couples are practicing some form of birth control. At monthly town meetings, each man is asked what he has done about birth control that month—and then the next month's supply of condoms and pills is handed out.

Why the contrast? Several things appear to contribute to it. For one thing, the Hindus of Banjar Kangin have much more open and permissive attitudes toward sex than do the Moslem Pakistanis. (But even Moslem areas of Indonesia do better than Pakistan.) For another, the administrative structure of the village is much stronger. But perhaps most important of all is that the village economic structure is such that children are perceived as liabilities, not assets. Even with these successes, though, Indonesia's population is expected to soar from 132 million in 1978 to 215 million in 2000.

Source: The descriptions of the programs in Pakistan and Indonesia are based on Bill Peterson, ''Battling the Birth Boom—Small Wins, Big Failures,'' *Washington Post,* May 19, 1978, p. A-1. India's story is based in part on Barry Kramer, ''The Politics of Birth Control,'' *Wall Street Journal,* May 8, 1978, and in part on William Borders, ''Birth Control Slows in India,'' *New York Times,* February 6, 1978, p. A-2.

FOOD AND DEVELOPMENT[3]

Hunger

The aspect of economic development that causes the greatest concern of all is the problem of hunger. Hunger comes in varying degrees. People are said to be undernourished if they suffer from a quantitative lack of calories. They are said to suffer from malnutrition if the food they do get contains insufficient protein and other nutrients, even if energy requirements are met. Undernourishment leads to actual starvation. In recent years it has been a major problem in the countries just south of the Sahara in Africa; in India, Bangladesh, and Sri Lanka in Asia; and in Bolivia, Haiti, and El Salvador in the Americas, to list only a few. Malnutrition is much more widespread and has long-run effects that are hardly less devastating. A protein insufficiency in the diets of young children and breast-feeding women is especially dangerous, because it retards brain development. People who survive a malnourished childhood are likely to suffer from lethargy and lack of productive ability in later life. These are hardly the traits required for the labor forces of poor countries struggling to achieve development.

Accurate statistics on world hunger are hard to come by. Definitions vary, and the governments of some of the worst-hit countries are reluctant to supply information. Some who have studied the problem believe that as many as

[3]This section draws on many points in the useful survey, *World of Hunger,* by Jonathan Power and Anne-Marie Holenstein (London: Temple Smith, 1976). Used by permission.

two-thirds of the world's population may suffer from undernourishment or malnutrition in some form. The data in Exhibit 21.7 are based on much more conservative methods of estimation, but they still show an appallingly serious problem.

Hunger and Population

The relationship between hunger and population is complex. It is natural to think of overpopulation causing hunger, with a Malthusian growth of numbers of people outstripping food production. Hunger can be a spur to population growth, too, however. Malnutrition leads to high infant mortality. High infant mortality in turn leads to the desire to have a large family, so that at least some children will survive. Perhaps the relationship between malnutrition and desired family size is part of the reason why birthrates have fallen earliest in those countries that have distributed the benefits of development widely among their populations.

When the world food problem is presented as a race between production and growth of demand, the results are sobering. Information presented at the World Food Conference in 1974 placed seventy-one less developed countries in three groups according to food and population trends during the period 1953–1971. In twenty-four of these countries, the rate of increase in food production fell short of population growth. In an additional seventeen, the rate of increase of food production exceeded the rate of population growth but fell short of the growth rate of domestic demand. Because rising incomes permitted people to eat more, these countries had to increase food imports (or decrease food exports), thereby making things harder yet for the countries in the first group. In the thirty remaining countries, the growth rate of food output exceeded the growth rate of demand, but even some of these countries

Exhibit 21.7

Estimated numbers of people with insufficient protein/energy supply, by regions, 1970

According to the relatively conservative estimates reported in this table, some 388 million people had less than minimum standards of nutrition in 1970. Some observers think that nearly two-thirds of the world's population may suffer from malnutrition to some extent.

Region	Population (billions)	Percentage below Lower Limit	Number below Lower Limit (millions)
Developed regions	1.07	3	28
Developing regions (excluding Asian centrally planned economies)	1.75	20	360
Latin America	0.28	13	37
Far East	1.02	22	221
Near East	0.17	20	34
Africa	0.28	25	68
World (excluding Asian centrally planned economies)	2.83	14	388

Source: Jonathan Power and Anne-Marie Holenstein, *World of Hunger* (London: Temple Smith, 1976). Reprinted by permission.

experienced regional problems because of maldistribution within their borders.[4]

What can be done about the world food problem? The remainder of this section will examine some possible approaches.

Food Aid

In 1954, the U.S. Congress passed the Agricultural Trade Development and Assistance Act, commonly known as PL480. This act has been the heart of world food aid efforts. During the 1960s, the United States gave up to 84 percent of all world food aid. The less developed countries were able to rely on food aid for 30 to 45 percent of their food imports.

Under Title 1 of PL480, food was sold on favorable terms to governments. Under Title 2, food went free to governments and to the United Nations World Food Program. Title 2 food aid was aimed at the especially underprivileged and at disaster relief. At the same time the populations of less developed countries were benefiting from PL480, U.S. farmers were also benefiting. The program was thus a combination of idealism and self-interest, but the combination for a long time seemed to work well.

Despite the very substantial benefits to countries receiving food aid, PL480 and the food aid programs of other governments have had their critics. It is important to realize why food aid alone is not likely to provide a long-run answer to the world food problem.

First of all, U.S. food aid is a somewhat uncomfortable mixture of charity and self-interest. As such, it is liable to disruption from the self-interest side. In periods when U.S. farmers produce large grain surpluses, voters and consumers are happy to see the surpluses given away. In the early 1970s, however, a combination of circumstances caused U.S. food surpluses suddenly to disappear. This put upward pressure on domestic food prices, and exports began to meet opposition from consumer groups. By 1974, the amount of food delivered under aid programs fell to a third of its 1972 level. PL480 thus proved least reliable just when it was needed most.

There is a second serious problem in the tendency of some receiver governments to rely on food aid as a substitute for domestic agricultural development. In some cases, the motivation has been political. Necessary agricultural reforms would have threatened the privileges of entrenched ruling classes, so U.S. aid seemed like an easy way out. In other cases, food aid has disrupted domestic markets. It has, for example, kept prices low in the less developed countries; this is fine for the landless poor, but it greatly reduces incentives to farmers. Sometimes, the effect of food aid on relative prices has made the growth of nonfood cash crops more attractive than food crops.

Finally, some critics of food aid are unhappy about the standards by which recipients have been selected. Food aid recipients have often been chosen more with political than with nutritional considerations in mind. As a result, say the critics, too small a portion of total food aid has gone to the countries where hunger and malnutrition are the most serious.

---

[4]Preliminary Assessment of the World Food Situation, World Food Conference, 1974, UNIE/Conf. 65/Prep./6. Data also presented as Table 7 in Power and Holenstein, *World of Hunger*, pp. 41–43.

Need for Rural Development

Throughout the world, less developed countries are urbanizing rapidly—far more rapidly than today's developed countries did at comparable stages of their own growth. The reasons for this urbanization are complex. Partly the modernity and the promise of a better life in the city attract people. Partly the problem is education systems that do not emphasize agricultural topics. Whatever the causes, cities are not able to meet the aspirations of all those who arrive in them. Urban unemployment rates are very high. Many people who are employed work in tertiary services—from shining shoes to hustling—that contribute little to economic development or to the development of the individuals. Huge shantytowns surrounding third world cities are the rule rather than the exception.

Current rates of urbanization far exceed the potential for industrial development in most poor countries. One study calculated that, just to keep urban unemployment from rising in a typical less developed country, industrial output would have to grow at 18 percent per year.[5] Even in Brazil, which has had outstanding success with industrialization and urban development, industrial growth has run at only 15 percent per year. To get rid of the 20 to 25 percent unemployment common in cities of less developed countries, industry would have to grow at something like 30 to 35 percent per year for a decade.

When urban unemployment and the food problem are considered together, it is not surprising that many development economists believe that the real hope for the less developed countries lies in the countryside. The hope is to hold people on the land and to make them productive there within a meaningful community structure. If the third world nations can do that, they may be able to feed themselves, distribute what little they have more equitably, meet the nonmaterial aspirations of their populations, and retain their independence. That, at least, is what the advocates of rural development say. They all recognize that there are problems, though.

Technological Problems Rural development does not mean just the introduction of new agricultural methods. It also means the growth of small-scale industry in villages and towns, which is necessary to meet local needs and provide employment for those whom even the most ambitious land reform program would leave landless. Is the technological basis for such development available?

In some respects, technological progress has been remarkable. The most talked-about development is the appearance of new, high-yield varieties of wheat and rice. Under laboratory conditions, these new varieties can triple food output per acre. They provide the best hope for less developed countries to escape from the sheer shortage of land.

Unfortunately, high-yield wheat, rice, and other grains cannot just be stuck in the ground and expected to do their magic. The secret of their success lies in their ability to absorb huge quantities of fertilizer. If ordinary varieties of grain are overfertilized, they produce only luxuriant growth of stems and leaves or

---

[5] David Turnham, *The Employment Problem in Less Developed Countries* (Paris: Organization for Economic Cooperation and Development, 1971), as cited by Power and Holenstein, *World of Hunger*, pp. 74–75.

**William Arthur Lewis
(1915–   )**

**Theodore W. Schultz
(1902–   )**

In October 1979, the Royal Swedish Academy awarded the Nobel Memorial Prize in Economic Science jointly to two men noted for their work in the economics of development. The two—Sir William Arthur Lewis, professor of economics at Princeton University, and Theodore Schultz, professor of economics at the University of Chicago—had never worked together directly. Their writings, however, shared a common theme: the importance of the agricultural sector in the development process, and the hazards of a development strategy overemphasizing industrialization.

Lewis was born on the island of St. Lucia in the British West Indies. He was educated in London and lectured at the University of London from 1938 to 1948. Before coming to Princeton in 1963, he served for several years as vice-chancellor of the University of the West Indies and was knighted by Queen Elizabeth for this work. The author of a number of books on development and development planning, he is best known for *The Theory of Economic Growth,* published in 1955. Lewis has served as an adviser to the governments of many developing nations, to the British government, and to the United Nations. It was this practical experience in particular that led him to recognize the central importance of agriculture in the economies of the less developed countries.

Theodore Schultz grew up on a farm in South Dakota in a community of German settlers. In 1930, he received a Ph.D. from the University of Wisconsin; in that same year, he joined the faculty at Iowa State College. During the 1930s and 1940s, Schultz worked to make agricultural economics a branch of general economics that would benefit from advances in other parts of the discipline. The numerous New Deal farm programs of the period provided many opportunities for research, and he published a series of books on U.S. agricultural policy. At the same time, he developed an interest in the process of economic growth—in particular, the contribution of investment in human capital to growth and development. This line of research led eventually to the publication, in 1964, of his book *Transforming Traditional Agriculture.* In this book, he argued that traditional farmers were efficient in the use of whatever resources they had available and would quickly adopt new methods of production when given the chance to do so. The popularity among third-world farmers of the new, high-yield crop varieties stands as a case in point.

Both men continue to be active scholars and advocates of their common point of view. The Nobel award will no doubt act as a further spur to their work in the economics of agricultural development.

seedheads so heavy that they break the stalk of the plant. With high-yield varieties, extra fertilization produces growth where it is needed. Without such fertilization, the new varieties actually produce less than traditional crops. (In many cases, heavy use of pesticides and irrigation is needed as well.)

As the use of high-yield varieties has spread, less developed countries have become more dependent on imported fertilizers. They now produce barely half their own fertilizer needs. What is worse, fertilizer production depends critically on oil. This is particularly true of nitrogen fertilizers, which make up half the total used. These are made almost entirely from natural gas and petroleum products. The "green revolution" has been extremely hard hit by high oil prices, because outside the Middle East, few less developed countries have their own oil supplies.

Rural industrial development faces technological problems that are, if anything, greater than those faced by agricultural development. Western industrial research has developed technology designed to use cheap capital and save expensive labor. The opposite conditions prevail in rural areas of the third world. Too little research has gone into the development of simple but sophisticated labor-intensive ways of doing things.

Institutional Problems A number of institutional problems also threaten rural development. Chief among them are the problem of land reform and the problem of supplying credit to rural areas.

Advocates of rural development support land reform, which involves buying (or sometimes confiscating) the large holdings of absentee landlords and distributing the land in the smallest feasible parcels among those who actually till the soil. The effects of land reform, if it works, are threefold. First, a small landowner has a greater incentive than a tenant farmer to improve the land and introduce better production techniques. Second, wide distribution of ownership means wide distribution of the product, with all the benefits this is believed to bring. Third, land reform can lead to more stable rural community structures, which help stop the rush to the city. They also help provide the dignity and sense of personal worth that are part of the process of depauperization.

Many countries have carried out thorough land reforms, but many others have not. Two problems hold back further land reform. One major problem is political. The land-owning classes often dominate the political structures of less developed countries and are reluctant to relinquish their hold. The second problem is economic. Under some circumstances, technological considerations may make it more productive to consolidate land holdings into bigger farms to realize economies of scale. To some extent, land reform can involve a trade-off between growth and depauperization.

The other major institutional weakness that holds back small-scale rural development is a weakness of credit markets. In many less developed countries, small farmers have no access to banks and other modern credit facilities. They must rely on local money lenders or merchants, who charge extremely high interest rates.

High-yield crops have made the credit problem more serious than ever. The green revolution can actually work against the small farmer. Higher yields drive land rents up and put downward pressure on output prices. The new varieties cannot be used without expensive fertilizers and pesticides, but buying these goods puts the small farmer more at the mercy of the money lender. Thus, if land reform is carried out without credit reform, it can in fact retard the introduction of new techniques.

CONCLUSIONS

The tone of much of this chapter has been pessimistic. There is no doubt that the problems of the less developed countries will be very difficult to surmount and that some countries will fail. There is every doubt of the ability and the will of the industrialized countries to carry the burden of development. Nonetheless, there are places where things are going right rather than wrong. It is fitting to end this chapter with one of these success stories.

Case 21.2
Daniel Benor's Agricultural Revolution

In India, Turkey, Thailand, Nepal, Sri Lanka, and Indonesia, Daniel Benor, a slender, balding Israeli, is producing a remarkable agricultural revolution. His revolution, sponsored by the World Bank, is quite different from the highly technological green revolution that has been so widely publicized. And it works. Small farmers are doubling and tripling their crop yields wherever the system is tried.

Benor's program is deceptively simple. It is based on what he calls the "T&V" (training and visitation) system of passing information from top experts to farmers in the field. The key link in the system consists of a network of village level extension workers whose responsibility it is to pass carefully limited and digestible doses of information along to a limited group of farmers. The extension worker visits each assigned village on a regular schedule, each week to two weeks. The emphasis is on such labor-intensive basics as proper spacing, weeding, and the use of the most promising seeds.

Even more importantly, in some cases, the program guards against misuse of the green revolution technologies. Take insecticides, for example. In the Gujarat area of India, cotton is the principal crop. The hybrid variety most widely grown responds well to good fertilization and care, but it is vulnerable to insect pests. The farmers' instinctive reaction was to spray heavily with insecticides. They sprayed so heavily, in fact, that they not only increased costs but upset the entire regional ecology. The pest problem actually got worse, not better.

Benor's solution to this problem was to put his T&V system to work teaching farmers when *not* to spray. He trained special "scouts," armed with magnifying glasses, to count the number of pests per plant. The fields would be sprayed only when a threshold—say twenty pests per plant—was reached. As soon as the number started to decline, spraying stopped. Using this simple approach, one agricultural cooperative of two hundred members increased its profits by a third in a single year. Elsewhere, the same principle is applied to prevent overfertilization.

Benor has become a hero to Asian farmers. Traditional development specialists were skeptical of his method at first, but it has now been so widely validated that they too are convinced of its effectiveness. World Bank President Robert S. McNamara, once a skeptic, is now one of Benor's biggest boosters. Countries all over the world are now eager to try the T&V system in the hope that as agricultural yields rise, the race between population and food may one day be won by food.

Source: Based on Hobart Rowen, "Poorest of Poor's Crop Yield Soars," *Washington Post*, November 12, 1978, p. K-1. © 1978 The Washington Post. Used by permission.

SUMMARY

1. Economic development is a complex phenomenon, a major part of which is sheer economic growth—increasing the size of GNP as a whole. Development also means industrialization. In countries that have already developed, industry has grown more rapidly than agriculture. In extreme cases, such as that of the Soviet Union, the agricultural sector has actually been stripped of resources to aid the more rapid growth of industry. A third aspect of economic development is depauperization—not only growing but distributing the benefits of growth to the poorest classes. An industry-first growth strategy may hamper depauperization.

2. A population grows whenever its crude birthrate exceeds its crude death rate. In a finite environment, living populations cannot grow indefinitely. If the birthrate does not fall to the death rate, overcrowding will force the death rate up to the birthrate. Population growth in developed countries has undergone a process known as the demographic transition. In preindustrial society, both birth and death rates were high. As industrialization began, death rates fell and a period of rapid population growth began. Economic growth was even more rapid than population growth, however, so per capita incomes rose. This brought birthrates down and reduced the rate of population growth.

3. Virtually all less developed countries face serious population pressures. Modern death control techniques have been introduced to all corners of the globe, no matter how poor. Where birthrates are still high, population growth rates are more rapid than they ever were during the demographic transition in developed countries. If the growth rate of GNP does not keep up with the growth of population, a country may be caught in a population trap. In order to complete the demographic transition successfully, many countries will have to find a way of lowering birthrates while per capita incomes are still at a very low level.

4. Some observers believe that as many as two-thirds of the world's people suffer from undernourishment or malnutrition in some form. In many developing countries, population growth is outstripping food production, thereby making the problem worse. In the past, food aid has been an important stopgap measure, but food aid alone is not the long-run solution. Rural development is needed if less developed countries are to be able to feed themselves. Technological advances, including high-yield grains, provide a potential basis for rural development. Economic and institutional problems remain, however. Some way must be found to provide the fertilizers, pesticides, and capital needed to make the best use of high-yield grains. Land reform and credit reform are also necessary parts of successful rural development.

DISCUSSION QUESTIONS

1. In what ways are the problems faced by the less developed countries similar to the problems faced by the United States one hundred or two hundred years ago? In what ways are they different? Will today's less developed countries follow a similar path to economic development, or is a different route more promising? Explain.

2. In early phases of industrialization, urbanization seems to be a major factor in bringing birthrates down. Today, birthrates are still falling in the United States, even though the degree of urbanization is no longer changing rapidly. What other factors do you think are at work causing the continued decline in birthrates?

3. Less developed countries are short on capital. Foreign firms are often willing to invest in such countries. Is foreign investment a good way for the countries to solve their capital shortage? What are the advantages and disadvantages to the countries of such foreign investment?

4. Less developed countries tend to have less equally distributed incomes than do developed countries. Why do you think this is so? Why does development sometimes increase rather than reduce inequality?

5. Do you see any similarity between the dual economy of some less developed countries and the dual labor market that some economists believe exists in the United States?

6. People in the United States eat huge quantities of meat. Each pound of meat requires up to ten pounds of grain to produce. It is sometimes said that the world food problem could be solved in part simply by people eating less meat. Suppose that this advice were taken to heart, and meat consumption in the United States were cut in half, with more bread eaten instead. Would the grain thus saved ever actually reach the hungry poor in the developing countries? If so, explain how shifts in market prices and changes in supply and demand conditions would operate to get it there. If not, explain why the market would fail to move the grain in the desired direction.

7. It is sometimes said that it is pointless to give money to developing countries to buy food, because this money will just end up lining the pockets of Kansas farmers without doing the less developed countries themselves any real good. Is this concern wholly justified, partly justified, or wholly unjustified? Why?

SUGGESTIONS FOR FURTHER READING

Bogue, Donald J., and Ong Tsui, Amy. "Zero World Population Growth." *Public Interest*, no. 55 (Spring 1979): 99–113.
A report on recent declines in fertility in many countries that are disproving some of the more pessimistic population forecasts made only a few years ago. The authors suggest that the "population bomb" may turn out to be a dud.

Ehrlich, Paul, and Ehrlich, Ann. *Population, Resources, and Environment.* 2d ed. San Francisco: W. H. Freeman, 1972.
A good introduction to population arithmetic, the debate over optimal population size, and population control techniques.

Johnson, D. Gale. *World Food Problems and Prospects.* Washington, D.C.: American Enterprise Institute, 1975.
A survey of the world food outlook from the perspective of 1975.

Meier, Gerald M., ed. *Leading Issues in Economic Development.* 3rd ed. New York: Oxford University Press, 1976.
A good introduction to the field of development economics.

PART FIVE
THE WORLD ECONOMY

C H A P T E R 22

INTERNATIONAL TRADE AND COMPARATIVE ADVANTAGE

WHAT YOU WILL LEARN IN THIS CHAPTER

This chapter introduces some important microeconomic principles of international trade. It shows how worldwide efficiency and productivity can be enhanced when every country specializes in producing and exporting the goods that it can produce at lower opportunity cost than its trading partners. At the same time, it explains why not every individual in every country will necessarily gain from international trade, even though, on the average, consumers in all countries will gain. The possibility that some consumers or workers may be harmed by changes in patterns of international trade lies at the root of most political controversies over trade policy.

FOR REVIEW

Here are some important terms and concepts that will be put to use in this chapter. If you do not understand them, review them before proceeding.
- *Opportunity cost (Chapter 1)*
- *Distributive justice (Chapter 1)*
- *Monopoly (Chapter 9)*
- *Monopsony (Chapter 15)*

Up to this point, economics has been studied solely within the context of a single national economy. A whole area of economic theory—the theory of international trade—has received hardly a mention.

The first question to be asked about this area of economics is why a separate theory of international trade is necessary. Does it really make that much difference that buyers and sellers in certain markets live on opposite sides of national boundaries? The answer is that the differences between international and national markets are small enough that most of the familiar tools of analysis apply to both; yet there are enough differences to require that the tools be applied in new ways and to new problems. A separate body of theory is therefore justified.

From a microeconomic point of view, the distinguishing feature of international markets is that finished products tend to move more easily in them than do factors of production. Land, with its natural resource deposits and associated climate factors, is the most immobile of factors. Labor also tends to be fairly immobile because of cultural, political, and linguistic barriers. Capital tends to be the most internationally mobile factor of production, but even it does not move as unrestrictedly between countries as within.

Factor immobility matters because it causes persistent differences in relative and absolute costs of production among nations. With factors immobile, goods that make intense use of labor tend to be cheaper in countries where labor is relatively abundant, agricultural commodities tend to be cheaper in countries with good climates, and so on. Were factors more mobile, countries with high labor costs would hire more foreign workers until their costs for labor-intensive products had fallen. Countries with bad growing conditions would import soil and sunlight to equalize the costs of agricultural production. In general, internation differences in production costs would be minimized.

From a macroeconomic point of view, the main point distinguishing international from national economics is the fact that different countries have different currencies, which fluctuate in value relative to one another. Different currencies make it possible for countries to pursue independent macroeconomic policies. This can mean inflation in one country and deflation across its border, differences in economic growth rates, and a variety of other things. When it comes to studying problems of international currency markets and the balance of payments, these differences become crucial.

This chapter will discuss the microeconomic aspects of international trade. Then, Chapter 23 will turn to the macro view of international economics.

THE THEORY OF COMPARATIVE ADVANTAGE

The study of international trade from a microeconomic point of view must begin with the theory of comparative advantage. In a sense, international trade theory starts here historically as well as logically. The theory of comparative advantage was first clearly set forth by David Ricardo early in the nineteenth century. Ricardo wanted to show why it would be to England's advantage to maintain active trade with other countries. To do so, he used an example very much like the following.

An Example

Imagine two countries called (for the sake of the example) Norway and Spain. Both have farms and offshore fishing beds, but the moderate climate of Spain makes both the farms and the fishing beds more productive. The number of labor hours required to produce a ton of each product in the two countries is shown in Exhibit 22.1. For simplicity, only labor costs are considered in this example. Other costs can be thought of as proportional to labor costs. Also, per unit labor costs are assumed to be constant for all levels of output.

Exhibit 22.1 reveals two kinds of differences in the cost structure of the two countries. First, both fish and grain require fewer labor hours to produce in Spain. Spain is thus said to have an **absolute advantage** in the production of both goods.

Absolute advantage In international trade theory, the ability of a country to produce a good at lower cost, measured in terms of factor inputs, than its trading partners'.

	Spain	Norway
Fish	4	5
Grain	2	5

Exhibit 22.1
Labor hours per ton of output in Spain and Norway
The figures in this table show the number of labor hours required to produce each ton of fish and grain in Spain and Norway. Spain has an absolute advantage in the production of both goods. Norway has a comparative advantage in fish, and Spain has a comparative advantage in grain.

David Ricardo, the greatest of the classical economists, was born in 1772. His father, a Jewish immigrant, was a member of the London stock exchange. Ricardo's education was rather haphazard, and he entered his father's business at the age of fourteen. In 1793, he married, abandoned strict Jewish orthodoxy, and went into business on his own. These were years of war and financial disturbance. The young Ricardo developed a reputation for remarkable astuteness and quickly made a large fortune.

David Ricardo (1772–1823)

In 1799, Ricardo read *The Wealth of Nations* and developed an interest in questions of political economy. In 1809, his first writings on economics appeared. They were a series of newspaper articles on "The High Price of Bullion," which appeared the next year as an influential pamphlet. Several other short works added to his reputation in this area. In 1814, he retired from business to devote all his time to political economy.

Ricardo's major work is *Principles of Political Economy and Taxation,* first published in 1817. This work contains, among other things, a pioneering statement of the principle of comparative advantage as applied to international trade. With a lucid numerical example, Ricardo shows why it is to the mutual advantage of both countries for England to export wool to Portugal and to import wine in return, even though both products can be produced at absolutely lower costs in Portugal.

But international trade is only a sidelight of Ricardo's *Principles.* The book covers the whole of economics as then known, beginning with value theory and progressing to a theory of economic growth and evolution. Ricardo, like his friend Malthus and his later follower John Stuart Mill, held that the economy was growing toward a future "steady state." In this state, economic growth would come to a halt, and the wage rate would be depressed to the subsistence level.

Ricardo's book was extraordinarily influential. For more than half a century thereafter, much of economics as written in England was an elaboration of or commentary on Ricardo's work. The most famous of all economists to fall under the influence of Ricardo's theory and method was Karl Marx. Although Marx eventually reached revolutionary conclusions that differed radically from any views Ricardo held, his starting point was Ricardo's labor theory of value and method of analyzing economic growth.

Second, there are differences in the opportunity costs between the two countries. Consider the cost of each good in each country not in terms of labor hours but in terms of the other good. In Norway, producing a ton of fish means forgoing the opportunity to use five labor hours in the fields. A ton of fish thus has an opportunity cost of one ton of grain there. In Spain, producing a ton of fish means giving up the opportunity to produce two tons of grain. In terms of opportunity costs, then, fish is cheaper in Norway than in Spain, and grain is cheaper in Spain than in Norway. The country in which the opportunity cost of a good is lower is said to have a **comparative advantage** in producing that good.

Comparative advantage In international trade theory, the ability of a country to produce a good at a lower opportunity cost, in terms of other goods, than its trading partners'.

Pretrade Equilibrium If no trade takes place between Norway and Spain, equilibrium in fish and grain markets in the two countries will be established independently. This example has simplified things by ignoring all costs but labor costs and by assuming these costs to be constant. In pretrade equilibrium, the ratio of the price of fish to the price of grain in each country will thus be equal to the ratio of labor inputs needed to produce the goods. In Norway, where a ton of grain and a ton of fish both take the same labor to produce, the price of fish will be equal to the price of grain. In Spain, where a ton of fish takes twice as much labor to produce as a ton of grain, the equilibrium price of fish will be twice the price of grain.

Suppose that each country has 1,000 labor hours available for the production of fish and grain. The way these labor hours are divided between the two products in each country depends on demand and consumer tastes. Suppose that demand conditions are such that in Norway 100 tons of grain and 100 tons of fish are produced, while in Spain 350 tons of grain are grown and 75 tons of fish are caught. The quantities produced and consumed in pretrade equilibrium are noted in Exhibit 22.2.

The Possibility of Trade The stage is now set to consider the possibilities for trade between Norway and Spain. A superficial look at labor costs in the two countries might suggest that there were no possibilities for trade. Norwegians might like to get their hands on some of those cheap Spanish goods, but why should the Spanish be interested? After all, couldn't they produce everything at home more cheaply than it could be produced abroad? If so, how could they gain from trade? But a closer analysis shows that this superficial view is incorrect. Absolute advantage turns out to be unimportant in determining patterns of trade. Only comparative advantage matters.

To see that possibilities for trade between the two countries do exist, imagine that an enterprising Norwegian fishing party decides to sail into a Spanish port with a ton of its catch. Spanish merchants in the port will have been used to giving 2 tons of grain, or its equivalent, for a ton of fish. The Norwegians will have been accustomed to getting only 1 ton of grain for each ton of fish. Any exchange ratio between 1 and 2 tons of grain per ton of fish will seem more than normally attractive to both parties. For instance, a trade of 1.5 tons of grain for a ton of fish will make both the Spanish merchants and the Norwegian fishing party better off than they would have been had they traded only with others from their own country.

Gains from Specialization The opening of trade between Spain and Norway will soon begin to have an effect on patterns of production in the two countries. In Norway, farmers will discover that instead of working five hours to raise a ton of grain from their own rocky soil, they can fish for five hours instead and trade their catch to the Spaniards for 1.5 tons of grain. In Spain, people will find it is no longer worth their while to spend four hours to catch a ton of fish. Instead, they can work just three hours in the fields. The 1.5 tons of grain that they grow will get them a ton of fish from the Norwegians. In short, the Norwegians will find it worth their while to specialize in fish, and the Spanish will find it worth their while to specialize in grain.

Suppose now that trade continues at the rate of 1.5 tons of grain per ton of

	Spain	Norway	World Total
Fish	75	100	175
Grain	350	100	450

Exhibit 22.2
Pretrade equilibrium outputs of fish and grain in Spain and Norway
If Spain and Norway do not engage in trade, each country will have to meet all its needs from its own resources. The quantities of goods each produces will depend on the strength of domestic demand. The relative prices of the two goods in each country will be determined by their labor costs, as shown in Exhibit 22.1.

Exhibit 22.3
Posttrade production and consumption of fish and grain in Spain and Norway
This table assumes that Spain and Norway have traded fish for grain at the rate of 1.5 tons of grain per ton of fish. Both countries have become entirely specialized. When this table is compared with the table in Exhibit 22.2, it is clear that consumers in both countries have the same amount of the product they export and more of the product they import than they did in the absence of trade. Also, total world production of fish has risen from 175 to 200 tons, and total world production of grain has risen from 450 to 500 tons.

		Spain	Norway	World Total
Fish	Production	0	200	200
	Consumption	100	100	200
Grain	Production	500	0	500
	Consumption	350	150	500

fish until both countries have become completely specialized. Spain no longer produces any fish, and Norway no longer produces any grain. Norwegians catch 200 tons of fish, half of which is exported to Spain. The Spanish grow 500 tons of grain, 150 tons of which are exported to Norway. Exhibit 22.3 summarizes this posttrade situation.

A comparison of this table with Exhibit 22.2 reveals three noteworthy things. First, Norwegians are better off than before; they have just as much fish to eat and 50 tons more grain than in the pretrade equilibrium. Second, Spaniards are also better off; they have just as much grain to consume as ever—and more fish. Finally, total world output of both grain and fish has risen as a result of trade. Everyone is better off, and no one is worse off.

Generalized Mutual Advantage The principle of mutual advantage from international trade is perfectly general. It applies to any situation where one country has a comparative advantage over another in producing some good. Wherever there is a comparative advantage, international specialization can increase both consumption in each trading country and world output as a whole.

A complete analysis of international trade would add many details. It would have to allow for cases in which only one country or neither country became fully specialized and for cases in which the constant cost assumption did not hold. No part of the more detailed theory, however, would undermine the basic conclusion: International trade and specialization promote world economic efficiency and generate mutual advantages to all trading nations.

PROTECTIONISM AND TRADE POLICY

Free Trade Challenged

There is a strong theoretical case that free international trade promotes world efficiency and consumer welfare. Nonetheless, many nations pursue policies that actively thwart such trade. Policies that interfere with international trade are referred to by the general term **protectionism.** The most common protectionist policies are the imposition of **tariffs,** which are taxes levied on imported goods, and **import quotas,** which are limitations on quantities imported. The U.S. government imposes tariffs and quotas on a number of goods.

Protectionism Policies of shielding domestic industry from foreign competition.

Tariff A tax levied on imported goods.

Import quota A limitation on the quantity of a good that can be imported in a given time period.

The sections that follow will look at some of the more commonly heard arguments in favor of protectionism. Some of them are altogether false. Others are partly valid in terms of positive economics. Still others focus primarily on normative considerations.

Cheap Foreign Labor One common argument against free trade sees a threat in imports from countries where wages are lower than in the country being considered. At the same time, though, workers in the low-wage countries fear competition from the country that is backed by heavy capital investment. If one argument were true, both ought to be. If both were true, then trade must be making everyone worse off.

Fortunately, both arguments are false. It is exactly such differences in factor supplies and comparative costs that create opportunities for mutual advantage. The fallacious cheap foreign labor argument implies that trade is best conducted with countries differing as little as possible from one's own. The theory of comparative advantage suggests, in contrast, that trade with such countries is likely to offer the least benefit. There is sometimes (but not always) an element of truth in the cheap foreign labor argument if it is applied to specific groups of workers, as will be shown below. But applied to average standards of living, as it often is, it is false.

Infant Industries The famous infant industry argument is a second weapon in the protectionist arsenal. It runs like this: Suppose a certain country has a comparative disadvantage in the production of automobiles but wishes to establish a domestic auto industry. To do so, it prohibits imports. This permits the domestic auto industry to expand and mature. Production costs fall, and efficiency increases. Eventually, the country achieves a true comparative advantage in cars. At that time, consumers will recoup the losses they suffered while the industry was growing up.

This sequence of events is not, in fact, wholly impossible. Nonetheless, it does not justify protection. If the present value of future gains to consumers more than offsets near-term losses, the auto industry ought to be able to grow without protection. It can borrow money to cover short-term operating losses while it competes with cheap foreign auto makers. Eventually, when the industry matures and gains its comparative advantage, it can pay off the loans and have some money left over. No special protection is needed to ensure the emergence of a domestic auto industry.

Suppose, though, that such borrowing will not be profitable for the auto industry. That, then, will be a sign that the future gains are so small or so distant that they do not offset current losses. In that case, to protect the industry is to promote misallocation of resources over time. Sometimes it is suggested that imperfections in the credit market may make it difficult for an infant industry to borrow the funds it needs to finance expansion. But if true, this at most creates a case for government sponsored loans to the infant industry. It still does not constitute a case for tariffs.

Terms of Trade A third well-known protectionist theory is the terms-of-trade argument, which has some respectable basis in positive economics. The argument applies to a country that exercises monopoly or monopsony power in the international market. For example, suppose that the United States is the world's largest exporter of wheat and the largest importer of textiles. Restricting wheat exports and textile imports drives the world market price of wheat up and the world market price of textiles down. If the price movement is great enough, the improved terms of trade more than compensate for the decrease in the volume of trade.

The terms-of-trade argument is valid (at least as a possibility) as it stands. Two things should be noted about it, however. First, it does not quite challenge the doctrine of comparative advantage head-on. What it really says is that by clever market manipulation, a country may be able to get a larger share of the gains from trade than it would if international markets operated unrestrictedly. Second, it cannot be applied to both sides of a market at once. If all countries try to play the terms-of-trade game, all of them lose; and for one to play it openly invites mutually self-defeating retaliation.

Macroeconomics Another partially valid protectionist argument suggests that trade may not be beneficial in times of macroeconomic disequilibrium. The basic idea is this: When a country is experiencing widespread unemployment, cutting off imports in a key sector may increase domestic employment. This may prime the pump, putting the economy on the road to macroeconomic recovery at the expense of only small microeconomic losses. The best rejoinder to this argument is that there are more sophisticated tools of macroeconomic policy that can do the same job with less microeconomic damage.

International Trade with More than One Factor of Production

The discussion up to this point has been limited to an economy in which there is only one factor of production—labor. Removing this assumption has some interesting implications. A modification of the earlier Spain-Norway example will illustrate some of them.

Assume from now on that fishing requires a relatively large capital investment per worker and farming a relatively small one. In the accepted terminology, fishing is said to be capital intensive and farming labor intensive. Assume, as before, that in the absence of trade, the opportunity cost of fish will be higher in Spain than in Norway. The theory of comparative advantage still applies, regardless of the number of factors of production under consideration. International trade will still make it possible for total world production of both fish and grain to increase. It will still enable the quantities of both goods available for consumption in both countries to increase. But now, a new question arises concerning the gains from trade. How will they be distributed within each country?

Internal Distribution To answer this question, one must look at what happens in factor markets as trade brings about increasing specialization in each country. In Norway, production shifts from farming to fishing. As grain production is phased out, large quantities of labor and relatively small quantities of capital are released. The shift in production thus creates a surplus of labor and a shortage of capital. Factor markets can return to equilibrium only when wages fall relative to the rate of return on capital. Only then will fisheries adopt relatively more labor-intensive methods of production. Meanwhile, in Spain, an opposite process occurs. The shift from fishing to farming depresses the rate of return on capital and increases the wage rate. This causes Spanish farmers to use more capital per worker than before.

These changes in relative factor prices determine how the gains from trade are distributed among the people of each country. Spanish workers and Norwegian ship owners will gain doubly from trade. They will gain first because trade increases the size of the pie (the total available quantity of goods) and second because the factor price shifts give them a relatively larger slice of the larger pie. For Norwegian workers and Spanish farm owners, in contrast, one of these effects works against the other. They still benefit from the growth of the pie, but they get a relatively smaller piece of it than before. They may or may not end up better off on balance as a result of the trade.

Suppose that the comparative advantage in the pretrade situation were large and the difference in factor intensity between the two countries were small. Norwegian workers and Spanish farm owners would then still gain from trade in an absolute sense, even though they would lose ground relative to others in their own country. If conditions were not so favorable, however, they could end up absolutely worse off than before trade began.

The Importance of Mobility The preceding section considered only two broadly defined factors of production—labor and capital. What was said there applies even more forcefully to narrowly defined factors of production. If one thinks in terms not of labor in general but of farmers and fishermen and in terms not of capital in general but of boat owners and tractor owners, then it becomes even more likely that trade will have a strongly uneven impact on incomes. The more specialized and less mobile the factors of production are, the more relative factor prices will shift as a result of trade and the more likely it will be that some specific groups will be harmed by trade.

Take an example nearer to home than that of Norwegian farmers and Spanish fishers. Consider instead the effects on the U.S. economy of increased imports of Chinese textiles. The impact of increased textile imports can be divided into three parts. First, all consumers in the United States will benefit because textiles will be cheaper than before. Second, the Chinese will increase their purchases of U.S. goods. This will benefit workers in U.S. export oriented industries. Finally, U.S. textile workers and manufacturers will suffer a decreased demand for their products.

Those with relatively mobile skills or assets can escape most of the impact by moving to other industries. For example, a truck driver working for a textile firm can switch to hauling peaches, or a plant making shirt boxes can switch to making shoe boxes. Some workers, however, are less mobile because of their personal circumstances or the specialization of their skills. They are likely to suffer a loss of income that will more than offset the benefits they receive as consumers from cheaper textiles. Imagine, for example, a middle-aged highly specialized spinning machine operator who has all his savings tied up in a house in a small textile town. He will derive slim consolation from being able to buy a cheap Chinese raincoat to wear on his weekly visits to the unemployment office.

In aggregate terms, the loss to the group adversely affected is more than offset by the gains to others in the economy. But this fact is not likely to make much impression on unemployed textile workers. They will see free trade as a threat and will campaign for protection. The government will then have a hard political decision to make. Which group of interests should it look after? How much weight should it place on the widespread gains from trade and how much on the complaints of particular people who do not share in those gains? Is there any way to reconcile these conflicting interests?

Balancing Gains and Losses These are questions of normative economics. If the people who lose from free trade are more deserving than those who gain, then the principle of distributive justice may call for protection. Protection will not necessarily advance distributive justice, however. The immediate impact points in that direction, but a number of things must be taken into account before a balanced judgment can be made.

First, to protect textiles would benefit textile workers. Suppose that these workers were relatively low paid and had lower than average mobility. If the idea of distributive justice emphasized support for the incomes of low paid workers, the impact of a protectionist policy would be beneficial.

Second, the tariff or quota would also benefit the owners of other factors used in the textile industry. These owners would include stockholders, other investors, executives, and owners of real estate in textile communities. On the average, ownership of nonlabor resources tends to be concentrated in the hands of people with relatively high incomes. It is hard to say whether these other factor owners would gain more or less from protection than workers would. That could be discovered only by empirical study. But it is very likely that this part of the impact, considered separately, would tend to increase inequality.

Third, protecting textiles would hurt consumers at large by raising textile prices. Again, it is hard to be sure about the distributional impact without a detailed study of whether high or low income groups tend to spend the greater share of their incomes on textile products. A seat-of-the-pants guess is that the pinch of higher textile prices would be felt more keenly by low income groups.

Finally, even if it is determined that the benefits of protection are concentrated on groups meriting special consideration and adverse effects are concentrated on less meritorious groups, one difficulty remains. The dollar losses to those harmed by protection will be greater in aggregate than the benefits to those helped. Does the gain in equality, if any, more than offset the loss in efficiency? In short, protecting a certain industry may improve things from the point of view of distributive justice, but this result is far from certain.

Alternative Policies

Suppose, for the sake of argument, that the distributional impact of protecting textiles is positive. Suppose even that this favorable result outweighs the necessary loss in efficiency. Does this mean protectionism should be supported? Not yet. Before any definite conclusion can be reached, the policy of protection must be compared with any alternative policies that may have the same distributive effects. One such alternative may be to subsidize the retraining and relocation of textile workers who lose their jobs. Another may be simply to offer these workers cash compensation.

How do these alternatives rate? In terms of efficiency, they are not perfect, but probably they are better than tariffs or quotas. In terms of distributive justice, they seem to offer two advantages. One is that benefits are more precisely concentrated on the people who want to get them. The other is that the tax burden required to fund the alternative program is likely to be distributed more equitably than the burden of high textile prices would be.

CONCLUSIONS

The debate over the merits of free trade versus protectionism has gone on for centuries. Adam Smith himself—with his doctrine that a highly developed division of labor depends on the widest possible market—was one of the early advocates of free trade. Since his time, protectionism has never been widely popular in the economics profession. Among politicians and the general public, however, the pendulum has swung back and forth several times. There have been great eras of free trade alternating with severe tariff wars. At present, free traders appear to be somewhat on the defensive, as the following case study suggests.

Case 22.1
The Wall Street Journal Polls Protectionist Sentiment

In 1978, at a time when people in the United States were becoming increasingly concerned about the ability of U.S. goods to compete in world markets, the *Wall Street Journal* conducted a two-part survey of U.S. attitudes toward protectionism and free trade. In one part, a Washington based survey research firm contacted 209 randomly selected persons by telephone. In the second part, the *Wall Street Journal* staff selected a sixteen-member panel of people thought to have representative views for an intensive two-hour discussion.

The telephone survey revealed clear doubts about U.S. competitiveness: 56 percent of the respondents thought U.S. economic power was declining, while only 6 percent thought it was increasing; 46 percent thought the quality of foreign products was improving, while just 21 percent thought it was declining. (However, by a narrow margin of 34 to 28 percent, those polled thought the quality of U.S. goods was still superior.)

Faced with this perceived decline in competitiveness, respondents to the poll favored protectionist measures: 58 percent thought the government should take action to restrict the quantity of foreign-made products sold in the United States, while just 32 percent favored free trade. Asked specifically about tariffs, 64 percent favored increases, and only 26 percent did not.

The in-depth panel revealed some of what lay behind the differences in opinion. As might be expected, union members and officials tended to be protectionists. The president of a Steelworkers local undoubtedly spoke for many unionists when he said: "I think foreign trade is good, but we're going to have to keep it competitive and not let foreign products cost us jobs. It puts our people on welfare, which means you people who work in nonunion places will have to support my people. So I think the idea is maybe to tax the imports to make them competitive."

Among younger adults and professional people, however, free trade sentiment apparently tends to prevail. A foreign exchange dealer on the panel characterized protectionist measures as a "costly luxury." If certain industries could not compete, he saw no sense in supporting them artificially. People working in those industries should shift to other occupations. A further source of antiprotectionist feeling was concern over inflation. "As a consumer," one panelist said, "my first criterion in purchasing is quality and price, and I just won't allow myself to look at that label and see where it's made."

SUMMARY

1. A country is said to have a comparative advantage in the production of any good that it can produce at a lower opportunity cost than that of its trading partners. Trading nations can realize mutual benefits if each specializes in products for which it has a comparative advantage. Such specialization can give consumers in each country more of all goods than they would have without international trade.

2. Some arguments against free trade are based on considerations of positive economics. Of these, the cheap foreign labor and infant industry arguments have little merit. The terms of trade argument establishes that a country with monopoly or monopsony power in international markets can gain by imposing tariffs on imported goods—but only if its trading partners do not retaliate. Trade restrictions are sometimes used to combat domestic unemployment in periods of macroeconomic disturbance, but conventional tools of macro policy are likely to be better for such a purpose.

3. Other protectionist arguments emphasize normative considerations. In a world of multiple factors of production, many of which are highly specialized, certain groups of workers or capitalists can gain by the exclusion of foreign competition. However, their gains are more than offset in dollar terms by losses to some of their fellow citizens.

DISCUSSION QUESTIONS

1. Suppose you learned that Vladimir Horowitz, the great pianist, was also an amazingly proficient typist. Knowing this, would it surprise you to learn also that he hired a secretary to type his correspondence even though he could do the job better and faster himself? What does this have to do with comparative advantage?

2. Turn to Exhibit 22.1. Suppose that new, high-yield grains were introduced in Norway and that the number of labor hours needed to grow a ton of grain there were cut from 5 hours to 2.5 hours. What would happen to trade between Norway and Spain? Would it still pay for Norwegians to import their grain from Spain? If the labor hours per ton of grain in Norway fell all the way to 2, what would happen to the pattern of trade?

3. One of the people interviewed in the *Wall Street Journal* poll (see Case 22.1) made the following statement: "We may still be No. 1, but I don't think we will be much longer. The Common Market, Japan, Russia, all areas of the world are catching up. . . . It's no longer economical for us to produce anything." On the basis of what you have learned about the principle of comparative advantage, do you think it is really possible to reach a point in time when it is no longer economical to produce anything—that is, when it is economical to import everything?

4. Suppose you, a convinced advocate of free trade, became president of the United States. Would your policy be to cut off all U.S. tariffs and quotas at once, or would you bargain with your trading partners, saying that you would cut U.S. tariffs only if they cut their own tariffs? Why would a mutual reduction be better than a one-sided reduction?

5. Simple trade theory suggests that countries will export goods in which they have a comparative advantage and import goods in which they have a comparative disadvantage. In fact, countries often import the same kinds of goods they export. For example, most countries that are big exporters of automobiles are also big importers of automobiles. Why do you think that happens?

SUGGESTIONS FOR FURTHER READING

Ricardo, David. *Principles of Political Economy and Taxation*. London, 1817. (Available in a modern paperback edition from Pelican Books, 1971.)
Chapter 7, "On Foreign Trade," is generally credited with being the first clear exposition of the theory of comparative advantage.

Snider, Delbert A. *Introduction to International Economics*. 6th ed. Homewood, Ill.: Richard D. Irwin, 1975.
A useful basic text on international trade theory, covering in depth the topics treated in this chapter.

C H A P T E R 23

THE BALANCE OF PAYMENTS AND THE INTERNATIONAL MONETARY SYSTEM

WHAT YOU WILL LEARN IN THIS CHAPTER

This chapter introduces the world of international monetary economics. First, it explains how international transactions can be organized into simplified balance of payment accounts. Next, it shows how exchange rate movements can be interpreted in terms of supply and demand. Then, it discusses the major factors influencing supply and demand curves in foreign exchange markets in both the long run and short run. Finally, it examines problems of international monetary policy and evaluates the advantages and disadvantages of alternative sets of rules for the international monetary game.

FOR REVIEW

Here are some important terms and concepts that will be put to use in this chapter. If you do not understand them, review them before proceeding.
- *Elasticity of supply and demand (Chapter 3)*
- *Tariffs and quotas (Chapter 12)*

Of all the economic news that makes the headlines, that involving the balance of international payments is probably the least understood. Even well-informed people who have a basic understanding of what is going on and who read news reports of inflation and unemployment may have only the haziest idea of how the international monetary system works.

There was a time when this relative ignorance of international monetary affairs could be explained by the sheer strength and self-sufficiency of the U.S. economy. This was especially true during the first two decades following World War II, when the United States was less dependent on foreign trade than any of its major trading partners. The country consistently exported more than it imported, and its goods set standards for quality and technology in a broad range of world markets. Furthermore, the U.S. dollar was the undisputed world standard of value. But in recent years all this has been changing. During the 1970s, U.S. readers began being exposed to the same kind of economic news that had long been familiar to readers in other countries, and policy makers began struggling to find the right response to developments.

Consider, for example, the three-year period from 1976 through 1978. During that period, the U.S. balance of exports and imports swung from its traditional surplus position to a series of record breaking deficits. The U.S.

dollar lost 16 percent of its value against a weighted average of the currencies of trading partners—and lost much more than that in relation to certain key currencies. The West German mark, for example, gained more than a third in value, rising from $.38 in June 1976 to $.53 by September 1978. These events are detailed in Exhibit 23.1. Although the balance of payments recovered to the point of showing a small surplus in the first quarter of 1979 and the value of the dollar was stabilized, the international monetary events of 1978 left a strong impression on the U.S. public. A Gallup poll taken in November 1978 showed that keeping up the value of the dollar was the number 1 foreign policy concern of those polled. It outranked even such traditional concerns as

Exhibit 23.1

Recent trends in the balance of payments and in currency values

In the late 1970s, international monetary developments were very much in the news. During 1977 and 1978, the U.S. balance of payments shifted from its traditional surplus position to that of a sharp deficit. The value of the dollar fell in relation to a weighted average of the values of the currencies of major U.S. trading partners, and the value of certain strong currencies—most notably the West German mark—rose to record levels.

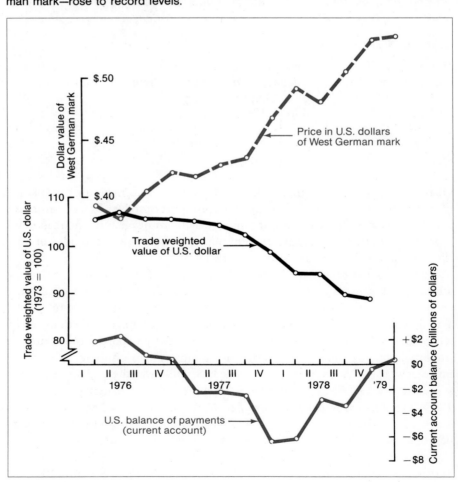

securing adequate energy supplies, containing communism, and defending the security of U.S. allies.[1]

Against the background of the just mentioned world events, this chapter faces the difficult job of explaining in a few short pages a subject that is worthy of a whole book. It will try to accomplish this goal by limiting objectives, sticking to the basics, and omitting all but a bare minimum of technicalities.

THE BALANCE OF PAYMENTS AND FOREIGN EXCHANGE MARKETS

Any discussion of an economy's balance of international payments is complicated by the fact that thousands of different kinds of international payments are made every day. Payments for goods and services exported and imported are probably the first that come to mind, but there are many others. Equally important are long- and short-term loans made to finance imports and exports and payments made in connection with purchases or sales of assets such as securities or real estate in international markets. In addition, governments and private individuals make many kinds of unilateral transfer payments to residents of other countries. They include outright gifts, pension payments, and official foreign aid. Finally, the U.S. Federal Reserve System and foreign central banks engage in many important kinds of official transactions with each other. The complexities of international payments are too great to be tackled all at once. They are best explained step by step, beginning with simplified situations in which only limited kinds of payments take place.

Foreign Exchange Markets and the Current Account

The first category of international payments to be discussed is that of payments on **current account**—payments for imports and exports of goods and services plus private payments and government transfer payments. For the moment, it is assumed that no other kinds of transactions occur among the citizens of the various countries of the world.

Current account payments in international trade differ from otherwise similar payments within a country in one important respect: The two countries have different national currencies. Because of this, each international transaction involves a visit to the **foreign exchange market**—the whole complex of institutions (including banks, specialized foreign exchange dealers, and official government agencies) through which the currency of one country can be exchanged for that of another.

Suppose, for example, that a West German clothing importer wants to buy a shipment of Levis. The importer plans to finance the purchase with West German marks held in a Frankfurt bank account. However, the U.S. manufacturer wants to be paid in dollars, which can be used to meet payrolls and buy materials in the United States. The German's bank sells the necessary quantity of marks on the foreign exchange market, receiving dollars in return. The dollars are then forwarded to the U.S. manufacturer to pay for the Levis.

Current account The account whose transactions include imports and exports of goods and services plus international unilateral transfer payments.

Foreign exchange market The whole complex of institutions—including banks, specialized foreign exchange dealers, and official government agencies—through which the currency of one country can be exchanged for that of another.

---

[1]Survey by the American Institute of Public Opinion (The Gallup Poll) for the Chicago Council on Foreign Relations, November 17–26, 1978, reported in *Public Opinion* 2 (March–May 1979):24.

The Supply and Demand for Foreign Exchange Meanwhile, thousands of other people in the United States and Germany are also buying and selling dollars and marks for their own purposes. The overall activity in the foreign exchange market, like that in any other market, can be characterized in terms of supply and demand curves, such as those shown in Exhibit 23.2. This market, as drawn, shows the supply and demand for dollars, with the price (the exchange rate) in terms of marks per dollar. But it could equally well have been drawn to show the supply and demand for marks, with the price in dollars per mark. The ratios of dollars to marks and marks to dollars are two ways of expressing the same thing; there is just one exchange rate.

Look first at the demand curve for dollars that appears in this market. Under the assumption that only current account transactions take place, the shape and position of the demand curve depends on how German demand for U.S. goods varies as the exchange rate varies, other things being equal. It is easy to see that the demand curve will normally be downward sloping, as drawn. Suppose, for example, that Levis sell in the United States for $10 a pair. At an exchange rate of 2 marks per dollar, German consumers would have to pay 20 marks per pair. They might buy a total of, say, 1 million pairs per year, thereby generating a demand for $10 million in the foreign exchange market. If the exchange rate fell to 1.8 marks per dollar while the U.S. price remained unchanged, German consumers would be able to buy Levis more cheaply—for 18 marks per pair. At the lower price, the Germans would presumably buy a greater quantity, say 1.25 million pairs. The demand for dollars on the foreign exchange market would thus increase to $12.5 million.

The supply curve for dollars in Exhibit 23.2 is drawn with an upward slope, indicating that more dollars will be supplied to the foreign exchange market as the price of dollars, in terms of marks, rises. This will be the case whenever U.S. demand for German goods is elastic—that is, whenever a 1 percent change in the price of German goods causes a greater than 1 percent change in the

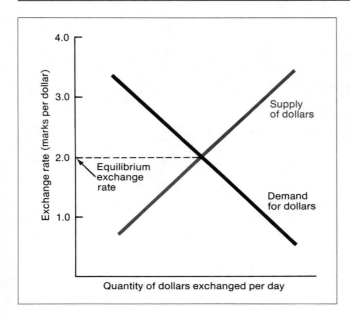

Exhibit 23.2

The foreign exchange market: Elastic demand for foreign goods

In this exhibit, the foreign exchange market is represented in terms of supply and demand curves for the dollar, with the price (exchange rate) stated in terms of the West German mark. The demand curve slopes downward because a lower exchange rate for the dollar, other things being equal, makes U.S. goods cheaper for Germans. That situation stimulates the export of goods, and more dollars are demanded to pay for them. The upward slope of the supply curve drawn here results from an assumed elastic demand in the United States for German goods. An increase in the exchange rate makes imports cheaper for people in the United States; and with elastic demand, they spend more total dollars on the larger quantity of goods.

quantity demanded. An example will show why the slope of the dollar supply curve depends on the elasticity of U.S. demand for German goods. Suppose that a certain model of the German BMW automobile has a price of 20,000 marks. At an exchange rate of 2 marks per dollar, the car would sell for $10,000 in the United States (not including shipping costs and other charges). If 5,000 BMWs per year were sold at that price, U.S. buyers would have to supply $50 million to the foreign exchange market in order to get the 100 million marks needed to pay the German manufacturer. Suppose that the exchange rate rose to 2.5 marks per dollar, so that U.S. buyers could get the car for just $8,000 (a 20 percent decrease in the dollar price). In keeping with the assumption of an elastic demand for BMWs, assume that the quantity imported would rise by 50 percent to 7,500 per year as a result of the change in the dollar price. In order to obtain 7,500 cars at 20,000 marks per car and an exchange rate of 2.5 marks per dollar, U.S. buyers would have to supply $60 million to the exchange markets. The quantity of dollars supplied to the foreign exchange markets would have increased in response to an increase in the price of the dollar in terms of marks, as shown in the diagram.

Supply with Inelastic Demand for Foreign Goods If U.S. demand for foreign goods were inelastic rather than elastic, the supply curve of dollars on the foreign exchange markets would have a negative slope, as shown in Exhibit 23.3. An inelastic demand means that a 1 percent change in the U.S. price of German goods would cause less than a 1 percent change in the quantity demanded. The BMW example can easily be changed to illustrate this. Suppose that when the exchange rate rises from 2 to 2.5 marks per dollar (bringing the U.S. price of BMWs down by 20 percent from $10,000 to $8,000), only 500 additional cars are sold (just a 10 percent increase). To get the German currency needed to buy 5,500 cars at 20,000 marks per car and an exchange rate of 2.5 marks per dollar, U.S. buyers would have to supply only

Exhibit 23.3

The foreign exchange market: Inelastic demand for foreign goods

In this exhibit, the foreign exchange market is shown as it might look with inelastic demand by the United States for German goods. Here, when the exchange rate goes up, German goods become cheaper for people in the United States, as before. However, because the quantity demanded changes by a smaller percentage than the change in price, fewer dollars are needed to purchase the increased quantity of imports. The quantity of dollars supplied in exchange for marks thus decreases as the price of dollars in terms of marks increases.

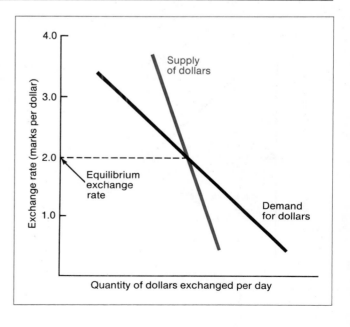

$44 million to the foreign exchange markets. An increase in the price of dollars in terms of marks would thus reduce the supply of dollars.[2]

Equilibrium—Current Account Only It is now possible to show how equilibrium is maintained in the foreign exchange markets in a world where the only international transactions are those that take place on current account. As Exhibit 23.4 is drawn, the foreign exchange market is initially in equilibrium at an exchange rate of 2 marks per dollar. Suppose that some change in current account payment occurs—say that individuals or government agencies in the United States increase transfer payments to Germany. To get marks that they can give to the German recipients of the transfers, the U.S. donors must give up more dollars on the foreign exchange markets. This is shown in the exhibit as a shift in the dollar supply curve from S_1 to S_2. The shift in the supply curve initially creates an excess supply of dollars, which tends to depress the exchange rate. As the rate falls, U.S. goods become cheaper for Germans to buy, which encourages a greater demand for dollars. This situation is represented by a movement down along the demand curve. At the same time, German goods become more expensive for U.S. buyers, which decreases somewhat the quantity of dollars supplied. This situation appears as a downward movement along the new dollar supply curve.

As the figure is drawn, the supply and demand for dollars come into equilibrium again at an exchange rate of 1.8 marks per dollar. The results of the increase in U.S. transfer payments to Germany have been the depression of the exchange rate, the stimulation of U.S. exports of goods and services, and the discouragement of U.S. imports of goods and services.

---

[2] As long as the negatively-sloped supply curve intersects the demand curve from the left as the price rises—as shown in Exhibit 23.3—the foreign exchange markets will function normally. It is theoretically possible, however, that the demand curve could be so steeply sloped that the supply curve would cross it from right to left as the price of the dollar, in terms of marks, increased. The complications that would arise in this situation will be discussed later in the chapter.

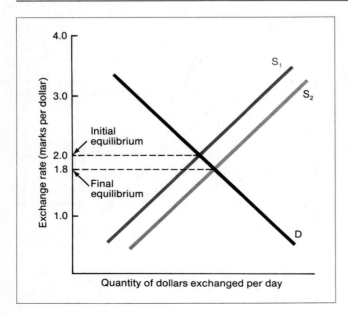

Exhibit 23.4
Maintaining equilibrium in the foreign exchange market
When only current account transactions are taken into account, the process by which equilibrium is maintained in the foreign exchange market is very simple. Suppose that an increase in transfers from the United States to Germany shifts the supply curve for dollars to the right, from S_1 to S_2. This situation creates an excess supply of dollars and puts downward pressure on the exchange rate. As the exchange rate falls, Germans are induced to spend more on U.S. goods and people in the United States spend less on German goods. The exchange rate reaches a new equilibrium at 1.8 marks per dollar.

In the terminology of foreign exchange markets, the dollar is said to **depreciate** when its price falls in terms of foreign currency, as in the example above. Seen from the German point of view, a fall in the price of the dollar in terms of marks is equivalent to a rise in the price of marks in terms of dollars. At the same time the dollar depreciates, then, the mark can be said to **appreciate** against the dollar.

Foreign Exchange Markets with Current and Capital Accounts

Current account transactions are not the only ones that take place among residents of different countries. International lending and borrowing and international sales and purchases of assets are just as important in determining exchange rates. A U.S. company, for example, might obtain a short-term loan from a London bank to finance the purchase of a shipload of beer for import to the United States. The Brazilian government might get a long-term loan from Citibank of New York to help finance construction of a hydroelectric project. A U.S. millionaire might open an account in a Swiss bank. An oil-rich Middle Easterner might purchase Iowa farmland or stock in a U.S. corporation.

All these transactions, and others like them, are called transactions on **capital account.** Purchases of U.S. assets by foreigners and borrowing by those in the United States from foreigners create flows of dollars into the United States and are thus called **capital inflows.** These inflows contribute to the demand for dollars in foreign exchange markets. Purchases of foreign assets by U.S. residents or loans by U.S. residents to foreigners create flows of dollars away from the United States and are thus called **capital outflows.** These outflows contribute to the supply of dollars in foreign exchange markets.

Relationships between Current and Capital Accounts When only current account transactions are considered, equilibrium in foreign exchange markets requires that imports of goods and services and unilateral transfers to foreign residents and governments be financed only by exporting goods and services and by unilateral transfers from abroad. Once capital account transactions are introduced, however, new means of financing these transactions are available. Imports of goods and services can now be paid for either by exports or by capital inflows—that is, by borrowing from foreigners or by selling assets to foreigners. Similarly, a country can export more goods and services than it imports, so long as it provides its trading partners with the means to pay for them by making loans to or buying assets from the trading partners.

Consider the hypothetical case shown in Exhibit 23.5. In the year for which these accounts are drawn up, the United States is shown as importing more goods and services than it exports and running a current account deficit of $30 billion. (All flows of dollars away from the United States are shown as −, and all flows of dollars toward the United States are shown as +.) At the same time, however, borrowing from foreigners plus sales of U.S. assets to foreigners (capital inflows) exceed loans to foreigners plus purchases of foreign assets (capital outflows) by $30 billion. The United States thus has a $30 billion capital account surplus that exactly balances the current account deficit.

It is not necessary to draw a new set of foreign exchange supply and demand curves to take both current and capital transactions into account. There are

Depreciation A fall in the price (exchange rate) of the currency of one country in terms of the currency of another country.

Appreciation A rise in the price (exchange rate) of the currency of one country in terms of the currency of another country.

Capital account The account whose transactions include all international borrowing and lending and all international purchases and sales of assets for investment purposes.

Capital inflow Purchases of domestic assets by foreigners and borrowing by domestic residents from foreigners.

Capital outflow Purchases of foreign assets by domestic residents and borrowing by foreigners from domestic sources.

Exports	+$120	
Imports	−150	
Unilateral transfers	0	
Current account deficit		−$30
Sales of U.S. assets to foreigners and borrowing from foreigners	+$60	
Purchases of foreign assets and loans to foreigners	−30	
Capital account surplus		+$30

Exhibit 23.5

Hypothetical balance of payments accounts: Current and capital accounts only (billions of U.S. dollars)
In a world where the only international transactions are those taking place on current and capital accounts, any current account deficit must be balanced by a capital account surplus and vice versa. In this hypothetical example, the United States is shown importing more than it exports, thereby running a current account deficit. This deficit is financed by a capital inflow—that is, by borrowing from abroad or by sales of U.S. assets to foreigners. Note that all outflows of dollars are listed with a minus and all inflows with a plus.

still just one supply curve of dollars, one demand curve for dollars, and one exchange rate for the dollar in terms of any other currency (such as the German mark). However, there are now additional sources of shifts in the supply and demand curves. Consider, for example, the effects of a rise in U.S. interest rates, other things being equal. One immediate effect is to make U.S. securities more attractive than before to foreign buyers. Their increased demand for dollars with which to buy these securities shows up as a rightward shift in the demand for dollars in the foreign exchange markets, which tends to cause the dollar to appreciate against the mark. Similarly, a rise in German interest rates, other things being equal, causes a rightward shift in the supply curve for dollars, which tends to cause the dollar to depreciate against the mark.

The Official Reserve Account

One important category of international transactions has yet to be explained: the sales and purchases of foreign currency reserves held by the Federal Reserve in the United States and the corresponding central banks of other countries. These sales and purchases are not included in the current account because they are not made to pay for imports or exports or to make unilateral transfers. They are not included in the capital account, because they are not necessarily made for investment purposes. Often, sales and purchases of foreign currency reserves by central banks are made instead to offset an excess supply or demand of dollars or other currencies, thereby preventing or moderating exchange rate fluctuations that would otherwise take place. These sales and purchases are referred to as transactions on the **official reserve account.**[3]

An example of how official reserve transactions might affect exchange rates appears in Exhibit 23.6. This diagram begins with the same scenario as did Exhibit 23.4: Initially, the market is in equilibrium at an exchange rate of 2 marks per dollar. This is shown by the intersection of D_1 and S_1. Next, an increase in U.S. transfer payments causes a rightward shift in the dollar supply

Official reserve account The account whose transactions include purchases and sales of reserves of foreign currency by central banks.

---

[3]In practice, it is impossible to distinguish clearly between central bank transactions made for investment purposes and those made for purposes of intervention in the foreign exchange markets. For example, when the Saudi Arabian government buys U.S. securities, it may be acting from ordinary business motives—looking for a good investment for its oil earnings—and at the same time may recognize and welcome the fact that the action helps stabilize the value of the dollar. In what follows, however, the focus is on the intervention motive for reserve account transactions.

Exhibit 23.6

Official intervention in the foreign exchange market
This exhibit begins with the same scenario shown in
Exhibit 23.4. Starting from an exchange rate of two
marks per dollar at the intersection of D_1 and S_1, an
increase in transfers from the United States shifts the
dollar supply curve to the right, to S_2. That shift creates
a surplus of dollars and puts downward pressure on the
exchange rate. To prevent the exchange rate from falling, the U.S. or German government begins official reserve purchases of dollars. These purchases shift the
demand curve for dollars to the right, to D_2, until the
demand curve intersects the new supply curve at the
old exchange rate.

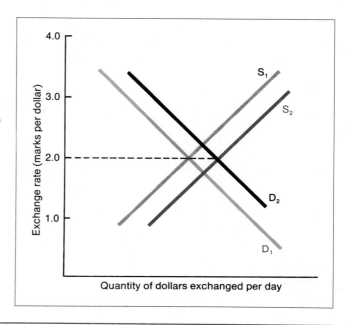

Quantity of dollars exchanged per day

---

curve to S_2, which creates an excess supply of dollars at the original exchange
rate. Normally, this would cause the dollar to depreciate against the mark.
Instead of permitting the exchange rate to fall, however, the Federal Reserve
could decide to use some of the German marks it holds as part of its foreign
currency reserves to purchase the surplus dollars. Alternatively, the German
central bank might sell marks in order to build up its reserves of dollars, or
both central banks might act together, coordinating their efforts. In any event,
the transactions would show up on the exchange market diagram as a rightward shift in the demand curve for dollars. As Exhibit 23.6 is drawn, sufficient
official reserve purchases of dollars are made to shift the demand curve all the
way to Position D_2. The entire excess supply of dollars is thus soaked up, and
the exchange rate does not change.

Relationships of the Three Accounts

Once the official reserve account is introduced, it no longer need be true, as in
Exhibit 23.5, that the capital account deficit or surplus will exactly offset the
current account deficit or surplus. However, the total of the current account,
capital account, and official reserve account balances must add to zero. The
reason is that every purchase of a dollar on the foreign exchange markets by
one party must correspond to a sale of a dollar by some other party, and all sales
and purchases appear in one or another of the three accounts.

Exhibit 23.7, which shows the main elements of the U.S. balance of payments accounts for 1977, illustrates the relationships between the current,
capital, and official reserve accounts. In that year, the United States ran a
current account deficit of $15.2 billion. Rather than being offset by a capital
inflow, this deficit was compounded by a $19 billion capital account deficit.
The capital account deficit was the result of a much more rapid increase in
U.S. holdings of foreign assets than of foreign holdings of U.S. assets. The
combined balance of payments deficit on current plus capital accounts was

Merchandise exports	$120.0	
Merchandise imports	−151.1	
Net exports of services	20.6	
Net unilateral transfers	−4.7	
Current account deficit		−$15.2
Purchases of foreign assets and loans to foreigners	−$34.4	
Sales of assets to foreigners and borrowing from foreigners	15.4	
Capital account deficit		−$19.0
Change in foreign official reserve holdings of U.S. assets	$35.4	
Change in U.S. official reserve holdings of foreign assets	−0.2	
Surplus on official reserve account		+$35.2
Statistical discrepancy		1.0
Grand total	0	0

Totals may be off slightly because of rounding.
Source: President's Council of Economic Advisers, *Economic Report of the President* (Washington, D.C.: Government Printing Office, 1979), Table B–97.

Exhibit 23.7
U.S. balance of payments accounts, 1977 (billions of U.S. dollars)
This exhibit shows, in simplified form, the actual U.S. balance of payments accounts for 1977. In that year, the United States ran both a current account deficit and a capital account deficit. The deficits were offset by transactions on the official reserve account, chiefly purchases of dollars by foreign central banks.

thus $34.2 billion. The deficit was offset by transactions on the official reserve account, where foreign central banks made some $35.4 billion of dollar purchases.

In principle, the sum of the current, capital, and reserve accounts shown in Exhibit 23.7 should be exactly zero. However, statistical sources and techniques are imperfect, and the items therefore do not quite balance. The total of the various errors and omissions in the three accounts, which is $1 billion for 1977, appears in the table under the heading "statistical discrepancy."

THE DETERMINANTS OF EXCHANGE RATES

So far, only the mechanics of exchange rate determination have been discussed; exchange rates, like other prices, are determined by supply and demand. The next step is to look beyond the supply and demand curves for a theory explaining why, at any particular time, the curves intersect at one exchange rate rather than another. Once that step has been taken, the next section will discuss the important policy issues of how and why governments use reserve transactions to intervene in foreign exchange markets.

The Long Run: Purchasing Power Parity

Purchasing power parity theory (of exchange rates) The theory holding that the price of a unit of Currency A in terms of Currency B will, in the long run, tend to be equal to the ratio of the price level in Country B to the price level in Country A.

The leading theory of exchange rate determination in the long run is the so-called **purchasing power parity theory.** According to this theory, the price of a unit of Currency A in terms of Currency B (that is, the exchange rate) will, in the long run, tend to equal the ratio of the price level in Country B to the price level in Country A.

In a world where all goods and services were traded internationally, with no transportation costs or other barriers to trade, the purchasing power parity theory would presumably hold exactly. Suppose, for example, that the U.S. and

German domestic price levels are such that $100 will buy exactly twice as large a market basket of goods in the United States as can be bought for 100 marks in Germany. The purchasing power parity theory will then imply that the exchange rate must be 2 marks per dollar. If a dollar could be exchanged for more than 2 marks, U.S. consumers would all try to turn in their dollars and do their shopping in Germany. Their attempt to do so would immediately drive the price of the dollar back down to 2 marks. Similarly, if a dollar could be purchased for less than 2 marks, Germans would try to turn in all their marks for dollars and shop in the United States. This would quickly push the price of the dollar up to 2 marks. In such a world, in fact, the expressions "100 dollars" and "200 marks" would simply be different names given in Germany and the United States to equal-sized lumps of abstract purchasing power.

In practice, exchange rates do not always reflect purchasing power parities exactly. According to a study by economist Irving B. Kravis, for example, in 1978, $1 in the United States had as much purchasing power as 3.12 marks in Germany, even though the official exchange rate was 2.08 marks per dollar.[4] The difference can be explained in part by the fact that purchasing power parities reflect the prices of all goods and services, while exchange rates tend to reflect the value of goods and services traded internationally. For example, Kravis estimated that a dollar in the U.S. would buy 3.8 times as much telephone service as a mark would buy in Germany—but telephone calls are not an internationally traded service.

Also, deviations of exchange values from present purchasing power parities may reflect future expectations as much as current realities. For example, if participants in foreign exchange markets come to expect U.S. inflation in the future consistently to average higher in relation to German inflation than they thought in the past, they may shift out of dollar denominated assets into mark denominated assets. These capital account transactions can depress the value of the dollar even before enough actual inflation takes place to justify the new exchange rate in terms of purchasing power parities. Similarly, if participants in foreign exchange markets judge that future real economic growth will cause the demand for a country's exports to increase more rapidly than its demand for imports, the present exchange rate for its currency may be bid up in anticipation of the expected future improvement in its current account balance.

Short-Run Exchange Rate Fluctuations

With the necessary reservations, as noted, the purchasing power parity theory can be thought of as determining exchange rates in the long run. In the short run, exchange rates vary from day to day and month to month for reasons that are related only indirectly, if at all, to long-run changes in relative purchasing power and inflation rates. Among the important short-run factors influencing exchange rates are changes in aggregate economic activity, in interest rates, and in inflationary expectations.

Aggregate Economic Activity The national economies of the United States and other countries do not grow at the same steady rate year after year.

---

[4]Based on unpublished research by Kravis, reported by Alfred Malabre, Jr., "Despite the Dollar's Decline, U.S. Retains Top Living Standards," *Wall Street Journal*, May 1, 1979, p. 48.

Instead, there tend to be periods in which real output expands more rapidly than the long-run growth rate of potential real output alternating with periods in which real output grows more slowly or actually contracts. Furthermore, expansionary and contractionary episodes in various countries are not perfectly synchronized. This lack of synchronization creates short-run variations in the pattern of international trade and hence in exchange rates.

In a country where real aggregate demand is expanding relatively rapidly, part of the growth is met by an increase in imports of goods from abroad, which tends to move the country's balance of payments on current account from surplus toward deficit. Similarly, a country experiencing slowly growing real aggregate demand, or actual recession, tends to move from current account deficit toward surplus. Other things being equal, then, a nation's currency can be expected to depreciate as its real growth rate accelerates relative to that of its trading partners and to appreciate as its real growth rate lags behind that of its trading partners.

Interest Rates As shown in the previous section, exchange rates are sensitive not only to transactions taking place on current account but also to transactions taking place on capital account. In today's world economy, investment funds tend to be highly mobile among countries. Individuals, international corporations, and even national governments face the problem of balancing their portfolios among assets of numerous countries, all having various risks, liquidities, and expected rates of return. Other things being equal, an increase in the interest rate in any country will tend to attract internationally mobile funds, which will tend to move that country's capital account balance toward surplus and to cause its currency to appreciate. Similarly, a country in which the interest rate falls, other things being equal, will tend to experience a capital outflow and a depreciation of its currency.

Inflationary Expectations In saying that high interest rates attract internationally mobile funds, other things being equal, one of the things held equal is the relative riskiness of assets. In a given country, high nominal interest rates that simply reflect a high rate of domestic inflation are thus not necessarily attractive to international investors. As shown earlier, in the long run, the purchasing power parity theory suggests that such a country's currency will depreciate. It follows that for a given nominal interest rate, a country is likely to experience a capital outflow as the result of any development that makes international investors expect its inflation rate to accelerate relative to the rates of its trading partners.

EXCHANGE RATE POLICY

Two Possible International Monetary Systems

The long-run and short-run fluctuations in exchange rates discussed in the previous section are the result of current and capital account transactions. This section turns again to the official reserve account and the use of sales and purchases of foreign currency reserves as an instrument of policy. It begins by distinguishing two idealized international monetary systems, each characterized by a set of rules for governments to follow in the conduct of official reserve transactions.

Fixed Rates The first system is one of fixed exchange rates. Under this system, a group of countries (in the idealized form of this system, all countries) meet and agree on a set of "par" values for their currencies. The West German mark may be set at a par value of $.50, the British pound at a par value of $2, and so on. The countries then agree to hold substantial foreign currency reserves and to buy and sell from these reserves when necessary to offset potential deviations of exchange rates from their par values. Suppose, for example, that developments in the current or capital accounts led to an excess demand for marks, putting upward pressure on the international value of that currency relative to the U.S. dollar. Under the terms of the agreement, the German central bank would be obligated to sell marks and buy dollars in sufficient quantity to meet the excess demand at the par value of $.50. Or suppose that an excess supply of British pounds developed, putting downward pressure on that currency. The Bank of England would then step in and buy enough pounds to soak up the excess supply, paying for them with dollars from its foreign currency reserves. As long as all countries played by the rules, then, the actual exchange rates of all currencies would remain fixed at their par values.[5]

Floating Rates The alternative system is one of completely flexible or "floating" exchange rates. In terms of policy, this system is just the opposite of a fixed rate system. Under it, all governments agree to a hands-off policy on exchange rates. They conduct no official reserve transactions for intervention purposes. Exchange rates fluctuate up or down in accordance with supply and demand generated on the current and capital accounts alone.

The current world monetary system is a hybrid that fits neither of the idealized patterns perfectly. Before the current system and its evolution are described, however, some of the claimed advantages and disadvantages of the idealized fixed and floating exchange rate regimes will be discussed.

The Case for Fixed Rates

The case that can be made for a system of fixed exchange rates can be reduced to four principal arguments.

Real Effects of Currency Disturbances The first point made by proponents of fixed rates is that variations in exchange rates have significant real effects on the economy. When a country's currency appreciates, its export industries find it harder to compete in world markets. At the same time, industries that face import competition find it difficult to compete in domestic markets. When a country's currency depreciates, in contrast, export- and import-competing industries boom, but industries that rely on imported energy or raw materials suffer. If the appreciation or depreciation in question reflects fundamental long-term changes in patterns of world trade, these adjustments in import and export industries may be necessary and desirable. But it is argued that short-term random, cyclical, or speculative changes in exchange rates should not be allowed to disturb the domestic economy. After all, labor

---

[5] One extreme form of fixed exchange rate system, no longer in use, is a *gold standard*. Under such a system, different currencies—such as the dollar or the mark—are only local names for gold coins (or other gold backed currency) of different sizes.

and other factors of production cannot make costless moves from sector to sector at a moment's notice.

The "J-Curve" Effect   A second reason frequently advanced for fixing exchange rates is that in the short run, the depreciation of a country's currency may worsen rather than improve its balance of payments on current account. To understand how this can happen, recall the earlier discussion of how the elasticity of demand for imports and exports affects the slope of the foreign exchange market supply and demand curves in a world where only current account transactions take place. The supply curve for dollars in Exhibit 23.2 was drawn with a positive slope on the assumption of elastic demand for imported goods. Exhibit 23.3 showed how the dollar supply curve would have a negative slope if domestic demand for imported goods were inelastic. Suppose now that both the domestic demand for imported goods and the foreign demand for U.S. exports are inelastic, creating the supply and demand curves shown in Exhibit 23.8. Here, the supply curve crosses the demand curve from right to left as the price rises. The market is in equilibrium at an exchange rate of 2 marks per dollar; however, the equilibrium is unstable. If the dollar depreciates to, say, 1.5 marks, an excess supply of dollars appears. This puts additional downward pressure on the exchange rate. Fluctuations in the exchange rate are thus not self-correcting in the short run, insofar as the current account is concerned.

A possible real-world result of the hypothetical situation shown in Exhibit 23.8 is the so-called **J-curve effect.** This effect, shown in Exhibit 23.9, occurs because import and export demands tend to be inelastic in the short run, although they are elastic in the longer run. When a country's currency first depreciates, few additional export sales are made immediately, and importers do not or cannot immediately reduce the quantity of goods they purchase. At the lower exchange rate, however, importers do have to offer

J-curve effect The tendency for the depreciation of a country's currency to worsen its current account deficit in the short run and to improve it only after a lag.

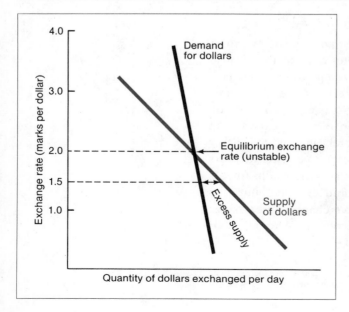

Exhibit 23.8
Foreign exchange market with extremely inelastic demand for imports and exports
This exhibit shows the dollar-mark foreign exchange market as it might look with extremely inelastic demand for U.S. goods in Germany and for German goods in the United States. The inelastic demand for U.S. goods in Germany makes the demand curve for dollars very steep. The inelastic U.S. demand for German goods gives the supply curve for dollars enough of a negative slope that it cuts the demand curve from the right as the exchange rate rises. The equilibrium exchange rate is 2 marks per dollar as the curves are drawn, but this equilibrium is unstable. For example, a depreciation of the dollar to 1.5 marks would create an excess supply (not an excess demand, as normally). This would put further downward pressure on the dollar rather than upward pressure toward equilibrium.

Exhibit 23.9
The J-curve effect
The so-called J-curve effect occurs when the demand for imports and exports is inelastic in the short run and elastic in the long run. As a result, a devaluation may initially worsen a country's balance of payments on its current account before eventually improving it. Here, the country has been experiencing a moderate current account deficit for some time. At the point shown, it devalues its currency. At first, the current account drops farther into deficit, but eventually it rises into surplus, following the J-shaped path shown.

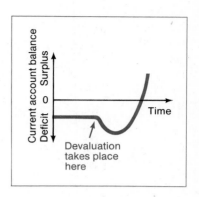

greater quantities of the domestic currency in order to buy the foreign currency they need to buy the unchanged physical quantity of imports. The current account balance thus moves toward deficit, putting further downward pressure on the exchange rate. Eventually, the lower exchange rate attracts new export buyers and encourages importers to find domestic substitutes. The current account balance then improves. The result is a pattern of events that, over a period of time, traces out a J-shaped curve—hence the name.

Proponents of fixed exchange rates argue that because of the J-curve effect, short-term fluctuations in exchange rates may not be self-correcting. If a disturbance in the exchange rate is expected to be only temporary, they say, why not short-circuit the J-curve by keeping the exchange rate fixed in the first place?

Inflationary Effects   A third argument in favor of fixed exchange rates is based on the relationship between exchange rate variations and inflation. The previous section argued that countries experiencing relatively rapid inflation can expect their currencies to depreciate—in accordance with the purchasing power parity theory. However, the causation may also run the other way; a currency depreciation may cause domestic cost-push inflation. This occurs in part directly, because the prices of imported goods and raw materials rise, and in part indirectly, because domestic import-competing industries feel free to raise their prices when the prices of imports rise.

Under the proper conditions, a vicious cycle that runs something like this can be touched off: Inflation in, say, the United States causes the dollar to depreciate. Depreciation brings a round of cost-push inflation. International asset holders see the worsening inflation and react by pulling their funds out of U.S. banks and securities, thereby creating a capital account deficit. Especially if the J-curve effect of the depreciation is creating a current account deficit at the same time, the value of the dollar can plunge out of control in the absence of official intervention.

Meanwhile, a less inflationary country, say Switzerland, enters a "virtuous" cycle that is the mirror image of the vicious cycle described for the United States. Currency appreciation lowers import prices, further dampening inflation. International investors rush to put their funds in the ultra-safe Swiss franc, thereby creating a capital account surplus that causes further appreciation. But while the banks of Zurich grow fat, Swiss watchmakers find themselves increasingly priced out of the world market on which their livelihood depends.

The way to prevent such runaway vicious-virtuous cycles, it is said, is to prevent exchange rate fluctuations in the first place. Rather than letting differential rates of inflation disturb exchange markets, countries should use the time gained by exchange rate intervention to undertake domestic policies to control inflation.

Automatic Monetary Policy This leads to the fourth argument in favor of fixed exchange rates: The act of exchange market intervention itself automatically institutes the correct anti-inflationary monetary policy. Suppose, for example, that inflation begins to accelerate in the United States, putting downward pressure on the international value of the dollar. Under a fixed exchange rate system, the Fed would be obligated to go to the exchange markets to buy dollars, paying for them with foreign currency reserves. These dollars would go into the Fed's own accounts, thus disappearing from the money supply.

This contractionary monetary policy has several beneficial effects that help correct the original exchange market imbalance. First, interest rates tend to rise, encouraging a capital inflow. Second, international investors anticipate that the contractionary monetary policy will dampen inflation, which makes the dollar a less risky currency and further encourages capital inflow. Finally, aggregate demand in the United States is moderated, which moderates the demand for imports and improves the current account. All of this happens because the Fed's action in buying dollars through its "foreign desk" is a perfect substitute for buying dollars (that is, selling bonds) through its "open market desk."

Under floating rates, in contrast, central banks are not subject to the same kind of international discipline and may feel free to create more inflation. Fixed exchange rate advocates blame part of the increase in worldwide inflation over the last decade on the move toward floating rates.

The Case for Floating Rates

Advocates of floating rates remain unconvinced by the arguments in favor of fixed rates. They offer counterarguments to each of the four points just raised and provide some additional arguments of their own.

Counterarguments Floating rate advocates begin by pointing out that fixed rates do not truly protect the domestic economy from the real effects of international disturbances. For example, if inflation occurs under a fixed rate system, foreign competition may prevent prices from rising in industries facing strong international competition. As costs and prices rise in other sectors of the domestic economy, the industries facing foreign competition will be squeezed and resource allocation will consequently be disturbed.

Next, while acknowledging the J-curve effect as a short-run possibility for the current account, floating rate advocates believe it does not justify fixed rates. Why should it matter, they say, if devaluation temporarily causes a current account deficit if that deficit can be offset by a surplus on capital account? They dismiss the possibility that supply and demand curves for the foreign exchange market as a whole—including both current and capital accounts—can cross in the unstable configuration shown in Exhibit 23.8. It is nonsense, they say, to suggest that exchange rates shoot off to zero or infinity at the slightest disturbance; instability of that type simply does not exist.

Floating rate advocates are similarly unconvinced by the argument that currency depreciation creates a vicious cycle through cost-push inflation. The impact of exchange rate fluctuations on domestic inflation depends on whether the domestic money stock is held constant or increased. If the money stock is held constant—instead of being increased to accommodate the inflationary impact of currency depreciation—price increases in some markets will tend to be offset by price decreases elsewhere. Floating rate advocates concede that in a floating rate world, central banks would not always have the necessary discipline to avoid inflationary monetary policy, but they suggest that the blame should be placed on the banks, not on the monetary system.

Playing by the Rules In addition to disputing the arguments in favor of fixed rates, floating rate advocates advance a further argument of their own. The real trouble with a system of fixed exchange rates, they say, is that governments refuse to play by the rules. The rules call for exchange market intervention to be used only to iron out temporary fluctuations in exchange rates. Long-term variations, especially those arising from differential rates of inflation, are supposed to be handled by domestic macroeconomic policy.

In particular, governments tend to balk at subjecting themselves to the discipline of the automatic monetary policy that a fixed rate system implies. Suppose, for example, that a fixed rate system is in force, and, for some reason or other, downward pressure develops on the dollar. The Fed obediently buys dollars through its foreign desk, thereby propping up the exchange rate. But various domestic interest groups are immediately offended. The housing industry starts to squawk about high interest rates. Labor unions rebel at the threat of rising unemployment. The administration sees an election coming up and pressures the Fed to pursue expansionary domestic monetary policy. So at the same time the Fed buys dollars through its foreign market desk, it puts them right back into circulation through its open market desk. The continuing inflation pushes the current and capital accounts farther and farther into deficit. The U.S. government leans on its allies and trading partners to join it in defending the dollar through massive official reserve account purchases. But as long as the fundamental inflationary imbalance remains uncorrected, this effort only buys time and makes the crisis bigger when it comes.

But it is not necessary to deal in hypothetical cases to show the problems of a fixed rate system. It is time to turn from theory to a review of the postwar history of the international monetary system.

Bretton Woods

After World War II, the major trading nations of the world met under United Nations auspices at Bretton Woods, New Hampshire, to forge a new world monetary system of the fixed rate variety. The Bretton Woods conference also set up the International Monetary Fund (IMF), with headquarters in Washington, D.C., to administer the system. The rules of the international monetary game as it was played under the Bretton Woods system are presented here.

It was not quite an ideal fixed rate system. Instead, it featured what might best be called an "adjustable peg." Par values for each currency were established in terms of the U.S. dollar. Exchange rates were pegged at the par values; thus they were allowed to fluctuate under the influence of supply and demand within a narrow range of 2.25 percent above par to 2.25 percent below par. (The limits were only 1 percent until December 1971.) When the value of a currency rose to the upper limit or fell to the lower one, the government of the country in question was obligated under IMF rules to intervene and prevent further movement. A government faced with an excess demand for its currency at the limit rate had to sell enough of its own currency in exchange for dollars to soak up the excess demand. A government faced with an excess supply of its currency had to buy it in exchange for dollars if necessary to keep its price from slipping below the limit.

Although governments were supposed to intervene in exchange markets to counteract temporary disturbances, they had another option if they felt the disturbances reflected fundamental long-term changes. In the face of such changes, they could adjust the peg—change the par values of their currencies. This could be done in either of two slightly different ways. One way was to declare immediately a new par value above or below the initial value. The other was to float the currency temporarily, letting it find a new equilibrium value under the influence of supply and demand without government intervention. A new par value would later be fixed at the market determined rate when things seemed to have settled down. (A few countries, notably Canada, let their currencies float for years at a time in the postwar period. This, however, was considered to be a violation of at least the spirit, if not the letter, of IMF rules.)

Problems of the Bretton Woods System

Resisting Adjustment Under the Bretton Woods system, a country whose currency fell to the lower limit of the permissible range either was supposed to let automatic monetary policy do its job until the imbalance was corrected or was supposed to adjust the peg, make a new start at a new par value, and try to keep serious imbalances from arising again in the future. Unfortunately, governments often did neither when faced with downward pressure on their currencies. Fearing unemployment and high interest rates, they short-circuited the monetary adjustment mechanism. And concerned about possible sectoral effects, they resisted downward adjustment of their par value. In desperate attempts to prop up their currencies, they engaged in all sorts of trade restrictions. They imposed tariffs and quotas to try to improve current account balances, and they slapped on foreign exchange controls to prevent free international movements of capital, all in the hope of improving the capital account. But these mechanisms usually did little more than postpone the day of reckoning.

Crises Because adjustments were seldom fully automatic, the system was crisis-prone. Governments often resisted making small adjustments when the adjustments would have been only slightly painful. Instead, they waited for pressures to build up, and these pressures eventually tore the system apart.

Here is the scenario for the kind of international monetary crisis that repeatedly occurred under the Bretton Woods rules. Some country, say the United Kingdom, runs a persistent balance of payments deficit. A chronic excess supply of British pounds sterling appears on the world's exchange markets. The British government is forced to support the pound. It resists monetary restraint. Gradually, dollar reserves are run dangerously low, and the British government is forced to borrow from the IMF or the U.S. Treasury. It may try imposing exchange controls or other trade restrictions, but its efforts are met with threats of retaliation and domestic political resistence. It becomes harder and harder to keep the pound from breaking through the floor.

Speculation At this point, speculation enters the picture. Speculators are active all the time in international currency markets. Under the Bretton Woods rules, if I were a speculator, my game would work like this: Suppose the pound is floating between its upper limit of $2.45 and its lower limit of $2.35, changing a bit from day to day. If I buy 100,000 pounds today at $2.40, and tomorrow the vagaries of supply and demand carry the rate up to $2.41, I can change them back into dollars and pocket a clear profit of $1,000. The problem is that in normal times no one can be sure whether the pound is on its way up or on its way down. I might just as easily lose $1,000. Heads I win, tails I lose. Speculators are professional risk takers who perform a number of useful economic functions. In normal times, though, they do not play a very big role in the international payments picture.

But back to the scenario of the British government hanging desperately on the brink of a forced devaluation. At this point, I am faced with the kind of situation speculators are always looking for but are rarely lucky enough to find: the situation where heads I win, tails I break even. The question is: Will the pound hold at $2.35, or will it be devalued? Suppose I sell all the pounds I can get my hands on, borrowing them if necessary. If the pound is devalued to $2.10 tomorrow, I can buy pounds back to pay off the loans and make a huge profit. If the British government somehow muddles through, and the pound holds, I lose practically nothing. At the very worst, the pound will rise a cent or two off its floor and I will have to pay a few days' or weeks' interest on the loans.

The final scene in the sterling crisis is set when speculators start to pour hundreds of millions of pounds into the foreign exchange markets. The excess supply of sterling becomes overwhelming, and the last straw forcing an actual devaluation is the speculative pressure occurring in anticipation of the devaluation.

The End of the Bretton Woods System

In early 1973, an especially severe crisis occurred, involving the U.S. dollar, the German mark, and the Japanese yen. In response to this crisis, the major trading nations took the bold step of abandoning the adjustable peg and allowing their currencies to float relative to each other. The relative values of the yen, the dollar, and the mark were allowed to find their own levels under the influence of supply and demand.

The international monetary system that emerged from the crisis of 1973 is still a mixed system. It contains a number of features that do not conform exactly to a pure floating rate system. Although it is much more flexible than the adjustable peg, two important restrictions must be kept in mind.

First, not every currency floats against every other currency. Rather, the system is one in which major blocks of currencies float against one another. A number of Western European countries have attempted to peg their currencies against one another in an arrangement known as the European Monetary Union. Countries with strong trading ties to the United States have pegged their currencies to the dollar. Those with strong ties to Britain have pegged theirs to the pound. Movements between blocks have been substantial, though. Because increased flexibility has been introduced, several currencies have swung by as much as 20 to 30 percent. Occasionally there have been swings of 2 or 3 percent in a single day.

Second, governments have not taken a strictly hands-off attitude toward exchange rates. Instead, they have frequently intervened in foreign exchange markets to damp what they perceive to be temporary or unjustified fluctuations in exchange rates. This intervention is, however, not guided by any specific rules, as under the Bretton Woods agreements. The present mixture of floating rates and sporadic intervention is often referred to as a "dirty float."

The following case study illustrates the present international monetary system in action. The events it describes highlight a number of the features of the system that have just been discussed in theoretical terms.

Case 23.1
Carter's Dollar Rescue, 1978

As noted at the beginning of this chapter, international monetary events were very prominent in the news during 1977 and 1978. Exhibit 23.1 shows some of the important trends during that period—a swing in the current account balance from surplus to deficit, a decline in the trade-weighted value of the dollar on the foreign exchange markets, and a dramatic appreciation of certain "strong" currencies, notably the West German mark and the Japanese yen (the latter not shown).

Throughout the period, a substantial deficit on capital account added to downward pressure on the dollar. This deficit was most frequently attributed to the high rate of inflation in the United States compared with that of its major trading partners. In 1977, the United States experienced a 6.5 percent inflation rate while inflation in Germany was only 3.9 percent. Inflation in Japan was over 8 percent in 1977; but, importantly, it was on its way down from higher levels, while U.S. inflation was clearly on its way up. In Switzerland, not a major U.S. trading partner but a crucial international financial center, inflation had virtually been eliminated.

As long as the decline in the value of the dollar was gradual, the Carter administration did little to intervene in exchange markets. It was content to see heavy official reserve purchases of dollars by foreign central banks soak up the excess dollars created by the U.S. current and capital account deficits. Meanwhile, it hoped that the moderate depreciation would soon improve the current account balance. By the third quarter of 1978, however, the downward trend in the value of the dollar began to accelerate. The hoped-for improvement in the current account proved very slow in coming. It became increasingly difficult to convince international asset holders that anything serious was being done about inflation.

By October, the Carter administration saw it was time to act. On October 24, the president went on national television to announce a renewed anti-inflation policy featuring voluntary wage and price guidelines. He also pledged to reduce the budget deficit as a further anti-inflationary measure. International financial circles were disturbed, however, by the absence of any mention of monetary policy in the talk. They apparently decided that the anti-inflation package was just window dressing for domestic consumption. The run on the dollar continued.

Prompted by this further pressure on the dollar, the administration and the Federal Reserve finally took decisive monetary action on November 1. A dramatic new policy package to rescue the dollar was announced. Its main features were the tightening of monetary policy and the assembly of massive foreign currency reserves for exchange market intervention. The monetary policy was signaled by a full percentage point increase in the discount rate and a half percentage point increase in the federal funds rate. From November 1 through March 1979, the growth rate of the money supply slowed almost to a stop. The intervention package included drawing on the U.S. reserve position at the IMF, borrowing reserves from Germany and Japan through currency "swaps," and, for the first time ever, selling U.S. government securities denominated in German marks and Japanese yen directly to residents of those countries.

Effects of the November 1 initiative were felt immediately. Within a week, the dollar had climbed 7.7 percent from its low point at the close of trading on October 30. The gains held through the winter and into the spring of 1979. By the first quarter of 1979, the current account had swung back into surplus.

CONCLUSIONS

As the international economy enters the 1980s, the world of Bretton Woods fades more and more into history. The academic debates over fixed versus floating rates that characterized the fifties and sixties have been overtaken by events. At present, it is clear that the dirty float is here to stay for quite a while.

A floating rate world has not proved to be the promised land that some academic enthusiasts once thought it would be. It has not brought a halt to world inflation. It has not led to a dismantling of tariffs, quotas, and other barriers to free trade. It has not protected domestic economies from internationally generated disturbances. But, say floating rate advocates, it has not halted crime or illiteracy either; such expectations, in other words, were unrealistic to begin with. Something like the present system appears to be the only one possible in today's world. It is at least robust. It is hard to imagine, for example, that the Bretton Woods system could ever have accommodated the enormous international financial disturbances brought on by the rise of the OPEC oil cartel. And as long as the present system prevails, international monetary economics will continue to be a lively and exciting field of study.

SUMMARY

1. The many kinds of international transactions that take place in the world economy can conveniently be classified into three "accounts." The first is the current account, which comprises imports and exports of goods and services and unilateral transfers. The second is the capital account, which includes all international borrowing and lending and all international purchases and sales of assets for investment purposes. The third is the official reserve account, which is made up of central bank purchases and sales of foreign currency reserves. Because all international transactions are included in one account or another, the sum of the surpluses or deficits on these three accounts must always be zero (except for unavoidable statistical discrepancies).

2. The foreign exchange markets are made up of a whole complex of banks, specialized currency dealers, and government agencies through which currencies are exchanged for one another. Like other markets, they can be represented by supply and demand curves. A currency is said to depreciate when its value on the foreign exchange markets falls and to appreciate when its value rises. Fluctuations in exchange rates can result from shifts in supply

or demand arising in either the current or capital accounts. Often governments use official reserve account transactions to offset such currency fluctuations.

3. In the long run, international exchange rates tend to reflect, at least approximately, changes in the purchasing power parity of various national currencies. In the short run, changes in the growth of aggregate demand, in interest rates, and in inflationary expectations can cause substantial deviations from purchasing power parity exchange rates.

4. From 1944 to 1973, the international monetary system operated under a system of fixed exchange rates. Many observers of the international economy continue to favor such a system. They argue (a) that it shields the domestic economy from international financial disturbances, (b) that under flexible rates, depreciation of a currency does not necessarily improve the current account balance in the short run, (c) that a depreciating exchange rate can cause as well as be caused by inflation, thereby creating the danger of a vicious-virtuous cycle, and (d) that fixed rates impose automatic monetary discipline on inflationary countries.

5. Advocates of floating rates dispute each of these arguments and contend that fixed rate proponents exaggerate the inherent instability of the international economy. They see the unwillingness of governments to play by the rules of the game as a fatal flaw in all fixed rate systems. Experience under the Bretton Woods system appears to have justified this second criticism. At present, a floating rate system of some sort seems to be the only workable possibility.

DISCUSSION QUESTIONS

1. In your library, locate two copies of a good financial newspaper, such as the *New York Times* or *Wall Street Journal*—a current copy and one a year old (the latter probably on microfilm). In the daily table of international exchange rates, check the values of the West German mark, the Japanese yen, the British pound, and the Swiss franc. Are they currently moving up or down? How have they changed from a year previously? For a more ambitious research project, pick one of these currencies, and try to explain its movements in terms of the ideas presented in this chapter.

2. As another research project, try updating Case 23.1. A good place to start is with a general news index, such as the *New York Times Index*, beginning with March 1979.

SUGGESTIONS FOR FURTHER READING

Kindleberger, Charles, and Lindert, Peter. *International Economics.* 6th ed. Homewood, Ill.: Richard D. Irwin, 1978.
A comprehensive text on international economics; Chapters 13 to 22 deal with the issues of theory and policy raised in this chapter.

President's Council of Economic Advisers. *Economic Report of the President.* Washington, D.C.: Government Printing Office, annually.
Each year's report contains an up-to-date analysis of international economic developments and a discussion of policy alternatives facing the U.S. government in the year ahead.

Riehl, Heinz, and Rodriguez, Rita. *Foreign Exchange Markets: A Guide to Foreign Currency Operations.* New York: McGraw-Hill, 1977.
A nuts-and-bolts guide to how foreign exchange markets work.

Schmidt, Wilson E. *The U.S. Balance of Payments and the Sinking Dollar.* New York: New York University Press, 1979.

Discusses the balance of payments accounts and explains why, in the author's view, the balance of payments should not be a major policy concern under a floating exchange rate regime.

Yeager, Leland. *International Monetary Relationships.* New York: Harper & Row, 1976.

The historical chapters of this book provide a good discussion of exchange rate experience under various institutional arrangements in the past.

C H A P T E R 24

CAPITALISM VERSUS SOCIALISM

WHAT YOU WILL LEARN IN THIS CHAPTER

Beyond all the particular issues of economic policies lies the wider issue of capitalism versus socialism. This chapter begins by defining the two terms and distinguishing several particular varieties of each type of economic system. Next, it surveys major elements of the long-standing debate over the relative merits of capitalism and socialism, first from the point of view of efficiency and then from the point of view of equity.

FOR REVIEW

Here are some important terms and concepts that will be put to use in this chapter. If you do not understand them, review them before proceeding.
- *Market justice and distributive justice (Chapter 1)*
- *Managerial and market coordination (Chapter 6)*
- *Efficiency and perfect competition (Chapter 9)*
- *Functional distribution of income (Chapter 15)*

The term *economic system* refers to the whole pattern of economic institutions that determine the way resources are allocated in a society. In most branches of economics, systems and institutions are among the givens. For example, macroeconomics develops theories about how an increase in the money supply will affect prices and interest rates, assuming a given institutional structure of the banking system and credit markets. Sometimes it examines the effects of the change in one particular institution while assuming that others do not change. An example is the study of the effects of fixed versus flexible exchange rates on world trade. In the branch of economics called comparative economic systems, though, the scope of analysis is much broader. Institutions and whole systems of institutions become the variables rather than the givens of analysis.

Economic systems can be grouped into broad categories on the basis of certain common traits. One way to classify them is on the basis of property rights. Property can be owned privately, owned cooperatively by voluntary associations of individuals, or owned by the government. In practice, examples of each kind of ownership can be found in almost every economic system, but often one form or another predominates. In economies called capitalist, for example, there is widespread private ownership of nonlabor factors of production. In socialist economies, cooperative or government ownership prevails.

Economic systems can also be classified in terms of their organizational structure. Chapter 7 introduced two general principles by which the division of labor in an economy can be coordinated. One is the managerial principle, which depends on centralized decision making; coordination is accomplished by means of orders passed from superiors to subordinates within a hierarchical organization. The other is the market principle, which depends on decentralized decision making and the use of the price system as a means of coordination. In capitalist economies, there is a tendency for managerial coordination to be confined to the internal business of individual firms. Relationships among firms are coordinated on a market basis. In socialist economies, there is usually an attempt to introduce managerial coordination on a larger scale, in the form of national economic planning.

This chapter will show how the two bases of classification can be used in various combinations to identify a variety of different subtypes of capitalist and socialist economies. It will also enter briefly into the general debate on the relative merits of the various systems. Chapter 25 will take a more detailed look at one of the largest socialist economies—that of the Soviet Union.

CAPITALISM

Capitalism Any economic system based on private ownership of all factors of production in which owners of capital act as entrepreneurs and coordinate their activity through use of the market.

The discussion of capitalism begins with a formal definition. **Capitalism** is any economic system based on private ownership of all factors of production in which owners of capital act as entrepreneurs and coordinate their activity through use of the market. Under capitalism, the principle of managerial coordination is limited to the internal workings of firms. Capitalism is sometimes also referred to as a *free enterprise system* because production and consumption activities are carried out on the basis of free contracts and voluntary exchange. The rules of the game under which capitalism operates formally prohibit the use of force, violence, threats, and fraud in market transactions.

The term *capitalism* has been applied to so many economic systems that it is necessary to distinguish several different varieties. The following sections will discuss three kinds of capitalism that differ from one another in terms of the economic role played by government. This role can range from nothing at all to very substantial.

Classical Liberal Capitalism

Classical liberal capitalism A capitalist economic system in which government performs only the limited role of protecting property rights and settling private disputes.

Under the tenets of **classical liberal capitalism,** the government plays an important, but strictly limited, role in the economy. In the classical liberal conception, government is a referee that enforces the rules of the game. It has just two functions: (1) to maintain a police force, a system of courts, and, if necessary, a military establishment to protect property rights against criminal activity and foreign aggression; and (2) to provide a court system for the peaceable settlement of disputes that arise over the terms of private contracts. Marxist opponents of capitalism say that this means that the government simply acts as the "executive committee" of the capitalist class and settles all disputes in favor of the owners of capital. Classical liberals deny the executive committee doctrine. Their ideal is a government that is impartial—one that is as vigilant in protecting the personal and property rights of consumers and workers as in protecting those of capitalists.

Under classical liberal capitalism, the government has a monopoly on the legitimate use of force, but it uses its coercive powers only against those who violate the personal and property rights of others. The sole exception is that the government can force private citizens to pay whatever minimal taxes are needed to finance its defense and law enforcement agencies.

Anarcho-capitalism

Some supporters of capitalism are even more strongly opposed to the use of force in economic affairs and even more strongly in favor of the free market than are the classical liberals. They believe that even the limited government of classical liberalism is too much. If it is right to protect private property, then the government need have no monopoly in this field. Furthermore, if it is wrong to use force in economic life, then the use of force by the government to collect taxes is also wrong. Following this reasoning, society should dispense with the institution of government altogether. This combination of a radical attack on government (anarchism) with a defense of private property (capitalism) is called **anarcho-capitalism,** or, alternatively, **radical libertarianism.**

    Radical libertarians believe that in an anarcho-capitalist society, profit-seeking private firms would take over all the legitimate functions now performed by government. Like classical liberals, they believe that private firms could deliver the mail, dispose of garbage, and collect tolls from motorists to pay for the construction and repair of highways. Unlike classical liberals, they believe that private arbitration firms could settle disputes between parties to business contracts, that private insurance companies could provide protection against criminal activity, and that the criminals themselves could be tracked down by private detectives (hired by the insurance companies) and locked up in privately run jails. A few hours spent with a radical libertarian tract such as Murray Rothbard's *For a New Liberty* have convinced many a skeptic that the principles of private enterprise are much more widely applicable than they ever imagined.[1]

Anarcho-capitalism (radical libertarianism) A capitalist system under which no state exists and all goods and services—including defense, police, and court services—are supplied by private firms.

State Capitalism

At the opposite end of the capitalist spectrum from radical libertarianism are systems that are basically capitalist but in which government plays a much larger role than just enforcing the rules of the game. The term **state capitalism** serves to describe these systems.

    Under state capitalism, government provides an alternative to the market as a means by which individuals and firms can win control over resources. If a firm wishes to increase its profits, it can cut costs and improve its product. Alternatively, it can lobby the government for regulations that will drive its competitors out of business and permit it to charge monopoly prices. If homeowners want to improve the value of their houses, they can buy larger lots to build on. Alternatively, they can persuade local zoning officials to force their neighbors to buy larger lots for their houses. If people want to live comfortably in retirement, they can save from their own wages during their working lifetimes. Alternatively, they can arrange that other people's wages be taxed to pay them social security.

    In effect, in every sphere of economic life under state capitalism, the

State capitalism A capitalist system under which government intervenes widely in the market and provides an alternative to the market as a means by which individuals and firms can win control over resources.

---

[1]Murray N. Rothbard, *For a New Liberty* (New York: Macmillan, 1972).

government and the market provide parallel structures for resource allocation. To the extent that most factors of production continue to be privately owned, such a system can still legitimately be called capitalist. Clearly, though, it is a rather different form of capitalism than that envisioned by classical liberals.

SOCIALISM

The doctrines and systems that have been called socialist are so diverse that any short definition is bound to offend at least some people who call themselves socialists. If these cautionary words are kept in mind, however, there is no reason not to at least try a definition. As the term is used here, **socialism** means any of a number of doctrines that include two tenets: (1) that some major share of nonlabor factors of production ought to be owned in common or by the state; and (2) that justice requires incomes to be distributed at least somewhat more equally than under classical liberal capitalism. No more will be said here about socialism in general; instead, the chapter will turn to a number of particular types of socialism.

Socialism Any of a number of doctrines that include the following tenets: (1) that some major share of nonlabor factors of production ought to be owned in common or by the state, and (2) that justice requires incomes to be distributed at least somewhat more equally than under classical liberal capitalism.

Centralized Socialism

Perhaps the most widely discussed variety of socialism—and, to many, the only "pure" variety—is **centralized socialism.** In such a system, all capital and natural resources are government owned. The government sets up some kind of central planning board that coordinates all production according to managerial principles. The board issues plans that have binding force on all individual units where production is actually carried out. In a literal sense, the entire economy is one big firm.

Centralized socialism A socialist system under which all capital and natural resources are owned by the government, which plans all production as if the economy were one big firm.

In the most commonly described form of centralized socialism, planning is carried out in physical terms. The plans drawn up by the central planning board specify the number of tons of steel or number of yards of cloth or whatever to be made in each factory. The plans also specify the number of tons of coal or pounds of yarn or whatever to be used up in producing the output. Labor is the only factor of production not directly owned by the state. Workers are free to choose their own jobs within the framework of the plans. (Forms of centralized socialism in which workers are assigned to specific jobs are by no means unknown, however.) Governments that have espoused centralized socialism have generally tried to bring agriculture as well as industry under the sway of central planning.

Socialism as an economic system is inseparably associated with the name of Karl Marx. Although Marx was notoriously reluctant to draw up blueprints for the socialist future he foresaw, a careful study of his writings suggests that he thought of the socialist economy in centralized terms. As will be shown in the next chapter, that has certainly been the interpretation placed on Marxism by ideological authorities in the Soviet Union. Today, however, one often encounters people who think of themselves as Marxian socialists without being strict centralists on economic matters. Many Eastern European reformers and Western Marxist radicals are noncentralists.

Lange's Market Socialism

From the early days of this century, one aspect of centralized socialism has been consistently criticized by economists: the principle of planning in physi-

Karl Marx—German philosopher, international revolutionary, and patron saint of Soviet communism—was also a prominent member of the British classical school of economics. His study of economics began in earnest when he moved to London in 1849 at the age of thirty-one. As it was for his contemporary, John Stuart Mill, the study of economics for Marx was first and foremost the study of the works of David Ricardo. But whereas other economists of the classical school were for the most part sympathetic to the capitalist system, Marx took the tools of Ricardian economic analysis and turned them against the social system that had spawned them.

The keystone of classical economics was the labor theory of value—the doctrine that the values and relative prices of various goods are determined primarily by the number of labor hours that go into their production. For Ricardo, the labor theory had been just a description of how the economy worked; but Marx went on to argue that if labor is the source of all value, workers ought to receive the whole product of their labor. Instead, under capitalism, a large part of that product was siphoned off into the pockets of capitalists in the form of profits or "surplus value."

Marx did not limit himself to exposing the inner workings of the capitalist system and condemning it as unjust. In addition, he attempted in his massive work, *Capital,* to prove that capitalism was headed for an inevitable breakdown, to be followed by a socialist revolution. Marx worked all his life with international revolutionary groups to prepare the way for this coming revolution.

Karl Marx (1818–1883)

Despite his faith in the inevitability of the socialist revolution, Marx had practically nothing to say about the operation of a socialist economy. The few remarks he did make suggest, however, that the socialism he envisioned would be of a centralized variety in which the "planning principle" would replace the "anarchy of the market." The rest he left to be worked out by future socialists in the course of their practical experience.

---

cal terms. Opponents of socialism have argued that it is beyond the capacity of central planners to specify the physical quantities of the millions of inputs required for thousands of firms. Even if workable sets of plans could be drawn up, planners could not guarantee that they had found the most efficient combination of inputs for production of the given outputs and the most efficient pattern of outputs to satisfy consumer demands.

During the 1930s, economist Oskar Lange issued a justly famous reply to these critics. In a series of articles entitled "On the Economic Theory of Socialism," Lange claimed that central planning in physical terms was neither the only nor the best way of running a socialist economy. Instead, he proposed a system—**market socialism**—in which the socialist managers of individual firms would mimic the behavior of managers under perfectly competitive capitalism. A central planning board would exist, but its major function would no longer be to issue commands; instead, it would set prices for goods and factors of production. Managers would take these prices into account and would conduct the actual operation of their firms according to two rules:

Market socialism A socialist system in which details of resource allocation are made through market mechanisms rather than through central planning.

1. The quantity of output produced by each firm would be the quantity that would make the marginal cost of production equal to the assigned price of the product.
2. A combination of factor inputs would be chosen to produce each product; this would make the marginal physical product per dollar's worth of each factor equal to the marginal physical product per dollar's worth of any other factor.

Managers would requisition whatever quantities of factors of production they needed to produce according to these rules. They would produce whatever

Oskar Lange (1904–1965)

In his sixty-one years, Oskar Lange achieved not one but two distinguished careers as an economist. Born in Tomaszow, Poland, he came to the United States to study at the University of California and Stanford University. He remained in the United States to teach at the University of Michigan, Stanford University, and the University of Chicago. His famous article, "On the Economic Theory of Socialism," appeared in the *Review of Economic Studies* in 1937 and gave him an international reputation.

Lange's interests as an economist went beyond the question of the economics of socialism. He was a pioneer in econometrics and did important early work in macroeconomics as well. In 1944, he wrote *Price Flexibility and Full Employment*, in which he attempted to establish Keynes's employment theory as a special case within a general equilibrium theory.

By this time, Lange had acquired U.S. citizenship. In 1945, however, he renounced it to become the Polish ambassador to the United States. After serving as ambassador, he became Poland's delegate to the United Nations. Finally, in 1947, he returned to Poland to begin the second phase of his career as an economist. He held various positions in the Communist Party and government and in 1957 became the chairman of the Polish Economic Council.

As a leading economist in communist Poland, Lange turned to electronic computers and cybernetics to reconcile his earlier views on market socialism with Soviet-type central planning. He described the market as a cumbersome and slow-working servo-mechanism—the best available in the days before computers, but now obsolete. Without repudiating his earlier work, he characterized its proposed trial-and-error system as quaintly out of date. He continued to write on econometrics and economic cybernetics until his death in 1965.

quantities of outputs the rules required. In any particular period, the uncoordinated actions of individual firms might result in a surplus or shortage of some goods or factors. If this were to occur, the central planning board would correct any imbalances. It would raise the prices of any factors or goods of which there was a shortage, thereby discouraging their use. Similarly, it would lower the prices of any goods or factors of which there was a surplus, thereby encouraging greater use. In this way, production and use would be brought into equilibrium and the plans of individual firms coordinated.

Lange's system, of which this is only the barest sketch, immediately caught the imagination of his readers. It appeared to offer two major advantages over centralized socialism with physical planning. First, the burden of work on central planners would be lessened because they would be responsible only for prices. Individual managers would do their own planning of physical input and output requirements. Second, Lange's rules for managers closely resembled the rules of managerial calculation under perfect competition. That resemblance made it seem likely that inputs and outputs would be chosen more efficiently than under a regime of physical planning. (These points will be discussed in more detail later in the chapter.)

Participatory Socialism

Participatory socialism A socialist system under which the means of production are owned collectively by the workers of individual firms, who participate democratically in the process of management and share the profits of their firms.

Under **participatory socialism,** the third socialist system to be looked at, the means of production belong neither to the state nor to private capitalists. Instead, they are owned in common by the workers who actually operate them. The workers of each firm participate democratically in management; hence the name. Relationships among firms and between firms and consumers are coordinated by markets, as in a capitalist economy. The role of the government need not be greater than under state capitalism.

Under participatory socialism, workers, not capital owners, are the entrepreneurs. If successful, they share in the profits. The functional distribution of income is determined by marginal productivity principles, much as under capitalism; but the principles that govern the personal distribution of income are quite different. The ownership of nonlabor factors of production is not highly concentrated, as it is under capitalism; instead, it is widely shared by all workers. As a result, workers receive in addition to their wages a bonus or "social dividend" that represents their share of the profits and of the product of resources owned in common. To the extent necessary, of course, this principle of distribution can be supplemented by social insurance to meet the needs of the elderly, the disabled, and the nonworkers.

Participatory Socialism in Yugoslavia Participatory socialism is not just a creature of abstract theory. An entire national economy, that of Yugoslavia, has operated under a system of worker management since the early 1950s. In the Yugoslav economy, a new firm can be created by central or local government, by an existing firm, or by a group of individuals. Once it comes into being, it takes on an independent life of its own, entering into market relationships with its customers and suppliers. The basic governing unit of a Yugoslav firm is the workers' council, in which all workers participate. The council directly reviews and approves basic long-run policy decisions, including the important decision regarding distribution of the firm's income. The council also elects a smaller executive council and a director to handle the day-to-day business of the firm. Although Yugoslavia's communist government claims to find authority in Marx's writings for this brand of socialism, the system could hardly be in greater contrast to the centralized blueprint of official Soviet doctrine.

In many respects, participatory socialism has worked well in Yugoslavia. Although the country was very nearly the poorest one in Europe at the end of World War II, over the next two decades it enjoyed one of the fastest economic growth rates in Europe. Furthermore, Yugoslavs have enjoyed a far greater degree of political and personal freedom than their comrades in other Eastern European countries. This fact is by no means unrelated to the difference in economic systems. Yugoslavia has its share of economic problems, ranging from high inflation and regional disparities in income to complaints that workers spend too much time at factory meetings and not enough on the production line. Nonetheless, it is a system from which there is much to be learned in both the East and the West.

European Social Democracy

The fourth kind of socialism to be looked at is European social democracy. Social democratic parties have either held power or been a strong opposition party in most countries of Western Europe and Scandinavia since World War II. Although there are important differences among the parties of various countries, the main principles of social democracy can be illustrated with the example of the British Labour Party. The defining characteristics of British social democracy are an overriding concern for the poor and a belief in equality. By equality, in the words of a leading member of the Labour Party, "we mean more than a simple redistribution of income. We want a wider social equality embracing the distribution of property, the educational system, social class relationships, power and privilege in industry—indeed, all that is enshrined in the age-old socialist dream of classless society." [2] In pursuit of this goal of equality, the Labour Party, like its counterparts on the continent of Europe, instituted wide-ranging "welfare state" policies. These policies are supposed to guarantee to every citizen, as a matter of political right, minimum standards of health care, education, food, and housing. At the other end of the scale, confiscatory rates of taxation were imposed on people with inherited wealth (or even simply high earned incomes). Great Britain's Labour governments also made strong efforts to reduce selectivity in education in an attempt to eliminate an important source of class distinction.

On the matter of ownership of the means of production, the more moderate Labour Party leaders are not dogmatists. The same person just quoted writes that a "mixed economy is essential to social democracy. For while a substantial public sector is clearly needed to give us the necessary control over the economy, complete state collectivism is without question incompatible with liberty and democracy." [3] Great Britain's public sector is indeed substantial by U.S. standards. In its various periods in power, Labour governments extensively nationalized steel, coal, railroads, shipbuilding, aircraft, automobiles, and several other important industries, although still leaving a large part of the private sector. British nationalized industries are supposed to be run on competitive business principles and are supposed to turn a profit to help finance the government's welfare state policies. In practice, though, the managers of nationalized industry have complained of capricious political interference in their affairs. Many of the largest nationalized industries have operated at a loss and have required heavy subsidies from the taxpayers. The new Conservative government elected in 1979 pledged to return some nationalized industry to private hands and to improve management of the rest.

As economic systems, social democracy and state capitalism are not far apart. Although they lie to the "left" of any major U.S. political groupings, the European social democrats represent the "right" within the broad spectrum of possible socialisms.

SOCIALISM: PRO AND CON

Having made this catalog of capitalist and socialist economic systems, the chapter turns now to a brief survey of the ongoing debate over the relative merits of various systems. Socialist slogans have long proclaimed the superiority of socialism over capitalism. Socialism, it has been said, replaces the "anarchy of the market" with the "planning principle." It also replaces "production for profit" with "production for use" and replaces capitalist exploitation of the working classes with a system in which the whole product goes to the real producers. Such slogans are impressive to hear but difficult to evaluate. What exactly is the planning principle? What is the difference between production for profit and production for use? And what is meant by "exploitation"? Can a discussion in terms of mundane economic standards shed some light on the merits of socialism?

---

[2] Anthony Crosland, *Social Democracy in Europe*, Fabian Tract 438 (London: Fabian Society, 1975), p. 1.
[3] Ibid.

Static Efficiency

The first standard that can be used for comparing economic systems is static efficiency. In comparative economics, static efficiency is the efficiency of resource allocation under hypothetical conditions of universal equilibrium. In this system, resources, production technologies, and consumer tastes are known to everyone and are forever unchanging.

Lange's Claims for the Static Efficiency of Socialism Under perfect competition, a capitalist economy can, in principle, operate with complete static efficiency. If claims are to be made for socialism on grounds of static efficiency, then, it must be shown that it can do at least as well as capitalism under the same ideal conditions. That is what Oskar Lange set out to prove. He accepted the idea that any kind of socialism relying on central planning in physical terms would score poorly in terms of static efficiency. In his own system, however, efficiency would be guaranteed. Managers would be instructed to make the proper adjustments in marginal costs and marginal products, while central planners would be instructed to adjust prices to market-clearing, equilibrium levels.

That was only a starting point. It was not enough for Lange to show that under ideal circumstances, his socialist system could function at least as efficiently as capitalism. He went on to argue that under the circumstances that actually prevailed in the real world, his system would do better. First, he claimed that his system solved the problem of monopoly. Under capitalism, in an industry with only one or a few firms, managers tend to equate marginal cost with marginal revenue rather than with price. That tendency violates static efficiency conditions. In Lange's system, in contrast, managers would be instructed to follow the same rule—marginal cost equals price—no matter how few firms there were in a market.

Furthermore, Lange pointed out that even competitive markets would not operate efficiently when pollution or other distorting factors caused private costs to deviate from opportunity costs. Under his system, central planners could automatically correct for such things. They would simply build the appropriate incentives or penalties into the prices they set.

Counterclaims Lange's claims for the superior static efficiency of his system have brought forth three kinds of counterclaims. First, some critics have attacked the system directly in Lange's own terms. They have suggested, for example, that the trial-and-error pricing system that Lange's central planners were to use would be too time-consuming and might even be unstable. Also, they have pointed out that it is not clear how the trial-and-error method for finding market-clearing prices could be applied to goods that were custom-made, as much important industrial equipment is. Finally, they have argued that Lange's system would do poorly where considerations of time and risk played an important role in the pricing process.

A second, rather different, kind of criticism comes from advocates of state capitalism and moderate social democrats. They argue that a full transition to socialism is not necessary to achieve the desired gains in static efficiency. Instead, it would make more sense to keep a market economy and to introduce ad hoc corrections to deal with problems such as monopoly and pollution where necessary.

Finally, the most important of all the criticisms of Lange's system is a simple rejection of static efficiency as a standard of evaluation. Any gains in static efficiency from Lange's system, according to the critics, would be offset by disadvantages. This rejection raises the issues of dynamic efficiency and economic growth, to which the chapter now turns.

Dynamic Efficiency and Economic Growth

Dynamic efficiency and economic growth are standards for evaluating economic systems that accept the world as it is, with changing technologies, resource availabilities, and consumer preferences. The two standards are closely related. Economic growth measures the overall rate of expansion of the output of goods and services. Part of any increase in economic growth that occurs may be attributable to increased supplies of factors of production. More capital is accumulated through saving, more labor through population growth or more hours of work per capita, and more natural resources through mineral discoveries or territorial expansion. Dynamic efficiency refers to the growth rate that can be sustained with a given rate of expansion of factor supplies. High dynamic efficiency depends partly on the ability of a system to generate scientific and technical advances. It depends even more on the ability of its entrepreneurs to take advantage of opportunities as they emerge, quickly and effectively.

Claims for the Dynamic Efficiency of Socialism Some claims have been made for socialism on the ground of dynamic efficiency. One such claim is that the absence of private patent rights under socialism speeds the spread of innovations. Another is that monopolistic firms under capitalism consciously obstruct technological progress because they have vested interests in traditional products and methods of production. More commonly, though, the emphasis of socialist writers has been on the ability of their systems to raise the rate of economic growth through better mobilization of the factors of production.

One way socialist planners can increase the rate of economic growth is by diverting a larger share of national product into saving and investment than would be forthcoming under a free market system. It was once popular to claim that individual consumers had a "faulty telescopic facility." Thus people underrated the value of increased future incomes that could be earned by saving more now and overrated the value of present consumption. Socialist planners could feel justified in cutting present consumption to increase investment, because whether consumers realized it or not, such policies would make them better off in the long run.

Socialist planners have pursued other policies as well to increase factor supplies. These policies have included encouragement of long work hours, increased labor force participation by women, mobilization of surplus rural labor for work in industry, and intensified exploitation of new agricultural land and mineral resources. Socialists of almost every variety have advocated some policies to accelerate economic growth. Lange thought that his socialists should opt for more investment. The Yugoslav government has taken a variety of steps to ensure that the country's labor managed enterprises do not distribute too large a share of their revenues among workers for current consumption. As will be shown in the next chapter, though, it is the advocates of centralized socialism who have placed the greatest emphasis on growth. In fact, the ability of centralized socialism to mobilize massive factor supplies is sometimes said to more than outweigh the inferior static and dynamic efficiency of that system. Factor mobilization is alleged to give centralized socialism an edge over all alternatives in terms of economic growth.

Counterclaims Critics have long claimed that dynamic efficiency is the area of socialism's greatest economic weakness. This was brought out very early in the protracted "socialist controversy," to which Lange's famous papers were a contribution. The beginning of the controversy is usually given as 1922, the year the Austrian economist, Ludwig von Mises, published a paper in German, entitled "Economic Calculation in the Socialist Commonwealth."[4] In this paper, Mises attacked socialism for what he saw as its inability, in the absence of markets and a price system, to put collectively owned means of production to efficient use in pursuing the socialist planners' chosen ends. Lange began his own defense of socialism by acknowledging that Mises had identified an important weakness in the writings of socialists of his day. He went so far as to suggest that in the future socialist commonwealth, a statue should be erected in Mises's honor, so no one would forget that prices and markets would be essential under socialism too. Lange then set forth his own proposals, as described earlier.

Mises and his Austrian colleague, Friedrich von Hayek, were by no means satisfied with Lange's solution to the problem of resource allocation under socialism. What Lange had done, they said, was only to solve the problem of managerial calculation under socialism. But Lange completely neglected to deal with the even more important problem of entrepreneurship. As Mises put it:

The cardinal fallacy implied in this and all kindred proposals is that they look at the economic problem from the perspective of the subaltern clerk whose intellectual horizon does not extend beyond subordinate tasks. They consider the structure of industrial production and the allocation of capital to the various branches and production aggregates as rigid, and do not take into account the necessity of altering this structure in order to adjust it to changes in conditions. What they have in mind is a world in which no further changes occur and economic history has reached its final stage.[5]

Hayek added to the force of Mises's criticism with his insights into the role of the market as a mechanism for using knowledge. Effective entrepreneurship requires making use of particular knowledge of time and place as well as general knowledge of the opportunity cost of widely marketed goods. The existence of a price system makes the general information on opportunity costs available to people on the spot. Perhaps Lange's artificial price system would also be able to serve this purpose. To make use of the equally important particular knowledge of time and place, though, the people on the spot need independence of action and adequate incentives.

Under capitalism, the necessary independence is provided by private ownership of the means of production. The necessary incentives are provided by the opportunity to earn profits when decisions are taken correctly and the responsibility for bearing losses when things go wrong. Under socialism, the

---

[4]Translated in Friedrich A. von Hayek, ed., *Collectivist Economic Planning*, 6th ed. (London: Routledge & Kegan Paul, 1963).
[5]Ludwig von Mises, *Human Action* (New Haven: Yale University Press, 1949), p. 703.

Ludwig von Mises (1881–1973)

Ludwig von Mises was born when the "marginal revolution" that established modern economics was just getting under way, and he lived to celebrate the centenary of that revolution. In the meantime, he became one of the foremost economists of the twentieth century.

Mises was born in Lemberg, Austria, and was educated at the University of Vienna. He taught at the University of Vienna until the Nazis arrived and then moved to Switzerland. In 1940, he came to the United States, and in 1946, he became a U.S. citizen. In 1945, he joined the faculty of New York University, where he remained until his retirement in 1969, at the age of eighty-eight.

Mises's most original theoretical work is his *Theory of Money and Credit,* published in German in 1912. In that work, he became the first to apply the general principle of consumer choice to explain the demand for cash balances. He went on to use the principle as an explanation of expansions and contractions in economic activity. This pioneering insight, that macroeconomic fluctuations have their roots in microeconomic behavior, was lost sight of by mainstream economists during the Keynesian era. Today, however, the importance of the phenomena about which Mises wrote is widely recognized.

In 1922, Mises set forth his famous critique of socialism, "Economic Calculation in the Socialist Commonwealth." This work had a major influence on socialist writers of the day. Oskar Lange in the United States and Abba Lerner in England took Mises's criticism very seriously, and they set out to create a new market socialism that would solve the allocation problem as elegantly and accurately as any capitalist market. Mises, however, was unimpressed. To him, it was impossible to separate the market as an allocational mechanism from the real-world striving of owners after rents and entrepreneurs after profits. He dismissed Lange's and Lerner's work as that of "men playing at markets as boys play at trains."

In 1949, Mises published his monumental *Human Action.* This work is a treatise on all of economics, a grand work on the scale of Adam Smith's *Wealth of Nations* and John Stuart Mill's *Principles.* In *Human Action,* Mises elaborated on all his views on theory, methodology, and policy at great length. Throughout the book, and indeed throughout his whole career, he championed the libertarian doctrine that all government intervention in the economy is to be regarded with intense suspicion. Mises was a great teacher, and his influence lives on through the many students he taught over the years.

---

person on the spot is inevitably an economic civil servant whose independence in the economic hierarchy is limited. Furthermore, the civil servant's incentives operate in the direction of playing it safe and not rocking the boat.

The critics do not deny, for the most part, that a socialist economy can achieve a high rate of economic growth despite low dynamic efficiency by means of forced savings and, in some cases, forced labor mobilization. Such growth, however, may be growth at too high a price. This point is underlined by the fact that high saving and growth rates can, if desired, be achieved under state capitalism (as in Japan) and without any substantial sacrifice of dynamic efficiency.

CONCLUSIONS

It would be very misleading to think that socialism owes its widespread support solely to its purportedly superior economic performance. There are many socialists for whom the problems of production are secondary to the problems of economic justice. Economic justice, of course, means different things to different people, but here are at least some of the things it means to socialists.

First, socialists conceive of economic justice as equality. In their time-honored phrase, it means "from each according to ability, to each according to need." Some socialists are willing to accept the degree of inequality of labor income that would result from wage payments proportional to marginal productivity. Even these people, however, advocate supplementing wages with some kind of equalizing social dividend or social wage to be paid for with the interest, rent, and profits earned by collectively owned nonlabor factors.

Second, socialist economic justice is supposed to mean an end to exploitation. In this view, the profits, rents, and interest earned by nonworkers under capitalism do not reflect any real productive contribution of inanimate factors of production. They are instead unfairly deducted from the just earnings of labor. Socialists thus often oppose the nonwage earnings even of small-scale shopkeepers, landlords, and moneylenders, despite the fact that these earnings may not raise their recipients very high up the ladder of income distribution.

Finally, many socialists hold that economic justice requires not only that workers get a fair share of the product but also that they have some voice in the actual management of business affairs. Some socialists pay only lip service to this principle. They promote systems in which workers end up as remote from the functions of the central planning bureaucracies as they are from board-room management under capitalism. Others—the participatory socialists—make this the first and foremost element of economic justice.

Whatever the specific content given to the concept of economic justice, any argument that a socialist economy is inefficient can always, in the last resort, be met by the reply that one can afford to tolerate inefficiency in the name of equity.

Two kinds of counterclaims are advanced against the contention that socialism is necessary to achieve economic justice. One comes from left-wing state capitalists of the kind widely represented among liberal Democrats and Republicans in the United States. These people are basically in sympathy with the egalitarian aims of socialism. They simply argue that the government of a capitalist country can, if it has the will to do so, use tax and transfer policies to distribute income however desired. As mentioned earlier, this variety of opinion merges imperceptibly at some point with the position taken by moderate European social democrats.

The less moderate view on capitalism, socialism, and economic justice is heard from classical liberals and radical libertarians. These people conceive of economic justice primarily in terms of what has been called market justice. What economic justice requires, they say, is a system in which all people are able to devote their own energies and abilities exclusively to the pursuit of their own chosen objectives, without coercive intervention by anyone. In this view, the first requirement is a free market in which workers, consumers, and resource owners can participate on a purely voluntary basis. In such a system, no person has a right to demand that another turn over property or produce without offering a fair exchange. Nationalization of the means of production and redistributive taxation are thus unjust per se; equality has nothing to do with the matter.

SUMMARY

1. Any market economy in which all factors of production are privately owned and in which the owners of capital for the most part play the role of entrepreneurs can be called a capitalist economy. In both theory and

practice, there is a broad range of kinds of capitalism. The U.S. economy is a form of state capitalism in which government intervenes widely in the affairs of the market. Classical liberals advocate limiting the role of government to the provision of police, defense, and court services. Anarcho-capitalists favor reducing the role of government all the way to zero, with even the minimal functions of the classical liberal state being performed by private firms.

2. Any system can be called socialist if at least substantial parts of nonlabor factors of production are collectively owned and if an attempt is made to distribute incomes more equally than under classical liberal capitalism. Socialist systems differ widely from one another in the role they assign to the market. Centralized socialism envisions an economy run as one big firm in which the market plays no role at all. Lange's socialist economy, participatory socialism, and European-style social democracy all depend heavily on the market as a mechanism of resource allocation but use redistribution policies to modify the personal distribution of income.

3. The static efficiency of an economy is its theoretical efficiency under idealized conditions in which resources, production technologies, and consumer tastes are completely known and unchanging. A capitalist economy could achieve complete static efficiency under perfect competition. Centralized socialism is widely thought to score poorly in terms of static efficiency. Lange built the case for his own brand of socialism largely on consideration of static efficiency. He argued that under ideal conditions his system would operate as well as a capitalist market economy and that under real-world conditions it could achieve higher static efficiency.

4. Dynamic efficiency and economic growth are additional standards by which to judge the performance of an economic system. Centralized socialism claims a superior growth potential because of its ability to mobilize resources of capital and labor and focus them on the task of economic expansion. Questionable dynamic efficiency is seen as a major weakness of Lange's system.

5. Socialists claim that their systems provide greater economic justice than does capitalism. By economic justice, they mean distributive justice. Some state capitalists claim that the welfare state can achieve distributive justice without socialism. Other critics of socialism emphasize the standard of market justice and see capitalism as superior to socialism according to that standard.

DISCUSSION QUESTIONS

1. Why is it that owners of capital so often perform the entrepreneurial function in an economy where factors of production are privately owned? Why should land owners not play this role? Why not workers? Why not people who own no resources at all but who hire everything they need on a contract basis? Can you think of exceptions to the rule that entrepreneurs are also owners of capital? Explain.

2. What position do you think an advocate of classical liberal capitalism would take on each of the following issues that were discussed in earlier chapters: Antitrust policy? Regulation? Poverty? Pollution? Protectionism? How would the classical liberal position on these issues differ from the anarcho-capitalist position—if at all?

3. Of all the kinds of economic systems discussed in this chapter, which kind would you expect U.S. "big businesses" to favor? Why? On what evidence do you base your answer?

4. Explain just what it means to say that under centralized socialism the whole economy is run as one big firm. In an anarcho-capitalist economy, which would entirely lack any government antitrust policy, do you think private businesses would grow and merge with one another to the point that the whole economy would become one big private firm? Explain.

5. There are no serious legal barriers to the emergence of participatory socialist firms in the U.S. economy. If the workers in a private firm pooled all their resources (perhaps making temporary sacrifices to increase their rate of saving), they could buy up the firm's stock share by share until they owned a controlling interest. They would then be in more or less the same position as the worker-owners of a Yugoslav firm. Why do workers so rarely do this in the U.S. economy? Do you know of any example of worker-owned and operated firms in the U.S. economy? Explain.

SUGGESTIONS FOR FURTHER READING

Crosland, Anthony. *Social Democracy in Europe*, Fabian Tract 438. London: Fabian Society, 1975.
An articulate defense of European social democracy by a leading British Labour Party spokesman.

Friedman, Milton. *Capitalism and Freedom*. Chicago: University of Chicago Press, 1972.
A classic defense of classical liberal capitalism.

Lange, Oskar, and Taylor, Fred M. *On the Economic Theory of Socialism*. New York: McGraw-Hill, 1964.
This volume conveniently reprints Lange's classical articles of the 1930s together with a closely related essay by Taylor.

Rothbard, Murray N. *For a New Liberty*. New York: Macmillan, 1973.
An exposition of the theory of anarcho-capitalism by the leading proponent of that economic system.

Vanek, Jaroslav. *The Participatory Economy*. Ithaca, N.Y.: Cornell University Press, 1971.
A discussion of participatory socialism, both as a general concept and as practiced in Yugoslavia.

CHAPTER 25
THE SOVIET ECONOMY

WHAT YOU WILL LEARN IN THIS CHAPTER
This chapter surveys the economic problems and achievements of the Soviet economy, the largest experiment ever in centrally planned socialism. The chapter begins with a discussion of the ideological origins and early history of the Soviet economy. It then surveys the formal structure of the Soviet planning system and points out that the informal structure of the system also plays an important role in how it works. Next, it reviews the Soviet growth record and discusses the Soviet Union's prospects for the future. The chapter concludes with some comments on economic reform in the Soviet system.

FOR REVIEW
Here are some important terms and concepts that will be put to use in this chapter. If you do not understand them, review them before proceeding.
- *Centralized socialism (Chapter 24)*
- *Managerial and market coordination (Chapter 6)*

The last chapter discussed many different kinds of economic systems, including several varieties of socialism. This chapter turns from theoretical comparisons to an extended case study of one kind of socialism—the centralized socialism of the Soviet Union. The very size of the Soviet Union as an industrial, political, and military power makes it worth taking a close look at the Soviet economic system. Another reason for studying it is to learn more about the general problem of resource allocation and what must be done to solve it successfully. Following is a survey of the origins, structure, and performance of the Soviet economy.

ORIGINS

Marxism-Leninism
The discussion of the Soviet economy begins with an explanation of its ideological origins as a system founded on the principles of Marxism-Leninism. The voluminous writings of Karl Marx are devoted largely to the evolution and structure of capitalism. Marx wanted to pave the way for revolution by demonstrating that capitalism was headed for a breakdown, but he did not attempt to draw a detailed blueprint for the coming socialist economy. There is little doubt, though, that he envisioned the socialist economy in highly

centralized terms. Private ownership of nonlabor factors of production would be abolished, and planning would replace the market as the primary means of resource allocation.

V. I. Lenin, the leader of the Russian Revolution, was, if anything, more of a centralist than Marx himself. The secret of Lenin's political success in Russia was the highly centralized, disciplined structure of the Bolshevik Communist Party he led. It was natural for him to apply the same methods of administration to the economy. In a book written just before he came to power, Lenin likened the task of running the economy to that of running the post office or any other bureaucratic administrative agency. The important thing would be a strong party leadership to define economic goals clearly and to provide the discipline and the will necessary to carry them out.

War Communism

Within months of the revolution of October 1917, the Bolsheviks were engaged in a civil war with their White Russian opponents. From the beginning of the civil war, the market economy was abandoned. Trade between the city and countryside was replaced with forced requisitioning of agricultural products. Virtually all industry was nationalized, including many small-scale businesses. Retail trade was also nationalized, although a substantial black market soon emerged. Industrial labor was put under semimilitary discipline, with workers sent to jobs wherever the need was most pressing. As a final blow to the market, a massive outpouring of paper currency from the new government sent inflation spiraling so high that money became useless. Workers in essential positions were paid in food or other goods. Party ideologists proudly proclaimed that socialism had come to the Russian economy.

Either the civil war or the government's radical policies taken one at a time would have produced economic chaos. In combination, they were a disaster. Militarily, the Bolsheviks scraped through against the odd assortment of White Russians and Western armies of intervention who opposed them. By 1921, however, with the war over, the economy was in sad shape. Agricultural production was down by one-third, and industrial workers had fled to the countryside in search of food. It was time for a change of direction.

The NEP

With the threat of war removed, Lenin launched his New Economic Policy, known as the NEP. It was a step backward, taken, as he put it, in order to prepare for two steps forward. Lenin had endorsed the centralist and antimarket policies of war communism, which fitted closely the views he had expressed before the revolution.[1] Now he set those policies aside in order to get production back on its feet. Trade and small industry went back to private hands. Buying replaced forced requisitioning in agriculture. The peasants once again found it worth their while to sow the fields they had let go fallow. Currency reform put the brake on inflation, and the money economy reappeared. The "commanding heights"—heavy industry, transportation, banking, and foreign trade—remained in government hands, while the rest of the

---

[1]On Lenin's attitude toward war communism, see Paul Craig Roberts, *Alienation and the Soviet Economy* (Albuquerque, N.M.: University of New Mexico Press, 1971), chap. 2.

economy followed its own course. Planning was reduced to the issuance of "control figures," which were not directives but merely forecasts intended to help guide investment decisions.

An an instrument for economic recovery, the NEP was a great success. By 1928, prewar production levels had been surpassed in both industry and agriculture. Lenin died in 1924, and Stalin was busy consolidating his power in the party. It was time to take the two steps forward that Lenin had promised.

Collectivization and the Five-Year Plan

The two steps forward taken in 1928 were the Five-Year Plan for industry and the policy of collectivization in agriculture. These steps were designed to overcome two features of the NEP that Stalin saw as serious defects. First, as long as the NEP was in force, central authorities were altogether unable to control the direction of the market economy. Events went their own way while the nominal planners sat on the side and collected statistics after the fact. Second, the NEP provided no mechanism for transferring resources from agriculture to industry. The party needed such a transfer in order to pursue its industry first development strategy. Higher taxes, lower agricultural prices, or forced requisitioning of grain would result only in a withdrawal of effort by the peasants, as during the civil war.

In industry, the Five-Year Plan was, for the first time, supposed to set the course of development in advance. Annual operational plans were to be drawn up in accordance with it. These plans were to include assignments of the necessary raw materials to producers on a nonmarket basis. Above all, the Five-Year Plan envisioned a massive program of capital investment.

Industrial growth was to be financed by obtaining more agricultural produce. Collectivization was the technique used to make sure that the needed grain moved from the country to the city. Between 1928 and 1932, some 15 million peasant households—about two-thirds of the rural population—were formed into 211,000 collective farms. On the collectives, land and livestock were owned in common, while agricultural machinery was supplied by independent machine-tractor stations. Land was worked in common too, and a complex system of payment to collective farmers was introduced. Party control over the peasantry was immeasurably strengthened. Party policy could be imposed on the collectives in a way that had never been possible while agriculture was in private hands.

Collectivization was at least a qualified success. The policy wreaked havoc with agricultural production. The number of livestock fell nearly by half as peasants slaughtered them rather than turn them over to the collectives. Grain output also fell sharply, both because of the general chaos accompanying collectivization and because the incentive structure of the collectives themselves discouraged effort. Despite the disruption of production, though, the flow of goods from the countryside to the city increased; and that, after all, had been a major objective of the policy.

The increased flow to the cities occurred partly because collectivization put the grain where party authorities could get their hands on the first share, before the remainder was distributed to the peasants, and partly because there were fewer livestock left to eat it in the countryside. There were fewer people in the countryside too. Several millions died in the initial turmoil of collectivization and the subsequent famine of 1932–1934.

Emerging Outlines

Out of the disorder of the early 1930s emerged an economic system that displayed most of the major features of the Soviet economy today. Industry, trade, banking, transportation, and foreign commerce were all completely nationalized—with only the most trivial exceptions. Agriculture was almost entirely collectivized. At the top of the system sat Gosplan, the state planning agency. This agency and the ruling party guided the economy with a development strategy emphasizing centralization and planning in physical terms.

The next section of this chapter will look at some details of the structure and functioning of this system. Then, the final section will evaluate its performance.

STRUCTURE

Central Hierarchy

According to the official party handbook, *Fundamentals of Marxism-Leninism*, the Soviet economy functions as a single enterprise, directed by a single will. At the top of the economic hierarchy are the highest political organs of the Soviet government—the Supreme Soviet and its Council of Ministers. Under the Council of Ministers come a number of specialized agencies, including Gosplan, the Central Statistical Administration, and the State Bank. Also under the Council of Ministers are a long list of ministries with specific industrial responsibilities, such as coal, railroads, and ferrous metallurgy. Subordinate to these ministries are numerous regional agencies that act as intermediaries between the central government and the individual firms that stand at the bottom of the hierarchy.

Parallel to the government administrative structure is a Communist Party hierarchy, which also has important economic responsibilities. One of them is to observe, check, and report to the party leadership what is going on in firms and administrative agencies throughout the economy. A second responsibility is to control appointments to administrative and managerial posts at all levels. A third is to mobilize and exhort the labor force to greater efforts in service of the plan. In addition to these specific responsibilities, local party officials consult and participate in many kinds of managerial decision making at the enterprise level.

Enterprise Status

Operation of the individual Soviet enterprise is governed by a so-called technical-industrial-financial plan. This plan, issued annually, is broken down into quarterly and monthly segments. Its most important part is the production plan, which specifies how much output is to be produced, what assortment of products is to be included in total output, and when output is to be delivered. Other parts of the plan specify the quantities of labor and material inputs allotted to individual firms. A financial section gives targets for costs, wage bills, profits, use of short-term credit, and so on. In all, the plan may contain two dozen or more specific physical and financial targets that a particular firm is to meet.

The plan has the binding force of law on enterprise management. In principle, criminal penalties can be imposed for failure to fulfill the plan, although administrative penalties such as demotion or transfer to less desirable jobs are more commonly used. Positive incentives are also provided. Very substantial bonuses are given to managers who successfully fulfill or overfulfill the various parts of their plans.

Planning Procedures

The heart of the planning process is a set of material balances—summaries of the sources and uses of two hundred or three hundred of the most important industrial commodities—drawn up by Gosplan. The purpose of each balance is to ensure that the sources (supply) and uses (demands) for each good are equal and that there will be no shortages or surpluses.

In a simplified form, the process by which material balances are drawn up works something like this. As soon as Gosplan receives directives from the political authorities indicating the general rate of projected development and the most important priorities, work begins on a preliminary set of balances called control figures. These figures show roughly how much of each good must be produced and how much must be used in each sector of the economy if the overall goals are to be met. The next step is to pass the control figures down through the planning hierarchy, where the main balances are broken down into requirements for each region of the country and finally for each enterprise.

When enterprise managers receive these preliminary control figures, they are supposed to suggest ways they can increase outputs or reduce inputs to achieve more ambitious targets. They also have an opportunity to complain if they think the plans exceed their capacity for output or do not provide sufficient inputs. Enterprise responses to the control figures are then sent back up through the hierarchy to Gosplan at the center.

When the original control figures are corrected in the light of information collected from below, it is likely that the sources and uses of materials will no longer balance. People actually responsible for carrying out the plans will often have tried to make their jobs easier by asking for reduced output targets or increased supplies of inputs. What follows is a complex procedure of adjustment and bargaining in which Gosplan tries to eliminate threatened material shortages without sacrificing overall targets. In some cases, shortages may be covered by imports or by drawing down reserve inventories. More commonly, Gosplan responds by tightening the plan—putting pressure on producers to accomplish more with less. If the tightening process goes too far, the result will be a balance on paper only. The plan will contain concealed shortages that will emerge during its execution.

The final balances are then broken down again. In addition to the crucial two hundred or three hundred materials subject to central balancing, individual ministries or regional authorities will in the meanwhile have prepared balances on thousands of other goods that are not of economy-wide significance. These material balances together eventually become the technical-industrial-financial plans for all firms through the economy. This is a very time-consuming process. Often the final plans are not completed until the planned year is several weeks or even months underway.

Labor Planning

The planning process for one important resource needs special treatment. Allocating labor is partly a matter of how goods are to be produced and partly a matter of who is to do any particular job. Indirectly, the decisions made on the hows and whos also affect income distribution.

Roughly speaking, the how is decided by central planners. Gosplan draws up labor balances for various kinds of work in much the same way that material balances are drawn up. Basic policy on how much labor each enterprise is to use to accomplish the tasks is specified in the technical-industrial-financial plan.

The who of labor allocation, in contrast, is handled largely by markets. For the most part, individual workers are free to choose their occupation and place of work. Two methods are used by the central authorities to ensure that the right number of workers is available in each sector of the economy. One method is to offer substantial wage differentials, paying premiums for skilled work or for work that is unattractive. The other is to manipulate the labor supply through education and training programs.

Individual enterprises are able to exercise some degree of control over the wages they pay. They do this both by adding bonus payments to standard wages and by deciding the skill bracket to which any particular worker is assigned. The overall result is a system where variations in wages are used to ensure a balance between the supply and demand for labor. This is the most important instance of the use of the market for resource allocation in the Soviet economy.

The Informal Structure

The formal administrative structure of the Soviet economy exactly fits the model of centralized socialism. Communications follow vertical paths up and down the planning hierarchy. The messages passed to enterprise management have the binding force of law. Managers are rewarded or reprimanded in accordance with their degree of obedience to the plan. Only the method of assigning particular workers to particular jobs provides a major exception.

A close study of the informal structure of the Soviet economy, however, shows that central control is not absolute. A good deal of informal "horizontal" communication and exchange occurs among firms. Plans are not always treated as binding; sometimes they are treated as only one among a number of factors influencing management behavior. And the attainment of a comfortable and prosperous life for a Soviet manager is not always just a matter of obeying commands to the letter.

The Safety Factor Soviet managers do not passively wait for plans to arrive from above and then do the best they can to fulfill them. Instead, they direct considerable efforts to making sure that they have a safety factor that will cushion them against the danger of being assigned impossible tasks and then being punished for failing to achieve them.

Safety factors often take the form of large inventories of inputs or semifinished products. Inventories have always been a problem in the Soviet Union. Sometimes, when there are shortages, inventories get squeezed so low that any break in deliveries disrupts production. At other times, when an enterprise manages to get its hands on more than it needs of some essential material, it hoards the scarce material as a safety factor against future shortages.

A rather different safety factor takes the form of deliberately concealed productive capacity. By hiding its true capacity, an enterprise hopes to get an easy plan. Suppose that when provisional control figures come down to some textile mill, they call for an output of, say, 100,000 yards of fabric in the next year. The manager knows that this is just about all the enterprise can squeeze out, given the inputs the control figures say will be available. It does not pay to let Gosplan know that, however. Instead, the manager complains that it will not be possible to produce more than 90,000 yards unless the labor force is substantially increased and the enterprise is given a bigger allotment of synthetic yarn. The easy 90,000-yard plan provides the needed safety factor. The target will be met even if something goes wrong during the year.

Of course, the people in Gosplan know that managers always try to develop a safety factor of some kind. They act on that knowledge when they are juggling their material balances to make them come out even. They do not hesitate to tighten up the plan even when told from below that it cannot be done. The whole thing develops into a sort of game, which greatly increases the degree of uncertainty involved in the planning process.

Procurement According to the formal structure of the Soviet economic system, individual enterprise managers are not responsible for procuring their own raw materials, energy supplies, equipment, or other inputs. As part of the plan, each user of, say, copper tubing is given a schedule of expected deliveries. At the same time, some supplier is given a corresponding schedule of deliveries to make. The user and supplier do not even need to communicate directly with one another. The necessary plans are all supposed to be set up on the basis of information passed vertically to higher authorities.

In practice, however, managers who passively wait for carloads of copper tubing to roll up to their factory gate are likely to be in trouble. Instead, they must be concerned that either their assigned supplies may be behind schedule on their production plan or that the suppliers may be trying to tuck away a hoard of tubing as a safety factor against future demand. Managers of the user enterprises take appropriate measures to deal with this problem. For one thing, they keep on their payrolls people colorfully known as "pushers." The pushers' job is to go around wining and dining and wheedling suppliers, much as the salespeople of a capitalist firm go after potential buyers. Of course, technical-industrial-financial plans do not allow for funds to hire pushers. They have to be worked in under the title of consulting engineer or something of the sort.

Sometimes all pushers have to do to get supplies moving on time is to twist a few arms. Other times they may have to pay outright bribes. On still other occasions they may have to work out a black market barter deal under which one firm will come up with a hoarded carload of copper tubing in exchange for a desperately needed crate of ball bearings. All in all, the telephone lines are always busy, despite the fact that such things are theoretically unnecessary in a centrally planned economy.

Selective Fulfillment The plan specifies not one but many targets for each enterprise. There are targets for total production, for assortment of production, for cost reduction, for technological improvements, and for numerous other things. Sometimes the end result of issuing so many different targets is to give managers more, rather than less, freedom to maneuver. This happens when it becomes impossible to fulfill all targets at once, so managers must decide which part of the plan will be most impressive to fulfill. The following much-repeated anecdote illustrates the nature of the problem.

Case 25.1
Fulfilling the Plan in a Soviet Nail Factory

There was once a factory whose business it was to manufacture nails for use in the construction trade. In a certain year, the plant was assigned the task of producing x tons of nails, which were to be distributed among a variety of sizes according to the needs of Soviet carpenters. Before the planned year was far underway, the unfortunate manager of the enterprise realized that he could not achieve his target for total output if he kept to the planned assortment. His past experience had taught him that the authorities were much more interested in the total output than in the assortment plan, so he decided on an ingenious strategy. He gave up making little nails, which were a bother to produce and weighed hardly anything, and concentrated on enormous spikes. In that year, he turned out far more than x tons of output. He was gloriously rewarded for overfulfilling the plan.

Naturally, the long-suffering Soviet carpenters complained. They had no way of fastening together anything smaller than two railroad ties! An ingenious Gosplan official hit on a solution. The next year, when the plan was issued, the total output target for the enterprise was stated not in tons but in number of nails, by count. The reader can guess how the enterprise manager responded. He gave up entirely on huge spikes, which took altogether too much hard-to-produce steel. Instead, he concentrated on producing the tiniest pins and brads, which used hardly any metal and counted millions to the ton.

Naturally, the long-suffering Soviet carpenters complained.

Perhaps this anecdote has become exaggerated with the telling, but not by much. In real-life Soviet stores, one finds the assortment of shoe sizes out of step with the assortment of feet, because big sizes take too much leather and bonuses are based on the number of pairs produced. One finds paint mixed so thinly that two coats are needed instead of one, because bonuses are paid on the basis of number of gallons. One finds new models and styles very rarely, because the innovation plan is less important than the output plan. All in all, the very multiplicity of plan targets reduces the real degree of control the planners achieve over what is actually produced.

Planners' Reactions

Naturally, the central authorities are not unaware of the games managers play. They know that the letter of the law is sometimes broken, that reserves are hidden, and that some parts of the plan are less important than others. They could crack down severely on managerial independence, but they do not. They know that the economy could not function if they did. Planners know that the best plans they can make are full of inconsistencies and contradictions. They have to rely on local initiative and ingenuity to overcome these defects, even if the local initiative involves breaking the law. As a result, the authorities take a pragmatic attitude of selective toleration toward the independent behavior of enterprise managers. If a manager acting on local initiative manages to fulfill the plan, nothing is said. Bonuses are paid, and all is well. Only if illegal methods are used and the plan still is not fulfilled is the manager liable to be called on the carpet. In short, it is recognized that the pushers, the bribes, and the safety factors are the grease that keep an imperfectly fashioned machine running.

PERFORMANCE

Growth Record

Soviet leaders, and indeed ordinary Soviet citizens, are extremely proud of one aspect of their economy's performance: its growth record. Within the lifetimes of millions, Russia has been transformed from an economic backwater into one of the world's leading industrial powers. In 1917, Russia had achieved only something like the level of economic development of today's Brazil. It had only a small industrial sector set against a backdrop of vast rural poverty. Today, Soviet living standards are comparable to those of, say, Italy. Soviet industrial capacity exceeds that of West Germany; and in certain particular fields, such as steel output and military technology, it equals or surpasses that of the United States.

Exhibit 25.1 presents the Soviet growth record and compares it to growth in the United States. In the upper figure, representing economic growth in the Soviet Union, two sets of data are presented. The official Soviet statistics show an enormous surge of growth during the 1930s, interrupted by the devastation of World War II and continuing at very high, but gradually declining, rates thereafter. On the same chart, a Western estimate of Soviet growth also shows very respectable growth rates in the earlier periods, but by no means so spectacular a growth as the official Soviet figures show. In the 1970s, both Soviet and Western estimates indicate a slowdown.

Explaining Differing Estimates Why do Western and official Soviet estimates of early Soviet growth differ so much? The answer is largely a matter

---

Exhibit 25.1

Growth rates of GNP: The Soviet Union and the United States

The Soviet Union has a very impressive record of economic growth. Western and Soviet estimates of this growth use different methods and arrive at different numbers; but even by Western measures, growth has consistently been more rapid in the Soviet Union than in the United States until quite recently.

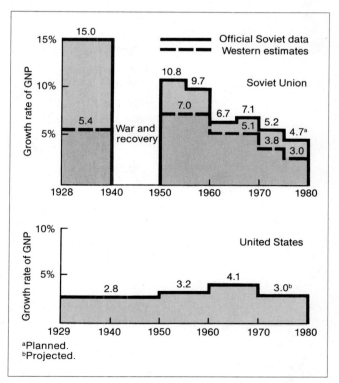

Sources: From Paul R. Gregory and Robert C. Stuart. *Soviet Economic Structure and Performance* (New York: Harper & Row, 1974), p. 378. (Soviet data recomputed from Abram Bergson.) Also from ''Breznhev's Russia,'' *Economist*, February 14, 1976, p. 63 All Soviet official data from published sources. Early Western estimates from Abram Bergson, *Real National Income of Soviet Russia since 1928* (Cambridge, Mass.: Harvard University Press, 1961), pp. 180, 210, 261. Most recent estimates from U.S. Joint Economic Committee. *Western Perceptions of Soviet Economic Trends* (Washington D.C., Government Printing Office, 1978), pp. 3–4.

of the accounting conventions used. Real GNP statistics are always derived by using some index of prices to adjust nominal GNP data in a way that will make it possible to compare data for different years. It turns out to make a great deal of difference which base year is chosen for the index. Choice of an early base year gives rise to numbers that exaggerate the growth rate, especially for an economy that is undergoing rapid structural changes. Soviet statisticians like to use the earliest possible year. The 15 percent growth rates of the 1930s reflect the use of 1928 prices as a basis for calculations. Western practice makes use of a later base year. Soviet accounting practices differ from Western ones in other ways as well, including the way output of services is measured, the way introduction of new kinds of products is taken into account, and the way agricultural harvests are computed.

In many cases, it is not a matter of Soviet statistics being wrong and Western calculations of Soviet performance being right; it is merely a matter of arbitrary choices of accounting convention. What is important for comparative purposes is to express the growth performance of different countries by using conventions that are as nearly the same as possible. It is the Western estimates of Soviet growth that ought to be compared with the figures given for the United States in the lower part of Exhibit 25.1.

Explaining the Slowdown Soviet economic growth, according to Western estimates, slowed markedly during the 1970s and is unlikely to recover to earlier rates during the 1980s. Over the next decade, Soviet growth is judged unlikely to exceed 3.5 percent, with 2.5 percent a realistic possibility. Various explanations are offered for the slowdown. For one thing, the growth rate of the Soviet labor force is slowing, and population growth in the relatively little industrialized Central Asian republics is exceeding that in the industrialized areas. The Soviet energy outlook also is not bright. The U.S. Central Intelligence Agency projects a decline in Soviet oil and natural gas production in the 1980s; the Soviet Union may be forced to stop oil exports to Eastern Europe and in the worst case may even become a net oil importer. This would drain scarce reserves of Western currency away from much-needed industrial imports. Finally, weather conditions for Soviet agriculture are not likely to be as favorable on the average during the 1980s as during the 1970s. Comparing these projections of Soviet economic growth with the estimated 3 percent growth rate of potential real GNP in the United States, one can see that the historic gap between Soviet and U.S. growth rates may be drawing to an end.

Sources of Soviet Economic Growth

In the past, the major source of rapid economic growth in the Soviet Union was the ability of the centrally planned economy to mobilize vast new supplies of factor inputs. In the decades immediately before and after World War II, the number of labor hours employed in the Soviet economy increased at a rate of 2.2 percent per year, while they were increasing at only 0.5 percent per year in the United States. Even more impressive, the Soviet capital stock grew at a rate of 7.4 percent per year, compared with just 1 percent per year in the U.S. economy. These very rapid growth rates of factor supplies more than compensated for the inferior dynamic efficiency of centralized socialism. The type of growth experienced by the Soviet Union, based primarily on expansion of inputs, is often called **extensive growth;** the type of growth experienced in the United States, based on better utilization of inputs, is called **intensive growth.**

Extensive growth is just as effective as intensive growth in adding to the economic power and prestige of a nation as a political unit, but it has certain disadvantages for individual citizens. Most important, a much larger share of GNP has been diverted from consumption into investment in the Soviet Union than in the United States. The figures for 1964 were 35 percent versus 17 percent. As a result, Soviet consumption per capita is only about a third that of the United States, even though GNP per capita is nearly half. It is also worth noting that Japan, the only noncommunist industrial nation to invest as high a fraction of GNP as the Soviet Union, has grown twice as fast in recent years. The Japanese experience shows what can be accomplished when rapid growth of inputs is combined with high dynamic efficiency rather than employed as a substitute for it.

Extensive growth Growth based predominantly on the mobilization of increasing quantities of factor inputs.

Intensive growth Growth based predominantly on improvements in the quality of factor inputs and in the efficiency with which they are utilized.

Pricing and Efficiency

As nearly as it can be measured (which is, in fact, only very roughly), the Soviet economy is inefficient in static terms as well as in dynamic terms. Western estimates indicate that it gets only about half as much output per unit of input as does the U.S. economy. There are a number of reasons for this. It may have to do with the structure of managerial incentives, and it may have to do with the motivation and work attitudes of Soviet workers in industry and agriculture. But it is likely that the major source of the Soviet economy's poor static efficiency is the lack of a price system capable of communicating information on opportunity cost to the economy's decision makers.

Consider two functions performed by the price system in a capitalist economy. The first is an accounting function. Prices make it possible to add apples and oranges and come up with a total expressed in dollars' worth of fruit. The second is an allocative function. The prices of inputs measure the opportunity cost of doing a thing or doing it in a certain way, and the prices of outputs measure the value of doing it.

In the Soviet economy, the price system performs the first of these functions but not the second. Industrial goods and consumer goods are all given prices so that industrial accountants can turn in reports on the number of rubles' worth of output produced. The prices, however, are based on custom and arbitrary accounting conventions that have little relationship to opportunity costs. Without knowledge of opportunity costs as reflected in a price system, Soviet planners often have difficulty deciding what to produce and how to produce it. Exact economic calculations are, in fact, impossible. In their place, Soviet planners can use one of three methods of deciding the what and how of resource allocation. First, they can give up calculations in terms of prices altogether and employ rough rules-of-thumb based strictly on engineering considerations. Second, they can do profit-and-loss calculations in terms of their own imperfect prices, even though the answers will at best be only approximately right. Third, they can imitate Western practice. As the following case study shows, though, none of these methods is foolproof.

Case 25.2
The Great Dieselization Blunder

During the 1950s, Soviet planners were faced with a classic problem in resource allocation. The problem was to decide what proportion of truck and tractor engines should be diesel-powered and what proportion gasoline-powered. The decision taken was in favor of massive dieselization. It is revealing to look at the considerations that influenced this important decision.

First, from a strictly engineering point of view, diesels seemed quite attractive. They offer substantially higher mechanical efficiency and are in many ways more elegant and technically sophisticated devices than gasoline engines. Second, the price of diesel fuel in the Soviet economy was low relative to gasoline—about 30 rubles a ton for diesel compared with 60 to 100 rubles for gasoline in the late 1950s. Finally, an examination of Western experience showed extensive dieselization of transportation equipment and heavy tractors.

Far from being a wise piece of economic calculation, though, the dieselization program turned out to be a great blunder. For one thing, diesels require greater initial costs. In part, then, the diesel versus gasoline decision is a matter of proper capital budgeting, in which higher initial costs must be balanced against discounted future gains. One defect in the Soviet price system is that the discount rate used by planners in such decisions is too low. Because the discount rate is, in effect, the "price" of future gains in terms of present costs, there is a bias in favor of techniques involving efficiently large initial costs. This no doubt played a part in the dieselization blunder.

What is more, available evidence indicates that the official Soviet price for diesel oil was too low in comparison to gasoline in the 1950s. Thus the price far underestimated the relative opportunity cost of the heavier fuel. In the United States, the refinery price of diesel is very little less than that of gasoline.

Finally, imitation of Western experience failed to take into account the special circumstances of the Soviet economy. The kinds of crude oil available in the Soviet Union are less suitable than those available in the United States for making diesel fuel. In order to provide fuel for all the new diesel engines, refineries were given plans that they could fulfill only by letting the quality of diesel fuel decline. The oil they used to make diesel should have been made into kerosene or furnace oil. Even worse, they allowed the sulfur content of diesel fuel to rise substantially. Cylinders and pistons wore out quickly when fed a diet of inferior fuel. Under these circumstances, the operating cost of diesel engines turned out to be higher than that of gasoline engines, not lower.

In the 1960s, planners realized their mistake and reversed their earlier decision. A program of de-dieselization began, and perhaps the right ratio of the two kinds of engines has now been reached. If so, the discovery was made not as a result of rational economic calculation but as a result of an enormously expensive process of trial and error.

Source: Based on Robert W. Campbell, *The Economics of Soviet Oil and Gas,* Resources for the Future Series (Baltimore: Johns Hopkins University Press, 1968), pp. 164–167.

Soviet Agriculture

If rapid industrial growth is the Soviet Union's proudest accomplishment, agriculture is its most distressing failure. While Soviet industry grew at a rate of 6.5 percent per year in the first half of the 1970s, agriculture crept ahead at only 2 percent (both official figures). In 1961, then-Premier Nikita Khrushchev set a target of 302 million tons of grain for 1980. In 1975, with three-quarters of Khrushchev's allotted time span elapsed, output was a mere 140 million tons.

That was an exceptionally bad year, to be sure, but even the official 1980 target has been scaled down to 218 million tons.

The roots of Soviet agricultural problems date from the earliest days of collectivization. In the Stalin era, agriculture was a cow to be milked for the benefit of industrial development. Now that it has become a serious constraint on industrial development, it is proving difficult to reverse the effects of decades of neglect.

The heart of the Soviet agricultural system is the collective farm, or **kolkhoz.** On paper, the kolkhoz is a cooperative, not very different from such participatory social institutions as the Yugoslav worker managed firm or the Israeli kibbutz. In practice, the collective farm is a far cry from the ideal. Three institutions exercise close control over it from outside. First, the Communist Party controls the selection of collective farm management and directs internal decision making. Second, the kolkhoz, like the industrial enterprise, is subject to a plan specifying inputs, outputs, production methods, capital investment projects, and dozens of other details. Third, until 1958, collective farms did not own their agricultural machinery but instead depended on rural "machine-tractor stations." These stations were able to use their monopoly on equipment to control the collective's affairs even further.

In the 1930s, the whole structure of agricultural administration was aimed at one purpose only: moving the indispensable minimum of grain from farm to city. To that end, delivery targets for the kolkhoz were set not at a percentage of output but at a fixed rate per acre sown. If bad weather brought yields down, the collective farmers bore the entire burden of the shortfall. The state and industry were guaranteed their share. Although it would seem that this would create a strong incentive for the collective to work hard to avoid shortfalls, the effect was blunted by a complex and inefficient system of distributing collective income among kolkhoz members. The system left individuals with few incentives to contribute to the common effort.

Khrushchev must be credited with recognizing that the agricultural problem needed a solution. He abolished the hated machine-tractor stations and made important changes in internal work organizations and management systems. Unfortunately, he diverted much energy and resources into ill-conceived crusades that soaked up resources and offered few long-term results. One crusade was the famous "virgin lands" campaign that put millions of acres of semidesert to the plow for the first time ever. Another was the attempt to introduce the growing of corn, which followed his trip to the United States in 1955. Even more than dieselization (which was also touted as a boon to agriculture), the corn campaign was a naive imitation of foreign practice with little attention paid to radical differences in local conditions.

Agricultural policy in the last decade, like so much else under the Brezhnev leadership, has been characterized by caution mixed with sober determination. Agricultural investment rose from 14 percent of all investment in 1960 to 31 percent in 1976. In the next five years, the farms were to be flooded with some 2 million new tractors and a half million harvesters. Unfortunately, this investment has not been accompanied by the further radical institutional reforms that seem necessary to raise the appallingly low level of agricultural productivity. Nearly a quarter of the entire Soviet labor force still works in agriculture. Productivity per worker is only about a fifth of the U.S. level.

Kolkhoz A Soviet collective farm.

CONCLUSIONS

What sort of future does the Soviet economy face? Since the early 1960s, there has been a great amount of talk, both in the Soviet Union and in the West, about economic reform. To many, the declining Soviet growth rate indicates a necessity to switch from an extensive to an intensive growth strategy, and that cannot be done within current economic institutions. These institutions were designed to mobilize resources and to implement vast structural changes, not to use scarce resources as efficiently as possible.

Reform proposals have centered on three areas. First, there is a need to reform managerial incentives so that, in the Soviet phrase, the interests of management will coincide with the interests of the national economy. The most important part of reforming incentives must be to make profit replace the dozens of indicators of output, assortment, cost, and productivity. Second, there must be a radical price reform. Profit cannot be used as an indicator of economic performance unless industrial prices reflect opportunity costs. Third, there is a need for decentralizing some decision making and establishing direct links among firms, bypassing the cumbersome planning bureaucracy.

The Soviet government has responded to these reform proposals by encouraging discussion, but it has done little else. Compared to the radical changes envisioned by some reformers, what has actually been accomplished is very little. Two official sets of reforms have been attempted. In 1965, Premier Aleksei Kosygin announced one set of reforms: to reduce the number of plan targets for each enterprise from two dozen or more to about eight and to place profit high among the eight as a source of managerial bonuses. In a related group of reforms, there was an attempt to restructure industrial prices during the years 1966 and 1967.

These reforms have eliminated some of the worst previous abuses. The old practice under which plants were rewarded for their achievements in gross output regardless of whether the output could be sold has been replaced by an emphasis on realized output, or actual sales. This practice helps reduce such problems as the production of shoes all of one size that rot in a warehouse for lack of users. Price reform did make some progress in bringing prices in line with average production costs. This eliminated the need to pay enormous subsidies to some firms whose output had always been undervalued. For the most part, though, the reforms have been very limited. A system with eight separate and often conflicting plan targets is a long way from introduction of profits as a single indicator. (Furthermore, since 1971, the direction of change has shifted, with the number of plan indicators increasing again.) By the same token, making prices equal to average cost is by no means the same as making them equal to opportunity cost on the marginal unit.

Explanations for the slow pace of reform vary. Some blame the political conservatism of the Brezhnev regime and the opposition of vested interests within the economic bureaucracy. Others say there is a fear that if economic reforms are introduced, political reforms will have to follow. Still others point out that reform is just not easy. You cannot reform incentives until you have reformed prices, you cannot reform prices until you have greater managerial independence, and you cannot give managers greater independence until you have rationalized their incentives. But, then, you cannot do everything at once either, so you end up doing nothing and hoping for the best!

What the future will bring is a matter of speculation. The most hopeful sign is the great amount of reform and experimentation being carried out in Eastern Europe. Every country in Eastern Europe except Albania has introduced reforms that go far beyond anything tried in the Soviet Union. Each set of reforms is different from the others. Perhaps when a new, more daring leadership comes on the scene in the Soviet Union, it will find in one or another of these experiments a path worth following.

SUMMARY

1. The origins of the Soviet economic system are found first in the Marxist-Leninist ideology and second in the practical experience of the first years of Soviet rule. After the 1917 revolution, an overambitious attempt to abolish the market economy all at once (war communism) was followed by a temporary restoration of the market (the new economic policy). The main features of what is now known as the Soviet-type economy—central planning in physical terms plus collectivization of agriculture—were established around 1928. They were designed to serve the government's objectives of complete political control of the economy and extensive, industry-first economic growth. The combination of planning plus collectivization was effective in achieving those objectives.

2. In its formal structure, the Soviet economy is a fully centralized hierarchy. Individual firms receive plans that specify inputs and outputs in physical terms, along with many other targets. These plans are legally binding on firms. In practice, managers of Soviet firms have considerable room to maneuver in fulfilling their plans. They bargain for safety factors, exercise initiative in procuring scarce inputs, and fulfill plans selectively. Central authorities tend to tolerate a certain degree of managerial independence as long as independent action results in fulfillment of the most important plan objectives.

3. The outstanding feature of Soviet economic performance has been rapid economic growth. The rate of growth, has, however, slowed in recent years. The need to switch from a strategy of extensive growth to one of intensive growth has focused attention on the inefficiency of the Soviet system. Soviet economic efficiency is hampered by inadequate managerial incentives and a price system that does not reflect opportunity costs. Many proposals have been put forward for reforming the system, but there has been little practical progress with reform in the Soviet Union. In the Soviet-type economies of Eastern Europe, however, a number of interesting and far-reaching reform experiments have been carried out.

DISCUSSION QUESTIONS

1. During the early war communism period of the Soviet Union, many leading economists seriously proposed the complete abolition of money as part of the transition to a centralized socialist system. Money was restored during the NEP, however, and no further attempt was made to abolish it after central planning began in earnest in the 1930s. Why does even a centrally planned socialist economy find it difficult to get along without money?
2. Any economist who has studied the Soviet economy closely can supply dozens of horror stories like that of the famous nail factory (Case 25.1). What kind of horror

stories involving flagrant misallocation of resources do you know for the U.S. economy? Would you look for such stories in independent private enterprise? In regulated industries? In government itself? Explain.

3. How can you be certain that the right proportion of gasoline and diesel engines are used in the U.S. economy? Or can you? Explain.

4. In the Soviet Union, market mechanisms are used to match workers to jobs, and wage differentials between jobs and regions are largely determined by supply and demand considerations. Do you think this means that labor resources are likely to be more efficiently allocated than other factors of production in the Soviet Union? Explain. In answering this question, you may wish to compare the determinants of labor demand curves in the U.S. and Soviet economies.

5. In reforming a Soviet-type economy, why is it difficult to introduce profit as the major success indicator for management before there has been a thoroughgoing price reform? Why is it difficult to reform prices before managerial incentives have been reformed?

6. In what ways do you think a centralized socialist economy of the Soviet type might be better equipped than a capitalist economy to deal with problems of population, resources, and pollution? In what ways is it less well equipped?

SUGGESTIONS FOR FURTHER READING

Gregory, Paul R., and Stuart, Robert C. *Soviet Economic Structure and Performance.* New York: Harper & Row, 1974.
A short textbook on the Soviet economy, covering all major aspects of history, structure, and performance.

U.S. Congress, Joint Economic Committee.
The Joint Economic Committee publishes numerous reports annually on the economies of the Soviet Union, China, and other Communist countries.

GLOSSARY

Absolute advantage In international trade theory, the ability of a country to produce a good at lower cost, measured in terms of factor inputs, than its trading partners'.

Accommodating monetary policy A policy under which the Federal Reserve System expands the money supply in an attempt to keep interest rates from rising when the Treasury sells bonds to cover a budget deficit.

Accounting profit Total revenue minus explicit costs.

Acreage controls Policies designed to raise agricultural prices by limiting the acreage on which certain crops can be grown.

Adaptive expectations Expectations about the rate of inflation or other future economic events formed primarily on the basis of experience in the recent past.

Aggregate A term used in economics to describe any quantity that is a grand total for the whole economy.

Aggregate demand The total value of all planned expenditures of all buyers in the economy.

Aggregate nominal demand schedule A graph showing the relationship between aggregate nominal demand (the nominal value of total planned expenditure) and nominal national income.

Aggregate supply The total value of all goods and services supplied in the economy; identical to national product.

Aggregate nominal supply schedule A graph showing the relationship between aggregate nominal supply (nominal national product) and nominal national income. The schedule has the form of a 45 degree line passing through the origin.

Agricultural marketing orders Agreements authorized by the Agricultural Marketing Agreement Act of 1937 that allow farmers collectively to control the quantities of particular farm products flowing to particular markets.

Anarcho-capitalism (radical libertarianism) A capitalist system under which no state exists and all goods and services—including defense, police, and court services—are supplied by private firms.

Antitrust laws A set of laws, including the Sherman Act of 1890 and the Clayton Act of 1914, that seek to control market structure and the competitive behavior of firms.

Appreciation A rise in the price (exchange rate) of the currency of one country in terms of the currency of another country.

Arbitrage The activity of earning a profit by buying a good for a low price in one market and reselling it for a higher price in another market.

Assets All the things to which a bank, other firm, or household holds legal claim.

Automatic stabilizers Changes in taxes, transfers, and government purchases that occur automatically as nominal GNP rises or falls.

Autonomous consumption The level of consumption shown by a consumption schedule for a zero disposable income level.

Balanced budget multiplier A multiplier showing how much equilibrium nominal national income will change in response to a change in government purchases matched dollar for dollar by an offsetting change in net taxes. The value of the balanced budget multiplier is always 1.

Benefit reduction rate The amount by which transfer benefits are reduced per dollar of earned income.

Bilateral monopoly A market in which both buyer and seller exercise monopoly power and neither passively accepts the demands of the other.

Birthrate *See* Crude birthrate.

Budget line A line showing the various combinations of goods that can be purchased at given prices within a given budget.

Capital As a factor of production, all means of production that are created by people, including such things as tools, industrial equipment, structures, and improvements to land.

Capital account The account whose transactions include all international borrowing and lending and all international purchases and sales of assets for investment purposes.

Capital inflow Purchases of domestic assets by foreigners and borrowing by domestic residents from foreigners.

Capitalism Any economic system based on private ownership of all factors of production in which owners of capital act as entrepreneurs and coordinate their activity through use of the market.

Capitalized value (of a rent) The amount equal to the value of the sum of money that would earn a periodic interest return equal to the rent if invested at the current market rate of interest.

Capital outflow Purchases of foreign assets by domestic residents and borrowing by foreigners from domestic sources.

Cartel An agreement among a number of independent suppliers of a product to coordinate their supply decisions so all of them will earn monopoly profits.

Centralized socialism A socialist system under which all capital and natural resources are owned by the government, which plans all production as if the economy were one big firm.

Circular flow of income and product The flow of goods from firms to households and factor services from households to firms, counterbalanced by the flow of expenditures from households to firms and factor payments from firms to households.

Civilian labor force All members of the noninstitutionalized adult civilian population who are either officially employed or officially unemployed.

Classical liberal capitalism A capitalist economic system in which government performs only the limited role of protecting property rights and settling private disputes.

Commodity inflation A variety of cost-push inflation in which a spontaneous increase in commodity prices is the initial source of general price increases.

Comparative advantage In international trade theory, the ability of a country to produce a good at a lower opportunity cost, in terms of other goods, than its trading partners'.

Complements A pair of goods for which an increase in the price of one causes a decrease in the demand for the other, other things being equal.

Concentration ratio The percentage of all sales contributed by the four or eight largest firms in a market.

Conglomerate mergers Mergers between firms that operate in unrelated markets.

Constant returns to scale A phenomenon said to occur when there are neither economies nor diseconomies of scale.

Consumer equilibrium A state of affairs in which consumers cannot increase the total utility they obtain from a given budget by shifting expenditure from one good to another. (In consumer equilibrium, the marginal utility of a dollar's worth of one good must be equal to the marginal utility of a dollar's worth of any other good.)

Consumer price index (CPI) A measure of the price level based on a weighted average of the prices of goods purchased by a typical urban consumer.

Consumption schedule A graphical or numerical representation of how nominal consumption expenditure varies as nominal income varies, other things being equal.

Contractionary gap The gap between planned expenditures and national product at the target level of national income when aggregate supply exceeds aggregate demand at that level.

Corporation A firm in which the ownership is divided into equal parts called shares, with each shareholder's liability limited to the amount of his or her investment in the firm.

Cost-push illusion The phenomenon that demand-pull inflation often looks like cost-push inflation to those caught up in it, because inventories cushion the immediate impact of demand on prices at each link in the chain of distribution from producers to retailers.

Cost-push inflation Inflation that is touched off by a spontaneous rise in wages, profit margins, commodity prices, or other elements of cost during a period of slack aggregate demand.

Craft union A union of skilled workers all practicing the same trade.

Crowding out effect The tendency of expansionary fiscal policy to cause a drop in private planned investment expenditure as a result of a rise in the interest rate.

Crude birthrate The number of people born into a population per thousand per year.

Crude death rate The number of people in a population who die per thousand per year.

Currency Coins and paper money.

Current account The account whose transactions include imports and exports of goods and services plus international unilateral transfer payments.

Death rate *See* Crude death rate.

Deficit In referring to government budgets, an excess of government purchases over net taxes.

Demand curve A graphical representation of the relationship between the price of a good and the quantity of it demanded.

Demand deposits Commercial bank deposits that depositors can withdraw by writing checks; commonly known as checking accounts.

Demand, law of *See* Law of demand.

Demand-pull inflation Inflation that is initially touched off by an increase in aggregate demand.

Demand schedule A table showing the quantity of a good demanded at various prices.

Demographic transition A population cycle that accompanies economic development, beginning with a fall in the death rate, continuing with a phase of rapid population growth, and concluding with a decline in the birthrate.

Depauperization Economic development of a kind that benefits the poorest of the poor, providing them not only with the material necessities of life but also with access to education, status, security, self-expression, and power.

Depreciation A fall in the price (exchange rate) of the currency of one country in terms of the currency of another country.

Diminishing marginal utility, principle of *See* Principle of diminishing marginal utility.

Diminishing returns, law of *See* Law of diminishing returns.

Discount rate The rate of interest charged by the Federal Reserve to member banks for reserves borrowed from the Fed.

Discretionary fiscal policy Changes in the levels of taxes, transfers, or government purchases made for the specific purpose of economic stabilization.

Diseconomies of scale A phenomenon said to occur whenever long-run average cost increases as output increases.

Disintermediation The large-scale withdrawal of funds from financial intermediaries by depositors in search of higher interest rates obtainable elsewhere.

Disposable personal income (disposable income) Personal income minus personal taxes.

Dissaving Negative saving—the difference between disposable income and consumption expenditure when consumption exceeds disposable income.

Distributive justice The principle of distribution according to innate merit. Roughly, the principle of "from each according to abilities, to each according to needs."

Dual economy An economy that is sharply divided into a modern, westernized industrial sector capable of rapid growth and a traditional rural sector that remains stagnant.

Dual labor market The division of the labor market into a primary sector, containing good jobs with established firms, and a secondary sector, containing low-paid, unstable jobs with marginal firms.

Dynamic efficiency The ability of an economy to increase consumer satisfaction through growth and innovation.

Econometrician A specialist in the statistical analysis of economic data.

Economic ideology A set of judgments and beliefs concerning efficiency, market justice, and distributive justice as goals of economic policy, together with a set of prejudices or beliefs concerning matters of positive economics.

Economies of scale A phenomenon said to occur whenever long-run average cost decreases as output increases.

Effective demand The quantity of a good that purchasers are willing and able to buy at a particular price.

Effective marginal tax rate The percentage of each dollar of additional earned income that a household loses through all explicit taxes and benefit reductions combined.

Efficiency The property of producing or acting with a minimum of expense, waste, and effort.

Elastic demand The situation where quantity changes by a larger percentage than price along the demand curve, so that total revenue increases as price decreases.

Empirical Term referring to data or methods based on observation of actual past experience or on controlled experiments.

Employed Officially, any person who works at least one hour per week for pay or at least fifteen hours per week as an unpaid worker in a family business.

Employment rate The ratio of the number of people employed to the number of people in the noninstitutional adult civilian population.

Entrepreneurship The aspect of economic decision making that consists of exploring for new alternatives, inventing new ways of doing things, being alert to new opportunities, taking risks, overcoming constraints, and experimenting with new objectives.

Event conditioned transfers Social insurance programs under which transfer payments are available to all citizens, regardless of income level, upon the occurrence of a specified event such as retirement, unemployment, or disability.

Excess quantity demanded The amount by which the quantity of a good demanded exceeds the quantity supplied when the price of the good is below the equilibrium level.

Excess quantity supplied The amount by which the quantity of a good supplied exceeds the quantity demanded when the price of the good is above the equilibrium level.

Excess reserves Reserves held by commercial banks in excess of required reserves.

Expansionary gap The gap between planned expenditures and national product at the target level of national income when aggregate demand exceeds aggregate supply at that level.

Expected real rate of interest The nominal rate of interest minus the expected rate of inflation.

Expected real rate of return The annual real net improvement in a firm's cost or revenue that it expects to obtain by making an investment; it is expressed as a percentage of the sum invested.

Expenditure approach A method of estimating aggregate economic activity by adding together the nominal expenditure of all economic units on newly produced final goods and services.

Explicit costs Costs taking the form of explicit payments to nonowners of a firm.

Extensive growth Growth based predominantly on the mobilization of increasing quantities of factor inputs.

Factor markets The markets in which the factors of production—labor, natural resources, and capital—are bought and sold.

Factors of production The basic inputs of natural resources, labor, and capital used in producing all goods and services.

Featherbedding The practice of negotiating purposefully inefficient work rules so that more workers will be needed to do a job.

Federal funds market A credit market in which banks can borrow reserves from one another for periods as short as twenty-four hours.

Final goods and services Goods and services sold directly for household consumption, business investment, or government purchase. Excludes intermediate goods sold for use as inputs in the production of other goods.

Financial intermediary Any financial institution that performs the function of channeling funds from savers to investors.

Fiscal policy The aggregate of policies that determine the levels of government purchases and net taxes.

Fixed inputs Inputs to the production process that cannot easily be increased or decreased in a short period of time (the quantity of fixed inputs employed by a firm defines the size of the firm's plant).

Fixed investment Purchases by firms of newly produced capital goods, such as production machinery, newly built structures, and office equipment.

Flows Processes occurring continuously through time, measured in units per time period.

Foreign exchange market The whole complex of institutions—including banks, specialized foreign exchange dealers, and official government agencies—through which the currency of one country can be exchanged for that of another.

Franchised monopoly A monopoly protected from competition by a government grant of monopoly privilege, such as an exclusive license, permit, or patent.

Frictional unemployment That portion of unemployment accounted for by people spending relatively short periods between jobs.

Full employment balanced budget rule A rule under which taxes and spending policy would be adjusted so that the federal budget would be in balance if the economy were at full employment.

Functional distribution of income The distribution of income according to factor ownership—that is, the distribution among workers, natural resource owners, and owners of capital.

General equilibrium analysis An approach to the study of markets along the lines of: If Event X occurs, the effect on Market Y will be Z, provided that other markets also adjust fully to the event in question.

GNP deflator A measure of the price level equal to the ratio of current year nominal GNP to current year real GNP times 100.

Government purchases of goods and services (government purchases) Expenditures made by federal, state, and local governments to purchase goods from private firms and to hire the services of government employees.

Gross national product (GNP) The dollar value at current market prices of all final goods and services produced annually by the nation's economy.

Homogeneous Having the property that every unit is just like every other unit.

Horizontal mergers Mergers between firms that are direct competitors in the same market.

Humphrey-Hawkins Act An act amending the Employment Act of 1946 by adding specific numerical policy targets for unemployment and inflation and by attempting to improve coordination of stabilization policies pursued by various branches of the federal government. Formally known as the Full Employment and Balanced Growth Act of 1978.

Hyperinflation Very rapid and sustained inflation.

Implicit costs The opportunity costs to a firm of using resources owned by the firm itself or contributed by owners of the firm.

Import quota A limitation on the quantity of a good that can be imported in a given time period.

Income approach A method of estimating aggregate economic activity by adding together the incomes earned by all households.

Income conditioned transfers Welfare or public charity programs under which transfer payments are available to citizens who meet some specified low income criterion.

Income effect The part of the change in quantity demanded of a good whose price has fallen that is attributable to the change in real income resulting from the price change.

Income elasticity of demand The ratio of the percentage change in the demand for a good to the percentage change in the income of buyers.

Incomes policy A policy that attempts to control wages, salaries, earnings, and prices directly in order to fight inflation.

Income velocity of money (velocity) The ratio of nominal income to the quantity of money.

Indexing The practice of automatically adjusting wages, salaries, or other payments to compensate for changes in the price level.

Indifference curve A graphical representation of an indifference set.

Indifference map A representative selection of indifference curves for a single consumer and pair of goods.

Indifference set A set of consumption alternatives each of which yields the same utility, so that no member of the set is preferred to any other.

Industrial union A union of all workers in an industry, including both skilled and unskilled workers and workers practicing various trades.

Inelastic demand The situation where quantity changes by a smaller percentage than price along the demand curve, so that total revenue decreases as price decreases.

Inferior good A good for which an increase in the income of buyers causes a leftward shift in the demand curve.

Inflationary recession A period of rising unemployment during which the rate of inflation remains high or even continues to rise.

Injections The part of total expenditures on domestically produced goods and services that does not originate from domestic households—that is, investment, government purchases, and exports.

Inside lag The delay between the time a policy action is needed and the time it is taken.

Intensive growth Growth based predominantly on improvements in the quality of factor inputs and in the efficiency with which they are utilized.

Inventory investment Changes in the stocks of finished products and raw materials that firms keep on hand. If stocks are increasing, inventory investment is positive; if they are decreasing, it is negative.

Investment The sum of fixed investment and inventory investment.

J-curve effect The tendency for the depreciation of a country's currency to worsen its current account deficit in the short run and to improve it only after a lag.

Keynesian cross A figure formed by the intersection of the aggregate nominal demand and aggregate nominal supply schedules.

Kolkhoz A Soviet collective farm.

Labor As a factor of production, the contributions to production made by people working with their minds and muscles.

Labor force See Civilian labor force.

Laffer curve A curve showing the relationship between a tax rate and the total revenue raised by the tax. At a zero or 100 percent tax rate, no revenue is raised; at some intermediate rate, tax revenue reaches a maximum.

Law of demand The law that the quantity of a good demanded by buyers tends to increase as the price of the good decreases and tends to decrease as the price increases, other things being equal.

Law of diminishing returns The law stating that as the quantity of one variable input used in a production process is increased (with the quantities of all other inputs remaining fixed), a point will eventually be reached beyond which the quantity of output added per unit of added variable input (that is, the marginal physical product of the variable input) begins to decrease.

Leakages The part of national income not devoted to consumption (saving plus net taxes) plus domestic expenditures on foreign-made goods (imports).

Liabilities Financial claims against a bank, other firm, or household by outsiders.

Liquid Description of an asset that can be used as a means of payment or easily converted to a means of payment without risk of gain or loss in nominal value.

Long run A time perspective long enough to permit changes in the quantities of all inputs, both fixed and variable.

Lump sum taxes Taxes that do not vary as income varies.

M_1 The measure of the money supply, defined as currency plus demand deposits.

M_2 M_1 plus savings and time deposits at commercial banks.

Macroeconomics The branch of economics devoted to the study of unemployment, inflation, economic growth, and stabilization policy.

Managerial coordination Coordination of economic activity through directives from managers to subordinates.

Margin, marginal Terms referring to the effects of making a small increase in any economic activity.

Marginal average rule The rule that marginal cost must be equal to average cost when average cost is at its minimum.

Marginal cost The increase in cost required to increase output of some good or service by one unit.

Marginal cost of pollution abatement The added cost of reducing a given kind of pollution by one unit.

Marginal factor cost The amount by which a firm's total factor cost must increase in order for it to obtain an additional unit of that factor.

Marginal physical product (of an input) The quantity of output, expressed in physical units, produced by each added unit of the input.

Marginal productivity theory of distribution A theory of the functional distribution of income according to which each factor receives a payment equal to its marginal revenue product.

Marginal propensity to consume The fraction of each added dollar of disposable income that goes to added consumption.

Marginal propensity to save The fraction of each added dollar of disposable income that is not consumed.

Marginal rate of substitution The rate at which one good can be substituted for another without gain or loss in satisfaction (equal to the slope of an indifference curve at any point).

Marginal revenue The amount by which total revenue increases as the result of a one-unit increase in quantity.

Marginal revenue product (of a factor) The change in revenue resulting from the sale of the product produced by one additional unit of factor input.

Marginal social cost of pollution The total additional cost to all members of society of an additional unit of pollution.

Marginal tax rate The percentage of each added dollar of income paid in taxes.

Marginal utility The amount of added utility obtained from a one-unit increase in consumption of a good.

Market coordination Coordination of economic activity using the price system to transmit information and provide incentives.

Market equilibrium A condition in which the separately formulated plans of buyers and sellers of some good exactly mesh when tested in the marketplace, so that the quantity supplied is exactly equal to the quantity demanded at the prevailing price.

Market justice The principle of distribution according to acquired merit. The observance of property rights and the honoring of contracts. Roughly, the principle of "value for value."

Markets All the various arrangements people have for trading with one another.

Market socialism A socialist system in which details of resource allocation are made through market mechanisms rather than through central planning.

Market structure Important characteristics of a market, including the number of firms that operate in it, the extent to which the products of different firms are diverse or homogeneous, and the ease of entry into and exit from the market.

Microeconomics The branch of economics devoted to the study of the behavior of individual households and firms and to the determination of the relative prices of individual goods and services.

Minimum efficient scale The level of output at which economies of scale are exhausted.

Monetarists Economists who believe that movements in the money supply are the primary causes of ups and downs in business activity.

Money Anything that serves as a unit of account, a medium of exchange, and a store of purchasing power.

Money demand schedule A schedule showing the quantity of money that people desire to hold in their portfolios given various values for the interest rate and the level of nominal income.

Money multiplier The ratio of the quantity of money to the total reserves in a banking system. Various money multipliers can be defined, depending on the definition of money used. For the U.S. banking system, the money multiplier is the M_1-to-total-reserves multiplier.

Monopolistic competition A market structure in which a large number of firms offer products that are relatively close substitutes for one another.

Monopoly power A seller's power to raise the price of a product without losing all, or nearly all, customers.

Monopsony A market in which there is only one buyer; from the Greek words *mono* ("single") and *opsonia* ("buying").

Multiplier effect The ability of a one dollar shift in the aggregate nominal demand schedule to induce a change of more than one dollar in the equilibrium level of nominal national income.

National income The total of all incomes, including wages, rents, interest payments, and profits received by households.

National product The total value of all goods and services supplied in the economy.

Natural monopoly A monopoly protected from competition by technological barriers to entry or by ownership of unique national resources.

Natural rate of unemployment The rate of unemployment that would prevail if the expected rate of inflation were equal to the actual rate of inflation.

Natural resources As a factor of production, everything useful as a productive input in its natural state, including agricultural land, building sites, forests, and mineral deposits.

Near monies Assets that are less than perfectly liquid but still liquid enough to be reasonably good substitutions for money.

Negative income tax A general name for transfer systems that emphasize cash benefits, beginning with a basic benefit available to households with zero earned income that is then subject to a benefit reduction rate of substantially less than 100 percent.

Net exports Total exports minus total imports.

Net national product (NNP) A measure of national product adjusted to exclude the value of investment expenditures that merely replace worn-out or obsolete capital goods. Officially, NNP equals GNP minus the capital consumption allowance.

Net reproduction rate The inherent long-term growth rate of a population, measured as the average number of daughters born to each female child over her lifetime.

Net taxes Total tax revenues collected by government at all levels minus total transfer payments disbursed.

Net tax multiplier A multiplier showing how much equilibrium nominal national income will change in response to a change in net taxes. The formula for the net tax multiplier is $-MPC/MPS$.

Net worth The assets of a bank, other firm, or household minus its liabilities.

Nominal rate of interest The rate of interest measured in the ordinary way, without adjustment for inflation.

Nominal values Measurements of economic values made in terms of actual market prices at which goods are sold.

Normal good A good for which an increase in the income of buyers causes a rightward shift in the demand curve.

Normal rate of return to capital The opportunity cost of capital to a firm—that is, the rate of return necessary to attract funds for investment from their best alternative uses.

Normative economics The part of economics devoted to making value judgments about what economic policies or conditions are good or bad.

Official reserve account The account whose transactions include purchases and sales of reserves of foreign currency by central banks.

Okun's law A rule of thumb according to which for each three percentage points by which real economic growth exceeds (or falls short of) the growth rate of potential real GNP in any year, the unemployment rate will tend to fall (or rise) by one percentage point.

Oligopolistic interdependence The necessity, in an oligopolistic market, for each firm to pay close attention to the behavior and likely reactions of its rivals when planning its own market strategy.

Oligopoly A market structure in which there are two or more firms, at least one of which has a large share of total sales.

Open market operation A purchase of securities from the public or a sale of securities to the public made by the Federal

Reserve for the purpose of altering the quantity of reserves available to member banks.

Opportunity cost The cost of doing something measured in terms of the loss of the opportunity to pursue the best alternative activity with the same time or resources.

Outside lag The delay between the time a policy action is taken and the time its effects on the economy are felt.

Parity price ratio The ratio of an index of prices that farmers receive to an index that farmers pay, using the years 1910–1914 as a base period.

Partial equilibrium analysis An approach to the study of markets along the lines of: If Event X occurs, the effect on Market Y will be Z, provided that the equilibrium of other markets is not disturbed.

Participatory socialism A socialist system under which the means of production are owned collectively by the workers of individual firms, who participate democratically in the process of management and share the profits of their firms.

Partnership A firm formed by two or more persons to carry on a business as co-owners. Each partner bears full legal liability for the debts of the firm.

Perfect competition A market structure characterized by a large number of relatively small firms, a homogeneous product, good distribution of information among all market participants, and freedom of entry and exit.

Perfectly elastic demand The situation where the demand curve is a horizontal line.

Perfectly inelastic demand The situation where the demand curve is a vertical line.

Personal distribution of income The distribution of income among individuals, taking into account both the functional distribution of income and the distribution of factor ownership among persons.

Personal income The total of all income, including transfer payments, actually received by households before payment of personal income taxes.

Phillips curve A curve showing the relationship between the rate of inflation and the level of unemployment. Inflation, usually placed on the vertical axis of such a figure, can be measured in terms of either the rate of change in wages or the rate of change in a price index.

Planned investment schedule A graphical representation of how the rate of planned investment for the economy as a whole varies as the expected real rate of interest varies, other things being equal.

Population trap A situation in which the rate of population growth rises above the rate of economic growth, halting the growth of per capita income and aborting the demographic transition.

Portfolio balance The idea that people try to maintain a balance among the various kinds of assets they own—including money, consumer durables, stocks, and bonds—shifting from one kind of asset to another as economic conditions change.

Positive economics The part of economics limited to making scientific predictions and purely descriptive statements.

Potential real GNP (potential real output) The level of real GNP that the economy could, in principle, produce if resources were fully employed.

Precautionary motive A motive for holding money arising from its usefulness as a reserve of liquid funds for use in emergencies or in taking advantage of unexpected opportunities.

Price discrimination The practice of charging more than one price for different units of a single product, when the price differences are not justified by differences in the cost of serving different customers.

Price elasticity of demand (elasticity of demand) The ratio of the percentage change in the quantity of a good demanded to the percentage change in the price of the good.

Price elasticity of supply (elasticity of supply) The ratio of the percentage change in the quantity of a good supplied to the percentage change in its price.

Price leadership A situation in an oligopolistic market where increases or decreases in price by one dominant firm, known as the price leader, are matched by all or most other firms in the market.

Price support A program under which the government guarantees a certain minimum price to farmers by undertaking to buy any surplus that cannot be sold to private buyers at the support price.

Price taker A firm that sells its outputs at fixed prices that are determined entirely by forces outside its own control.

Principle of diminishing marginal utility The principle that the greater the rate of consumption of some good, the smaller the increase in utility from a unit increase in the rate of consumption.

Producer price index A measure of the price level based on a weighted average of prices of crude, semi-finished, and finished producer goods bought and sold by private firms.

Production possibility frontier A curve showing the possible combinations of goods that can be produced by an economy, given the quantity and quality of factors of production available.

Profit-push inflation A variety of cost-push inflation in which a spontaneous increase in profit margins is the initial source of price increases.

Progressive tax A tax that takes a larger percentage of income from people whose incomes are high.

Protectionism Policies of shielding domestic industry from foreign competition.

Public goods Goods or services having the properties that (1) they cannot be provided to one citizen without being supplied also to that person's neighbors, and (2) once they are provided for one citizen, the cost of providing them to others is zero.

Purchasing power parity theory (of exchange rates) The theory holding that the price of a unit of Currency A in terms of Currency B will, in the long run, tend to be equal to the ratio of the price level in Country B to the price level in Country A.

Pure economic profit The sum remaining after both explicit and implicit costs are subtracted from total revenue.

Pure economic rent The income earned by any factor of production that is in perfectly inelastic supply.

Pure economizing The aspect of economic decision making that consists of choosing a pattern of activities from among a given set of alternative activities that will best serve a well-defined objective, subject to known constraints.

Pure monopoly A market structure in which one firm accounts for 100 percent of industry sales.

Rate of natural increase The current growth rate of a population calculated as the crude birthrate minus the crude death rate.

Rational expectations Expectations about the rate of inflation or other future economic events based on a rational weighing of all available evidence, including evidence on the probable effects of present and future economic policy.

Realized real rate of interest The nominal rate of interest minus the actual rate of inflation.

Real values Measurements of economic values that include adjustments for changes in prices between one year and another.

Reflation An expansion of aggregate demand after a period of high unemployment and decelerating inflation, bringing substantial short-term gains in employment with little or no inflationary penalty.

Regressive tax A tax that takes a larger percentage of income from people whose incomes are low.

Repurchase agreements Arrangements under which financial and nonfinancial firms sell securities subject to agreement to buy them back, often as soon as the next day.

Required reserve ratio The fraction of each type of deposit that the Federal Reserve System requires member banks to hold in the form of non-interest-bearing assets.

Reservation wage The wage (adjusted for nonmonetary advantages and disadvantages of a job) below which a person will not accept a job offer.

Residual charges Charges of a fixed amount per unit of waste imposed on all sources that discharge a given kind of waste into the environment.

Saving schedule A graphical or numerical representation of how nominal saving varies as nominal disposable income varies, other things being equal.

Savings deposits Deposits at commercial banks or thrift institutions subject to withdrawal at any time upon presentation of a passbook.

Scientific prediction A conditional prediction having the form "if A, then B, other things being equal."

Shortage As used in economics, an excess quantity demanded.

Short run A time perspective within which output can be adjusted only by changing the quantities of variable inputs within a plant of fixed size. *See also* Very short run.

Simple multiplier The ratio of an induced change in the equilibrium level of nominal national income to an initial shift in the aggregate nominal demand schedule. Using MPC to stand for the marginal propensity to consume, the value of the simple multiplier is given by the formula $1/(1 - MPC)$.

Socialism Any of a number of doctrines that include the following tenets: (1) that some major share of nonlabor factors of production ought to be owned in common or by the state, and (2) that justice requires incomes to be distributed at least somewhat more equally than under classical liberal capitalism.

Sole proprietorship A firm owned and usually managed by a single person, who receives all profits of the firm and who personally bears all of the firm's liabilities.

Speculative motive A motive for holding money arising from its fixed nominal value, when the nominal value of alternative assets is expected to decline.

State capitalism A capitalist system under which government intervenes widely in the market and provides an alternative to the market as a means by which individuals and firms can win control over resources.

Static efficiency The ability of an economy to get the greatest consumer satisfaction from given resources and technology.

Stocks Accumulated quantities existing at a particular time, measured in terms of simple units.

Stop-go policy A cycle of acceleration, inflationary recession, deceleration, and reflation brought about by alternating political pressures to do something first about inflation and then about unemployment.

Substitutes A pair of goods for which an increase in the price of one causes an increase in the demand for the other, other things being equal.

Substitution effect The part of the increase in quantity demanded of a good whose price has fallen that is attributable to the tendency of consumers to substitute relatively cheap goods for relatively expensive ones.

Supply curve A graphical representation of the relationship between the price of a good and the quantity of it supplied.

Supply schedule A table showing the quantity of a good supplied at various prices.

Surplus As used in economics, an excess quantity supplied. In referring to government budgets, an excess of net taxes over government purchases.

Target level of nominal national income (income target) The level of nominal national income judged by policy makers to be most nearly compatible with the goals of full employment, price stability, and real economic growth.

Target price A price guaranteed to farmers by the government; if the market price falls below the target price, the government pays the farmers the difference.

Tariff A tax levied on imported goods.

Tax-based incomes policy (TIP) An incomes policy employing tax incentives (penalties or rebates) to secure compliance with otherwise voluntary wage and price guidelines.

Theory of the mine The branch of economics concerned with the allocation over time of nonrenewable natural resources.

Thrift institutions Nonbank financial intermediaries primarily serving the interests of small savers and nonbusiness borrowers; thrift institutions include savings and loan associations, mutual savings banks, and credit unions.

Time deposits Deposits at commercial banks or thrift institutions subject to withdrawal without penalty only at the end of a specified period.

Total rate of return to capital The opportunity cost of capital plus pure economic profit, expressed as a percentage of the capital invested in a firm.

Transactions costs All costs of finding buyers or sellers to transact business with and of negotiating terms of exchanges, drawing up contracts, guarding against involuntary default or foul play, and so on.

Transactions motive A motive for holding money arising from the convenience of using it as a means of payment for day-to-day transactions.

Transfer payments All payments made by government to individuals that are not made in return for goods or services currently supplied. Social security benefits, welfare payments, and unemployment compensation are major forms of transfer payments.

Transitivity The situation where if A is preferred to B and B is preferred to C, then A must be preferred to C.

Unemployed Officially, any person without a job but actively looking for one.

Unemployment rate The percentage of the civilian labor force not employed.

Unit elastic demand The situation where price and quantity change by the same percentage along the demand curve, so that total revenue remains unchanged.

Utility The economist's term for the pleasure, satisfaction, and need fulfillment that people get from the consumption of material goods and services.

Variable inputs Inputs to the production process that can quickly and easily be varied to increase or decrease output within a plant of a given size.

Vertical mergers Mergers between firms that stand in a supplier-purchaser relationship to one another.

Very short run A time horizon so short that producers are unable to make any changes in input or output quantities in response to changing prices.

Wage-push inflation A variety of cost-push inflation in which a spontaneous increase in nominal wage rates is the initial source of price increases.

I N D E X